STUDIES IN THE SERMON ON THE MOUNT

Studies in the
SERMON *on the* MOUNT

One-Volume Edition

D. MARTYN LLOYD-JONES

WILLIAM B. EERDMANS PUBLISHING COMPANY
GRAND RAPIDS, MICHIGAN / CAMBRIDGE, U.K.

First Edition (in two volumes) 1959-60
Second edition (in one volume) 1971, 1976

Published by
Wm. B. Eerdmans Publishing Company
255 Jefferson Ave. S.E., Grand Rapids, Michigan 49503

Printed in the United States of America

11 10 09 08 07 06 05   23 22 21 20 19 18 17

ISBN 0-8028-0036-X

www.eerdmans.com

Contents

VOLUME TWO: MATTHEW 6 AND 7

Contents

VOLUME ONE

Preface

THIS volume consists of thirty sermons preached for the most part on successive Sunday mornings in the course of my regular ministry at Westminster Chapel. It is being published for one reason only, namely, that I can no longer resist the pressure brought to bear on me by large numbers of people, some
of whom heard the sermons when delivered and others who have read some of
them in our church magazine. Such readers will need no word of explanation as
to the form in which these sermons are published, but it may well be necessary
in the case of others.

These chapters are reports of sermons taken down in shorthand (no tape-
recording machine being available at that time). They have been subjected to a
minimum amount of correction and alteration, and no attempt has been made
to conceal, still less to expunge, the sermonic form. This has been quite deliberate and for several reasons.

I am profoundly convinced that the greatest need of the Church today is a
return to expository preaching. I would emphasize both words and especially
the latter. A sermon is not an essay and is not meant, primarily, for publication,
but to be heard and to have an immediate impact upon the listeners. This implies, of necessity, that it will have certain characteristics which are not found
and are not desirable in written studies. To prune it of these, if it should be sub-
sequently published, seems to me to be quite wrong, for it then ceases to be a
sermon and becomes something quite nondescript. I have a suspicion that what
accounts for the dearth of preaching at the present time is the fact that the majority of printed books of sermons have clearly been prepared for a reading
rather than a listening public. Their flavour and form are literary rather than
sermonic.

Another characteristic of expository preaching is that it is not merely an exposition of a verse or passage, or a running commentary on it; what turns it into preaching is that it becomes a message and that it has a distinct form and pattern.

Furthermore, it must always be applied and its relevance shown to the contemporary situation.

I am constantly being asked to give lectures on expository preaching. I rarely accede to such requests, believing that the best way of doing this is to give examples of such preaching in actual practice. It is my hope that this volume with its many faults may help somewhat in that respect, but it could not possibly have done so if drastic excisions, and an attempt to produce a literary form, had been made.

Here they are then, 'warts and all'. Those who are not interested in exposition, and those who have no taste for preaching as such, will probably be irritated by stylistic blemishes, 'the art of repetition' for the sake of emphasis, and what are termed 'pulpit mannerisms' (as if they were worse than any other kind of mannerism!). All I ask is that they be read and considered for what they are and for what they set out to do.

My greatest hope and desire is that they may in some small way stimulate a new interest in expository preaching. It may encourage preachers to know that such sermons, lasting on an average forty minutes on Sunday mornings, can be preached in what is called a 'down-town church' even in these days.

The two people who are most responsible for the appearance of the volume in print are Mrs. F. Hutchings who, almost miraculously, was able to take down the sermons in shorthand as they were delivered, and my daughter, Elizabeth Catherwood. Like many of my fellow preachers I acknowledge that my best and severest critic is my wife.

Westminster Chapel,
Buckingham Gate, London

D. M. Lloyd-Jones
March 1959

Chapter One

General Introduction

I T is a wise rule in the examination of any teaching to proceed from the general to the particular. This is the only way of avoiding the danger of 'missing the wood because of the trees'. This rule is of particular importance in connection with the Sermon on the Mount. We must realize, therefore, that at the outset certain general questions have to be asked about this famous Sermon and its place in the life, thought and outlook of Christian people.

The obvious question with which to start is this: Why should we consider the Sermon on the Mount at all? Why should I call your attention to it and to its teaching? Well, I do not know that it is a part of the business of a preacher to explain the processes of his own mind and his own heart, but clearly no man should preach unless he has felt that God has given him a message. It is the business of any man who tries to preach and expound the Scriptures to wait upon God for leading and guidance. I suppose fundamentally, therefore, my main reason for preaching on the Sermon on the Mount was that I had felt this persuasion, this compulsion, this leading of the Spirit. I say that deliberately, because if I had been left to my own choice I would not have chosen to preach a series of sermons on the Sermon on the Mount. And as I understand this sense of compulsion, I feel the particular reason for doing so is the peculiar condition of the life of the Christian Church in general at the present time.

I do not think it is a harsh judgment to say that the most obvious feature of the life of the Christian Church today is, alas, its superficiality. That judgment is based not only on contemporary observation, but still more on contemporary observation in the light of previous epochs and eras in the life of the Church. There is nothing that is more salutary to the Christian life than to read the history of the Church, to read again of the great movements of God's Spirit, and to observe what has happened in the Church at various times. Now I think that anyone who looks at the present state of the Christian Church in the light of that background will be driven to the reluctant conclusion that the outstanding characteristic of the life of the Church today is, as I have said, its superficiality. When I say that, I am thinking not only of the life and activity of the Church in an evangelistic sense. In that particular respect I think everybody would agree that superficiality is the most obvious characteristic. But I am thinking not only of modern evangelistic activities as compared and contrasted with the great evangelistic efforts of the Church in the past — the present-day tendency to boisterousness, for example, and the use of means which would have horrified and shocked our fathers; but I also have in mind the life of the Church in general where the same thing is true, even in such matters as her conception of holiness and her whole approach to the doctrine of sanctification.

The important thing for us is to discover the causes of this. For myself I would suggest that one main cause is our attitude to the Bible, our failure to take it seriously, our failure to take it as it is and to allow it to speak to us. Coupled with that, perhaps, is our invariable tendency to go from one extreme to the other. But the main thing, I feel, is our attitude towards the Scriptures. Let me explain in a little more detail what I mean by that.

There is nothing more important in the Christian life than the way in which we approach the Bible, and the way in which we read it. It is our textbook, it is our only source, it is our only authority. We know nothing about God and about the Christian life in a true sense apart from the Bible. We can draw various deductions from nature (and possibly from various mystical experiences) by which we can arrive at a belief in a supreme Creator. But I think it is agreed by most Christians, and it has been traditional throughout the long history of the Church, that we have no authority save this Book. We cannot rely solely upon subjective experiences because there are evil spirits as well as good spirits; there are counterfeit experiences. Here, in the Bible, is our sole authority.

Very well; it is obviously important that we should approach this Book in the right manner. We must start by agreeing that merely to read the Bible is not enough in and of itself. It is possible for us to read the Bible in such a mechanical manner that we derive no benefit from doing so. That is why I think we have to be careful with every kind of rule and regulation in the matter of discipline in the spiritual life. It is a good thing to read the Bible daily, but it can be quite profitless if we merely do so for the sake of being able to say we read the Bible daily. I am a great advocate of schemes of Bible reading, but we have to be careful that in our use of such schemes we are not content just to read the portion for the day and then to rush off without thought and meditation. That can be quite profitless. Our approach to the Bible is something which is of vital importance.

Now the Bible itself tells us this. You remember the apostle Peter's famous remark with regard to the writings of the apostle Paul. He says that there are things in them which are 'hard to be understood, which they that are unlearned and unstable wrest . . . unto their own destruction'. What he means is this. They read these Epistles of Paul, yes; but they are twisting them, they are wresting them to their own destruction. You can easily read these Epistles and be no wiser at the end than you were at the beginning because of what you have been reading into what Paul says, wresting them to your own destruction. Now that is something which we must always bear in mind with regard to the whole of the Bible. I can be seated with the Bible in front of me; I can be reading its words and going through its chapters; and yet I may be drawing a conclusion which is quite false to the pages in front of me.

There can be no doubt at all that the commonest cause of all this is our tendency so often to approach the Bible with a theory. We go to our Bibles with this theory, and everything we read is controlled by it. Now we are all quite familiar with that. There is a sense in which it is true to say that you can prove anything you like from the Bible. That is how heresies have arisen. The heretics were never dishonest men; they were mistaken men. They should not be thought of as men who were deliberately setting out to go wrong and to teach something that is wrong; they have been some of the most sincere men that the Church has ever known. What was the matter with them? Their trouble was this: they evolved a theory and they were rather pleased with it; then they went back with this theory to the Bible, and they seemed to find it everywhere. If you read half a verse and emphasize over-much some other half verse elsewhere, your theory is soon proved. Now obviously this is something of which we have to be very wary. There is nothing so dangerous as to come to the Bible with a theory, with preconceived ideas, with some pet idea of our own, because the moment we do so, we shall be tempted to over-emphasize one aspect and under-emphasize another.

Now this particular danger tends chiefly to manifest itself in the matter of the relationship between law and grace. That has always been true in the Church from the very beginning and it is still true today. Some so emphasize the law as to turn the gospel of Jesus Christ with its glorious liberty into nothing but a collection of moral maxims. It is all law to them and there is no grace left. They so talk of the Christian life as something that we have to do in order to make ourselves Christian that it becomes pure legalism and there is really no grace in it. But let us remember also that it is equally possible so to over-emphasize grace at the expense of law as, again, to have something which is not the gospel of the New Testament.

Let me give you a classical illustration of that. The apostle Paul, of all men, constantly had to be facing this difficulty. There was never a man whose preaching, with its mighty emphasis upon grace, was so frequently misunderstood. You remember the deduction some people had been drawing in Rome and in other places. They said, 'Now then, in view of the teaching of this man Paul, let us do evil that grace may abound, for, surely, this teaching is something that leads to that conclusion and to no other. Paul has just been saying, "Where sin abounded grace did much more abound"; very well, let us continue in sin that more and more grace may abound.' 'God forbid', says Paul; and he is constantly having to say that. To say that because we are under grace we therefore have nothing at all to do with law and can forget it, is not the teaching of the Scriptures. We certainly are no longer under the law but are under grace. Yet that does not mean that we need not keep the law. We are not under the law in the sense that it condemns us; it no longer pronounces judgment or condemnation on us. No! but we are meant to live it, and we are even meant to go beyond it. The argument of the apostle Paul is that I should live, not as a man who is under the law, but as Christ's free man. Christ kept the law, He lived the law; as this very Sermon on the Mount emphasizes, our righteousness must exceed that of the scribes and Pharisees. Indeed, He has not come to abolish the law; every jot and tittle has to be fulfilled and perfected. Now that is something which we very frequently find forgotten in this attempt to put up law and grace as antitheses, and the result is that men and women often completely and entirely ignore the law.

But let me put it in this way. Is it not true to say of many of us that in actual practice our view of the doctrine of grace is such that we scarcely ever take the plain teaching of the Lord Jesus Christ seriously? We have so emphasized the teaching that all is of grace and that we ought not to try to imitate His example in order to make ourselves Christians, that we are virtually in the position of ignoring His teaching altogether and of saying that it has nothing to do with us because we are under grace. Now I wonder how seriously we take the gospel of our Lord and Saviour Jesus Christ. The best way of concentrating on that question is, I think, to face the Sermon on the Mount. What is our view, I wonder, of this Sermon? Supposing that at this point I suggested that we should all write down on paper our answers to the following questions: What does the Sermon on the Mount mean to us? Where does it come in our lives and what is its place in our thinking and outlook? What is our relationship to this extraordinary Sermon that has such a prominent position in these three chapters in the Gospel according to St. Matthew? I think you would find the result would be very interesting and perhaps very surprising. Oh, yes, we know all about the doctrine of grace and forgiveness, and we are looking to Christ. But here in these documents, which we claim to be authoritative, is this Sermon. Where does it come in our scheme?

Now that is what I mean by background and introduction. However, let us take it a step further, by facing together another vital question. For whom is the Sermon on the Mount intended? To whom does it apply? What is really the purpose of this Sermon; what is its relevance? Now, here, there have been a number of conflicting opinions. There was once the so-called 'social gospel' view of the Sermon on the Mount. What it comes to is this, that the Sermon is in reality the only thing that matters in the New Testament, that there, in it, is the basis of the so-called social gospel. The principles, it was said, were there laid down as to how life should be lived by men, and all we have to do is to apply the Sermon on the Mount. We can thereby produce the kingdom of God on earth, war will be banished and all our troubles will be ended. That is the typical social gospel view, but we do not need to waste time with it. It has already become outmoded; it is to be found only amongst certain people whom I can describe as remnants and relics of the mentality of thirty years ago. The two world wars have shaken that view to its very foundation. Critical as we may be in many respects of the Barthian movement in theology, let us pay it this tribute: it has once and for ever made the social gospel look utterly ridiculous. But of course the real answer to this view of the Sermon on the Mount is that it has always ignored the Beatitudes, those statements with which the Sermon begins — 'Blessed are the poor in spirit'; 'Blessed are they that mourn.' As I hope to show you, these statements mean that no man can live the Sermon on the Mount in and of himself, and unaided. The advocates of the social gospel, having conveniently ignored the Beatitudes, have then rushed on to a consideration of the detailed injunctions, and have said, 'This is the gospel.'

Another view, which is perhaps a little more serious for us, is that which regards the Sermon on the Mount as nothing but an elaboration or an exposition of the Mosaic law. Our Lord, it is maintained, realized that the Pharisees and scribes and other teachers of the people were misinterpreting the law, as given by God to the people through Moses; what He does, therefore, in the Sermon on the Mount is to elaborate and expound the Mosaic law, giving it a higher spiritual content. That is a more serious view, obviously; and yet I feel it is totally inadequate if for no other reason than that it, also, fails to take account of the Beatitudes. The Beatitudes immediately take us into a realm that is beyond the law of Moses completely. The Sermon on the Mount does expound and explain the law at certain points — but it goes beyond it.

Then the next view I want to mention is what we may call the 'dispensational' view of the Sermon on the Mount. Probably many of you are familiar with it. It has been popularized in certain 'Bibles'. (I never like these adjectives; there is only one Bible, but we unfortunately tend to talk about 'So-and-so's Bible'.) There are, then, certain teachings which have been made popular in this way, and which teach a dispensational view of the Sermon on the Mount, saying that it has nothing whatsoever to do with modern Christians. They say our Lord began to preach about the kingdom of God, and the preaching of the Sermon on the Mount was in connection with the inauguration of this kingdom. Unfortunately, they continue, the Jews did not believe His teaching. So our Lord could not establish the kingdom, and therefore, almost as a kind of afterthought, the death on the cross came in, and as another afterthought the whole Church and the whole Church age came in, and that will persist up to a certain point in history. Then our Lord will return with the kingdom and again the Sermon on the Mount will be introduced. That is the teaching; it says, in effect, that the Sermon on the Mount has nothing to do with us. It is meant 'for the kingdom age'. It was meant for the people to whom He was preaching; it will be meant again in the millennial age. It is the law of that age and of the kingdom of heaven, and has nothing whatsoever to do with Christians in the meantime.

Now obviously this is a serious matter for us. This view is right or else it is not. According to this view I need not read the Sermon on the Mount; I need not be concerned about its precepts; I need not feel condemned because I am not doing certain things; it has no relevance for me. It seems to me that the answer to all that can be put like this. The Sermon on the Mount was preached primarily and specifically to the disciples. 'When he was set, his disciples came unto him: and he opened his mouth, and taught them, saying . . .' Now the whole presupposition is that it is preached to them. Take, for instance, the words which He spoke to them when He said, 'Ye are the salt of the earth'; 'Ye are the light of the world.' If the Sermon on the Mount has nothing to do with Christian people now, we must never say that we are the salt of the earth, or that we are the light of the world, for that does not apply to us. It applied to the first disciples; it will apply to some people later on. But, in the meantime, it has nothing to do with us. We must likewise ignore the gracious promises in this Sermon. We must not say that we must let our light so shine before men that they may see our good works and glorify our Father which is in heaven. If the whole Sermon on the Mount is inapplicable to modern Christians, all that is irrelevant. But clearly our Lord was preaching to these men and telling them what they were to do in this world, not only while He was here, but after He had gone. It was preached to people who were meant to practise it at that time and ever afterwards.

Not only that. To me another very important consideration is that there is no teaching to be found in the Sermon on the Mount which is not also found in the various New Testament Epistles. Make a list of the teachings of the Sermon on the Mount; then read your Epistles. You will find that the teaching of the

Sermon on the Mount is there also. Now all the Epistles are meant for Christians today; so if their teaching is the same as that of the Sermon on the Mount, clearly its teaching also is meant for Christians today. That is a weighty and important argument. But perhaps I can put it best like this. The Sermon on the Mount is nothing but a great and grand and perfect elaboration of what our Lord called His 'new commandment'. His new commandment was that we love one another even as He has loved us. The Sermon on the Mount is nothing but a grand elaboration of that. If we are Christ's, and our Lord has meant that word for us, that we should love one another even as He loved us, here we are shown how to do it.

The dispensational view is based on a wrong conception of the kingdom of God. This is where the confusion arises. I agree, of course, that the kingdom of God in one sense has not been established on the earth yet. It is a kingdom which is to come; yes. But it is also a kingdom which has come. 'The kingdom of God is among you', and 'within you'; the kingdom of God is in every true Christian, and in the Church. It means 'the reign of God', 'the reign of Christ'; and Christ is reigning today in every true Christian. He reigns in the Church when she acknowledges Him truly. The kingdom has come, the kingdom is coming, the kingdom is yet to come. Now we must always bear that in mind. Whenever Christ is enthroned as King, the kingdom of God is come, so that, while we cannot say that He is ruling over all in the world at the present time, He is certainly ruling in that way in the hearts and lives of all His people.

There is nothing, therefore, so dangerous as to say that the Sermon on the Mount has nothing to do with modern Christians. Indeed, I will put it like this: it is something which is meant for all Christian people. It is a perfect picture of the life of the kingdom of God. Now I have no doubt at all in my own mind that that is why Matthew put it in his Gospel at the beginning. It is agreed that Matthew was writing his Gospel especially for the Jews. That was his set desire. Hence all this emphasis upon the kingdom of heaven. And what was Matthew out to emphasize? Surely it was this. The Jews had a false, materialistic conception of the kingdom. They thought the Messiah was one who was coming to give them political emancipation. They were looking forward to someone who would deliver them from the bondage and yoke of the Roman Empire. They always thought of the kingdom in an external sense, a mechanical, military, materialistic sense. So Matthew puts the true teaching concerning the kingdom in the very forefront of his Gospel, for the great purpose of this Sermon is to give an exposition of the kingdom as something which is essentially spiritual. The kingdom is primarily something 'within you'. It is that which governs and controls the heart and mind and outlook. Far from being something which leads to great military power, it is to be 'poor in spirit'. In other words, we are not told in the Sermon on the Mount, 'Live like this and you will become Christian'; rather we are told, 'Because you are Christian live like this.' This is how Christians ought to live; this is how Christians are meant to live.

But to complete this part of our argument we must face another difficulty. Some say, 'Surely the Sermon on the Mount teaches that we have our sins forgiven only if we forgive others? Doesn't our Lord say, "If ye forgive not men their trespasses, neither will your Father forgive your trespasses"? Is not that law? Where is grace there? To be told that if we do not forgive, we shall not be forgiven, is not grace.' Thus they seem to be able to prove that the Sermon on the Mount does not apply to us. But if you say that, you will have to take almost the whole of Christianity out of the gospel. Remember also that our Lord taught exactly the same thing in His parable, recorded at the end of Matthew 18, of the steward who committed an offence against his master. This man went to his master and pleaded with him to forgive him; and his master forgave him. But he refused to forgive an underling who was likewise in debt to him, with the result that his master withdrew his forgiveness and punished him. Our Lord comments on this: 'So likewise shall my heavenly Father do also unto you, if ye from your hearts forgive not every one his brother their trespasses.' That is exactly the same teaching. But does it teach that I am forgiven only because I have forgiven? No, the teaching is, and we have to take this teaching seriously, that if I do not forgive, I am not forgiven. I explain it like this: the man who has seen himself as a guilty, vile sinner before God knows his only hope of heaven is that God has forgiven him freely. The man who truly sees and knows and believes that, is one who cannot refuse to forgive another. So the man who does not forgive another does not know forgiveness himself. If my heart has been broken in the presence of God I cannot refuse to forgive; and, therefore, I say to any man who is imagining fondly that his sins are to be forgiven by Christ, though he does not forgive anybody else, Beware, my friend, lest you wake up in eternity and find Him saying to you, 'Depart from me; I never knew you.' You are misinterpreting the doctrine, the glorious doctrine of the grace of God. The man who is truly forgiven and knows it, is a man who forgives. That is the meaning of the Sermon on the Mount at this point.

We shall be going into this in detail later. Here let me just put one last question. Having considered the people to whom the Sermon on the Mount applies, let us ask ourselves this: Why should we study it? Why should we try to live it? Let me give you a list of answers. The Lord Jesus Christ died to enable us to live the Sermon on the Mount. He died. Why? 'That he might . . . purify unto himself a peculiar people, zealous of good works,' says the apostle Paul — the apostle of grace (see Titus 2:14). What does he mean? He means that He died in order that I might now live the Sermon on the Mount. He has made this possible for me.

The second reason for studying it is that nothing shows me the absolute need of the new birth, and of the Holy Spirit and His work within, so much as the Sermon on the Mount. These Beatitudes crush me to the ground. They show me my utter helplessness. Were it not for the new birth, I am undone. Read and study it, face yourself in the light of it. It will drive you to see your ultimate need of the rebirth and the gracious operation of the Holy Spirit. There is nothing that so leads to the gospel and its grace as the Sermon on the Mount.

Another reason is this. The more we live and try to practise this Sermon on the Mount, the more shall we experience blessing. Look at the blessings that are promised to those who do practise it. The trouble with much holiness teaching is that it leaves out the Sermon on the Mount, and asks us to experience sanctification. That is not the biblical method. If you want to have power in your life and to be blessed, go straight to the Sermon on the Mount. Live and practise it and give yourself to it, and as you do so the promised blessings will come. 'Blessed are they which do hunger and thirst after righteousness: for they shall be filled.' If you want to be filled, don't seek some mystic blessing; don't rush to meetings hoping you will get it. Face the Sermon on the Mount and its implications and demands, see your utter need, and then you will get it. It is the direct road to blessing.

But this is what I want to leave in your minds. I suggest to you it is the best means of evangelism. Surely we all ought to be urgently concerned about this at the present time. The world today is looking for, and desperately needs, true Christians. I am never tired of saying that what the Church needs to do is not to organize evangelistic campaigns to attract outside people, but to begin herself to live the Christian life. If she did that, men and women would be crowding into our buildings. They would say, 'What is the secret of this?' Almost every day we read that the real secret of communism at the present time is that it seems to be doing something and giving people something. I am told repeatedly, as I talk to young people and read books, that communism is conquering as it is in the modern world because people feel that its adherents are doing things and are sacrificing for what they believe. That is how they are gaining their members. Now there is only one way to counter that, and that is to show we have something infinitely bigger and greater. It has been my privilege to meet comparatively recently more than one person converted from communism, and in each case it has not been as a result of some intellectual sermon or argument but as the result of this communist seeing in some simple Christian a more thorough-going practice of self-abnegation and concern for others than he or she had ever thought of.

Let me enforce this by quoting something I read some time ago. A one-time Law Minister in the Indian Government was a great man called Dr. Ambedkar, an outcaste himself and a leader of the outcastes in India. At the time of which I am speaking he was taking a great interest in the teachings of Buddhism, and attended a great Conference of twenty-seven countries in Ceylon which had met together to inaugurate a world fellowship of Buddhists. He gave as his chief reason for attending the Conference, his desire to discover to what extent the religion of Buddha was a live thing. He said at the Conference, 'I am here to find out to what extent there is dynamic in the Buddhist religion as far as the people of this country are concerned.' There was the leader of the outcastes turning to Buddhism, and examining it. He said, 'I want to find if it is alive. Has it something to give to these masses of my fellow outcastes? Has it dynamic in it? Is it something that can uplift people?' But the real tragedy about this able, learned man is that he had already spent much time in America and Great Britain studying Christianity. And it was because he had found it was not a live thing, because he had found an absence of dynamic in it, that he was now turning to Buddhism. Though he had not accepted Buddhism, yet he was seeking to find whether this was the power he was looking for. That is the challenge that comes to you and to me. We know Buddhism is not the answer. We claim to believe that the Son of God has come into the world and has sent His own Holy Spirit into us, His own absolute power that will reside in men and make them live a quality of life like His own. He came, I say, and lived and died and rose again and sent the Holy Spirit in order that you and I might live the Sermon on the Mount.

Do not say it has nothing to do with us. Why, it has everything to do with us! If only all of us were living the Sermon on the Mount, men would know that there is dynamic in the Christian gospel; they would know that this is a live thing; they would not go looking for anything else. They would say, 'Here it is.' And if you read the history of the Church you will find it has always been when men and women have taken this Sermon seriously and faced themselves in the light of it, that true revival has come. And when the world sees the truly Christian man, it not only feels condemned, it is drawn, it is attracted. Then let us carefully study this Sermon that claims to show what we ought to be. Let us consider it that we may see what we can be. For it not only states the demand; it points to the supply, to the source of power. God give us grace to face the Sermon on the Mount seriously and honestly and prayerfully until we become living examples of it, and exemplifiers of its glorious teaching.

Chapter Two

General View and Analysis

IN the last chapter we considered the background and introduction to the Sermon on the Mount. Although I want to advance from that now, we must again consider it as a whole before we come to its details and to its specific statements. It seems to me to be a very good thing indeed, and a very vital thing, to do this. I do not mean by that, that I am about to embark on a study of what we may call the technicalities. Learned authorities are very fond of discussing, for example, whether the Sermon on the Mount as recorded in Matthew 5, 6 and 7 is identical with that which is recorded in Luke 6. Many of you are probably familiar with all the arguments about that. For myself I am frankly not very concerned: indeed, I do not hesitate to say, I am not very interested. I am not decrying the value of a careful discussion and study of the Scriptures in that way; but I do feel constantly the need to warn myself and everybody else against becoming so immersed in the mechanics of Scripture that we miss its *message*. While we should be concerned about the harmony of the Gospels and similar problems, God forbid, I say, that we should regard the four Gospels as some kind of intellectual puzzle. The Gospels are not here for us to try to draw out our perfect schemes and classifications; they are here for us to read in order that we may apply them, that we may live them and practise them. I do not intend, therefore, to spend time considering such technical questions. There have been various classifications and subdivisions of the Sermon as recorded in these three chapters; there has been much argument and disputation on this kind of question — how many Beatitudes are there, seven, eight or nine? Others can spend their time on such problems if they like, but it seems to me that the important thing is not the numericals, as it were, but that we face the Beatitudes themselves. Thus I trust I shall not disappoint anyone who is interested in that kind of study.

I can never forget, in this connection, a man who, whenever I met him, always impressed upon me the fact that he was a great Bible student. I suppose in one sense he was, but his life was unfortunately very far removed from that which one finds described in the pages of the New Testament. Yet Bible study was his hobby and that is the thing of which I am afraid. You can be a Bible student in that mechanical sense. As people spend their time in analysing Shakespeare, so some people spend their time in analysing the Scriptures. An analysis of Scripture is all right as long as it is in a very subordinate position, and as long as we are careful it does not so grip us, that we become interested only in an objective, intellectual sense. It is a unique Word, and it must not be approached just as any other book is approached. I do increasingly understand those Fathers and saints of the Church in the past who used to say that we should never read the Bible except on our knees. We need this constant reminder as we approach the Word of God, that it is indeed and in truth the Word of God speaking directly to us.

The reason, then, why I believe it is important for us to take the Sermon as a whole before we come to the details, is this constant danger of 'missing the wood because of the trees'. We are all of us ready to fix on certain particular statements, and to concentrate on them at the expense of others. The way to correct that tendency, I believe, is to realize that no part of this Sermon can be understood truly except in the light of the whole. Some good friends have already said to me, 'I am going to be most interested when you come to state exactly what is meant by "Give to him that asketh thee"', etc. That is a betrayal of a false attitude to the Sermon on the Mount. They have jumped to particular statements. There is a great danger at this point. The Sermon on the Mount, if I may use such a comparison, is like a great musical composition, a symphony if you like. Now the whole is greater than a collection of the parts, and we must never lose sight of this wholeness. I do not hesitate to say that, unless we have understood and grasped the Sermon on the Mount as a whole, we cannot understand properly any one of its particular injunctions. I mean that it is idle and useless and quite futile to confront anybody with any particular injunction in the Sermon on the Mount unless such a person has already believed, and accepted, and has indeed already conformed to, and is living, the Beatitudes.

That is where the so-called 'social application of the Sermon on the Mount to modern needs' idea is such a complete fallacy and such a heresy. People have often applied it in this way. For example, they will select this matter of 'turning the other cheek'. They take that out of the Sermon and isolate it, and, on the basis of that, they have denounced all forms of war as being unchristian. I do not want to discuss the question of pacifism now; all I am concerned to show is this, that you cannot take that particular injunction and hold it up to an individual, or to a nation, or to the world, unless that particular individual, or that particular nation, or the whole world is already living and practising and conforming to the Beatitudes. All the particular injunctions which we shall consider follow the Beatitudes with which the Sermon starts. That is what I mean when I say that we must start by a kind of synoptic, general view of the whole before we even begin to consider the particular parts. In other words, everything in this Sermon, if we treat it rightly, and if we are to derive benefit from considering it, must be taken in its setting; and, as I have just been emphasizing, the order in which the statements come in the Sermon is really of supreme importance. The Beatitudes do not come at the end, they come at the beginning, and I do not hesitate to say that unless we are perfectly clear about them we should go no further. We have no right to go further.

There is a kind of logical sequence in this Sermon. Not only that, there is certainly a spiritual order and sequence. Our Lord does not say these things accidentally; the whole thing is deliberate. Certain postulates are laid down, and on the basis of those, certain other things follow. Thus I never discuss any particular injunction of the Sermon with a person until I am perfectly happy and clear in my mind that that person is a Christian. It is wrong to ask anybody who is not first a Christian to try to live or practise the Sermon on the Mount. To expect Christian conduct from a person who is not born again is heresy. The appeals of the gospel in terms of conduct and ethics and morality are always based on the assumption that the people to whom the injunctions are addressed are Christian.

Now that is obvious in any one of the Epistles, and it is equally obvious here. Take any Epistle you like. You will find that the subdivision in each one of them is the same; always doctrine first, then deductions from doctrine. The great principles are laid down and a description is given of the Christians to whom the letter is written. Then, because of that, or because they believe that, 'therefore' they are exhorted to do certain things. We always tend to forget that every New Testament letter was written to Christians and not to non-Christians; and the appeals in terms of ethics in every Epistle are always addressed only to those who are believers, to those who are new men and women in Christ Jesus. This Sermon on the Mount is exactly the same.

Very well; let us try to give a kind of general division of the contents of the Sermon on the Mount. Here again you will find it is almost true to say that every man has his own classification and subdivision. In a sense, why shouldn't he? There is nothing more futile than to ask, 'What is the correct subdivision and classification of the contents of this Sermon?' There are various ways in which it can be subdivided. The one that commends itself to me is as follows. I would divide the Sermon up into *general* and *particular*. The general part of the Sermon occupies verse 3 to verse 16. There you have certain broad statements with regard to the Christian. Then the remainder of the Sermon is concerned with particular aspects of his life and conduct. First the general theme, and then an illustration of this theme in particular.

But we can subdivide it a little further for the sake of convenience. In verses 3-10 you have the character of the Christian described in and of itself. That is, more or less, the Beatitudes which are a description of the character of the Christian in general. Then verses 11 and 12, I would say, show us the character of the Christian as proved by the reaction of the world to him. We are told, 'Blessed are ye, when men shall revile you, and persecute you, and shall say all manner of evil against you falsely, for my sake. Rejoice, and be exceeding glad: for great is your reward in heaven: for so persecuted they the prophets which were before you.' In other words, the character of the Christian is described positively and negatively. First we see the sort of man he is, and then we are told, because he is that, certain things happen to him. Yet it is still a general description. Then, obviously, verses 13-16 are an account of the relationship of the Christian to the world, or, if you prefer it, these verses are descriptive of the function of the Christian in society and in the world, and these descriptions of him are emphasized and elaborated, and then are summed up, as it were, in exhortation: 'Let your light so shine before men, that they may see your good works, and glorify your Father which is in heaven.'

There, then, is a general account of the Christian. From there on, I suggest, we come to what I may call the particular examples and illustrations of how such a man lives in a world like this. Here we can subdivide like this. In verses 17-48 we have the Christian facing the law of God and its demands. You will remember the various subdivisions. A general description of his righteousness is given. Then we are told of his relationship towards such matters as murder, adultery and divorce; then how he should speak and then his position with regard to the whole question of retaliation and self-defence, and his attitude towards his neighbour. The principle involved is that the Christian is primarily concerned about the spirit rather than the letter. This does not mean that he ignores the letter, but he is more concerned about the spirit. The whole error of the Pharisees and the scribes was that they were interested only in the mechanical. The Christian view of the law is one that is concerned about the spirit, and is interested in the details only as they are an expression of the spirit. That is worked out in terms of a number of particular examples and illustrations.

The whole of chapter 6, I suggest, relates to the Christian as living his life in the presence of God, in active submission to Him, and in entire dependence upon Him. If you read chapter 6 at your leisure I think you will come to that conclusion. It is all along concerned about the Christian in his relationship to the Father. Take, for instance, the first verse: 'Take heed that ye do not your alms before men, to be seen of them: otherwise ye have no reward of your Father which is in heaven.' It continues like that from beginning to end, and at the end we are told practically the same thing. 'Therefore take no thought, saying, What shall we eat? . . . or, Wherewithal shall we be clothed? (for after all these things do the Gentiles seek:) for your heavenly Father knoweth that ye have need of all these things. But seek ye first the kingdom of God, and his righteousness; and all these things shall be added unto you.' There, I say, is a description of the Christian as a man who knows he is always in the presence of God, so that what he is interested in is not the impression he makes on other men, but his relationship to God. Thus, when he prays, he is not interested in what other people are thinking, whether they are praising his prayers or criticizing them; he knows he is in the presence of the Father, and he is praying to God. Also, when he does his alms, it is God he has in mind all along. Furthermore, as he meets problems in life, his need of food and clothing, his reaction to external events, all are viewed in the light of this relationship which he bears to the Father. This is a very important principle with regard to the Christian life.

Then chapter 7 can be regarded in general as an account of the Christian as one who lives always under the judgment of God, and in the fear of God. 'Judge not, that ye be not judged.' 'Enter ye in at the strait gate.' 'Beware of false prophets.' 'Not every one that saith unto me, Lord, Lord, shall enter into the kingdom of heaven; but he that doeth the will of my Father which is in heaven.' Moreover the Christian is likened to a man who builds a house which he knows is going to be tested.

There, I think, we have not only a general analysis of the Sermon on the Mount, but also a very complete portrayal and representation of the Christian. Certain things always characterize the Christian, and these are certainly the three most important principles. The Christian is a man who of necessity must be concerned about keeping God's law. I mentioned in chapter one the fatal tendency to put up law and grace as antitheses in the wrong sense. We are not 'under the law' but we are still meant to keep it; the 'righteousness of the law' is meant to be 'fulfilled in us', says the apostle Paul in writing to the Romans. Christ coming 'in the likeness of sinful flesh, . . . condemned sin in the flesh'. Well; why? 'That the righteousness of the law might be fulfilled in us, who walk not after the flesh, but after the Spirit' (Rom. 8:3, 4). So the Christian is a man who is always concerned about living and keeping the law of God. Here he is reminded how that is to be done.

Again one of the essential and most obvious things about a Christian is that he is a man who lives always realizing he is in the presence of God. The world does not live in this way; that is the big difference between the Christian and the non-Christian. The Christian is a man whose every action should be performed in the light of this intimate relationship to God. He is not, as it were, a free agent. He is a child of God, so that everything he does, he does from this standpoint of being well-pleasing in His sight. That is why the Christian man, of necessity, should view everything that happens to him in this world entirely differently from everybody else. The New Testament emphasizes that every-where. The Christian is not worried about food and drink and housing and clothing. It is not that he says these things do not matter, but they are not his main concern, they are not the things for which he lives. The Christian sits loosely to this world and its affairs. Why? Because he belongs to another king-dom and another way. He does not go out of the world; that was the Roman Catholic error of monasticism. The Sermon on the Mount does not tell you to go out of life in order to live the Christian life. But it does say that your attitude is entirely different from that of a non-Christian, because of your relationship to God and because of your utter dependence upon Him. The Christian there-fore should never worry about his circumstances in this world because of his relationship to God. That, again, is fundamental about the Christian.

The third thing is equally true and fundamental. The Christian is a man who always walks in the fear of God — not craven fear, because 'perfect love casteth out' that fear. Not only does he approach God in terms of the Epistle to the Hebrews, 'with reverence and godly fear', but he lives his whole life like that. The Christian is the only man in the world who does live always with and under this sense of judgment. He must do so because our Lord tells him to do so. He tells him his building is going to be judged, the test of life is going to come. He tells him not to say, 'Lord, Lord,' nor to rely upon his activities in the Church as being of necessity sufficient, because judgment is coming, and judgment by One who sees the heart. He does not look at the sheep's clothing outside but at the inward parts. Now the Christian is a man who always remembers that. I said earlier that the final charge that will be laid against us modern Christians is the charge of superficiality and glibness. This is manifested at this point more than anywhere else, and that is why it is a good thing for us to read about Christians living in past ages. These New Testament people lived in the fear of God. They all accepted the teaching of the apostle Paul when he said, 'We must all appear before the judgment seat of Christ; that every one may receive the things done in his body, according to that he hath done, whether it be good or bad' (2 Cor. 5:10). That is addressed to Christians. Yet the modern Christian does not like that; he says he will have nothing to do with it. But that is the teaching of the apostle Paul as it is the teaching of the Sermon on the Mount. 'We must all appear before the judgment seat of Christ'; 'Knowing, therefore, the terror of the Lord.' Judgment is coming and it is going to 'begin at the house of God', where it should begin, because of the claim we make. It is all impressed upon us here in the final section of the Sermon on the Mount. We should always be living and walking, distrustful of the flesh, distrustful of ourselves, knowing we have to appear before God and be judged by Him. It is a 'strait gate', it is a 'narrow way', this way that leads to life which is life indeed.

How important it is, then, to look at this Sermon in general before we begin to argue with one another about what it means when it tells us to turn the other cheek, and so on. People always jump to these particulars and it is an utterly false approach to the Sermon.

Let me now lay down a number of controlling principles which should govern the interpretation of this Sermon. What is of supreme importance is that we must always remember that the Sermon on the Mount is a description of character and not a code of ethics or of morals. It is not to be regarded as law — a kind of new 'Ten Commandments' or set of rules and regulations which are to be carried out by us — but rather as a description of what we Christians are meant to be, illustrated in certain particular respects. It is as if our Lord says, 'Because you are what you are, this is how you will face the law and how you will live it.' It follows from this that each particular injunction is not to be considered and then applied mechanically or by rule of thumb, for that would of necessity make it ridiculous. People come to this Sermon and say something like this: 'Take that injunction, "if any man will sue thee at the law, and take away thy coat, let him have thy cloke also." If you did that you would soon have nothing left in the wardrobe.' That is the kind of approach that must not be made. You must not take separate injunctions and say, 'This is to be applied.' That is not the way to look at it. What is inculcated is that I should be in such a spirit that under certain circumstances and conditions, I must do just that — throw in the cloke, or go the second mile. This is no mechanical rule to be applied; but I am such a person that, if it is God's will and for His glory, I do so readily. All I am and have are His, and are no longer mine. It is a particular illustration of a general principle and attitude.

I find this relationship of the general to the particular something which is very difficult to put into words. Indeed I suppose one of the most difficult things in any realm or department of thought is to define what this relationship is. The nearest I can get to my own satisfaction is to put it like this. The relation of any particular injunction to the whole life of the soul is the relationship, I think, of the artist to the particular rules and laws that govern what he is doing. Take, for example, the realm of music. A man may play a piece of great music quite accurately; he may make no mistakes at all. And yet it may be true to say of him that he did not really play Beethoven's Moonlight Sonata. He played the notes correctly, but it was not the Sonata. What was he doing? He was mechanically striking the right notes, but missing the soul and the real interpretation. He wasn't doing what Beethoven intended and meant. That, I think, is the relationship between the whole and the parts. The artist, the true artist, is always correct. Even the greatest artist cannot afford to neglect rules and regulations. But that is not what makes him the great artist. It is this something extra, the expression; it is the spirit, it is the life, it is 'the whole' that he is able to convey. There, it seems to me, is the relationship of the particular to the general in the Sermon on the Mount. You cannot divorce, you cannot separate them. The Christian, while he puts his emphasis upon the spirit, is also concerned about the letter. But he is not concerned only about the letter, and he must never consider the letter apart from the spirit.

Let me, then, try to summarize it in this way. Here are some negative tests to apply. If you find yourself arguing with the Sermon on the Mount at any point, it means either that there is something wrong with you or else that your interpretation of the Sermon is wrong. I find that very valuable. As I read this Sermon something hits me and I want to argue with it. Well, I repeat, it means either that my whole spirit is wrong and I am not living and exemplifying the Beatitudes: or else I am interpreting that particular injunction in a wrong and false way. It is a very terrible sermon, this Sermon on the Mount. Be very careful as you read it, and especially when you talk about it. If you criticize this Sermon at any point you are really saying a great deal about yourself. Let us, therefore, in the words of James, 'be swift to hear, slow to speak, slow to wrath'.

Again, if our interpretation makes any injunction appear to be ridiculous then we can be certain our interpretation is wrong. You see the argument; I have already mentioned it earlier in the illustration of the coat and the cloak. Such an interpretation, I repeat, must be wrong, for nothing that our Lord ever taught can be ridiculous.

Finally, if you regard any particular injunction in this Sermon as impossible, once more your interpretation and understanding of it must be wrong. Let me put it like this. Our Lord taught these things, and He expects us to live them. His last injunction, you remember, to these men whom He sent out to preach was, 'Go ye therefore, and teach all nations, baptizing them in the name of the Father, and of the Son, and of the Holy Ghost: teaching them to observe all things whatsoever I have commanded you.' Now here in this Sermon are those very things. He meant them to be taught, He meant them to be practised. Our Lord Himself lived the Sermon on the Mount. The apostles lived the Sermon on the Mount, and if you take the trouble to read the lives of the saints down the centuries, and the men who have been most greatly used of God, you will find that, every time, they have been men who have taken the Sermon on the Mount not only seriously but literally. You read the life of a man like Hudson Taylor and you will find he literally lived it, and he is not the only one. These things were taught by the Lord and were meant for us, His people. This is how the Christian is meant to live.

There was a time when the designation applied to the Christian was that he was a 'God-fearing' man. I do not think you can ever improve on that — a 'God-fearing' man. It does not mean craven fear, it does not mean 'the fear that hath torment', but it is a wonderful description of the true Christian. He is of necessity, as we are reminded very forcibly in the seventh chapter of this Gospel, a man who lives in the fear of God. We can say of our blessed Lord Himself that His life was a God-fearing life. You see how important that view of the Christian is. So often, as I have been pointing out, modern Christians, who may be able to give very bright and apparently thrilling testimonies of some experience they have had, do not suggest that they are God-fearing people, but give the impression of being men of the world, both in dress and appearance, and in a kind of boisterousness and easy confidence.

So we must not only take the injunctions of the Sermon seriously. We must also check our particular interpretation in the light of the principles I have given. Beware of the spirit of arguing against them; beware of making them ridiculous; and beware of so interpreting them as to regard any one of them as impossible. Here is the life to which we are called, and I maintain again that if only every Christian in the Church today were living the Sermon on the Mount, the great revival for which we are praying and longing would already have started. Amazing and astounding things would happen; the world would be shocked, and men and women would be drawn and attracted to our Lord and Saviour Jesus Christ.

May God give us grace to consider this Sermon on the Mount and to remember that we are not to sit in judgment on it, but that we ourselves are under judgment, and that the building we are erecting in this world and in this life will have to face His final test and the ultimate scrutiny of the eye of the Lamb of God that once was slain.

Chapter Three

An Introduction to the Beatitudes

W E have now finished our general analysis of the Sermon and so can begin to consider this first section, the Beatitudes, this delineation of the Christian man in his essential features and characteristics. I am not, as I have said, concerned with the argument whether there are seven, eight or nine Beatitudes. What matters is not how many Beatitudes there are, but that we should be perfectly clear as to what is said about the Christian. First I want to look at this in general, because again I feel there are certain aspects of this truth which can only be grasped as we take it as a whole. In biblical study, it should invariably be the rule that you must start with the whole before you begin to pay attention to the parts. There is nothing so likely to lead to heresy and error as to start with the parts rather than the whole. The only man who is at all capable of carrying out the injunctions of the Sermon on the Mount is the man who is perfectly clear in his mind with regard to the essential character of the Christian. Our Lord says that this is the only kind of person who is truly 'blessed', that is, 'happy'. Someone has suggested that it might be put like this; this is the sort of man who is to be congratulated, this is the sort of man to be envied, for he alone is truly happy.

Happiness is the great question confronting mankind. The whole world is longing for happiness and it is tragic to observe the ways in which people are seeking it. The vast majority, alas, are doing so in a way that is bound to produce misery. Anything which, by evading the difficulties, merely makes people happy for the time being, is ultimately going to add to their misery and problems. That is where the utter deceitfulness of sin comes in; it is always offering happiness, and it always leads to unhappiness and to final misery and wretchedness. The Sermon on the Mount says, however, that if you really want to be happy, here is the way. This and this alone is the type of person who is truly happy, who is really blessed. This is the sort of person who is to be congratulated. Let us look at him, then, in general, by taking a kind of synoptic view of these Beatitudes before we come to deal with them one by one. It will be seen that I am adopting a somewhat leisurely procedure with this Sermon and I am doing so quite deliberately. I have already referred to the people who are anxiously wanting to know what is going to be said about 'going the second mile', for example. No; we need to spend a long time with 'the poor in spirit' and 'the meek' and terms such as these before we go on to those interesting questions which are so thrilling and exciting. We are to be interested primarily in character before we consider conduct.

There are certain general lessons, I suggest, to be drawn from the Beatitudes. First, *all Christians are to be like this.* Read the Beatitudes, and there you have a description of what every Christian is meant to be. It is not merely the description of some exceptional Christians. Our Lord does not say here that He is going to paint a picture of what certain outstanding characters are going to be and can be in this world. It is His description of every single Christian.

I pause with that for just a moment, and emphasize it, because I think we must all agree that the fatal tendency introduced by the Roman Catholic Church, and indeed by every branch of the Church that likes to use the term 'Catholic', is the fatal tendency to divide Christians into two groups — the religious and the laity, exceptional Christians and ordinary Christians, the one who makes a vocation of the Christian life and the man who is engaged in secular affairs. That tendency is not only utterly and completely unscriptural; it is destructive ultimately of true piety, and is in many ways a negation of the gospel of our Lord Jesus Christ. There is no such distinction in the Bible. There are distinctions in offices — apostles, prophets, teachers, pastors, evangelists, and so on. But these Beatitudes are not a description of offices; they are a description of character. And from the standpoint of character, and of what we are meant to be, there is no difference between one Christian and another. Let me put it like this. It is the Roman Catholic Church that canonizes certain people, not the New Testament. Read the introduction to almost any New Testament Epistle and you will find all believers addressed as in the Epistle to the Church at Corinth, 'called to be saints'. All are 'canonized', if you want to use the term, not some Christians only. The idea that this height of the Christian life is meant only for a chosen few, and that the rest of us are meant to live on the dull plains, is an entire denial of the Sermon on the Mount, and of the Beatitudes in particular. We are all meant to exemplify everything that is contained here in these Beatitudes. Therefore let us once and for ever get rid of that false notion. This is not merely a description of the Hudson Taylors or the George Müllers or the

Whitefields or Wesleys of this world; it is a description of every Christian. We are all of us meant to conform to its pattern and to rise to its standard.

The second principle I would put in this form; *all Christians are meant to manifest all of these characteristics.* Not only are they meant for all Christians, but of necessity, therefore, all Christians are meant to manifest all of them. In other words it is not that some are to manifest one characteristic and others to manifest another. It is not right to say some are meant to be 'poor in spirit', and some are meant to 'mourn', and some are meant to be 'meek', and some are meant to be 'peacemakers', and so on. No; every Christian is meant to be all of them, and to manifest all of them, at the same time. Now I think it is true and right to say that in some Christians some will be more manifest than others; but that is not because it is *meant* to be so. It is just due to the imperfections that still remain in us. When Christians are finally perfect, they will all manifest all these characteristics fully; but here in this world, and in time, there is a variation to be seen. I am not justifying it; I am simply recognizing it. The point I am emphasizing is that we are every one of us meant to manifest all of them together and at the same time. Indeed, I think we can even go further and say that the character of this detailed description is such, that it becomes quite obvious, the moment we analyse each Beatitude, that each one of necessity implies the other. For instance, you cannot be 'poor in spirit' without 'mourning' in this sense; and you cannot mourn without 'hungering and thirsting after righteousness'; and you cannot do that without being one who is 'meek' and a 'peacemaker'. Each one of these in a sense demands the others. It is impossible truly to manifest one of these graces, and to conform to the blessing that is pronounced upon it, without at the same time inevitably showing the others also. The Beatitudes are a complete whole and you cannot divide them; so that, whereas one of them may be more manifest perhaps in one person than in another, all of them are there. The relative proportions may vary, but they are all present, and they are all meant to be present at the same time.

That is a vitally important principle. But the third is perhaps even more important. *None of these descriptions refers to what we may call a natural tendency.* Each one of them is wholly a disposition which is produced by grace alone and the operation of the Holy Spirit upon us. I cannot emphasize this too strongly. No man naturally conforms to the descriptions here given in the Beatitudes, and we must be very careful to draw a sharp distinction between the spiritual qualities that are here described and material ones which appear to be like them. Let me put it like this. There are some people who appear to be naturally 'poor in spirit'; that is not what is described here by our Lord. There are people who appear to be naturally 'meek'; when we deal with that statement I hope to be able to show you that the meekness which Christ talks about is not that which appears to be natural meekness in an ordinary unregenerate person. These are not natural qualities; nobody by birth and by nature is like this.

This is a rather subtle matter and people are often in difficulty about it in this way. They say, 'I know a person who does not claim to be a Christian, never goes to a place of worship, never reads the Bible, never prays, and frankly tells us he is not interested in these things at all. But, you know, I have a feeling that he is more of a Christian than many people who do go to a place of worship and who do pray. He is always nice and polite, never says a harsh word or expresses an unkind judgment, and is always doing good.' Such people look at certain characteristics in the person they are considering and say, 'There are the Beatitudes obviously staring me in the face; this person must be a Christian though he denies the entire faith.' That is the kind of confusion that often arises through failure to be clear at this particular point. In other words, it will be our business to show that what we have here in each individual case is not a description of a natural temper, it is rather a disposition that is produced by grace.

Take this man who by nature appears to be such a fine Christian. If that is really a condition or a state which conforms to the Beatitudes, I suggest it is quite unfair, for it is a matter of natural temperament. Now a man does not determine his natural temperament, though he governs it up to a point. Some of us are born aggressive, others are quiet; some are alert and fiery, others are slow. We find ourselves as we are, and these nice people who are so frequently brought forward as an argument against the evangelical faith are in no sense responsible for being like that. The explanation of their condition is something biological; it has nothing to do with spirituality, and nothing to do with man's relationship to God. It is purely animal and physical. As people differ in their physical appearance, so they differ in temperament; and if that is what determines whether a man is a Christian or not, I say it is totally unfair.

But, thank God, that is not the position at all. Any one of us, every one of us, whatever we may be by birth and nature, is meant as a Christian to be like this. And not only are we meant to be like this; we can be like this. That is the central glory of the gospel. It can take the proudest man by nature and make him a man who is poor in spirit. There have been some wonderful and glorious examples of that. I would suggest there has never been a naturally prouder man than John Wesley; but he became a man who was poor in spirit. No; we are not concerned about natural dispositions or what is purely physical and animal, or what appears to simulate the Christian character. I am hoping to be able to show you this when we come to an analysis of these things, and I think you will very soon see the essential difference between them. Here are characteristics and dispositions that are the result of grace, the product of the Holy Spirit, and therefore possible for all. They cut right across all natural states and natural dispositions. That, I think you will agree, is a vital and essential principle, so that as we come to look at these individual descriptions, not only must we not confuse them with natural tempers, but we must be very careful at the same time not to define them in such terms. All along we must be drawing our distinction in a spiritual manner and on the basis of the New Testament teaching.

Let us now consider the next principle. These descriptions, I suggest, indicate clearly (perhaps more clearly than anything else in the entire realm of Scripture) *the essential, utter difference between the Christian and the non-Christian.* This is the thing that should really concern us; and that is why I say it is most important to consider this Sermon on the Mount. This is not just a description of what a man does; the real point is this difference between the Christian and the non-Christian. The New Testament regards that as something absolutely basic and fundamental; and, as I see things at the present time, the first need in the Church is a clear understanding of this essential difference. It has become blurred; the world has come into the Church and the Church has become worldly. The line is not as distinct as it was. There were times when the distinction was clear-cut, and those have always been the greatest eras in the history of the Church. We know, however, the arguments that have been put forward. We have been told that we have to make the Church attractive to the man outside, and the idea is to become as much like him as we can. There were certain popular padres during the First World War who mixed with their men, and smoked with them, and did this, that, and the other with them, in order to encourage them. Some people thought that, as a result, when the war was over, the ex-servicemen would be crowding into the churches. Yet it did not happen, and it never has happened that way. The glory of the gospel is that when the Church is absolutely different from the world, she invariably attracts it. It is then that the world is made to listen to her message, though it may hate it at first. That is how revival comes. That must also be true of us as individuals. It should not be our ambition to be as much like everybody else as we can, though we happen to be Christian, but rather to be as different from everybody who is not a Christian as we can possibly be. Our ambition should be to be like Christ, the more like Him the better, and the more like Him we become, the more we shall be unlike everybody who is not a Christian.

Let me show you this in detail. The Christian and the non-Christian are absolutely different in what they admire. The Christian admires the man who is 'poor in spirit', while the Greek philosophers despised such a man, and all who follow Greek philosophy, whether intellectually or practically, still do exactly the same thing. What the world says about the true Christian is that he is a weakling, an apology for a man, or that he isn't manly. Those are its expressions. The world believes in self-confidence, self-expression and the mastery of life; the Christian believes in being 'poor in spirit'. Take the newspapers and see the kind of person the world admires. You will never find anything that is further removed from the Beatitudes than that which appeals to the natural man and the man of the world. What calls forth his admiration is the very antithesis of what you find here. The natural man likes an element of boastfulness, but that is the very thing that is condemned in the Beatitudes.

Then, obviously, they must be different in what they seek. 'Blessed are they which do hunger and thirst.' After what? Wealth, money, status, position, publicity? Not at all. 'Righteousness.' And righteousness is being right with God. Take any man who does not claim to be a Christian and who is not interested in Christianity. Find out what he is seeking and what he really wants, and you will see it is always different from this.

Then, of course, they are absolutely different in what they do. That follows of necessity. If they admire and seek different things, they very clearly do different things. The result is that the life which is lived by the Christian must be an essentially different life from that of the man who is not a Christian. The non-Christian is absolutely consistent. He says he lives for this world. 'This', he says, 'is the only world, and I am going to get all I can out of it.' Now the Christian starts by saying he is not living for this world; he regards this world as but the way of entry into something vast and eternal and glorious. His whole outlook and ambition is different. He feels, therefore, that he must be living in a different way. As the man of the world is consistent, so the Christian also ought to be consistent. If he is, he will be very different from the other man; he cannot help it. Peter puts it perfectly in the second chapter of his first Epistle when he says that if we truly believe that we are a people who have been called 'out of darkness into his marvellous light', we must believe that this has happened to us in order that we might show forth His praises. Then he goes on to say: 'I beseech you as strangers and pilgrims (those of you who are in this world), abstain from fleshly lusts, which war against the soul; having your conversation honest among the Gentiles: that, whereas they speak against you as evildoers, they may by your good works, which they shall behold, glorify God in the day of visitation' (1 Pet. 2:11, 12). That is nothing but an appeal to their sense of logic.

Another essential difference between men is in their belief as to what they *can* do. The man of the world is very confident as to his own capacity and is prepared to do anything. The Christian is a man, and the only man in the world, who is truly aware of his own limitations.

I hope to deal with these things in detail in later chapters, but these are some of the essential, obvious, surface differences between the Christian and the non-Christian. There is nothing, surely, which exhorts us more than this Sermon on the Mount to be what we are meant to be, and to live as we are meant to live; to be like Christ by being a complete contrast to everyone who does not belong to Christ. I trust, therefore, that any of us who may have been guilty of trying to be like the man of the world in any respect will not do so any longer and will see what an utter contradiction it is of our faith.

Perhaps I can put it all finally in this concept. The truth is that *the Christian and the non-Christian belong to two entirely different realms.* You will notice the first Beatitude and the last Beatitude promise the same reward, 'for theirs is the kingdom of heaven.' What does this mean? Our Lord starts and ends with it because it is His way of saying that the first thing you have to realize about yourself is that you belong to a different kingdom. You are not only different in essence; you are living in two absolutely different worlds. You are in this world; but you are not of it. You are among those other people, yes; but you are citizens of another kingdom. This is the vital thing that is emphasized everywhere in this passage.

What is meant by this kingdom of heaven? You will find certain people saying that there is a difference between the 'kingdom of heaven' and the 'kingdom of God'; but my difficulty is to know what the difference is. Why does Matthew talk about the kingdom of heaven rather than the kingdom of God? Surely the answer is that he was writing primarily for the Jews, and to the Jews, and his chief object, perhaps, was to correct the Jewish conception of the kingdom of God or the kingdom of heaven. They had got into this materialistic way of looking at the kingdom; they were thinking of it politically and in a military sense, and our Lord's whole object here is to show that His kingdom is primarily a spiritual one. In other words He says to them, 'You must not think of this kingdom primarily as anything earthly. It is a kingdom in the heavens, which is certainly going to affect the earth in many different ways, but it is essentially spiritual. It belongs to the heavenly rather than to the earthly and human sphere.' What is this kingdom, then? It means, in its essence, Christ's rule or the sphere and realm in which He is reigning. It can be considered in three ways as follows. Many times when He was here in the days of His flesh our Lord said that the kingdom of heaven was already present. Wherever He was present and exercising authority, the kingdom of heaven was there. You remember how on one occasion, when they charged Him with casting out devils by the power of Beelzebub, He showed them the utter folly of that, and then went on to say, 'If I cast out devils by the Spirit of God, then the kingdom of God is come unto you' (Matt. 12: 28). Here is the kingdom of God. His authority, His reign was actually in practice. Then there is His phrase when He said to the Pharisees, 'the kingdom of God is within you', or, 'the kingdom of God is among you'. It was as though He were saying, 'It is being manifested in your midst. Don't say "look here" or "look there". Get rid of this materialistic view. I am here amongst you; I am doing things. It is here.' Wherever the reign of Christ is being manifested, the kingdom of God is there. And when He sent out His disciples to preach, He told them to tell the cities which received them not, 'Be ye sure of this, that the kingdom of God is come nigh unto you.'

It means that; but it also means that the kingdom of God is present at this moment in all who are true believers. The Roman Catholic Church has tended to identify this kingdom with the Church, but that is not right, because the Church contains a mixed multitude. The kingdom of God is only present in the Church in the hearts of true believers, in the hearts of those who have submitted to Christ and in whom and among whom He reigns. You remember how the apostle Paul puts it in language reminiscent of that of Peter. In writing to the Colossians he gives thanks to the Father 'who hath delivered us from the power of darkness, and hath translated us into the kingdom of his dear Son' (Col. 1:13). The 'kingdom of his dear Son' is 'the kingdom of God', it is 'the kingdom of heaven', it is this new kingdom into which we have entered. Or, again, in his letter to the Philippians he says, 'Our conversation is in heaven,' or, 'Our citizenship is in heaven.' We are here on earth, we obey the powers that be, we live our lives in this way. Yes; but 'our citizenship is in heaven; from whence also we wait for a Saviour' (Phil. 3:20, RV). We who recognize Christ as our Lord, and in whose lives He is reigning and ruling at this moment, are in the kingdom of heaven and the kingdom of heaven is in us. We have been translated into the 'kingdom of his dear Son'; we have become a 'kingdom of priests'.

The third and last way of looking at the kingdom is this. There is a sense in which it is yet to come. It has come; it is coming; it is to come. It was here when He was exercising authority; it is here in us now; and yet it is to come. It will come when this rule and reign of Christ will be established over the whole world even in a physical and material sense.

The day is coming when the kingdoms of this world will have become 'the kingdoms of our Lord, and of his Christ', when

Jesus shall reign where'er the sun
Doth his successive journeys run;
His kingdom stretch from shore to shore,
Till moons shall wax and wane no more.

It will then have come, completely and entirely, and everything will be under His dominion and sway. Evil and Satan will be entirely removed; there will be 'new heavens and a new earth, wherein dwelleth righteousness' (2 Pet. 3:13), and then the kingdom of heaven will have come in that material way. The spiritual and the material will become one in a sense, and all things will be subject to His sway, that 'at the name of Jesus every knee should bow, of things in heaven, and things in earth, and things under the earth; and that every tongue should confess that Jesus Christ is Lord, to the glory of God the Father' (Phil. 2:10, 11).

There, then, is the general account of the Christian which is given in the Beatitudes. Do you see how essentially different he is from the non-Christian? The vital questions which we therefore ask ourselves are these. Do we belong to this kingdom? Are we ruled by Christ? Is He our King and our Lord? Are we manifesting these qualities in our daily lives? Is it our ambition to do so? Do we see that this is what we are meant to be? Are we truly blessed? Are we happy? Have we been filled? Have we got peace? I ask, as we have looked together at the general description, what do we find ourselves to be? It is only the man who is like that who is truly happy, the man who is truly blessed. It is a simple question. My immediate reaction to these Beatitudes proclaims exactly what I am. If I feel they are harsh and hard, if I feel that they are against the grain and depict a character and type of life which I dislike, I am afraid it just means I am not a Christian. If I do not want to be like this, I must be 'dead in trespasses and sins'; I can never have received new life. But if I feel that I am unworthy and yet I want to be like that, well, however unworthy I may be, if this is my desire and my ambition, there must be new life in me, I must be a child of God, I must be a citizen of the kingdom of heaven and of God's dear Son.

Let every man examine himself.

Chapter Four

Blessed Are the Poor in Spirit

W E come now to a consideration of the first of the Beatitudes, 'Blessed are the poor in spirit: for theirs is the kingdom of heaven.' As I have already indicated in our last study, it is not surprising that this is the first, because it is obviously, as I think we shall see, the key to all that follows. There is, beyond any question, a very definite order in these Beatitudes. Our Lord does not place them in their respective positions haphazardly or accidentally; there is what we may describe as a spiritual logical sequence to be found here. This, of necessity, is the one which must come at the beginning for the good reason that there is no entry into the kingdom of heaven, or the kingdom of God, apart from it. There is no one in the kingdom of God who is not *poor in spirit*. It is the fundamental characteristic of the Christian and of the citizen of the kingdom of heaven, and all the other characteristics are in a sense the result of this one. As we go on to expound it, we shall see that it really means an emptying, while the others are a manifestation of a fullness. We cannot be filled until we are first empty. You cannot fill with new wine a vessel which is partly filled already with old wine, until the old wine has been poured out. This, then, is one of those statements which remind us that there has to be a kind of emptying before there can be a filling. There are always these two sides to the gospel; there is a pulling down and a raising up. You remember the words of the ancient Simeon concerning our Lord and Saviour when he held Him as an Infant in his arms. He said, 'this child is set for the fall and rising again of many.' The fall comes before the rising again. It is an essential part of the gospel that conviction must always precede conversion; the gospel of Christ condemns before it releases. Now that is obviously something which is fundamental. If you prefer me to put it in a more theological and doctrinal form, I would say that there is no more perfect statement of the doctrine of justification by faith only than this Beatitude:

33

'Blessed are the poor in spirit: for theirs (and theirs only) is the kingdom of heaven.' Very well then, this is the foundation of everything else.

But not only that. It is obviously, therefore, a very searching test for every one of us, not only as we face ourselves, but especially as we come to face the whole message of the Sermon on the Mount. You see, it at once condemns every idea of the Sermon on the Mount which thinks of it in terms of something that you and I can do ourselves, something that you and I can carry out. It negatives that at the very beginning. That is where it is such an obvious condemnation of all those views which we considered earlier, which think of it as being a new law, or in terms of bringing in a kingdom amongst men. We do not hear so much of that talk now, but it still lingers and it was very popular in the early part of this century. Men talked about 'bringing in the kingdom', and always used as their text the Sermon on the Mount. They thought of the Sermon as something that can be applied. You have to preach it and then men immediately proceed to put it into practice. But this view is not only dangerous, it is an utter denial of the Sermon itself, which starts with this fundamental proposition about being 'poor in spirit'. The Sermon on the Mount, in other words, comes to us and says, 'There is the mountain that you have to scale, the heights you have to climb; and the first thing you must realize, as you look at that mountain which you are told you must ascend, is that you cannot do it, that you are utterly incapable in and of yourself, and that any attempt to do it in your own strength is proof positive that you have not understood it.' It condemns at the very outset the view which regards it as a programme for man to put into operation immediately, just as he is.

Before we go on to deal with it from what we might call a more spiritual standpoint, there is one matter concerning the rendering of this verse which has to be considered. There are those who tell us that it should read 'Blessed in spirit are the poor'. They seem to derive a certain amount of justification for that from the parallel passage in Luke 6:20, where you will read, 'Blessed be ye poor' without any mention of 'poor in spirit'. So they would regard it as a commendation of poverty. But surely that must be entirely wrong. The Bible nowhere teaches that poverty as such is a good thing. The poor man is no nearer to the kingdom of heaven than the rich man, speaking of them as natural men. There is no merit or advantage in being poor. Poverty does not guarantee spirituality. Clearly, therefore, the passage cannot mean that. And if you take the whole paragraph in Luke 6, I think it becomes perfectly clear that our Lord was even there speaking of 'poor' as meaning 'not being possessed by the worldly spirit', poor in the sense, if you like, that you do not rely upon riches. That is the thing that is condemned, this reliance on riches as such. And obviously there are many poor people who rely upon riches exactly as many rich people do. They say, 'If only I had so-and-so', and they are jealous of those who have it. Now if they are in that condition they are not blessed. So it cannot be poverty as such.

I have had to emphasize this point because most of the Roman Catholic commentators and their imitators in Anglicanism are very fond of interpreting this statement in that sense. They regard it as scriptural authority for the assumption of voluntary poverty. Their patron saint is Francis of Assisi and they regard him and his type as those who alone conform to the statement of this Beatitude. They say that it refers to those who have deliberately made themselves poor, and turned their backs upon wealth. You will find that the late Bishop Gore in his book on the Sermon on the Mount definitely teaches that. It is the characteristic 'Catholic' interpretation of this particular statement. But obviously, for the reasons I have been deducing, that is to do violence to Scripture.

What our Lord is concerned about here is the spirit; it is poverty *of spirit*. In other words, it is ultimately a man's attitude towards himself. That is the thing that matters, not whether he is wealthy or poor. Now here we have a perfect illustration of one of those general principles that we laid down earlier when we said that these Beatitudes indicate more clearly than anything else in Scripture the utter and essential difference between the natural man and the Christian. We saw that there is a clear-cut division between these two kingdoms — the kingdom of God and the kingdom of this world, the Christian man and the natural — a complete, absolute distinction and division. Now there is perhaps no statement that underlines and emphasizes that difference more than this 'Blessed are the poor in spirit'. Let me show you the contrast. This is something which is not only not admired by the world; it is despised by it. You will never find a greater antithesis to the worldly spirit and outlook than that which you find in this verse. What emphasis the world places on its belief in self-reliance, self-confidence and self-expression! Look at its literature. If you want to get on in this world, it says, believe in yourself. That idea is absolutely controlling the life of men at the present time. Indeed I would say it is controlling the whole of life outside the Christian message. What, for instance, is the essence of good salesmanship according to modern ideas? It is giving the impression of confidence and assurance. If you want to impress your customer that is the way you must do it. The same idea is put into practice in every realm. If you want to succeed in a profession, the great thing is to give the impression that you are a success, so you suggest that you are more successful than you actually are, and people say, 'That is the man to go to'. That is the whole principle on which life is run at the present time — express yourself, believe in yourself, realize the powers that are innate in yourself and let the whole world see and know them. Self-confidence, assurance, self-reliance. And it is in terms of that fundamental belief that men think they can bring in the kingdom; it is the whole basis of the fatal assumption that by Acts of Parliament alone you can produce a perfect society. Everywhere we see displayed this tragic confidence in the power of education and knowledge as such to save men, to transform them and make them into decent human beings.

Now in this verse we are confronted by something which is in utter and absolute contrast to that, and it is tragic to see how people view this kind of statement. Let me quote the criticism which a man offered a few years ago on that famous hymn of Charles Wesley, 'Jesu, Lover of my soul'. You will remember the verse in which Wesley says:

> Just and holy is Thy name,
>   I am all unrighteousness;
> Vile and full of sin I am,
>   Thou art full of truth and grace.

This he ridiculed and asked, 'What man desiring a post or job would dream of going to an employer and saying to him, "Vile and full of sin I am"? Ridiculous!' And he said it, alas, in the name of what he regards as Christianity. You see what a complete misunderstanding of this first Beatitude that reveals. As I am going to show you, we are not looking at men confronting one another, but we are looking at men face-to-face with God. And if one feels anything in the presence of God save an utter poverty of spirit, it ultimately means that you have never faced Him. That is the meaning of this Beatitude.

But neither is this Beatitude popular in the Church today. It was this I had in mind earlier when I regretted the amazing and obvious contrast between so much that is true of the Church now and that which was true in past ages, especially in the Puritan era. There is nothing so unchristian in the Church today as this foolish talk about 'personality'. Have you noticed it — this tendency to talk about the 'personality' of speakers and to use such phrases as 'What a wonderful personality that man has'? Incidentally, it is tragic to observe the way in which those who speak thus seem to define personality. It is generally something purely fleshly and carnal, and a matter of physical appearance.

But, and this is still more serious, this attitude is generally based upon a confusion between self-confidence, self-assurance and self-expression on the one hand, and true personality on the other. Indeed, I have noticed at times a tendency even to fail to appreciate what is regarded by the Bible as the greatest virtue of all, namely, humility. I have heard people on a Committee discuss a certain candidate and say, 'Yes, very good; but he is rather lacking in personality,' when my opinion of that particular candidate was that he was humble. There is a tendency rather to exalt a certain aggressiveness and self-assurance, and to justify a man's making use of himself and his own personality and trying to put it forward, or as the horrible phrase has it, 'to put it across'. The advertisements that are being increasingly used in connection with Christian work proclaim this tendency very loudly. You read the old records of the activities of God's greatest workers, the great evangelists and others, and you observe how self-effacing they were. But, today, we are experiencing something that is almost a complete reversal of this. Advertisements and photographs[1] are being put into the foreground.

What does it mean? 'We preach not ourselves,' says Paul, 'but Christ Jesus the Lord.' When he went to Corinth, he tells us, he went 'in weakness, and in fear, and in much trembling'. He did not step onto the platform with confidence and assurance and ease, and give the impression of a great personality. Rather, the people said of him, 'His appearance is weak and his speech contemptible.' How far we tend to wander from the truth and the pattern of the Scriptures. Alas! How the Church is allowing the world and its methods to influence and control her outlook and life. To be 'poor in spirit' is not as popular even in the Church as it once was and always should be. Christian people must rethink these matters. Let us not take things on their face value; let us above all avoid being captivated by this worldly psychology; and let us realize from the outset that we are in the realm of a kingdom which is unlike everything that belongs to this 'present evil world'.

Let us come more positively to this subject, however. What does it mean to be poor in spirit? Once more let me give you certain negatives. To be 'poor in spirit' does not mean that we should be diffident or nervous, nor does it mean that we should be retiring, weak or lacking in courage. There are certain people, it is true, who, reacting against this self-assertion which the world and the Church foolishly describe as 'personality', think that it does mean just that. We have all met those naturally unobtrusive people who, far from pushing themselves forward, always stand in the background. They are born like that and may even be naturally weak, retiring and lacking in a sense of courage. We emphasized earlier the fact that none of the things which are indicated in the Beat-

1. I was interested to observe, since stating the above, Bishop Frank Houghton's tribute in *The Christian* to the late Miss Amy Carmichael. He points out how one who made such free use of pictures and photographs in all her books never once inserted a photograph of herself.

itudes are natural qualities. To be 'poor in spirit', therefore, does not mean that you are born like that. Let us get rid of that idea once and for ever.

Neither does it mean that we are to become what I can best describe as imitators of Uriah Heep. Many, again, have mistaken being 'poor in spirit' for that. I remember once having to go to preach at a certain town. When I arrived on the Saturday evening, a man met me at the station and immediately asked for my bag, indeed he almost took it from my hand by force. Then he talked to me like this. 'I am a deacon in the church where you are preaching tomorrow', he said, and then added, 'You know, I am a mere nobody, a very unimportant man, really. I do not count; I am not a great man in the Church; I am just one of those men who carry the bag for the minister.' He was anxious that I should know what a humble man he was, how 'poor in spirit'. Yet by his anxiety to make it known he was denying the very thing he was trying to establish. Uriah Heep — the man who thus, as it were, glories in his poverty of spirit and thereby proves he is not humble. It is an affectation of something which he obviously does not feel. This is a danger which confronts many people, though not as much today as once it did. There was a time when it was the curse of the Church, and affected men's very appearance and even their gait! It did great harm to the cause of Christ, and the moderns have reacted violently against it, and in some cases have obviously gone to the other extreme. I am far from being a defender of clerical dress; but if I had to defend either it or the attire of a man who deliberately goes out of his way to avoid giving the impression that he is a minister, I should undoubtedly defend clerical dress. I heard a man describing a minister of religion the other day and he seemed to be greatly impressed by the fact that the minister did not look like one. 'He does not look like a preacher,' he said. 'He looks like a prosperous man of affairs.' I am not interested in men's personal appearance, but I am suggesting that a man of God should not look like a 'prosperous man of affairs', and he certainly should not go out of his way to give that impression. That but shows that he has far too great a concern about himself and the impression he is making. No, no; we are not to be concerned about these things; we are to be concerned about the spirit. The man who is truly 'poor in spirit' need not worry so much about his personal appearance and the impression he makes; he will always give the right impression.

Then again, to be 'poor in spirit' is not a matter of the suppression of personality. This also is very important. There are those who would agree with all we have been saying but who would then interpret being 'poor in spirit' in that way and would urge the necessity for a man to repress his true personality. This is a great subject which can best be illustrated here by taking one example. The type of thing we are considering is seen in the story of Lawrence of Arabia. You will remember that in his attempt to efface himself and to suppress his own personality he went to the extent of even changing his name and becoming 'Aircraftman Shaw' — just an ordinary man in the Royal Air Force. You recall how he met his death tragically in a bicycle accident, and how he was hailed as a wonderful example of humility and self-abnegation. Now to be poor in spirit does not mean that you have to do that sort of thing. It does not mean that you have to change your name and falsely crucify yourself or assume another character and personality in life. That is utterly unscriptural and quite unchristian. That kind of behaviour often impresses the world, and even impresses Christians also, for they regard it as wonderfully humble. You will find that there is always this subtle temptation to think that the only man who is truly 'poor in spirit' is the man who makes a great sacrifice, or, after the manner of the monks, retires out of life and its difficulties and responsibilities. But that is not the biblical way. You do not have to go out of life in order to be 'poor in spirit'; you do not have to change your name. No; it is something in the realm of your spirit.

We can go one step further and say that to be 'poor in spirit' is not even to be humble in the sense in which we speak of the humility of great scholars. Generally speaking, the truly great thinker is a humble man. It is 'a little learning' that 'is a dangerous thing'. Now to be 'poor in spirit' does not mean that, because that humility is produced by an awareness of the vastness of knowledge and is not of necessity a true humility of spirit in the scriptural sense.

If those are the negatives then what is the positive aspect of being 'poor in spirit'? I think the best way to answer that question is to put it in terms of Scripture. It is what Isaiah said (57:15): 'For thus saith the high and lofty One that inhabiteth eternity, whose name is Holy; I dwell in the high and holy place, with him also that is of a contrite and humble spirit, to revive the spirit of the humble, and to revive the heart of the contrite ones.' That is the quality of spirit, and you have endless illustrations of it in the Old Testament. It was the spirit of a man like Gideon, for instance, who, when the Lord sent an angel to him to tell him the great thing he was to do, said, 'No, no, this is impossible; I belong to the lowest tribe and to the lowest family in the tribe.' That was not Uriah Heep, it was a man who really believed what he said and who shrank from the very thought of greatness and honour, and thought it was incredible. It was the spirit of Moses, who felt deeply unworthy of the task that was laid upon him and was conscious of his insufficiency and inadequacy. You find it in David, when he said, 'Lord, who am I that thou shouldst come to me?' The thing was incredible to him; he was astonished by it. You get it in Isaiah in exactly the same way. Having had a vision, he said, 'I am a man of unclean lips'. That is to be 'poor in spirit', and it can be seen right through the Old Testament.

But let us look at it in the New Testament. You see it perfectly, for instance, in a man like the apostle Peter who was naturally aggressive, self-assertive, and self-confident — a typical modern man of the world, brimful of this confidence and believing in himself. But look at him when he truly sees the Lord. He says, 'Depart from me; for I am a sinful man, O Lord.' Look at him afterwards as he pays his tribute to the apostle Paul, in 2 Peter 3:15, 16. But observe that he never ceases to be a bold man; he does not become nervous and diffident. No, he does not change in that way. The essential personality remains; and yet he is 'poor in spirit' at the same time. Or look at it as you see it in the apostle Paul. Here was a man, again with great powers, and obviously, as a natural man, fully aware of them. But in reading his Epistles you will find that the fight he had to wage to the end of his life was the fight against pride. That is why he kept on using the word 'boasting'. Any man gifted with powers is generally aware of them; he knows he can do things, and Paul knew this. He has told us in that great third chapter of the Epistle to the Philippians about his confidence in the flesh. If it is a question of competition, he seems to say, he fears no one; and then he gives us a list of the things of which he can boast. But having once seen the risen Lord on the road to Damascus all that became 'loss', and this man, possessed of such tremendous powers, appeared in Corinth, as I have already reminded you, 'in weakness and fear and much trembling'. That is the position right through, and as he goes on with the task of evangelism, he asks, 'Who is sufficient for these things?' If any man had a right to feel 'sufficient' it was Paul. Yet he felt insufficient because he was 'poor in spirit'.

But, of course, we see this most of all as we look at the life of our Lord Himself. He became a Man, He took upon Him 'the likeness of sinful flesh'. Though He was equal with God He did not clutch at the prerogatives of His Godhead. He decided that while He was here on earth He would live as a man, though He was still God. And this was the result. He said, 'I can do nothing of myself.' It is the God-Man speaking. 'I can do nothing of myself.' He said also, 'The words that I speak unto you I speak not of myself: but the Father that dwelleth in me, he doeth the works' (John 14:10). 'I can do nothing, I am utterly dependent upon Him.' That is it. And look at His prayer life. It is as you watch Him praying, and realize the hours He spent in prayer, that you see His poverty of spirit and His reliance upon God.

That, then, is what is meant by being 'poor in spirit'. It means a complete absence of pride, a complete absence of self-assurance and of self-reliance. It means a consciousness that we are nothing in the presence of God. It is nothing, then, that we can produce; it is nothing that we can do in ourselves. It is just this tremendous awareness of our utter nothingness as we come face-to-face with God. That is to be 'poor in spirit'. Let me put it as strongly as I can, and I do so on the basis of the teaching of the Bible. It means this, that if we are truly Christian we shall not rely upon our natural birth. We shall not rely upon the fact that we belong to certain families; we shall not boast that we belong to certain nations or nationalities. We shall not build upon our natural temperament. We shall not believe in and rely upon our natural position in life, or any powers that may have been given to us. We shall not rely upon money or any wealth we may have. The thing about which we shall boast will not be the education we have received, or the particular school or college to which we may have been. No, all that is what Paul came to regard as 'dung', and a hindrance to this greater thing because it tended to master and control him. We shall not rely upon any gifts like that of natural 'personality', or intelligence or general or special ability. We shall not rely upon our own morality and conduct and good behaviour. We shall not bank to the slightest extent on the life we have lived or are trying to live. No; we shall regard all that as Paul regarded it. That is 'poverty of spirit'. There must be a complete deliverance from and absence of all that. I say again, it is to feel that we are nothing, and that we have nothing, and that we look to God in utter submission to Him and in utter dependence upon Him and His grace and mercy. It is, I say, to experience to some extent what Isaiah experienced when, having seen the vision, he said, 'Woe is me! . . . I am a man of unclean lips' — that is 'poverty of spirit'. As we find ourselves in competition with other men in this world we say, 'I am a match for them'. Well, that is all right in that realm, if you like. But when a man has some conception of God, he of necessity feels 'as one dead', as did the apostle John on the Isle of Patmos, and we must feel like that in the presence of God. Any natural spirit that is in us goes out, because it is not only exposed in its smallness and weakness, but its sinfulness and foulness become apparent at the same time.

Let us then ask ourselves these questions. Am I like that, am I poor in spirit? How do I really feel about myself as I think of myself in terms of God, and in the presence of God? And as I live my life, what are the things I am saying, what are the things I am praying about, what are the things I like to think of with regard to myself? What a poor thing it is, this boasting of the things that are accidental and for which I am not responsible, this boasting of things that are artificial and that will count as nothing at the great day when we stand in the presence of God. This poor self! That hymn of Lavater's puts it perfectly: 'Make this poor self grow less and less', and 'O Jesus Christ, grow Thou in me.'

How does one therefore become 'poor in spirit'? The answer is that you do not look at yourself or begin by trying to do things to yourself. That was the whole error of monasticism. Those poor men in their desire to do this said, 'I must go out of society, I must scarify my flesh and suffer hardship, I must mutilate my body.' No, no, the more you do that the more conscious will you be of yourself, and the less 'poor in spirit'. The way to become poor in spirit is to look at God. Read this Book about Him, read His law, look at what He expects from us, contemplate standing before Him. It is also to look at the Lord Jesus Christ and to view Him as we see Him in the Gospels. The more we do that the more we shall understand the reaction of the apostles when, looking at Him and something He had just done, they said, 'Lord, increase our faith.' Their faith, they felt, was nothing. They felt it was so weak and so poor. 'Lord, increase our faith. We thought we had something because we had cast out devils and preached Thy word, but now we feel we have nothing; increase our faith.' Look at Him; and the more we look at Him, the more hopeless shall we feel by ourselves, and in and of ourselves, and the more shall we become 'poor in spirit'. Look at Him, keep looking at Him. Look at the saints, look at the men who have been most filled with the Spirit and used. But above all, look again at Him, and then you will have nothing to do to yourself. It will be done. You cannot truly look at Him without feeling your absolute poverty, and emptiness. Then you say to Him,

> Nothing in my hand I bring,
> Simply to Thy cross I cling.

Empty, hopeless, naked, vile. But *He* is the all-sufficient One —

> Yea, all I need, in Thee to find,
> O Lamb of God, I come.

Chapter Five

Blessed Are They That Mourn

WE come now to a consideration of the second Beatitude — 'Blessed (or happy) are they that mourn: for they shall be comforted.' This, like the first, stands out at once, and marks off the Christian as being quite unlike the man who is not a Christian and who belongs to the world. Indeed the world would, and does, regard a statement like this as utterly ridiculous — Happy are those who mourn! The one thing the world tries to shun is mourning; its whole organization is based on the supposition that that is something to avoid. The philosophy of the world is, Forget your troubles, turn your back upon them, do everything you can not to face them. Things are bad enough as they are without your going to look for troubles, says the world; therefore be as happy as you can. The whole organization of life, the pleasure mania, the money, energy and enthusiasm that are expended in entertaining people, are all just an expression of the great aim of the world to get away from this idea of mourning and this spirit of mourning. But the gospel says, 'Happy are they that mourn.' Indeed they are the only ones who are happy! If you turn to the parallel passage in Luke 6 you will find it is put in a still more striking manner, because there the negative is employed. 'Woe unto you that laugh now!' our Lord says, 'for ye shall mourn and weep.' This saying condemns the apparent laughter, joviality and happiness of the world by pronouncing a woe upon it. But it promises blessing and happiness, joy and peace to those who mourn. These preliminary statements, then, concerning the Christian are obviously of primary importance.

Once more it is clear, that we have here something which is entirely spiritual in its meaning. Our Lord did not say that those who mourn in a natural sense are happy, meaning by 'mourning', the sorrow experienced because of the death of someone. No, this is a spiritual mourning. As we saw that poverty of spirit was not something financial, but something essentially spiritual, so this

43

<u>again is something entirely spiritual and has nothing to do with our natural life</u> <u>in this world</u>. <u>All these Beatitudes have reference to a spiritual condition and to a spiritual attitude</u>. Those who are commended are those who mourn in spirit; they, says our Lord, are the happy people.

This, as we have seen, is something which is never found in the world, and it presents a striking contrast to what is found there. But, again, I am constrained to say that this is something which is not as evident in the Church today as it once was and as it is in the New Testament. In a sense, as I said earlier, that is really our main reason for considering this Sermon on the Mount. We are concerned about the state and life of the Church at the present time. I have no hesitation again in asserting that the failure of the Church to have a greater impact upon the life of men and women in the world today is due entirely to the fact that her own life is not in order. To me there is nothing more tragic or shortsighted or lacking in insight than the assumption, made by so many, that the Church herself is all right and all she has to do is to evangelize the world outside. Every revival proves clearly that men who are outside the Church always become attracted when the Church herself begins to function truly as the Christian Church, and as individual Christians approximate to the description here given in these Beatitudes. So we must start with ourselves, and see why, unfortunately, this description of the Christian as one who 'mourns' is one that makes us feel that somehow or another this is not as evident in the Church today as it once was.

The explanation of this is fairly obvious. It is partly a reaction against the kind of false puritanism (I say *false* puritanism, not puritanism) which, let us be frank, was too much in evidence towards the end of the last century and the beginning of the present one. It often manifested itself in an assumed piety. It was not natural; it did not come from within; but people affected and assumed a pious appearance. It almost gave the impression that to be religious was to be miserable; it turned its back upon many things that are perfectly natural and legitimate. In that way a picture was given of the Christian man that was not attractive, and, I think, there has been a violent reaction against it, a reaction so violent that it has gone to the other extreme.

But I also think that another explanation of this is the idea which has gained currency that if we as Christians are to attract those who are not Christian we must deliberately affect an appearance of brightness and joviality. Thus many try to assume a kind of joy and happiness which is not something that rises from within, but is something which is put on. Now probably that is the main explanation of the absence of this characteristic of mourning in the life of the Church today. It is this superficiality, this glibness or joviality that is almost unintelligent. It is this endeavour to appear to be something and to cut a certain figure, instead of a life arising from within, which controls and determines the whole of our appearance and behaviour.

I sometimes think, however, that the ultimate explanation of it all is something still deeper and still more serious. I cannot help feeling that the final explanation of the state of the Church today is a defective sense of sin and a defective doctrine of sin. Coupled with that, of course, is a failure to understand the true nature of Christian joy. There is the double failure. There is not the real, deep conviction of sin as was once the case; and on the other hand there is this superficial conception of joy and happiness which is very different indeed from that which we find in the New Testament. Thus the defective doctrine of sin and the shallow idea of joy, working together, of necessity produce a superficial kind of person and a very inadequate kind of Christian life.

Now this is obviously extremely important, especially as regards the matter of evangelism. It is not surprising that the Church is failing in her mission if her dual conception of sin and joy are thus defective and inadequate. And, therefore, it comes to pass that so much evangelism, whether organized on a large or a small scale (in spite of all that is claimed for it in figures and results), is obviously not affecting the life of the Church deeply. Indeed, the very statistics prove the failure in this respect. For this reason it is surely a very fundamental subject for us to consider. That is why it is so important that we should approach it all in terms of this Sermon on the Mount, which starts with negatives. We have to be poor in spirit before we can be filled with the Holy Spirit. Negative, before positive. And here again is another example of exactly the same thing — conviction must of necessity precede conversion, a real sense of sin must come before there can be a true joy of salvation. Now that is the whole essence of the gospel. So many people spend all their lives in trying to find this Christian joy. They say they would give the whole world if they could only find it, or could be like some other person who has it. Well, I suggest that in ninety-nine cases out of a hundred this is the explanation. They have failed to see that they must be convicted of sin before they can ever experience joy. They do not like the doctrine of sin. They dislike it intensely and they object to its being preached. They want joy apart from the conviction of sin. But that is impossible; it can never be obtained. Those who are going to be converted and who wish to be truly happy and blessed are those who first of all mourn. Conviction is an essential preliminary to true conversion.

It is of the greatest importance, then, that we should know exactly what our Lord means when He thus says, 'Happy are those who mourn.' We shall discover the answer as we look at the teaching of the New Testament in general with regard to this subject. Let us start, for instance, with our Lord Himself. We, as Christians, are made, we are told by the Bible, after the image and the pattern of the Lord Himself. A Christian is one who is to be like the Lord Jesus Christ. He is 'the first-born among many brethren'; that is the ultimate standard of what you and I are to be like. Very well; let us look at Him. What do we find?

One thing we observe is that we have no record anywhere that He ever laughed. We are told He was angry; we are told that He suffered from hunger and thirst; but there is actually no record of laughter in His life. I know an argument from silence can be a dangerous one, and yet we must pay due attention to that fact. We remember the prophecy concerning Him in the book of the prophet Isaiah, where we are told He was to be a 'man of sorrows, and acquainted with grief', that His visage would be so marred that none would desire Him. That is the prophecy concerning Him, and as you look at these accounts of Him in the New Testament Gospels you will see that the prophecy was literally fulfilled. There is an indication in John 8:57, that our Lord looked very much older than He actually was. You remember He had said, 'Abraham rejoiced to see my day' and they looked at Him and said, 'Thou art not yet fifty years old, and hast thou seen Abraham?' This was spoken to one just over thirty, and I tend to agree with the interpreters who argue from this statement that our Lord looked much older than He really was. There is, then, no record of laughter in His life. But we are told that He wept at the grave of Lazarus (John 11:35). That was not because His friend was dead, because He had gone to raise Him from the dead. He knew that in a moment Lazarus was going to live again. No, it is something very different, something we are going to consider together. We are told also that He wept over Jerusalem as He looked at the city just before the end (see Luke 19:41-44). That is the picture which you find as you look at our Lord in these Gospels, and we are meant to be like Him. Compare it, not only with the world, but also with this assumed brightness and joviality which so many Christians seem to think is the right portrait of the Christian. I think you will see at once the amazing and striking contrast. There is nothing of that in our Lord.

Again, let us look at the teaching of the apostle Paul as it is to be seen, for example, in Romans 7. We are to be like this apostle, and like the other apostles and the saints of all centuries, if we are to be truly Christian. Let us remember, then, that the Christian is a man who knows what it is to cry out, 'O wretched man that I am! who shall deliver me from the body of this death?' That tells us something of what is meant by mourning. Here is a man who was so grief-stricken about himself that he cries out in that agony. All Christians are meant to be like that. A Christian man knows that experience of feeling utterly hopeless about himself, and says about himself, as did Paul, 'In me (that is, in my flesh,) dwelleth no good thing'. He knows the experience of being able to say, 'the good that I would I do not: but the evil which I would not, that I do'. He is fully aware of this conflict between the law in the mind and the law in the members, and all this wretched struggling and striving. But listen again to what Paul says in Romans 8. You know there are some people who consider that what is described in Romans 7 was only a phase in Paul's experience, and that he left it, turned over a new leaf and went to the eighth chapter of Romans where he no longer knew what it was to mourn. But this is what I read in verse 23 of that chapter, 'And not only they, but ourselves also, which have the firstfruits of the Spirit, even we ourselves groan within ourselves, waiting for the adoption, to wit, the redemption of our body.' Or, again, writing in 2 Corinthians 5, he says that 'we that are in this tabernacle do groan, being burdened': he describes himself as 'earnestly desiring to be clothed upon with our house which is from heaven'. He puts all this even more explicitly in the Pastoral Epistles, in which he writes to Timothy and Titus to tell them how they are to teach other people. He says that 'the aged men' are to be 'sober, grave, temperate'. Indeed even 'the young men' are to be 'sober minded'. There is none of your glib joviality and brightness here. Even young Christians ought not to affect this appearance of such a wonderful joy that they always wear a bright smile on their face in order to show the world how happy they are.

I have selected these few passages at random. I could supplement them from the writings of the other New Testament writers. What does it all mean? I think the best way we can put it is this. To 'mourn' is something that follows of necessity from being 'poor in spirit'. It is quite inevitable. As I confront God and His holiness, and contemplate the life that I am meant to live, I see myself, my utter helplessness and hopelessness. I discover my quality of spirit and immediately that makes me mourn. I must mourn about the fact that I am like that. But obviously it does not stop there. A man who truly faces himself, and examines himself and his life, is a man who must of necessity mourn for his sins also, for the things he does. Now the great experts in the life of the spirit have always recommended self-examination. They all recommend and practise it themselves. They say it is a good thing for every man to pause at the end of the day and meditate upon himself, to run quickly over his life, and ask, 'What have I done, what have I said, what have I thought, how have I behaved with respect to others?' Now if you do that any night of your life, you will find that you have done things which you should not have done, you will be conscious of having harboured thoughts and ideas and feelings which are quite unworthy. And, as he realizes these things, any man who is at all Christian is smitten with a sense of grief and sorrow that he was ever capable of such things in action or in thought, and that makes him mourn. But he does not stop merely at things he has done, he meditates upon and contemplates his actions and his state and condition of

47

sinfulness, and as he thus examines himself he must go through that experience of Romans 7. He must become aware of these evil principles that are within him. He must ask himself, 'What is it in me that makes me behave like that? Why should I be irritable? Why should I be bad tempered? Why am I not able to control myself? Why do I harbour that unkind, jealous and envious thought? What is it in me?' And he discovers this war in his members, and he hates it and mourns because of it. It is quite inevitable. Now this is not imagination; it is actual experience and true to fact. It is a very thoroughgoing test. If I object to this kind of teaching, it just means that I do not mourn and therefore I am not one of the people who, our Lord says, are blessed. If I regard this as nothing but morbidity, something a man should not do, then I am simply proclaiming the fact that I am not spiritual, and that I am unlike the apostle Paul and all the saints, and I am contradicting the teaching of the Lord Jesus Christ Himself. But if I bemoan these things in myself, I am truly mourning.

Yet the Christian does not stop even at that. The man who is truly Christian is a man who mourns also because of the sins of others. He does not stop at himself. He sees the same thing in others. He is concerned about the state of society, and the state of the world, and as he reads his newspaper he does not stop at what he sees or simply express disgust at it. He mourns because of it, because men can so spend their life in this world. He mourns because of the sins of others. Indeed, he goes beyond that and mourns over the state of the whole world as he sees the moral muddle and unhappiness and suffering of mankind, and reads of wars and rumours of wars. He sees that the whole world is in an unhealthy and unhappy condition. He knows that it is all due to sin; and he mourns because of it.

That is why our Lord Himself mourned, that is why He was 'a man of sorrows, and acquainted with grief'; that is why He wept at the grave of Lazarus. He saw this horrid, ugly, foul thing called sin which had come into life and introduced death into life, and had upset life and made life unhappy. He wept because of that; He groaned in His spirit. And as He saw the city of Jerusalem rejecting Him and bringing upon itself its own damnation, He wept because of it. He mourned over it and so does His true follower, the one who has received His nature. In other words, he must mourn because of the very nature of sin itself, because it has ever entered into the world and has led to these terrible results. Indeed he mourns because he has some understanding of what sin means to God, of God's utter abhorrence and hatred of it, this terrible thing that would stab, as it were, into the heart of God, if it could, this rebelliousness and arrogance of man, the result of listening to Satan. It grieves him and he mourns because of it.

There, then, is the New Testament teaching with respect to this matter.

That is what is meant by mourning in this spiritual sense in the New Testament. Perhaps we can best put it like this. It is the very antithesis of the spirit and mind and outlook of the world, which, as our Lord puts it, 'laughs now'. Look at the world outside, even in a time of war. It still tries to go on not looking at the true situation, ignoring it and being happy. 'Let us eat, drink, and be merry', is its motto. It laughs, and says, 'Don't dwell too much upon these things'. To mourn is the exact opposite. The Christian man's attitude is essentially different.

We do not stop at this point, however, otherwise our description of the Christian is going to be an incomplete one. Our Lord in these Beatitudes makes a complete statement and it must be taken as such. 'Blessed are they that mourn', He says, 'for they shall be comforted.' The man who mourns is really happy, says Christ; that is the paradox. In what respect is he happy? Well, he becomes happy in a personal sense. The man who truly mourns because of his sinful state and condition is a man who is going to repent; he is, indeed, actually repenting already. And the man who truly repents as the result of the work of the Holy Spirit upon him, is a man who is certain to be led to the Lord Jesus Christ. Having seen his utter sinfulness and hopelessness, he looks for a Saviour, and he finds Him in Christ. No one can truly know Him as his personal Saviour and Redeemer unless he has first of all known what it is to mourn. It is only the man who cries out, 'O wretched man that I am! who shall deliver me?' who can go on to say, 'I thank God through Jesus Christ our Lord.' Now this is something that follows as the night the day. If we truly mourn, we shall rejoice, we shall be made happy, we shall be comforted. For it is when a man sees himself in this unutterable hopelessness that the Holy Spirit reveals unto him the Lord Jesus Christ as his perfect satisfaction. Through the Spirit he sees that Christ has died for his sins and is standing as his advocate in the presence of God. He sees in Him the perfect provision that God has made and immediately he is comforted. That is the astounding thing about the Christian life. Your great sorrow leads to joy, and without the sorrow there is no joy.

Now this is not only true at conversion; it is something that continues to be true about the Christian. He finds himself guilty of sin, and at first it casts him down and makes him mourn. But that in turn drives him back to Christ; and the moment he goes back to Christ, his peace and happiness return and he is comforted. So that here is something that is fulfilled at once. The man who mourns truly is comforted and is happy; and thus the Christian life is spent in this way, mourning and joy, sorrow and happiness, and the one should lead to the other immediately.

But there is not only this immediate comfort offered to the Christian.

There is another comfort, that which we may call 'the blessed hope', elaborated by the apostle Paul in Romans 8 to which we have already made reference. He says that at the present moment even we who 'have the firstfruits of the Spirit, even we ourselves groan within ourselves, waiting for the adoption, to wit, the redemption of our body'. 'For we are saved by hope', he continues, and we are confident that 'the sufferings of this present time are not worthy to be compared with the glory which shall be revealed'. In other words, as the Christian looks at the world, and even as he looks at himself, he is unhappy. He groans in spirit; he knows something of the burden of sin as seen in the world which was felt by the apostles and by the Lord Himself. But he is immediately comforted. He knows there is a glory coming; he knows that a day will dawn when Christ will return, and sin will be banished from the earth. There will be 'new heavens and a new earth, wherein dwelleth righteousness'. O blessed hope! 'Blessed are they that mourn: for they shall be comforted.'

But what hope has the man who does not believe these things? What hope has the man who is not a Christian? Look at your world; read your newspaper. What can you bank upon? Fifty years ago they used to bank on the fact that man was rapidly improving and getting better. You cannot do that now. You cannot bank on education; you cannot bank on the United Nations any more than you could on the League of Nations. All that has been tried and failed. What hope is there for the world? There is none. There is no comfort for the world now. But for the Christian man who mourns because of sin and because of the state of the world, there is this comfort — the comfort of the blessed hope, the glory that yet remains. So that even here, though he is groaning, he is happy at the same time because of the hope that is set before him. There is this ultimate hope in eternity. In that eternal state we shall be wholly and entirely blessed, there will be nothing to mar life, nothing to detract from it, nothing to spoil it. Sorrow and sighing shall be no more; all tears shall be wiped away; and we shall bask for ever and ever in the eternal sunshine, and experience joy and bliss and glory unmixed and unspoiled. 'Happy are they that mourn: for they shall be comforted.' How true it is. Unless we know that, we are not Christian. If we are Christian, we do know it, this joy of sins forgiven and the knowledge of it; the joy of reconciliation; the joy of knowing that God takes us back when we have fallen away from Him; the joy and contemplation of the glory that is set before us; the joy that comes from anticipation of the eternal state.

Let us, then, try to define this man who mourns. What sort of a man is he? He is a sorrowful man, but he is not morose. He is a sorrowful man, but he is not a miserable man. He is a serious man, but he is not a solemn man. He is a sober-minded man, but he is not a sullen man. He is a grave man, but he is never cold or prohibitive. There is with his gravity a warmth and attraction. This man, in other words, is always serious; but he does not have to affect the seriousness. The true Christian is never a man who has to put on an appearance of either sadness or joviality. No, no; he is a man who looks at life seriously; he contemplates it spiritually, and he sees in it sin and its effects. He is a serious, soberminded man. His outlook is always serious, but because of these views which he has, and his understanding of truth, he also has 'a joy unspeakable and full of glory'. So he is like the apostle Paul, 'groaning within himself', and yet happy because of his experience of Christ and the glory that is to come. The Christian is not superficial in any sense, but is fundamentally serious and fundamentally happy. You see, the joy of the Christian is a holy joy, the happiness of the Christian is a serious happiness. None of that superficial appearance of happiness and joy! No, no; it is a solemn joy, it is a holy joy, it is a serious happiness; so that, though he is grave and sober-minded and serious, he is never cold and prohibitive. Indeed, he is like our Lord Himself, groaning, weeping, and yet, 'for the joy that was set before him' enduring the cross, despising the shame.

That is the man who mourns; that is the Christian. That is the type of Christian seen in the Church in ages past, when the doctrine of sin was preached and emphasized, and men were not merely urged to take a sudden decision. A deep doctrine of sin, a high doctrine of joy, and the two together produce this blessed, happy man who mourns, and who at the same time is comforted. The way to experience that, obviously, is to read the Scriptures, to study and meditate upon them, to pray to God for His Spirit to reveal sin in us to ourselves, and then to reveal to us the Lord Jesus Christ in all His fullness. 'Blessed are they that mourn: for they shall be comforted.'

Chapter Six

Blessed Are the Meek

I N our consideration of the Beatitudes as a whole, we have already found that there are certain general characteristics which apply to them all. As we come to study each Beatitude separately we find that this proves to be so in detail. Here once more, therefore, we must point out that this Beatitude, this particular description of the Christian, causes real surprise because it is so completely and entirely opposed to everything which the natural man thinks. 'Blessed are the meek: for they shall inherit the earth.' World conquest — possession of the whole universe — given to the meek, of all people! The world thinks in terms of strength and power, of ability, self-assurance and aggressiveness. That is the world's idea of conquest and possession. The more you assert yourself and express yourself, the more you organize and manifest your powers and ability, the more likely you are to succeed and get on. But here comes this astounding statement, 'Blessed are the meek: for they shall inherit the earth' — and they alone. Once more, then, we are reminded at the very beginning that the Christian is altogether different from the world. It is a difference in quality, an essential difference. He is a new man, a new creation; he belongs to an entirely different kingdom. And not only is the world unlike him; it cannot possibly understand him. He is an enigma to the world. And if you and I are not, in this primary sense, problems and enigmas to the non-Christians around us, then this tells us a great deal about our profession of the Christian faith.

This statement must have come as a great shock to the Jews of our Lord's own day; and there can be no doubt, as we agreed at the beginning, that Matthew was writing primarily for the Jews. He places the Beatitudes in the forefront of the Gospel for that reason. They had ideas of the kingdom which, you remember, were not only materialistic but military also, and to them the Messiah was one who was going to lead them to victory. So they were thinking in terms of conquest and fighting in a material sense, and immediately our Lord dismisses all that. It is as though He says, 'No, no, that is not the way. I am not like that, and my kingdom is not like that.' — 'Blessed are the meek: for they shall inherit the earth.' It is a great contrast to the Jews' way of thinking.

But further, this Beatitude comes, alas, in the form of a very striking contrast to much thinking within the Christian Church at the present time. For is there not a rather pathetic tendency to think in terms of fighting the world, and sin, and the things that are opposed to Christ, by means of great organizations? Am I wrong when I suggest that the controlling and prevailing thought of the Christian Church throughout the world seems to be the very opposite of what is indicated in this text? 'There', they say, 'is the powerful enemy set against us, and here is the divided Christian Church. We must all get together, we must have one huge organization to face that organized enemy. Then we shall make an impact, and then we shall conquer.' But 'Blessed are the *meek*', not those who trust to their own organizing, not those who trust to their own powers and abilities and their own institutions. Rather it is the very reverse of that. And this is true, not only here, but in the whole message of the Bible. You get it in that perfect story of Gideon where God went on reducing the numbers, not adding to them. That is the spiritual method, and here it is once more emphasized in this amazing statement in the Sermon on the Mount.

As we approach this statement let us first of all try to look at it in its relationship to the other Beatitudes. Clearly it follows on from what has gone before. There is an obvious logical connection between these different Beatitudes. Each one suggests the next and leads to the next. They are not spoken haphazardly. There is first of all that fundamental postulate about being 'poor in spirit'. That is the primary fundamental spirit that leads in turn to a condition of mourning as we become aware of our sin; and that in turn leads to this spirit of meekness. But — and I want to emphasize this — we not only find this logical connection between them. I would point out, also, that these Beatitudes as they proceed become increasingly difficult. In other words, what we are now considering is more searching, more difficult, more humbling and even more humiliating than anything we have looked at hitherto in our consideration of this Sermon on the Mount. We can look at it like this. The first Beatitude asks us to realize our own weakness and our own inability. It confronts us with the fact that we have to face God, not only in the Ten Commandments and the moral law, but also in the Sermon on the Mount, and in the life of Christ Himself. Anybody who feels that he, by his own strength, can accomplish all that, has not started to be a Christian. No, it makes us feel we have nothing; we become 'poor in spirit', we are truly helpless. Anyone who thinks that he can live the Christian life himself is proclaiming that he is not a Christian. When we realize truly what we have to be, and what we have to do, we become inevitably 'poor in spirit'. That in turn leads to that second state in which, realizing our own sinfulness and our own true nature, realizing that we are so helpless because of the indwelling of sin within us, and seeing the sin even in our best actions, thoughts and desires, we mourn and we cry out with the great apostle, 'O wretched man that I am! who shall deliver me from the body of this death?' But here, I say, is something which is still more searching — 'Blessed are the meek'.

Now why is this? Because here we are reaching a point at which we begin to be concerned about other people. Let me put it like this. I can see my own utter nothingness and helplessness face-to-face with the demands of the gospel and the law of God. I am aware, when I am honest with myself, of the sin and the evil that are within me, and that drag me down. And I am ready to face both these things. But how much more difficult it is to allow other people to say things like that about me! I instinctively resent it. We all of us prefer to condemn ourselves than to allow somebody else to condemn us. I say of myself that I am a sinner, but instinctively I do not like anybody else to say I am a sinner. That is the principle that is introduced at this point. So far, I myself have been looking at myself. Now, other people are looking at me, and I am in a relationship to them, and they are doing certain things to me. How do I react to that? That is the matter which is dealt with at this point. I think you will agree that this is more humbling and more humiliating than everything that has gone before. It is to allow other people to put the searchlight upon me instead of my doing it myself.

Perhaps the best way of approaching this is to look at it in terms of certain examples. Who is this meek person? What is he like? Well, there are many illustrations one can give. I have merely selected some which I regard as the most important and striking. Take certain of the Old Testament characters, for instance. Look at the portrait of that great gentleman — in many ways, I think, the greatest gentleman in the Old Testament — Abraham, and as you look at him you see a great and wonderful portrait of meekness. It is the great characteristic of his life. You remember his behaviour with respect to Lot, and how he allows the younger man to assert himself and take the first choice and does it without a murmur and without a complaint — that is meekness. You see it again in Moses, who is actually described as the meekest man on the face of the earth. Examine his character and you see the same thing, this lowly conception of himself, this readiness not to assert himself but rather to humble and to abase himself — meekness. There were wonderful possibilities ahead of him, all the possibility of the court of Egypt and his position as the son of Pharaoh's daughter. But how truly he evaluated it all, saw it as it was, and humbled himself completely to God and His will.

The same is true of David, especially in his relations with Saul. David knew he was to be king. He had been informed, he had been anointed; and yet how he suffered Saul and Saul's unjust and unkind treatment of him! Read the story of David again and you will see meekness exemplified in a most extraordinary manner. Again, take Jeremiah and the unpopular message that was given to him. He was called upon to speak the truth to the people — not the thing he wanted to do — while the other prophets were saying smooth and easy things. He was isolated. He was an individualist — non-cooperative they would call him today — because he did not say what everybody else was saying. He felt it all bitterly. But read his story. See how he suffered it all and allowed the unkind things to be said about him behind his back, and how he went on delivering his message. It is a wonderful example of meekness.

Come, however, to the New Testament, and here you will see it again and again. Look at the portrait of Stephen and you will see this text illustrated. Look at it in the case of Paul, that mighty man of God. Consider what he suffered at the hands of these different churches and at the hands of his own countrymen and various other people. As you read his letters you will see this quality of meekness coming out, and especially as he writes to the members of the church at Corinth who had been saying such unkind and disparaging things about him. It is again a wonderful example of meekness. But of course we must come to the supreme example, and stand and look at our Lord Himself. 'Come unto me,' He said, 'all ye that labour . . . and I will give you rest . . . I am meek and lowly in heart.' You see it in the whole of His life. You see it in His reaction to other people, you see it especially in the way He suffered persecution and scorn, sarcasm and derision. Rightly was it said of Him, 'A bruised reed shall he not break, and smoking flax shall he not quench.' His attitude towards His enemies, but perhaps still more His utter submission to His Father, show His meekness. He said, 'The words that I speak unto you, I speak not of myself', and 'the Father that dwelleth in me, he doeth the works'. Look at Him in the Garden of Gethsemane. Look at the portrait of Him which we find in Philippians 2 where Paul tells us that He did not regard His equality with God as a prerogative at which to clutch or something to hold on to at all costs. No, He decided to live as a Man, and He did. He humbled Himself, became as a servant and even went to the death on the cross. That is meekness; that is lowliness; that is true humility; that is the quality which He Himself is teaching at this point.

Well then, what is meekness? We have looked at the examples. What do we see in them? First, let us notice again that it is not a natural quality. It is not a matter of a natural disposition, because all Christians are meant to be like this. It is not only some Christians. Every Christian, whatever his natural temperament or psychology may be, is meant to be like this. Now we can prove that very easily. Take these various characters whom I have mentioned, apart from our Lord Himself, and I think you will find that in every case we have a man who was not like this by nature. Think of the powerful, extraordinary nature of a man like David, and yet observe his meekness. Jeremiah similarly lets us into the secret. He says he was almost like a boiling cauldron, and yet he was still meek. Look at a man like the apostle Paul, a master mind, an extraordinary personality, a strong character; yet consider his utter humility and meekness. No, it is not a matter of natural disposition; it is something that is produced by the Spirit of God.

Let me emphasize it by putting it like this. Meekness does not mean indolence. There are people who appear to be meek in a natural sense; but they are not meek at all, they are indolent. That is not the quality of which the Bible is speaking. Nor does it mean flabbiness — I use the term advisedly. There are people who are easygoing, and you tend to say how meek they are. But it is not meekness; it is flabbiness. Nor does it mean niceness. There are people who seem to be born naturally nice. That is not what the Lord means when He says, 'Blessed are the meek.' That is something purely biological, the kind of thing you get in animals. One dog is nicer than another, one cat is nicer than another. That is not meekness. So it does not mean to be naturally nice or easy to get on with. Nor does it mean weakness in personality or character. Still less does it mean a spirit of compromise or 'peace at any price'. How often are these things mistaken. How often is the man regarded as meek who says, 'Anything rather than have a disagreement. Let's agree, let's try to break down these distinctions and divisions; let's smooth over these little things that divide; let's all be nice and joyful and happy.'

No, no, it is not that. Meekness is compatible with great strength. Meekness is compatible with great authority and power. These people we have looked at have been great defenders of the truth. The meek man is one who may so believe in standing for the truth that he will die for it if necessary. The martyrs were meek, but they were never weak; strong men, yet meek men. God forbid that we should ever confuse this noble quality, one of the noblest of all the qualities, with something merely animal or physical or natural.

My last negative would be that meekness is not merely a matter of outward manner, but also, and still more, of inward spirit. A well-known hymn which inculcates the spirit of meekness tells us to 'stay the angry blow', and of course it is right. But if we are to be truly meek we must not only 'stay the angry blow', we must get into that state and condition in which we do not feel like doing it at all.

We must control the lips and the mouth, and not say the things we feel like saying. You cannot spend time with a verse like this without its humbling you. It is true Christianity; it is the thing for which we are called and for which we are meant.

What, then, is meekness? I think we can sum it up in this way. Meekness is essentially a true view of oneself, expressing itself in attitude and conduct with respect to others. It is therefore two things. It is my attitude towards myself; and it is an expression of that in my relationship to others. You see how inevitably it follows being 'poor in spirit' and 'mourning'. A man can never be meek unless he is poor in spirit. A man can never be meek unless he has seen himself as a vile sinner. These other things must come first. But when I have that true view of myself in terms of poverty of spirit, and mourning because of my sinfulness, I am led on to see that there must be an absence of pride. The meek man is not proud of himself, he does not in any sense glory in himself. He feels that there is nothing in himself of which he can boast. It also means that he does not assert himself. You see, it is a negation of the popular psychology of the day which says 'assert yourself', 'express your personality'. The man who is meek does not want to do so; he is so ashamed of it. The meek man likewise does not demand anything for himself. He does not take all his rights as claims. He does not make demands for his position, his privileges, his possessions, his status in life. No, he is like the man depicted by Paul in Philippians 2. 'Let this mind be in you, which was also in Christ Jesus.' Christ did not assert that right to equality with God; He deliberately did not. And that is the point to which you and I have to come.

Then let me go further; the man who is meek is not even sensitive about himself. He is not always watching himself and his own interests. He is not always on the defensive. We all know about this, do we not? Is it not one of the greatest curses in life as a result of the fall — this sensitivity about self? We spend the whole of our lives watching ourselves. But when a man becomes meek he has finished with all that; he no longer worries about himself and what other people say. To be truly meek means we no longer protect ourselves, because we see there is nothing worth defending. So we are not on the defensive; all that is gone. The man who is truly meek never pities himself, he is never sorry for himself. He never talks to himself and says, 'You are having a hard time, how unkind these people are not to understand you'. He never thinks: 'How wonderful I really am, if only other people gave me a chance.' Self-pity! What hours and years we waste in this! But the man who has become meek has finished with all that. To be meek, in other words, means that you have finished with yourself altogether, and you come to see you have no rights or deserts at all. You come to realize that nobody can harm you. John Bunyan puts it perfectly. 'He that is down need fear no fall.' When a man truly sees himself, he knows nobody can say anything about him that is too bad. You need not worry about what men may say or do; you know you deserve it all and more. Once again, therefore, I would define meekness like this. The man who is truly meek is the one who is amazed that God and man can think of him as well as they do and treat him as well as they do. That, it seems to me, is its essential quality.

It must then go on and express itself in our whole demeanour and in our behaviour with respect to others. It does so like this. A person who is of the type that I have been describing must of necessity be mild. Think again of the examples; think again of the Lord Jesus Christ. Mild, gentle, lowly— those are the terms. Quiet, of a quiet spirit — I have already quoted the terms — 'meek and lowly'. In a sense the most approachable Person this world has ever seen was the Lord Jesus Christ. But it also means that there will be a complete absence of the spirit of retaliation, having our own back or seeing that the other person pays for it. It also means, therefore, that we shall be patient and long-suffering, especially when we suffer unjustly. You remember how Peter puts that in the second chapter of his first Epistle, that we should 'follow his steps: who did no sin, neither was guile found in his mouth: who, when he was reviled, reviled not again; when he suffered, he threatened not; but committed himself to him that judgeth righteously'. It means patience and long-suffering even when we are suffering unjustly. There is no credit, Peter argues in that chapter, if, when we are buffeted for our faults, we take it patiently; but if we do well and suffer for it and take it patiently, then that is the thing that is praiseworthy in the sight of God. That is meekness. But it also means that we are ready to listen and to learn; that we have such a poor idea of ourselves and our own capabilities that we are ready to listen to others. Above all we must be ready to be taught by the Spirit, and led by the Lord Jesus Christ Himself. Meekness always implies a teachable spirit. It is what we see again in the case of our Lord Himself. Though he was the Second Person in the blessed Holy Trinity, He became man, He deliberately humbled Himself to the extent that He was dependent entirely upon what God gave Him, what God taught Him and what God told Him to do. He humbled Himself to that, and that is what is meant by being meek. We must be ready to learn and listen and especially must we surrender ourselves to the Spirit.

Finally, I would put it like this. We are to leave everything — ourselves, our rights, our cause, our whole future — in the hands of God, and especially so if we feel we are suffering unjustly. We learn to say with the apostle Paul that our policy must be this, 'Vengeance is mine; I will repay, saith the Lord'. We need not repay, we just deliver ourselves into the hands of God. The Lord will revenge; He will repay. We have nothing to do. We leave ourselves and our cause, and our rights and everything with God, with a quietness in spirit and in mind and heart. Now all this, we shall see later, is something that is abundantly illustrated in the various detailed teachings of this Sermon on the Mount.

Now notice what happens to the man who is like this. 'Blessed are the meek; *for they shall inherit the earth.*' What does that mean? We can summarize it very briefly. The meek already inherit the earth in this life, in this way. A man who is truly meek is a man who is always satisfied, he is a man who is already content. Goldsmith expresses it well when he says: 'Having nothing yet hath all.' The apostle Paul has put it still better, for he says, 'as having nothing, and yet possessing all things.' Again, in writing to the Philippians, he says in effect, 'Thank you for sending your present. I like it, not because I wanted anything, but I like the spirit that made you send it. Yet as for myself, I have all things and abound.' He has already said to them, 'I know both how to be abased, and I know how to abound' and 'I can do all things through Christ which strengtheneth me'. Notice, too, the striking way in which he expresses the same thought in 1 Corinthians 3. After telling his readers that they need not be jealous or concerned about these things, he says, 'All things are yours', everything; 'whether Paul, or Apollos, or Cephas, or the world, or life, or death, or things present, or things to come; all are yours; and ye are Christ's; and Christ is God's.' All things are yours if you are meek and truly Christian; you have already inherited the earth.

But obviously it has a future reference also. 'Do ye not know', says Paul again to these Corinthians, in 1 Corinthians 6, 'do ye not know that the saints shall judge the world?' You are going to judge the world, you are going to judge angels. You will then have inherited the earth. In Romans 8, he puts it this way. We are children, 'and if children, then heirs; heirs of God, and joint-heirs with Christ.' That is it; we are going to inherit the earth. 'If we suffer', he says to Timothy, 'we shall also reign with him.' In other words, 'Do not be worried about your suffering, Timothy. You be meek and suffer and you shall reign with Him. You are going to inherit the earth with Him.' But I think it is all to be found in those words of our Lord in Luke 14:11: 'Whosoever exalteth himself shall be abased; and he that humbleth himself shall be exalted.'

There, then, is what is meant by being meek. Need I emphasize again that this is obviously something that is quite impossible to the natural man? We shall never make ourselves meek. The poor people who went off and made themselves monks were trying to make themselves meek. We shall never do it. It cannot be done. Nothing but the Holy Spirit can humble us, nothing but the Holy Spirit can make us poor in spirit and make us mourn because of our sinfulness and produce in us this true, right view of self and give us this very mind of Christ Himself. But this is a serious matter. Those of us who claim to be Christian claim of necessity that we have already received the Holy Spirit. Therefore we have no excuse for not being meek. The man who is outside has an excuse, for it is impossible to him. But if we truly claim that we have received the Holy Spirit, and this is the claim of every Christian, we have no excuse if we are not meek. It is not something that you do and I do. It is a character that is produced in us by the Spirit. It is the direct fruit of the Spirit. It is offered to us and it is possible for us all. What have we to do? We must face this Sermon on the Mount; we must meditate upon this statement about being meek; we must look at the examples; above all we must look at the Lord Himself. Then we must humble ourselves and confess with shame, not only the smallness of our stature, but our utter imperfection. Then we must finish with that self which is the cause of all our troubles, so that He who has bought us at such a price may come in and possess us wholly.

Chapter Seven

Righteousness and Blessedness

T HE Christian's concern is to view life in this world in the light of the gospel; and, according to the gospel, the trouble with mankind is not any one particular manifestation of sin, but rather sin itself. If you are anxious about the state of the world and the threat of possible wars, then I assure you that the most direct way of avoiding such calamities is to observe words such as these which we are now considering, 'Blessed are they which do hunger and thirst after righteousness: for they shall be filled.' If every man and woman in this world knew what it was to 'hunger and thirst after righteousness' there would be no danger of war. Here is the only way to real peace. All other considerations eventually do not touch the problem, and all the denunciations that are so constantly made of various countries and peoples and persons will not have the slightest effect upon the international situation. Thus we often waste our time, and God's time, in expressing our human thoughts and sentiments instead of considering His Word. If every human being knew what it was to 'hunger and thirst after righteousness', the problem would be solved. The greatest need in the world now is for a greater number of Christians, individual Christians. If all nations consisted of individual Christians there would be no need to fear atomic power or anything else. So the gospel, which seems to be so remote and indirect in its approach, is actually the most direct way of solving the problem. One of the greatest tragedies in the life of the Church today is the way in which so many are content with these vague, general, useless statements about war and peace instead of preaching the gospel in all its simplicity and purity. It is righteousness that exalts a nation, and the most important thing for all of us is to discover what righteousness means.

In this particular statement in the Sermon on the Mount we are looking at another of the characteristics of the Christian, a further description of the

Christian man. Now, as we have seen, it is very important that we should take it in its logical place in the series of statements that have been made by our Lord. This Beatitude again follows logically from the previous ones; it is a statement to which all the others lead. It is the logical conclusion to which they come, and it is something for which we should all be profoundly thankful and grateful to God. I do not know of a better test that anyone can apply to himself or herself in this whole matter of the Christian profession than a verse like this. If this verse is to you one of the most blessed statements of the whole of Scripture you can be quite certain you are a Christian; if it is not, then you had better examine the foundations again.

Here is an answer to the things we have been considering. We have been told that we must be 'poor in spirit', that we must 'mourn', and that we must be 'meek'. Now here is the answer to all that. For, even though this Beatitude belongs logically to all the others that have gone before, it is nonetheless true to say that it introduces a slight change into the whole approach. It is a little less negative and more positive. There is a negative element here, as we shall see, but there is a more positive element. The others, as it were, have been causing us to look at ourselves and to examine ourselves; here we begin to look for a solution, and thus there is a slight change in the emphasis. We have been looking at our own utter helplessness and weakness, our utter poverty of spirit, our bankruptcy in these spiritual matters. And having looked at ourselves, we have seen the sin that is within us and that mars God's perfect creation of man. Then we saw the delineation of meekness and all that it represents. All along, we were concerned with this terrible problem of the self — that self-concern, and interest, that self-reliance which leads to our miseries and which is the ultimate cause of war, whether between individuals or nations, that selfishness and self-centredness that turns in upon self and deifies self, that horrible thing that is the cause of all unhappiness ultimately. And we have seen that the Christian man is one who bemoans and regrets and hates it all. Here we turn and look for the solution, for the deliverance from self for which we long.

In this verse we have one of the most notable statements of the Christian gospel and everything that it has to give us. Let me describe it as the great charter for every seeking soul, the outstanding declaration of the Christian gospel to all who are unhappy about themselves and their spiritual state, and who long for an order and quality of life that they have not hitherto enjoyed. We can also describe it as one of the most typical statements of the gospel. It is very doctrinal; it emphasizes one of the most fundamental doctrines of the gospel, namely, that our salvation is entirely of grace or by grace, that it is entirely the free gift of God. This is its great emphasis.

The simplest way, perhaps, to approach the text is just to look at its terms. It is one of those texts that divides itself for us, and all we have to do is to look at the meaning of the various terms which are used. Obviously therefore the one to start with is the term 'righteousness'. 'Blessed — or happy — are they which do hunger and thirst after righteousness.' They are the only truly happy people. Now the whole world is seeking for happiness; there is no question about that. Everybody wants to be happy. That is the great motive behind every act and ambition, behind all work and all striving and effort. Everything is designed for happiness. But the great tragedy of the world is that, though it gives itself to seek for happiness, it never seems to be able to find it. The present state of the world reminds us of that very forcibly. What is the matter? I think the answer is that we have never understood this text as we should have done. 'Blessed are they which do hunger and thirst after righteousness.' What does it mean? Let me put it negatively like this. We are not to hunger and thirst after blessedness; we are not to hunger and thirst after happiness. But that is what most people are doing. We put happiness and blessedness as the one thing that we desire, and thus we always miss it; it always eludes us. According to the Scriptures happiness is never something that should be sought directly; it is always something that results from seeking something else.

Now this is true of those outside the Church and of many inside the Church as well. It is obviously the tragedy of those who are outside the Church. The world is seeking for happiness. That is the meaning of its pleasure mania, that is the meaning of everything men and women do, not only in their work but still more in their pleasures. They are trying to find happiness, they are making it their goal, their one objective. But they do not find it because, whenever you put happiness before righteousness, you will be doomed to misery. That is the great message of the Bible from beginning to end. They alone are truly happy who are seeking to be righteous. Put happiness in the place of righteousness and you will never get it.

The world, it is obvious, has fallen into this primary and fundamental error, an error which one could illustrate in many different ways. Think of a man who is suffering from some painful disease. Generally the one desire of such a patient is to be relieved of his pain, and one can understand that very well. No-one likes suffering pain. The one idea of this patient, therefore, is to do anything which will relieve him of it. Yes; but if the doctor who is attending this patient is also only concerned about relieving this man's pain he is a very bad doctor. His primary duty is to discover the cause of the pain and to treat that. Pain is a wonderful symptom which is provided by nature to call attention to disease, and the ultimate treatment for pain is to treat the disease, not the pain. So if a doctor merely treats the pain without discovering the cause of the pain, he is not only acting contrary to nature, he is doing something that is extremely dangerous to the life of the patient. The patient may be out of pain, and seems to be well; but the cause of the trouble is still there. Now that is the folly of which the world is guilty. It says, 'I want to get rid of my pain, so I will run to the pictures, or drink, or do anything to help me forget my pain.' But the question is, What is the cause of the pain and the unhappiness and the wretchedness? They are not happy who hunger and thirst after happiness and blessedness. No. 'Blessed are they which do hunger and thirst after righteousness: for they shall be filled.'

This is equally true, however, of many within the Church. There are large numbers of people in the Christian Church who seem to spend the whole of their life seeking something which they can never find, seeking for some kind of happiness and blessedness. They go round from meeting to meeting, and convention to convention, always hoping they are going to get this wonderful thing, this experience that is going to fill them with joy, and flood them with some ecstasy. They see that other people have had it, but they themselves do not seem to get it. So they seek it and covet it, always hungering and thirsting; but they never get it.

Now that is not surprising. We are not meant to hunger and thirst after experiences; we are not meant to hunger and thirst after blessedness. If we want to be truly happy and blessed, we must hunger and thirst after righteousness. We must not put blessedness or happiness or experience in the first place. No, that is something that God gives to those who seek righteousness. Oh, the tragedy that we do not follow the simple teaching and instruction of the Word of God, but are always coveting and seeking this experience which we hope we are going to have. The experiences are the gift of God; what you and I are to covet and to seek and to hunger and thirst for is *righteousness*. Very well, that is a very important negative. But there are others.

What does this righteousness mean? It does not mean, of course, what is talked about so much at the present time, a sort of general righteousness or morality between nations. There is a great deal of talk about the sanctity of international contracts, and the honouring of bonds, and keeping your word, and straight dealing and fair play and all the rest of it. Well, it is not for me to denounce all that. It is all right as far as it goes; that is the kind of morality that was taught by the Greek pagan philosophers and it is very good. But the Christian gospel does not stop at that; its righteousness is not that at all. There are men who can talk eloquently about that kind of righteousness who know very little, it seems to me, about personal righteousness. Men can wax eloquent about how countries threaten the peace of the world and break their contracts, who at the same time are disloyal to their wives and disloyal to their own marriage contracts and the solemn vows they have taken. The gospel is not interested in that kind of talk; its conception of righteousness is much deeper than that. Neither does righteousness mean merely a general respectability or a general morality. I cannot stop with these various points; I merely mention them in passing.

Much more important and much more serious from the truly Christian standpoint is, I think, the fact that it is not right to define righteousness in this connection even as justification. There are those who turn up their concordance and look at this word 'righteousness' (and of course you will find it in many places) and say it stands for justification. The apostle Paul uses it like that in the Epistle to the Romans, where he writes about 'the righteousness of God which is by faith'. There, he is talking about justification, and in such cases the context will generally make it perfectly plain to us. Very often it does mean justification; but here, I suggest, it means more. The very context in which we find it (and especially its relation to the three Beatitudes that have gone before) insists, it seems to me, that righteousness here includes not only justification but sanctification also. In other words, the desire for righteousness, the act of hungering and thirsting for it, means ultimately the desire to be free from sin in all its forms and in its every manifestation.

Let me divide that a little. It means a desire to be free from sin, because sin separates us from God. Therefore, positively, it means a desire to be right with God; and that, after all, is the fundamental thing. All the trouble in the world today is due to the fact that man is not right with God, for it is because he is not right with God that he has gone wrong everywhere else. That is the teaching of the Bible everywhere. So the desire for righteousness is a desire to be right with God, a desire to get rid of sin, because sin is that which comes between us and God, keeping us from a knowledge of God, and all that is possible to us and for us with God and from God. So I must put that first. The man who hungers and thirsts after righteousness is the man who sees that sin and rebellion have separated him from the face of God, and longs to get back into that old relationship, the original relationship of righteousness in the presence of God. Our first parents were made righteous in the presence of God. They dwelt and walked with Him. That is the relationship such a man desires.

But it also means of necessity a desire to be free from the power of sin. Having realized what it means to be poor in spirit and to mourn because of sin within, we naturally come to the stage of longing to be free from the power of sin. The man we have been looking at in terms of these Beatitudes is a man who has come to see that the world in which he lives is controlled by sin and Satan; he sees that he is under the control of a malign influence, he has been walking 'according to the prince of the power of the air, the spirit that now worketh in the children of disobedience'. He sees that 'the god of this world' has been blinding him to various things, and now he longs to be free from it. He wants to get away from this power that drags him down in spite of himself, that 'law in his members' of which Paul speaks in Romans 7. He wants to be free from the power and the tyranny and the thraldom of sin. You see how much further and how much deeper it goes than vague general talk, of a relationship between nation and nation, and things of that kind.

But it goes further still. It means a desire to be free from the very desire for sin, because we find that the man who truly examines himself in the light of the Scriptures not only discovers that he is in the bondage of sin; still more horrible is the fact that he likes it, that he wants it. Even after he has seen it is wrong, he still wants it. But now the man who hungers and thirsts after righteousness is a man who wants to get rid of that desire for sin, not only outside, but inside as well. In other words, he longs for deliverance from what you may call the pollution of sin. Sin is something that pollutes the very essence of our being and of our nature. The Christian is one who desires to be free from all that.

Perhaps we can sum it all up like this. To hunger and thirst after righteousness is to desire to be free from self in all its horrible manifestations, in all its forms. When we considered the man who is meek, we saw that all that really means is that he is free from self in its every shape and form — self-concern, pride, boasting, self-protection, sensitiveness, always imagining people are against him, a desire to protect self and glorify self. That is what leads to quarrels between individuals, that is what leads to quarrels between nations; self-assertion. Now the man who hungers and thirsts after righteousness is a man who longs to be free from all that; he wants to be emancipated from self-concern in every shape and form.

Until now I have been putting it rather negatively; but let me put it positively like this. To hunger and thirst after righteousness is nothing but the longing to be positively holy. I cannot think of a better way of defining it. The man who hungers and thirsts after righteousness is the man who wants to exemplify the Beatitudes in his daily life. He is a man who wants to show the fruit of the Spirit in his every action and in the whole of his life and activity. To hunger and thirst after righteousness is to long to be like the New Testament man, the new man in Christ Jesus. That is what it means, that the whole of my being and the whole of my life shall be like that. Let me go further. It means that one's supreme desire in life is to know God and to be in fellowship with Him, to walk with God the Father, the Son and the Holy Spirit in the light. 'Our fellowship', says John, 'is with the Father, and with his Son Jesus Christ.' He also says, 'God is light, and in him is no darkness at all'. To be in fellowship with God means to be walking with God the Father, Son and Holy Spirit in the light, in that blessed purity and holiness. The man who hungers and thirsts after righteousness is the man who longs for that above everything else. And in the end that is nothing but a longing and desire to be like the Lord Jesus Christ Himself. Look at Him; look at His portrait in these Gospels; look at Him when He was here on earth in His incarnate state; look at Him in His positive obedience to God's holy law; look at Him in His reaction to other people, His kindness, His compassion, His sensitive nature; look at Him in His reaction to His enemies and all that they did to Him. There is the portrait, and you and I, according to the New Testament doctrine, have been born again and have been fashioned anew after that pattern and image. The man, therefore, who hungers and thirsts after righteousness, is the man who wants to be like that. His supreme desire is to be like Christ.

Very well, if that is righteousness, let us look at the other term, 'Blessed are they which do *hunger and thirst* after righteousness.' Now this is most important because it brings us to the practical aspect of this matter. What does it mean to 'hunger and thirst'? Obviously it does not mean that we feel we can attain unto this righteousness by our own efforts and endeavour. That is the worldly view of righteousness which concentrates on man himself and leads to the individual pride of the Pharisee, or to the pride of one nation as against other nations regarding itself as being better and superior. It leads to those things which the apostle Paul lists in Philippians 3 and which he there dismisses as 'dung', all self-confidence, all belief in self. 'To hunger and thirst' cannot mean that, because the first Beatitude tells us that we must be 'poor in spirit' which is a negation of every form of self-reliance.

Well, what does it mean? It obviously means some simple things like these. It means a consciousness of our need, of our deep need. I go further, it means a consciousness of our desperate need; it means a deep consciousness of our great need even to the point of pain. It means something that keeps on until it is satisfied. It does not mean just a passing feeling, a passing desire. You remember how Hosea says to the nation of Israel that she is always, as it were, coming forward to the penitent form and then going back to sin. Her righteousness, he says, is as 'a morning cloud' — it is here one minute and gone the next. The right way he indicates in the words — 'then shall we know, if we follow on to know the Lord.' 'Hunger' and 'thirst'; these are not passing feelings. Hunger is something deep and profound that goes on until it is satisfied. It hurts, it is painful; it is like actual, physical hunger and thirst. It is something that goes on increasing and makes one feel desperate. It is something that causes suffering and agony.

Let me suggest another comparison. To hunger and thirst is to be like a man who wants a position. He is restless, he cannot keep still; he is working and plodding; he thinks about it, and dreams about it; his ambition is the controlling passion of his life. To 'hunger and thirst' is like that; the man 'hungers and thirsts' after that position. Or it is like a longing for a person. There is always a great hunger and thirst in love. The chief desire of the one who loves is to be with the object of his love. If they are separated he is not at rest until they are together again. 'Hungering and thirsting'. I need not use these illustrations. The Psalmist has summed it up perfectly in a classical phrase: 'As the hart panteth after the water brooks, so panteth my soul after thee, O God. My soul thirsteth for God, for the living God.' He is hungering and thirsting after Him — that is it. Let me quote some words of the great J. N. Darby which I think put this exceedingly well. He says, 'To be hungry is not enough; I must be really starving to know what is in His heart towards me.' Then comes the perfect statement of the whole thing. He says, 'When the prodigal son was hungry he went to feed upon husks, but when he was starving, he turned to his father.' Now that is the whole position. To hunger and thirst really means to be desperate, to be starving, to feel life is ebbing out, to realize my urgent need of help. 'Hungering and thirsting after righteousness' — 'as the hart panteth after the water brooks, so panteth — so thirsteth — my soul after thee, O God.'

Lastly, let us look briefly at what is promised to the people who are like that. It is one of the most gracious, glorious statements to be found in the entire Bible. 'Happy, happy', 'blessed', 'to be congratulated' are those who thus hunger and thirst after righteousness. Why? Well, 'they shall be filled', they shall be given what they desire. The whole gospel is there. That is where the gospel of grace comes in; it is entirely the gift of God. You will never fill yourself with righteousness, you will never find blessedness apart from Him. To obtain this, 'all the fitness He requireth, is to see your need of Him', nothing more. When you and I know our need, this hunger and starvation, this death that is within us, then God will fill us, He will give us this blessed gift. 'Him that cometh to me I will in no wise cast out.' Now this is an absolute promise, so if you really are hungering and thirsting after righteousness you will be filled. There is no question about it. Make sure you are not hungering and thirsting after blessedness. Hunger and thirst after righteousness, long to be like Christ, and then you will have that and the blessedness.

How does it happen? It happens — and this is the glory of the gospel — it happens immediately, thank God. 'They shall be filled' at once, in this way — that immediately we desire this truly, we are justified by Christ and His righteousness and the barrier of sin and guilt between us and God is removed. I trust there is no-one who is uncertain or unhappy about that. If you believe truly on the Lord Jesus Christ, if you believe that on that cross He was dying for you and for your sin, you have been forgiven; you have no need to ask for forgiveness, you have been forgiven. You have to thank God for it, you are filled with that righteousness immediately, the righteousness of Christ is imputed to you. God looks at you in the righteousness of Christ and He no longer sees the sin. He sees you as a sinner whom He has forgiven. You are no longer under the law, you are under grace; you are filled with the righteousness of Christ in this whole matter of your standing before God and your justification — glorious, wondrous truth. The Christian, therefore, should always be a man who knows that his sins are forgiven. He should not be seeking it, he should know he has it, that he is justified in Christ freely by the grace of God, that he stands righteous at this moment in the presence of the Father. So he can say with Augustus Toplady:

> The terrors of law and of God
> With me can have nothing to do;
> My Saviour's obedience and blood
> Hide all my transgressions from view.

Thank God it happens immediately.

But it is also a continuing process. By this I mean that the Holy Spirit, as already shown, begins within us His great work of delivering us from the power of sin and from the pollution of sin. We have to hunger and thirst for this deliverance, from the power and from the pollution. And if you hunger and thirst for that you will get it. The Holy Spirit will come into you and He will work in you 'both to will and to do of his good pleasure'. Christ will come into you, He will live in you; and as He lives in you, you will be delivered increasingly from the power of sin and from its pollution. You will be able to be more than conqueror over all these things that assail you, so that not only do you get this answer and blessing immediately, it goes on continuously as you walk with God and with Christ, with the Holy Spirit living in you. You will be enabled to resist Satan, and he will flee from you; you will be able to stand against him and all his fiery darts, and the whole time the work of getting rid of the pollution will be going on within you.

But of course, finally, this promise is fulfilled perfectly and absolutely in eternity. There is a day coming when all who are in Christ and belong to Him shall stand in the presence of God, faultless, blameless, without spot and without wrinkle. All blemishes will have gone. A new and perfect man in a perfect body. Even this body of my humiliation shall be transformed and glorified and be like the glorified body of Christ. We shall stand in the presence of God, absolutely perfect in body, soul and spirit, the whole man filled with a perfect, complete and entire righteousness which we shall have received from the Lord Jesus Christ. In other words we have a paradox once more. Have you noticed the apparent contradiction in Philippians 3? Paul says, 'Not as though I had already attained, either were already perfect', and then a few verses further on he says, 'Let us therefore, as many as be perfect.' Is it a contradiction of what he has just been saying? Not at all; you see the Christian is perfect, and yet he is to become perfect. 'Of him', he says in writing to the Corinthians, 'are ye in Christ Jesus, who of God is made unto us wisdom, and righteousness, and sanctification, and redemption.' At this moment I am perfect in Christ, and yet I am being made perfect. 'Not as though I had already attained, either were already perfect; but I follow after . . . I press toward the mark.' Yes, he is addressing those who are Christians, those who are already perfect in this matter of understanding concerning the way of righteousness and justification. Yet his exhortation to them in a sense is, 'let us therefore go on to perfection.'

I do not know what you feel about this, but to me it is fascinating. You see the Christian is one who at one and the same time is hungering and thirsting, and yet he is filled. And the more he is filled the more he hungers and thirsts. That is the blessedness of this Christian life. It goes on. You reach a certain stage in sanctification, but you do not rest upon that for the rest of your life. You go on changing from glory into glory 'till in heaven we take our place'. 'Of his fullness have we received and grace upon grace', grace added to grace. It goes on and on; perfect, yet not perfect; hungering, thirsting, yet filled and satisfied, but longing for more, never having enough because it is so glorious and so wondrous; fully satisfied by Him and yet a supreme desire to 'know him, and the power of his resurrection, and the fellowship of his sufferings, being made conformable unto his death; if by any means I might attain unto the resurrection of the dead.'

Are you filled? are you blessed in this sense? are you hungering and thirsting? Those are the questions. This is the gracious, glorious promise of God to all such: 'Blessed are they which do hunger and thirst after righteousness: for they shall be filled.'

Chapter Eight

The Tests of Spiritual Appetite

W E dealt with verse 6 in general in the last chapter. I propose to continue our study of it in this, because I feel that what we considered then is not enough. We can never exhaust this great statement, and certainly if we are to derive anything approaching the full benefit from a consideration of it, we must also look at it in a slightly more practical manner than we have done so far. I do so because in many ways this is one of the key Beatitudes, it is one of the most vital of all.

We have realized that in this Beatitude we begin to turn away from an examination of self, to God. This is, of course, a vital matter, for it is this whole question of how to turn to God that causes so many to stumble. We are entitled, therefore, to say that this is the only way of blessing. Unless we 'hunger and thirst' after righteousness, we shall never have it, we shall never know the fullness which is here promised to us. Therefore, because it is such a vital matter, we must come back to it. I suggested earlier that the very essence of the Christian salvation is given us in this verse. It is a perfect statement of the doctrine of salvation by grace only.

Furthermore, this Beatitude is of exceptional value because it provides us with a perfect test which we can apply to ourselves, a test not only of our condition at any given time, but also of our whole position. It operates in two main ways. It is a very wonderful test of our doctrine, and also a very thoroughgoing, practical test of where, exactly, we stand.

Let us consider it, first, as a test of our doctrine. This one Beatitude deals with what I would describe as the two commonest objections to the Christian doctrine of salvation. It is very interesting to observe how people, when they have the gospel presented to them, generally have two main objections to it, and

71

what is still more interesting is that the two objections are so often found in the same people. They tend to change their position from one to the other. First of all, when they hear this announcement, 'Blessed are they which do hunger and thirst after righteousness: for they shall be filled', when they are told that salvation is altogether of grace, that it is something that is given by God, which they cannot merit, which they can never deserve, and about which they can do nothing except receive it, they immediately begin to object and say, 'But that is making the thing much too easy. You say that we receive this as a gift, that we receive forgiveness and life, and ourselves do nothing. But surely,' they say, 'salvation cannot be as easy as that.' That is the first statement.

Then, when one points out to them that it must be like that because of the character of the righteousness about which the text speaks, they begin to object and to say that that is making it much too difficult, indeed so difficult as to make it impossible. When one tells them that one has to receive this salvation as a free gift, because what is required is that we should be fit to stand in the presence of God, who is light, and in whom is no darkness at all, when they hear that we should be like the Lord Jesus Christ Himself and that we should conform to these various Beatitudes, they say, 'Now that is making it impossible for us'. They go astray, you see, about this whole question of righteousness. Righteousness to them means just being decent and moral up to a certain level. But we saw in our last chapter that that is a totally wrong definition of it. Righteousness ultimately means being like the Lord Jesus Christ. That is the standard. If we want to face God and spend eternity in His holy presence, we must be like Him. No one can be in the presence of God who has any vestige of sin remaining in him; a righteousness is demanded that is absolutely perfect. That is what we have to attain unto. And, of course, the moment we realize that, then we see that it is something we ourselves cannot do, and realize that we must therefore receive it as helpless paupers, as those who have nothing in our hands at all, as those who take it entirely as a free gift.

Now this one statement deals with both those aspects. It deals with those people who object to the fact that this evangelical presentation of the gospel makes it too easy, those people who tend to say, as I once heard someone say who had just been listening to a sermon which emphasized human activity in this matter of salvation, 'Thank God there is something for us to do after all'. It shows that that kind of person just admits that he or she has never understood the meaning of this righteousness, has never seen the real nature of sin within, and has never seen the standard with which God confronts us. Those who have really understood what righteousness means never object to the fact that the gospel 'makes it too easy'; they realize that apart from it they would be left entirely without hope, utterly lost. 'Nothing in my hand I bring, Simply to Thy cross I cling' — is the statement of everyone who has truly seen the position. Therefore, to object to the gospel because it 'makes things too easy', or to object to it because it makes things too difficult, is just virtually to confess that we are not Christians at all. The Christian is one who admits that the statements and the demands of the gospel are impossible, but thanks God that the gospel does the impossible for us and gives us salvation as a free gift. 'Blessed are they', therefore, 'which do hunger and thirst after righteousness: for they shall be filled.' They can do nothing, but as they hunger and thirst for it, they shall be filled by it. There, then, is the test of our doctrinal position. And it is a very thoroughgoing test. But let us ever remember that the two aspects of the test must always be applied together.

Let us now consider the practical test. This is one of those statements which reveal to us exactly where we are in this Christian life. The statement is categorical — they who hunger and thirst after righteousness 'shall be filled', and therefore they are happy, they are the people to be congratulated, they are the truly blessed. That means, as we saw in the last chapter, that we are filled immediately, in one sense, namely that we are no longer seeking forgiveness. We know we have had it. The Christian is a man who knows he has been forgiven; he knows he is covered by the righteousness of Jesus Christ, and he says, 'Therefore being justified by faith, we have peace with God'. Not, we are *hoping* to have it. We have it. The Christian has this immediate filling; he is completely satisfied concerning the matter of his standing in the presence of God; he knows that the righteousness of Christ is thus imputed to him and that his sins have been forgiven. He also knows that Christ, by the Holy Spirit, has come to dwell within him. His essential problem of sanctification is also solved. He knows that Christ has been made unto him of God 'wisdom, and righteousness, and sanctification, and redemption'. He knows that he is already complete in Christ so that he is no longer hopeless even about his sanctification. There is an immediate sense of satisfaction about that also; and he knows that the Holy Spirit is in him and that He will continue to work in him 'both to will and to do of his good pleasure'. Therefore he looks forward, as we saw, to that ultimate, final state of perfection without spot or wrinkle or blemish or any such thing, when we shall see Him as He is and we shall be like Him, when we shall indeed be perfect, when even this body which is 'the body of our humiliation' shall have been glorified and we shall be in a state of absolute perfection.

Very well then; if that is the meaning of filling, we must surely ask ourselves questions such as these: Are we filled? Have we got this satisfaction? Are we aware of this dealing of God with us? Is the fruit of the Spirit being manifested in our lives? Are we concerned about that? Are we experiencing love to God and to other people, joy and peace? Are we manifesting long-suffering, goodness, gentleness, meekness, faith and temperance? They that do hunger and thirst after righteousness shall be filled. They are filled, and they are being filled. Are we, therefore, I ask, enjoying these things? Do we know that we have received the life of God? Are we enjoying the life of God in our souls? Are we aware of the Holy Spirit and all His mighty working within, forming Christ in us more and more? If we claim to be Christian, then we should be able to say yes to all these questions. Those who are truly Christian are filled in this sense. Are we thus filled? Are we enjoying our Christian life and experience? Do we know that our sins are forgiven? Are we rejoicing in that fact, or are we still trying to make ourselves Christian, trying somehow to make ourselves righteous? Is it all a vain effort? Are we enjoying peace with God? Do we rejoice in the Lord alway? Those are the tests that we must apply. If we are not enjoying these things, the only explanation of that fact is that we are not truly hungering and thirsting after righteousness. For if we do hunger and thirst we shall be filled. There is no qualification at all, it is an absolute statement, it is an absolute promise — 'Blessed are they which do hunger and thirst after righteousness: for they shall be filled.'

The question that now remains is obviously this: How can we tell whether we *are* hungering and thirsting after righteousness? That is the vital thing; that is all we have to be concerned about. I suggest the way to discover the answer is to study the Scriptures, as, for example, Hebrews 11, because there we have some great and glorious examples of people who did hunger and thirst after righteousness and were filled. Go through the whole of the Bible and you will discover the meaning of this, especially in the New Testament itself. Then you can supplement scriptural biography by reading about some of the great saints who have adorned the Church of Christ. There is ample literature concerning this matter. Read the Confessions of St. Augustine, or the lives of Luther, of Calvin, and of John Knox. Read the lives of some of the outstanding Puritans and the great Pascal. Read the lives of those mighty men of God of 200 years ago in the evangelical awakening, for example the first volume of John Wesley's Journal, or the astounding biography of George Whitefield. Read the life of John Fletcher of Madeley. I have not time to mention them all: there are men who enjoyed this fullness, and whose holy lives were a manifestation of it. Now the question is, how did they arrive at that? If we want to know what hungering and thirsting means, we must study the Scriptures and then go on to see it more on our own level by reading the lives of such people, and if we do so, we come to the conclusion that there are certain tests which we can apply to ourselves to discover whether we are hungering and thirsting after righteousness or not.

The first test is this: Do we see through all our own false righteousness?

That would be the first indication that a man is hungering and thirsting after righteousness. Until he has come to see that his own righteousness is nothing, is, as the Scripture puts it, but 'filthy rags', or, to use a stronger term, the particular term that the apostle Paul used and which some people think should not be used from a Christian pulpit, the term used in Philippians 3, where Paul speaks of all the wonderful things he had been doing and then tells us that he counts them all as 'dung' — dung, refuse, putrefying refuse. That is the first test. We are not hungering and thirsting after righteousness as long as we are holding with any sense of self-satisfaction to anything that is in us, or to anything that we have ever done. The man who hungers and thirsts after righteousness is the man who knows what it is to say with Paul, 'In me (that is, in my flesh) dwelleth no good thing'. If we still want to pat ourselves on the back, and feel a sense of satisfaction in the things we have done, it indicates perfectly clearly that we are still trusting and holding on to our own righteousness. If we are in any sense prone to defend ourselves, well, that means that we are just holding on still to some righteousness of our own. And as long as we do that we shall never be blessed. We see that to be hungering and thirsting in this sense is, as John Darby puts it, to be starving, to realize we are dying because we have nothing. That is the first step, seeing all false righteousness of our own as 'filthy rags' and as 'refuse'.

But it also means that we have a deep awareness of our need of deliverance and our need of a Saviour; that we see how desperate we are, and realize that unless a Saviour and salvation are provided, we really are entirely without hope. We must recognize our utter helplessness, and see that, if someone does not come and take hold of us, or do something to us, we are altogether lost. Or let me put it like this. It means that we must have a desire within us to be like those saints to whom I have made reference. That is a very good way of testing ourselves. Do we long to be like Moses or Abraham or Daniel or any of those men who lived in the subsequent history of the Church to whom I have referred? I must add a warning, however, because it is possible for us to want to be like these people in the wrong way. We may desire to enjoy the blessings which they enjoyed without really desiring to be like them. Now, there is a classical example of this in the story of that false prophet, Balaam. You remember he said, 'Let me die the death of the righteous, and let my last end be like his!' Balaam wanted to die like the righteous but, as a wise old Puritan pointed out, he did not want to live like the righteous. That, indeed, is true of many of us. We want the blessings of the righteous; we want to die like them. Of course we do not want to be unhappy on our deathbed. We want to enjoy the blessings of this glorious salvation. Yes; but if we want to die like the righteous we must also want to live like the righteous. These two things go together. 'Let me die like the righteous.' If I could but see the heavens open and yet go on living as I am, I should be happy! But it does not work like that. I must long to live like them if I want to die like them.

There, then, are some of the preliminary tests. But if I leave it like that we may come to the conclusion that we have nothing to do but to be entirely passive, and to wait quietly for something to happen. That, however, it seems to me, is to do much violence to these terms, 'hungering and thirsting'. There is an active element in them. People who really want something always give some evidence of that fact. People who really desire something with the whole of their being do not sit down, passively waiting for it to come. And that applies to us in this matter. So I am going to apply some more detailed tests as to whether we are truly hungering and thirsting after righteousness. Here is one of them. The person who is truly hungering and thirsting after righteousness obviously avoids everything that is opposed to such a righteousness. I cannot obtain it myself, but I can refrain from doing things that are obviously opposed to it. I can never make myself like Jesus Christ, but I can stop walking in the gutters of life. That is a part of hungering and thirsting.

Let us subdivide that. There are certain things in this life that are patently opposed to God and His righteousness. There is no question about that at all. We know they are bad; we know they are harmful; we know they are sinful. I say that to hunger and thirst after righteousness means avoiding such things just as we would avoid the very plague itself. If we know there is an infection in a house, we avoid that house. We segregate the patient who has a fever, because it is infectious, and obviously we avoid such persons. The same is equally true in the spiritual realm.

But it does not stop at that. I suggest that if we are truly hungering and thirsting after righteousness we shall not only avoid things that we know to be bad and harmful, we shall even avoid things that tend to dull or take the edge off our spiritual appetites. There are so many things like that, things that are quite harmless in themselves and which are perfectly legitimate. Yet if you find that you are spending much of your time with them, and that you desire the things of God less, you must avoid them. This question of appetite is a very delicate one. We all know how, in the physical sense, we can easily spoil our appetite, dull its edge, so to speak, by eating things between meals. Now it is like that in the spiritual realm. There are so many things that I cannot condemn in and of themselves. But if I find I spend too much of my time with them, and that somehow I want God and spiritual things less and less, then, if I am hungering and thirsting after righteousness, I shall avoid them. I think it is a common-sense argument.

Let me give another positive test. To hunger and thirst after righteousness means we shall remind ourselves of this righteousness actively. We shall so discipline our lives as to keep it constantly before us. This subject of discipline is of vital importance. I am suggesting that unless we day by day voluntarily and deliberately remind ourselves of this righteousness which we need, we are not very likely to be hungering and thirsting after it. The man who truly hungers and thirsts after it makes himself look at it every day. 'But', you say, 'I am so tremendously busy. Look at my agenda. Where have I time?' I say, if you are hungering and thirsting after righteousness you will find time. You will order your life, you will say, 'First things must come first; there is a priority in these matters, and though I have to do this, that and the other, I cannot afford to neglect this because my soul is in bondage.' 'Where there is a will there is a way.' It is amazing how we find time to do the things we want to do. If you and I are hungering and thirsting after righteousness, a good deal of time every day will be spent in considering it.

But let us go further. The next test I would apply is this. The man who is hungering and thirsting after righteousness always puts himself in the way of getting it. You cannot create it yourself; you cannot produce it. But at any rate you do know there are certain ways in which it seems to have come to these people about whom you have been reading, so you begin to imitate their example. You remember that blind man, Bartimaeus. He could not heal himself. He was blind; do what he would and what others would, he could not get back his sight. But he went and put himself in the way of getting it. He heard that Jesus of Nazareth was going that way, so he took up his stand on the high road. He got as near as he could. He could not give himself sight, but he put himself in the way of getting it. And the man who hungers and thirsts after righteousness is the man who never misses an opportunity of being in those certain places where people seem to find this righteousness. Take, for example, the house of God, where we meet to consider these things. I meet people who talk to me about their spiritual problems. They have these difficulties; they so want to be Christian, they say. But somehow or other something is lacking. Quite frequently I find that they do not often go to the house of God, or that they are very haphazard in their attendance. They do not know what it is to hunger and thirst after righteousness. The man who really wants it says, 'I cannot afford to lose any opportunity; wherever this is being talked about I want to be there.' It is common sense. And then, of course, he seeks the society of people who have this righteousness. He says, 'The oftener I am in the presence of godly and saintly men the better it is for me. I see that person has it; well, I want to talk to that person, I want to spend my time with such a person. I do not want to spend so much time with others who do me no good.

But these people, who have this righteousness, I am going to keep close to them.'

Then, reading the Bible. Here is the great textbook on this matter. I ask a simple question again. I wonder whether we spend as much time with this Book as we do with the newspaper or with the novels or with the films and all other entertainments — wireless, television and all these things. I am not condemning these things as such. I want to make it completely clear that that is not my argument. My argument is that the man who is hungering and thirsting after righteousness and has time for such things should have more time for this — that is all I am saying. Study and read this Book. Try to understand it; read books about it.

And then, prayer. It is God alone who can give us this gift. Do we ask Him for it? How much time do we spend in His presence? I have referred to the biographies of these men of God. If you read them, and if you are like me, you will feel ashamed of yourself. You will find that these saints spent four or five hours daily in prayer, not just saying their prayers at night when they were almost too weary to do so. They gave the best time of their day to God; and people who hunger and thirst after righteousness know what it is to spend time in prayer and meditation reminding themselves of what they are in this life and world and what is awaiting them.

And then, as I have already said, there is the need for reading the biographies of the saints and all the literature you can lay your hands on about these things. This is how the man acts who really wants righteousness, as I have proved by the examples I have given. To hunger and thirst after righteousness is to do all that and, having done it, to realize that it is not enough, that it will never produce it. The people who hunger and thirst after righteousness are frantic. They do all these things; they are seeking righteousness everywhere; and yet they know that their efforts are never going to lead to it. They are like Bartimaeus or like the importunate widow of whom our Lord spoke. They come back to the same person until they get it. They are like Jacob struggling with the angel. They are like Luther, fasting, sweating, praying, not finding; but going on increasingly in his helplessness until God gave it to him. The same is true of all the saints of all ages and countries. It does not matter whom you look at. It seems to work out like this: it is only as you seek this righteousness with the whole of your being that you can truly discover it. You can never find it yourself. Yet the people who sit back and do nothing never seem to get it. That is God's method. God, as it were, leads us on. We have done everything, and having done all we are still miserable sinners: and then we see that, as little children, we are to receive it as the free gift of God.

Very well; these are the ways in which we prove whether we are hungering and thirsting after this righteousness or not. Is it the greatest desire of our life? Is it the deepest longing of our being? Can I say quite honestly and truly that I desire above everything else in this world truly to know God and to be like the Lord Jesus Christ, to be rid of self in every shape and form, and to live only, always and entirely to His glory and to His honour?

Let me conclude this chapter with just a word in this practical sense. Why should this be the greatest desire of every one of us? I answer the question in this way. All who lack this righteousness of God remain under the wrath of God and are facing perdition. Anybody who dies in this world without being clothed with the righteousness of Jesus Christ goes on to utter hopelessness and wretchedness. That is the teaching of the Bible, that is what the Bible says. 'The wrath of God abideth on him.' It is only this righteousness that can fit us to be right with God and to go to heaven and to be with Him and to spend eternity in His holy presence. Without this righteousness we are lost and damned and doomed. How amazing it is that this is not the supreme desire in the life of everybody! It is the only way to blessing in this life and to blessing in eternity. Let me put to you the argument of the utter hatefulness of sin, this thing that is so dishonouring to God, this thing that is dishonouring in itself, and dishonouring even to us. If only we saw the things of which we are guilty so continually in the sight of God, and in the sight of utter holiness, we should hate them even as God Himself does. That is a great reason for hungering and thirsting after righteousness — the hatefulness of sin.

But lastly I put it in a positive form. If only we knew something of the glory and the wonder of this new life of righteousness, we should desire nothing else. Therefore let us look at the Lord Jesus Christ. That is how life should be lived, that is what we should be like. If only we really saw it. Look at the lives of His followers. Wouldn't you really like to live like those men, wouldn't you like to die like them? Is there any other life that is in any way comparable to it — holy, clean, pure, with the fruit of the Spirit manifesting itself as 'love, joy, peace, long-suffering, gentleness, goodness, faith, meekness, temperance'. What a life, what a character. That is a man worthy of the name of man; that is life as it should be. And if we see these things truly, we shall desire nothing less; we shall become like the apostle Paul and we shall say, 'That I may know him, and the power of his resurrection, and the fellowship of his sufferings, being made conformable unto his death; if by any means I might attain unto the resurrection of the dead.' Is that your desire? Very well, 'Ask, and it shall be given you; seek, and ye shall find; knock (and go on knocking), and it shall be opened unto you.' 'Blessed are they which do hunger and thirst after righteousness: for they shall be filled' — with 'all the fullness of God'.

Chapter Nine

Blessed Are the Merciful

THIS particular statement, 'Blessed are the merciful: for they shall obtain mercy', is a further stage forward in the description, given in these Beatitudes, of the Christian man. I say deliberately that it is a further stage forward because there is again a change in the type and kind of description. In a sense we have so far been looking at the Christian in terms of his need, of his consciousness of his need. But here there is a kind of turning point. Now we are concerned more with his disposition, which results from everything that has gone before. That is true, of course, of the subsequent Beatitudes also. We have already seen some of the results which follow when a man has truly seen himself, and especially when he has seen himself in his relationship to God. Here, now, are some further consequences which must inevitably be manifested when one is truly Christian. So that again we can emphasize the fact that our Lord clearly chose these Beatitudes carefully. He did not speak haphazardly. There is a definite progression in the thought; there is a logical sequence. This particular Beatitude comes out of all the others, and especially is it to be noted that it is in a very sharp and well-defined logical connection with the immediately preceding one, 'Blessed are they which do hunger and thirst after righteousness: for they shall be filled.' I would emphasize once more that it is idle to take any statement of the Sermon on the Mount at random, and to try to understand it, without taking it in the context of the whole, and especially in the context of these descriptions which are here given of the character and the disposition of the Christian man.

'Blessed are the merciful.' What a searching statement that is! What a test of each one of us, of our whole standing and of our profession of the Christian faith! Those are the happy people, says Christ, those are the people to be congratulated. That is what man should be like — merciful. This is perhaps a convenient point at which to emphasize once more the searching character of the whole of this statement which we call the Beatitudes. Our Lord is depicting and delineating the Christian man and the Christian character. He is obviously searching us and testing us, and it is good that we should realize that, if we take the Beatitudes as a whole, it is a kind of general test to which we are being subjected. How are we reacting to these searching tests and probings? They really tell us everything about our Christian profession. And if I dislike this kind of thing, if I am impatient with it, if I want instead to be talking about communism, if I dislike this personal analysis and probing and testing, it simply means that my position is entirely contrary to that of the New Testament man. But if I feel, on the other hand, that though these things do search and hurt me, nevertheless they are essential and good for me, if I feel it is good for me to be humbled, and that it is a good thing for me to be held face-to-face with this mirror, which not only shows me what I am, but what I am in the light of God's pattern for the Christian man, then I have a right to be hopeful about my state and condition. A man who is truly Christian, as we have already seen, never objects to being humbled. The first thing that is here said about him is that he should be 'poor in spirit', and if he objects to being shown that there is nothing in him, then that is not true of him. So these Beatitudes taken as a whole do provide a very searching test.

They are searching also, I think, in another way, a fact which is borne out very strikingly in the particular Beatitude we are looking at now. They remind us of certain primary, central truths about the whole Christian position. The first is this. The Christian gospel places all its primary emphasis upon being, rather than doing. The gospel puts a greater weight upon our attitude than upon our actions. In the first instance its main stress is on what you and I essentially are rather than on what we do. Throughout the Sermon our Lord is concerned about disposition. Later, He is going to talk about actions; but before He does that He describes character and disposition. And that of course is, as I am trying to show, essentially the New Testament teaching. A Christian *is* something before he does anything; and we have to *be* Christian before we can act as Christians. Now that is a fundamental point. Being is more important than doing, attitude is more significant than action. Primarily it is our essential character that matters. Or let me put it like this. We are not called upon as Christians to be, or to try to be, Christian in various respects. To be Christian, I say, is to possess a certain character and therefore to be a certain type of person. So often that is misinterpreted and people think that what the New Testament exhorts us to do is to try to be Christian in this and that respect, and to try to live as a Christian here and there. Not at all: we *are* Christians and our actions are the outcome of that.

Going a step further, we can put it like this. We are not meant to control our Christianity; our Christianity is rather meant to control us. From the standpoint of the Beatitudes, as indeed from the standpoint of the whole of the New Testament, it is an entire fallacy to think in any other way, and to say, for example, 'To be truly Christian I must take up and use Christian teaching and then apply it.' That is not the way our Lord puts it. The position rather is that my Christianity controls me; I am to be dominated by the truth because I have been made a Christian by the operation of the Holy Spirit within. Again I quote that striking statement of the apostle Paul which surely puts it so perfectly — 'I live; yet not I, but Christ liveth in me.' He is in control, not I; so that I must not think of myself as a natural man who is controlling his attitude and trying to be Christian in various ways. No; His Spirit controls me at the very centre of my life, controls the very spring of my being, the source of my every activity. You cannot read these Beatitudes without coming to that conclusion. The Christian faith is not something on the surface of a man's life, it is not merely a kind of coating or veneer. No, it is something that has been happening in the very centre of his personality. That is why the New Testament talks about rebirth and being born again, about a new creation and about receiving a new nature. It is something that happens to a man in the very centre of his being; it controls all his thoughts, all his outlook, all his imagination, and, as a result, all his actions as well. All our activities, therefore, are the result of this new nature, this new disposition which we have received from God through the Holy Spirit.

That is why these Beatitudes are so searching. They tell us, in effect, that as we live our ordinary lives we are declaring all the time exactly what we are. That is what makes this matter so serious. By the way we react we manifest our spirit; and it is the spirit that proclaims the man in terms of Christianity. There are people, of course, who as a result of a strong human will can control their actions very largely. Yet in these other respects they are always proclaiming what they are. All of us are proclaiming whether we are 'poor in spirit', whether we 'mourn', whether we are 'meek', whether we 'hunger and thirst', whether we are 'merciful', or whether we are not. The whole of our life is an expression and a proclamation of what we really are. And as we confront a list like this, or as we look at this extraordinary portrait of the Christian drawn by our Lord, we are forced to look at ourselves and examine ourselves and ask ourselves these questions.

The particular question here is: Are we merciful? The Christian, according to our Lord, is not only what we have seen him to be already, but he is also merciful. Here is the blessed man, here is the man to be congratulated; one who is merciful. What does our Lord mean by this? First let me just mention one negative which is of importance. It does not mean that we should be 'easygoing', as we put it. There are so many people today who think that being merciful means to be easygoing, not to see things, or if we do see them, to pretend we have not. That, of course, is a particular danger in an age like this which does not believe in law or discipline, and in a sense does not believe in justice or righteousness. The idea today is that man should be absolutely free minded, that he has the right to do just what he likes. The merciful person, many people think, is one who smiles at transgression and law breaking. He says, 'What does it matter? Let's carry on.' He is a flabby kind of person, easygoing, easy to get on with, to whom it does not matter whether laws are broken or not, who is not concerned about keeping them.

Now that, obviously, is not what is meant by our Lord's description of the Christian at this point, and for very good reasons. You may recall that when we considered these Beatitudes as a whole, we laid great stress upon the fact that none of them must ever be interpreted in terms of natural disposition, because if you start thinking of these Beatitudes in such terms you will find they are grossly unfair. Some are born like this, some are not; and the man who is born with this easygoing temperament has a great advantage over the man who is not. But that is a denial of the whole of biblical teaching. This is not a gospel for certain temperaments; nobody has an advantage over anybody else when they are face-to-face with God. 'All have come short of the glory of God', 'every mouth has been stopped' before God. That is the New Testament teaching, so that natural disposition must never be the basis of our interpretation of any one of the Beatitudes.

There is, however, a very much stronger reason than that for saying that what is meant by 'merciful' is not being easygoing. For when we interpret this term we must remember that it is an adjective that is applied specially and specifically to God Himself. So that whatever I may decide as to the meaning of 'merciful' is true also of God, and the moment you look at it like that you see that this easygoing attitude that doesn't care about breaking the law is unthinkable when we are talking about God. God is merciful; but God is righteous, God is holy, God is just: and whatever our interpretation of merciful may be it must include all that. 'Mercy and truth are met together', and if I can think of mercy only at the expense of truth and law, it is not true mercy, it is a false understanding of the term.

What is mercy? I think perhaps the best way of approaching it is to compare it with grace. You notice in the introduction to the so-called Pastoral Epistles that the apostle brings in a new term. Most of his other Epistles start by saying 'grace and peace' from God the Father and the Lord Jesus Christ; but in his Pastoral

Epistles he says, 'grace, mercy, and peace', and there is thus an interesting distinction implied between grace and mercy. The best definition of the two that I have ever encountered is this: 'Grace is especially associated with men in their sins; mercy is especially associated with men in their misery.' In other words, while grace looks down upon sin as a whole, mercy looks especially upon the miserable consequences of sin. So that mercy really means a sense of pity plus a desire to relieve the suffering. That is the essential meaning of being merciful; it is pity plus the action. So the Christian has a feeling of pity. His concern about the misery of men and women leads to an anxiety to relieve it. There are many ways in which one could illustrate that. For example, to have a merciful spirit means the spirit that is displayed when you suddenly find yourself in the position of having in your power someone who has transgressed against you. Now the way to know whether you are merciful or not is to consider how you feel towards that person. Are you going to say, 'Well now, I am going to exert my rights at this point; I am going to be legal. This person has transgressed against me; very well, here comes my opportunity'? That is the very antithesis of being merciful. This person is in your power; is there a vindictive spirit, or is there a spirit of pity and sorrow, a spirit, if you like, of kindness to your enemies in distress? Or, again, we can describe it as inward sympathy and outward acts in relation to the sorrows and sufferings of others. Perhaps an example is the best way of illustrating this. The great New Testament illustration of being merciful is the parable of the Good Samaritan. On his journey he sees this poor man who has been in the hands of robbers, stops, and goes across the road to where he is lying. The others have seen the man but have gone on. They may have felt compassion and pity yet they have not done anything about it. But here is a man who is merciful; he is sorry for the victim, goes across the road, dresses the wounds, takes the man with him and makes provision for him. That is being merciful. It does not mean only feeling pity; it means a great desire, and indeed an endeavour, to do something to relieve the situation.

But let us go from that to the supreme example of all. The perfect and central example of mercy and being merciful is the sending by God of His only begotten Son into this world, and the coming of the Son. Why? Because there is mercy with Him. He saw our pitiable estate, He saw the suffering, and, in spite of the law breaking, this was the thing that moved Him to action. So the Son came and dealt with our condition. Hence the whole necessity for the doctrine of the atonement. There is no contradiction between justice and mercy, or mercy and truth. They have met together. Indeed John the Baptist's father put this very clearly when, having understood what was happening by the birth of his son, he thanked God that at last the mercy promised to the fathers had arrived, and then proceeded to thank God that the Messiah had come 'through the tender mercy of our God'. That is the idea, and he realized it at the very beginning. It is all a matter of mercy. It is God, I say, looking down upon man in his pitiful condition as the result of sin, and having pity upon him. The grace that is there in regard to sin in general now becomes mercy in particular as God looks at the consequences of sin. And, of course, it is something that is to be observed constantly in the life and behaviour of our blessed Lord Himself.

That, then, is more or less a definition of what is meant by being merciful. The real problem, however, in this Beatitude is raised by the promise, 'for they shall obtain mercy'; and perhaps there is no other Beatitude that has been misunderstood quite so frequently as this one. For there are people who would interpret it like this. They say, 'If I am merciful towards others, God will be merciful towards me; if I forgive, I shall be forgiven. The condition of my being forgiven is that I forgive.' Now the best way to approach this problem is to take it with two parallel statements. First there is that well-known statement in the Lord's Prayer which is an exact parallel to this, 'Forgive us our trespasses, as we forgive them that trespass against us', or, 'Forgive us our debts, as we forgive our debtors'. There are those who interpret this as meaning that if you forgive, you will be forgiven, if you do not, you will not be forgiven. Some people refuse to recite the Lord's Prayer for this reason.

Then there is a similar statement recorded in the parable of the debtors in Matthew 18. Here a cruel servant who was in debt was asked by his master for payment. The man did not have the money to pay so he besought his master to forgive him his debt. His master had mercy upon him and forgave him all that he owed. But, you remember, this man went outside and demanded payment from somebody under himself who owed him a comparatively trivial debt. That man in turn prayed and besought him and said, 'Have patience with me, and I will pay thee all'. But he would not listen and cast him into prison until he could pay him the utmost farthing. But other servants, seeing this, reported it to their lord. On hearing their account he called for this cruel and unjust servant and said to him in effect, 'Very well; in view of your action I am going to repeal what I said to you'; and he cast him into prison, saying he should remain there until he had paid the utmost farthing. Our Lord ends the parable by saying, 'So likewise shall my heavenly Father do also unto you, if ye from your hearts forgive not every one his brother their trespasses.'

Here again people at once begin to say, 'Well; does not that clearly teach that I am forgiven by God only as I forgive others and to the extent that I forgive others?' It is an amazing thing to me that anybody could ever arrive at such an interpretation, and that for two main reasons. First, if you and I were to be judged strictly on those terms, it is very certain that not one of us would be forgiven and not one of us would ever see heaven. If the passage is to be interpreted in that strictly legal manner forgiveness is impossible. It is amazing that people can think like that, not realizing they are condemning themselves as they do so.

The second reason is still more striking. If that is the interpretation of this Beatitude and the parallel passages, then we must cancel the whole doctrine of grace from the New Testament. We must never again say that we are saved by grace through faith, and that not of ourselves; we must never read those glorious passages which tell us that 'while we were yet sinners, Christ died for us', even 'when we were enemies, we were reconciled to God', or 'God was in Christ, reconciling the world unto himself'. They must all go; they are all nonsense; and they are all untrue. Scripture, you see, must be interpreted by Scripture; we must never interpret any Scripture in such a manner as to contradict other Scriptures. We must 'rightly divide the word of truth', and we must see that there is a conformity of doctrine to doctrine.

When we apply this to the statement before us, the explanation is perfectly simple. Our Lord is really saying that I am only truly forgiven when I am truly repentant. To be truly repentant means that I realize I deserve nothing but punishment, and that if I am forgiven it is to be attributed entirely to the love of God and to His mercy and grace, and to nothing else at all. But I go further; it means this. If I am truly repentant and realize my position before God, and realize that I am only forgiven in that way, then of necessity I shall forgive those who trespass against me.

Let me put it like this. I have taken the trouble to point out in each case how every one of these Beatitudes follows the previous one. This principle was never more important than it is here. This Beatitude follows all the others; therefore I put it in this form. I am poor in spirit; I realize that I have no righteousness; I realize that face-to-face with God and His righteousness I am utterly helpless; I can do nothing. Not only that. I mourn because of the sin that is within me; I have come to see, as the result of the operation of the Holy Spirit, the blackness of my own heart. I know what it is to cry out, 'O wretched man that I am! who shall deliver me?' and desire to be rid of this vileness that is within me. Not only that. I am meek, which means that now that I have experienced this true view of myself, nobody else can hurt me, nobody else can insult me, nobody can ever say anything too bad about me. I have seen myself, and my greatest enemy does not know the worst about me. I have seen myself as something truly hateful, and it is because of this that I have hungered and thirsted after righteousness. I have longed for it. I have seen that I cannot create or produce it, and that nobody else can. I have seen my desperate position in the sight of God. I have hungered and thirsted for that righteousness which will put me right with God, that will reconcile me to God, and give me a new nature and life. And I have seen it in Christ. I have been filled; I have received it all as a free gift.

Does it not follow inevitably that, if I have seen and experienced all that, my attitude towards everybody else must be completely and entirely changed? If all that is true of me, I no longer see men as I used to see them. I see them now with a Christian eye. I see them as the dupes and the victims and the slaves of sin and Satan and of the way of the world. I have come to see them not simply as men whom I dislike but as men to be pitied. I have come to see them as being governed by the god of this world, as being still where once I was, and would be yet but for the grace of God. So I am sorry for them. I do not merely see them and what they do. I see them as the slaves of hell and of Satan, and my whole attitude toward them is changed. And because of that, of course, I can be and must be merciful with respect to them. I differentiate between the sinner and his sin. I see everybody who is in a state of sin as one who is to be pitied.

But I would take you again to the supreme example. Look at Him there upon the cross, who never sinned, who never did any harm to anyone, who came and preached the truth, who came to seek and save that which was lost. There He is, nailed and suffering agonies on that cross, and yet what does He say as He looks upon the people who are responsible for it? 'Father, forgive them.' Why? 'For they know not what they do.' It is not they, it is Satan; they are the victims; they are being governed and dominated by sin. 'Father, forgive them; for they know not what they do.' Now you and I are to become like that. Look at Stephen the martyr attaining to that. As they are stoning him, what does he say? He prays to his heavenly Father and cries, 'Lay not this sin to their charge.' 'They do not know what they are doing, Lord', says Stephen; 'they are mad. They are mad because of sin; they do not understand me as Thy servant; they do not understand my Lord and Master; they are blinded by the god of this world; they do not know what they are doing. Lay not this sin to their charge. They are not responsible.' He has pity upon them and is merciful with respect to them. And that, I say, is to be the condition of every one who is truly Christian. We are to feel a sense of sorrow for all who are helpless slaves of sin. That is to be our attitude towards people.

I wonder whether we have recognized this as the Christian position even when people were using us despitefully and maligning us. As we shall see later in this Sermon on the Mount, even when they are doing that, we are still to be merciful. Do you not know something about this in experience? Have you not felt sorry for people who show from the expression on their faces the bitterness and the anger they feel? They are to be pitied. Look at the things about which they get angry, showing that their whole central spirit is wrong; so unlike

Christ, so unlike God who has forgiven them everything. We should feel a great sorrow for them, we should be praying to God for them and asking Him to have mercy upon them. I say that all this follows of necessity if we have truly experienced what it means to be forgiven. If I know that I am a debtor to mercy alone, if I know that I am a Christian solely because of that free grace of God, there should be no pride left in me, there should be nothing vindictive, there should be no insisting upon my rights. Rather, as I look out upon others, if there is anything in them that is unworthy, or that is a manifestation of sin, I should have this great sorrow for them in my heart.

All these things then follow inevitably and automatically. That is what our Lord is saying here. If you are merciful, you have mercy in this way. You already have it, but you will have it every time you sin, because when you realize what you have done you will come back to God and say, 'Have mercy upon me, O God.' But remember this. If, when you sin, you see it and in repentance go to God, and there on your knees immediately realize that you are not forgiving somebody else, you will have no confidence in your prayers; you will despise yourself. As David puts it, 'If I regard iniquity in my heart, the Lord will not hear me.' If you are not forgiving your brother, you can ask God for forgiveness, but you will have no confidence in your prayer, and your prayer will not be answered. That is what this Beatitude says. That is what our Lord said in the parable of the unjust steward. If that unrighteous, cruel servant would not forgive the servant who was under him, he was a man who had never understood forgiveness or his relationship to his master. Therefore he was not forgiven. For the one condition of forgiveness is repentance. Repentance means, among other things, that I realize that I have no claim upon God at all, and that it is only His grace and mercy that forgive. And it follows as the night the day that the man who truly realizes his position face-to-face with God, and his relationship to God, is the man who must of necessity be merciful with respect to others.

It is a solemn, serious and, in a sense, terrible thing to say that you cannot be truly forgiven unless there is a forgiving spirit in you. For the operation of the grace of God is such, that when it comes into our hearts with forgiveness it makes us merciful. We proclaim, therefore, whether we have received forgiveness or not by whether we forgive or not. If I am forgiven, I shall forgive. None of us has by nature a forgiving spirit. And if you now have such a spirit, you have it for one reason only. You have seen what God has done for you in spite of what you deserve, and you say, 'I know that I am truly forgiven; therefore, I truly forgive.' 'Blessed are the merciful: for they shall obtain mercy.' Because they have already obtained mercy, therefore they are merciful. As we go on through the world we fall into sin. The moment we do so we need this mercy and we get it. And remember the end. In 2 Timothy 1:16-18 Paul inserts a note about Onesiphorus whom he recalls as one who had compassion on him and who visited him when he was a prisoner in Rome. Then he adds: 'The Lord grant unto him that he may find mercy of the Lord in that day.' Oh yes, we shall need it then; we shall need it at the end, at the day of judgment when every one of us stands before the judgment seat of Christ and has to give an account of the deeds done in the body. For certain, there will be things which are wrong and sinful, and we shall need mercy in that day. And, thank God, if the grace of Christ is in us, if the spirit of the Lord is in us, and we are merciful, we shall obtain mercy in that day. What makes me merciful is the grace of God. But the grace of God *does* make me merciful. So it comes to this. If I am not merciful there is only one explanation; I have never understood the grace and the mercy of God; I am outside Christ; I am yet in my sins, and I am unforgiven.

'Let every man examine himself.' I am not asking you what sort of life you are living. I am not asking whether you do this, that or the other. I am not asking whether you have some general interest in the kingdom of God and His house. I am simply asking this. Are you merciful? Are you sorry for every sinner even though that sinner offends you? Have you pity upon all who are the victims and the dupes of the world and the flesh and the devil? That is the test. 'Blessed — happy — are the merciful: for they shall obtain mercy.'

Chapter Ten

Blessed Are the Pure in Heart

WE come now to what is undoubtedly one of the greatest utterances to be found anywhere in the whole realm of Holy Scripture. Anyone who realizes even something of the meaning of the words, 'Blessed are the pure in heart: for they shall see God', can approach them only with a sense of awe and of complete inadequacy. This statement, of course, has engaged the attention of God's people ever since it was first uttered, and many great volumes have been written in an attempt to expound it. Obviously, therefore, one cannot hope to deal with it in any exhaustive sense in just one chapter. Indeed, no one can ever exhaust this verse. In spite of all that has been written and preached, it still eludes us. Our best plan, perhaps, is just to, try to grasp something of its central meaning and emphasis.

Once again it is important, I feel, to consider it in its setting, and to study its relationship to the other Beatitudes. As we have seen, our Lord did not select these statements at random. Clearly there was a definite sequence of thought, and it is our business to try to discover this. Of course we must always be very careful as we do that. It is interesting to try to discover the order and the sequence in Scripture; but it is very easy to impose upon the sacred text our own ideas as to order and sequence. An analysis of the books of the Bible can be a very useful thing indeed. But there is always the danger that, by imposing our analysis on the Scripture, we shall thereby distort its message. As we seek in this way to discover the order we must bear that warning in mind.

I suggest that the following is a possible way of understanding the sequence. The first question which must be answered is, why is this statement put here? You would have thought, perhaps, that it should have come at the beginning, because the vision of God has always been regarded by God's people as the *summum bonum*. It is the ultimate goal of every endeavour. To 'see God' is the whole purpose of all religion. And yet here it is, not at the beginning, not at the end, not even in the exact middle. That, at once, must raise the question in our minds, why does it come just here? A possible analysis, which commends itself to me, is as follows. I regard the sixth verse as providing the explanation. It comes, as I think we saw when we dealt with it, in the centre; the first three Beatitudes lead up to it and these other Beatitudes follow it. If we regard verse six as a kind of watershed, I think it helps us to understand why this particular statement comes at this point.

Now the first three Beatitudes were concerned with our need, our consciousness of need — poor in spirit, mourning because of our sinfulness, meek as the result of a true understanding of the nature of self and its great egocentricity, that terrible thing that has ruined the whole of life. These three emphasize the vital importance of a deep awareness of need. Then comes the great statement of the satisfaction of the need, God's provision for it, 'Blessed are they which do hunger and thirst after righteousness: for they shall be filled.' Having realized the need, we hunger and thirst, and then God comes with His wondrous answer that we shall be filled, fully satisfied. From there on we are looking at the result of that satisfaction, the result of being filled. We become merciful, pure in heart, peacemakers. After that, there is the outcome of all this, 'persecuted for righteousness' sake'. That, I suggest, is the way of approach to this passage. It leads up to the central statement about hungering and thirsting and then describes the results that follow. In the first three we are going up one side of the mountain, as it were. We reach the summit in the fourth, and then we come down on the other side.

But there is a closer correspondence even than that. It seems to me that the three Beatitudes which follow the central statement in verse six correspond to the first three that lead up to it. The merciful are those who realize their poverty of spirit; they realize that they have nothing in themselves at all. As we have seen, that is the most essential step to becoming merciful. It is only when a man has reached that view of himself that he will have the right view of others. So we find that the man who realizes he is poor in spirit and who is utterly dependent upon God, is the man who is merciful to others. It follows from that, that this second statement which we are now considering, namely, 'blessed are the pure in heart', also corresponds to the second statement in the first group, which was, 'blessed are they that mourn'. What did they mourn about? We saw that they were mourning about the state of their hearts; they were mourning about their sinfulness; they were mourning, not only because they did things that were wrong, but still more because they ever wanted to do wrong. They realized the central perversion in their character and personality; it was that which caused them to mourn. Very well then; here is something which corresponds to that —

'blessed are the pure in heart.' Who are the pure in heart? Essentially, as I am going to show you, they are those who are mourning about the impurity of their hearts. Because the only way to have a pure heart is to realize you have an impure heart, and to mourn about it to such an extent that you do that which alone can lead to cleansing and purity. And in exactly the same way, when we come to discuss the 'peacemakers' we shall find that the peacemakers are those that are meek. If a person is not meek he is not likely to be a peacemaker.

I do not want to stay longer with this matter of order, but I think it is a possible way of discovering what underlies the precise arrangement which our Lord adopted. We take the three steps in order of need; then we come to the satisfaction; then we look at the results that follow and find that they correspond precisely to the three that lead up to it. This means that, in this amazing and glorious statement about 'blessed are the pure in heart: for they shall see God' which comes at this particular point, the emphasis is upon the purity of heart and not upon the promise. If we look at it from that standpoint, I think it will enable us to see why our Lord took this precise order.

Here, then, we are face-to-face with one of the most magnificent, and yet one of the most solemnizing and searching, statements which can be found anywhere in Scripture. It is, of course, the very essence of the Christian position and of the Christian teaching. 'Blessed are the pure in heart.' That is what Christianity is about, that is its message. Perhaps the best way of considering it is once more to take the various terms and to examine them one by one.

We begin of course with the 'heart'. Here, I repeat, is something which is very characteristic of the gospel. The gospel of Jesus Christ is concerned about the heart: all its emphasis is upon the heart. Read the accounts which we have in the Gospels of the teaching of our blessed Lord, and you will find that all along He is talking about the heart. The same is true in the Old Testament. Our Lord undoubtedly put this emphasis here because of the Pharisees. It was His great charge against them always that they were interested in the outside of the pots and platters and ignored the inside. Looked at externally, they were without spot. But their inward parts were full of ravening and wickedness. They were most concerned about the external injunctions of religion; but they forgot the weightier matters of the law, namely, love to God and the love of one's neighbour. So here our Lord puts this great emphasis upon it again. The heart is the whole centre of His teaching.

Let us for a moment consider this emphasis in terms of a few negatives. He puts His emphasis upon the heart and not upon the head. 'Blessed are the pure in heart.' He does not commend those who are intellectual; His interest is in the heart. In other words we have to remind ourselves again that the Christian faith is ultimately not only a matter of doctrine or understanding or of intellect, it is a condition of the heart. Let me hasten to add that the doctrine is absolutely essential; the intellectual apprehension is absolutely essential; understanding is vital. But it is not only that. We must ever beware lest we stop at giving only an intellectual assent to the faith or to a given number of propositions. We have to do that, but the terrible danger is that we stop at that. When people have had merely an intellectual interest in these matters it has oftentimes been a curse to the Church. This applies not only to doctrine and theology. You can have a purely mechanical interest in the Word of God, so that merely to be a student of the Bible does not mean that all is well. Those who are interested only in the mechanics of exposition are in no better position than the purely academic theologians. Our Lord says that this is not essentially a matter of the head. It is that, but it is not only that.

But again, why is it that He puts His emphasis upon the heart rather than upon externalities and conduct? The Pharisees, you will remember, were always ready to reduce the way of life and righteousness to a mere matter of conduct, ethics and behaviour. How this gospel finds us all out! Those of you who dislike the intellectual emphasis were probably saying 'Amen', as I emphasized that first point. 'Yes, that is quite right', you said, 'it is not intellectual, it is the life that matters.' Be careful! for Christianity is also not primarily a matter of conduct and external behaviour. It starts with this question: What is the state of the heart?

What is meant by this term, 'the heart'? According to the general scriptural usage of the term, the heart means the centre of the personality. It does not merely mean the seat of the affections and the emotions. This Beatitude is not a statement to the effect that the Christian faith is something primarily emotional, not intellectual or pertaining to the will. Not at all. The heart in Scripture includes the three. It is the centre of man's being and personality; it is the fount out of which everything else comes. It includes the mind; it includes the will; it includes the heart. It is the total man; and that is the thing which our Lord emphasizes. 'Blessed are the pure in *heart*'; blessed are those who are pure, not merely on the surface but in the centre of their being and at the source of their every activity. It is as deep as that. Now that is the first thing; the gospel always emphasizes that. It starts with the heart.

Then, secondly, it emphasizes that the heart is always the seat of all our troubles. You remember how our Lord put it, 'Out of the heart proceed evil thoughts, murders, adulteries, fornications, thefts, false witness, blasphemies'. The terrible, tragic fallacy of the last hundred years has been to think that all man's troubles are due to his environment, and that to change the man you have nothing to do but to change his environment. That is a tragic fallacy. It overlooks the fact that it was in Paradise that man fell. It was in a perfect environment that he first went wrong, so to put man in a perfect environment cannot solve his problems. No, no; it is out of 'the heart' that these things arise. Take any problem in life, anything that leads to wretchedness; find out its cause, and you will always discover that it comes from the heart somewhere, from some unworthy desire in somebody, in an individual, in a group or in a nation. All our troubles arise out of this human heart which, we are told by Jeremiah, is 'deceitful above all things, and desperately wicked: who can know it?' In other words, the gospel not only tells us that all these problems arise out of the heart, but that they do so because the heart of man, as the result of the fall and as the result of sin, is, as Scripture puts it, desperately wicked and deceitful. Man's troubles, in other words, are at the very centre of his being, so that merely to develop his intellect is not going to solve his problems. We should all be aware that education alone does not make a good man; a man may be highly educated and yet be an utterly wicked person. The problem is in the centre, so that mere schemes for intellectual development cannot put us right. Neither can these efforts to improve the environment do so alone. Our tragic failure to realize this is responsible for the state of the world at this moment. The trouble is in the heart, and the heart is desperately wicked and deceitful. That is the problem.

Now we come to the second term. 'Blessed', says our Lord, 'are the *pure* in heart', and you see again how packed with doctrine these Beatitudes are. We have just been looking at the human heart. Is anybody prepared to say in the light of that, that man can make himself a Christian? You can see God only when you are pure in heart, and we have just seen what we are by nature. It is a complete antithesis; nothing could be further removed from God. What the gospel proposes to do is to bring us out of the terrible pit and to raise us up to the heavens. It is supernatural. Therefore let us look at it in terms of definition. What does our Lord mean by '*pure* in heart'? It is generally agreed that the word has at any rate two main meanings. One meaning is that it is without hypocrisy; it means, if you like, 'single'. You remember our Lord talks about the evil eye later on in this Sermon on the Mount. He says, 'If therefore thine eye be single, thy whole body shall be full of light. But if thine eye be evil, thy whole body shall be full of darkness.' This pureness of heart, therefore, corresponds to 'singleness'. It means, if you like, 'without folds'; it is open, nothing hidden. You can describe it as sincerity; it means single-minded, or single-eyed devotion. One of the best definitions of purity is given in Psalm 86:11, 'Unite my heart to fear thy name'. The trouble with us is our divided heart. Is not that my whole problem face-to - face with God? One part of me wants to know God and worship God and please

God; but another part wants something else. You remember the way Paul expresses it in Romans 7; 'For I delight in the law of God after the inward man: but I see another law in my members, warring against the law of my mind, and bringing me into captivity to the law of sin which is in my members.' Now the pure heart is the heart that is no longer divided, and that is why the Psalmist, having understood his trouble, prayed the Lord to 'unite my heart to fear thy name'. 'Make it one', he seems to say; 'make it single, take out the pleats and the folds, let it be whole, let it be one, let it be sincere, let it be entirely free from any hypocrisy.'

But that is not the only meaning of this term 'purity'. It also obviously carries the further meaning of 'cleansed', 'without defilement'. In Revelation 21:27 John tells us concerning the people who are to be admitted into the heavenly Jerusalem that is to come, that 'there shall in no wise enter into it any thing that defileth, neither whatsoever worketh abomination, or maketh a lie: but they which are written in the Lamb's book of life'.

In Revelation 22:14 we read, 'Blessed are they that do his commandments, that they may have right to the tree of life, and may enter in through the gates into the city. For without are dogs, and sorcerers, and whoremongers, and murderers, and idolaters, and whosoever loveth and maketh a lie.' Nothing that is unclean or impure, or has any defiling touch about it, shall enter into the heavenly Jerusalem.

But perhaps we can perfectly express it by saying that being pure in heart means to be like the Lord Jesus Christ Himself, 'who did no sin, neither was guile found in his mouth' — perfect and spotless and pure and entire. Analysing it a little we can say that it means we have an undivided love which regards God as our highest good, and which is concerned only about loving God. To be pure in heart, in other words, means to keep 'the first and great commandment', which is that 'Thou shalt love the Lord thy God with all thy heart, and with all thy soul, and with all thy mind.'

Reducing it still further, it means that we should live to the glory of God in every respect, and that that should be the supreme desire of our life. It means that we desire God, that we desire to know Him, that we desire to love Him and to serve Him. And our Lord states here that only those who are like that shall see God. That is why I say that this is one of the most solemnizing statements in Holy Scripture. There is a parallel one in the Epistle to the Hebrews which speaks of 'holiness, without which no man shall see the Lord'. I cannot understand people who object to the preaching of holiness (I am not referring to the theories about it; I am talking about preaching holiness itself in the New Testament sense), because we have this plain, obvious statement of Scripture that without it 'no man shall see the Lord'. Now we have been looking at what holiness really means. I ask once more, therefore, whether there is any folly greater than the folly of imagining that you can ever make yourself a Christian. The whole object of Christianity is to bring us to the vision of God, to see God.

What then is necessary before I can see God? Here is the answer. Holiness, a pure heart, an unmixed condition of being. Yet men and women would reduce all this to just a little matter of decency, of morality or an intellectual interest in the doctrines of the Christian faith. But nothing less than the whole person is involved. 'God is light, and in him is no darkness at all.' In the spiritual realm you cannot mix light and darkness, you cannot mix black and white, you cannot mix Christ and Belial. There is no connection between them. Obviously, therefore, only those who are like Him can see God and be in His presence. That is why we must be pure in heart before we can see God.

What is meant by the vision of God? What is meant by saying we shall 'see' God? Here again is a matter which has been often written about throughout the long history of the Christian Church. Some of the great Fathers and the early teachers in the Church were much attracted by it and gave a great deal of thought to the problem. Did it really mean that in the glorified state we should see God with the naked eye or not? That was their great problem. Was it objective and visible, or was it purely spiritual? Now it seems to me that, ultimately, that is a question that cannot be answered. I can only put evidence before you. There are statements made in Scripture which seem to indicate one or the other. But at any rate we can say this much. You remember what happened to Moses. On one occasion God took him aside and placed him in the cleft of a rock and said He was going to give Moses a vision of Himself, but told him that he should see only His back parts, suggesting, surely, that to see God is impossible. The theophanies of the Old Testament, namely, those occasions when the Angel of the Covenant appeared in the form of man, surely suggest that this seeing is impossible in a physical sense.

Then you remember the statements made by our Lord Himself. He turned to the people and said on one occasion, 'Ye have neither heard his voice at any time, nor seen his shape' — suggesting that there is a 'shape'. Again He said, 'Not that any man hath seen the Father, save he which is of God, he hath seen the Father.' 'You have not seen the Father,' said our Lord in effect to the people; 'but I who am of God have seen the Father.' 'No man hath seen God at any time; the only begotten Son, which is in the bosom of the Father, he hath declared him.' There are the statements by which we are confronted. Then you remember, on another occasion He said, 'He that hath seen me hath seen the Father', one of the most cryptic of all the statements. This is what Scripture says on the matter, and it does seem to me that, on the whole, it is unprofitable to spend our time on it. We just do not know. The very Being of God is so transcendent and eternal that all our efforts to arrive at an understanding are doomed at the very outset to failure. Scripture itself, it seems to me — I say it with reverence — does not attempt to give us an adequate conception of the Being of God. Why? Because of the glory of God. Our terms are so inadequate, and our minds are so small and finite, that there is a danger in any attempt at a description of God and His glory. All we know is that there is this glorious promise that, in some way or other, the pure in heart shall see God.

I suggest, therefore, that it means something like this. As with all the other Beatitudes, the promise is partly fulfilled here and now. In a sense there is a vision of God even while we are in this world. Christian people can see God in a sense that nobody else can. The Christian can see God in nature, whereas the non-Christian cannot. The Christian sees God in the events of history. There is a vision possible to the eye of faith that no one else has. But there is a seeing also in the sense of knowing Him, a sense of feeling He is near, and enjoying His presence. You remember what we are told about Moses in that great eleventh chapter of the Epistle to the Hebrews. Moses endured 'as seeing him who is invisible'. That is a part of it, and that is something that is possible to us here and now. 'Blessed are the pure in heart.' Imperfect as we are, we can claim that even now we are seeing God in that sense; we are 'seeing him who is invisible'. Another way we see Him is in our own experience, in His gracious dealings with us. Do we not say we see the hand of our Lord upon us in this and that? That is part of the seeing of God.

But of course that is a mere nothing as compared with what is yet to be. 'Now we see through a glass, darkly.' We see in a way we had not seen before, but it is all still much of an enigma. But then we shall see 'face-to-face'. 'Beloved, now are we the sons of God,' John says, 'and it doth not yet appear what we shall be: but we know that, when he shall appear, we shall be like him; for we shall see him as he is.' This is surely the most amazing thing that has ever been said to man, that you and I, such as we are, pressed with all the problems and troubles of this modern world, are going to see Him face-to-face. If we but grasped this, it would revolutionize our lives. You and I are meant for the audience chamber of God; you and I are being prepared to enter into the presence of the King of kings. Do you believe it, do you know it as true of you? Do you realize that a day is coming when you are going to see the blessed God face-to-face? Not as in a glass, darkly; but face-to-face. Surely the moment we grasp this, everything else pales into insignificance. You and I are going to enjoy God, and to spend our eternity in His glorious and eternal presence. Read the book of the Revelation, and listen to the redeemed of the Lord as they praise Him and ascribe all glory to Him. The blessedness is inconceivable, beyond our imagination. And we are destined for that. 'The pure in heart shall see God', nothing less than that. How foolish we are to rob ourselves of these glories that are here held out before our wondering gaze. Have you in a partial sense already seen God? Do you realize you are being prepared for this, and do you set your affection on it? 'Set your affection on things above, not on things on the earth.' Are you looking at these things which are unseen and eternal? Do you spend time in meditating upon the glory that yet awaits you? If you do, the greatest concern of your life will be to have a pure heart.

But how can our hearts become pure? Here again is a great theme which has occupied attention throughout the centuries. There are two great ideas. First there are those who say there is only one thing to do, that we must become monks and segregate ourselves from the world. 'It is a whole-time job', they say. 'If I am going to have this pure heart, I have not time for anything else.' There you have the whole idea of monasticism. We must not stay with that, but I would simply point out in passing that it is utterly unscriptural. It is not to be found in the New Testament, for it is something you and I can never do. All such efforts at self-cleansing are doomed to failure. The way of the Scriptures is rather this. All you and I can do is to realize the blackness of our hearts as they are by nature, and as we do so we shall join David in the prayer, 'Create in me a clean heart, O God; and renew a right spirit within me'. We shall join Joseph Hart in saying:

> 'Tis thine to cleanse the heart,
>   To sanctify the soul,
> To pour fresh life in every part
>   And new create the whole.

You can start trying to clean your heart, but at the end of your long life it will be as black as it was at the beginning, perhaps blacker. No! it is God alone who can do it, and, thank God, He has promised to do it. The only way in which we can have a clean heart is for the Holy Spirit to enter into us and to cleanse it for us. Only His indwelling and working within can purify the heart, and He does it by working in us 'both to will and to do of his good pleasure'. Paul's confidence was this, that 'he which hath begun a good work in you will perform it until the day of Jesus Christ'. That is my only hope. I am in His hands, and the process is going on. God is dealing with me, and my heart is being cleansed. God has set His hand to this task, and I know, because of that, that a day is coming when I shall be faultless and blameless, without spot or wrinkle, without any defilement. I shall be able to enter into the gate of the holy city, leaving everything that is unclean outside, solely because He is doing it.

That does not mean that I therefore remain passive in the matter. I believe that the work is God's; but I also believe what James says, 'Draw nigh to God, and he will draw nigh to you.' I want God to draw nigh to me, because, if He does not, my heart will remain black. How is God going to draw nigh to me? You 'draw nigh to God, and he will draw nigh to you', says James. 'Cleanse your hands, ye sinners; and purify your hearts, ye double minded.' The fact that I know that I cannot ultimately purify and cleanse my heart in an absolute sense does not mean that I should walk in the gutters of life waiting for God to cleanse me. I must do everything I can and still know it is not enough, and that He must do it finally. Or listen again to what Paul says: 'It is God which worketh in you both to will and to do of his good pleasure.' Yes, but 'mortify therefore your members which are upon the earth'. Strangle them, get rid of them, get rid of everything that stands between you and the goal you are aiming at. 'Mortify', put it to death. 'If ye through the Spirit', he says again to the Romans, 'do mortify the deeds of the body, ye shall live.'

All I have tried to say can be put like this. You are going to see God! Do you not agree that this is the biggest, the most momentous, the most tremendous thing that you can ever be told? Is it your supreme object, desire and ambition to see God? If it is, and if you believe this gospel, you must agree with John, 'Every man that hath this hope in him purifieth himself, even as he is pure.' The time is short, you and I have not long to prepare. The Great Reception is at hand; in a sense the ceremonial is all prepared; you and I are waiting for the audience with the King. Are you looking forward to it? Are you preparing yourself for it? Don't you feel ashamed at this moment that you are wasting your time on things that not only will be of no value to you on that great occasion, but of which you will then be ashamed. You and I, creatures of time as we appear to be, are going to see God and bask in His eternal glory for ever and ever. Our one confidence is that He is working in us and preparing us for that. But let us also work and purify ourselves 'even as he is pure'.

Chapter Eleven

Blessed Are the Peacemakers

A S we come to consider this further characteristic of the Christian man, we are once more constrained to suggest that there is nothing in the whole range of Scripture which so tests and examines and humbles us as these Beatitudes. Here in this statement, 'Blessed are the peacemakers,' we have a further outcome and outworking of being filled by God. According to the scheme which we outlined in the last chapter we can see how this corresponds to 'blessed are the meek'. I suggested there that there was this correspondence between the Beatitudes which preceded and followed the statement in verse 6 — poverty of spirit and being merciful can be regarded together, the mourning for sin and being pure in heart are similarly connected, and, in exactly the same way, the meekness and being peacemakers correspond to each other; and the link between them is always that waiting upon God for that fullness which He alone can give.

Here, then, we are reminded once more that the outworking in the Christian of the Christian life is altogether and entirely different from everything that can be known by any man who is not a Christian. That is the message which recurs in every one of these Beatitudes and which, obviously, our Lord desired to emphasize. He was establishing an entirely new and different kingdom. As we have seen in all our previous studies, there is nothing more fatal than for the natural man to think that he can take the Beatitudes and try to put them into practice. Here once more this particular Beatitude reminds us that this is utterly impossible. Only a new man can live this new life.

We can see that this statement must have come as a very great shock to the Jews. They had the idea that the coming kingdom of the Messiah was to be a military one, a national, materialistic one. People are always ready to materialize the great promises of Scripture (they are still doing it) and the Jews fell into that fatal error. Here our Lord reminded them again at the very beginning that their whole idea was a complete fallacy. They thought the Messiah when He came would set Himself up as a great King, and that He would deliver them from all their bondage and would thus establish the Jews above everybody else as the conquering and the master race. You remember that even John the Baptist seems to have clung to that conception when he sent his two disciples and asked his famous question, 'Art thou he that should come? or look we for another?' 'I know all about these miracles', he seems to say, 'but when is the big thing going to take place?' And you remember how the people were so impressed after our Lord had performed that great miracle of the feeding of the five thousand that they began to say, 'This is He undoubtedly', and then they went, we are told, and tried to 'take him by force, to make him a king'. It was always like that. But here our Lord says to them, in effect, 'No, no; you do not understand. Blessed are the peacemakers. My kingdom is not of this world. If it were, then My citizens would be fighting for this sort of thing. But it is not that; you are entirely wrong in your whole outlook upon it.' And then He gives them this Beatitude and stresses that principle once more.

Surely this should impress us at the present time. Never, perhaps, was there a more appropriate word for this modern world of ours than this Beatitude which we are studying together. There is perhaps no clearer pronouncement of what the Scriptures, and the New Testament gospel especially, have to say about the world, and life in this world, than this. And of course, as I have been trying to point out as we have faced each of these Beatitudes, it is a very highly theological statement. Now I say that again deliberately, for there is no section of the New Testament that has been so misunderstood and abused as the Sermon on the Mount. You remember how it used to be the habit (especially in the early years of this century, and it still lingers) for certain people to say that they had no interest in theology at all, that they utterly disliked the apostle Paul and regarded it as a calamity that he had ever become a Christian; 'that Jew', they said, 'with his legalistic notions, who came along and foisted his legalism upon the glorious, delightful and simple gospel of Jesus of Nazareth.' They were not interested in the New Testament Epistles at all, but they were tremendously interested, they said, in the Sermon on the Mount. That was the great need of the world. All that was needed was to take seriously this beautiful idealism thus presented by the Master Teacher of Galilee. All we had to do was to study it and to try to persuade one another to put it into practice. 'Not theology', they said; 'that has been the curse of the Church. What is needed is this beautiful ethical teaching, this marvellous, moral uplift which is to be found here in the Sermon on the Mount.' The Sermon on the Mount was their favourite portion of Scripture because they maintained it was so un-theological, so utterly lacking in doctrine and dogma and all such wasteful interest.

We are reminded here of the utter folly and futility of such a view of this glorious portion of Scripture. Let me put it like this. Why are peacemakers blessed? The answer is that they are blessed because they are so absolutely unlike everybody else. The peacemakers are blessed because they are the people who stand out as being different from the rest of the world, and they are different because they are the children of God. In other words, I say, we are again plunged immediately into New Testament theology and doctrine.

Let me vary my question. Why are there wars in the world? Why is there this constant international tension? What is the matter with the world? Why have we had these world wars in this century? Why is there a threat of further war and all this unhappiness and turmoil and discord amongst men? According to this Beatitude, there is only one answer to these questions — sin. Nothing else; it is just sin. So immediately you are back at the doctrine of man and the doctrine of sin — theology, in fact. The peacemaker, you see, has become different from what he was; there again is essential theology. The explanation of all our troubles is human lust, greed, selfishness, self-centredness; it is the cause of all the trouble and the discord, whether between individuals, or between groups within a nation, or between nations themselves. So you cannot begin to understand the problem of the modern world unless you accept the New Testament doctrine with regard to man and sin, and here it is at once suggested to us.

Or look at it in this way. Why is there so much trouble and difficulty in maintaining peace in the world? Think of all the endless international conferences that have been held in this present century to try to produce peace. Why have they all failed and why are we now coming to the state when very few of us seem to have any confidence in any conference that men may choose to hold? What is the explanation of all this? Why did the League of Nations fail? Why does the United Nations Organization seem to be failing? What is the matter? Now I suggest to you that there is only one adequate answer to that question; it is not political, it is not economic, it is not social. The answer once more is essentially and primarily theological and doctrinal. And it is because the world in its folly and blindness will not recognize this, that it wastes so much time. The trouble, according to the Scripture, is in the heart of man, and until the heart of man is changed, you will never solve his problem by trying to make manipulations on the surface. If the source of the trouble is in the fountain and the origin from which the stream comes, is it not obviously a waste of time and money and energy to be pouring chemicals into the stream in an attempt to cure the condition? You must go to the source. There is the essential trouble; none of these things can possibly work while man remains what he is. The tragic folly of this twentieth century is our failure to see that. And, alas, it is not only the failure which is found in the world, it is a failure to be found even in the Church herself. How often has the Church been preaching nothing but these human efforts and endeavours, preaching the League of Nations and the United Nations. It is a contradiction of biblical doctrine. Do not misunderstand me. I am not saying you should not make all these efforts internationally; but I am saying that the man who pins his faith to these things is a man who is not regarding life and the world from the standpoint of Scripture. According to the Scripture, the trouble is in the heart of man and nothing but a new heart, nothing but a new man can possibly deal with the problem. It is 'out of the heart' that evil thoughts, murders, adultery, fornication, jealousy, envy, malice and all these other things proceed; and while men are like that there will be no peace. What is in, will inevitably come out. I say once more, therefore, that there is nothing I know of in Scripture which so utterly condemns humanism and idealism as this Sermon on the Mount, which has always apparently been the humanists' favourite passage of Scripture. Clearly they have never understood it. They have evacuated it of its doctrine, and have turned it into something which is entirely different.

This teaching, then, is something which is of prime importance at the present hour, because it is only as we see our modern world in proper perspective through these New Testament eyes that we shall even begin to understand it. Are you surprised that there are wars and rumours of wars? You should not be if you are a Christian; indeed you should regard it as a strange and extraordinary confirmation of the biblical teaching. I remember some twenty years ago shocking certain nice Christian people because I could not be very enthusiastic about what was then called the Kellogg pact. I happened to be at a Christian meeting when the news came through of the Kellogg pact, and I remember a very worthy deacon in that meeting getting up and proposing that the meeting should not take its customary form of sharing experiences and considering problems of the spiritual life, but that the whole meeting ought to be given to talking about this Kellogg pact. To him it was such a wonderful thing, it was something that was going to outlaw war for ever, and he was amazed at my lack of enthusiasm. I think I need say no more. Our approach must be doctrinal and theological. The trouble is in the heart of man, and while it is there, these manipulations on the surface cannot possibly deal with the problem in any final sense.

Bearing all that in mind, let us look at this great word positively. The great need of the world today is for a number of peacemakers. If only we were all peacemakers there would be no problems, there would be no troubles. What then is a peacemaker? Obviously again, it is not a matter of natural disposition. It does not mean an easygoing person, it does not mean your 'peace at any price' person. It does not mean the sort of man who says, 'Anything to avoid trouble'. It cannot mean that. Have we not agreed all along that none of the Beatitudes describe natural dispositions? But not only that. These easygoing, peace-at-any-price people are often lacking in a sense of justice and righteousness; they do not stand where they should stand; they are flabby. They appear to be nice; but if the whole world were run on such principles and by such people it would be even worse than it is today. So I would add that your true peacemaker is not an 'appeaser', as we say today. You can postpone war by appeasement; but it generally means that you are doing something that is unjust and unrighteous in order to avoid war. The mere avoidance of war does not make peace, it does not solve the problem. This generation ought to know that with particular certainty. No; it is not appeasement.

What is it, then, to be a peacemaker? He is one about whom we can say two main things. Passively, we can say that he is peaceable, for a quarrelsome person cannot be a peacemaker. Then, actively, this person must be pacific, he must be one who makes peace actively. He is not content to 'let sleeping dogs lie', he is not concerned about maintaining the *status quo*. He desires peace, and he does all he can to produce peace and to maintain it. He is a man who actively sees that there should be peace between man and man, and group and group, and nation and nation. Obviously, therefore, I think we can argue that he is a man who is finally and ultimately concerned about the fact that all men should be at peace with God. There, essentially, is the peacemaker, both passively and actively, negatively and positively pacific, one who not only does not make trouble, but who goes out of his way to produce peace.

What does this involve and imply? Clearly, in view of what I have been saying, it implies the necessity of an entirely new outlook. It must involve a new nature. To sum it up in a phrase, it means a new heart, a pure heart. There is, as we have seen, a logical order in these matters. It is only the man of a pure heart who can be a peacemaker because, you remember, we saw that the person who did not have a pure heart, who had a heart which was filled with envy, jealousy and all such horrible things, could never be a peacemaker. The heart must be cleansed of all that before one can possibly make peace. But we do not even stop at that. To be a peacemaker obviously means that one must have an entirely new view of self, and here you see how it links up with our definition of the meek. Before one can be a peacemaker one really must be entirely delivered from self, from self-interest, from self-concern. Before you can be a peacemaker you really must be entirely forgetful of self because as long as you are thinking about yourself, and shielding yourself, you cannot be doing the work properly.

To be a peacemaker you must be, as it were, absolutely neutral so that you can bring the two sides together. You must not be sensitive, you must not be touchy, you must not be on the defensive. If you are, you will not be a very good peacemaker.

Perhaps I can best explain it like this. The peacemaker is one who is not always looking at everything in terms of the effect it has upon himself. Now is not that the whole trouble with us by nature? We look at everything as it affects us. 'What is the reaction upon me? What is this going to mean to me?' And the moment we think like that there is of necessity war, because everybody else is doing the same thing. That is the explanation of all the quarrelling and discord. Everybody looks at it from the self-centred point of view. 'Is this fair to me? Am I having my rights and dues?' They are not interested in the causes they should be serving, or the great thing that brings them all together, this Church, Society, or Organization. It is, 'How is this affecting me? What is this doing to me?' Now that is the spirit that always leads to quarrels, misunderstandings and disputes, and it is a negation of being a peacemaker.

The first thing, therefore, we must say about the peacemaker is that he has an entirely new view of himself, a new view which really amounts to this. He has seen himself and has come to see that in a sense this miserable, wretched self is not worth bothering about at all. It is so wretched; it has no rights or privileges; it does not deserve anything. If you have seen yourself as poor in spirit, if you have mourned because of the blackness of your heart, if you have truly seen yourself and have hungered and thirsted after righteousness, you will not stand any longer on your rights and privileges, you will not be asking, 'What about me in this?' You will have forgotten this self. Indeed, can we not agree that one of the best tests of whether we are truly Christian or not is just this: Do I hate my natural self? Our Lord said, 'He that loveth his life (in this world) shall lose it.' By this He meant loving ourselves, the natural man, the natural life. That is one of the best tests of whether we are Christian or not. Have you come to hate yourself, your natural self? Can you say with Paul, 'O wretched man that I am'? If you have not, and if you cannot, you will not be a peacemaker.

The Christian is a man who has two men in him, the old and the new. He hates the old and says to him, 'Silence! leave me alone! I have finished with you.' He has a new view of life, and this obviously implies that he has a new view of others also. He is concerned about them; he has come to see them objectively, and is now trying to see them in the light of the biblical teaching. The peacemaker is the man who does not talk about people when they are offensive and difficult. He does not ask, 'Why are they like that?' He says, 'They are like that because they are still being governed by the god of this world, "the spirit that now worketh in the children of disobedience." That poor person is a victim of self and of Satan; he is hell bound; I must have pity and mercy upon him.' The moment he begins to look at him like that he is in a position to help him, and he is likely to make peace with him. So you must have an entirely new view of the other person.

It also means an entirely new view of the world. The peacemaker has only one concern, and it is the glory of God amongst men. That was the Lord Jesus Christ's only concern. His one interest in life was not Himself, but the glory of God. And the peacemaker is the man whose central concern is the glory of God, and who spends his life in trying to minister to that glory. He knows that God made man perfect, and that the world was meant to be Paradise, so when he sees individual and international disputes and quarrelling, he sees something that is detracting from the glory of God. This is the thing that concerns him, nothing else. Very well; with these three new views this is what follows. He is a man who is ready to humble himself, and he is ready to do anything and everything in order that the glory of God may be promoted. He so desires this that he is prepared to suffer in order to bring it to pass. He is even prepared to suffer wrong and injustice in order that peace may be produced and God's glory magnified. You see he has finished with himself and with self-interest and self-concern. He says, 'What matters is the glory of God and the manifestation of that amongst men.' So that if his suffering is going to lead to that, he will endure it.

Now that is the theory. But what about the practice? This is very important, because to be a peacemaker does not mean that you sit in a study and theoretically work out this principle. It is in practice that you prove whether you are a peacemaker or not. So I do not apologize for putting it very simply, indeed in almost an elementary manner. How does this work out in practice? First and foremost it means that you learn not to speak. If only we could all control our tongues there would be much less discord in this world. James, with his practical turn of mind, puts it perfectly: 'Be swift to hear, slow to speak, slow to wrath.' That, I say, is one of the best ways of being a peacemaker, that you just learn not to speak. When, for example, something is said to you, and the temptation is to reply, do not do it. Not only that; do not repeat things when you know they are going to do harm. You are not a true friend when you tell your friend something unkind that was said about him by somebody else. It does not help; it is a false friendship. Moreover, apart from anything else, unworthy and unkind things are not worth repeating. We must control our tongues and our lips. The peacemaker is a man who does not say things. He often feels like saying them, but for the sake of peace he does not. The natural man is so strong in us. You often hear Christian people say, 'I must express my mind'. What if everybody were like that! No; you must not excuse yourself or talk in terms of what you are by nature. As Christians you are meant to be new men, made after the image and pattern of the Lord Jesus Christ, 'swift to hear, slow to speak, slow to wrath.' If I were preaching on the international situation my one main comment at the present time would be this. I believe there is far too much talking going on in the international realm; I cannot see it does any good to be constantly black-guarding another nation. It is never a good thing to say these unkind, unpleasant things. You can organize for war; you can organize for peace; but stop talking. One of the first things in making peace is to know when not to speak.

The next thing I would say is that we should always view any and every situation in the light of the gospel. When you face a situation that tends to lead to trouble, not only must you not speak, you must think. You must take the situation and put it into the context of the gospel and ask, 'What are the implications of this? It is not only I who am involved. What about the Cause? what about the Church? what about the Organization? what about all the people who are dependent? what about the people who are right outside?' The moment you think of it like that you are beginning to make peace. But as long as you are thinking of it in a personal sense there will be war.

The next principle which I would ask you to apply would be this. You must now become positive and go out of your way to look for means and methods of making peace. You remember that mighty word, 'If thine enemy hunger, feed him.' There is your enemy, who has been saying terrible things about you. Well, you have not answered him, you have controlled your tongue. Not only that, you have said, 'I can see it is the Devil that is in him and therefore I must not answer him. I must have pity and pray that God will deliver him and show him himself as the dupe of Satan.' Good; that is the second step. But you must go beyond that. He is hungry, things have gone wrong for him. Now you begin to seek for ways of relieving him. You are becoming positive and active. It may mean sometimes that you, as we put it so foolishly, have to humble yourself and approach the other person. You have to take the initiative in speaking to him, perhaps apologizing to him, trying to be friendly, doing everything you can to produce peace.

And the last thing in the practical realm is that, as peacemakers, we should be endeavouring to diffuse peace wherever we are. We do this by being selfless, by being lovable, by being approachable and by not standing on our dignity. If we do not think of self at all, people will feel, 'I can approach that person, I know I shall get sympathy and understanding, I know I shall get an outlook which is based upon the New Testament.' Let us be such people that all will come to us, that even those who have a bitter spirit within them will somehow feel condemned when they look at us, and perhaps may be led to speak to us about themselves and their problems. The Christian is to be a man like that.

Let me sum it all up like this: the benediction pronounced on such people is that they 'shall be called the children of God'. Called means 'owned'. 'Blessed are the peacemakers: for they shall be "owned" as the children of God.' Who is going to own them? God is going to own them as His children. It means that the peacemaker is a child of God and that he is like his Father. One of the most glorious definitions of the being and character of God in the Bible is contained in the words, 'the God of peace, that brought again from the dead our Lord Jesus' (Heb. 13:20). And Paul, in his Epistle to the Romans, speaks twice of 'the God of peace' and prays that his readers will themselves be granted peace by God the Father. What is the meaning of the advent? Why did the Son of God ever come into this world? Because God, though He is holy and just and righteous and absolute in all His qualities, is a God of peace. That is why He sent His Son. Where did war come from? From man, from sin, from Satan. Discord was brought into the world in that way. But this blessed God of peace has not, I say it with reverence, 'stood upon His dignity'; He has come, He has done something. God has made peace. He has humbled Himself in His Son to produce it. That is why the peacemakers are 'children of God'. What they do is to repeat what God has done. If God stood upon His rights and dignity, upon His Person, every one of us, and the whole of mankind, would be consigned to hell and absolute perdition. It is because God is a 'God of peace' that He sent His Son, and thus provided a way of salvation for us. To be a peacemaker is to be like God, and like the Son of God. He is called, you will remember, 'the Prince of Peace', and you know what He did as the Prince of Peace. Though He counted it not robbery to be equal with God, He humbled Himself. There was no need for Him to come. He came deliberately because He is the Prince of Peace.

But beyond that, how has He made peace? Paul, in writing to the Colossians, says 'having made peace through the blood of his cross'. He gave Himself that you and I might be at peace with God, that we might have peace within and that we might have peace with one another. Take that glorious statement of the second chapter of Ephesians, 'For he is our peace, who hath made both one, and hath broken down the middle wall of partition between us; having abolished in his flesh the enmity, even the law of commandments contained in ordinances; for to make in himself of twain one new man, so making peace.' It is all there, and that is why I kept that to the end, that we might remember, whatever else we may forget, that to be a peacemaker is to be like that. He did not clutch at His rights; He did not hold on to the prerogative of deity and of eternity. He humbled Himself; He came in the likeness of a man, He humbled Himself even to the death of the cross. Why? He was not thinking of Himself at all. 'Let this mind be in you, which was also in Christ Jesus.' 'Look not every man on his own things, but every man also on the things of others.' That is the New Testament teaching. You finish with self, and then you begin to follow Jesus Christ. You realize what He did for you in order that you might enjoy that blessed peace of God, and you begin to desire that everybody else should have it. So, forgetting self, and humbling self, you follow in His steps 'who did no sin, neither was guile found in his mouth: who, when he was reviled, reviled not again; when he suffered, he threatened not; but committed himself to him that judgeth righteously.' That is it. God give us grace to see this blessed, glorious truth, and make us reflections, reproducers of the Prince of Peace, and truly children of 'the God of peace'.

Chapter Twelve

The Christian and Persecution

W E come in verse 10 to the last of the Beatitudes, 'Blessed are they which are persecuted for righteousness' sake.' It is generally agreed that verses 11 and 12 are a kind of elaboration of this Beatitude, and perhaps an application of its truth and message to the disciples in particular. In other words, our Lord has finished the general portrayal of the characteristics of the Christian man by the end of verse 10, and He then applies this last statement in particular to the disciples.

At first, this Beatitude seems to be rather different from all the others in that it is not so much a positive description of the Christian as an account of what is likely to result because of what has gone before and because the Christian is what we have seen him to be. Yet ultimately it is not different because it is still an account and description of the Christian. He is persecuted because he is a certain type of person and because he behaves in a certain manner. The best way of putting it, therefore, would be to say that, whereas all the others have been a direct description, this one is indirect. 'This is what is going to happen to you because you are a Christian', says Christ.

Now it is interesting to observe that this particular Beatitude follows immediately the reference to the peacemakers. In a sense it is because the Christian is a peacemaker that he is persecuted. What a wealth of insight and understanding that gives us into the nature and character of the Christian life! I do not think you will ever find the biblical doctrines of sin and the world put more perfectly or precisely anywhere in Scripture than in just these two Beatitudes — 'Blessed are the peacemakers', and 'Blessed are they which are persecuted for righteousness' sake'. If a Christian man is a peacemaker this is what happens to him.

Another preliminary point of interest is that the promise attached to this

Beatitude is the same as the promise attached to the first, 'theirs is the kingdom of heaven'. That is, if you like, a further and additional proof of the fact that this is the last Beatitude. You start with the kingdom of heaven and you end with it. It is not, of course, that the various blessings which have been attached to the other Beatitudes do not belong to those who are in the kingdom of heaven, or that they do not get blessings. They all get blessings; but our Lord started and ended with this particular promise in order to impress upon His listeners that the important thing was membership of the kingdom of heaven. As we have seen, the Jews had a false notion about the kingdom. 'But,' our Lord says in effect, 'I am not talking of this kind of kingdom. The important thing is that you should realize what My kingdom is, and you should know how to become members of it.' So He starts and ends with it. Over and above all these particular blessings which we receive, and which we are to receive in greater measure and greater fullness, the great thing is that we are citizens of the kingdom of heaven and thus belong to that spiritual realm.

Here, again, I think we are entitled to say that we are confronted by one of the most searching tests that can ever face us. Let no one imagine that this Beatitude is a kind of appendix to the others. In its way it is as positive a description as any that precede it, though it may be indirect; and it is one of the most searching of all. 'Blessed are they which are persecuted for righteousness' sake.' What an amazing, astounding and unexpected statement. Yet remember that it is part of the description of the Christian quite as much as being pure in heart, quite as much as being peacemakers, quite as much as being merciful. This is one of the characteristics of the Christian, as I am going to remind you, and that is why it is one of the most searching tests that we can ever face. All these Beatitudes have been searching, but there are ways in which this is even more searching than the others. But let me hasten to add that perhaps there is no Beatitude where we have to be quite so careful, there is no Beatitude that is so liable to misconstruction and misunderstanding. There is certainly no Beatitude that has been so frequently misunderstood and misapplied. Therefore we must approach it with great circumspection and care. It is a vital statement, an essential and integral part of the whole teaching of the New Testament. You will find it right through the Gospels and the Epistles. Indeed, we can go so far as to say that it is one of the great characteristic messages of the whole Bible, which carries its inevitable implication with it. I suggest, therefore, that the most important thing to emphasize is this phrase, 'for righteousness' sake'. It does not merely say, 'blessed are they which are persecuted', but 'blessed are they which are persecuted for righteousness' sake'.

Now I need not, I am sure, take any time in pointing out what a relevant statement this is for Christian people in every country at this moment. There is more persecution of Christians today, some would say, than there has been since the first centuries of the Christian era; and I think a good case can be made out for that statement. There have been grievous periods of persecution at various epochs in the long history of the Church, but they have generally been more or less localized. Now, however, persecution has spread throughout the world. There are Christian people who are being actively and bitterly persecuted in many countries at this very moment, and there may well be a strong case for saying that this may be the most important verse in your life and mine. There are so many indications that the Church may indeed be facing that fiery trial of which the apostle Peter writes and speaks. He was thinking primarily, of course, of one that was coming in his own day. But it may well be that we in this country, in apparent safety and ease, may know and experience something of the fiery trial and furnace of affliction and of persecution. Let us be clear, then, that we understand this verse and know exactly what it does say.

To that end let us start with a few negatives. It does not say, 'Blessed are those who are persecuted because they are objectionable.' It does not say, 'Blessed are those who are having a hard time in their Christian life because they are being difficult.' It does not say, 'Blessed are those who are being persecuted as Christians because they are seriously lacking in wisdom and are really foolish and unwise in what they regard as being their testimony.' It is not that. There is no need for one to elaborate this, but so often one has known Christian people who are suffering mild persecution entirely because of their own folly, because of something either in themselves or in what they are doing. But the promise does not apply to such people. It is *for righteousness' sake.* Let us be very clear about that. We can bring endless suffering upon ourselves, we can create difficulties for ourselves which are quite unnecessary, because we have some rather foolish notion of witnessing and testifying, or because, in a spirit of self-righteousness, we really do call it down on our own heads. We are often so foolish in these matters. We are slow to realize the difference between prejudice and principle; and we are so slow to understand the difference between being offensive, in a natural sense, because of our particular makeup and temperament, and causing offence because we are righteous.

So let me put another negative. We are not told, 'Blessed are the persecuted because they are fanatical.' Neither does it say, 'Blessed are the persecuted because they are overzealous.' Fanaticism can lead to persecution; but fanaticism is never commended in the New Testament. There are so many temptations that tend to come to us in the spiritual and Christian life. Some people, even in worship, seem to think that they must say their 'Amen' in a particular way, or must say it often. Thinking that this is a sign of spirituality, they make themselves a nuisance at times to others and so get into trouble about that. That is not commended in Scripture; it is a false notion of worship. The spirit of fanaticism has also very often led people into grievous difficulties. I once remember a poor man who not only brought suffering upon himself, but also upon his wife on account of his zeal. He was overzealous, and he was not facing some of the injunctions given by our Lord Himself, because he was so anxious to be testifying. Now let us be careful that we do not bring unnecessary suffering upon ourselves. We are to be 'wise as serpents, and harmless as doves'. God forbid that any of us should suffer because we fail to remember that. In other words we are not told, 'Blessed are they who are persecuted because they are doing something wrong,' or because they themselves are wrong in some respect. You remember how Peter put it in his wisdom, 'let none of you suffer as a murderer, or as a thief, or as an evildoer'. Let us notice, also, what he put into the same category as murderers, evildoers, thieves and so on — *busybodies in other men's matters* (see 1 Pet. 4:15).

Let me now add another negative from a different category. This text surely does not even mean 'blessed are they that are persecuted for a cause'. This is a little subtle and we must be careful. I say that there is a difference between being persecuted for righteousness' sake and being persecuted for a cause. I know that the two things often become one, and many of the great martyrs and confessors were at one and the same time suffering for righteousness' sake and for a cause. But it does not follow by any means that the two are always identical. Now I think that this is one of the most vital points for us to bear in mind just at this present moment. I think that in the last twenty years there have been men, some of them very well known, who have suffered, and have even been put into prisons and concentration camps, for religion. But they have not been suffering for righteousness' sake. We have to be careful about that very distinction. There is always this danger of our developing the martyr spirit. There are some people who seem anxious for martyrdom; they almost court it. That is not the thing about which our Lord is talking.

We must also realize that it does not mean suffering persecution for religio-political reasons. Now it is the simple truth to say that there were Christian people in Nazi Germany who were not only ready to practise and live the Christian faith but who preached it in the open air and yet were not molested. But we know of certain others who were put into prisons and concentration camps, and we should be careful to see why this happened to them. And I think if you draw that distinction you will find it was generally something political. I need not point out that I am not attempting to excuse Hitlerism; but I am trying to remind every Christian person of this vital distinction. If you and I begin to mix our religion and politics, then we must not be surprised if we receive persecution. But I suggest that it will not of necessity be persecution for righteousness' sake. This is something very distinct and particular, and one of the greatest dangers confronting us is that of not discriminating between these two things. There are Christian people in China and on the Continent at the present time to whom this is the most acute problem of all. Are they standing for righteousness' sake, or for a cause? After all, they have their political views and ideas. They are citizens of that particular country. I am not saying that a man should not stand for his political principles; I am simply reminding you that the promise attached to this Beatitude does not apply to that. If you choose to suffer politically, go on and do so. But do not have a grudge against God if you find that this Beatitude, this promise, is not verified in your life. The Beatitude and the promise refer specifically to suffering for righteousness' sake. May God give us grace and wisdom and understanding to discriminate between our political prejudices and our spiritual principles.

There is much confusion on this very matter at the present time. Much talk which appears to be, and is said to be, Christian, in its denunciation of certain things that are happening in the world, is, I believe, nothing but the expression of political prejudices. My desire is that we might all be saved from this serious and sad misinterpretation of Scripture, which may lead to such needless and unnecessary suffering. Another great danger in these days is that this pure Christian faith should be thought of by those who are outside in terms of certain political and social views. They are eternally distinct and have nothing to do with one another. Let me illustrate this; the Christian faith as such is not anti-communism, and I trust that none of us will be foolish enough and ignorant enough to allow the Roman Catholic Church, or any other interest, to delude and mislead us. As Christians we are to be concerned for the souls of communists, and their salvation, in exactly the same way as we are concerned about all other people. And if once we give them the impression that Christianity is just anti-communism we are ourselves shutting and barring the doors, and almost preventing them from listening to our gospel message of salvation. Let us be very careful, Christian people, and take the words of Scripture as they are.

Let us look at one final negative; this Beatitude does not even say, Blessed are they that are persecuted for being good, or noble, or self-sacrificing. There again, of course, is another vital and, it seems to some people, subtle distinction. The Beatitude does not say we are blessed if we suffer for being good or noble, for the excellent reason that you will probably not be persecuted for being good. I doubt very much also if you will ever be persecuted for being noble. The world, as a matter of fact, generally praises and admires and loves the good and the noble; it only persecutes the righteous. There are people who have made great sacrifices, those who have given up careers, prospects and wealth and who sometimes have even sacrificed their lives; and the world has thought of them as great heroes and has praised them. So we should suspect immediately that that is not true righteousness. There are certain men today who are acclaimed as very great Christians by the world simply because they have made such sacrifices. That, I suggest, should raise at once a query in our minds as to whether they are really practising the Christian faith, or whether it is not just something else — perhaps a general nobility of character.

What, then, does this Beatitude mean? Let me put it like this. Being righteous, practising righteousness, really means being like the Lord Jesus Christ. Therefore they are blessed who are persecuted for being like Him. What is more, those who are like Him always will be persecuted. Let me show this first of all from the teaching of the Bible. Listen to the way in which our Lord Himself puts it. 'If the world hate you, ye know that it hated me before it hated you. If ye were of the world, the world would love his own: but because ye are not of the world, but I have chosen you out of the world, therefore the world hateth you. Remember the word that I said unto you, The servant is not greater than his lord. If they have persecuted me, they will also persecute you' (John 1:18-20). Now there is no qualification, it is a categorical statement. Listen to His servant Paul putting it in this way, 'Yea', says Paul, writing to Timothy, who did not understand this teaching and was therefore unhappy because he was being persecuted, 'Yea, and all that will live godly in Christ Jesus shall suffer persecution' (2 Tim. 3:12). It is again a categorical statement. That is why I said at the beginning that I sometimes think this is the most searching of all the Beatitudes. Are you suffering persecution?

That is the teaching. Let us look at its outworking right through the Bible. For instance, Abel was persecuted by his brother Cain. Moses received grievous persecution. Look at the way in which David was persecuted by Saul, and at the terrible persecution that Elijah and Jeremiah had to endure. Do you remember the story of Daniel, and how he was persecuted? These are some of the most outstanding righteous men of the Old Testament, and every one of them verifies the biblical teaching. They were persecuted, not because they were difficult, or overzealous, but simply because they were righteous. In the New Testament we find exactly the same thing. Think of the apostles, and the persecution they had to endure. I wonder whether any man has ever suffered more than the apostle Paul, in spite of his gentleness and kindness and righteousness. Read his occasional descriptions of the sufferings that he had to endure. It is not surprising that he said that 'all that will live godly in Christ Jesus shall suffer persecution'. He had known and experienced it. But, of course, the supreme example is our Lord Himself. Here He is in all His utter, absolute perfection, and His gentleness and meekness, of whom it can be said that 'a bruised reed shall he not break, and smoking flax shall he not quench'. Never was anyone so gentle and so kind. But look at what happened to Him and at what the world did to Him. Read also the long history of the Christian Church and you will find that this statement has been verified endlessly. Read the lives of the martyrs, of John Huss, or the Covenanters, or the Protestant Fathers. Read about it also in more modern times and observe the persecution endured by the leaders of the Evangelical Awakening in the eighteenth century. Not many men have known what it is to suffer as did Hudson Taylor, who lived into our century. He knew what it was to undergo at times grievous persecution. It is just a verification of the statement of this Beatitude.

By whom are the righteous persecuted? You will find as you go through the Scriptures, and as you study the history of the Church, that the persecution is not confined to the world. Some of the most grievous persecution has been suffered by the righteous at the hands of the Church herself, and at the hands of religious people. It has often come from nominal Christians. Take our Lord Himself. Who were His chief persecutors? The Pharisees and scribes and the doctors of the Law! The first Christians, too, were persecuted most bitterly of all by the Jews. Then read the history of the Church, and watch it in the Roman Catholic persecution of some of those men in the Middle Ages who had seen the pure truth and were trying to live it out quietly. How they were persecuted by nominal, religious people! That was also the story of the Puritan Fathers. This is the teaching of the Bible, and it has been substantiated by the history of the Church, that the persecution may come, not from the outside but from within. There are ideas of Christianity far removed from the New Testament which are held by many and which cause them to persecute those who are trying in sincerity and truth to follow the Lord Jesus Christ along the narrow way. You may well find it in your own personal experience. I have often been told by converts that they get much more opposition from supposedly Christian people than they do from the man of the world outside, who is often glad to see them changed and wants to know something about it. Formal Christianity is often the greatest enemy of the pure faith.

But let me ask another question. Why are the righteous thus persecuted? And, especially, why is it that the righteous are persecuted rather than the good and noble? The answer, I think, is quite simple. The good and noble are very rarely persecuted because we all have the feeling that they are just like ourselves at our best. We think, 'I am capable of that myself if I only put my mind to it,' and we admire them because it is a way of paying a compliment to ourselves. But the righteous are persecuted because they are different. That was why the Pharisees and the scribes hated our Lord. It was not because He was good; it was because He was different. There was something about Him that condemned them. They felt all their righteousness was being made to look very tawdry. That was what they disliked. The righteous may not say anything; they do not condemn us in words. But just because they are what they are, they do in fact condemn us, they make us feel unhappy, and we shrivel into nothing. So we hate them for it and try to find fault with them. 'You know,' people say, 'I believe in being a Christian; but that is much too much, that is going too far.' That was the explanation of Daniel's persecution. He suffered all he did because he was righteous. He did not make a show of it, he did it quietly in his own way. But they said, 'This man condemns us by what he is doing; we shall have to catch him.' That is always the trouble, and that was the explanation in the case of our Lord Himself. The Pharisees and others hated Him just because of His utter, absolute holiness and righteousness and truth. And that is why you find gentle, loving, lovable people like Hudson Taylor, to whom I have already referred, suffering terrible and bitter persecution sometimes at the hands of ostensible Christians.

Obviously, then, we can draw certain conclusions from all this. For one thing, it tells us a great deal about our ideas concerning the Person of the Lord Jesus Christ. If our conception of Him is such that He can be admired and applauded by the non-Christian, we have a wrong view of Him. The effect of Jesus Christ upon His contemporaries was that many threw stones at Him. They hated Him; and finally, choosing a murderer instead of Him, they put Him to death. This is the effect Jesus Christ always has upon the world. But you see there are other ideas about Him. There are worldly people who tell us they admire Jesus Christ, but that is because they have never seen Him. If they saw Him, they would hate Him as His contemporaries did. He does not change; man does not change. So let us be careful that our ideas about Christ are such that the natural man cannot easily admire or applaud.

That leads to the second conclusion. This Beatitude tests our ideas as to what the Christian is. The Christian is like his Lord, and this is what our Lord said about him. 'Woe unto you, when all men shall speak well of you! for so did their fathers to the false prophets' (Luke 6:26). And yet is not our idea of what we call the perfect Christian nearly always that he is a nice, popular man who never offends anybody, and is so easy to get on with? But if this Beatitude is true, that is not the real Christian, because the real Christian is a man who is not praised by everybody. They did not praise our Lord, and they will never praise the man who is like Him. 'Woe unto you, when all men shall speak well of you!' That is what they did to the false prophets; they did not do that to Christ Himself.

117

So I draw my next deduction. It concerns the natural, unregenerate man, and it is this. The natural mind, as Paul says, 'is enmity against God'. Though he talks about God, he really hates God. And when the Son of God came on earth he hated and crucified Him. And that is the attitude of the world towards Him now.

This leads to the last deduction, which is that the new birth is an absolute necessity before anybody can become a Christian. To be Christian, ultimately, is to be like Christ; and one can never be like Christ without being entirely changed. We must get rid of the old nature that hates Christ and hates righteousness; we need a new nature that will love these things and love Him and thus become like Him. If you try to imitate Christ the world will praise you; if you become Christlike it will hate you.

Finally, let us ask ourselves this question: Do we know what it is to be persecuted for righteousness' sake? To become like Him we have to become light; light always exposes darkness, and the darkness therefore always hates the light. We are not to be offensive; we are not to be foolish; we are not to be unwise; we are not even to parade the Christian faith. We are not to do anything that calls for persecution. But by just being like Christ persecution becomes inevitable. But that is the glorious thing. Rejoice in this, say Peter and James. And our Lord Himself says, 'Blessed are ye, happy are ye, if you are like that.' Because if ever you find yourself persecuted for Christ and for righteousness' sake, you have in a sense got the final proof of the fact that you are a Christian, that you are a citizen of the kingdom of heaven. 'Unto you,' says Paul to the Philippians, 'unto you it is given in the behalf of Christ, not only to believe on him, but also to suffer for his sake' (Phil. 1:29). And I look at those first Christians persecuted by the authorities and I hear them thanking God that at last they had been accounted worthy to suffer for the Name's sake.

May God through His Holy Spirit give us great wisdom, discrimination, knowledge and understanding in these things, so that if ever we are called upon to suffer, we may know for certain that it is for righteousness' sake, and may have the full comfort and consolation of this glorious Beatitude.

Chapter Thirteen

Rejoicing in Tribulation

A S we suggested in the last chapter, verses 11 and 12 are an extension of the statement in verse 10. They extend and apply that Beatitude to the particular condition of the disciples whom our Lord was addressing at that time, and through them, of course, to all other Christians in every subsequent age of the Church. Yet there is a sense, also, in which we can say that this amplification of the Beatitude adds somewhat to its meaning and thereby brings out certain further truths about the Christian.

As we have seen, all these Beatitudes when taken together are meant to be a delineation of the Christian man. They present a composite picture, so that each one of them should show a part of the Christian character. The Christian is a difficult man to describe, and undoubtedly the best way of doing so is to depict the various qualities that he manifests.

In this amplification of the last Beatitude our Lord again throws much light upon the character of the Christian. As we have seen repeatedly, there are two main ways of looking at him. You can look at him as he is, in and of himself, and you can also look at him in his reaction to the various things that happen to him in this life and world. There are certain positive statements you can always make about the Christian. But you learn still more about him when you look at him in his contact with people and in his behaviour with respect to them. The two verses we are now considering belong to that second class, for we see the Christian's reactions to this matter of persecution. There are three principles with regard to the Christian which emerge very clearly from what our Lord tells us here. They are quite obvious; and yet I think that often we must all plead guilty to the fact that we forget them.

The first is once again that *he is unlike everybody who is not a Christian*. We have repeated that many times already because it is surely the principle that our Lord wished to stress above everything else. He Himself said, you remember, 'Think not that I am come to send peace on earth: I came not to send peace, but a sword' (Matt. 10:34). In other words, 'The effect of My ministry is going to be a division, a division even between the father and the son, and the mother and the daughter; and a man's foes may very well be those of his own household.' The gospel of Jesus Christ creates a clear-cut division and distinction between the Christian and the non-Christian. The non-Christian himself proves that by persecuting the Christian. The way in which he persecutes him does not matter; the fact is, that in some shape or form, he is almost certain to do so. There is an antagonism in the non-Christian towards the true Christian. That is why, as we saw in our last chapter, the last Beatitude is such a subtle and profound test of the Christian. There is something, as we saw, about the Christian character, due to its being like the character of our Lord Himself, which always calls forth this persecution. No one was ever so persecuted in this world as the Son of God Himself, and 'the servant is not greater than his lord'. So he experiences the same fate. That, then, can be seen here as a very clear and striking principle. The non-Christian tends to revile, to persecute, and to speak all manner of evil falsely against the Christian. Why? Because he is fundamentally different, and the non-Christian recognizes this. The Christian is not just like everybody else with a slight difference. He is essentially different; he has a different nature and he is a different man.

The second principle is that *the Christian's life is controlled and dominated by Jesus Christ*, by his loyalty to Christ, and by his concern to do everything for Christ's sake. 'Blessed are ye, when men shall revile you, and persecute you, and shall say all manner of evil against you falsely, for my sake.' Why are they persecuted? Because they are living for Christ's sake. From this I deduce that the whole object of the Christian should be to live for Christ's sake and no longer to live for his own. People are unpleasant to one another and may persecute one another, even when they are not Christian, but that is not for Christ's sake. The peculiar thing about the persecution of the Christian is that it is 'for Christ's sake'. The Christian's life should always be controlled and dominated by the Lord Jesus Christ, and by considerations of what will be well-pleasing in His sight. That is something which you find everywhere in the New Testament. The Christian, being a new man, having received new life from Christ, realizing that he owes everything to Christ and His perfect work, and particularly to His death upon the cross, says to himself, 'I am not my own; I have been bought with a price'. He therefore wants to live his whole life to the glory of Him who has thus died for him, and bought him, and risen again. So he desires to present himself, 'body, soul and spirit', everything to

Christ. This, you will agree, is something that was not only taught by our Lord; it is emphasized everywhere in all the New Testament Epistles. 'For Christ's sake' is the motive, the great controlling motive in the life of the Christian. Here is something that differentiates us from everybody else and provides a thorough test of our profession of the Christian faith. If we are truly Christian, our desire must be, however much we may fail in practice, to live for Christ, to glory in His name and to live to glorify Him.

The third general characteristic of the Christian is that *his life should be controlled by thoughts of heaven and of the world to come.* 'Rejoice, and be exceeding glad: for great is your reward in heaven: for so persecuted they the prophets which were before you.' This again is something that is all a part of the warp and woof of the New Testament teaching. It is vital and is, indeed, to be found everywhere. Look at that marvellous summary of the Old Testament in Hebrews 11. Consider these men, the author is saying, these heroes of the faith. What was their secret? It was just that they said, 'Here we have no continuing city, but we seek one to come.' They were all men who were looking 'for a city which hath foundations, whose builder and maker is God'. That is the secret. It must therefore be an essential part of the differentia of the Christian man, as we are reminded here. Again you see this obvious difference between the Christian and the non-Christian. The non-Christian does everything he can not to think of the world beyond. That is the whole meaning of the pleasure mania of today. It is just a great conspiracy and effort to stop thinking, and especially to avoid thinking of death and the world to come. That is typical of the non-Christian; there is nothing he so hates as talking about death and eternity. But the Christian, on the other hand, is a man who thinks a great deal about these things, and dwells upon them; they are great controlling principles and factors in the whole of his life and outlook.

Let us now see how all these three principles are illustrated in terms of the way in which the Christian faces persecution. That is how our Lord presents it. In showing how the Christian faces persecution He makes three specific statements. As we look at them together, let us remind ourselves again that these verses apply only to those who are really being persecuted falsely for Christ's sake and for no other reason. Our Lord was so concerned about it that He repeats it. The blessings of the Christian life are promised only to those who obey the conditions, and there is always a condition attached to every promise. The condition that is attached here is that the persecution must not in any sense be because of what we are as natural men; it is because of what we are as new men in Christ Jesus.

Let us look first of all at the way in which the Christian should face persecution. Again we need not waste any time in considering the form the persecution may take. We are all familiar with that. It may be violent; it may mean being arrested and thrown into prison or concentration camp. That is happening to thousands of our fellow Christians in this world today. It can take the form of men actually being shot, or murdered in some other way. It may take the form of a man losing his post. It may manifest itself just by sneering and jeering and laughter as he enters the room. It may take the form of a kind of whispering campaign. There is no end to the ways in which the persecuted may suffer. But that is not what matters. What really matters is the way in which the Christian faces these things. Our Lord tells us here how we are to do so.

We can put it first of all negatively. The Christian must not retaliate. It is very difficult not to do so, and more difficult for some of us than for others. But our Lord did not do so, and we who are His followers are to be like Him. So we must 'stay the angry word'; we must not reply. To retaliate is just to be like the natural man who always does reply; by nature he has the instinct of self-preservation and the desire to get his own back. But the Christian is different, different in nature; so he must not do that.

Furthermore, not only must he not retaliate; he must also not feel resentment. That is much more difficult. The first thing you do is to control your actions, the actual reply. But our Lord is not content with that, because to be truly Christian is not simply to live in a state of repression. You have to go beyond that; you have to get into the state in which you do not even resent persecution. I think you will all know from experience the difference between these two things. We may have come to see long ago that to lose our temper over a thing, or to manifest annoyance, is dishonouring to our Lord. But we still may feel it, and feel it intensely, and be hurt about it and resent it bitterly. Now the Christian teaching is that we must get beyond that. We see in Philippians 1 how the apostle Paul had done so. He was a very sensitive man — his Epistles make that plain — and he could be grievously hurt and wounded. His feelings had been hurt, as he shows quite clearly, by the Corinthians, the Galatians and others; and yet he has now come to the state in which he really is no longer affected by these things. He says he does not even judge his own self; he has committed the judgment to God.

We must therefore not even resent what is done to us. But we must go further, because these things are very subtle. If we know the psychology of our own souls, and the psychology of the Christian life — using the term 'psychology' in its real sense and not in its modern, perverted sense — we must realize that we must go a step beyond that. The third negative is that we must never be depressed by persecution. After you have done the first two, you may still find that the thing is casting you down and making you feel generally unhappy. Not the thing itself, perhaps; but somehow a sense of depression or oppression covers your soul and spirit. It is not that you feel any resentment to a particular person; but you say to yourself, 'Why should it be like this? Why am I being treated thus?' So a feeling of depression in your spiritual life seems to settle down upon you, and you tend to lose control of your Christian living. That again is something which our Lord denounces. He puts it positively by saying explicitly, 'Rejoice, and be exceeding glad.' We have seen frequently in our consideration of these Beatitudes, that they do show more clearly than anything else perhaps in the New Testament the utter fallacy and futility of imagining that men can make themselves Christian by their own efforts. This is what it means to be a Christian. When you are persecuted and people are saying all manner of evil against you falsely, you 'rejoice' and are 'exceeding glad'. Now that to the natural man is an utter impossibility. He cannot even control his spirit of retaliation. Still less can he rid himself of a sense of resentment. But to 'rejoice and be exceeding glad' in such circumstances is something he will never do. That, however, is the position to which the Christian is called. Our Lord says we must become like Him in these matters. The author of the Epistle to the Hebrews puts it in one verse. 'Who for the joy that was set before him endured the cross, despising the shame.'

That, then, is our first proposition. We have looked at the way in which the Christian, in actual practice, faces persecution. Now let us ask a second question. Why is the Christian to rejoice like this, and how is it possible for him to do so? Here we come to the heart of the matter. Obviously the Christian is not to rejoice at the mere fact of persecution. That is always something which is to be regretted. Yet you will find as you read Christian biographies that certain saints have faced that temptation very definitely. They have rejoiced wrongly in their persecution for its own sake. Now that, surely, was the spirit of the Pharisees, and is something which we should never do. If we rejoice in the persecution in and of itself, if we say, 'Ah, well; I rejoice and am exceeding glad that I am so much better than those other people, and that is why they are persecuting me', immediately we become Pharisees. Persecution is something that the Christian should always regret; it should be to him a source of great grief that men and women, because of sin, and because they are so dominated by Satan, should behave in such an inhuman and devilish manner. The Christian is, in a sense, one who must feel his heart breaking at the effect of sin in others that makes them do this. So he never rejoices in the fact of persecution as such.

Why then does he rejoice in it? Why should he be exceeding glad? Here are our Lord's answers. The first is that this persecution which he is receiving for

Christ's sake is proof to the Christian of who he is and what he is. 'Rejoice, and be exceeding glad: for great is your reward in heaven: for so persecuted they the prophets which were before you.' So if you find you are being persecuted and maligned falsely for Christ's sake, you know you are like the prophets, who were God's chosen servants, and who are now with God, rejoicing in glory. Now that is something to rejoice about. This is one of the ways in which our Lord turns everything into a victory. In a sense He makes even the devil a cause of blessing. The devil through his agencies persecutes the Christian and makes him unhappy. But if you look at it in the right way, you will find a cause for rejoicing, and will turn to Satan and say, 'Thank you; you are giving me proof that I am a child of God, otherwise I should never be persecuted like this for Christ's sake.' James, in his Epistle, argues likewise that this is proof of your calling and sonship; it is something which makes you know for certain you are a child of God.

Or, take the second argument to prove this. It means, of course, that we have become identified with Christ. If we are thus being maligned falsely and persecuted for His sake, it must mean that our lives have become like His. We are being treated as our Lord was treated, and therefore we have proof positive that we do indeed belong to Him. As we saw, He Himself prophesied before His going that this was going to happen and this teaching is found everywhere in the New Testament. The apostle Paul, for example, says, 'Unto you it is given in the behalf of Christ, not only to believe on him, but also to suffer for his sake.' So that, as the Christian receives this kind of persecution, he finds that second proof of the fact that he has indeed become a child of God. It has established who he is and what he is, and in that he rejoices.

The second cause of rejoicing and of joy is, of course, that this persecution is proof also of where we are going. 'Rejoice, and be exceeding glad.' Why? 'For great is your reward in heaven.' Here is one of these great central principles that you find running all the way through the Bible. It is this consideration of the end, our final destiny. If this happens to you, says Christ in effect, it is just the hallmark of the fact that you are destined for heaven. It means you have a label on; it means your ultimate destiny is fixed. By thus persecuting you the world is just telling you that you do not belong to it, that you are a man apart; you belong to another realm, thus proving the fact that you are going to heaven. And that, according to Christ, is something which causes us always to rejoice and be exceeding glad. Here another great test of the Christian life and profession emerges. As I have already pointed out, the question we ask ourselves is whether that is a cause of rejoicing, whether this proof, given by the world, that we are going to heaven and to God, is something that does truly fill us with this sense of joyful anticipation. Let me put it like this. Do you believe the cause of the gladness and the rejoicing should be our consciousness of the reward that awaits us? 'Rejoice, and be exceeding glad: for great is your reward in heaven.'

Let us look at it in this way. According to this argument, my whole outlook upon everything that happens to me should be governed by these three things: my realization of who I am, my consciousness of where I am going, and my knowledge of what awaits me when I get there. You will find this argument in many places in the Scriptures. The apostle Paul once put it like this, 'Our light affliction, which is but for a moment, worketh for us a far more exceeding and eternal weight of glory; while we look not at the things which are seen, but at the things which are not seen: for the things which are seen are temporal; but the things which are not seen are eternal' (2 Cor. 4:17, 18). The Christian should always be looking at that.

But let me consider certain objections at this point. Someone may ask, Is this idea of a reward a right one for the Christian to entertain? Should a Christian ever be governed in his motives by a thought concerning the reward that remains for him in heaven? You know it was the tendency, particularly in the early part of this century (one does not hear it quite so often now), for people to say, 'I do not like these ideas of seeking a reward and of fearing punishment. I believe that the Christian life should be lived for its own sake.' Such people say that they are not interested in heaven and hell; it is this wonderful life of Christianity itself that they are interested in. You remember they used to tell the story of the woman who was to be seen walking in an Eastern country carrying a bucket of water in one hand and a bucket of fuel with live coals of fire in the other hand. Somebody asked her what she was going to do, and she said she was going to drown hell with one and burn up heaven with the other. This idea, that you are not interested in reward or fear of punishment, but are just wonderful people who, with no ulterior motive, are enjoying a pure joy in Christian living, appeals to many.

Now these people consider themselves to be exceptional Christians. But the answer we give them is that their attitude is quite unscriptural, and any teaching that goes beyond the Scriptures is always wrong, however wonderful it may seem to be. Everything must be tested by the teaching of the Bible: and here it is in this one verse — 'Rejoice, and be exceeding glad: for great is your reward in heaven.' Are we not even told by the author of the Epistle to the Hebrews, as I have already reminded you, that Christ endured the cross, and despised the shame 'for the joy that was set before him'? It was by looking beyond it to what was coming that He endured.

We find this everywhere. The apostle Paul says in 1 Corinthians 3 that what really controlled his whole life, and especially his ministry, was the fact that in the day that was coming every man's work would be tried 'as by fire'. 'I am very careful what I build on this one and only foundation,' he says, in effect; 'whether I build wood, or hay, or stubble, or precious metal. The day is coming and will declare it. Every man's work shall be judged and every man shall be rewarded according to his work' (see 1 Cor. 3:10-15). The reward counted a great deal in the life of this man. Again, in 2 Corinthians 5, he writes, 'We must all appear before the judgment seat of Christ; that every one may receive the things done in his body, according to that he hath done, whether it be good or bad. Knowing therefore the terror of the Lord, we persuade men' (2 Cor. 5:10, 11). And when, in his second Epistle to Timothy, he comes to look back across his life, he thinks about the crown that is laid up for him, that wonderful crown which the blessed Lord is going to put upon his brow. That is the scriptural teaching. Thank God for it. These things are written for our encouragement. The gospel is not impersonal, it is not inhuman. This whole idea of the reward is there, and we are meant to think about these things, and to meditate upon them. Let us be careful that we do not set up an idealistic philosophy in the place of the Scripture and its plain teaching.

But someone may ask a second question. 'How is this reward possible? I thought that all was of grace and man was saved by grace; why speak of reward?' The answer of Scripture seems to be that even the reward itself is of grace. It does not mean that we merit or deserve salvation. It just means that God treats us as a Father. The father tells the child that there are certain things he wants him to do, and that it is his duty to do them. He also tells him that if he does them he will give him a reward. It is not that the child merits a reward. It is given of grace, and it is the expression of the father's love. So God, of His infinite grace, 'throws these things into the bargain' as it were, and encourages us, and fills us with a sense of love and of gratitude. It is not that any man will ever deserve or merit heaven; but the teaching is, I say, that God does reward His people. We can even go further and say that there are differences in the reward. Take that reference in Luke 12 where we read of the servants who are beaten with many and with few stripes. It is a great mystery, but it is clear teaching to the effect that there are rewards. No one will have a sense of loss or of lack and yet there is a difference. Let us never lose sight of 'the recompense of the reward'.

The Christian is a man who should always be thinking of the end. He does not look at the things which are seen, but at the things which are not seen. That was the secret of those men in the eleventh chapter of Hebrews. Why did Moses not continue as the child of Pharaoh's daughter? Because he chose 'rather to suffer affliction with the people of God, than to enjoy the pleasures of sin for a season'. He had his eye upon the end, 'the recompense of the reward'. He did not stop at thoughts of this life; he looked at death and eternity. He saw the things that abide, he saw 'him who is invisible'. That is how he went on. That is how they all went on. 'Set your affection on things above, not on things on the earth' writes Paul to the Colossians. Does not this word condemn us all? Does it not make foolish the way we look so much at this world and all it has? We know perfectly well that it is all vanishing and disappearing, yet how little we look at those other things. 'Rejoice,' says Christ, 'and be exceeding glad: for great is your reward in heaven.'

What is this reward? Well, the Bible does not tell us much about it, for a very good reason. It is so glorious and wonderful that our human language is of necessity almost bound to detract from its glory. You see even our very language is polluted. Take the word 'love'. It has become debased, and we have a wrong impression of it. The same is true of many other expressions such as 'glory', 'brightness', and 'joy'. So there is a sense in which even the Bible cannot tell us about heaven because we should misunderstand it. But it does tell us something like this. We shall see Him as He is, and worship in His glorious presence. Our very bodies will be changed, and glorified, with no sickness or disease. There will be no sorrow, no sighing; all tears shall be wiped away. All will be perpetual glory. No wars or rumours of wars; no separation, no unhappiness, nothing that drags a man down and makes him unhappy, even for a second!

Unmixed joy, and glory, and holiness, and purity and wonder! That is what is awaiting us. That is your destiny and mine in Christ as certainly as we are alive at this moment. How foolish we are that we do not spend our time in thinking about that. Oh, how we cling to this unhappy, wretched world, and fail to think on these things and to meditate upon them. We are all going on to that, if we are Christians, to that amazing glory and purity and happiness and joy. 'Rejoice, and be exceeding glad.' And if people are unkind and cruel and spiteful, and if we are being persecuted, well then we must say to ourselves, Ah, unhappy people; they are doing this because they do not know Him, and they do not understand me. They are incidentally proving to me that I belong to Him, that I am going to be with Him and share in that joy with Him. Therefore, far from resenting it, and wanting to hit back, or being depressed by it, it makes me realize all the more what is awaiting me. I have a joy unspeakable and full of glory awaiting me. All this is but temporary and passing; it cannot affect that. I therefore must thank God for it, because, as Paul puts it, it 'worketh for us a far more exceeding and eternal weight of glory'.

How often do you think of heaven and rejoice as you think of it? Does it give you a sense of strangeness and of fear, and a desire, as it were, to avoid it? If it does so to any degree, I fear we must plead guilty that we are living on too low a level. Thoughts of heaven ought to make us rejoice and be exceeding glad.

True Christian living is to be like Paul and to say, 'to me to live is Christ, and to die is gain.' Why? Because it means, 'to be with Christ; which is far better,' to see Him and to be like Him. Let us think more about these things, realizing increasingly, and reminding ourselves constantly, that if we are in Christ these things are awaiting us. We should desire them above everything else. Therefore, 'Rejoice, and be exceeding glad: for great is your reward in heaven.'

Chapter Fourteen

The Salt of the Earth

WE now come to a new and fresh section in the Sermon on the Mount. In verses 3-12 our Lord and Saviour has been delineating the Christian character. Here at verse 13 He moves forward and applies His description. Having seen what the Christian is, we now come to consider how the Christian should manifest this. Or, if you prefer it, having realized what we are, we must now go on to consider what we must be.

The Christian is not someone who lives in isolation. He is in the world, though he is not of it; and he bears a relationship to that world. In the Scriptures you always find these two things going together. The Christian is told that he must be otherworldly in his mind and outlook; but that never means that he retires out of the world. That was the whole error of monasticism which taught that living the Christian life meant, of necessity, separating oneself from society and living a life of contemplation. Now that is something which is denied everywhere in the Scriptures, and nowhere more completely than in this verse which we are now studying, where our Lord draws out the implications of what He has already been saying. You notice that in the second chapter of his first Epistle, Peter does exactly the same thing. He says, 'Ye are a chosen generation, a royal priesthood, an holy nation, a peculiar people; that ye should shew forth the praises of him who hath called you out of darkness into his marvellous light.' *[handwritten: Peter 2:9]*

It is exactly the same here. We are poor in spirit, and merciful, and meek, and hungering and thirsting after righteousness in order, in a sense, that we may be 'the salt of the earth'. We pass, therefore, from the contemplation of the character of the Christian to a consideration of the function and purpose of the Christian in this world in the mind and the purpose of God. In other words, in these verses that immediately follow, we are told very clearly the relationship of the Christian to the world in general.

There are certain senses in which we can say that this question of the function of the Christian in the world as it is today is one of the most urgent matters confronting the Church and the individual Christian at this present time. It is obviously a very large subject, and in many ways an apparently difficult one. But it is dealt with very clearly in the Scriptures. In the verse we are now considering we have a very characteristic exposition of the typical biblical teaching with regard to it. I say it is important because of the world situation. As we saw in our consideration of verses 10 and 11, it may very well become the most urgent problem for many of us. We saw there that we are likely to experience persecution, that, as the sin that is in the world becomes aggravated, the persecution of the Church is likely to be increased. Indeed, as we know, there are many Christian people in the world today who are already experiencing this. Whatever our conditions may be here, therefore, it behooves us to think this matter through very carefully in order that we may be able to pray intelligently for our brethren, and to help them by means of advice and instruction. Quite apart from the fact of persecution, however, this really is a most urgent question, because it arises even here and now for us in this country. What is to be the relationship of Christian people to society and the world? We are in the world; we cannot contract out of it. But the vital question is, what are we to do about it, what are we called to do as Christians in such a situation? This surely is an essential subject for us to consider. In this verse we have the answer to the question. First of all we shall consider what our text says about the world, and then we can consider what it has to say about the Christian in the world.

'Ye are the salt of the earth.' Now that is not only a description of the Christian; it is a description by implication of the world in which he finds himself. It really stands here for humanity at large, for mankind which is not Christian. What, then, is the biblical attitude towards the world? There can really be no uncertainty with regard to the biblical teaching on this matter. Here we come to what is, in many ways, the crucial problem of this twentieth century, undoubtedly one of the most interesting periods that the world has ever known. I do not hesitate to claim that there has never been a century which has so proved the truth of the biblical teaching as this one. It is a tragic century, and it is tragic very largely because its own life has completely disproved and demolished its own favourite philosophy.

As you know, there never was a period of which so much was expected. It is indeed pathetic to read the prognostications of the thinkers (so-called), the philosophers and poets and leaders, towards the end of the last century. How sad to note that easy, confident optimism of theirs, the things they expected from the twentieth century, the golden era that was to come. It was all based upon the theory of evolution, not only in a biological sense, but still more in a philosophical sense. The controlling idea was that the whole of life was advancing, developing and going upwards. That was what we were told in a purely biological sense; man had risen out of the animal and had arrived at a certain stage of development. But still more was this advance emphasized in terms of the mind and the thought and the outlook of man. Wars were going to be abolished, diseases were being cured, suffering was going to be not only ameliorated but finally eradicated. It was to be an amazing century. Most of the problems were going to be solved, for man had at last really begun to think. The masses, through education, would cease giving themselves to drink and immorality and vice. And as all the nations were thus educated to think and to hold conferences instead of rushing to war, the whole world was very soon going to be Paradise. That is not caricaturing the situation; it was believed confidently. By Acts of Parliament, and by international conferences, all problems would be solved now that man had begun at last to use his mind.

There are not many people living in the world today, however, who believe that. You still find an element of this teaching occasionally appearing in certain places, but surely this question no longer needs to be argued. I remember many years ago when I first began to preach, and when I began to say this kind of thing in public, I was often regarded as an oddity, as a pessimist, and as one who believed in some outmoded theology. For liberal optimism was then very prevalent, in spite of the First World War. But that is no longer so. The fallacy of it all has by now been recognized by all serious thinkers, and book after book is coming out just to explode the whole confident idea of that inevitable progress.

Now the Bible has always taught that, and it is put perfectly by our Lord when He says, 'Ye are the salt of the earth.' What does that imply? It clearly implies rottenness in the earth; it implies a tendency to pollution and to becoming foul and offensive. That is what the Bible has to say about this world. It is fallen, sinful and bad. Its tendency is to evil and to wars. It is like meat which has a tendency to putrefy and to become polluted. It is like something which can only be kept wholesome by means of a preservative or antiseptic. As the result of sin and the fall, life in the world in general tends to get into a putrid state. That, according to the Bible, is the only sane and right view to take of humanity. Far from there being a tendency in life and the world to go upwards, it is the exact opposite. The world, left to itself, is something that tends to fester. There are these germs of evil, these microbes, these infective agents and organisms in the very body of humanity, and unless checked, they cause disease. This is something which is obviously primary and fundamental. Our outlook with regard to the future must be determined by it. And if you bear this in mind you will see very clearly what has been happening during the present century. There is a sense, therefore, in which no Christian should be in the least surprised at what has taken place. If this scriptural position is right, then the surprising thing is that the world is as good as it is now, because within its own very life and nature there is this tendency to putrefaction.

The Bible is full of endless illustrations of this. You see it manifesting itself in the very first book. Though God had made the world perfect, because sin entered, this evil, polluting element at once began to show itself. Read the sixth chapter of Genesis and you find God saying, 'My Spirit shall not always strive with man'. The pollution has become so terrible that God has to send the flood. After that there is a new start; but this evil principle still manifests itself and you come to Sodom and Gomorrah with their almost unthinkable sinfulness. That is the story which the Bible is constantly putting before us. This persistent tendency to putrefaction is ever showing itself.

Now that, obviously, must control all our thinking and proposals with regard to life in this world, and with regard to the future. The question in the minds of so many people today is, What lies ahead of us? Clearly if we do not start by holding this biblical doctrine at the centre of our thinking, our prophecy must of necessity be false. The world is bad, sinful and evil; and any optimism with regard to it is not only thoroughly unscriptural but has actually been falsified by history itself.

Let us turn, however, to the second aspect of this statement which is still more important. What does this have to say about the Christian who is in the world, the kind of world at which we have been looking? It tells him he is to be as salt; 'ye, and ye alone' — for that is the emphasis of the text — 'are the salt of the earth'. What does this tell us? The first thing is that which we have been reminded of in considering the Beatitudes. We are to be unlike the world. There is no need to stress that, it is perfectly obvious. Salt is essentially different from the medium in which it is placed and in a sense it exercises all its qualities by being different. As our Lord puts it here — 'If the salt have lost his savour, wherewith shall it be salted? it is thenceforth good for nothing, but to be cast out, and to be trodden under foot of men.' The very characteristic of saltness proclaims a difference, for a small amount of salt in a large medium is at once apparent. Unless we are clear about this we have not even begun to think correctly about the Christian life. The Christian is a man who is essentially different from everybody else. He is as different as the salt is from the meat into which it is rubbed. He is as different as the salt is from the wound into which it is put. This external difference still needs to be emphasized and stressed.

The Christian is not only to be different, he is to glory in this difference. He is to be as different from other people as the Lord Jesus Christ was clearly different from the world in which He lived. The Christian is a separate, unique, outstanding kind of individual; there is to be in him something which marks him out, and which is to be obvious and clearly recognized. Let every man, then, examine himself.

But let us go on to consider more directly the function of the Christian. This is where the matter becomes slightly difficult and often controversial. It seems to me that the first thing which is emphasized by our Lord is that one of the Christian's main functions with respect to society is a purely negative one. Now what is the function of salt? There are those who would say that it is to give health, that it is health- or life-giving. But that seems to me to be a serious misunderstanding of the function of salt. Its business is not to provide health; it is to prevent putrefaction. The principal function of salt is to preserve and to act as an antiseptic. Take, for instance, a piece of meat. There are certain germs on its surface, perhaps in its very substance, which have been derived from the animal, or from the atmosphere, and there is the danger of its becoming putrid. The business of the salt which is rubbed into that meat is to preserve it against those agencies that are tending to its putrefaction. Salt's main function, therefore, is surely negative rather than positive. Now clearly this is a very fundamental postulate. It is not the only function of the Christian in the world, because, as we shall see later, we are also to be the light of the world, but in the first instance this is to be our effect as Christians. I wonder how often we conceive of ourselves in this way, as agents in the world meant to prevent this particular process of putrefaction and decay?

Another subsidiary function of salt is to provide savour, or to prevent food from being insipid. That is undoubtedly a further function of salt (whether a right one or not it is not for me to argue) and it is very interesting to look at it. According to this statement, therefore, life without Christianity is insipid. Does not the world today prove that? Look at the pleasure mania. Clearly people are finding life dull and boring, so they must be rushing out to this entertainment or that. But the Christian does not need these entertainments because he has a savour in life — his Christian faith. Take Christianity out of life and the world, and what an insipid thing life becomes, especially when one gets old or is on one's deathbed. It is utterly tasteless and men have to drug themselves in various ways because they feel their need of a savour.

The Christian, then, first and foremost, should function in that way. But how is he to do this? Here you find the great answer. Let me put it first in what I regard as the positive teaching of the New Testament. Then we can consider certain criticisms. Here, I think, the vital distinction is between the Church as such and the individual Christian. There are those who say that the Christian should act as salt in the earth by means of the Church's making pronouncements about the general situation of the world, about political, economic and international affairs and other such subjects. Undoubtedly in many churches, if not in the vast majority, that is how this text would be interpreted. People denounce communism, and talk about war, the international situation, and other similar problems. They say that the Christian functions as salt in the earth in this general way, by making these comments upon the world situation.

Now, as I see it, that is a most serious misunderstanding of scriptural teaching. I would challenge anybody to show me such teaching in the New Testament. 'Ah,' they say, 'but you get it in the prophets of the Old Testament.' Yes; but the answer is that in the Old Testament the Church was the nation of Israel, and there was no distinction between Church and state. The prophets had therefore to address the whole nation and to speak about its entire life. But the Church in the New Testament is not identified with any nation or nations. The result is that you never find the apostle Paul or any other apostle commenting upon the government of the Roman Empire; you never find them sending up resolutions to the Imperial Court to do this or not to do that. No; that is never found in the Church as displayed in the New Testament.

I suggest to you, therefore, that the Christian is to function as the salt of the earth in a much more individual sense. He does so by his individual life and character, by just being the man that he is in every sphere in which he finds himself. For instance, a number of people may be talking together in a rather unworthy manner. Suddenly a Christian enters into the company, and immediately his presence has an effect. He does not say a word, but people begin to modify their language. He is already acting as salt, he is already controlling the tendency to putrefaction and pollution. Just by being a Christian man, because of his life and character and general deportment, he is already controlling that evil that was manifesting itself, and he does so in every sphere and in every situation. He can do this, not only in a private capacity in his home, his workshop or office, or wherever he may happen to be, but also as a citizen in the country in which he lives. This is where the distinction becomes really important, for we tend to swing from one extreme error to the other in these matters. There are those who say, 'Yes, you are quite right, it is not the business of the Church as a Church to intervene in political, economic or social conditions. What I say is that the Christian should have nothing whatsoever to do with these things; the Christian must not register his vote, he must have nothing to do in the control of affairs and society.' That, it seems to me, is an equal fallacy; for the Christian as an individual, as a citizen in a state, is to be concerned about these things. Think of great men, like the Earl of Shaftesbury and others, who, as private Christians and as citizens, worked so hard in connection with the Factory Acts. Think also of William Wilberforce and all that he did with regard to the abolition of slavery. As Christians we are citizens of a country, and it is our business to play our part as citizens, and thereby act as salt indirectly in innumerable respects. But that is a very different thing from the Church's doing so.

Someone may ask, 'Why do you draw this distinction?' Let me answer that question. The primary task of the Church is to evangelize and to preach the gospel. Look at it like this. If the Christian Church today spends most of her time in denouncing communism, it seems to me that the main result will be that communists will not be likely to listen to the preaching of the gospel. If the Church is always denouncing one particular section of society, she is shutting the evangelistic door upon that section. If we take the New Testament view of these matters we must believe that the communist has a soul to be saved in exactly the same way as everybody else. It is my business as a preacher of the gospel, and a representative of the Church, to evangelize all kinds and conditions and classes of men and women. The moment the Church begins to intervene in these political, social and economic matters, therefore, she is hampering and hindering herself in her God-appointed task of evangelism. She can no longer say that she 'knows no man after the flesh', and thereby she is sinning. Let the individual play his part as a citizen, and belong to any political party that he may choose. That is something for the individual to decide. The Church is not concerned as a Church about these things. Our business is to preach the gospel and to bring this message of salvation to all. And, thank God, communists can be converted and can be saved. The Church is to be concerned about sin in all its manifestations, and sin can be as terrible in a capitalist as in a communist; it can be as terrible in a rich man as in a poor man; it can manifest itself in all classes and in all types and in all groups.

Another way in which this principle works is seen in the fact that, after every great awakening and reformation in the Church, the whole of society has reaped the benefit. Read the accounts of all the great revivals and you will find this. For example, in the revival which took place under Richard Baxter at Kidderminster, not only were the people of the Church revived, but many from the world outside were converted and came into the Church. Furthermore, the whole life of that town was affected, and evil and sin and vice were controlled. This happened not by the Church denouncing these things, not by the Church persuading the government to pass Acts of Parliament, but by the sheer influence of Christian individuals. And it has always been like that. It happened in the same way in the seventeenth and eighteenth centuries and at the beginning of this century in the revival which took place in 1904-5. Christians, by being Christian, influence society almost automatically.

You find proof of this in the Bible and also in the history of the Church. In the Old Testament after every reformation and revival there was this general benefit to society. Look also at the Protestant Reformation and you will find at once that the whole of life was affected by it. The same is true of the Puritan Reformation. I am not referring to the Acts of Parliament which were passed by the Puritans, but to their general manner of life. Most competent historians are agreed in saying that what undoubtedly saved this country from a revolution such as was experienced in France at the end of the eighteenth century was nothing but the Evangelical Revival. This was not because anything was done directly, but because masses of individuals had become Christian, and were living this better life and had this higher outlook. The whole political situation was affected, and the great Acts of Parliament which were passed in the last century were mostly due to the fact that there were such large numbers of individual Christians to be found in this land.

Finally, is not the present state of society and of the world a perfect proof of this principle? I think it is true to say that during the last fifty years the Christian Church has paid more direct attention to politics and to social and economic questions than in the whole of the previous hundred years. We have had all this talk about the social application of Christianity. Pronouncements have been made and resolutions have been sent from Church Assemblies and the General Assemblies of the various denominations to the governments. We have all been so tremendously interested in the practical application. But what is the result? No one can dispute it. The result is that we are living in a society which is much more immoral than it was fifty years ago, in which vice and lawbreaking and lawlessness are rampant. Is it not clear that you cannot do these things except in the biblical way? Though we try to bring them about directly by applying principles, we find that we cannot do so. The main trouble is that there are far too few Christian people, and that those of us who are Christian are not sufficiently salt. By that I do not mean aggressive; I mean Christian in the true sense. Also, we must admit that it is not true of us that when we enter a room people are immediately controlled in their language and their general conversation because we have arrived. That is where we fail lamentably. One truly saintly man radiates his influence; it will permeate any group in which he happens to be. The trouble is that the salt has lost its saltness in so many instances; and we are not controlling our fellows by being 'saints' in the way we should. Though the Church makes her great pronouncements about war and politics, and other major issues, the average man is not affected. But if you have a man working at a bench who is a true Christian, and whose life has been saved and transformed by the Holy Spirit, it does affect others all around him.

That is the way in which we can act as salt in the earth at a time like this. It is not something to be done by the Church in general; it is something to be done by the individual Christian. It is the principle of cellular infiltration. Just a little salt can affect the great mass. Because of its essential quality it somehow or another permeates everything. That, it seems to me, is the great call to us at a time like this. Look at life; look at society in this world. Is it not obviously rotten? Look at the decay that is setting in amongst all classes of people. Look at these horrible divorces and separations, this joking about the sanctities of life, this increase in drink and pilfering. There are your problems, and it is obvious that men by passing Acts of Parliament cannot deal with them. Newspaper articles do not seem to touch them. Indeed nothing ever will, save the presence of an increasing number of individual Christians who will control the putrefaction, and the pollution, and the rottenness, and the evil, and the vice. Every one of us in our circle has thus to control this process, and so the whole lump, the whole mass, will be preserved.

May God give us grace to examine ourselves in the light of this simple proposition. The great hope for society today is an increasing number of individual Christians. Let the Church of God concentrate on that and not waste her time and energy on matters outside her province. Let the individual Christian be certain that this essential quality of saltness is in him, that because he is what he is, he is a check, a control, an antiseptic in society, preserving it from unspeakable foulness, preserving it, perhaps, from a return to a dark age. Before the Methodist Revival, life in London, as you can see in books written at the time and since, was almost unthinkable with its drink and vice and immorality. Is there not a danger that we are going back to that? Is not our whole generation going down visibly? It is you and I and others like us, Christian people, who alone can prevent that. God give us grace to do so. God stir up the gift within us, and make us such that we shall indeed be like the Son of God Himself and influence all who come into contact with us.

Chapter Fifteen

The Light of the World

I N verse 14 we have, surely, one of the most astounding and extraordinary statements about the Christian that was ever made, even by our Lord and Saviour Jesus Christ Himself. When you consider the setting, and remember the people to whom our Lord uttered these words, they do indeed become most remarkable. It is a statement full of significance and profound implications with regard to an understanding of the nature of the Christian life. It is a great characteristic of scriptural truth that it can compress, as it were, the whole content of our entire position into a pregnant verse such as this. 'Ye', said our Lord, looking out upon those simple people, those entirely unimportant people from the standpoint of the world, 'Ye are the light of the world.' It is one of those statements which should always have the effect upon us of making us lift up our heads, causing us to realize once more what a remarkable and glorious thing it is to be a Christian. And of course it thus becomes, as all such statements inevitably become, a very good and thorough test as to our position and our experience. All these statements that are thus made about the Christian always come back to us in that form, and we should always be careful to see that they do this for us. The 'ye' referred to in this statement means simply ourselves. The danger always is that we may read a statement like this and think about somebody else, the first Christians, or Christian people in general. But it is ourselves to whom it refers if we truly claim to be Christian.

A statement such as this, then, obviously calls for a detailed analysis. Before attempting this, however, we shall consider it in general and try to draw out from it some of its most obvious implications.

First of all let us look at its negative import or claim. For the real force of the statement is this: 'Ye, and ye alone, are the light of the world'; the 'ye' is emphatic and it carries that suggestion. Now at once you see there are certain things implied. The first is that the world is in a state of darkness. This, indeed, is always one of the first statements that the Christian gospel has to make. There is no point, perhaps, at which we see this striking contrast between the Christian view of life and all other views more clearly than in a verse such as this. The world is always talking about its enlightenment. That is one of its favourite phrases, particularly since the Renaissance of the fifteenth and sixteenth centuries when men began to take a new interest in knowledge. That is regarded by all thinkers as a great turning point in history, a great watershed which divides the history of civilizations, and all are agreed that modern civilization, as you and I know it, really did begin then. There was a kind of rebirth of knowledge and learning. The Greek classics were rediscovered; and their teaching and knowledge, in a purely philosophical sense, and still more in a scientific sense, really emerged and began to control the outlook and the lives of many.

Then there was, as you know, a similar revival in the eighteenth century, which actually gave itself this very name of the 'Enlightenment'. Any who are interested in the history of the Christian Church and of the Christian faith must reckon with that movement. It was the beginning, in a sense, of the attack upon the authority of the Bible, for it put philosophy and human thought in the position of the authoritative divine revelation and the declaration of God's truth to man. Now that has continued up to this present hour, and the point I am emphasizing is that it always represents itself in terms of light, and men who are interested in that kind of movement always refer to it as 'enlightenment'. Knowledge, they say, is that which brings light, and, of course, in so many respects it does. It would be foolish to dispute that. The increase in knowledge about the processes of nature and about physical illnesses and diseases and many other subjects has been truly phenomenal. New knowledge has also thrown greater light upon the working of the whole cosmos, and has given greater understanding with regard to so many different aspects of life. That is why people commonly talk about being 'enlightened' as the result of knowledge and of culture. And yet, in spite of all that, this is still the scriptural statement: 'Ye, and ye alone, are the light of the world.'

Scripture still proclaims that the world as such is in a state of gross darkness, and the moment you begin to look at things seriously you can easily prove that this is nothing but the simple truth. The tragedy of our century has been that we have concentrated solely upon one aspect of knowledge. Our knowledge has been a knowledge of things, mechanical things, scientific things, a knowledge of life in a more or less purely biological or mechanical sense. But our knowledge of the real factors that make life life, has not increased at all. That is why the world is in such a predicament today. For, as has often been pointed out, in spite of our having discovered all this great and new knowledge, we have failed to discover the most important thing of all, namely, what to do with our knowledge. That is the essence of the whole problem with regard to atomic power at this moment. There is nothing wrong in discovering atomic power. The tragedy is that we have not yet a sufficient knowledge of ourselves to be able to know what to do with this power now that we have discovered it.

That is the difficulty. Our knowledge has been mechanical and scientific in that pure sense. But when you come back to the great basic and fundamental problems of life and living, of being and existence, is it not obvious that our Lord's statement is still true, that the world is in a state of terrible darkness? Think of it in the realm of personal life and conduct and behaviour. There are many men with great knowledge in many departments of thought who are just tragic failures in their own personal lives. Look at it in the realm of relationships between person and person. At the very time when we have been boasting of our enlightenment and knowledge and understanding, there is this tragic breakdown in personal relationships. It is one of the major moral and social problems of society. Observe how we have multiplied our institutions and organizations. We have to give instruction now concerning things about which people were never instructed in the past. For instance, we now have to have Marriage Guidance classes. Up to this century men and women were married without this expert advice which now seems to be so essential. It all proclaims very eloquently that as regards the great momentous questions of how to live, how to avoid evil, and sin, and all that is base and unworthy, how to be clean, and straight, and pure, and chaste, and wholesome, there is gross darkness. Then, as you come up the scale and look at the relationships between group and group, there is obviously again the same condition and so we have these great industrial and economic problems. On a still higher level, look at the relationships between nation and nation. This century, of all centuries, when we talk so much about our knowledge and enlightenment, is proving that the world is in a state of unutterable darkness with regard to these vital and fundamental problems.

We must go even further than that, however. Our Lord not only pronounces that the world is in a state of darkness, He goes so far as to say that nobody but a Christian can give any helpful advice, knowledge or instruction with respect to it. That is our proud claim and boast as Christian people. The greatest thinkers and philosophers are completely baffled at this present time and I could easily give you many quotations from their writings to prove that. I care not where you look in the realm of pure science or philosophy with regard to these ultimate questions; the writers are completely at a loss to explain or understand their own century. This is because their controlling theory was that all man needed was more knowledge. They believed that if man had knowledge he would inevitably apply it to the solution of his difficulties. But, patently, man is not doing that. He has the knowledge, but he is not applying it; and that is ex-actly where the 'thinkers' are baffled. They do not understand the real problem of man; they are not able to tell us what is responsible for the present state of the world, and still less, therefore, are they able to tell us what can be done about it.

I remember some years ago, reading a review by a well-known teacher of philosophy in this country of a book which was meant to deal with these prob-lems. He put it very significantly like this. 'This book as regards analysis is very good, but it does not go beyond analysis and therefore it does not help. We can all analyse, but the vital question we want answered is, What is the ultimate source of the trouble? What can be done about it? There it has nothing to say,' he said, 'though it bears the imposing title of *The Condition of Man*.' Now that is very true. You can turn today to the greatest philosophers and thinkers and again and again you will find they will never take you beyond analysis. They are very good at laying out the problem and showing the various factors which op-erate. But when you ask them what is ultimately responsible for this, and what they propose to do, they just leave you unanswered. Clearly they have nothing to say. There is obviously no light at all in this world apart from the light that is provided by Christian people and the Christian faith. That is no exaggeration. I am suggesting that if we want to be realistic we just have to face that, and realize that when our Lord spoke, nearly two thousand years ago, He not only spoke the simple, startling truth about His own age, but He also spoke the truth with regard to every subsequent age. Let us never forget that Plato, Socrates, Aris-totle, and the rest, had given their full teaching several centuries before these words were uttered. It was after that amazing flowering of the mind and the in-tellect that our Lord made this statement. He looked at this band of ordinary, insignificant people and said, 'You and you alone are the light of the world.' Now this is a tremendous and most thrilling statement; and I would say again that there are many respects in which I thank God that I am preaching this gos-pel today and not a hundred years ago. If I had made that statement a hundred years ago people would have smiled, but they do not smile today. History itself is now proving, more and more, the truth of the gospel. The darkness of the world has never been more evident than it is now, and here comes this astonish-ing and startling statement. That, then, is the negative implication of our text.

Now let us consider its positive implications. It says 'ye'. In other words its claim is that the ordinary Christian, though he may never have read any philosophy at all, knows and understands more about life than the greatest expert who is not a Christian. This is one of the great major themes of the New Testament. The apostle Paul in writing to the Corinthians puts it quite explicitly when he says, 'the world by wisdom knew not God,' and therefore 'it pleased God by the foolishness of preaching to save them that believe'. This thing that appears to be utterly ridiculous to the world is the pure wisdom of God. This is the extraordinary paradox with which we are confronted. Its implication must be quite obvious; it shows that we are called to do something positive. This is the second statement which our Lord makes with regard to the function of the Christian in this world. Having described the Christian in general in the Beatitudes, the first thing He then says is, 'You are the salt of the earth.' Now He says, 'You are the light of the world, and you alone.' But let us always remember that it is a statement concerning the ordinary, average Christian, not certain Christians only. It is applicable to all who rightly claim this name.

Immediately the question arises, How, then, is it to become true of us? Once again we are led immediately into the teaching concerning the nature of the Christian man. The best way to understand it, I think, is this. The Lord who said, 'Ye are the light of the world,' also said, 'I am the light of the world.' These two statements must always be taken together, since the Christian is only 'the light of the world' because of his relationship to Him who is Himself 'the light of the world'. Our Lord's claim was that He had come to bring light. His promise is that 'he that followeth me shall not walk in darkness, but shall have the light of life'. Here, however, He also says, 'ye are the light of the world.' It comes to this, therefore, that He and He alone gives us this vital light with respect to life. But He does not stop at that; He also makes us 'light'. You remember how the apostle Paul put it in Ephesians v, where he says, 'For ye were sometimes darkness, but now are ye light in the Lord'. So not only have we received light, we have been made light; we become transmitters of light. In other words, it is this extraordinary teaching of the mystical union between the believer and his Lord. His nature enters into us so that we become, in a sense, what He Himself is. It is essential that we bear in mind both aspects of this matter. As those who believe the gospel we have received light and knowledge and instruction. *But,* in addition, it has become part of us. It has become our life, so that we thus become reflectors of it. The remarkable thing, therefore, of which we are reminded here is our intimate relationship with Him. The Christian is a man who has received and has become a partaker of the divine nature. The light that is Christ Himself, the light that is ultimately God, is the light that is in the Christian. 'God is light, and in him is no darkness at all.' 'I am the light of the world.' 'Ye are the light of the world.' The way to understand this is to grasp our Lord's teaching concerning the Holy Spirit in John 14-16 where He says, in effect, 'The result of His coming will be this: My Father and I will take up Our abode in you; We will be in you and you will be in Us.' God, who is 'the Father of lights', is the light that is in us; He is in us, and we are in Him, and thus it can be said of the Christian, 'Ye are the light of the world.'

It is interesting to observe that, according to our Lord, this is the second great result of our being the kind of Christian man He has already described in the Beatitudes. We should consider also the order in which these statements are made. The first thing our Lord said of us was, 'Ye are the salt of the earth'; and it is only after this that He says, 'Ye are the light of the world'. Why does He put it in that order instead of the reverse? This is a very interesting and important practical point. The first effect of the Christian on the world is a general one; in other words, it is more or less negative. Here is a man who has become a Christian; he lives in society, in his office or workshop. Because he is a Christian he immediately has a certain effect, a controlling effect, which we considered together earlier. It is only after that, that he has this specific and particular function of acting as light. In other words Scripture, in dealing with the Christian, always emphasizes first what he *is,* before it begins to speak of what he *does.* As a Christian, I should always have this general effect upon men before I have this specific effect. Wherever I may find myself, immediately that 'something different' about me should have its effect; and that in turn ought to lead men and women to look at me and to say, 'There is something unusual about that man.' Then, as they watch my conduct and behaviour, they begin to ask me questions. Here, the element of 'light' comes out; I am able to speak and to teach them. Far too often we Christians tend to reverse the order. We have spoken in a very enlightened manner, but we have not always lived as the salt of the earth. Whether we like it or not, our lives should always be the first thing to speak; and if our lips speak more than our lives it will avail very little. So often the tragedy has been that people proclaim the gospel in words, but their whole life and demeanour has been a denial of it. The world does not pay much attention to them. Let us never forget this order deliberately chosen by our Lord; 'the salt of the earth' before 'the light of the world'. We *are* something before we begin to *act* as something. The two things should always go together, but the order and sequence should be the one which He sets down here.

Bearing that in mind, let us now look at it practically. How is the Christian to show that he is indeed 'the light of the world'? That resolves itself into a simple question: What is the effect of light? What does it really do? There can be no doubt that the first thing light does is to expose the darkness and the things that belong to darkness. Imagine a room in darkness, and then suddenly the light is switched on. Or think of the headlights of a motorcar coming along a dark country road. As the Scripture puts it, 'Whatsoever doth make manifest is light'.

There is a sense in which we are not truly aware of darkness until the light appears, and this is something that is fundamental. Speaking of the coming of the Lord into this world, Matthew says, 'The people which sat in darkness saw great light'. The coming of Christ and the gospel is so fundamental that it can be put in that way; and the first effect of His coming into the world is that He has exposed the darkness of the life of the world. That is something that is always, and inevitably, done by any good or saintly person. We always need something to show us the difference, and the best way of revealing a thing is to provide a contrast. The gospel does that, and everyone who is a Christian does that. As the apostle Paul puts it, the light exposes 'the hidden things of darkness', and so he says, 'They that be drunken are drunken in the night.' The whole world is divided into 'children of light' and 'children of darkness'. So much of the life of the world is life under a kind of shroud of darkness. The worst things always happen under cover of darkness; even the natural man, degenerate and in a state of sin, would be ashamed of such things in the glare of light. Why? Because light exposes; 'Whatsoever doth make manifest is light.'

Now the Christian is 'the light of the world' in that way. It is quite inevitable, he cannot help it. Just by being Christian he shows a different type of life, and that immediately reveals the true character and nature of the other way of living. In the world, therefore, he is like a light being put on, and immediately people begin to think, and wonder, and feel ashamed. The more saintly the person, of course, the more obviously will this take place. He need not say a word; just by being what he is he makes people feel ashamed of what they are doing, and in that way he is truly functioning as light. He is providing a standard, he is showing that there is another kind of life which is possible to mankind. He therefore brings out the error and the failure of man's way of thinking and of living. As we saw in dealing with the Christian as 'the salt of the earth', the same thing can be said of him as 'the light of the world'. Every true revival has always had this effect. A number of Christian people in any district or society will tend to affect the life of the whole. Whether other people agree with their principles or not, they just make them feel that the Christian way is right after all, and the other way unworthy. The world has discovered that 'honesty is the best policy'. As someone puts it, that is the kind of tribute that hypocrisy always pays to truth; it has to admit in its heart of hearts that truth is right. The influence the Christian has as light in the world is to show that these other things belong to darkness. They thrive in darkness, and somehow or other they cannot stand the light. This is stated explicitly in John 3, where the apostle says, 'This is the condemnation, that light is come into the world, and men loved darkness rather than light, because their deeds were evil.' Our Lord goes on to say that such men do not come into the light because they know that, if they do, their deeds will be reproved, and they do not want that.

That, of course, was really the ultimate cause of the antagonism of the Pharisees and the scribes to our Lord and Saviour Jesus Christ. Here were these men, who were teachers of the law, these men who were experts, in a sense, on the religious life. Why did they so hate and persecute Him? The only adequate explanation is His utter purity, His utter holiness. Without His saying a word against them at the beginning — for He did not denounce them until the end — His purity made them see themselves as they really were, and they hated Him for it. Thus they persecuted Him, and finally crucified Him, just because He was 'the light of the world'. It revealed and manifested the hidden things of darkness that were within them. Now you and I have to be like that in this world: by just living the Christian life we are to have that effect.

Let us now go a step further and say that light not only reveals the hidden things of darkness, it also explains the cause of the darkness. That is where it becomes so practical and important at the present time. I have already reminded you that the best and greatest academic thinkers in the world today are entirely baffled with regard to what is wrong with the world. Two lectures were broadcast some years ago on the wireless by men who were described as humanists, Dr. Julian Huxley and Professor Gilbert Murray. Both admitted quite frankly in their talks that they could not explain life as it is. Dr. Julian Huxley said he could not see any end or purpose in life. The whole thing to him was fortuitous. Professor Gilbert Murray, also, could not explain the Second World War and the failure of the League of Nations. He had nothing to offer as a corrective but the 'culture' that has been available for centuries, and which has already failed.

It is just here that we Christians have the light which explains the situation. The sole cause of the troubles of the world at this moment, from the personal to the international level, is nothing but man's estrangement from God. That is the light which only Christians have, and which they can give to the world. Man has been so made by God that he cannot truly live unless he is in the right relationship to God. He was made like that. He was made by God; he was made for God. And God has put certain rules in his nature and being and existence, and unless he conforms to them he is bound to go wrong. That is the whole cause of the trouble. Every difficulty in the world today can be traced back, in the last analysis, to sin, selfishness and self-seeking. All the quarrels, disputes and misunderstandings, all the jealousy, envy and malice, all these things come back to that and nothing else. So we are 'the light of the world' in a very real sense at this present time; we alone have an adequate explanation of the cause of the state of the world. It can all be traced to the fall; the whole trouble arises from that. I want to quote again John 3:19: 'This is the condemnation, that light is come into the world, and men loved darkness rather than light, because their deeds were evil.' 'This is the condemnation' and nothing else. This is the cause of the trouble. What, then, is the matter? If light is come into the world in the face of Jesus Christ, what is wrong with the world in the middle of this twentieth century? The verse we have just quoted gives the answer. In spite of all the knowledge that has been amassed in the last two hundred years since the beginning of the enlightenment halfway through the eighteenth century, fallen man by nature still 'loves darkness rather than light'. The result is that, though he knows what is right, he prefers and does what is evil. He has a conscience which warns him before he does anything he knows to be wrong. Nevertheless he does it. He may regret it, but he still does it. Why? Because he likes it. The trouble with man is not in his intellect, it is in his nature — the passions and the lusts. That is the dominating factor. And though you try to educate and control man it will avail nothing as long as his nature is sinful and fallen and he is a creature of passion and dishonour.

That, then, is the condemnation; and there is no one to warn the modern world except the Christian. The philosopher not only does not speak; he resents such teaching. Such a man does not like to be told that he, with his wide knowledge, is still nothing but a lump of ordinary human clay like everybody else, and that he himself is a creature of passions and lusts and desires. But that is the simple truth concerning him. As was the case in the time of our Lord with many of those philosophers in that ancient world, who went out of life by that forbidden gate of suicide, so it is often the case today. Baffled, bewildered, feeling frustrated, having tried all their psychological and other treatments, but still going from bad to worse, men give up in despair. The gospel offends in that it makes a man face himself, and it always tells him that selfsame thing, 'The fault, dear Brutus, is not in our stars, but in ourselves, that we are underlings.' 'Men love darkness rather than light', that is the trouble, and the gospel alone proclaims it. It stands as a light in the heavens and it should be revealing itself through all of us amidst the problems of this dark, miserable, unhappy world of men.

But thank God we do not stop at that. Light not only exposes the darkness; it shows and provides the only way out of the darkness. This is where every Christian should be jumping to the task. The problem of man is the problem of a fallen, sinful, polluted nature. Can nothing be done about it? We have tried knowledge, we have tried education, we have tried political enactments, we have tried international conferences, we have tried them all but nothing avails. Is there no hope? Yes, there is abundant and everlasting hope: 'Ye must be born again'. What man needs is not more light; he needs a nature that will love the light and hate the darkness — the exact opposite of his loving the darkness and hating the light. Man needs to be taken hold of, and he needs to get back to God. It is not enough just to tell him that, because, if we do, we are leaving him in a still greater state of hopelessness. He will never find his way to God, try as he may. But the Christian is here to tell him that there is a way to God, a very simple one. It is to know one Person called Jesus Christ of Nazareth. He is the Son of God and He came from heaven to earth to 'seek and to save that which was lost'. He came to illumine the darkness, to expose the cause of the darkness, and to make a new and living way out of it all back to God and to heaven. He has not only borne the guilt of this terrible sinfulness that has involved us in such trouble, He offers us new life and a new nature. He does not merely give us new teaching or a new understanding of the problem; He does not merely procure pardon for our past sins; He makes us new men with new desires, new aspirations, a new outlook and a new orientation. But above all He gives us that new life, the life that loves the light and hates the darkness, instead of loving the darkness and hating the light.

Christian people, you and I are living in the midst of men and women who are in a state of gross darkness. They will never have any light anywhere in this world except from you and from me and the gospel we believe and teach. They are watching us. Do they see something different about us? Are our lives a silent rebuke to them? Do we so live as to lead them to come and ask us, 'Why do you always look so peaceful? How is it you are so balanced? How can you stand up to things as you do? Why is it you are not dependent upon artificial aids and pleasures as we are? What is this thing that you have got?' If they do we can then tell them that wondrous, amazing, but tragically neglected news, that 'Christ Jesus came into the world to save sinners', and to give men a new nature and a new life and to make them children of God. Christian people alone are the light of the world today. Let us live and function as children of the light.

Chapter Sixteen

Let Your Light So Shine

IN the last two chapters we have considered the two positive statements which our Lord made about the Christian: he is the 'salt of the earth' and the 'light of the world'. But He was not content with making merely a positive statement. To Him, evidently, this matter was so important that He must emphasize it, as was customary with Him, by means of certain negatives. He was anxious that those people to whom He was actually speaking, and, indeed, all Christians in every age, should see clearly that we are what He has made us in order that we may become something. That is the great argument which you find running right through the Scriptures. It is seen perfectly in that statement of the apostle Peter, 'Ye are a chosen generation, a royal priesthood, an holy nation, a peculiar people; that ye should shew forth the praises of him who hath called you out of darkness into his marvellous light' (1 Pet. 2:9). That is the argument, in a sense, in every New Testament Epistle, which again shows the utter folly of regarding this Sermon on the Mount as merely meant for some Christians who are yet to live in some future age or dispensation. For the teaching of the apostles, as we saw in our general introduction to the Sermon, is just an elaboration of what we have here. Their letters provide many examples of the working out of this very matter we are considering. In Philippians 2, the apostle Paul describes Christians as 'luminaries' or 'lights' in the world, and he exhorts them to 'hold forth the word of life' for that reason. He makes constant use of the comparison of light and darkness in order to show how the Christian functions in society because he is a Christian. Our Lord seems very anxious to impress this upon us. We are to be the salt of the earth. Very well; but remember, 'If the salt have lost his savour, wherewith shall it be salted? it is thenceforth good for nothing, but to be cast out, and to be trodden under foot of men.' We are 'the light of the world'. Yes; but let us remember that 'a city that is set on an hill cannot be hid.

Neither do men light a candle, and put it under a bushel, but on a candlestick; and it giveth light unto all that are in the house.' Then we have this final summing up of it all again: 'Let your light so shine before men, that they may see your good works, and glorify your Father which is in heaven.'

In view of the way in which our Lord emphasizes this it is obvious that we must consider it also. It is not enough just to remember that we are to act as salt in the earth or as the light of the world. We also have to grasp the fact that it must become the biggest thing in the whole of our life, for the reasons which we shall consider. Perhaps the best way of doing so is to put it in the form of a number of statements or propositions.

The first thing to consider is why we as Christians should be like salt and light, and why we should desire to be so. It seems to me that our Lord has three main arguments there. The first is that, by definition, we were meant to be such. His very comparisons convey that teaching. The business of salt is to be salt, just that. The characteristic of salt is saltness. It is exactly the same with light. The whole function and purpose of light is to give light. We must start there and realize that these things are self-evident and need no illustration. Yet the moment we put it like that, does it not tend to come as a rebuke to us all? How prone we are to forget these essential functions of salt and light. As we proceed with the argument, I think you will agree that this is something of which we need constantly to be reminded. A lamp, as our Lord puts it — and He is just appealing to ordinary, natural common sense — a lamp is lit in order that it may give light to all that are in the house. There is no other purpose in lighting a lamp but that. The whole object is that light may be disseminated and diffused in that particular area. That, therefore, is our first statement. We have to realize what a Christian is by definition, and this is our Lord's own definition of him. So that, at the very outset, when we start describing a Christian in our own terms, our definition must never be less than that. These are the essential things about him: 'salt'; 'light'.

But let us come to the second argument, which seems to me to be that our position becomes not only contradictory but even ridiculous if we do not act in this way. We are to be like 'a city that is set on an hill', and 'a city that is set on an hill cannot be hid'. In other words, if we are truly Christian we cannot be hid. Put in a different way, the contrast between us and others is something which is to be quite self-evident and perfectly obvious. But our Lord does not leave it at that; He presses it still further. He asks us, in effect, to imagine a man lighting a light and then putting it under a bushel instead of putting it on a candlestick. Now, in the past, commentators have spent a good deal of their time in defining what is meant by a 'bushel', sometimes with amusing results. To me the important thing is that it covers the light, and it does not matter very much what it is as long as it does that. What our Lord is saying is that it is a ridiculous and contradictory procedure. The whole purpose of lighting a light is that it may give light. And for a foolish man to cover it with something which prevents that quality from manifesting itself is, we are all agreed, utterly ridiculous. Yes; but remember that our Lord is speaking about us. There is obviously a danger, or at least a temptation, that the Christian may behave in this completely ridiculous and futile manner, and that is why He emphasizes the matter in this way. He seems to be saying, 'I have made you something that is meant to be like a light, like a city set upon a hill which cannot be hid. Are you deliberately concealing it? Well, if you are, apart from anything else, it is something which is completely ridiculous and foolish.'

But come to the last step in His argument here. To do this, according to our Lord, is to render ourselves utterly useless. Now this is very striking, and there is no doubt that He uses these two comparisons in order to bring out this particular point. Salt without its savour is quite useless. In other words, as I said at the beginning, there is only one essential quality of salt and that is saltness. And when salt has lost its saltness it is of no use at all. Now that is not true of everything. Take flowers, for example; when they are alive they are very beautiful and they may have an aroma; but when the flower dies it does not become quite useless. You can throw it on to the compost heap and it may be useful as compost. So with many other things; they do not become useless when their primary function ceases to operate. You can still make some secondary or subsidiary use of them. But the extraordinary thing about salt is that the moment it loses its saltness it is really no use at all: 'it is thenceforth good for nothing, but to be cast out, and to be trodden under foot of men.' It is very difficult to know what to do with it; you cannot throw it on a compost heap, it does harm there. It just has no function or value at all, and the only thing to do is to get rid of it. Nothing is left once it loses the essential quality and purpose for which it has been made. The same is true of light. The essential characteristic of light is that it is light, and gives light, and it really has no other function whatsoever. In other words, the moment it ceases to act as light it has no value. Its essential quality is its only quality, and once it loses that, it becomes entirely useless.

According to our Lord's argument that is the truth concerning the Christian. As I understand it, and it seems to me to be an inevitable piece of logic and interpretation, there is nothing in God's universe that is so utterly useless as a merely formal Christian. I mean by that, one who has the name but not the quality of a Christian. The apostle Paul describes this when he speaks of certain people 'having a form of godliness, but denying the power thereof'. They appear to be Christian but they are not. They want to appear as Christians, but they are not functioning as Christians. They are salt without savour, light with-out light, if you can imagine such a thing. You can do so most easily, perhaps, when you think of the illustration of the light being hid by the bushel. If you test this by observation and experience you will have to agree that it is the sim-ple truth. The formal Christian is a man who knows enough about Christianity to spoil the world for him; but he does not know enough about it for it to be of any positive value. He does not go with the world because he knows just enough about it to be afraid of certain things; and the people who live right in the world know that he is trying to be different and that he cannot be whole-heartedly with them. On the other hand he has no real fellowship with the Christian. He has enough 'Christianity' to spoil everything else, but not enough to give him real happiness, peace and joy and abundance of life. I think such people are the most pathetic people in the world. Our Lord certainly says they are the most useless people in the world. They do not function as worldlings or as Christians. They are nothing, neither salt nor light, neither one thing nor the other. And as a matter of actual fact, they are cast out; cast out, as it were, by the world and cast out by the Church. They refuse to regard themselves as of the world, while on the other hand they do not enter truly into the life of the Church. They feel it themselves, and others feel it. There is always this barrier. They are finally outsiders. They are more outside, in a sense, than the man who is entirely worldly and makes no claim or profession, because he at least has his own society.

Of all people, then, these are the most pathetic and the most tragic, and the solemn warning which we have in this verse is the warning of our Lord against getting into such a state and condition. It is reinforced by those parables in Matthew 25 where we are told again of this final shutting out of such people, like salt that is thrown out. To their amazement they will eventually find them-selves shut outside the door, trodden under foot of men. This has been proved historically. There have been certain churches which, having lost their savour, or having ceased to give out the true light, have just been trodden under foot. There was once a powerful Christian church in North Africa, a flourishing church that produced many of those early giants, including the great St. Augus-tine. But it lost its savour and its true light, and because of that it was literally trodden under foot and has ceased to be. It has happened in other countries. God give us grace to take this solemn warning unto ourselves. A mere formal profession of Christianity is something that will ultimately always suffer that fate.

Perhaps we can sum it all up in this way. The true Christian cannot be hid, he cannot escape notice. A man truly living and functioning as a Christian will stand out. He will be like salt; he will be like a city set upon a hill, a candle set

151

upon a candlestick. But we can also add this further word. The true Christian does not even desire to hide his light. He sees how ridiculous it is to claim to be a Christian and yet deliberately to try to hide the fact. A man who truly realizes what it means to be a Christian, who realizes all that the grace of God has meant to him and done for him, and understands that, ultimately, God has done this in order that he may influence others, is a man who cannot conceal it. Not only that; he does not desire to conceal it, because he argues thus, 'Ultimately the object and purpose of it all is that I might be functioning in this way.'

These comparisons and illustrations, then, are meant by our Lord to show us that any desire which we may find in ourselves to hide the fact that we are Christian is not only to be regarded as ridiculous and contradictory, it is, if we indulge it and persist in it, something which (though I do not understand the doctrine at this point) may lead to a final casting out. Let me put it in this way. If we find in ourselves a tendency to put the light under a bushel, we must begin to examine ourselves and make sure that it really is 'light'. It seems to be a fact about salt and light that they want to manifest their essential quality, so if there is any uncertainty about this, we should examine ourselves and discover again the cause of this illogical and contradictory position. Let us put it, therefore, in this simple form. The next time I find myself with any sort of tendency to cover over the fact that I am a Christian, in order, maybe, to ingratiate myself with somebody else or to avoid persecution, I am just to think of the man lighting his candle and then covering it with a bushel. The moment I think of it like that and see how ridiculous it is, I shall recognize that the subtle thing which offered me that bushel is the hand of the devil. I shall therefore reject it, and shine still more brightly.

That is the first statement. Let us now come to the second, which is a very practical one. How are we to ensure that we really do function as salt and as light? In a sense both illustrations put this point, but the second is perhaps the simpler of the two. Our Lord talks about the difficulty, the impossibility, of a man ever restoring the quality of saltness to salt. Again the commentators are most interested in that and give an illustration of a man who had once, on a journey, found some sort of salt which had lost its saltness. How foolish we can become when we begin to study Scripture in terms of words instead of doctrine! We need not go to the East to try to find salt without saltness; our Lord's sole purpose here is to show how ridiculous the whole thing is.

The second of the two illustrations is the more definite. Two things only are necessary to the lamp — the oil and the wick — and the two things always go together. You will find, of course, that some people talk only about the oil, others only about the wick. But without the oil and the wick you will never have a light. The two are absolutely essential, and so we are to pay attention to them both. The parable of the ten virgins again helps us to remember that. The oil is absolutely essential and vital; we can do nothing without it and the whole point of the Beatitudes, in a sense, is just to emphasize that fact. We have to receive this life, this divine life. We cannot function as light without it. We are only 'the light of the world' as He who is 'the light of the world' works in and through us. The first thing, then, which we must ask ourselves is, Have I received this life divine? Do I know that Christ is dwelling in me? Paul prays for the Ephesians that Christ may dwell in their hearts richly by faith, that they may be filled with all the fullness of God. The whole doctrine concerning the work of the Holy Spirit is essentially that. It is not to give particular gifts, such as tongues or the various other things about which people get so excited. His purpose is to give life and the graces of the Spirit, which is 'a more excellent way'. Am I sure that I have the oil, the life, that which the Holy Spirit of God alone can give to me?

The first exhortation, then, must be that we must seek this constantly. That means, of course, prayer, which is the action of going to receive it. We so often tend to think that these gracious invitations of our Lord are something which are given once and for ever. He says, 'Come unto me' if you want the water of life, 'Come unto me' if you want the bread of life. But we tend to think that once and for ever we come to Christ and thereafter we have this permanent supply. Not at all. It is a supply that we have to renew; we have to go back and receive it constantly. We are to live in contact with Him, and it is only as we constantly receive this life from Him that we shall function as salt and as light.

But, of course, it not only means constant prayer, it means what our Lord Himself describes as 'hungering and thirsting after righteousness'. You will remember we interpreted that as being something that goes on continuously. We are filled, yes; but we always want more. We are never static, we never rest upon our oars, we never say, 'Once and for ever.' Not at all. We go on hungering and thirsting; we go on realizing our perpetual need of Him and of this supply of life and of everything He has to give. So we continue to read the Word of God where we can learn about Him and this life which He offers us. The supply of oil is essential. Read the biographies of the men who have obviously been like cities set upon a hill which cannot be hid. You will find that they did not say, 'I have come to Christ once and for all; here is the one great climactic experience of life that will last for ever afterwards.' Not at all; they tell us that they found it an absolute necessity to spend hours in prayer and Bible study and meditation. They never ceased drawing the oil and receiving the supply.

The second essential is the wick. We must attend to this also. To keep that lamp burning brightly the oil is not enough, you must keep on trimming the wick. That is our Lord's illustration. Many of us today have never known anything other than this modern world of electricity. But some of us remember how the wick had to be given special attention. Once it began to smoke, it did not give the light, so the wick had to be trimmed. And a very delicate process it was. What does this mean in practice for us? I think it means that we constantly have to remind ourselves of the Beatitudes. We should read them every day. I ought to remind myself daily that I am to be poor in spirit, merciful, meek, a peacemaker, pure in heart, and so on. There is nothing that is better calculated to keep the wick in order and trimmed than just to remind myself of what I am by the grace of God, and of what I am meant to be. That, I suggest, is something for us to do in the morning before we start our day. In everything I do and say, I am to be like that man I see in the Beatitudes. Let us start with that and concentrate on it.

But not only are we to remind ourselves of the Beatitudes, we are to live accordingly. What does this mean? It means that we are to avoid everything that is opposed to this character, we are to be entirely unlike the world. It is a tragic thing to me that so many Christians, because they do not want to be different or to suffer persecution, seem to be living as near as they can to the world. But this is again a contradiction in terms. There is no mean between light and darkness; it is either one or the other, and there is no communion between them. Either it is light or it is not. And the Christian is to be like that in the earth. Far from being like the world, we should concentrate on being as different as we can.

Positively, however, it means that we should show this difference in our lives, and that, of course, can be done in a thousand and one ways. I cannot attempt to give a complete list; all I do know is that it means, at the very minimum, living a separated life. The world is becoming more and more rude; rougher, uglier, louder. I think all will agree with that. As the Christian influence is diminishing in this country the whole tone of society is becoming more gross; the decencies, yes, even the little politenesses, are less and less in evidence. The Christian is not to live in that way. We are far too prone these days just to say, 'I am a Christian', or 'Isn't it wonderful to be a Christian?' and then sometimes to be rude and inconsiderate. Let us remember that these are the things which proclaim what we are — 'the manner doth proclaim the man'. We are to be humble, peaceable, peacemaking in all our talk and behaviour, and especially in our reactions to the behaviour of other persons. I believe that the individual Christian is having a greater opportunity today than he has had for many a century, owing to the whole state of the world and of society. I believe that people are watching us very closely because we claim to be Christian; and they are watching our reactions to people and to the things they say and do to us. Do we flare up? The non-Christian does; the Christian should not. He is like the man in the Beatitudes, so he reacts differently. And when confronted with world events, with wars and rumours of wars, with calamities, pestilences and all these other things, he is not overanxious, troubled and irritable. The world is; the Christian is not. He is essentially different.

The last principle is the supreme importance of doing all this in the right way. We have considered why we are to be like salt; we have considered why we are to be like light. We have considered how to be so, how to ensure that we are. But it must be done in the right way. 'Let your light so shine before men', — the great word there is 'so' — 'that they may see your good works, and glorify your Father which is in heaven.' You see, there is to be a complete absence of ostentation and display. It is a little difficult in practice, is it not, to draw the line between truly functioning as salt and light, and still not to be guilty of display or ostentation? Yet that is what we are told to do. We are so to live that men may see our good works, but glorify our Father which is in heaven. How difficult to function truly as an active Christian, and yet not to have any showmanship. This is true even in our listening to the gospel, quite apart from our preaching of it! As we produce and reveal it in our daily lives, we must remember that the Christian does not call attention to himself. Self has been forgotten in this poverty of spirit, in the meekness and all the other things. In other words, we are to do everything for God's sake, and for His glory. Self is to be absent, and must be utterly crushed in all its subtlety, for His sake, for His glory.

It follows from this that we are to do these things in such a way as to lead other men to glorify Him, and glory in Him, and give themselves to Him. 'Let your light so shine before men, that they may see your good works.' Yes; and so see them that they will themselves glorify your Father which is in heaven. Not only are you to glorify your Father; you are to do so in order that these other people may glorify Him also.

That in turn leads to the fact that, because we are truly Christian, we are to have great sorrow in our hearts for those other people. We are to realize that they are in darkness, and in a state of pollution. In other words, the more we draw our life from Him, the more we shall become like Him; and He had a great compassion for the people. He saw them as sheep without a shepherd. He had great sorrow for them in His heart, and it was that which determined His conduct and behaviour. He was not concerned about Himself; He had compassion for the multitude. And that is the way in which you and I are to live and to regard these matters. In other words, in all our work and Christian living these three things should always be uppermost. We shall always do it for His sake and His glory. We shall lead men to Him and to glorify Him. And all will be based upon a love for them and a compassion for them in their lost condition.

That, then, is the way in which our Lord exhorts us to show what He has made of us. We must function as men and women who have received from Him life divine. He ridicules the opposite. He puts before us this wondrous picture of becoming like Himself in this world. It was as men and women saw Him that they were led to think of God. Have you noticed how often, after His miracles, we read that the people 'gave glory unto God'? They said, 'We have never seen things like this before'; and they glorified the Father. You and I are to live like that. In other words, we are to live in such a way that, as men and women look at us, we shall become a problem to them. They will ask, 'What is it? Why are these people so different in every way, different in their conduct and behaviour, different in their reactions? There is something about them which we do not understand; we cannot explain it.' And they will be driven to the only real explanation, which is that we are the people of God, children of God, 'heirs of God, and joint-heirs with Christ'. We have become reflectors of Christ, reproducers of Christ. As He is 'the light of the world' so we have become 'the light of the world'.

Chapter Seventeen

Christ and the Old Testament

'T HINK not that I am come to destroy the law, or the prophets: I am not come to destroy, but to fulfil. For verily I say unto you, Till heaven and earth pass, one jot or one tittle shall in no wise pass from the law, till all be fulfilled.' These verses, although they are a continuation of what has gone before, nevertheless mark the beginning of a new section in the Sermon. Hitherto we have seen that our Lord has been concerned to describe the Christian. First we have been reminded of what we are; then we have been told that, this being so, we must ever remember it and let our life be such that it will always be a manifestation of this essential being of ours. It is like the parent saying to the child who is going away from home to a party, 'Now remember who you are. You must behave in such a way that you reflect glory and honour upon your family and your parents.' Or the same appeal is made to children in the name of the school or to its citizens by a country.

That is what our Lord has been saying. We are children of God and citizens of the kingdom of heaven. Because of that, we have to manifest the characteristics of such people. We do this in order to manifest His glory, and so that others may be brought to glorify Him.

The question then arises as to how this is to be done. That is the subject which now confronts us. The answer, in a word, can be put like this: we are to live a life of righteousness. That is the one word that sums up Christian living, 'righteousness'. And the theme of the remainder of the Sermon on the Mount is in many ways just that, the kind of life of righteousness which the Christian is to live. Until you come to 7:14 that is the great theme which is expounded in various ways.

What is this righteousness which we have to manifest, what is its character?

Verses 17 to 20 in this fifth chapter are a kind of general introduction to that subject. Here our Lord introduces this whole question of the righteousness and the righteous life which are to characterize the Christian. You observe His method. Before He comes to the details, He lays down certain general princi- ples. He has an introduction before He really begins to explain and expound His subject. Some people, I gather, do not like introductions. In that case they do not like our Lord's method! It is always vital to start with principles. The people who go wrong in practice are always those who are not sure of their principles. It seems to me that this is most vital today. We live in an age of spe- cialists, and the specialist is almost invariably a man who is so lost in details that he often forgets principles. Most of the breakdown in life today is due to the fact that certain basic principles have been forgotten. In other words if only everybody lived a godly life we should have no need for this multiplicity of con- ferences and organizations.

The method of starting with basic principles is something we see here as our Lord goes on to deal with this question of righteousness. He does so by lay- ing down in this paragraph two categorical propositions. In the first, in verses 17 and 18, He says that everything He is going to teach is in absolute harmony with the entire teaching of the Old Testament Scriptures. There is nothing in this teaching which in any way contradicts them.

The second proposition, which He lays down in verses 19 and 20, is that this teaching of His which is in such harmony with the Old Testament is in complete disharmony with, and an utter contradiction of, the teaching of the Pharisees and scribes.

Those are two great pronouncements and they are important, because we shall never understand the record of our Lord's life which we have in the four Gospels, unless we grasp these two principles. Here we have an explanation of all the antagonism towards Him which was displayed by the Pharisees, the scribes, the doctors of the law and various other people. Here is the explanation of all the troubles that He had to endure, and the misunderstanding to which He was so constantly subjected.

Another general observation is that our Lord was not content with making pos- itive statements only; He made negative ones also. He was not content with just stating His doctrine. He also criticized other doctrines. I am emphasizing that again in passing because, as I have pointed out repeatedly in dealing with this Sermon, for some extraordinary reason a peculiar flabbiness — intellectual and moral — seems to have entered into many people, Evangelicals included. Many, alas, seem to object in these days to negative teaching. 'Let us have positive teaching', they say. 'You need not criticize other views.' But our Lord definitely did criticize the teaching of the Pharisees and scribes. He exposed and denounced it frequently. And it is essential, of course, that we should do the same. We are all talking about ecumenicity, and the argument is put forward that, because of a certain common danger, it is not the time to be arguing about points of doctrine; rather we should all be friendly and pull together. Not at all, according to our Lord. The fact that the Roman Catholic and Greek Orthodox churches are called Christian is no reason why we should not expose the corruptness and the dangerous errors of their systems.

Our Lord, then, does not stop with the positive; and that, in turn, leads to another question. Why did He do this? Why this kind of introduction to the detailed part of the Sermon? I think the answer is very plain. As we read the four Gospels we see clearly that there was much confusion with regard to our Lord's teaching. He was undoubtedly a great problem to His contemporaries. There were so many unusual things about Him. He Himself, for instance, was unusual. He was not a Pharisee and He had not been trained as a Pharisee. He had not been to the customary schools, so they looked at Him and said, 'Who is this fellow, this man who teaches and makes these dogmatic pronouncements? What is this?' He did not come into His position as a teacher along the usual lines or through the customary channels, and that at once created a problem. The leaders and the people were rather perplexed about it. But not only that. As I have been reminding you, He deliberately criticized the Pharisees and the scribes, and their teaching. Now they were the acknowledged leaders and religious teachers, and everyone was prepared to do what they said. They were quite outstanding in the nation. But, suddenly, here was a Man who did not belong to their schools, who not only taught, but also denounced their authoritative teaching. Then, over and above that, He did not spend all His time in expounding the law. He preached an extraordinary doctrine of grace and of the love of God which introduced such things as the parable of the Prodigal Son. But, even worse, He mixed with publicans and sinners, sitting down and eating with them. Not only did he not seem to observe all the rules and regulations; He actually seemed to be deliberately breaking them. In His words He criticized their official teaching, and in practice He did the same.

So questions began to arise at once because of His theory and because of His practice. 'Does this new Teacher not believe the Holy Writings? The Pharisees and the scribes claim to be the exponents and the expounders of the Holy Scripture; does this Jesus of Nazareth, therefore, not believe it? Has He come to do away with it? Is His teaching absolutely new? Is it denouncing the law and the prophets? Is He teaching that there is some new way to God, some new way of pleasing God? Is He turning His back resolutely upon the whole of the past?' Now those were the questions which our Lord well knew were bound to arise because of His personal character and because of what He taught. So, here, at the very introduction to the detailed teaching, He met the criticism beforehand. In particular He warned His disciples lest they should be confounded and influenced by the talk and criticism which they were so likely to hear. He prepared their mind and outlook by laying down these two fundamental postulates.

Our Lord had already told them in general what they were to be like and the kind of righteousness they were to manifest. Now, as He came to detailed and specific questions, He wanted them to understand the whole setting. I am calling attention to this not out of a theoretical interest and not merely because it is a fresh section of this Sermon which we must expound. I am doing so because it is a very urgent and practical question for every one of us who is in any way concerned about the Christian life. For this is not merely an old problem; it is also a very modern one. It is not something theoretical, for there are large numbers of people who are still in trouble on this very question. There are those who stumble at Christ and His salvation because of this very point of His relationship to the law; and therefore I say that it is vital we should look at it. Indeed there are some who say that this verse we are considering actually increases their problem instead of diminishing it.

There are two main difficulties which are raised with regard to this. There is one school which believes that all our Lord Himself did was to continue the teaching of the law. You know the school, although it is not quite as popular now as it was some thirty years ago or more. Its followers say that they see a great difference between the four Gospels and the New Testament Epistles. The Gospels are nothing but a very wonderful exposition of the ancient law, and Jesus of Nazareth was only a Teacher of the Law. The real founder of so-called Christianity, they continue, was the man we know as the apostle Paul with all his doctrine and legalism. The four Gospels are nothing but law, ethical teaching and moral instruction; and there is nothing in them about the doctrine of justification by faith, sanctification and such things. That is the work of the apostle Paul with his theology. The real tragedy, they say, is that the simple, glorious gospel of Jesus was turned by this other man into what has become Christianity, which is entirely different from the religion of Jesus. Those who are old enough will remember that towards the turn of the century and after there were several books written along that line, *The Religion of Jesus and the Faith of Paul*, and so on, which tried to show the great contrast between Jesus and Paul. That is one difficulty.

The second main difficulty is the exact opposite to that; and it is interesting to observe how heresies almost invariably cancel one another out. For the second view is that Christ abolished the law completely, and that He introduced grace in place of it. 'The law was given by Moses,' they quote, 'grace and truth came by Jesus Christ.' The Christian, therefore, has nothing to do with the law. They argue that the Bible says we are under grace, so we must never even mention the law. You remember we dealt with this argument in chapter one. We considered there the view which said that the Sermon on the Mount had nothing to do with us today, that it had reference to the people to whom it was preached, and will have reference to the Jews in the future kingdom age. It is interesting to note how these old troubles still persist.

Our Lord answers both at one and the same time in this vital statement in verses 17 and 18 which deals with this specific matter of His relationship to the law and to the prophets. What has He to say about it? Perhaps the best thing to do at this point is to define our terms, and to be perfectly clear that we understand their meaning. What is meant by 'the law' and 'the prophets'? The answer is, the whole of the Old Testament. You can turn up passages for yourself and you will find that wherever this expression is used it includes the entire Old Testament canon.

What, then, is meant by 'the law' in particular, at this point? It seems to me we must agree that the word, as used here, means the entire law. This, as given to the children of Israel, consisted of three parts, the moral, the judicial and the ceremonial. If you read again the books of Exodus, Leviticus and Numbers, you will find that this was how God gave it. The moral law consisted of the Ten Commandments and the great moral principles that were laid down once and for ever. Then there was the judicial law, which means the legislative law given for the nation of Israel in its peculiar circumstances at that time, which indicated how men were to order their behaviour in relationship to others and the various things they were and were not to do. Finally there was the ceremonial law concerning burnt offerings and sacrifices and all the ritual and ceremonial in connection with their worship in the temple and elsewhere. At this point we must assert that 'the law' includes all that; so that our Lord is here referring to everything that it teaches directly about life, conduct and behaviour.

We must remember also, however, that the law includes everything that is taught by the various types, the different offerings and all the details that are given concerning them in the Old Testament. Many Christian people say that they find the books of Exodus and Leviticus so boring. 'Why all this detail', they ask, 'about the meal and the salt and all these various other things?' Well, all these are just types, and they are all prophecy, in their way, of what was done perfectly once and for ever by our Lord and Saviour Jesus Christ. I say, therefore, that when we talk of the law we must remember that all this is included. Not only the positive, direct teaching of these books and their injunctions on how life should be lived; but also all that they suggest and foretell with regard to what was to come. The law, then, must be taken in its entirety. Actually, we shall find that, from verse 21 onwards, when our Lord speaks of the law He is speaking only of the moral section. But in this general statement here He is talking about it all.

What is meant by 'the prophets'? The term clearly means all that we have in the prophetic books of the Old Testament. There again we must never forget that there are two main aspects. The prophets actually taught the law, and they applied and interpreted it. They went to the nation and told them that the trouble with them was that they were not keeping God's law, their main endeavour being to call the people back to a true understanding of it. To this end they caused it to be read again and expounded. But, in addition, they did foretell the coming of the Messiah. They were 'forth-tellers', but at the same time they were foretellers. Both aspects are included in the prophetic message.

That leaves us with one final term, the term 'fulfil'. There has been a great deal of confusion with regard to its meaning, so we must point out at once that it does not mean to complete, to finish; it does not mean to add to something that has already been begun. This popular interpretation is an entire misunderstanding of the word. It has been said that the Old Testament began a certain teaching and that it carried on so far and up to a point. Then our Lord came and carried it a stage further, rounding it off and fulfilling it, as it were. That is not the true interpretation. The real meaning of the word 'fulfil' is to carry out, to fulfil in the sense of giving full obedience to it, literally carrying out everything that has been said and stated in the law and in the prophets.

Having defined our terms, let us now consider what our Lord is really saying to us. What is His actual teaching? I am going to put it in the form of two principles and, in order to do so, I am going to take verse 18 before verse 17. The two statements come together, and are connected by the word 'for'. 'Think not that I am come to destroy the law, or the prophets: I am not come to destroy, but to fulfil.' And here is the reason why. 'For verily I say unto you, Till heaven and earth pass, one jot or one tittle shall in no wise pass from the law, till all be fulfilled.'

The first proposition is that God's law is absolute; it can never be changed, not even modified to the slightest extent. It is absolute and eternal. Its demands are permanent, and can never be abrogated or reduced 'till heaven and earth pass'. That last expression means the end of the age. Heaven and earth are signs of permanence. While they are there, says our Lord, nothing shall pass away, not even a jot or a tittle. There is nothing smaller than these, the smallest letter in the Hebrew alphabet and the smallest point in the smallest letter. Heaven and earth shall not pass away until every minute detail shall be absolutely and entirely fulfilled. Now that is the pronouncement, and it is, of course, one of the most momentous and important pronouncements that has ever been made. Our Lord emphasizes it by the word 'for', which always calls attention to something and denotes seriousness and importance. Then He adds to the importance by saying, 'Verily I say unto you.' He is impressing the statement with all the authority He possesses. The law that God has laid down, and which you can read in the Old Testament, and everything that has been said by the prophets, is going to be fulfilled down to the minutest detail, and it will hold and stand until this absolute fulfilment has been entirely carried out. I do not think I need emphasize the vital importance of that any further.

Then, in the light of that, our Lord makes His second statement to the effect that obviously, therefore, He has not come to destroy, or indeed to modify even to the slightest extent, the teaching of the law or the prophets. He has come, He tells us, rather to fulfil and to carry them out, and to give them a perfect obedience. There, we see the central claim which is made by our Lord. It is, in other words, that all the law and all the prophets point to Him and will be fulfilled in Him down to the smallest detail. Everything that is in the law and the prophets culminates in Christ, and He is the fulfilment of them. It is the most stupendous claim that He ever made.

This is a theme which we must elaborate, but here, first, is the immediate deduction. Our Lord Jesus Christ in these two verses confirms the whole of the Old Testament. He puts His seal of authority, His *imprimatur,* upon the whole of the Old Testament canon, the whole of the law and the prophets. Read these four Gospels, and watch His quotations from the Old Testament. You can come to one conclusion only, namely, that He believed it all and not only certain parts of it! He quoted almost every part of it. To the Lord Jesus Christ the Old Testament was the Word of God; it was Scripture; it was something absolutely unique and apart; it had authority which nothing else has ever possessed nor can possess. Here, then, is a vital statement with regard to this whole matter of the authority of the Old Testament.

You will find so many people today who seem to think they can believe on the Lord Jesus Christ fully and yet more or less reject the Old Testament. It must be said, however, that the question of our attitude to the Old Testament inevitably raises the question of our attitude towards the Lord Jesus Christ. If we say that we do not believe in the account of the creation, or in Abraham as a person; if we do not believe that the law was given by God to Moses, but think that it was a very clever bit of Jewish legislation produced by a man who was a good leader, and who obviously had certain sound ideas about public health and hygiene — if we say that, we are in fact flatly contradicting everything our

Lord and Saviour Jesus Christ said about Himself, the law, and the prophets. Everything in the Old Testament, according to Him, is the Word of God. Not only that, it is all going to stand until it has all been fulfilled. Every jot and tittle, everything has meaning. Everything is going to be carried out down to the smallest detail imaginable. It is God's law, it is God's enactment.

Nor were the words of the prophets words of men who were simply poets, and who, having this poetic insight, saw a little further into life than other people, and, thus inspired, made wonderful statements about life and how to live it. Not at all. These were men of God who were given their message by Him. What they said is all true, and all will be fulfilled down to the smallest detail. It was all given with reference to Christ. He is the fulfilment of all these things, and it is only as they are fully carried out in Him that they can in any sense come to an end.

Now this, of course, is also of vital significance. People have often wondered why it was that the early Church decided to incorporate the Old Testament with the New Testament. So many people who are Christians say that they like reading the Gospels, but that they are not interested in the Old Testament, and that they do not think those five books of Moses and their message have anything to do with them. The early Church did not take that view, and for this reason: the one casts light upon the other, and each in a sense can only be understood in the light of the other. These two Testaments must always go together. As the great St. Augustine once put it, 'The New Testament is latent in the Old Testament and the Old Testament is patent in the New Testament.'

But, above all, here is this pronouncement by the Son of God Himself, in which He says that He has not come to supersede the Old Testament, the law and the prophets. 'No,' He seems to say, 'all this is of God, and I am come to carry it out and fulfil it.' He regarded it all as the Word of God and finally authoritative. And you and I, if we are to be true followers of Him and believers in Him, are to do the same. The moment you begin to question the authority of the Old Testament, you are of necessity questioning the authority of the Son of God Himself, and you will find yourself in endless trouble and difficulty. If you once begin to say that He was just a child of His age and was limited in certain respects because of that and liable to error, you are seriously qualifying the biblical doctrine as to His full, absolute and unique deity. You must be very careful, therefore, in what you say about the Scriptures. Watch His quotations from them — the quotations from the law and the prophets, the quotations from the Psalms. He quotes them everywhere. To Him they are always the Scripture which has been given, and which, He says, in John 10:35, 'cannot be broken'. It is God's own Word that is going to be fulfilled to the minutest detail and which will last while heaven and earth are in existence.

Chapter Eighteen

Christ Fulfilling the Law and the Prophets

W E have laid down our two main principles with regard to the relationship between the Old Testament Scriptures and the gospel and now we must consider this subject again in greater detail. First of all, let us see how our Lord 'fulfils' and carries out what has been written by the prophets in the Old Testament — a most important subject. You remember the use which the apostle Peter makes of that in his second Epistle. He is writing to comfort people who were living in very hard and difficult times and who were experiencing persecution. He is now an old man and realizes that he has not long to live. He wants, therefore, to give them some final comfort before he goes. He tells them various things; how, for instance, he and James and John had the privilege of seeing the transfiguration of our Lord and how they even heard that voice from the excellent glory which said, 'This is my beloved Son, hear him.' 'And yet', says Peter in effect, 'I have something even better than that to tell you. You need not place your confidence on my testimony and experience. There is the "more sure word of prophecy". Go back and read your Old Testament prophets. See their verification in Christ Jesus and you will have the strongest buttress of faith that man can ever obtain.' This, then, is something of vital importance. Our Lord claims that He is the fulfilment, in and of Himself, of that which was taught by the Old Testament prophets. The apostle Paul makes a great and comprehensive statement about this in 2 Corinthians 1:20 where he says, 'All the promises of God in him are yea, and in him Amen.' Now that is finality. All the promises of God are, in this wonderful Person, yea and amen. That, in effect, is what our Lord is saying here.

We cannot go into this fully; I must leave you to work out the details for yourself. The fulfilment of the prophecies is truly one of the most astounding and remarkable things that one can ever encounter, as has often been pointed

out. Think of the exact prophecies as to His birth, the place of His birth even —
Bethelehem-Judah; all these were fulfilled exactly. The extraordinary things
that are foretold of His Person make it almost incredible that the Jews should
ever have stumbled at Him. It was their own ideas which led them astray. They
should not have thought of the Messiah as a worldly king, or a political person-
age, because they had been told the opposite by their prophets. They had had
these prophets read to them, but they were blinded by prejudice, and instead of
looking at the words, they were looking at their own superimposed ideas — a
constant danger. But there we have the prophetic record down to the smallest
detail. Think of the extraordinarily accurate description of the type of life He
lived — 'a bruised reed shall he not break, and smoking flax shall he not
quench' — and that wonderful description of His Person and life in Isaiah 53.
Think of the accounts of what He was going to do, the foretelling of His miracles, His physical miracles, the kind of thing He was likely to do and the teaching involved in that. It is all there, and that is why it is always such an easy and
wonderful thing to preach the gospel out of the Old Testament. Some people
are still foolish enough to be amazed at it, but in a sense you can preach the gospel as well out of the Old Testament as out of the New. It is full of gospel.

Above everything else, however, you have the prophecy of His death and
even the mode of His death. Read Psalm 22 for instance, and you will find there
a literal, accurate description in detail of what actually happened on Calvary's
cross. Prophecy, you see, is found in the Psalms as well as in the prophets. He
fulfilled literally and completely what is foretold of Him there. In the same way
you find even the resurrection quite clearly foretold in the Old Testament together with much wonderful teaching about the kingdom which our Lord was
going to establish. Still more amazing, in a sense, are the prophecies concerning
the bringing in of the Gentiles. That is really remarkable when you remember
that these oracles of God were written in particular for one nation, the Jews,
and yet there are these clear prophecies regarding the spreading of the blessing
to the Gentiles in this extraordinary manner. In the same way, you will find
clear accounts of what happened on that great day of Pentecost at Jerusalem
when the Holy Spirit descended upon the infant Christian Church and people
were baffled and amazed. You remember how the apostle Peter faced it all and
said, 'You should not be surprised at this. This is that which was said by the
prophet Joel; it is nothing but a fulfilment of that.'

We could go on like this endlessly, just showing the extraordinary way in
which our Lord, in His Person and works and actions, in what happened to
Him, and in what resulted from these events, is in a sense doing nothing but
fulfilling the law and the prophets. We must never drive a wedge between the
Old Testament and the New. We must never feel that the New makes the Old

unnecessary. I feel increasingly that it is very regrettable that the New Testament should ever have been printed alone, because we tend to fall into the serious error of thinking that, because we are Christians, we do not need the Old Testament. It was the Holy Spirit who led the early Church, which was mainly Gentile, to incorporate the Old Testament Scriptures with their New Scriptures and to regard them all as one. They are indissolubly bound together, and there are many senses in which it can be said that the New Testament cannot be truly understood except in the light that is provided by the Old. For example, it is almost impossible to make anything of the Epistle to the Hebrews unless we know our Old Testament Scriptures.

Let us also observe, very hurriedly, how Christ fulfils the law. This again is something so wonderful that it should lead us to worship and adoration. First, He was 'made under the law'. 'When the fulness of the time was come, God sent forth his Son made of a woman, made under the law' (Gal. 4:4). It is very difficult for our finite minds to grasp what that means, but it is one of the essential truths concerning the incarnation that the eternal Son of God was made under the law. Though He is eternally above it, as Son of God He came and was made under the law, as one who had to carry it out. At no time has God shown more clearly the inviolable and absolute character of His own holy law than when He placed His own Son under it. It is an astounding conception; and yet, as you read the Gospels, you will find how perfectly true it is. Notice how very careful our Lord was to observe the law; He obeyed it down to the minutest detail. Not only that; He taught others to love the law and explained it to them, confirming it constantly and asserting the absolute necessity of obedience to it. That was why He could say at the end of His life that no one could find any wrong in Him, no one could bring any charge against Him. He defied them to do so. No one could arraign Him before the law. He had lived it fully and obeyed it perfectly. There was nothing, not a jot or a tittle, in connection with it which He had to the slightest extent broken or failed to fulfil. You see that in His life, as well as in His birth, He was made subject to the law.

Once more, however, we come to what is to us the centre of our whole faith — the cross on Calvary's hill. What is the meaning of that? Well, I suggest again that if we are not clear in our understanding of the law, we shall never understand the meaning of the cross. The essence of evangelism is not merely to talk about the cross but to proclaim the true doctrine of the cross. There are people who talk about it, but they do so in a purely sentimental manner. They are like the daughters of Jerusalem, whom our Lord Himself rebuked, weeping as they thought of what they called the tragedy of the cross. That is not the right way to view it. There are those who regard the cross as something which exercises a kind of moral influence upon us. They say that its whole purpose is to break down our hard hearts. But that is not the biblical teaching as to its meaning. The purpose of the cross is not to arouse pity in us, neither is it merely some general display of the love of God. Not at all! It is finally understood only in terms of the law. What was happening upon the cross was that our Lord and Saviour Jesus Christ, the Son of God, was enduring in His own holy body the penalty prescribed by the holy law of God for the sin of man. The law condemns sin, and the condemnation that it pronounces is death. 'The wages of sin is death.' The law pronounces that death must pass upon all who have sinned against God and broken His holy law. Christ says, 'Think not that I am come to destroy the law, or the prophets; I am not come to destroy, but to fulfil.' One of the ways in which the law has to be fulfilled is that its punishment of sin must be carried out. This punishment is death, and that was why He died. The law must be fulfilled. God cannot put it on one side in any respect, and the punishment cannot be put on one side. God in forgiving us — let us say so clearly — does not do so by deciding not to exact the punishment that He has decreed. That would imply a contradiction of His holy nature. Whatever God says must be brought to pass. He does not go back upon Himself and upon what He says. He has said that sin has to be punished by death, and you and I can be forgiven only because the punishment has been thus exacted. In respect of its punishment of sin God's law has been fulfilled absolutely, because He has punished sin in the holy, spotless, blameless body of His own Son there upon the cross on Calvary's hill. Christ is fulfilling the law on the cross, and unless you interpret the cross, and Christ's death upon it, in strict terms of the fulfilling of the law you have not the scriptural view of the death upon the cross.

We see also that, in a most extraordinary and wonderful manner, by so dying upon the cross and bearing in Himself and upon Himself the punishment due to sin, He has fulfilled all the Old Testament types. Go back again and read the books of Leviticus and Numbers; read all about the burnt offerings and sacrifices; read all about the tabernacle, and the temple ceremonial, all about the altar and the laver of washing and so on. Go back to those details and ask yourself, 'What do all these things mean? What are they for, the shewbread, and the high priest, and the vessels, and all these other things? What are they meant to do?' They are nothing but shadows, types, prophecies of what is going to be done fully and finally by the Lord Jesus Christ. He indeed has literally fulfilled and carried out and brought to pass every single one of those types. Some may be interested in this subject and there are certain books in which you may find out all the details[1]. But the principle, the great truth, is just this: Jesus Christ, by

---

1. See, for example, *The Typology of Scripture*, by P. Fairbairn.

His death and all He has done, is an absolute fulfilment of all these types and shadows. He is the high priest, He is the offering, He is the sacrifice, and He has presented His blood in heaven so that the whole of the ceremonial law has been fulfilled in Him. 'Think not that I am come to destroy the law, or the prophets: I am not come to destroy, but to fulfil.' By His death and resurrection, and the presentation of Himself in heaven, He has done all this.

But we go a step beyond this and say that He fulfils the law also in us and through us by means of the Holy Spirit. That is the argument of the apostle Paul in Romans 8:2-4. He tells us quite clearly that this is one of the explanations of why our Lord died. 'For the law of the Spirit of life in Christ Jesus hath made me free from the law of sin and death. For what the law could not do, in that it was weak through the flesh, God sending his own Son in the likeness of sinful flesh, and for sin, condemned sin in the flesh: that the righteousness of the law might be fulfilled in us, who walk not after the flesh, but after the Spirit.' This is most important and significant, for the apostle here links together two things: the way in which our Lord fulfilled the law Himself and the way in which He fulfils the law in us. That is precisely what our Lord is saying at this point in Matthew 5. He fulfils the righteousness of the law, and we are to do the same. The two go together. He does this in us by giving us the Holy Spirit, and the Holy Spirit gives us a love of the law and the power to live by it. 'The carnal mind is enmity against God: for it is not subject to the law of God, neither indeed can be', says the apostle Paul in that same eighth chapter of Romans. But we who have received the Spirit are not like that. We are not at enmity with God, and therefore we are also subject to the law. The natural man hates God and is not subject to His law; but the man who has received the Spirit loves God and is subject to the law. He wants to be so and is given power to be so: 'that the righteousness of the law might be fulfilled in us, who walk not after the flesh, but after the Spirit.' Look at it in this way. Through the prophet Jeremiah, God gave a great promise. He said, in effect, 'I am going to make a new covenant, and the difference between the new and the old will be this, that I am going to write My law in your minds and on your hearts. No longer will it be on tables of stone outside you, but on the fleshly tables of the heart.' The author of the Epistle to the Hebrews takes that up in the eighth chapter where he glories in the new covenant, the new relationship, because under it the law is within us, not outside us. It is because the law has been written in our minds and our hearts that we are anxious to fulfil it, and are enabled to do so.

Let me summarize all this by asking a question. What, then, is the position with regard to the law and the prophets? I have already tried to show you how the prophets have been fulfilled in and through our Lord Jesus Christ; and yet there still remains something to be fulfilled. What about the law? We can say with regard to the ceremonial law, as I have shown, that it has been already completely fulfilled. Our Lord observed it in His life while here on earth, and He exhorted the disciples to do the same. In His death, resurrection and ascension the whole of the ceremonial law has been entirely fulfilled. In confirmation of that, as it were, the temple was later destroyed. The veil of the temple had already been rent in twain at His death, and finally the temple and all that belonged to it were destroyed. So that, unless I see that the Lord Jesus Christ is the altar and the sacrifice and the laver of washing and the incense and everything else, I am still bound to that levitical order. Unless I see all this fulfilled in Christ, unless He is my burnt offering, my sacrifice, my everything, all this ceremonial law still applies to me, and I shall be held responsible unless I perform it. But seeing it all fulfilled and carried out in Him, I say I am fulfilling it all by believing in Him and by subjecting myself to Him. That is the position with regard to the ceremonial law.

What of the judicial law? This was primarily and especially for the nation of Israel, as God's theocracy, in its then special circumstances. But Israel is no longer the theocratic nation. You remember that at the end of His ministry our Lord turned to the Jews and said, 'Therefore say I unto you, The kingdom of God shall be taken from you, and given to a nation bringing forth the fruits thereof.' That is Matthew 21:43, one of the most crucial and important statements in the whole of Scripture with regard to prophecy. And the apostle Peter, in 1 Peter 2:9, 10, makes it abundantly clear that the new nation is the Church. There is then no longer a theocratic nation, so the judicial law has likewise been fulfilled.

That leaves us with the moral law. The position with regard to this is different, because here God is laying down something which is permanent and perpetual, the relationship which must always subsist between Himself and man. It is all to be found, of course, in what our Lord calls the first and greatest commandment. 'Thou shalt love the Lord thy God with all thy heart, and with all thy soul, and with all thy strength, and with all thy mind.' That is permanent. That is not for the theocratic nation only; it is for the whole of mankind. The second commandment, He says, 'is like unto it, Thou shalt love thy neighbour as thyself.' That again was not only for the theocratic nation of Israel; that was not merely the old ceremonial law. It is a permanent condition and part of our perpetual relationship to God. Thus the moral law, as interpreted by the New Testament, stands now as much as it has ever done, and will do so until the end of time and until we are perfected. In 1 John 3 the apostle is very careful to remind his readers that sin in Christian people is still 'a transgression of the law'. 'We still see our relationship to the law', says John in effect, 'for sin is a transgression of the law.' The law is still there, and when I sin I am breaking that law, though I am a Christian and though I have never been a Jew, and am a Gentile. So the moral law still applies to us. That, it seems to me, is the present position.

With regard to the future, I have simply two statements to make. The first is that the kingdom will eventually cover the whole earth. The stone that is spoken of in the second chapter of Daniel is going to fill the whole world; the kingdoms of this world shall become 'the kingdoms of our Lord, and of his Christ'. The process is going on, it will finally be completed. Every tittle of the law and the prophets will thus be completely carried out. The law breakers will finally be punished. Let us make no mistake about this. Those who die finally impenitent, and unbelieving in the Lord Jesus Christ, are under the condemnation of the law. And at the very end the pronouncement delivered upon them will be, 'Depart from me, ye cursed, into everlasting fire.' And it is the law that will condemn them to that. So that the law of God is going to be carried out fully in every respect. Those who do not avail themselves of what is offered in the Lord Jesus Christ will abide under the condemnation of the law which is the expression of the justice and righteousness of God.

The last question must be this. What then is the relationship of the Christian to the law? We can put our answer in this form. The Christian is no longer under the law in the sense that the law is a covenant of works. That is the whole argument in Galatians 3. The Christian is not under the law in that respect; his salvation does not depend upon his keeping of it. He has been delivered from the curse of the law; he is no longer under the law as a covenant relationship between himself and God. But that does not release him from it as a rule of life. Now I think the whole trouble tends to arise because we become confused in our minds as to the relationship between law and grace. Let me put it like this. We tend to have a wrong view of law and to think of it as something that is opposed to grace. But it is not. Law is only opposed to grace in the sense that there was once a covenant of law, and we are now under the covenant of grace. Nor must the law be thought of as being identical with grace. It was never meant to be something in and of itself. The law was never meant to save man, because it could not. Some people tend to think that God said to the nation, 'I am now giving you a law; you keep that law and it will save you.' But that is ridiculous because no man can save himself by keeping the law. No! the law was 'added because of transgressions'. It came in 430 years after the promise was given to Abraham and his seed in order that it might show the true character of God's demands, and that it might show 'the exceeding sinfulness of sin'. The law was given, in a sense, in order to show men that they could never justify themselves before God, and in order that we might be brought to Christ. In Paul's words it was meant to be 'our schoolmaster to bring us unto Christ'.

171

You see, therefore, that the law has a great deal of prophecy in it, and a great deal of the gospel. It is full of grace, leading me to Christ. We have already seen that all the sacrifices and the ceremonial in connection with the law were also designed to do the same thing. That is where the critics of the Old Testament, who say they are not interested in the burnt offerings and the ceremonial, who argue that these are but pagan rites which the Jews and others employed and which can therefore be explained away in terms of comparative religion, that is where such people are really denying the New Testament gospel of the grace of God in Christ. All the rites and ceremonial were given to Israel in detail by God. He called Moses up into the mount and said, 'See . . . that thou make all things according to the pattern shewed to thee in the mount.'

We must realize, therefore, that all these aspects of the law are but our schoolmaster to bring us to Christ, and we must beware lest we fall into a false view of the law. In the same way, people have a false view of grace. They think that grace is apart from law and has nothing to do with it. That is what is called antinomianism, the attitude of people who abuse the doctrine of grace in order to live a sinful, slack or indolent type of spiritual life. They say, 'I am not under the law, but under grace, and therefore it does not matter what I do.' Paul wrote his sixth chapter of Romans to deal with that: 'Shall we continue in sin, that grace may abound? God forbid', says Paul. That is an absolutely wrong and false view of grace. The whole purpose of grace, in a sense, is just to enable us to keep the law. Let me put it in this way. The trouble with us is that we so often have a wrong view of holiness at this point. There is nothing more fatal than to regard holiness and sanctification as experiences to be received. No; holiness means being righteous, and being righteous means keeping the law. Therefore if your so-called grace (which you say you have received) does not make you keep the law, you have not received grace. You may have received a psychological experience, but you have never received the grace of God. What is grace? It is that marvellous gift of God which, having delivered a man from the curse of the law, enables him to keep it and to be righteous as Christ was righteous, for He kept the law perfectly. Grace is that which brings me to love God; and if I love God, I long to keep His commandments. 'He that hath my commandments, and keepeth them,' Christ said, 'he it is that loveth me.'

We must never separate these two things. Grace is not sentimental; holiness is not an experience. We must have this new mind and disposition which leads us to love the law and to desire to keep it; and by His power He enables us to fulfil the law. That is why our Lord goes on to say in verse 19, 'Whosoever therefore shall break one of these least commandments, and shall teach men so, he shall be called the least in the kingdom of heaven: but whosoever shall do and teach them, the same shall be called great in the kingdom of heaven.' That was not spoken only to the disciples for the three short years they were to be with Christ until He died; it is permanent and everlasting. He enforces it again in Matthew 7, where He says, 'Not every one that saith unto me, Lord, Lord, shall enter into the kingdom of heaven; but he that doeth the will of my Father which is in heaven.' What is the will of the Father? The Ten Commandments and the moral law. They have never been abrogated. He 'gave himself for us,' says Paul to Titus, 'that he might . . . purify unto himself a peculiar people, zealous of good works.' 'Yea', says our Lord, as we hope to consider later, 'except your righteousness shall exceed the righteousness of the scribes and Pharisees, ye shall in no case enter into the kingdom of heaven.'

This study has been in some ways a difficult one but, at the same time, it has been concerned with a glorious truth. Looking at the law and the prophets and seeing them all fulfilled in Him, have you not seen an aspect of the grace of Christ that has given you a deeper view of it? Do you not see that it was the law of God that was being enacted upon the cross and that God has punished your sin there in the body of Christ? The substitutionary doctrine of the atonement emphasizes that He has carried out the law fully. He has submitted Himself to it absolutely, actively and passively, negatively and positively. All the types have been fulfilled in Him. And what yet remains of the prophecy will certainly be carried out. The effect of this glorious, redeeming work is not only to give forgiveness to us miserable, law-breaking rebels against God, but to make us sons of God — those who delight in the law of God, those indeed who 'hunger and thirst after righteousness' and who long to be holy, not in the sense of having a wonderful feeling or experience, but who long to live like Christ and to be like Him in every respect.

Chapter Nineteen

Righteousness Exceeding
That of the Scribes and Pharisees

W E turn now to deal particularly with the statement of verse 20 in which our Lord defines His attitude to the law and the prophets, and especially perhaps to the law. We have seen how vital this short paragraph, running from verses 17 to 20, is in His ministry, and how it must influence our whole outlook upon the Christian gospel. Nothing was more important than that He should state very clearly and explicitly, at the outset, the characteristics of His ministry. There were many reasons why men should harbour various misapprehensions with regard to that. He Himself was unusual; He did not belong to the order of the scribes and Pharisees; He was not an official doctor of the law. Yet here He was standing before them as a Teacher. Not only that, He was a Teacher who did not hesitate to criticize, as He did here, the teaching of the recognized, and, in a sense, authorized teachers of the people. Moreover, His conduct was strange at certain points. Far from avoiding the company of sinners, He went out of His way to choose it. He was known as 'the friend of publicans and sinners'. There was also an element in His teaching which emphasized the doctrine called 'grace'. All these things seemed to differentiate what He said from everything that the people had ever heard, so they were obviously liable to certain grave misunderstandings with regard to His message and its general import.

We have seen, therefore, that He defines it here by laying down two main principles. First, His teaching is in no way inconsistent with that of the law and the prophets; but, secondly, it is very different from the teaching of the scribes and Pharisees.

We have seen, too, that our attitude towards the law, therefore, is most important. Our Lord has not come to make it easier for us or to make it in any sense less stringent in its demands upon us. His purpose in coming was to en-

174

able us to keep the law, not to abrogate it. So He emphasizes here that we must know what the law is, and then must keep it: 'Whosoever therefore shall break one of these least commandments, and shall teach men so, he shall be called the least in the kingdom of heaven: but whosoever shall do and teach them, the same shall be called great in the kingdom of heaven.' Now we need not spend any time in considering what is meant by 'the least' and 'greatest' of the commandments. There is obviously a distinction in some sense between them. They are all the commandments of God, and, as He emphasizes here, even the least commandment is therefore of the most vital importance. Furthermore, as James reminds us, anyone who fails in one point of the law has failed in it all.

But all the same there is a kind of division of the law into two sections. The first section concerns our relationship to God; the second concerns our relationship to man. There is a relative difference in the importance therefore; our relationship to God is obviously of greater importance than our relationship to man. You remember when the scribe came to our Lord and asked Him which was the greatest commandment, our Lord did not turn to him and say, 'You must not talk about greater and lesser, you must not talk about first and second.' He said, 'The first commandment is this; Thou shalt love the Lord thy God with all thy heart, and with all thy soul, and with all thy mind, and with all thy strength. And the second is like, namely this, Thou shalt love thy neighbour as thyself.' Very well; as you read the law you can see there is a meaning in this distinction between the least and the greatest of the commandments. What our Lord says, therefore, is that we must keep every part and portion of the law, that we must do and teach it all.

It is at that point that He turns our thoughts to the teaching of the Pharisees and scribes, because if the law is thus vitally important to us, and if, in the last analysis, the whole purpose of the grace of God in Jesus Christ is to enable us to fulfil and to keep the righteousness of the law, then we must obviously be clear in our minds as to what the law is, and what it demands of us. We have seen that that is the biblical doctrine of holiness. Holiness is not an experience that we have; it means keeping and fulfilling the law of God. Experiences may help us to do that, but we cannot receive holiness and sanctification as experiences. Holiness is something we practise in our daily life. It is the honouring and the keeping of the law, as the Son of God Himself kept it while He was here on earth. It is being like Him. That is holiness. So you see it is intimately related to the law, and must always be thought of in terms of keeping the law. It is at that point that the Pharisees and the scribes come in, because they appeared to be most holy people. But our Lord is able to show very clearly that they were lacking in righteousness and holiness. That was true of them very largely because of their tragic misunderstanding and misinterpretation of the law. In the two verses which we are now considering, our Lord enforces His teaching by means of a negative, and the words in verse 20 must have come as a most surprising and almost shocking statement to the men and women to whom they were uttered. 'Do not imagine', says our Lord in effect, 'that I have come to make things easier by reducing the demands of the law. Far from doing that, I am here to tell you that unless your righteousness shall exceed that of the scribes and Pharisees, you have no hope of entering the kingdom of heaven at all, let alone being the least in it.'

Now what does this mean? We must remember that the scribes and Pharisees were in many senses the most outstanding people of the nation. The scribes were men who spent their time in teaching and expounding the law; they were the great authorities on the law of God. They gave their whole life to the study and illustration of it. They, more than anyone else, therefore, could claim to be concerned about it. They were the men who made copies of it, exercising great care as they did so. Their whole life was lived with the law, and everyone looked up to them for that reason.

The Pharisees were the men who were quite outstanding and famous for their sanctity, so-called. The very word 'Pharisee' means 'separatist'. They were people who set themselves apart, and they did so because they had formed a code of the ceremonial acts connected with the law which was more rigid than the law of Moses itself. They had drawn up rules and regulations for life and conduct which in their stringency went far beyond anything we find demanded in the Old Testament Scriptures. For example, in our Lord's picture of the Pharisee and the publican who went up to the temple to pray, the Pharisee said that he fasted twice in the week. Now there is no demand in the Old Testament that men should fast twice in the week. Indeed the Old Testament asked for only one fast in the year. But gradually these men had elaborated the system and had actually brought it to the point at which they exhorted and commanded the people to fast twice in the week, instead of only once in the year. It was in such ways that they formed their excessively stringent code of morals and behaviour and, as a result of that, everybody thought of the scribes and Pharisees as paragons of virtue. The average man said to himself, 'Ah, there is very little hope of my ever being as good as the scribes or the Pharisees. They are outstanding; they just live to be sanctified and holy. That is their profession; that is their whole aim and object in a religious, moral and spiritual sense.' But here comes our Lord; and He announces to these people that unless their righteousness shall exceed that of the scribes and Pharisees they shall in no wise enter into the kingdom of heaven.

This, then, is surely one of the most vital things we can ever consider. What is our conception of true holiness and sanctification? What is our idea of being religious? What is our conception of a Christian? Our Lord sets it down here as a postulate, that the righteousness of the Christian, the very least Christian, must exceed that of the scribes and Pharisees. Let us therefore examine our profession of the Christian faith in the light of this analysis of His. You must often have been struck by the fact that in the four Gospels a great deal of space is given to what our Lord had to say about the scribes and Pharisees. He was always, as it were, referring to them and dealing with them. That was not only because they criticized Him; it was chiefly because He knew that the common people depended upon these men and their teaching. In a sense, the one thing our Lord had to do was to show the hollowness of their teaching, and then present the people with the true teaching. That is what He does in these words.

Let us, then, glance at the religion of the Pharisees in order that we may see its defects, and in order that we may see what is demanded of us. One of the most convenient ways of doing this is to look at that picture which our Lord Himself drew of the Pharisee and the publican going up together to the temple to pray. The Pharisee, you remember, stood forward in a very prominent place, and thanked God he was not as other men, especially not as that publican. Then he began to say certain things about himself: he was not an extortioner, not unjust, not an adulterer, and not as that publican. Now those statements were true. Our Lord accepted them; that was why He repeated them. These men had that kind of external righteousness. Not only that, they fasted twice in the week, as I have reminded you. They also gave a tithe, a tenth, of all they possessed to God and to His cause. They tithed everything they had even down to their herbs, the mint and anise and cumin. But in addition to that they were highly religious, and most punctilious in their observance of certain religious services and ceremonials. All that was true of the Pharisees. They did not merely say it, they did it. Yet no one can read the four Gospels, even in a casual or cursory manner, without seeing that there was nothing that called forth such wrath from our blessed Lord as that very religion of the scribes and the Pharisees. Take the twenty-third chapter of Matthew's Gospel with its terrible pronouncement of woes upon the scribes and the Pharisees, and there you see in its essence our Lord's exposure of these people and His criticism of their whole attitude towards God and towards religion. It is because of all this that He says, 'except your righteousness shall exceed the righteousness of the scribes and Pharisees, ye shall in no case enter into the kingdom of heaven.'

We must realize that this is one of the most serious and important matters we can ever consider together. There is a real and terrible possibility of our deluding and fooling ourselves. The Pharisees and the scribes were denounced by our Lord as being hypocrites. Yes; but they were unconscious hypocrites. They did not realize it, they really thought all was well. You cannot read your Bible without constantly being reminded of that terrible danger. There is the possibility of our relying upon the wrong thing, of resting upon things that appertain to true worship rather than being in the position of true worship. And let me remind you tenderly, in passing, that it is something of which those of us who not only claim to be evangelical, but are proud to call ourselves such, may very easily be guilty.

Let us, then, follow our Lord's analysis of the religion of the scribes and Pharisees. I have tried to extract certain principles which I put to you in this form. The first and, in a sense, the basic charge against them is that their religion was entirely external and formal instead of being a religion of the heart. He turned to them one day and said, 'Ye are they which justify yourselves before men; but God knoweth your hearts: for that which is highly esteemed among men is abomination in the sight of God' (Luke 16:15). Now let us remember that all these statements which are thus made about the Pharisees by our Lord are judicial condemnations. There is no contradiction between the love of God and the wrath of God. The Lord Jesus Christ was so full of love that He never complained of anything done to Himself. But He denounced judicially the people who misrepresented God and religion. That does not imply any contradiction in His character. Holiness and love must go together; and it is a part of holy love to unmask the false and the spurious and to denounce the hypocritical.

On another occasion our Lord said something like this to them. Some of the Pharisees were rather surprised at the actions of His disciples who came in from the marketplace and immediately sat down at the table and began to eat without first washing their hands. 'Ah', He said in effect, 'how careful you Pharisees are about the outside, but how negligent you are about the inside. It is not that which goes into man which defiles him, but that which comes out. It is the heart that matters, for it is out of the heart that come evil thoughts, murders, adulteries, fornications, thefts, false witness and all these other things.' But you remember how the record puts it later in Matthew 23. Our Lord tells the Pharisees that they are like whited sepulchres; the outside seems to be all right, but look at the inside! It is possible for us to be highly regular in our attendance at the house of God and yet to be envious and spiteful. That is the thing our Lord denounces in the Pharisees. And unless our righteousness exceeds these external religious demands we do not belong to the kingdom of God. The kingdom of God is concerned about the heart; it is not my external actions, but what I am inside that is important. A man once said that the best definition of religion was this: 'Religion is that which a man does with his own solitude.' In other words, if you want to know what you really are, you can find the answer when you are alone with your thoughts and desires and imaginations. It is what you say to yourself that matters. How careful we are in what we say to others; but what do we say to ourselves? What a man does with his own solitude is what ultimately counts. The things that are within, which we hide from the outside world because we are ashamed of them, these proclaim finally what we really are.

The second charge which our Lord brought against the scribes and Pharisees was that they were obviously more concerned with the ceremonial than with the moral; and that, of course, always follows upon the first. These people were careful externally; they were most punctilious with the washing of hands and with the ceremonial aspects of the law. But they were not as careful with regard to the moral aspects of the law. Need I remind you that this is still a terrible danger? There is a type of religion — and, alas, it seems to me that it is becoming more common — which does not hesitate to teach that as long as you go to the house of God on Sunday morning it does not matter very much what you do with the rest of the day. I am not thinking only of those who say that all you need to do is to go to holy communion in the morning and then you are free to keep Sunday as you like. I wonder whether we are all perfectly happy in our consciences about this? There is, it seems to me, this increasing tendency to say, 'Of course it is the morning service that matters; I need the teaching and instruction. But the evening service is purely evangelistic, so I will spend the rest of my time writing my letters and reading.' That, I say, is to be guilty of the error of the Pharisees. The Lord's day is a day that is meant to be given as much as possible to God. We ought on this day to put everything aside as far as we can, that God may be honoured and glorified and that His cause may prosper and flourish. The Pharisee was quite content so long as he had done his external duty. Yes, he had been to the service and that for him was sufficient.

Another characteristic of the Pharisees' religion was that it was one of man-made rules and regulations which were based upon certain dispensations they had decided to grant to one another, and which really violated the law they pretended to keep. Some of them were even guilty of neglecting their duties as children. They said, 'Now, we have devoted that particular sum of money to the Lord, so we cannot very well give it to our parents to help to look after them and their needs.' 'Hypocrites', says our Lord in effect, 'that is just the way you have of avoiding the demands of the law that you should honour your father and your mother.' They worked by traditions, and most of these traditions were really nothing but very clever and subtle ways of evading the demands of the law. You avoided these demands by saying that you did it in this special way, which meant that you really did not do it at all. I think we all know something about that. We Protestants are highly critical of the Roman Catholics and especially its teachers in the Middle Ages who were called casuists. These men were experts in making fine and subtle distinctions, especially with regard to matters relating to the conscience and behaviour. They often appeared to be able to reconcile things that seemed hopelessly contradictory. You have probably observed it in the newspapers. You see that a Roman Catholic who does not believe in divorce has obtained one. How has it happened? It has probably been done by means of casuistry — some kind of explanation on paper that seems to satisfy the letter of the law. But, again, I am not simply concerned to denounce that Catholic type of religion. God knows we are all experts at this. We can all rationalize our own sins and explain them away, and excuse ourselves for the things we do and do not do. That was typical of the Pharisees.

The next charge which our Lord brings against them, however, is that they were clearly primarily concerned about themselves and their own righteousness, with the result that they were almost invariably self-satisfied. In other words the ultimate object of the Pharisee was to glorify not God, but himself. When he went about his religious duties he was really considering himself and his performance of the duty, not the glory and the honour of God. Our Lord shows, in that picture of the Pharisee and the publican praying in the temple, that the Pharisee did and said all without worshipping God at all. He said, 'I thank thee, that I am not as other men are.' It was an insult to God; there was no worship there. The man was full of his own activity, his own religious life and of what he was doing. Of course if you set out like that and you have your own standard, you select the things you think ought to be done. And as long as you conform to that particular list you are all right, you are satisfied. Now the Pharisees were self-satisfied and concentrated always upon their own achievements rather than on their relationship to God. I wonder whether we are not sometimes guilty of the same attitude? Is it not one of the besetting sins of those of us who are called Evangelicals? We see other men obviously denying the faith and living godless lives. How easy it is to become self-satisfied because we are better than such people — 'I thank God I am not as other men and especially as that modernist.' The trouble with us is that we never look at ourselves in the sight of God: we never remind ourselves of the character and the being and the nature of God. Our religion consists of a certain number of things we have decided to do; and having done them we think all is well. Smugness, glibness, self-satisfaction are surely far too much in evidence among us.

That leads us in turn to consider the Pharisee's regrettable and tragic attitude towards others. The ultimate condemnation of the Pharisee is that there is in his life a complete absence of the spirit delineated in the Beatitudes. That is the difference between him and the Christian. The Christian is a man who exemplifies the Beatitudes. He is 'poor in spirit', he is 'meek', he is 'merciful'. He is not satisfied because he has performed one prescribed task. No; he is 'hungering and thirsting after righteousness'. He longs to be like Christ. There is a profound lack of satisfaction within him. That is the test by which we must judge ourselves. In the last analysis our Lord condemns these Pharisees for completely failing to keep the law. The Pharisees, He says, tithe mint and anise and cumin, but they forget and ignore the weightier matters of the law, which are love of God and love of man. But that is the whole centre of religion and the whole purpose of our worship. May I remind you once more that what God demands of us is that we should love Him with all our heart, and with all our soul, and with all our strength, and with all our mind, and our neighbour as ourselves. The fact that you are tithing mint and anise and cumin, that you are pressing these matters of your tithe even down to the smallest detail, that is not sanctity. The test of sanctity is your relationship to God, your attitude to Him and your love for Him. How do you stand up to that particular test? To be holy does not just mean the mere avoidance of certain things, or even not thinking certain things; it means the ultimate attitude of the heart of man towards that holy, loving God, and, secondly, our attitude towards our fellow men and women.

The trouble with the Pharisees was that they were interested in details rather than principles, that they were interested in actions rather than in motives, and that they were interested in doing rather than in being. The remainder of this Sermon on the Mount is just an exposition of that. Our Lord said to them in effect, 'You are pleased with yourselves because you do not commit adultery; but if you even look with lust in your eyes, that is adultery.' It is the principle, not the action only, that matters; it is what you think and desire, it is the state of your heart that is important. You do not become Christian by just refraining from some actions and doing others; the Christian is a man who is in a particular relationship to God and whose supreme desire is to know Him better and to love Him more truly. That is not a part-time job, if I may so put it, it is not achieved by the religious observance of a part of Sunday; it demands all the time and attention we have. Read the lives of the great men of God and you will find that that is the principle that always emerges.

Now let me ask the question that is probably in your mind at this point. What then is our Lord teaching? Is He teaching salvation by works? Is He saying that we have to live a life better than that of the Pharisees in order to enter the kingdom? Patently not, because 'there is none righteous, no, not one'. The law of God given to Moses condemned the whole world; 'every mouth has been stopped'; all are 'guilty before God' and have 'come short of the glory of God'. Our Lord did not come to teach justification or salvation by works, or by our own righteousness. 'Very well,' says the opposite school; 'is He not teaching that salvation is by means of the righteousness of Christ alone, so that it does not matter at all what we may do? He has done it all and therefore we have nothing to do.' Now that is the other extreme, and the other error. That, I argue, is an impossible exposition of this verse because of the little word 'for' at the beginning of verse 20. It links up with verse 19 where He said, 'Whosoever therefore shall break one of these least commandments, and shall teach men so, he shall be called the least in the kingdom of heaven: but whosoever shall do and teach them, the same shall be called great in the kingdom of heaven.' He is emphasizing the practical carrying out of the law. That is the whole purpose of the paragraph. It is not to make it easy for us or to enable us to say, 'Christ has done it all for us and therefore it matters not what we do.' We always tend in our folly to consider things as antitheses which are meant to be complementary. Our Lord is teaching that the proof of our having truly received the grace of God in Jesus Christ is that we are living a righteous life. You know the old argument, of course, about faith and works. Some say the one is all important, some say the other. The Bible teaches that both these views are wrong: it is faith showing itself by works which is the mark of a true Christian.

Now lest you may think this is *my* doctrine, let me quote the apostle Paul, who of all others is the apostle of faith, and of grace. 'Be not deceived', he says — not to the world, but to church members at Corinth — 'be not deceived: neither fornicators, nor idolaters, nor adulterers . . . nor extortioners, shall inherit the kingdom of God.' 'It is no use saying, "Lord, Lord," unless you do the things that I command you', says Christ. It comes to this, that unless my life is a righteous life, I must be very careful before I claim that I am covered by the grace of God in Jesus Christ. For to receive the grace of God in Jesus Christ means not only that my sins are forgiven because of His death for me on the cross on Calvary's hill, but also that I have been given a new life and a new nature. It means that Christ is being formed in me, that I have become a partaker of the divine nature, that old things have passed away and all things have become new. It means that Christ is dwelling in me, and that the Spirit of God is in me. The man who has been born again, and who has the divine nature within him, is a man who is righteous and his righteousness does exceed that of the scribes and Pharisees. He is no longer living for self and his own attainments, he is no longer self-righteous and self-satisfied. He has become poor in spirit, meek, and merciful; he hungers and thirsts after righteousness; he has become a peacemaker. His heart is being purified. He loves God, yes unworthily, alas, but he loves Him and longs for His honour and glory. His desire is to glorify God and to keep and honour and fulfil His law. The commandments of God to such a man 'are not grievous'. He wants to keep them, for He loves them. He is no longer at enmity against God; but he now sees the holiness of the law and nothing so appeals to him as the living of this law and the exemplifying of it in his daily life. It is a righteousness that far exceeds the righteousness of the scribes and Pharisees.

Some of the most vital questions that can be asked, then, are these. Do you know God? Do you love God? Can you say honestly that the biggest and the first thing in your life is to glorify Him and that you so want to do this that you do not care what it may cost you in any sense? Do you feel that this must come first, not that you may be better than somebody else, but that you may honour and glorify and love that God who, though you have sinned against Him grievously, has sent His only begotten Son to the cross on Calvary's hill to die for you, that you might be forgiven and that He might restore you unto Himself? Let every man examine himself.

Chapter Twenty

The Letter and the Spirit

W E come now to the beginning of another new section. To understand the real import of this Sermon, it is essential that we should understand the precise connection between what our Lord begins to say at verse 21 and what has gone before. And of course it is a very direct connection. The danger in dealing with a part of Scripture such as this is that we shall become so immersed in a consideration of the details that we miss the essential teaching and the great principles which our Lord was enunciating. It will be good for us, therefore, to remind ourselves again of the general outline of the Sermon so that every part will be seen in relationship to the whole.

Our Lord is concerned to describe the citizens of the kingdom, the kingdom of God or the kingdom of heaven. First and foremost, He gives us in the Beatitudes a general description of the essential nature of the Christian man. Then He goes on to tell us about the function and the purpose of the Christian in this life and world. Then we have seen that that brings Him immediately to this whole question of the relationship of such a person to the law. It was essential that He should do that because the people to whom He was preaching were Jews who had been taught the law, and obviously they would evaluate any new teaching in terms of the law. So He had to show them the relationship of Himself and His teaching to the law, and He does that in verses 17-20, summing it up in the vital statement which we have just been studying.

Now here, at verse 21, He proceeds to expand that statement. He expounds the relationship of the Christian to the law in two respects. He gives us His own positive exposition of the law, and He also contrasts it with the false teaching of the scribes and Pharisees. Indeed, there is a sense in which it can be said that the whole of the remainder of this Sermon, from verse 21 right through to the end of chapter 7, is nothing but an elaboration of that fundamental proposition, that our righteousness must exceed that of the scribes and Pharisees if we are indeed to be citizens of the kingdom of heaven. This is something which our Lord does in a most interesting manner. Looking at it broadly we can say that in the remainder of chapter 5 He is concerned to do this in terms of a true exposition of the law over against the false exposition of the Pharisees and the scribes. His main concern in chapter 6 is to show the true nature of fellowship with God, again in contra-distinction to the Pharisaical teaching and practice. Then in chapter 7 He is concerned to show true righteousness as it views itself and others, once more contrasted with what was taught and practised by the Pharisees and the scribes. That is the essential analysis of the teaching which we must try to hold in our minds.

In verses 21-48, then, our Lord is concerned mainly to give a true account of the law. He does this by putting forward a series of six particular statements and we should look at these very carefully. The first is in verse 21: 'Ye have heard that it was said by them of old time, Thou shalt not kill.' The next comes in verse 27 where He says again: 'Ye have heard that it was said by them of old time, Thou shalt not commit adultery.' Then in verse 31 we read: 'It hath been said, Whosoever shall put away his wife, let him give her a writing of divorcement.' The next is in verse 33: 'Again, ye have heard that it hath been said by them of old time, Thou shalt not forswear thyself, but shalt perform unto the Lord thine oaths.' Then in verse 38 we read: 'Ye have heard that it hath been said, An eye for an eye, and a tooth for a tooth.' And the last is in verse 43: 'Ye have heard that it hath been said, Thou shalt love thy neighbour, and hate thine enemy.'

It is most important, before we come to deal with each of these statements separately and in particular, that we should consider them together as a whole, because, if you look at them, you will see at once that there are certain principles which are common to all six. Indeed, I do not hesitate to suggest that our Lord was really more concerned about these common principles than He was about the particulars. In other words, He lays down certain principles and then illustrates them. Obviously, therefore, we must make certain that we really grasp the principles first.

The first thing we must consider is the formula which He uses: 'Ye have heard that it was said by them of old time'. There is a slight variation in the form here and there, but that, essentially, is the way in which He introduces these six statements. We must be perfectly clear about this. You will find that certain translations put it like this: 'Ye have heard it was said to them of old time.' On purely linguistic grounds no one can tell whether it was 'by' or 'to' for, as usual, when you come to matters of linguistics, you find the authorities are divided, and you cannot be sure. Only a consideration of the context, therefore, can help us to determine exactly what our Lord meant to convey by this. Is He referring simply to the law of Moses, or is He referring to the teaching of the Pharisees and scribes? Those who would say it should read 'to them of old time' obviously must say that He is referring to the law of Moses given to the fathers; whereas those who would emphasize the 'by', as we have it in the Authorized Version, would say that it has reference to what was taught by the scribes and Pharisees.

It seems to me that certain considerations make it almost essential for us to take the second view, and to hold that what our Lord is really doing here is showing the true teaching of the law over against the false representations of it made by the Pharisees and the scribes. You remember that one of the great characteristics of their teaching was the significance which they attached to tradition. They were always quoting the fathers. That is what made the scribe a scribe; he was an authority on the pronouncements which had been made by the fathers. These had become the tradition. I suggest, therefore, that the verses must be interpreted in that way. Indeed, the wording used by our Lord more or less clinches the matter. He says: 'Ye have heard that it was said by them of old time.' He does not say 'You have read in the law of Moses', or 'It was written and you have read'. That is significant in this way. Perhaps we can best show it by means of an illustration. The condition of the Jews in our Lord's day was remarkably like that of people in this country before the Protestant Reformation. You remember that in those days the Scriptures were not translated into English, but were read Sunday by Sunday in Latin to people who did not understand Latin. The result was that the people were entirely dependent for their knowledge of the Scriptures upon the priests who read the Bible to them and who claimed to be expounding it. They were unable to read the Scriptures for themselves and to verify and confirm that which they were hearing from the various pulpits on Sundays and weekdays. What the Protestant Reformation did, in a sense, was to give the Bible to the people. It enabled them to read the Scriptures for themselves, and to see the false teaching and the false representations of the gospel which had been given to them.

Now the position when our Lord was speaking here was very similar to that. The children of Israel during their captivity in Babylon had ceased to know the Hebrew language. Their language when they came back, and at this time, was Aramaic. They were not familiar with Hebrew so they could not read the law of Moses as they had it in their own Hebrew Scriptures. The result was that they were dependent for any knowledge of the law upon the teaching of the Pharisees and the scribes. Our Lord, therefore, very rightly said, 'Ye have heard', or 'That is what you have been hearing; that is what has been said to you; that is the preaching that has been given to you as you have gone to your synagogues and listened to the instruction.' The result was that what these people thought of as the law was in reality not the law itself, but a representation of it given by the scribes and Pharisees. In particular it consisted of the various interpretations and traditions which had been added to the law during the centuries, and thus it was essential that these people should be given a true account of what the law really did say and teach. The Pharisees and scribes had added their own interpretations to it, and it was almost impossible at this time to tell which was law and which was interpretation. Again the analogy of what happened in this country before the Reformation will help us to see the exact position. The Roman Catholic teaching before the Protestant Reformation was a false representation of the gospel of Jesus Christ. It said you had to believe in the sacraments to be saved, and that apart from the Church and priesthood there was no salvation. That was how salvation was being taught. Tradition and various additions had beclouded the simple gospel. Our Lord's object, as I think we shall see as we work through these examples, was to show exactly what had been happening to the law of Moses as the result of the teaching of the scribes and Pharisees. So He is concerned to make clear to them exactly what the law has to say. That is the first principle which we must hold in mind.

Then we must also consider this other extraordinary statement: 'I say unto you'. This is, of course, one of the most crucial statements with regard to the doctrine of the Person of the Lord Jesus Christ. You see, He does not hesitate here to set Himself up as the authority. Obviously, also, it has real significance with regard to the previous statement. If you take the view that 'by them of old time' means just the law of Moses, then you are more or less forced into the position of believing that our Lord was saying: 'The law of Moses said . . . but I say . . .', which suggests that He was correcting the law of Moses. But that is not so. He is saying, rather, 'I am interpreting to you the law of Moses, and it is My interpretation that is true and not that of the Pharisees and scribes.' Indeed there is even more than that in it. There is a suggestion that He is saying something like this: 'I who am speaking to you am the very One who was responsible for the law of Moses; it was I who gave it to Moses, and it is I alone, therefore, who can truly interpret it.' You see, He does not hesitate here to claim for Himself a unique authority; He claims to speak as God. Regarding the law of Moses, as He does, as something which shall not pass away until every jot and tittle has been fulfilled, He does not hesitate, nevertheless, to say, 'But I say unto you.' He claims the authority of God; and that, of course, is the claim which is made for Him everywhere in the four Gospels and in the entire New Testament. It is vitally important, therefore, that we should realize the authority with which these words come to us. He was not a mere teacher, He was not a mere man; He was not a mere expounder of the law or just another scribe or Pharisee, or prophet. He was infinitely more than that, He was God the Son in the flesh presenting the truth of God. We might very well spend much time considering this great phrase, but I trust that we are all clear and all agreed about that. Everything we have in this Sermon on the Mount must be accepted as coming from the Son of God Himself. So we are confronted with this stupendous fact that here in this world of time the very Son of God has been amongst us; and though He came in the likeness of sinful flesh, He still speaks with this divine authority and His every word is of crucial importance to us.

That leads us on to the consideration of what He actually said. Here it is important that we should consider the statement as a whole before looking at the particular injunctions in detail. Let us once and for all get rid of the idea that our Lord came to set up a new law, or to announce a new code of ethics. As we consider the detailed statements we shall find that many people have dropped into that error. There are those who do not believe in the unique deity of the Lord Jesus Christ or in His atonement, and who do not worship Him as the Lord of glory, but who say that they are great believers in the Sermon on the Mount because they find there a code of ethics for this life and world. That, they say, is how life should be lived. I am, therefore, emphasizing the principles in order that we may see that to look at the Sermon in that way is to nullify its real purpose. It is not meant to be a detailed code of ethics; it is not a new kind of moral law which was given by Him. It was probably thought of in that way in His own day, so He constantly said something like this: 'I have come to found a new kingdom. I am the first of a new race of people, the first-born among many brethren; and the people of whom I am Head will be of a certain type and character, people who, because they conform to that description, are going to behave in a certain manner. Now I want to give you some illustrations of how they are going to behave.'

That is what our Lord is saying, and that is why He is concerned about the principles rather than the detailed examples. So if we take the illustrations and turn them into a law we are denying the very thing He was setting out to do. Now it is characteristic of human nature that we always prefer to have things cut and dried rather than have them in the form of principles. That is why certain forms of religion are always popular. The natural man likes to be given a definite list; then he feels that, as long as he conforms to the things stated in the list, all will be well. But that is not possible with the gospel; that is not possible at all in the kingdom of God. That was partly the position under the Old Dispensation, and even there it was carried too far by the Pharisees and scribes. But it is not at all like that under the New Testament dispensation. However, we still tend to like this sort of thing. It is very much easier, is it not, to think of holiness in terms of observing Lent for six weeks or so during the year, rather than to be living with a principle which demands and insists upon application day by day. We always like to have a set of routine rules and regulations. That is why I am pressing this point. If you take the Sermon on the Mount with these six detailed statements and say, 'As long as I do not commit adultery — and so on — I am all right', you have entirely missed our Lord's point. It is not a code of ethics. He is out to delineate a certain order and quality of life, and He says in effect: 'Look, I am illustrating this kind of life. It means this type of behaviour.' So we must hold on to the principle without turning the particular illustration into a law.

Let me put it again in this form. Any man in the ministry has to spend a good deal of his time answering the questions of people who come and want him to make particular pronouncements upon particular questions. There are certain problems which face us all in life, and there are people who always seem to want some kind of detailed statement so that when they are confronted by any particular problem, all they have to do is to turn up their textbook and there they find the answer. The Catholic types of religion are prepared to meet such people. The casuists of the Middle Ages, whom we have already mentioned, those so-called doctors of the Church, had thought out and discussed together the various moral and ethical problems likely to confront Christian people in this world, and they codified them and drew up their rules and regulations. When you were faced with a difficulty you immediately turned up your authority and found the appropriate answer. There are people who are always anxious for something like that in the spiritual realm. The final answer to them in terms of this Sermon can be put in this form. The gospel of Jesus Christ does not treat us like that. It does not treat us as children. It is not another law, but something which gives us life. It lays down certain principles and asks us to apply them. Its essential teaching is that we are given a new outlook and understanding which we must apply with respect to every detail of our lives. That is why the Christian, in a sense, is a man who is always walking on a kind of knife edge. He has no set regulations; instead he applies this central principle to every situation that may arise.

All this must be said in order to emphasize this point. If we take these six statements made by our Lord in terms of the formula 'Ye have heard' and 'I say unto you', we shall find that the principle He uses is exactly the same in each case. In one He is dealing with sex-morality, in the next with murder and in the next with divorce. But every single time the principle is the same. Our Lord as a great Teacher knew the importance of illustrating a principle, so here He gives six illustrations of the one truth. Let us now deal with this common principle which is to be found in the six, so that when we come to work each one out we shall always be holding this central principle in our minds. Our Lord's chief desire was to show the true meaning and intent of the law, and to correct the erroneous conclusions which had been drawn from it by the Pharisees and scribes and all the false notions which they had founded upon it. These, I suggest, are the principles.

First, it is the spirit of the law that matters primarily, not the letter only. The law was not meant to be mechanical, but living. The whole trouble with the Pharisees and the scribes was that they concentrated only on the letter, and they did so to the exclusion of the spirit. It is a great subject — this relationship between form and content. Spirit is always something that must be embodied in form, and that is where the difficulty arises. Man will ever concentrate on the form rather than on the content; upon the letter rather than upon the spirit. You remember that the apostle Paul stresses this in 2 Corinthians where he says: 'The letter killeth, but the spirit giveth life', and his whole emphasis in that chapter is that Israel was so constantly thinking of the letter that they lost the spirit. The whole purpose of the letter is to give body to the spirit; and the spirit is the thing that really matters, not the mere letter. Take, for example, this question of murder. As long as the Pharisees and scribes did not actually murder a man they thought they had kept the law perfectly. But they were missing the whole point and spirit of the law, which is not merely that I should literally not commit murder, but that my attitude towards my fellow men should be a right and loving one. Likewise with all these other illustrations. The mere fact that you do not commit adultery in an actual physical sense does not mean that you have kept the law. What is your spirit? What is your desire as you look, and so on? It is the spirit, not the letter, that counts.

It is clear, then, that if we rely only upon the letter we shall completely misunderstand the law. Let me emphasize that this applies not only to the law of Moses, but still more, in a sense, to this very Sermon on the Mount. There are people today who so look at the letter of the Sermon on the Mount as to miss its spirit. When we come to details we shall see that in practice. Take for instance the attitude of the Quakers with regard to taking the oath. They have taken the letter here literally, and, it seems to me, have not only denied the spirit, but have even made our Lord's statement almost ridiculous. There are people who do exactly the same with turning the other cheek, and giving to those who ask gifts of us, bringing the whole teaching into ridicule because they are constantly living on the letter, whereas our Lord's whole emphasis was upon the primary importance of the spirit. That does not mean of course that the letter does not matter; but it does mean that we must put the spirit before it and interpret the letter according to the spirit.

Now take a second principle, which is really another way of putting the first. Conformity to the law must not be thought of in terms of actions only. Thoughts, motives and desires are equally important. The law of God is concerned as much with what leads to the action as it is with the action itself. Again it does not mean that the action does not matter; but it does mean very definitely that it is not the action only that is important. This should be an obvious principle. The scribes and Pharisees were concerned only about the *act* of adultery or the *act* of murder. But our Lord was at pains to emphasize to them that it is the desire in man's heart and mind to do these things that is really and ultimately reprehensible in the sight of God. How often He said in this connection that it is out of the heart that evil thoughts and actions come. It is the heart of man that matters. So we must not think of this law of God and of pleasing God merely in terms of what we do or do not do; it is the inward condition and attitude that God is always observing. 'Ye are they which justify yourselves before men; but God knoweth your hearts: for that which is highly esteemed among men is abomination in the sight of God' (Luke 16:15).

The next principle we can put in this form. The law must be thought of not only in a negative manner, but also positively. The ultimate purpose of the law is not merely to prevent our doing certain things that are wrong; its real object is to lead us positively, not only to do that which is right, but also to love it. Here again is something which comes out clearly in these six illustrations. The whole Jewish conception of the law was a negative one. I must not commit adultery, I must not commit murder, and so on. But our Lord emphasizes all along that what God is really concerned about is that we should be lovers of righteousness. We should be hungering and thirsting after righteousness, not merely negatively avoiding that which is evil.

It is surely unnecessary that I should turn aside to show the practical relevance of each one of these points to our present condition. Alas, there are still people who seem to think of holiness and sanctification in this purely mechanical manner. They think that, as long as they are not guilty of drinking, gambling or going to theatres and cinemas, all is well. Their attitude is purely negative. It does not seem to matter if you are jealous, envious and spiteful. The fact that you are full of the pride of life seems to be of no account as long as you do not do certain things. That was the whole trouble with the scribes and Pharisees who perverted the law of God by regarding it purely in a negative manner.

The fourth principle is that the purpose of the law as expounded by Christ is not to keep us in a state of obedience to oppressive rules, but to promote the free development of our spiritual character. This is vitally important. We must not think of the holy life, the way of sanctification, as something hard and grievous which puts us into a state of servitude. Not at all. The glorious possibility that is offered us by the gospel of Christ is development as children of God and growing 'unto the measure of the stature of the fulness of Christ'. 'His commandments', says John in his first Epistle, 'are not grievous.' So if you and I regard the ethical teaching of the New Testament as something that cramps us, if we think of it as something narrow and restrictive, it means we have never understood it. The whole purpose of the gospel is to bring us into 'the glorious liberty of the children of God', and these special injunctions are simply particular illustrations of how we may arrive at that and enjoy it.

That, in turn, brings us to the fifth principle which is that the law of God, and all these ethical instructions of the Bible, must never be regarded as an end in themselves. We must never think of them as something to which we just have to try to conform. The ultimate objective of all this teaching is that you and I might come to know God. Now these Pharisees and scribes (and the apostle Paul said it was true of him too before he was truly converted) put, as it were, the Ten Commandments and the moral law on the wall, and having viewed them in this negative, restricted manner said: 'Well, now; I am not guilty of these various things, therefore I am all right. I am righteous, and all is well between me and God.' You see they viewed the law as something in and of itself. They codified it in this way, and as long as they kept to that code they said all was well. According to our Lord that is an utterly fallacious view of the law. The one test which you must always apply to yourself is this, 'What is my relationship to God? Do I know Him? Am I pleasing Him?' In other words, as you examine yourself before you go to bed, you do not just ask yourself if you have committed murder or adultery, or whether you have been guilty of this or that, and if you have not, thank God that all is well. No. You ask yourself rather, 'Has God been supreme in my life today? Have I lived to the glory and the honour of God? Do I know Him better? Have I a zeal for His honour and glory? Has there been anything in me that has been unlike Christ — thoughts, imaginations, desires, impulses?' That is the way. In other words, you examine yourself in the light of a living Person and not merely in terms of a mechanical code of rules and regulations. And as the law must not be thought of as an end in itself, neither must the Sermon on the Mount. These are simply agencies which are meant to bring us into that true and living relationship with God. We must always be very careful, therefore, lest we do with the Sermon on the Mount what the Pharisees and the scribes had been doing with the old moral law. These six examples chosen by our Lord are nothing but illustrations of principles. It is the spirit not the letter that matters; it is the intent, object and purpose that are important. The one thing we have to avoid above everything else in our Christian lives is this fatal tendency to live the Christian life apart from a direct, living, and true relationship to God.

Finally, we can illustrate it like this. Discipline in the Christian life is a good and essential thing. But if your main object and intent is to conform to the discipline that you have set for yourself it may very well be the greatest danger to your soul. Fasting and prayer are good things; but if you fast twice a week or pray at a particular hour every day merely in order to carry out your discipline, then you have missed the whole object of fasting and praying. There is no point in either of them, or in observing Lent, or in anything else that is meant to be an aid to the spiritual life, unless they bring us into a deeper relationship to God. I may stop smoking, I may stop drinking or gambling during these six weeks or at any other period. But if during that time my poverty of spirit is not greater, my sense of weakness is not deepened, my hunger and thirst after God and righteousness is not greatly increased, then I might just as well not have done it at all. Indeed I would say it would be very much better for me if I had not done it. All this is the fatal danger of making these things ends in themselves. We can be guilty of the same thing with public worship. If public worship becomes an end in itself, if my sole object in a pulpit is to preach a sermon and not to try to explain the blessed gospel of God that you and I, and all of us, may come to know and love Him better, my preaching is vain and it may be the thing that will damn my soul. These things are meant to be aids to help us, and illustrations of the Word. God forbid that we should turn them into a religion. 'The letter killeth, but the spirit giveth life.'

Chapter Twenty-one

Thou Shalt Not Kill

IN the paragraph comprising verses 21-26 we have the first of this series of six examples which our Lord gives of His interpretation of the law of God over and against that of the scribes and Pharisees. I would remind you that that is the way in which we interpret the remainder of this chapter, and indeed most of the remainder of this Sermon on the Mount. It is all, in a sense, an exposition of that amazing statement: 'Except your righteousness shall exceed the righteousness of the scribes and Pharisees, ye shall in no case enter into the kingdom of heaven.' The contrast, therefore, is not between the law given through Moses and the teaching of the Lord Jesus Christ; it is a contrast, rather, between the false interpretation of the law of Moses, and the true presentation of the law given by our Lord Himself. This distinction is made by the apostle Paul in Romans 7, where he says that once he thought he was keeping the law perfectly. Then he suddenly understood that the law said 'Thou shalt not covet', and at once he was convicted. 'When the commandment came, sin revived, and I died.' He had not realized that it was the spirit of the law that mattered, and that coveting is as reprehensible under the law as the actual doing of the deed itself. That is the kind of thing we have in principle running through the exposition of the law which is given here by our Lord.

Having thus defined His attitude towards the law, and announced that He has come to fulfil it, and having told His hearers that they must realize exactly what that means, our Lord proceeds now to give these practical illustrations. He presents us with six contrasts, each of which is introduced by the formula: 'Ye have heard it was said by them of old time . . . but I say unto you.' We now consider the first example.

The Pharisees and scribes were always guilty of reducing the meaning and even the demands of the law, and there is a perfect illustration of that here. He said: 'Ye have heard that it was said by them of old time, Thou shalt not kill; and whosoever shall kill shall be in danger of the judgment.' It is very important that we should approach that in the right way. 'Thou shalt not kill' is in the Ten Commandments, and if the Pharisees taught 'thou shalt not kill', surely they were teaching the law? What conceivable criticism can there be even of the Pharisees and scribes at that particular point? So we are tempted to speak and to ask. The answer is that they had added something to that: 'Thou shalt not kill; and whosoever shall kill shall be in danger of the judgment.' But, says someone again, does it not say in the law, 'whosoever shall kill shall be in danger of the judgment'? The answer is that the law did say so, and you will find it in Numbers 35:30, 31. What then is wrong with this? It is that the Pharisees, by putting these two things together in juxtaposition, had reduced the import of this commandment 'Thou shalt not kill' to just a question of committing actual murder. By immediately adding the second to the first they had weakened the whole injunction.

The second thing they did was to reduce and confine the sanctions with which this prohibition was associated, to mere punishment at the hands of the civil magistrates. 'Whosoever shall kill shall be in danger of the judgment.' The 'judgment' there means the local court. The result was that they were merely teaching, 'You must not do murder because if you do you will be in danger of being punished by the civil magistrate.' That was their full and complete interpretation of the great commandment which says: *Thou shalt not kill.* In other words they had evacuated it of its truly great content and had reduced it merely to a question of murder. Furthermore, they did not mention the judgment of God at all. It is only the judgment of the local court that seems to matter. They had made of it something purely legal, just a matter of the letter of a law which said: 'If you commit murder, certain consequences will follow.' The effect of this was that the Pharisees and scribes felt perfectly happy about the law on this point, so long as they were not guilty of murder. For a man to commit murder was, of course, a terrible thing to them, and if he did do so he should be arraigned before the court, and the judgment suitable to such a crime should be meted out to him. But, as long as one did not actually commit murder, all was well, and he could face the commandment, 'Thou shalt not kill', with equanimity and say to himself, 'I have kept and fulfilled the law.'

'No, no', says the Lord Jesus Christ in effect. 'It is just here that you see how the whole conception of righteousness and law which has characterized the teaching of these scribes and Pharisees has become an utter travesty. They have so reduced the law, and confined it, that it is no longer in fact the law of God. It does not convey the real injunction which God had in His mind when He promulgated this particular law. They have simply and very conveniently reduced it within bounds and measures designed to render them perfectly happy. And therefore they say that they have completely kept the law.'

We have seen earlier that we have here one of the guiding principles which enables us to understand this false interpretation of the law of which the Pharisees and scribes were guilty. We tried to point out also that it is something of which we still tend to be guilty ourselves. It is possible for us to face the law of God as we find it in the Bible, but so to interpret and define it, as to make it something which we can keep very easily because we only keep it negatively. So we may persuade ourselves that all is well. The apostle Paul, as we have already seen, as the result of that very process, thought before his conversion that he had kept the law perfectly. The rich young ruler thought he had kept the law because he likewise had been taught in this way and believed the same false interpretation. And as long as you and I accept the letter, and forget the whole spirit, content and meaning, we may persuade ourselves that we are perfectly righteous face-to-face with the law.

Now let us see how our Lord exposes that fallacy and shows us that to look at it like that is completely to misunderstand the meaning of God's holy law. He states His view and His exposition under three clear headings which we shall now consider.

The first principle is that *what matters is not merely the letter of the law but the spirit*. The law says: 'Thou shalt not kill'; but that does not just mean: 'Thou shalt not commit murder'. To interpret it like that is merely to define the law in a way which enables us to imagine that we escape it. Yet we may be guilty in a most grievous manner of breaking this very law. Our Lord proceeds to explain that. This commandment, He says, includes not only actual physical murder, but also causeless anger in our heart against a brother. The true way of understanding 'Thou shalt not kill' is this: 'Whosoever is angry with his brother without a cause shall be in danger of the judgment.' 'Do not listen', He says in effect, 'to these Pharisees and scribes who say you are only in danger of the judgment when you actually murder a man; I say unto you that if you are angry in your heart with a brother without a cause you are exposed to precisely the same demand and the same punishment of the law.' It is at this point we begin to see something of the real spiritual content of the law. It is at this point also that we must see, surely, the meaning of His words when He said that the law must be 'fulfilled'. In that ancient law given through Moses there was all this spiritual content. It was the tragedy of Israel that they missed it. Let us not imagine, therefore, that as Christians we have finished with the law of Moses. No, the old law asks a man not to feel a causeless anger in his heart against his brother. For us as Christians to feel enmity in our hearts is, according to our Lord Jesus Christ, to be guilty of something which, in the sight of God, is murder. To hate, to feel bitter, to have this unpleasant, unkind feeling of resentment towards a person without a cause is murder. Indeed, let me remind you that there are some authorities who say that this qualifying phrase 'without a cause' should not be there. In some of the manuscripts it is omitted. It is impossible to decide exactly on grounds of textual criticism whether it should be included or not. But even taking it as it is, it is a tremendous demand; and if we leave out the qualifying phrase it is still more so. You should not be angry with your brother. Anger in the heart towards any human being, and especially to those who belong to the household of faith, is, according to our Lord, something that is as reprehensible in the sight of God as murder.

But that is not all. Not only must we not feel this causeless anger; we must never even be guilty of expressions of contempt. 'Whosoever shall say to his brother, Raca, shall be in danger of the council.' 'Raca' means 'worthless fellow'. It is an attitude of contempt, that tendency which, alas, we are all aware of, within our hearts and spirits. To dismiss the brother, saying 'Raca', 'worthless fellow', is, according to our Lord, something which, in the sight of God, is terrible. And of course it is. Our Lord frequently pointed out this very thing. Have you ever noticed some of those lists of sins which He uses? Take that statement: 'Out of the heart proceed evil thoughts, murders, adulteries,' and so on. You see we are remarkably like these Pharisees and scribes in the way we talk about murder, and robbery, and drunkenness and certain particular sins. But our Lord always includes evil thoughts with murders, and such things as strife, enmity, deceit and many other things which we do not regard as being such terrible, foul sins. And, obviously, the moment we stop to think about it, and to analyse the position, we see how perfectly true it is. Contempt, a feeling of scorn and derision, is the very spirit that ultimately leads to murder. We may have various reasons for not allowing it to be expressed in actual committal of murder. But, alas, we have often murdered one another in mind and heart and thought, have we not? We have nursed thoughts against people which are as foul as murder. There has been this disturbance in the realm of the spirit and we have said of another, 'Raca'. Oh, yes, there are ways in which men can be destroyed short of murder. We can destroy a man's reputation, we can shake somebody else's confidence in him by whispering criticism or by deliberate fault finding. That is the kind of thing which our Lord is here indicating, and His whole purpose is to show that all that is included in this commandment: 'Thou shalt not kill.' Killing does not only mean destroying life physically, it means still more trying to destroy the spirit and the soul, destroying the person in any shape or form.

Our Lord then moves to the third point: 'But whosoever shall say, Thou fool, shall be in danger of hell fire.' This means an expression of abuse, the vilifying of a person. It means this bitterness and hatred in the heart finding its expression in words. I think that, as we follow this analysis, we can see, as was pointed out in chapter one, what a terrible and dangerous error it is for us as Christian people to feel that, because we are Christians, the Sermon on the Mount has nothing to do with us, or to feel that this is something which does not apply to present-day Christians. It speaks to us today; it searches us to the depths of our being. Here we are confronted not only with actual murder, but with all this within our hearts, feelings and sensibilities, and ultimately our spirit, that is regarded by God as murder.

Now this, obviously, is a very important statement. 'Does it mean', asks someone, 'that anger is always wrong? That anger is always prohibited?' 'Are there not illustrations', asks another, 'in the New Testament itself where our Lord spoke of these Pharisees in strong terms; when, for example, He referred to them as "blind" and as "hypocrites", and when He turned to the people and said, "O fools, and slow of heart to believe", and "Ye fools and blind"? How can He issue these prohibitions at this point, and then use such language Himself? How do you reconcile this teaching with Matthew 23 where He pronounces His woes upon the Pharisees?' Surely there is no real difficulty in that question. When our Lord pronounced those woes, He did so in a judicial manner. He did so as one given authority by God. Our Lord is pronouncing final judgment upon the Pharisees and the scribes. He, as the Messiah, is authorized to do so. He had offered the gospel to them; every opportunity had been given to them. But they had rejected it. Not only that, we must remember that He always utters these statements against false religion and hypocrisy. What He is really denouncing is the self-righteousness that rejects the grace of God and would even justify itself before God and reject Him. It is judicial, and if you and I can always claim that any such expression we may use is uttered in a similar sense, then we are free from this particular charge.

It is exactly the same with the so-called imprecatory Psalms which trouble so many people. The Psalmist, under the inspiration of the Holy Spirit, is pronouncing judgment against not only his own enemies, but the enemies of God and those who are abusing the Church and the kingdom of God as it is represented in him and in the nation. Let me put it like this. Our anger must only be against sin; we must never feel angry with the sinner, but only full of sorrow and compassion for him. 'Ye that love the Lord, hate evil', says the Psalmist. We should feel a sense of anger as we view sin, hypocrisy, unrighteousness, and everything that is evil. That is the way, of course, in which we fulfil the injunction of the apostle Paul to the Ephesians: 'Be ye angry, and sin not.' The two things are not incompatible at all. Our Lord's anger was always a righteous indignation, it was a holy anger, an expression of the wrath of God Himself. Let us remember that 'The wrath of God is revealed from heaven against all ungodliness and unrighteousness of men' (Rom. 1:18). 'Our God', against sin, 'is a consuming fire.' There is no question about this. God hates evil. God's anger is displayed against it, and His wrath will be poured out upon it. That is essentially a part of the biblical teaching.

The holier we become, the more anger we shall feel against sin. But we must never, I repeat, feel anger against the sinner. We must never feel angry with a person as such; we must draw a distinction between the person himself and what he does. We must never be guilty of a feeling of contempt or abhorrence, or of this expression of vilification. Thus I think we are enabled to draw lines of distinction between these things. 'Do not imagine you are clear with regard to this injunction,' says Christ in effect, 'simply because you have not committed murder.' What is the state of your heart? How do you react to things that happen? Do you find yourself flaring into a raging temper when a person has done something to you? Or do you sometimes feel anger against a person who really has done nothing to you at all? These are the things that matter. It is that which God meant when He said, 'Thou shalt not kill'. 'God seeth the heart', and is not concerned only with the external action. God forbid that we should produce a kind of self-righteousness by reducing the law of God to something which we know we have already kept, or which we feel sure we are not likely to transgress. 'Let every man examine himself.'

Let us now go on to the second statement. *Our attitude is meant to be not negative, but positive.* Our Lord puts it in these words. Having emphasized the negative He goes on to put it positively like this: 'Therefore if thou bring thy gift to the altar, and there rememberest that thy brother hath ought against thee; leave there thy gift before the altar, and go thy way; first be reconciled to thy brother, and then come and offer thy gift.' This is a most significant and important statement. Not only are we not to harbour murder and evil thoughts in our heart against another; but the commandment not to kill really means we should take positive steps to put ourselves right with our brother. The danger is that we may stop at the negative, and feel that, as long as we have not actually committed murder, all is well. But there is a second stage which we have forgotten. 'All right', we say, 'I must not actually commit murder, and I must not say these unkind things against people. I must put a guard upon my lips; though the thought is there I must not say it.' And there we tend to stop and say: 'As long as I do not say these things all is well.' But our Lord tells us that we must not stop even there, we must not even harbour the thought and the feeling in our heart.

That is the point at which so many stop. The moment these ugly, unworthy thoughts tend to come into their hearts they switch their minds to something positive and beautiful. That is quite all right as long as we do not stop at that. We must not only repress these unkind and unworthy thoughts, says Christ; we have to do more than that. We must actually take steps to remove the cause of the trouble; we must aim at a positive goal. We have to reach the stage in which there shall be nothing wrong even in spirit between our brother and ourselves.

Our Lord enforces that by reminding us in verses 23 and 24 of a very subtle danger in the spiritual life, the terrible danger of trying to atone for moral failure by balancing evil with good. I think we know something about this; we must all plead guilty to it. The danger is that of making certain ceremonial sacrifices to cover up moral failure. The Pharisees were expert at that. They went to the temple regularly; they were always punctilious in these matters of the details and minutiae of the law. But the whole time they were judging and condemning their fellows with contempt. They avoided every twinge of conscience by saying, 'After all I am worshipping God; I am taking my gift to the altar.' I think I can say again that we all know something about this tendency not to face directly the conviction which the Holy Spirit produces in our heart, but to say to ourselves: 'Well, now; I am doing this and that; I am making great sacrifices at this point; I am being helpful in that matter; I am busily engaged in that piece of Christian work.' The whole time we are not facing the jealousy we may feel against another Christian worker, or something in our personal, private life. We are balancing one thing with another, thinking that this good will make up for that evil. No, no, says our Lord. God is not like that: 'Ye are they which justify yourselves before men; but God knoweth your hearts: for that which is highly esteemed among men is abomination in the sight of God' (Luke 16:15). This matter, He tells us, is so important, that, even if I find myself at the altar with a gift I am going to offer to God, and there suddenly remember something I have said or done, something which is causing another person to stumble or go wrong somehow; if I find that I am harbouring unkind and unworthy thoughts about him or in any way hindering his life, then our Lord tells us (may I put it thus with reverence), we should, in a sense, even keep God waiting rather than stay. We must get right with our brother and then come back and offer the gift. In the sight of God there is no value whatsoever in an act of worship if we harbour a known sin.

The Psalmist puts it like this, 'If I regard iniquity in my heart, the Lord will not hear me.' If I, in the presence of God, and while trying to worship God actively, know there is sin in my heart which I have not dealt with and confessed, my worship is useless. There is no value in it at all. If you are in a state of conscious enmity against another, if you are not speaking to another person, or if you are harbouring these unkind thoughts and are a hindrance and an obstacle to that other, God's Word assures you that there is no value in your attempted act of worship. It will avail you nothing, the Lord will not hear you. Or take that statement which we read in 1 John 3:20, 'If our heart condemn us, God is greater than our heart, and knoweth all things.' There is no value or purpose in praying to God if you know in your own heart that you are not right with your brother. It is impossible for God to have any dealings with sin and iniquity. He is of such a pure countenance that He cannot even look upon it. According to our Lord the matter is so vital that you must even interrupt your prayer, you must, as it were, even keep God waiting. Go and put it right, He says; you cannot be right with God until you put yourself right with man.

Let me sum it all up by reminding you of the great illustration of all this which is found in the Old Testament in 1 Samuel 15. God has given His commandments and He means us to keep them. You remember on one occasion Saul was told by God to destroy the Amalekites entirely. But Saul thought to himself that he need not go as far as that and said, 'I will spare some of the people, and some of the beasts and cattle to sacrifice to God.' He thought all was well, and began to worship and to praise God. But suddenly Samuel the prophet arrived and asked: 'What have you been doing?' Saul replied, saying: 'I have just been carrying out the commandments of God.' 'If you have been carrying out the commandments of God', said Samuel, 'what is the meaning of the bleating of the sheep and the lowing of the cattle which I am hearing? What have you done?' 'I decided I would spare some of them', said Saul. Then Samuel uttered those momentous and terrifying words: 'Hath the Lord as great delight in burnt offerings and sacrifices, as in obeying the voice of the Lord? Behold, to obey is better than sactifice, and to hearken than the fat of rams.' I always feel sorry for king Saul because I understand him so well. You see, we do not do what God tells us; and when we thus put our limits upon the commandment, we somehow feel that to perform a great act of worship will cover it, and all will be well, thinking that the Lord has as great delight in burnt offerings and sacrifices as in obeying the voice of the Lord. Of course He has not! 'Behold, to obey is better than sacrifice.' Leave thy gift; run away and put it right with thy brother; get rid of the obstacle. Then come back; and then, and only then, is it of any value. 'To obey is better than sacrifice, and to hearken than the fat of rams.'

Just a word on the last principle. Let me impress upon you *the urgency of all this because of our relationship to God.* 'Agree with thine adversary quickly, whiles thou art in the way with him; lest at any time the adversary deliver thee to the judge, and the judge deliver thee to the officer, and thou be cast into prison. Verily I say unto thee, Thou shalt by no means come out thence, till thou hast paid the uttermost farthing.' Yes, says Christ, it is as urgent and as desperate as that. You must do it at once; delay not a moment, for that is your position. This is just His way of saying that we must always remember our relationship to God. We must not only think in terms of our brother whom we are offending, or with whom there is something wrong, we must always think of ourselves before God. God is the judge, God is the justifier. He is always making these demands upon us, and He has power over all the courts of heaven and earth. He is the judge, and His laws are absolute; and He has a right to demand the uttermost farthing. What then are we to do? Come to an agreement as quickly as we can with God. Christ says here that we are 'in the way'. We are in this world, we are in life, walking, as it were, along the road. But suddenly our adversary comes and says: 'What of that which you owe?' Well, says Christ, make an agreement with him at once or the processes of the law will be set going, and the uttermost farthing will be demanded of you. That is nothing but a picture. You and I are travelling through this world, and the law is there making its demands. It is the law of God. It says: 'What about that relationship between you and your brother, what about those things that are in your heart? You have not attended to them.' Settle it at once, says Christ. You may not be here tomorrow morning and you are going to eternity like that. 'Agree with thine adversary quickly, whiles thou art in the way with him.'

How do we feel at this point? As we have seen our Lord's exposition of this holy law, do we feel the demands of the law? Are we aware of the condemnation? What of the things we have said and thought, the things we have done? Are we aware of all this, the utter condemnation of it all? It is God making demands through His law. I thank God for the injunction that tells us to act as quickly as we are in the way. Thank God, His terms are very easy. They are just this, that I face and acknowledge this sin and confess it utterly and absolutely, that I stop any self-defence or self-justification, though there was provocation from this other person. I must just confess and admit it without any reservation to God. If there is something in actual practice that I can do about it I must do it at once. I must humble myself, make a fool of myself as it were, and let the other person gloat over me if necessary, as long as I have done everything I can to remove the barrier and the obstacle. Then He will tell me that all is right. 'I will settle with you', He will say, 'indeed I will forgive it all because, though you are a guilty and foul sinner before Me, and the bill you owe Me is one you can never pay, I have sent My Son into your world and He has paid it for you. He has cancelled it. He did not do it because you are loving and kind and good, He did not do it for you because you have done nothing against Me. It was while you were an enemy, hateful in yourself, hating Me and hating others. It was in spite of all your foulness and your unworthiness that I sent Him. And He came deliberately and gave Himself even unto death. It is because of all this that I forgive you utterly and freely and absolutely.' Thank God for such terms, such terms for bankrupt, foul sinners. Those are the terms, utter, absolute confession and repentance; everything we can do by way of restitution; and an acknowledgment that we are forgiven only as the result of the grace of God manifested perfectly in the loving, self-giving, self-sacrifice of the Son of God upon the cross. Come to a quick agreement. Do not delay. Whatever you may be convicted of at this moment, come, leave your gift, run away, put it right. 'Agree with thine adversary quickly, whiles thou art in the way with him.'

Chapter Twenty-two

The Exceeding Sinfulness of Sin

W E come now to verses 27-30, our Lord's second illustration of His teaching with respect to the law. 'Ye have heard that it was said by them of old time, Thou shalt not commit adultery: but I say unto you, That whosoever looketh on a woman to lust after her hath committed adultery with her already in his heart.' The Pharisees and scribes had reduced the commandment which prohibits adultery to the mere physical act of adultery; and again they imagined that, as long as they were not actually guilty of the act itself, the commandment had nothing to say to them and they were perfectly innocent as far as it was concerned. It is the same thing again. Once more they had taken the letter of the law and reduced it to one particular matter, and thereby had nullified it. In particular, they had forgotten the whole spirit of the law. As we have seen, this is something that is fundamentally vital to a true understanding of the New Testament gospel: 'the letter killeth, but the spirit giveth life.'

There is a very simple way of looking at this. The real trouble with the Pharisees and scribes was that they had never even read the Ten Commandments properly. If they had truly considered and studied them, they would have seen that you cannot take each one in isolation. For example, the tenth says that we must never covet our neighbour's wife, and that, obviously, should be taken in conjunction with this command not to commit adultery. The apostle Paul, in that striking statement of his in Romans 7, confesses that he himself had been guilty of that very error. He says that it was when he realized that the law said, 'Thou shalt not covet', that he began to understand the meaning of lust. Before that he had been thinking of the law in terms of action only; but the law of God does not stop at mere action, it says 'Thou shalt not covet'. The law had always stressed the importance of the heart, and these people, with their mechanical notions of worshipping God and their purely mechanical conception of obedience, had entirely forgotten that. Our Lord, therefore, is anxious to stress that important truth and to impress it upon His followers. Those who think they can worship God and obtain salvation in terms of their own actions are always guilty of this error. That is why they never truly understand the Christian way of salvation. They have never seen that ultimately it is a question of the heart, but think that, as long as they do not do certain things and as long as they try to do certain good works, they can put themselves right in the sight of God. To that, as we have seen already, our Lord replies always, 'Ye are they which justify yourselves before men; but God knoweth your hearts: for that which is highly esteemed among men is abomination in the sight of God.' Our Lord is concerned here to bring out that principle once more. They said in effect, 'As long as you do not commit adultery you have kept this law.' He says: 'Whosoever looketh on a woman to lust after her hath committed adultery with her already in his heart.'

Here again we have our Lord's teaching with regard to the nature of sin. The whole purpose of the law, as Paul reminds us, was to show the exceeding sinfulness of sin. But by misunderstanding it in this way the Pharisees had nullified it. Nowhere, perhaps, do we have such a terrible exposure of sin as it really is as in the words of our Lord at this particular point.

I know, of course, that the doctrine of sin is not popular today. People dislike the whole idea, and try to explain it away psychologically, in terms of development and temperament. Man has evolved out of the animal, they say, and he is just sloughing off very slowly these relics and remnants of his animal past and his animal nature. Thus the whole doctrine of sin is entirely denied and avoided. But, obviously, if that is our view and position, the Scriptures must be quite meaningless to us, because everywhere in the New Testament, as in the Old Testament also, this is something which is central. That is why we must consider it, for there is nothing at the present time which is more urgently necessary than that we should truly grasp the biblical doctrine with respect to sin. I assert that most of our failures and troubles in the Church, as well as in the world, are due to the fact that we have not really understood this doctrine. We have all been influenced by the idealism that has been controlling thought for the past hundred years, this idea that man was evolving towards perfection, and that education and culture were going to put us right. Thus we have never taken seriously this tremendous teaching which is found from beginning to end in the Bible; and most of our troubles arise from this source.

Let me illustrate what I mean. I suggest that unless we are clear about the doctrine of sin we shall never truly understand the New Testament way of salvation. Take, for instance, the death of our Lord Jesus Christ upon the cross.

Look at all the misunderstanding with regard to that. The great question one has to face is; Why did He die upon the cross? Why did He set His face steadfastly to go to Jerusalem and refuse to allow His followers to defend Him? Why did He say that, if He desired, He could command twelve legions of angels to protect Him, but that if He did so He could not fulfil all righteousness? What is the meaning of the death upon the cross? Now I maintain that if we do not understand the doctrine of sin, we shall never really know the answers to these questions. There is only one way to understand the death upon the cross and it is this:

> There was no other good enough
> To pay the price of sin;
> He only could unlock the gate
> Of heaven, and let us in.

It is the problem of sin that accounts for it. Indeed the incarnation would never have been necessary were it not for sin. The problem of sin is as profound as that. To tell mankind what to do is not enough. God had done that in the law given through Moses, but no one had kept it. 'There is none righteous, no, not one.' All the exhortations to men and women to live a better life had failed before ever Christ came. The Greek philosophers had all lived and taught before His birth. Knowledge and information and all these things are not enough. Why? Because of sin in the human heart. Thus the only way to understand the New Testament doctrine of salvation is to start with the doctrine of sin. Whatever else sin may be, it is at least something that could be dealt with only by the coming of the eternal Son of God from heaven into this world and by His actually going to the death of the cross. That had to happen; there was no other way. God, I say with reverence, would never have allowed His only-begotten, beloved Son to suffer in the way He did unless it was absolutely essential: and it was essential because of sin.

But the same is true of the New Testament doctrine of regeneration. Consider all the teaching about being born again, and the new creation, which is to be found right through the Gospels and Epistles. That is meaningless unless you understand the New Testament doctrine of sin. But if you do understand it, then you can see quite clearly that unless a man is born again, and given a new nature and a new heart, he cannot possibly be saved. But regeneration is meaningless to people who have a negative view of sin and do not realize its profundity. This, then, is the point at which we must start. So if you dislike the New Testament doctrine of sin, it simply means that you are not a Christian. For you cannot be one without believing that you must be born again and without realizing that nothing but the death of Christ upon the cross saves you and reconciles you to God. All who are trusting to their own efforts are denying the gospel, and the reason for that is always that they have never seen themselves as sinners or understood the New Testament doctrine of sin. This is a crucial matter.

This doctrine, therefore, is absolutely vital in determining our conception of true evangelism. There is no true evangelism without the doctrine of sin, and without an understanding of what sin is. I do not want to be unfair, but I say that a gospel which merely says 'Come to Jesus', and offers Him as a Friend, and offers a, marvellous new life, without convicting of sin, is not New Testament evangelism. The essence of evangelism is to start by preaching the law; and it is because the law has not been preached that we have had so much superficial evangelism. Go through the ministry of our Lord Himself and you cannot but get the impression that at times, far from pressing people to follow Him and to decide for Him, He put great obstacles in their way. He said in effect: 'Do you realize what you are doing? Have you counted the cost? Do you realize where it may lead you? Do you know that it means denying yourself, taking up your cross daily and following Me?' True evangelism, I say, because of this doctrine of sin, must always start by preaching the law. This means that we must explain that mankind is confronted by the holiness of God, by His demands, and also by the consequences of sin. It is the Son of God Himself who speaks about being cast into hell. If you do not like the doctrine of hell you are just disagreeing with Jesus Christ. He, the Son of God, believed in hell; and it is in His exposure of the true nature of sin that He teaches that sin ultimately lands men in hell. So evangelism must start with the holiness of God, the sinfulness of man, the demands of the law, the punishment meted out by the law and the eternal consequences of evil and wrongdoing. It is only the man who is brought to see his guilt in this way who flies to Christ for deliverance and redemption. Any belief in the Lord Jesus Christ which is not based on that is not a true belief in Him. You can have a psychological belief even in the Lord Jesus Christ; but a true belief sees in Him one who delivers us from the curse of the law. True evangelism starts like that, and obviously is primarily a call to repentance, 'repentance toward God, and faith toward our Lord Jesus Christ.'

In exactly the same way this doctrine of sin is also vital to a true conception of holiness; and here again I think we see its urgent relevance at the present time. Not only has our evangelism been superficial, our conception of holiness has been superficial also. Far too often there have been people who have been smug and glibly satisfied with themselves because they are not guilty of certain things

207

— adultery, for example — and therefore think that they are all right. But they have never examined their heart. Self-satisfaction, smugness and glibness are the very antithesis of the New Testament doctrine of holiness. Here we see holiness as a matter of the heart, and not merely a matter of conduct; it is not only a man's deeds that count but his desires; not only must we not commit, we must not even covet. It penetrates to the very depths, and thus this conception of holiness leads to constant watchfulness and self-examination. 'Watch ye', says the apostle Paul to the Corinthians. 'Examine yourselves, whether ye be in the faith; prove your own selves.' Search your own heart and discover whether there is any evil there. That is New Testament holiness. How much more disconcerting it is than that superficial conception of holiness which thinks only in terms of action.

Above all, this doctrine of sin leads us to see the absolute need of a power greater than ourselves to deliver us. It is a doctrine that makes a man run to Christ and rely upon Him; it makes him realize that without Him he can do nothing. So again I would say that the New Testament way of presenting holiness is not just to say, 'Would you like to live life with a capital "L"? Would you like to be permanently happy?' No, it is to preach this doctrine of sin, it is to reveal man to himself so that, having seen himself, he will abhor himself and become poor in spirit and meek, he will mourn, he will hunger and thirst after righteousness, he will fly to Christ and abide in Him. It is not an experience to be received so much as a life to be lived and a Christ to be followed.

Finally, it is surely only a true grasp of the New Testament doctrine of sin that enables us to realize the greatness of God's love to us. Do you feel that your love to God is weak and faint and that you do not love Him as much as you should? Let me remind you again that this is the ultimate test of our profession. We are meant to *love* God, not only to believe certain things about Him. These men of the New Testament loved Him and they loved the Lord Jesus Christ. Read the biographies of the saints and you will find that they had a love for God which became greater and greater. Why do not we love God as we should? It is because we have never realized what He has done for us in Christ, and this itself is because we have not realized the nature and the problem of sin. It is only as we see what sin really is in the sight of God, and realize that, nevertheless, He did not spare His only Son, that we begin to understand and to measure His love. So if you want to love God more, grasp this doctrine of sin, and as you realize what it meant to Him, and what He has done about it, you will see that His love is indeed 'so amazing, so divine'.

There, then, are the reasons for concentrating upon this doctrine of sin. But now let us look at what our Lord actually says about it. There is no true under-standing of the gospel of salvation, no true evangelism, no true holiness, no true knowledge of the love of God unless we realize what sin is. Well, what is it? Let us first attempt just a brief analysis of what our Lord says about it, and then we can go on to state what He says in these same verses about how we can be de-livered from it. It is no use talking about deliverance from sin until we know what sin is. There must be a radical diagnosis before we can begin to think of treatment. Here is the diagnosis.

The first thing our Lord emphasizes is what we may call *the depth or the power of sin.* 'Thou shalt not commit adultery.' He does not say 'As long as you do not do the act all is well'; rather 'I say unto you, That whosoever looketh on a woman to lust after her hath committed adultery with her already in his heart.' Sin is not merely a matter of actions and of deeds; it is something within the heart that leads to the action. In other words the teaching here is the character-istic teaching of the Bible everywhere about this subject, namely, that what we must really concentrate upon is not so much sins as sin. Sins are nothing but the symptoms of a disease called sin and it is not the symptoms that matter but the disease, for it is the disease that kills and not the symptoms. Symptoms can vary tremendously. I may see one person propped up in bed, breathing pain-fully, and in acute distress; and I say that person is desperately ill suffering from pneumonia or something like that. But I may see another person lying flat on his back in bed, no distress, no acute symptoms, no pain, no difficult breathing, lying apparently at ease and in comfort. And yet there may be some foul disease, some foul growth in that person's constitution eating away at the vitals, a dis-ease which will kill him as certainly and as surely as the other. It is not the mode but the fact of death that matters. It is not the symptoms that finally count, but the disease.

That is the truth which our Lord here impresses upon us. The fact that you have not committed the act of adultery does not mean you are guiltless. What about your heart? Is there disease there? And His teaching is that what matters is this fell and foul power that is in human nature as the result of sin and the fall. Man was not always like that, for God made him perfect. If you believe in the evolutionary theory, you are really saying that God never made man perfect, but is bringing him to perfection. Therefore there is no true sin. But the Bible teaching is that man was made perfect and that he fell from that perfection, with the result that this power, this canker, has entered human nature and is there as an evil force within. The consequence is that man desires and covets. Quite apart from what is happening round and about him, this thing is within him. I quote again, as I have quoted so often in this connection, that our Lord said it is 'out of the heart' that 'Proceed evil thoughts, murders, adulteries, . . .'

Now sin must be understood like this, as a terrible power. It is not so much that I do a thing, it is what makes me do it, what urges me to do it, that matters. There it is in all of us — and we must face it — the depth and the power of sin.

But let me say a word about *the subtlety of sin*. Sin is this terrible thing which so deludes and fools us as to make us feel quite happy and contented so long as we have not committed the act. 'Yes', I say, 'I was tempted, but thank God I did not fall.' That is all right up to a point, so long as I am not too content with that. If I am merely satisfied with the fact that I did not do the thing, I am all wrong. I ought to go on and ask: 'But why did I want to do it?' That is where the subtlety of sin comes in. It affects the whole constitution of man. It is not merely something in the animal part of our nature; it is in our mind and out-look, and it makes us think corruptly in that manner. Then think of the clever way in which it insinuates itself into the mind, and the terrible way in which we are guilty of sinning with the mind. There are highly respectable men and women who would never dream of committing an act of adultery, but look at the way in which they enjoy sinning in the mind and in the imagination. We are dealing with practical matters, we are dealing with life as it is. This is what I mean. You have never been guilty of adultery? All right. Would you then answer me this simple question. Why do you read all the details of divorce cases in the newspapers? Why do you do it? Why is it essential that you should read right through these reports? What is your interest? It is not a legal interest, is it? or a social one? What is it? There is only one answer: you are enjoying it. You would not dream of doing these things yourself, but you are doing them by proxy. You are sinning in your heart and mind and in your imagination, and you are there-fore guilty of adultery. That is what Christ says. How subtle this awful, terrible thing is! How often do men sin by reading novels and biographies. You read the reviews of a book and find that it contains something about a man's miscon-duct or behaviour, and you buy it. We pretend we have a general philosophical interest in life, and that we are sociologists reading out of pure interest. No, no; it is because we love the thing; we like it. It is sin in the heart; sin in the mind!

A further illustration of this state of sin is found in the way in which we al-ways try to explain away our failures in this respect in terms of eye and hand. We say: 'I was born like that. Look at that other man, he is not like that.' You do not know the other man; and in any case it is the subtlety of sin that would have you explain yourself away in terms of your particular nature — the hand, the foot, the eye or something like that. No, the trouble is in your heart. All else is but the expression. It is that which leads to the sin that matters.

Then there is the *perverting nature and effect of sin*. Sin is something that perverts. Wherefore, says our Lord, 'if thy right hand offend thee, cut it off, and cast it from thee.' How true that is of what sin does. It is such a devastating, perverting thing that it turns the very instruments that God has given me, and which were meant to minister to my good, into my enemies. There is nothing wrong with the instincts of human nature. They are all God-given; they are excellent. But these very instincts, because of sin, have become our enemies. The things which God put into man to make him man, and to enable him to function, have become the cause of his downfall. Why? Because sin twists everything, so that precious gifts such as the hand or the eye may become a nuisance to me, and I have, metaphorically, to cut them off and pluck them out. I have to get rid of them. Sin has perverted man, turning good itself into evil. Read again the way in which Paul expounded that. This, he says, is what sin has done to man; it has made the law of God, which is holy and just and good, into something that actually leads a man to sin (Rom. 7). The very fact that the law tells me not to do a thing makes me think of that thing. That then brings it to my imagination, and I end by doing it. But if the law had not forbidden me to do it, I would not have done so. 'Unto the pure all things are pure.' Yes, but if you are not pure, some things which are good in themselves may be harmful. That is why I never believe in giving sex-morality teaching to children in schools. You are introducing them to sin. You are telling them about things they never knew before, and they are not 'pure'. Therefore you cannot act on the assumption that such teaching will lead to good. That is the whole tragedy of modern education; it is based entirely on a psychological theory that does not recognize sin, instead of on New Testament teaching. There is that within us that drives us to sin. The law is right and good and pure. The trouble is in us and in our perverted natures.

Finally, sin is something which is destructive. 'If thy right eye offend thee, pluck it out, and cast it from thee.' Why? 'It is profitable for thee that one of thy members should perish, and not that thy whole body should be cast into hell.' Sin destroys man; it introduced death into the life of man and death into the world. It always leads to death, and ultimately to hell, suffering and punishment. It is hateful to God, it is abhorrent to Him. And I say with reverence that because God is God sin must lead to hell. 'The wages of sin is death.' God and sin are utterly incompatible, and therefore sin, of necessity, leads to hell. He is of such pure countenance that He cannot look upon sin — it is so utterly hateful to Him.

That is the biblical, the New Testament doctrine of sin. 'Thou shalt not commit adultery.' Of course not! But is it in our hearts? Is it in our imagination? Do we like it? God forbid that any of us should be able to look at this holy law of God and feel satisfied. If we do not feel unclean at this moment, God have mercy upon us. If we can conceivably be satisfied with our lives because we have never committed an act of adultery or of murder or any one of these things, I say that we do not know ourselves nor the blackness and the foulness of our own hearts. We must listen to the teaching of the blessed Son of God and examine ourselves, examine our thoughts, our desires, and our imagination. And unless we feel that we are vile and foul, and need to be washed and cleansed, unless we feel utterly helpless with a terrible poverty of spirit, and unless we are hungering and thirsting after righteousness, I say, God have mercy upon us.

I thank God that I have a gospel which tells me that Another who is spotless and pure and utterly holy has taken my sin and my guilt upon Himself. I am washed in His precious blood, and He has given me His own nature. When I realized that I needed a new heart, I found, thank God, that He had come to give it to me, and He has given it.

> Thy nature, gracious Lord, impart;
>   Come quickly from above;
> Write Thy new name upon my heart,
>   Thy new, best name of Love.

Let that be our prayer.

Chapter Twenty-three

The Mortification of Sin

W E have already considered verses 27-30 as a whole, in order that we might understand our Lord's view of sin over against the teaching of the Pharisees and scribes. Now let us look at verses 29 and 30 in particular. Our Lord, having dealt with the whole nature of sin, did not leave it at that point, for in thus describing it He also, in a sense, indicated the way in which we are to deal with it. He wants us to see the character of sin in such a way that we shall abhor and forsake it. It is this second aspect of the matter that we must now consider.

We must start first at the point of pure interpretation. What exactly is meant by the words: 'And if thy right eye offend thee, pluck it out, and cast it from thee: for it is profitable for thee that one of thy members should perish, and not that thy whole body should be cast into hell'? There are many who think that these extraordinary and startling statements should be interpreted like this. Our Lord, they maintain, has been emphasizing the importance of a clean heart; He says that it is not enough that you do not commit an *act* of adultery — it is the heart that matters. They imagine that at that point there was a kind of objection, perhaps expressed, or perhaps our Lord sensed it. Or perhaps He anticipated an objection which would be put like this: 'We are so constituted that our very faculties inevitably lead us to sin. We have eyes and we see, and as long as we have them it is no use telling us that we must have a clean heart. If I see with my right eye and that leads to certain consequences, what is the use of telling me to improve and clean it? It is an impossible demand. The trouble with me, really, is the fact that I have a right eye and a right hand.' Then they interpret this statement as meaning that our Lord replies to such an objection: 'Well, if you tell Me it is your right eye that leads to sin, pluck it out, and if you tell Me it is your right hand, cut it off.' In other words, they assert, He met the

213

objectors on their own level. 'The Pharisees', they say, 'try to evade the issue by saying that the trouble is not so much in their own desires and hearts, as in the very fact that they can see. That, inevitably, leads to temptation, and temptation leads to sin. It is an attempt again at an avoidance of His teaching. So He, as it were, turns back and says: "Very well, if you say your whole trouble is due to your right eye and hand, get rid of them".'

Furthermore, they would have us understand that by saying that, of course, our Lord is ridiculing that whole position because He only refers to the right eye and hand; whereas if a man plucks out his right eye he still has his left, and he sees the same thing with the left as with the right; and if he chops off the right hand he has not solved his problem because his left hand is still there. 'Thus', they say, 'our Lord ridicules this whole conception of holiness and the sanctified life which would regard it as a matter of our physical being, and shows that if a man is ever to have a clean and pure heart along that line, well, to put it absolutely plainly, both eyes must be plucked out, both hands, both feet must be cut off. He must mutilate himself in a sense until he is no longer a man.'

Now I do not want to reject that exposition entirely. There is undoubtedly true teaching in it. But whether or not it is an exact explanation of what our Lord says at this point I am not so certain. It seems to me that a better interpretation of this statement is that our Lord was anxious to teach at one and the same time the real and horrible nature of sin, the terrible danger in which sin involves us, and the importance of dealing with sin and getting rid of it. So He deliberately puts it in this way. He talks about the precious things, the eye and the hand, and He singles out in particular the right eye and the right hand. Why? At that time people held the view that the right eye and hand were more important than the left. It is not difficult to see why they believed that. We all know the importance of the right hand and the similar relative importance of the right eye. Now our Lord takes up that common, popular belief, and what He says in effect is this: 'If the most precious thing you have, in a sense, is the cause of sin, get rid of it.' Sin is as important as that in life; and its importance can be put in that way. It seems to me that that is a much more natural interpretation of this statement than the other. He is saying that, however valuable a thing may be to you in and of itself, if it is going to trap you and cause you to stumble, get rid of it, throw it away. Such is His way of emphasizing the importance of holiness, and the terrible danger which confronts us as the result of sin.

How, then, are we to deal with this problem of sin? I would remind you again that it is not merely a question of not committing certain acts; it is a question of dealing with the pollution of sin in the heart, this force that is within us, these powers which are resident in our very natures as the result of the fall.

These are the problems, and merely to deal with them in a negative manner is not enough. We are concerned about the state of our hearts. How are we to face these problems? Here our Lord indicates a number of points, which we must observe and grasp.

The first, obviously, is that *we must realize the nature of sin, and also its consequences.* We have already been looking at that and He Himself starts with it once more. There is no doubt whatever that an inadequate view of sin is the chief cause of a lack of holiness and sanctification, and indeed of most of the false teaching with respect to sanctification. All your antinomianisms throughout the centuries, all the tragedies that have ever followed the perfectionist movements, have really arisen because of false notions concerning sin, and a failure to see that not only is sin a power and something which leads to guilt, but that there is such a thing as the pollution of sin. Though a man does not do anything wrong he is still sinful. His nature is sinful. We must grasp the idea of 'sin' as distinct from 'sins'. We must see it as something that leads to the actions and that exists apart from them.

Perhaps the most convenient way of putting all this is to remind ourselves of Palm Sunday, a day which brings us right back to all the details of the earthly life of the Son of God. There He is going up to Jerusalem for the last time. What is the meaning of all this? Why is He going to that cross and to that death? There is only one answer to that question. Sin is the cause; and sin is something that can be dealt with in that way only, and in no other. Sin is something, let me say it with reverence, that has created a problem even in heaven. It is as profound a problem as that, and we must start by realizing this. Sin in you and in me is something that caused the Son of God to sweat drops of blood in the Garden of Gethsemane. It caused Him to endure all the agony and the suffering to which He was subjected. And finally it caused Him to die upon the cross. That is sin. We can never remind ourselves of that too frequently. Is it not our danger — I think we all must admit it — to think of sin merely in terms of ideas of morality, to catalogue sins and to divide them into great and small, and various other classifications? There is a sense, no doubt, in which there is some truth in these ideas: but there is another sense in which such classifications are all wrong and indeed dangerous. For sin is sin, and always sin; that is what our Lord is emphasizing. It is not, for example, only the *act* of adultery; it is the thought, and the desire also which is sinful.

That is the fact on which we must concentrate. We must realize what a terrible thing sin is. So let us cease to be so interested in our moral classifications, and let us cease to think even of actions in terms of moral catalogues. But let us think of everything in terms of the Son of God and what it meant for Him, and what it led to in His life and in His ministry. That is the way to think of sin. Of course, as long as we think of it only in these moral terms we may feel smug and contented because we have not done certain things. But that is an utterly false conception, and what we have to realize is that, because we are what we are, the Son of God had to come from heaven and go through all that, and even die that cruel death upon the cross. You and I are such that all that became necessary. Such is this pollution of sin that is in us. We can never look too often at the nature of sin and its consequences. One of the most direct roads to holiness, always, is to consider Him and His suffering and agony. Nowhere is the nature of sin displayed in such terrible and awful colours as in the death of the blessed Son of God.

The second thing we must realize is *the importance of the soul and its destiny.* 'It is profitable for thee that one of thy members should perish, and not that thy whole body should be cast into hell.' Notice that our Lord says this twice in order to emphasize it. The soul, He says, is so important that if your right eye is the cause of your being trapped by sin, you should pluck it out and get rid of it. Not, as I am going to show you, in a physical sense. There are many things in this life and world which, in and of themselves, are very good, right and profitable. But our Lord tells us here that if even those things trap us, we must put them on one side. He put it still more strongly on one occasion when He said, 'If any man . . . hate not his father, and mother, and wife, and children, and brethren, and sisters, yea, and his own life also, he cannot be my disciple' (Luke 14:26). This means that it does not matter who or what it is that comes between us and Him, if it is harmful to the soul, it must be hated and put on one side. It does not mean that a man who is a Christian has, of necessity, to hate his loved ones. Obviously not, for our Lord told us to love even our enemies. It simply means that anything which militates against the soul and its salvation is an enemy at that point, and must be dealt with as such. It is our misuse of these things, our putting them in the wrong position, that is wrong; and that is the point which He stresses here. If my faculties, propensities and abilities do lead me to sin, then I must forsake them and get rid of them. I must put even those on one side. If you examine your own experience, I think you will see at once what this means. The trouble is that because of sin we tend to pervert everything. 'Unto the pure all things are pure.' Yes; but, as we said earlier, we are not pure; and the result is that even pure things at times become impure. Our Lord here shows us that the importance of the soul and its destiny is such that everything must be subservient to it. Everything else must be secondary where this is concerned, and we must examine the whole of our life and see to it that this is ever in the forefront of our considerations. That is His message, and He puts it in this striking and emphatic manner. Your most important possession — your right eye, even — if it is trapping you, must be plucked out. Nothing must be allowed to come between you and your soul's eternal destiny.

That, then, is the second great principle. I wonder whether it is ever in the forefront in our considerations. Do we all realize that the most important thing we have to do in this world is to prepare ourselves for eternity? There is no question at all about that. This is not in any way to detract from the importance of life in this world. It is important. It is God's world, and we are to live a full life here. Yes; but only as those who are preparing themselves for eternity and for the glory that awaits us. 'It is profitable for thee that one of thy members should perish', that we should, as it were, be cripples while we are here, in order to make certain that when we get there we shall stand in His presence with joy and with glory. Oh, how sadly we neglect the culture of the soul, how negligent we are about our eternal destiny! We are all so very concerned about this life. But are we equally concerned about our soul and spirit and our eternal destiny? That is the question our Lord is asking us. It is tragic that we are so negligent about the eternal and are so concerned about that which must inevitably come to an end. It is better to be a cripple in this life, says our Lord, than to lose everything in the next. Put your soul and its eternal destiny before everything else. It may mean that you will not get promotion in your work or that you will not do as well as somebody else. Well, 'what shall it profit a man, if he shall gain the whole world, and lose his own soul?' That is the calculation. 'It is profitable for thee that one of thy members should perish, and not that thy whole body should be cast into hell.' 'Fear not them which kill the body, but are not able to kill the soul: but rather fear him which is able to destroy both soul and body in hell' (Matt. 10:28).

The third principle is that *we must hate sin, and do all we can to destroy it at all costs within ourselves.* You remember how the Psalmist puts it, 'Ye that love the Lord, hate evil.' We must train ourselves to hate sin. In other words we must study it and understand its working. I think we have been very negligent in this respect; and here we are in very striking and pathetic contrast to those great men whom we call the Puritans. They used to analyse sin and expose it, with the result that they were laughed at and were called specialists in sin. Let the world laugh if it likes; but that is the way to become holy. Look at it; read the biblical description of it; analyse it; and the more we do so the more we shall hate it and do all we can to get rid of it at all costs, and to destroy it out of our lives.

The next principle is that we must realize that *the ideal in this matter is to have a clean and pure heart, a heart that is free from lusts.* The idea is not simply that we be free from certain actions, but that our hearts should become pure. So we come back again to the Beatitudes: 'Blessed are the pure in heart: for they shall see God.' Our standard must always be a positive one. We must never think of holiness merely in terms of not doing certain things. Every type of holiness teaching which simply ends at that, and which tells us not to do certain things for a certain period in the year, is always negative. The true teaching, however, is always positive. Of course we must not do certain things. But the Pharisees were expert at that, and they stopped there. No, says our Lord; you must aim at a heart that is clean and pure:

> A heart in every thought renewed
> And filled with love divine,
> Perfect and right and pure and good;
> A copy, Lord, of Thine.

In other words, our ambition should be to have a heart which never knows bitterness, envy, jealousy, hate or spite, but is ever full of love. That is the standard; and again I think it is quite obvious that this is the point at which we often fail. We have only a negative conception of holiness, and therefore we feel self-satisfied. If we examined our heart, if we came to know what the Puritans always called 'the plague of our own heart', it would promote holiness. But we do not like examining our hearts. Far too often those of us who rejoice in the name of 'Evangelical' are perfectly happy because we are orthodox and because we are unlike those liberals or modernists and various other sections of the Church, which are obviously wrong. So we sit down complacent and satisfied, feeling that we have arrived, and that we have only to maintain our position. But that means that we do not know our own hearts, and our Lord calls for a pure heart. You can commit sin in your heart, He says, without anybody knowing it; and you may still look perfectly respectable, and nobody would guess what is going on in your imagination. But God sees it, and in the sight of God it is awful, foul, ugly, filthy. Sin in the heart!

The last principle is *the importance of the mortification of sin*. 'If thy right hand offend thee, cut it off, and cast it from thee.' Now mortification is a great subject. If you are interested in it you should read a book, *The Mortification of Sin*, by that great Puritan, Dr. John Owen. What does the term mean? There are two views on this subject. There is a false conception of mortification which says that we must literally cut off our hands and throw them away. It is the view which regards sin as being resident in the physical frame, and which therefore deals severely with the physical body as such. There were many in the early days of Christianity who literally cut off their hands, and thought they were carrying out the injunctions of the Sermon on the Mount by so doing. They interpreted our Lord's word here exactly as do others, whom we shall consider later, who have taken the teaching about 'turning the other cheek' in that literal, unintelligent manner. They say: 'It is the Word; there it is, and we must carry it out as it is.' But they were still left with the left eye and hand, and they still sinned. In the same way the idea that celibacy is essential to sanctification and holiness belongs to the same category. Any teaching that makes us live an unnatural life is not New Testament holiness. To argue thus is the negative view of mortification, and it is false.

What is the true view? It is to be found in many places in the New Testament. Take, for instance, Romans 8:13 where Paul says: 'For if ye live after the flesh, ye shall die: but if ye through the Spirit do mortify the deeds of the body, ye shall live.' And in 1 Corinthians 9:27 he expresses it thus: 'I keep under my body, and bring it into subjection: lest that by any means, when I have preached to others, I myself should be a castaway.' What does he mean? Well, this is what the authorities on the Greek words tell us. He punches his body and knocks it about until it is black and blue in order to keep it down. That is the mortification of the body. In Romans 13:14, he says: 'Make not provision for the flesh, to fulfil the lusts thereof.' Now these are things which we must do. Instead of, 'Let go and let God', or 'Receive this marvellous experience and then you will have nothing to do', we are rather told, 'Mortify therefore your members which are upon the earth' (Col. 3:5). That is the apostle's teaching. Mortify through the Spirit the deeds of the body. Keep under the body. And our Lord says: 'If thy right hand offend thee, cut it off.' It is the same principle everywhere.

These are things which we must do. What does it mean? Again, I am merely going to give some indication of the principles. First, *we must never 'feed the flesh'.* 'Make not provision for the flesh,' says Paul, 'to fulfil the lusts thereof.' There is a fire within you; never bring any oil anywhere near it, because if you do there will be a flame, and there will be trouble. Do not give it too much food; which being interpreted means this, among other things: never read anything that you know will do you harm. I referred to that earlier and I repeat it again, for these matters are very practical. Do not read those reports in the newspapers which are suggestive and insinuating and which you know always do you harm. Don't read them; 'pluck out your eye.' They are of no value to anybody; but alas, there they are in the paper and they pander to the public taste. The majority like that sort of thing, and you and I by nature like it. Well, then; don't read it, 'pluck out your eye.' The same is true of books, especially novels, radio programmes, television and also the cinema. We must come down to these details. These things are generally a source of temptation, and when you give time and attention to them you are making provision for the flesh, you are adding a little fuel to the flame, you are feeding the thing you know is wrong. And we must not do so. 'But', you say, 'it is educational. Some of those books are written by marvellous people, and if I do not know these things I shall be considered an ignoramus.' Our Lord's reply is that, for the sake of your soul, you had better be an ignoramus, if you know it does harm to know these things. Even the most valued thing must be sacrificed.

It also means avoidance of what the Bible calls 'foolish talking and, jesting' — stories and jokes thought to be clever but which are insinuating and polluting. You will often get that kind of thing with its cleverness, subtlety and wit, from highly intelligent men. The natural man admires it all; but it leaves a nasty taste in the mouth. Reject it; say you do not want it, that you are not interested. You may offend people by saying so. Well, offend them if that is their mentality and morality. Offend them, I say, for the sake of your soul. Again, we must be careful in the company that we keep. Let me put it like this. We must avoid everything that tends to tarnish and hinder our holiness. 'Abstain from all appearance of evil', which means, 'avoid every form of evil'. It does not matter what form it takes. Anything that I know does me harm, anything that arouses, and disturbs, and shakes my composure, no matter what it is, I must avoid it. I must 'keep under my body', I must 'mortify my members'. That is what it means; and we must be strictly honest with ourselves.

But someone may ask at this point: 'Are you not teaching a kind of morbid scrupulosity? Is not life going to be rather wretched and miserable?' Well, there are people who become morbid. But if you want to know the difference between them and what I am teaching, think of it in this way. Morbid scrupulosity is always concerned about itself, its state and condition, and its own achievements. True holiness, on the other hand, is always concerned about pleasing God, glorifying Him and ministering to the glory of Jesus Christ. If you and I keep that ever in the foreground of our minds we need not be very worried about becoming morbid. All that will be at once avoided if we do it for His sake, instead of spending the whole of our time feeling our spiritual pulse and taking our spiritual temperature.

The next principle I would lay down would be this, that *we must deliberately restrain the flesh* and deal with every suggestion and insinuation of evil. In other words, we must 'watch and pray'. We must all be concerned to do as the apostle Paul says, 'I keep under my body.' If Paul needed to do it, how much more so the rest of us.

Those are things that you and I have to do ourselves. They will not be done for us. I do not care what experience you have or may have had, nor how much you have been filled with the Spirit, if you read suggestive matter in the newspaper, you will probably be guilty of sin, you will sin in your heart. We are not machines; we are told that we ourselves must put these things into practice.

That, in turn, leads me to the last great principle, which I put in this form: *We must realize once more the price that had to be paid to deliver us from sin.* To the true Christian there is no greater stimulus and incentive in the fight to 'mortify the deeds of the body' than this. How frequently we are reminded that our Lord's object in coming into the world and enduring all the shame and the suffering of death upon the cross was 'to deliver us from this present evil world', to 'redeem us from all iniquity', and to separate 'unto himself a peculiar people, zealous of good works'. It was all designed in order that 'we should be holy and without blame before him in love'. If His love and His sufferings mean anything to us, they will inevitably lead us to agree with Isaac Watts that such love 'demands my soul, my life, my all'.

Finally, these considerations must have brought us to see our absolute need of the Holy Spirit. You and I have to do these things. Yes, but we need the power and the help that the Holy Spirit alone can give us. Paul put it like this: 'If ye *through the Spirit* do mortify the deeds of the body'. The Holy Spirit's power will be given to you. He has been given if you are a Christian. He is in you, He is working in you 'both to will and to do of his good pleasure'. If we realize the task we have to do, and long to do it, and are concerned about this purification; if we start with this process of mortification, He will empower us. That is the promise. So we must not do those things which we know to be wrong: we act as empowered by Him. Here it is all in one phrase: 'Work out your own salvation with fear and trembling. For it is God which worketh in you both to will and to do of his good pleasure.' The two sides are absolutely essential. If we try to mortify the flesh alone, in our own strength and power, we shall produce an utterly false type of sanctification which is not really sanctification at all. But if we realize the power and the true nature of sin; if we realize the awful grip it has on man, and its polluting effect; then we shall realize that we are poor in spirit and utterly feeble, and we shall plead constantly for that power which the Holy Spirit alone can give us. And with this power we shall proceed to 'pluck out the eye' and 'cut off the hand', 'mortify the flesh', and thus deal with the problem. In the meantime He is still working in us and we shall go on until finally we shall see Him face-to-face, and stand in His presence faultless and blameless, without spot and without rebuke.

Chapter Twenty-four

Christ's Teaching on Divorce

W E now come to consider our Lord's statement in verses 31 and 32 on the subject of divorce. Let me begin by pointing out that, when we come to a subject and passage like this, we see the value of a systematic study of the teaching of Scripture. How often do we hear an address on a text such as this? Is it not true to say that this is the kind of subject that preachers tend to avoid? And thereby, of course, we are guilty of sin. Is it not for us to study some parts of the Word of God and to ignore others; it is not for us to shy at difficulties. These verses that we are now considering are as much the Word of God as anything else which is to be found in the Scriptures. But because of our failure to expound the Bible systematically, because of our tendency to take texts out of their context and to choose what interests and pleases us, and to ignore and forget the rest, we become guilty of an unbalanced Christian life. That in turn leads, of course, to failure in actual practice. It is a very good thing, therefore, that we should work our way through the Sermon on the Mount in this manner, and so find ourselves face-to-face with this statement.

For some reason or another many commentators, even though they may have set out to write a commentary on the Sermon on the Mount, slide over this and do not deal with it. One can easily understand why people tend to avoid a subject like this; but that is no excuse for them. The gospel of Jesus Christ concerns every part and portion of our life, and we have no right to say that any part of our life is outside its scope. Everything that we need is here provided for us and we have clear teaching and instruction upon every aspect of our life and being. But at the same time, anyone who has ever troubled to read up on this subject and the various interpretations will realize that it is a matter that is surrounded by many difficulties. Most of these difficulties, however, are man-made, and can be traced ultimately to the particular teaching of the Roman Catholic Church about marriage as a sacrament. Having started by taking up that position she manipulates statements in Scripture to suit her theory. We should thank God, however, that we are not left to ourselves and our own ideas, but have this clear instruction and teaching. It is our business to face it honestly.

As we approach these verses, let us once more remind ourselves of their background or context. This statement is one of six statements made by our Lord in which He introduces the subject by the formula 'Ye have heard . . . but I say unto you'. It comes in the section of the Sermon on the Mount in which our Lord is showing the relationship of His kingdom and teaching to the law of God that was given through Moses to the children of Israel. He began by saying that He has not come to destroy but to fulfil; indeed He says, till heaven and earth pass, one jot or one tittle shall in no wise pass from the law till all be fulfilled. Then comes the following: 'Whosoever therefore shall break one of these least commandments, and shall teach men so, he shall be called the least in the kingdom of heaven: but whosoever shall do and teach them, the same shall be called great in the kingdom of heaven. For I say unto you, That except your righteousness shall exceed the righteousness of the scribes and Pharisees, ye shall in no case enter into the kingdom of heaven.' He then proceeds to display His teaching in the light of this background.

Bearing all that in mind, let us also remember that in these six contrasts which our Lord draws, He is comparing not the law of Moses, as such, with His own teaching, but rather the false interpretation of this law by the Pharisees and scribes. Our Lord obviously does not say that He had come to correct the law of Moses, because it was God's law, given by God Himself to Moses. No; our Lord's purpose was to correct the perversion, the false interpretation of the law which was being taught to the people by the Pharisees and scribes. He is therefore honouring the law of Moses and displaying it in its great fullness and glory. That, of course, is precisely what He does with regard to the question of divorce. He is especially concerned to expose the false teaching of the Pharisees and scribes with regard to this important matter.

The best way to approach the subject is to consider it under three headings. First of all we must be clear in our minds as to what the law of Moses really did teach about this matter. Then we must be clear as to what the Pharisees and scribes taught. Lastly we must consider what our Lord Himself teaches.

First, then, what did the law of Moses really teach concerning this problem? The answer is to be found in Deuteronomy 24, especially verses 1-4. In Matthew 19 our Lord again refers to that teaching and in a sense gives us a perfect summary of it, but it is important that we should look at the original statements. There is often a good deal of confusion about this. The first thing to notice is that in the old Mosaic dispensation the word adultery is not mentioned in the matter of divorce, for the good reason that under the law of Moses the punishment for adultery was death. Anybody under that old law who was found guilty of adultery was stoned to death, so there was no need to mention it. The marriage had come to an end; but it was not brought to an end by divorce but by punishment by death. That is a very important principle to have clearly in our minds.

What then was the object and purpose of the Mosaic legislation with regard to divorce? You see the answer at once, not only as you read Deuteronomy 24, but especially when you read our Lord's pronouncement upon, and exposition of, that legislation. The whole object of the Mosaic legislation in this matter was simply to control divorce. The position had become entirely chaotic. This is what was happening. In those days, you remember, the men generally held a very low and poor view of women, and they had come to believe that they had a right to divorce their wives for almost any and every kind of frivolous and unworthy reason. If a man, for any reason whatsoever, was anxious to get rid of his wife, he did so. He brought forward some trumpery excuse and on the basis of that he divorced her. Of course the ultimate cause of it all was nothing but lust and passion. It is interesting to observe how, in this Sermon on the Mount, our Lord introduces this subject in immediate connection with the subject that went before it, namely, the whole question of lust. In the Authorized Version of the Bible, these two things are put together in one paragraph. That may not be right, but it does remind us of the intimate connection between the two. The Mosaic legislation, therefore, was introduced in order to regularize and control a situation that had not only become chaotic, but was grossly unfair to the women, and which, in addition, led to untold and endless suffering on the part of both the women and the children.

In the main, it laid down three great principles. The first was that it limited divorce to certain causes. It was only to be permitted henceforth when there was some natural, moral or physical defect discovered in the wife. All the various excuses which men had been using and bringing forward were now prohibited. Before he could obtain a divorce a man had to establish that there was some very special cause, described under the title of uncleanness. He not only had to prove that, he had also to establish it in the sight of two witnesses. Therefore the Mosaic legislation, far from giving a number of excuses for divorce, greatly limited it. It dismissed all the frivolous, superficial and unjust reasons, restricting it to one particular matter.

The second thing it enforced was that any man who thus divorced his wife must give her a bill of divorcement. Before the Mosaic law, a man could say he no longer wanted his wife, and could turn her out of the house; and there she was, at the mercy of the whole world. She might be charged with unfaithfulness or adultery and so be liable to being stoned to death. Therefore, in order to protect the woman, this legislation provided that she should be given a bill of divorcement in which a statement was made that she had been dismissed, not because of unfaithfulness, but because of one of these reasons which had been discovered. It was to protect her, and the bill of divorcement was handed to her in the presence of two witnesses whom she could always call in any case of need and necessity. Divorce was made something formal, something serious, the idea being to impress upon the minds of those people that it was a solemn step and not something to be undertaken lightly in a moment of passion when a man suddenly felt he disliked his wife and wanted to get rid of her. In this way the seriousness of marriage was emphasized.

Then the third step in the Mosaic legislation was a very significant one, namely, that a man who divorces his wife and gives her a bill of divorcement is not allowed to marry her again. The case was put like this. Here is a man who has divorced his wife, and given her a bill of divorcement. With that in her hand she is entitled to marry somebody else. Now the second husband may also give her a bill of divorcement. Yes, says the law of Moses, but if that does happen and she is free to get married once more, she must not marry the first husband: The whole force of that enactment is again exactly the same; it is to make these people see that marriage is not something you can walk in and out of at will. It tells the first husband that, if he gives his wife a bill of divorcement, it is a permanent enactment.

When we examine it like that, we can see at once that the old Mosaic legislation is very far indeed from being what we thought it was, and especially what the Pharisees and scribes thought it to be. Its object was to reduce to a certain amount of order a situation that had become utterly chaotic. You will find that this was the characteristic of all the details of the Mosaic legislation. Take for example the matter of 'an eye for an eye, and a tooth for a tooth'. The Mosaic legislation enacted that. Yes, but what was the object of it? It was not to tell the people that if a man knocked out another man's eye, the victim must retaliate in the same way. No; its purpose was to say this: You are not entitled to kill a man for that offence; it is only an eye for an eye, or if a man knocks out another's tooth, all you are entitled to is a tooth. It is restoring order in a state of chaos, limiting the consequences and legislating for a particular condition. Now the law concerning divorce was exactly the same as that.

Next we must consider the teaching of the Pharisees and scribes because, as we have seen, it was to this especially that our Lord was referring. They said that the law of Moses commanded, indeed urged, a man to divorce his wife under certain conditions. Now, of course, it never said anything of the kind. The law of Moses never commanded anybody to divorce his wife; all it did was to say to a man: If you do want to divorce your wife you should do so only under these conditions. But the Pharisees and scribes, as our Lord makes particularly plain in Matthew 19 when He was speaking on this same subject, were teaching that Moses commanded divorce. And, of course, the next step was that they were again demanding divorce and insisting upon their right to it, for all kinds of inadequate reasons. They took that old Mosaic legislation with regard to this question of uncleanness and had their own interpretation as to what was meant by it. They actually taught that, if a man ceased to like his wife, or for any reason found her to be unsatisfactory to him, that, in a sense, was 'uncleanness'. How typical this is of the teaching of the Pharisees and scribes, and their method of interpreting the law! But in reality they were avoiding the law in principle as well as in letter. The result was that at the time of our Lord terrible injustices were again being done to many women who were being divorced for most unworthy and frivolous reasons. There was only one factor that really mattered to these men, and that was the legal one of giving a bill of divorcement. They were very punctilious about that, as they were careful about other legal details. They did not, however, state why they were divorcing her. That was unimportant. But what did matter supremely was that she be given a writing of divorcement! Our Lord puts it like this: 'It hath been said' — that is the sort of thing you have been hearing from the Pharisees and scribes. What is the important thing for 'whosoever shall put away his wife'? 'Let him give her a writing of divorcement.' Well, of course, that is important, and the law of Moses had enacted it. But you see that is not the main thing, or the thing to be stressed and emphasized. But it was in the centre of the picture as far as the Pharisees and scribes were concerned and, in emphasizing this, they had been failing to see the real meaning of marriage. They had failed to consider this whole question of divorce, and the reason for it, in a true, just and righteous manner. Such was the perversion by the Pharisees and scribes of the Mosaic teaching. They were avoiding it and circumventing it with their clever interpretations and traditions which they added to the law. The result was that the ultimate object of the Mosaic legislation had really been entirely concealed and nullified.

That brings us to our third and last main heading. What does our Lord say about this? 'But I say unto you, That whosoever shall put away his wife, saving for the cause of fornication, causeth her to commit adultery: and whosoever shall marry her that is divorced committeth adultery.' Now the statement in Matthew 19:3-9 is most important and helpful in interpreting this teaching, because it is a fuller explication of what our Lord puts here in a summarized form. The Pharisees and scribes said to Him — they were trying to trap Him — 'Is it lawful for a man to put away his wife for every cause?' They were really giving themselves away in asking such a question for they themselves were actually sanctioning this. And here is our Lord's answer. The first principle He emphasizes is that of the sanctity of marriage. 'Whosoever shall put away his wife, saving for the cause of fornication.' You notice that He goes back beyond the law of Moses to the law that was given by God at the very beginning. When God created woman to be a helpmeet for man He made that great pronouncement. He said, 'They twain shall be one flesh.' 'What therefore God hath joined together, let not man put asunder.' Marriage is not a civil contract, or a sacrament; marriage is something in which these two persons become one flesh. There is an indissolubility about it, and our Lord goes right back to that great principle. When God made woman for man that was His intention, that was what He indicated, and that was what He ordained. The law which God laid down was that a man should leave father and mother and be joined to his wife and that they should become one flesh. Something new and distinct has taken place, certain other ties are broken and this new one is formed. This aspect of 'one flesh' is all-important. You will find that it is a principle running right through Scripture whenever this subject is dealt with. It is seen in 1 Corinthians 6, where Paul says that the terrible thing about fornication is that a man becomes one flesh with a harlot — a most solemn and important teaching. Our Lord starts there. He goes back to the beginning, to God's own original view of marriage.

'If that is so', asks someone, 'how do you explain the law of Moses? If that is God's own view of marriage why did He allow divorce to take place on the conditions which we have just considered?' Our Lord again answered that question by saying that, because of the hardness of their hearts, God made a concession, as it were. He did not abrogate His original law with regard to marriage. No, He introduced a temporary legislation because of the conditions then prevailing. God controlled it. It was exactly the same as we have seen with regard to 'an eye for an eye, and a tooth for a tooth'. It was a tremendous innovation at that time; but in reality it was God leading the people back in the direction of His original pronouncement. 'Because of the hardness of your hearts', says our Lord, 'Moses gave you this concession.' It was not God advocating divorce, or commanding anybody to divorce his wife; it was God just reducing the chaos to a certain amount of order, regularizing what had become utterly irregular. We must keep in the forefront of our minds in these matters God's original object and intention with regard to this whole estate of marriage: the one flesh, the indissolubility, and the coming together in that way.

The first principle leads us to the second, which is that God has never anywhere commanded anybody to divorce. The Pharisees and scribes were suggesting that this was so with Moses' law. Yes; he certainly commanded them to write that bill of divorcement if there was to be a divorce. But that is not the same thing as commanding them to divorce. The idea taught by God's Word is not only that of the indissolubility of marriage, but that of the law of love and forgiveness. We must get rid of this legalistic approach which makes a man say, 'She has spoiled my life, therefore I must divorce her.' As unworthy and undeserving sinners we have all been forgiven by the grace of God, and that must enter into and control our view of everything that happens to us with respect to all other persons, and especially in the relationship of marriage.

The next principle is one which is of the utmost importance. There is only one legitimate cause and reason for divorce — that which is here called 'fornication'. Now I need not emphasize the urgent relevance of all this teaching. We are living in a country in which conditions have become chaotic in this matter of divorce, and there are still further bills proposed which are designed to make divorce easier and which would aggravate the position still further. Here is our Lord's teaching with regard to the subject. There is only one cause for divorce. There *is* one; but there is only one. And that is unfaithfulness by one party. This term 'fornication' is inclusive, and it really means unfaithfulness on the part of one party to a marriage. 'Whosoever shall put away his wife, saving for the cause of fornication, causeth her to commit adultery.' We must realize the importance of this principle. It was particularly important in the days of the early Church. If you read 1 Corinthians 7 you will find there that this matter is referred to again. In those early days the problem presented itself to many Christians in this form. Imagine a husband and wife. The husband is suddenly converted, the wife is not. Here is a man who has become a new creature in Christ Jesus, but his wife still remains a pagan. These people had been taught the doctrine about separation from the world and sin. They, therefore, immediately jumped to the conclusion which forced them to say, 'It is impossible for me to go on living with a woman like that who is a pagan. Surely, if I am to live the Christian life, I must divorce her because she is not a Christian.' And many a wife who had been converted and whose husband was not, was saying the same thing. But the apostle Paul taught these people that the husband was not to leave his wife because he was converted and she was not. You see, even that is not a ground for divorce. Take all this modern talk of incompatibility of temperament. Can you imagine anything more incompatible than a Christian and a non-Christian? And according to modern ideas, if ever there was cause for divorce surely there it is. But the plain teaching of Scripture is that even that is not a ground for divorce. Do not leave the unconverted one, says Paul. The wife who has been converted having an unbelieving husband sanctifies that husband. You need not worry about your children; if one party is Christian they are covered and have the privilege of Christian nurture within the life of the Church.

Now that is a most important and vital argument. It is the way of impressing upon us this great principle which is laid down by our Lord Himself. Nothing is a cause for divorce save fornication. It does not matter how difficult it may be, it does not matter what the stress or the strain, or whatever can be said about the incompatibility of temperament. Nothing is to dissolve this indissoluble bond save this one thing. But I emphasize again that this one thing does. Our Lord Himself says that this is a cause and a legitimate one for divorce. He says Moses granted certain concessions 'because of the hardness of your hearts'. But this is now laid down as a principle, not as a concession to weakness. He Himself tells us that unfaithfulness is a cause for divorce and the reason for this is surely obvious. It is this question of the 'one flesh' again; and the person who is guilty of adultery has broken the bond and has become united to another. The link has gone, the one flesh no longer obtains, and therefore divorce is legitimate. Let me emphasize again, it is not a commandment. But it is a ground for divorce, and a man who finds himself in that position is entitled to divorce his wife, and the wife is entitled to divorce the husband.

The next step makes this even clearer. Our Lord says that if you divorce your wife for any other reason you cause her to commit adultery. 'Whosoever shall put away his wife, saving for the cause of fornication, causeth her to commit adultery.' The argument is this: There is only one thing that can break this bond. Therefore, if you put away your wife for any other reason you are putting her away without breaking the bond. In this way you are making her break the bond if she should marry again; and she is therefore committing adultery. So that a man who divorces his wife for any reason but for this is thereby causing her to commit adultery. He is the cause, and the man who marries her is in like manner an adulterer. Thus our Lord enforces this great principle in this positive and clear manner. There is only one cause for divorce, and no other.

What, then, is the effect of this teaching? We can summarize it in this way. Our Lord here shows Himself to us as the great Law-giver. All law comes from Him; everything appertaining to this life and world has come from Him. There was temporary legislation for the children of Israel because of their peculiar circumstances. The Mosaic penalty for adultery was death by stoning. Our Lord abrogated that temporary legislation. The next thing He has done is to make divorce for the case of adultery legitimate; He has established the law on this matter. These are two main results of His teaching. From that time onwards men and women are not stoned and put to death for adultery. If you want to do anything you are entitled to a divorce. Out of that we may legitimately draw one very important and serious deduction. We can say not only that a person who thus has divorced his wife because of her adultery is entitled to do so. We can go further and say that the divorce has ended the marriage, and that this man is now free and as a free man he is entitled to remarriage. Divorce puts an end to this connection, our Lord Himself says so. His relationship to that woman is the same as if she were dead; and this innocent man is therefore entitled to remarriage. Even more than this, if he is a Christian, he is entitled to Christian remarriage. But he alone is in that position and she is not, or vice versa.

'Have you nothing to say about the others?' asks someone. All I would say about them is this, and I say it carefully and advisedly, and almost in fear lest I give even a semblance of a suggestion that I am saying anything that may encourage anyone to sin. But on the basis of the gospel and in the interest of truth I am compelled to say this: Even adultery is not the unforgivable sin. It is a terrible sin, but God forbid that there should be anyone who feels that he or she has sinned himself or herself outside the love of God or outside His kingdom because of adultery. No; if you truly repent and realize the enormity of your sin and cast yourself upon the boundless love and mercy and grace of God, you can be forgiven and I assure you of pardon. But hear the words of our blessed Lord: 'Go, and sin no more.'

There, then, is our Lord's teaching on this important subject. You see the state of the world and of society round about us today. Is it surprising that our world is as it is while men and women play fast and loose with God's Word in this vital matter? What right have we to expect nations to stand to their bonds and keep their vows if men and women do not do it even in this most solemn and sacred union of marriage? We must start with ourselves; we must start at the beginning, we must observe the law of God in our own personal, individual lives. And then, and then only, will we be entitled to trust nations and peoples, and to expect a different type of conduct and behaviour from the world at large.

Chapter Twenty-five

The Christian and the Taking of Oaths

WE consider now verses 33-37 containing the fourth of the six examples and illustrations which show what our Lord meant when He defined in verses 17-20 of this chapter the relationship of His teaching and kingdom to the law of God. Having laid down the principle, He proceeds thus to demonstrate and to illustrate it. But of course He is concerned not only to illustrate His principle, but also to give specific and positive teaching. In other words, all these detailed matters are of great importance in the Christian life.

There may be those who ask: 'Is it profitable for us, confronted as we are by vast problems in this modern world, to be considering this simple matter of our speech and how we should be speaking to one another?' The answer, according to the New Testament, is that everything that a Christian does is most important because of what he is, and because of his effect upon others. We must believe that if everybody in the world today were a Christian, then most of our major problems would simply vanish out of sight and there would be no need to fear war and such horrors. The question is, then, how are people to become Christian? One of the ways is that they observe Christian people. That is perhaps one of the most potent means of evangelism at the present time. We are all being watched and therefore everything we do is of tremendous importance.

Thus it comes to pass that in the various Epistles which are included in the New Testament canon (not only in those of the apostle Paul but in the others also) the writers invariably have laid down their doctrine with regard to the various details of life. In that great Epistle to the Ephesians, after Paul has risen to the heights and given us in the first chapters that amazing conception of God's ultimate purpose for the whole universe and has transported us into the heavenly places, suddenly he comes back to earth and looks at us and says to us in effect: 'Lie not to one another; speak the truth always.' But there is no contra-

231

diction there. The gospel is, as Wordsworth says of the skylark, 'true to the kindred points of heaven and home'. It always presents doctrine, and yet it is concerned about the smallest details of life and of living. In the words we are now going to consider we have an illustration of this.

As we have seen, this whole section of the Sermon on the Mount is framed by our Lord to expose the sham and the falseness of the Pharisees' and scribes' representation of the Mosaic law, and to contrast it with His own positive exposition. That is what we have here. He says: 'Ye have heard that it hath been said by them of old time, Thou shalt not forswear thyself, but shalt perform unto the Lord thine oaths.' Those exact words are not to be found anywhere in the Old Testament, which again is a proof that He was not dealing with the Mosaic law as such but with the Pharisaical perversion of it. Nevertheless, as was generally true of the teaching of the Pharisees and scribes, it was indirectly dependent upon certain Old Testament statements. For instance, they clearly had in mind the third commandment which reads like this: 'Thou shalt not take the name of the Lord thy God in vain'; also Deuteronomy 6:13: 'Thou shalt fear the Lord thy God, and serve him, and shalt swear by his name,' and also Leviticus 19:12, which reads: 'And ye shall not swear by my name falsely, neither shalt thou profane the name of thy God: I am the Lord.' The Pharisees and scribes were familiar with those Scriptures and out of them they had extracted this teaching: 'Thou shalt not forswear thyself, but shalt perform unto the Lord thine oaths.' Our Lord is concerned here to correct that false teaching, and not only to correct it, but to replace it with the true teaching. In so doing He brings out, as He always does, the real intent and object of the law as given to Moses by God, the law that is therefore binding upon all of us who are Christian and who are concerned about the honour and glory of God.

Once again we can approach the subject under three main headings. First let us look at the Mosaic legislation. What was the purpose of these various statements, such as those I have just quoted, with regard to this matter of forswearing or taking of oaths? The answer is, undoubtedly, that its main intent was to place a bridle upon man's proneness, as the result of sin and the fall, to lying. One of the greatest problems with which Moses had to deal was the tendency of people to lie to one another and deliberately to say things that were not true. Life was becoming chaotic because men could not rely upon one another's words and statements. So one of the chief purposes of the law at this point was to check that, to control it, and, as it were, to make life possible. The same principle was true, as we saw, of the commandment with regard to divorce where, in addition to the specific object, there was a more general one also.

Another object of this Mosaic legislation was to restrict oath-taking to serious and important matters. There was the tendency on the part of the people to take an oath about any trivial kind of matter. On the slightest pretext they would take an oath in the name of God. The object of the legislation was, therefore, to put an end to this indiscriminate, glib oath-taking, and to show that to take an oath is a very solemn matter, something that must be reserved only for those causes and conditions where a matter of exceptional gravity and unusual concern for the individual or for the nation was involved. In other words this enactment was concerned to remind them of the seriousness of the whole of their life; to remind these children of Israel, especially, of their relationship to God, and to stress that everything they did was under the eye of God, that God was over all, and that every part and portion of their life must be lived as unto Him.

That is one of the great principles of the law which is illustrated in particular at this point. We must always bear in mind, as we consider all these Mosaic commandments, the statement: 'I am the Lord your God: . . . ye shall be holy; for I am holy.' These people had to remember that everything they did was important. They were God's people and were reminded that even in their talk and conversation, and especially in the taking of oaths, everything must be done in such a way as to realize that God was looking upon them. They must therefore recognize the great seriousness of all these matters because of their relationship to Him.

The teaching of the Pharisees and scribes, however, which our Lord desired to expose and correct, said: 'Thou shalt not forswear thyself, but shalt perform unto the Lord thine oaths.' In our consideration of the general principle we saw that ultimately the trouble with the Pharisees and scribes was that their attitude was legalistic. They were more concerned about the letter of the law than the spirit. As long as they could persuade themselves that they were keeping the letter of the law they were perfectly happy. For example, as long as they were not guilty of physical adultery they were all right. And the same thing again applied to divorce. Now here it is once more. They had so construed the meaning and so turned and phrased it in a legal form that they allowed themselves ample scope to do many things that were utterly contradictory to the spirit of the law, yet they felt they were free because they had not actually broken the letter. In other words, they had confined the whole purpose of the enactment at this point to the one question of committing perjury. To commit perjury was to them a very serious and solemn matter; it was a terrible sin and they denounced it. You could, however, take all kinds of oaths, and do all sorts of things, but as long as you never committed perjury you were not guilty before the law.

You see the importance of all this. Legalism is still with us; all these matters are highly relevant to ourselves. It is not at all difficult to see this selfsame legalistic attitude towards religion and the Christian faith in large numbers of people today. It is to be found in certain types of religion and it is obvious on the surface in nearly all creeds. To illustrate the case let me point out how obvious it all is in the typical Roman Catholic attitude towards this matter. Take their view of divorce. Their attitude is stated in their written principles. But suddenly in the newspaper you see that a certain prominent Roman Catholic has been granted a divorce. How does it happen? It is a matter of interpretation, and their claim is that they are able to prove that no real marriage had taken place. By subtle arguments they seem to be able to prove anything. You find the same thing in every other type of religion, even, at times, among those who are strongly evangelical. What we do is to isolate a certain thing and say: 'To do that is sin, and as long as you are not doing it all is well.' How often have we indicated that this is the tragedy of the modern view of holiness. Holiness and worldliness are defined in a manner far removed from biblical usage. According to some people, to be worldly seems to mean going to a cinema, and that is the sum total of worldliness. As long as you do not do that you are not worldly. But they forget pride — the pride of life, the lust of the flesh, the lust of the eye; pride in ancestry and things like that. You isolate and confine the definition to one matter only. And as long as you are not guilty of that, all is well. That was the trouble with the Pharisees and scribes; they reduced the whole great question to one of perjury only. In other words, they thought there was no harm in a man taking an oath at any time as long as he did not forswear himself. As long as he did not do that he could take an oath by heaven, by Jerusalem and almost by anything. Thus they opened a door for men to multiply oaths at any time or with respect to any matter whatsoever.

The other characteristic of their false interpretation was that they drew a distinction between various oaths, saying that some were binding while others were not. If you took an oath by the temple, that was not binding; but if you took an oath by the gold of the temple, that was binding. If you took an oath by the altar you need not keep it; but if you took an oath by the gift that was on the altar then it was absolutely binding. You notice how in Matthew 23 our Lord poured His scorn and ridicule, not only upon the perversion of the law therein displayed, but also upon the utter dishonesty of it all. And it is good for us to observe that our Lord did do this. There are certain things in connection with the Christian faith which must be treated in that way. We have all become so uncertain of principles in this loose, effeminate age, that we are afraid of denunciations such as we read here, and are almost ready to condemn our Lord for having spoken about the Pharisees as He did. Shame on us! This utter, rank dishonesty in connection with the things of God is to be exposed and denounced for the thing it is. The Pharisees were guilty of this in distinguishing between oath and oath, saying that some were binding and some not, and the result of all this teaching of theirs was that solemn oaths were being used commonly and lightly in conversation and with respect to almost everything.

Let us now consider our Lord's teaching. The same contrast is here again: '. . . I say unto you'. Here is the Legislator Himself speaking. Here is the Law-Giver; here is one standing absolutely as a Man among men, yet He speaks with the whole authority of the Godhead. He says in effect: 'I who gave the old Law am saying this to you. I say, Swear not at all; neither by heaven; for it is God's throne: nor by the earth; for it is His footstool: neither by Jerusalem; for it is the city of the great King. Neither shalt thou swear by thy head, because thou canst not make one hair white or black. But let your communication be, Yea, yea; Nay, nay: for whatsoever is more than these cometh of evil.' What does this mean?

The first thing we must do, perhaps, is to deal with the situation as it confronts us in a concrete example. Members of the Society of Friends, commonly called the Quakers, have always had a great interest in this paragraph, and it is on the basis of this that they have always traditionally refused to take an oath even in a court of law. Their interpretation is that this is a complete and absolute ban upon the taking of an oath in every shape or form and under any circumstance whatsoever. They say that our Lord said: 'Swear not at all', and our business is to take His words as they are. We must examine this position, but not because the matter of taking oaths in a Law Court is that which is dealt with here. Indeed I am not at all sure but that those who interpret the passage thus have not quite unwittingly and unconsciously placed themselves almost in the ancient legalistic position of the Pharisees and scribes. If we reduce this whole paragraph to taking an oath in a court of law, then we have concentrated on the 'mint and anise and cumin' and have forgotten the 'weightier matters of the law'. I cannot possibly accept their interpretation for the following reasons.

The first is the Old Testament injunction in which God laid down legislation as to how and when oaths should be taken. Is it conceivable that God could ever do that if it was His will that man should never take an oath at all? But not only that, there is the Old Testament practice. When Abraham sent his servant to find a wife for Isaac, he first of all extracted an oath from him — Abraham, the friend of God. That holy man Jacob extracted an oath from Joseph, Joseph extracted an oath from his brethren and Jonathan asked an oath from David. You cannot read the Old Testament without seeing that, on certain special occasions, these holiest of men had to take an oath in a most solemn and serious manner. Indeed we have higher authority for this in the passage which describes our Lord's own trial. In Matthew 26:63, we are told that 'Jesus held his peace'. He was being tried by the high priest. 'And the high priest answered and said unto him, I adjure thee by the living God, that thou tell us whether thou be the Christ, the Son of God.' Our Lord did not say: 'You must not speak like that.' Not at all. He did not condemn his using the name of God in this manner. He did not denounce it on such an occasion, but seemed to regard it as perfectly legitimate. Then, and only then, in response to this solemn charge, did He reply.

However, let us also consider the custom practised by the apostles, who had been taught these matters by our Lord. You will find they frequently took oaths. The apostle Paul says in Romans 9:1: 'I say the truth in Christ, I lie not, my conscience also bearing me witness in the Holy Ghost'; and again in 2 Corinthians 1:23: 'I call God for a record upon my soul, that to spare you I came not as yet unto Corinth.' That was his practice and custom. But there is a very interesting argument based on this whole matter in Hebrews 6:16. The author at that point is trying to give his readers assurance and strong consolation, and his argument is that God has taken an oath in this matter. 'For men verily swear by the greater: and an oath for confirmation is to them an end of all strife.' God therefore 'confirmed it by an oath'. In other words, in referring to the practice of men taking an oath he shows how an oath is a confirmation to man, and puts an end to all strife. He does not say it is wrong; he accepts it as something which is right and customary and taught of God. Then he proceeds to argue that even God Himself has taken an oath, 'that by two immutable things, in which it was impossible for God to lie, we might have a strong consolation, who have fled for refuge to lay hold upon the hope set before us'. In the light of all this the case for not taking an oath in a Court of Law as based upon this Scripture is something which indeed seems unsatisfactory. The conclusion we can come to, based upon Scripture, is that, while oath-taking must be restricted, there are certain solemn, vital occasions when it is right, when it is not only legitimate, but actually adds a solemnity and an authority which nothing else can give.

That is the negative view of our Lord's teaching. But what does He teach positively? Clearly the first thing that our Lord wants to do is to forbid the use of the sacred title always in the matter of swearing or cursing. The name of God and of Christ must never be used in this way. You have only to walk the streets of a city or sit in its trains or buses to hear this being constantly done. It is utterly and absolutely condemned.

The second thing He absolutely forbids is swearing by any creature, because all belong to God. We must not swear by heaven or earth or by Jerusalem; we must not swear by our heads, or by anything but by the name of God Himself. So these discriminations and distinctions drawn by the Pharisees and scribes were utterly ridiculous. What is Jerusalem? It is the city of the great King. What is the earth? It is nothing but His footstool. You cannot even determine whether your hair be white or black. All these things are under God. Also the temple is the seat of God's presence, so you cannot differentiate between the temple and God in that way. His very presence is in that Shekinah glory. Those distinctions were quite false.

Furthermore, He forbids all oaths in ordinary conversation. There is no need to take an oath about an argument, and you must not do so. Indeed I go further and would remind you that He says no oaths or exaggerated avowals are ever necessary. It must either be *Yea, yea;* or *Nay, nay.* He calls for simple veracity, the speaking of truth always in all ordinary communications and conversations and speech. 'Let your communication be, Yea, yea; Nay, nay: for whatsoever is more than these cometh of evil.'

All this is a most solemn matter. We can see its relevance in this modern world and life of ours. Are not most of our troubles in life due to the fact that men and women are forgetting these things? What is the main trouble in the international sphere? Is it not just that we cannot believe what is being said — lying? Hitler based his whole policy upon it, and said it was the way to succeed in this world. If you want your nation to be great, you lie about it. And the more you lie the more likely you are to succeed. One country cannot believe another; the oaths, the solemn pledges no longer matter and no longer count.

But it is not only true in the international realm, it is equally true in our own country, and in some of the most sacred associations of life. One of the great scandals of life today is the appalling increase in divorce and infidelity. To what is it due? It is that men have forgotten the teaching of Christ with regard to vows and oaths, and common veracity and truth and honesty in speech. How like these Pharisees and scribes we are. Men on political platforms have waxed eloquent on the sanctity of international contracts. But, at the very time they were speaking, they were not loyal and true to their own marriage vows. When Hitler lied, we all held up our hands aghast; but we seem to think it is somehow different when we tell what we call a 'white lie' in order to get out of a difficulty. It is terrible, we think, to lie on the international level, but not, apparently, when it comes to a matter between husband and wife, or parents and children. Is not that the position?

It is the old fallacy. The temple — nothing; the gold of the temple — everything. The altar — nothing; the gift on the altar — tremendous. No, we must realize that this is a universal law and principle which runs from top to bottom and covers the whole of life. It applies to us also; the message comes right home to each one of us. We must not lie. And we are all given to it, if not always in a barefaced form. What a terrible thing perjury is to us. We should never dream of it. But surely to tell a lie is as bad as perjury, for, as Christians, we should always speak as in the presence of God. We are His people, and a lie which we may tell to a private individual may come between that individual's soul and its salvation in Christ Jesus. Everything we do is of tremendous importance. We must not exaggerate, or allow people to exaggerate for us, because exaggeration becomes a lie. It gives those who hear a false impression. All that is involved here. Once more: 'Let every man examine himself.' God have mercy upon us in that we are so like these Pharisees and scribes, trying to distinguish between big sins and little sins, lies and things which are not exactly lies. There is but one way to deal with all these things. I am not exhorting you to indulge in morbidity or encouraging what might be called morbid scrupulosity, but we must realize that we are always in the presence of God. We claim we are walking through this world in fellowship with Him and with His Son and that we are indwelt by the Holy Spirit. Very well, 'grieve not the Holy Spirit of God', says Paul. He sees and hears everything — every exaggeration, every suggested lie. He hears it all and it hurts and offends. Why? Because He is the 'Spirit of truth', and there is no lie anywhere near Him. Let us then listen to the command of our heavenly King, who is also our Lord and Saviour, who when He suffered, threatened not, and of whom we read, that 'there was no guile found in his mouth'. Let us follow in His steps and desire to be like Him in all things. Let us remember that everything in our lives and conversation is in His presence, and may indeed be the thing which will determine what others will think of Him. 'Swear not at all . . . let your communication be, Yea, yea; Nay, nay: for whatsoever is more than these cometh of evil.'

Chapter Twenty-six

An Eye for an Eye, and a Tooth for a Tooth

IN verses 38-42 we have our Lord's fifth illustration of the way in which His interpretation of the Mosaic law is contrasted with the perversion of it by the scribes and Pharisees. With that in mind, the best procedure is perhaps to adopt again the threefold division of the matter which we have used in our consideration of some of the previous illustrations. The first thing, therefore, is to look once more at the intent of the Mosaic enactment.

The Old Testament statement 'an eye for an eye, and a tooth for a tooth' is found in Exodus 21:24, Leviticus 24:20 and Deuteronomy 19:21. It was made to the children of Israel by Moses and the important thing now is to determine why this was so. The same principle obtains as in the matter of adultery and divorce, and in the taking of oaths. The main intent of the Mosaic legislation was to control excesses. In this case in particular, it was to control anger and violence and the desire for revenge. There is no need to elaborate this, because we are all unfortunately familiar with it. We are all guilty of it. If any harm is done to us, the immediate natural instinct is to hit back, and not only that, but to do more than hit back. That is what men and women were doing then, and it is what they still do. A slight injury, and the man injured will have his vengeance, including bodily injury to the other; he might even kill him. This whole tendency to wrath and anger, to retribution and retaliation is there at the very depths of human nature. Not only is nature 'red in tooth and claw', mankind is also. Look at children, for example. From our very earliest days we have this desire for revenge; it is one of the most hideous and ugly results of the fall of man, and of original sin.

Now this tendency was manifesting itself amongst the children of Israel and there are examples of it given in the Old Testament literature. The object, therefore, of this Mosaic legislation was to control and reduce this utterly chaotic condition to a certain amount of order. This, as we have seen, is a great fundamental principle. God, the Author of salvation, the Author of the way whereby mankind can be delivered from the bondage and the tyranny of sin, has also ordained that there shall be a check upon sin. The God of grace is also the God of law, and this is one of the illustrations of the law. God will not only ultimately destroy evil and sin and all its works entirely. He is also, in the meantime, controlling it and has set a bound upon it. We find this working out in the Book of Job, where even the devil cannot do certain things until he is given permission. He is ultimately under the control of God, and one of the manifestations of that control is that God gives laws. He gave this particular law which insists that a certain principle of equality and equity must enter into these matters. So, if a man knocks out another man's eye, he must not be killed for that — 'an eye for an eye'. Or if he knocks out the tooth of another, the victim is only entitled to knock out one of his teeth. The punishment must fit the crime and not be in excess of it.

That is the purpose of this Mosaic legislation. The principle of justice must come in, and justice is never excessive in its demands. There is a correspondence between the crime and the punishment, the thing done and what is to be done about it. The object of that law was not to urge men to take an eye for an eye and a tooth for a tooth, and to insist upon it every time; it was simply meant to avoid this horrible excess, this terrible spirit of revenge and demand for retribution, and to check it and hold it within bounds.

But perhaps the most important thing is that this enactment was not given to the individual, but rather to the judges who were responsible for law and order amongst the individuals. The system of judges was set up amongst the children of Israel, and when disputes and matters arose the people had to take them to these responsible authorities for judgment. It was the judges who were to see to it that it was an eye for an eye and a tooth for a tooth and no more. The legislation was for them, not for the private individuals — as in the law of our land at this moment. The law is carried out by the magistrate or the judge, by the one who is appointed in the nation to do this. That was the principle; and it is a true picture of the Mosaic legislation itself. Its main object was to introduce this element of justice and of righteousness into a chaotic condition and to take from man the tendency to take the law into his own hands and to do anything he likes.

As far as the teaching of the Pharisees and scribes is concerned, their main trouble was that they tended to ignore entirely the fact that this teaching was for the judges only. They made it a matter for personal application. Not only that, they regarded it, in their typical legalistic manner, as a matter of right and duty to have 'an eye for an eye, and a tooth for a tooth'. To them it was something to be insisted upon rather than something which should be restrained. It was a legalistic outlook which thought only of its rights — a kind of Shylock attitude. They were therefore guilty of two main errors at that point. They were turning a negative injunction into a positive one and, furthermore, were interpreting it and carrying it out themselves, and teaching others to do so, instead of seeing that it was something that was to be carried out only by the appointed judges who were responsible for law and order.

It is in the light of that background that our Lord's teaching is given, 'I say unto you, That ye resist not evil', together with the further statements that follow.

Clearly, we are face-to-face here with a subject which has often been debated, which has been frequently misunderstood, and which has always been the cause of much confusion. There is possibly no passage in Scripture which has produced as much heat and disputation as this very teaching which tells us not to resist evil and to be loving and forgiving. Pacifism is the cause of much wordy warfare and it often leads to a spirit which is as far removed as possible from that which is taught and inculcated here by our blessed Lord. It is of course one of those passages to which people rush the moment the Sermon on the Mount is mentioned. Many people, no doubt, have been longing for us to arrive at this point and now at last we have reached it, yet nothing is more important than that we should have taken all this time to come to it, because, as we have seen in these expositions, this kind of injunction can only be understood truly if it is always kept in its context and setting.

We saw at the beginning that there are certain principles of interpretation which must be observed if we want to know the truth concerning these matters. We should remind ourselves of some of them now. First, we must never regard the Sermon on the Mount as a code of ethics, or a set of rules to cover our conduct in detail. We must not think of it as being a new kind of law to replace the old Mosaic law; it is rather a matter of emphasizing the spirit of the law. So that we must not, if we are in trouble as to what to do at a particular point, rush to the Sermon on the Mount and turn up a particular passage. You do not get that in the New Testament. Is it not rather tragic that those of us who are under grace always seem to want to be under law? We ask one another, 'What is the exact teaching about this?' and if we cannot be given 'yes' or 'no' as an answer we say, 'It is all so vague and indefinite'.

Secondly, these teachings are never to be applied mechanically or as a kind of rule of thumb. It is the spirit rather than the letter. Not that we depreciate the letter, but it is the spirit that we must emphasize.

Thirdly, if our interpretation ever makes the teaching appear to be ridiculous or leads us to a ridiculous position, it is patently a wrong interpretation. And there are people who are guilty of this.

The next principle is this: If our interpretation makes the teaching appear to be impossible it also is wrong. Nothing our Lord teaches is ever impossible. There are people who do interpret certain things in the Sermon on the Mount in such a way and their interpretation must be false. Its teaching was meant for daily life.

Lastly, we must remember that if our interpretation of any one of these things contradicts the plain and obvious teaching of Scripture at another point, again it is obvious that our interpretation has gone astray. Scripture must be taken and compared with Scripture. There is no contradiction in biblical teaching.

Bearing all this in mind, let us consider what our Lord teaches. He says, 'I say unto you, That ye resist not evil.' They say, 'an eye for an eye, and a tooth for a tooth'. What does it mean? We must inevitably start with the negative which is that this statement is not to be taken literally. There are always people who say, 'Now what I say is this, you must take the Scripture exactly as it is, and Scripture says *resist not evil*. There you are; there is no more to be said.' We cannot deal now with that whole attitude towards Scripture interpretation; but it would be a very simple thing to show that if that is carried out in every respect, we should arrive at an interpretation which is not only ridiculous but impossible. There are, however, certain famous people in the history of the Church and Christian thought who insisted on our interpreting this particular statement in this way. Perhaps no man has more influenced men's thinking concerning these matters than that great writer Count Tolstoy, and he did not hesitate to say that these words of our Lord are to be taken at their face value. He said that to have soldiers, or police, or even magistrates, is unchristian. Evil, he maintained, is not to be resisted; for Christ's way is not to resist evil in any sense. He said that the statement is not qualified, that it does not say that this is true only under certain special conditions. It says, 'resist not evil'. Now policemen resist evil; therefore you must not have them. The same is true of soldiers, magistrates, judges and law courts. There should be no punishment for crime. 'Resist not evil.'

There are others who do not go quite so far as Tolstoy. These people say that we must have magistrates and courts and so on; but they do not believe in soldiers, in wars, or in capital punishment. They do not believe in killing in any sense, whether judicial or otherwise.

You are familiar with that kind of teaching and outlook; and it is part of the business of preaching and of interpreting the Scriptures to meet such an attitude when it is put forward honestly and sincerely. It seems to me that the answer to it is that we must remember once more the whole context and connection of these statements. This can never be emphasized too often. The Sermon on the Mount must be taken in the order in which it was preached and in which it is presented to us. We start not with this injunction, but with the Beatitudes. We start with those fundamental definitions and advance from them. We shall see the relevance of this later; but first we must deal with the paragraph in general.

The first main principle is that this teaching is not for nations or for the world. Indeed we can go further and say that this teaching has nothing whatever to do with a man who is not a Christian. Here we see the importance of the right order. 'This is the sort of way in which you must live', says our Lord to these people. To whom is He speaking? They are the people whom He has already described in the Beatitudes. The first thing He said about them was that they are 'poor in spirit'. In other words they are perfectly aware of their own utter inability. They are aware of the fact that they are sinners, and are absolutely helpless in the sight of God. They are those who are mourning because of their sins. They have come to understand sin as a principle within them that is vitiating the whole of their lives, and they mourn because of it. They are meek; they have a spirit in them that is the very antithesis of the spirit of the world. They are hungering and thirsting after righteousness, and so on. Now these particular injunctions which we are studying are meant only for such people.

We need not stress this point further. This teaching is utterly impossible for anyone who lacks such qualities. Our Lord never asks a man who is but a natural man, the dupe of sin and Satan, and under the dominion of hell, to live a life like this, for he cannot. We must be new men and born again before we can live such a life. Therefore to advocate this teaching as a policy for a country or a nation is no less than heresy. It is heretical in this way: if we ask a man who has not been born again, and who has not received the Holy Spirit, to live the Christian life, we are really saying that a man can justify himself by works, and that is heresy. We are suggesting that a man by his own efforts, and by putting his mind to it, can live this life. That is an absolute contradiction of the whole of the New Testament. Our Lord established that once and for ever in His interview with Nicodemus. Nicodemus was clearly on the point of asking, 'What have I to do in order that I may be like you?' 'My dear friend,' said our Lord to him in effect, 'Do not think of it in terms of what you can do; you cannot do anything; you must be born again.' Therefore to ask for Christian conduct from an individual who is not born again, let alone a nation or a group of nations or a world of nations, is both impossible and wrong.

For the world, and for a nation, and for non-Christians the law still applies, and it is the law which says 'an eye for an eye, and a tooth for a tooth'. These people are still under that justice which restrains and holds man back, preserving law and order and controlling excesses. In other words, that is why a Christian must believe in law and order, and why he must never be negligent of his duties as a citizen of a State. He knows that 'the powers that be are ordained of God', that lawlessness must be controlled, and vice and crime kept within bounds — 'an eye for an eye, and a tooth for a tooth,' justice and equity. In other words the New Testament teaches that, until a man comes under grace, he must be kept under the law. It is at this point that all this modern muddle and confusion has entered in. People who are not Christian talk vaguely about Christ's teaching concerning life, and interpret it as meaning that you must not punish a child when it does wrong, that there must be no law and order, and that we must first love everybody and make them nice. And now we are seeing the results! But this is heresy. It is 'an eye for an eye, and a tooth for a tooth' until the spirit of Christ enters into us. Then, something higher is expected of us, but not until then. The law exposes evil and keeps it within bounds and it is God Himself who has ordained this, and all 'the powers that be' that are to enforce it.

That is our first principle. This has nothing to do with nations or so-called Christian pacifism, Christian socialism and things like that. They cannot be based on this teaching; indeed they are a denial of it. That was the whole tragedy of Tolstoy, and alas, poor man, he himself became a tragedy at the end when he faced the utter uselessness of it all. That was quite inevitable from the beginning, as he would have seen had he truly understood the teaching.

Secondly, this teaching, which concerns the Christian individual and nobody else, applies to him only in his personal relationships and not in his relationships as a citizen of his country. This is the whole crux of the teaching. We all of us live in different realms. Here am I, a citizen of Great Britain with my relationship to the state, to the government and to other such organizations. Yes, but there are also certain more personal relationships, my relationship to my wife and children, my relationship as an individual to other people, my friendships, my membership of the Church and so on. All these are quite apart from my general relationship to the country to which I belong. Now here, I would repeat, our Lord's teaching concerns the behaviour of the Christian in his personal relationships only; indeed, in this saying, the Christian's relationship to the State is not even considered or mentioned. Here we have nothing but the reaction of the Christian as an individual to the things that are done to him personally. With regard to the Christian's relationship to the state and his general relationships, there is ample teaching in the Scriptures. If you are anxious about your relationship to the State or your attitude as a citizen do not stay with the Sermon on the Mount. Rather go on to other chapters that deal specifically with that subject, such as Romans 13 and 1 Peter 2. So that if I, as a young man, am considering my duty to the state in the matter of going into the Forces, I do not find the answer here. I must look for it elsewhere. This is only concerned about my personal relationships. And yet how often, when a man's duty towards the state is being considered, this passage is quoted. I suggest it has nothing whatsoever to do with it.

The third principle which controls the interpretation of this subject is, clearly, that the question of killing and taking of life is not considered as such in this teaching, whether it be regarded as capital punishment, or killing in war, or any other form of killing. Our Lord is considering this law of the Christian's personal reaction to the things that happen to him. Ultimately, of course, it will cover the whole question of killing, but that is not the principle that He puts in the forefront. Therefore, to interpret this paragraph in terms of pacifism and nothing else is to reduce this great and wonderful Christian teaching to a mere matter of legalism. And those who base their pacifism upon this paragraph — whether pacifism is right or wrong I am not concerned to say — are guilty of a kind of heresy. They have dropped back into the legalism of the Pharisees and scribes; and that is an utterly false interpretation.

What, then, is taught here? Surely there is but one principle in this teaching, and that is a man's attitude towards himself. We could discuss the Christian in terms of the state and war and all these things. But that is something very much easier than that which the Lord Jesus Christ asks us to face here. What He asks you to face is yourself, and it is very much easier to discuss pacifism than to face His clear teaching at this point. What is it? I suggest that the key to it is to be found in verse 42: 'Give to him that asketh thee, and from him that would borrow of thee turn not thou away.' That is most important. As you read this paragraph, your first feeling when you come to verse 42 is that it should not be there at all. 'Ye have heard that it hath been said, An eye for an eye, and a tooth for a tooth: But I say unto you, That ye resist not evil.' That is the theme, resisting evil, and therefore these questions of war and killing and capital punishment seem to arise. But then He goes on to say: 'but whosoever shall smite thee on thy right cheek, turn to him the other also. And if any man will sue thee at the law, and take away thy coat, let him have thy cloke also. And whosoever shall compel thee to go a mile, go with him twain.' Then suddenly: 'Give to him that asketh thee, and from him that would borrow of thee turn not thou away.' And at once we feel like asking, What has this question of borrowing to do with resisting evil and not hitting back, or with fighting and killing? How does this come in? There, we are given a clue to the understanding of the principles our Lord is here inculcating. He is concerned the whole time about this question of the 'self' and of our attitude towards ourselves. He is saying in effect that if we are to be truly Christian we must become dead to self. It is not a question of whether we should go into the army or anything else; it is a question of what I think of myself, and of my attitude towards myself.

It is very spiritual teaching, and it works out in the following respects. First, I must be right in my attitude towards myself and the spirit of self-defence that immediately rises when any wrong is done to me. I must also deal with the desire for revenge and the spirit of retaliation that is so characteristic of the natural self. Then there is the attitude of self towards injustices that are done to it and towards the demands that are made upon it by the community or by the State. And finally there is the attitude of self to personal possessions. Our Lord here is unveiling and exposing this horrible thing that controls the natural man — self, that terrible legacy that has come down from the fall of man and which makes man glorify himself and set himself up as a god. He protects this self all along and in every way. But he does it not only when he is attacked or when something is taken from him; he does it also in the matter of his possessions. If another wants to borrow from him, his instinctive response is: 'Why should I part with my goods and impoverish myself?' It is self the whole time.

The moment we see that, there is no contradiction between verse 42 and the others. It is not only a connection, it is an essential part of it. The tragedy of the Pharisees and scribes was that they interpreted 'An eye for an eye, and a tooth for a tooth' in a purely legal manner or as something physical and material. Men still do that. They reduce this amazing teaching just to the question of capital punishment or whether we should take part in war. 'No,' says Christ in effect, 'it is a matter of the spirit, it is a matter of your whole attitude, especially your attitude towards yourself; and I would have you see that if you are to be truly My disciples you must become dead to yourself.' He is saying, if you like: 'If any man would be My disciple, let him deny himself (and all his rights to himself and all the rights of self), and take up the cross, and follow Me.'

Chapter Twenty-seven

The Cloak and the Second Mile

W E have already dealt with verses 38-42 in general, and laid down certain great principles that it is essential to consider before we can even hope to understand the meaning of this challenging paragraph. How often do we tend to forget that the most important factor when we come to Scripture, and especially to a difficult statement like this, is the preparation of the spirit. It is not enough to come to Scripture with a mind, however clear, powerful or intellectual. In the understanding and the elucidation of Scripture, the spirit is very much more important even than the mind. Therefore it is fatal to rush at a statement like this in an argumentative or debating mood. That is why we have taken some time in painting in the background or, if you like, in preparing our spirits and making sure that our whole attitude is one which is set and prepared to receive the message.

We come now to deal with it in detail. It is not that our Lord is giving us here a complete list of what we have to do in every circumstance and condition which we are likely to meet in life. He tells us first that we have to die to self. What does this mean? This paragraph shows us how we can do that; it shows us some ways in which we can test ourselves as to whether we are dying to self or not. These are just three illustrations that He takes, as it were, almost at random, in order to illustrate the principle. It is not an exhaustive list. The New Testament does not provide us with detailed instructions of that kind. Rather, it says: 'You are called; remember you are God's men. Here are the principles; go and apply them.' Of course it is a good thing that we should discuss these things together. But let us be careful that we do not put ourselves back under the law. This needs to be stressed because there are many people who, though they object to Roman Catholicism and its casuistry, are very Catholic in their ideas and doctrine at this point. They think that it is the business of the Church to give them a detailed answer to every little question, and they are always worried about these things. We must get right out of that atmosphere into the realm of great principles.

The first principle is this whole question which we generally refer to as 'turning the other cheek'. 'I say unto you, That ye resist not evil: but whosoever shall smite thee on thy right cheek, turn to him the other also.' What does this mean in the light of the general principles we have enunciated earlier? It means that we must rid ourselves of the spirit of retaliation, of the desire to defend ourselves and to revenge ourselves for any injury or wrong that is done to us. Our Lord starts on the physical level. He imagines a man coming along and, without any provocation, striking us on the right cheek. Immediately the instinct is to hit back and punish him and to have vengeance. The moment I am hit I want to retaliate. That is what our Lord is concerned about, and He just says simply and categorically that we are not to do it. 'Vengeance is mine; I will repay, saith the Lord.'

Let me give you two illustrations of men who, we must all agree, put this teaching into practice. The first is about the famous Cornish evangelist, Billy Bray, who before his conversion was a pugilist, and a very good one. Billy Bray was converted; but one day, down in the mine, another man who used to live in mortal dread and terror of Billy Bray before Bray's conversion, knowing he was converted, thought he had at last found his opportunity. Without any provocation at all he struck Billy Bray, who could very easily have revenged himself upon him and laid him down unconscious on the ground. But instead of doing that Billy Bray looked at him and said, 'May God forgive you, even as I forgive you', and no more. The result was that that man endured for several days an agony of mind and spirit which led directly to his conversion. He knew what Billy Bray could do, and he knew what the natural man in Billy Bray wanted to do. But Billy Bray did not do it; and that is how God used him.

The other is a story of a very different man. Hudson Taylor, standing on a riverbank in China one evening, hailed a boat to take him across a river. Just as the boat was drawing near, a wealthy Chinese came along who did not recognize Hudson Taylor as a foreigner because he had affected native dress. So when the boat came he struck and thrust Hudson Taylor aside with such force that the latter fell into the mud. Hudson Taylor, however, said nothing; but the boatman refused to take his fellow-countryman, saying, 'No, that foreigner called me, and the boat is his, and he must go first.' The Chinese traveller was amazed and astounded when he realized he had blundered. Hudson Taylor did not complain but invited the man into the boat with him and began to tell him what it was in him that made him behave in such a manner. As a foreigner he could have resented such treatment; but he did not do so because of the grace of God in him. A conversation followed which Hudson Taylor had every reason to believe made a deep impression upon that man and upon his soul.

These are but two instances of men trying to implement and, indeed, succeeding in implementing, this particular injunction. What it means is this: we should not be concerned about personal injuries and insults, whether of a physical kind or any other. To be struck on the face is humiliating and insulting. But an insult can be given in many ways. It can be done with the tongue or by a look. Our Lord desires to produce in us a spirit that does not take offence easily at such things, that does not seek immediate means of retaliation. He wants us to reach a state in which we are indifferent to self and self-esteem. The apostle Paul, for instance, puts this perfectly in 1 Corinthians 4:3. He is writing to those Corinthians who have been saying some very unkind things about him. He had been the means of establishing the church, but rival factions had arisen within her. Some were boasting about Apollos and his wonderful preaching, while others were saying they were followers of Cephas. Many had been criticizing the great apostle in a most insulting manner. Notice what he says: 'With me it is a very small thing that I should be judged of you, or of man's judgment: yea, I judge not mine own self.' He means that he has become indifferent to personal criticism, insult and abuse, and to anything that men may do to him.

That is the broad principle which our Lord lays down. But let us be careful that we do not violate one of the principles of interpretation to which we drew attention earlier. This is not so much a qualification, as an elaboration of the teaching. Our Lord's teaching here does not mean that we should be unconcerned about the defence of law and order. To turn the other cheek does not mean that it does not matter at all what happens in national affairs, whether there is order or chaos. Not at all. That, as we saw, was the error of Tolstoy, who said that there should be no policemen, soldiers or magistrates. That is a complete travesty of the teaching. What our Lord says is that I am not to be concerned about myself, my own personal honour and so on. But that is a very different thing from being unconcerned about the maintenance of law and order, or about the defence of the weak and unprotected. While I must and should be prepared to suffer any personal insult or indignity that man can ever inflict upon me, I should at the same time believe in law and order. I assert on biblical authority that 'the powers that be are ordained of God', that the magistrate is a necessary power, that evil and sin must be restrained and restricted, and that I, as a citizen, am to be concerned about that. Therefore I must not construe our Lord's teaching at this point in that general way; it is a personal word to me. For example, it makes our Lord's teaching ridiculous to say that if a drunken man, or a violent lunatic, should happen to come along and strike me on the right cheek, I am immediately to turn the other cheek to him. For if a man in that intoxicated condition, or a lunatic, should so deal with me, what is happening is really not any personal insult or injury. This man who is not in control of his faculties is behaving like an animal and does not know what he is doing. What our Lord is concerned about is my spirit and my attitude towards such a man. Because of the alcohol, this poor man is not aware of what he is doing; he is not really concerned to insult me, he is a man who is doing harm to himself as well as to me and to others. He is, therefore, a man who is to be restrained. And, in the full spirit of this injunction, I should restrain him. Or if I see a man ill-treating or abusing a child I should do precisely the same thing. The teaching has reference to my concern about myself. 'I have been insulted, I have been struck; therefore I must defend myself, and my honour.' That is the spirit our Lord is anxious to banish from our lives.

The second illustration our Lord uses is this matter of the cloak and the coat. 'If any man will sue thee at the law, and take away thy coat, let him have thy cloke also.' Now what does this mean? It can be put as a principle in this way. Our Lord is concerned here with the tendency to insist upon our rights, our legal rights. He gives this example of a man coming and suing me in a court of law for my inner garment. Now according to Jewish law a man could never be sued for his outer garment, though it was legitimate to sue for an inner one. Yet our Lord says, 'If a man comes and sues thee for thy coat, instead of resisting him let him have thy cloak also.'

Here again is a very difficult matter, and the only way of dealing with the problem is to pay close attention to the principle, which is this tendency of men always to demand and insist upon their legal rights. We are all familiar with this at the present time. There are people who are never tired of telling us that the real problem in the world today is that everybody is talking about his rights instead of his duties. It is with this tendency that our Lord is dealing here. Men are always thinking of their rights and saying, 'I must have them.' That is the spirit of the world and of the natural man who must have his pound of flesh, and insists upon it. That, our Lord is concerned to show, is not the Christian spirit. He says we must not insist upon our legal rights even though we may at times suffer injustice as the result.

That is the bald statement of the principle, but once more we must elaborate it. There are passages of Scripture which are most important in this connection. Here we see most clearly the importance of taking Scripture with Scripture and of never interpreting it at one point in such a way that it contradicts the teaching at another point. Our Lord says here, 'If any man will sue thee at the law, and take away thy coat, let him have thy cloke also.' But He also said, 'Moreover if thy brother shall trespass against thee, go and tell him his fault between thee and him alone: if he shall hear thee, thou hast gained thy brother.' He also goes on to say, 'If he will not hear thee, then take with thee one or two more . . . And if he shall neglect to hear them, tell it unto the church: but if he neglect to hear the church, let him be unto thee as an heathen man and a publican' (Matt. 18:15-17). In other words, He does not seem to be telling us there to turn the other cheek or to throw in the cloak in addition to the coat.

Then again in John 18:22, 23 we read, 'And when he had thus spoken, one of the officers which stood by struck Jesus with the palm of his hand, saying, Answerest thou the high priest so? Jesus answered him, If I have spoken evil, bear witness of the evil: but if well, why smitest thou me?' He protests, you see, against the action of the officer.

Let me remind you, too, of what we are told of the apostle Paul in Acts 16:37. Paul and Silas had been thrown into prison at Philippi and their feet were made fast in the stocks. Then, next morning, after the earthquake and all the other events of that memorable night, the magistrates realized they had made a mistake and sent down an order that Paul and Silas should be set at liberty. But see the reply Paul gave: 'They have beaten us openly uncondemned, being Romans, and have cast us into prison; and now do they thrust us out privily? nay verily; but let them come themselves and fetch us out.' And the magistrate had to come down into the prison in order to release them.

How do we reconcile these things? Our Lord here in the Sermon on the Mount seems to be saying that invariably you must turn the other cheek, or if ever you are sued for your coat you must throw in your cloak as well. But He Himself, when He is smitten on the face, does not turn the other cheek, but registers a protest. And the apostle Paul insisted upon the magistrate coming down to release him. If we accept the original principle, there is no difficulty at all in reconciling the two sets of statements. It can be done in this way. These instances are not examples and illustrations of either our Lord or the apostle insisting upon personal rights. What our Lord did was to rebuke the breaking of the law and His protest was made in order to uphold the law. He said to these men, in effect: 'You know by striking me like this you are breaking the law.' He did not say: 'Why do you insult me?' He did not lose His temper or take it as a personal affront. He did not become angry, or show concern about Himself. But He was concerned to remind these men of the dignity and honour of the law. And the apostle Paul did exactly the same thing. He did not make a great protest about having been thrown into prison. His concern was that the magistrates should see that by throwing him into prison like that they were doing something that was illegal and were violating the law that they had been appointed to carry out. So he reminded them of the dignity and honour of that law.

251

The Christian is not to be concerned about personal insults and personal defence. But when it is a matter of honour and justice, righteousness and truth, he *must* be concerned and thus he makes his protest. When the law is not honoured, when it is flagrantly broken, not in any personal interest, not in any way to protect himself, he acts as a believer in God, as one who believes that all law ultimately derives from God. That was the tragic heresy of Tolstoy and others, though they did not realize they were being heretical. Law and laws ultimately come from God. It is He who has appointed the bounds of every nation; it is He who has appointed kings and governments and magistrates and those who are meant to maintain law and order. The Christian, therefore, must believe in observing the law. Thus, while he is prepared for anything to happen to himself personally, he must protest when injustices are being done.

It is obvious that these questions are all tremendously significant and important in the lives of large numbers of Christian people today in many countries. There are many Christians in China and in the countries behind the so-called 'iron curtain' who are facing these things. It may well be that we ourselves may have to face them also, so let us try to keep these principles clearly in our minds.

The next principle involves the question of going the second mile. 'And whosoever shall compel thee to go a mile, go with him twain.' That is to be explained in this way. This compelling to go a mile is a reference to a custom which was very common in the ancient world, by means of which a government had a right to commandeer a man in a matter of porterage or transport. A certain amount of baggage had to be moved from one place to another, so the authorities had the right to commandeer a man at any place and they would make him carry the baggage from that stage to the next. Then they took hold of someone else and made him take it to the next stage, and so on. This, of course, was a power that was especially exercised by any country that had conquered another, and at this time Palestine had been conquered by the Romans. The Roman army was in control of the life of the Jews, and they very frequently did this sort of thing. A man might be doing his own work when suddenly a band of soldiers would come and say to him, 'You must carry this baggage from here to the next stage. You must carry it for a mile.' That is the kind of thing our Lord had in mind and He says: 'When they come to you like that and compel you to go a mile, go with them the second mile.' Go beyond what they have demanded, 'go with them twain'.

Here again is a most important and a most practical matter. The principle is that, not only are we to do what is demanded of us, we are to go beyond it in the spirit of our Lord's teaching here. This passage is concerned with a man's natural resentment at the demands of government upon him. It has reference to our dislike and hatred of legislation of which we do not approve, to Acts of Parliament, for example, which we do not like and which we have opposed. 'Yes', we tend to say; 'they are passed by Parliament. But why should I obey? How can I get out of this?' That is the attitude our Lord is condemning. Let us be perfectly practical. Take the question of the payment of taxes. We may dislike and resent them, but the principle involved is exactly the same as in being willing to go a second mile. Our Lord says that not only must we not resent these things, we must do them willingly; and we must even be prepared to go beyond what is demanded of us. Any resentment that we may feel against the legitimate, authoritative government of our land is something which our Lord condemns. The government that is in power has a right to do these things, and it is our business to carry out the law. Even further, we must do so though we may entirely disagree with what is being done, and though we may regard it as unjust. If it has legal authority and sanction it is for us to do it.

Peter in his Epistle (1 Pet. 2) says, 'Servants, be subject to your masters . . .' and goes on to show the spirit of our Lord's teaching — 'not only to the good and gentle, but also to the froward.' Christian people are often heard quoting that about servants: 'Ah', they say, 'the trouble is that servants are always talking about their rights, never about their duties. They are all rebellious and do not do things in a good spirit. They do everything grudgingly and reluctantly. Men no longer believe in work', and so on. Yes; but the very same people speak about the government and about Acts of Parliament in exactly the same spirit which they condemn in servants. Their attitude towards income tax or the law at certain points is just the one they condemn. That has never occurred to them. But let us remember, if we are employers, that what Peter and our Lord say about the servant applies to all of us. For we are all servants of the state. The principle, therefore, can be put in this way. If we become excited about these matters, or lose our temper about them, if we are always talking about them and if they interfere with our loyalty to Christ or our devotion to Him, if these things are monopolizing the centre of our lives, we are living the Christian life, to put it mildly, at the very lowest level. No, says our Lord, if you are doing that job and this soldier comes along and says you have to carry his baggage for a mile, not only do it cheerfully, but go the second mile. The result will be that when you arrive this soldier will say: 'Who is this person? What is it about him that makes him act like this? He is doing it cheerfully, and is going beyond his duty.' And they will be driven to this conclusion: 'This man is different, he seems to be unconcerned about his own interests.' As Christians, our state of mind and spiritual condition should be such that no power can insult us.

There are thousands of Christian people who are in this position today in occupied countries, and we know not what may be coming to us. It may be that we shall be subjected ourselves some day to a tyrannous power which we naturally hate and which will compel us to do things we dislike. This is the way in which you are to behave in such circumstances, says Christ. You do not stand up for your rights; you do not show the bitterness of the natural man. You have another spirit. We must get into that spiritual state and condition in which we are invulnerable to these attacks which come upon us in different ways.

There is one qualification which must be added. This injunction does not say that we are not entitled to a change of government. But this must always be done by lawful means. Let us change the law if we can, as long as we do it constitutionally and in a lawful manner. It does not say that we must take no interest in politics and in the reform of law. Certainly, if reform seems necessary, let us seek to achieve it, but only within the framework of the law. If we believe that a particular law includes injustices, then in the name of justice, not for our own personal feelings, nor for our own private gain, let us try to change the law. Let us be certain however that our interest in the change is never personal and selfish, but that it is always done in the interest of government and justice and truth and righteousness.

The last point, which we can only touch upon, is the whole question of giving and lending. 'Give to him that asketh thee, and from him that would borrow of thee turn not thou away.' Of course, this again could be interpreted in a mechanical and literal manner so as to make it ridiculous. But what it really means can be put in this form. It is this denial of self once more. It is just our Lord's way of saying that the spirit which says, 'What I have I hold, and what is mine is mine; and I cannot listen to the request of those other people because ultimately I may suffer', is completely wrong. He is rebuking the wrong spirit of those who are always considering themselves, whether they are being struck on the face, or whether their coat is being taken, or whether they are compelled to carry the baggage or to give of their own goods and wealth to help someone in need.

Let us now go immediately to the qualification, realizing that that is the principle. Our Lord does not encourage us here to help frauds or professional beggars or drunkards. I put it like this plainly because we all have these experiences. A man comes to you under the influence of drink and asks you to give him some money. Although he says he wants it for a night's lodging you know he will go immediately and spend it upon drink. Our Lord does not tell us to encourage or help such a man. He is not even considering that. What He is considering is the tendency of a man because of self, and a self-centred spirit, not to help those who are in real need. It is this holding on to what is mine that He is concerned about. We can therefore put it like this. We must always be ready to listen and to give a man the benefit of the doubt. It is not something we do mechanically or thoughtlessly. We must think, and say: 'If this man is in need, it is my business to help him if I am in a position to do so. I may be taking a risk, but if he is in need I will help him.' The apostle John gives us a perfect exposition of this. 'But whoso hath this world's good, and seeth his brother have need, and shutteth up his bowels of compassion from him, how dwelleth the love of God in him? My little children, let us not love in word, neither in tongue; but in deed and in truth' (1 John 3:17, 18). That is the way we are to follow. 'Whoso hath this world's good, and seeth his brother have need.' The man under the influence of drink who asks us for money is not in need, neither is the man who lives by this sort of thing and is too lazy to work. Paul says of such: 'If any would not work, neither should he eat.' So your professional beggar is not in need and I do not give to him. But if I see that my brother is in need and I have this world's goods and am in a position to help him, I must not shut up the bowels of my compassion from him, because, if I do, the love of God is not in me. The love of God is a love that gives of itself in order to help and strengthen those who are in need.

Finally then, having simply studied these injunctions one by one and step by step, and having considered this teaching, we should see clearly that it takes a new man to live this kind of life. This is no theory for the world or for the non-Christian. No man can hope to live like this unless he is born again, unless he has received the Holy Spirit. Such people alone are Christian, and it is to such that our Lord addresses this noble, exalted and divine teaching. It is not comfortable teaching to consider and I can assure you that it is not an easy thing to spend a week with a text like this. But this is the Word of God, and this is what Christ would have us be. It deals with our whole personality, down to the little practical details of life. Holiness is not something to be received in a meeting; it is a life to be lived and to be lived in detail. We may be truly interested and moved as we listen to wonderful addresses about giving ourselves, and so on. But we must not forget our attitude towards legislation which we do not like, and the rates and taxes and the ordinary pinpricks of life. It is all a question of this attitude towards self. God have mercy upon us and fill us with His Spirit.

Chapter Twenty-eight

Denying Self and Following Christ

IN this chapter I want again to consider verses 38-42. We have already studied them twice. First, we looked at them in general, reminding ourselves of certain principles which govern the interpretation. Then we considered the statements one by one in detail, and saw that our Lord's concern is that we should be set free from all desire for personal revenge. There is nothing which is so tragic as the way in which many people, when they come to this paragraph, become so immersed in details, and are so ready to argue about the rightness or wrongness of doing this or that, that they completely lose sight of the great principle here expressed, which is the Christian's attitude towards himself. These illustrations are used by our Lord simply to bring out His teaching concerning that great central principle. 'You', He says in effect, 'must have a right view of yourselves. Your troubles arise because you tend to go wrong at that particular point.' In other words, our Lord's primary concern here is with what we are, rather than with what we do. What we do is important, because it is indicative of what we are. He illustrates that here, and says: 'If you are what you claim to be, this is how you will behave.' So we must concentrate not so much upon the action as upon the spirit that leads to the action. That is why, let us repeat it again, it is so essential that we should take the teaching of the Sermon on the Mount in the order in which it is given. We have no right to consider these particular injunctions unless we have already grasped, and mastered, and have submitted ourselves to, the teaching of the Beatitudes.

In this paragraph we have our attitude towards ourselves presented in a negative manner; in the paragraph that follows it is presented positively. There our Lord goes on to say: 'Ye have heard that it hath been said, Thou shalt love thy neighbour, and hate thine enemy. But I say unto you, Love your enemies, bless them that curse you, do good to them that hate you, and pray for them which despitefully use you, and persecute you.' But here we are concerned with the negative, and this teaching is of such central importance in the New Testament that we must consider it once more.

We have already found more than once that the Sermon on the Mount is full of doctrine. There is nothing quite so pathetic as the way in which people used to say some thirty or forty years ago (and some still say it) that the only part of the New Testament they really believed in and liked was the Sermon on the Mount, and that because it contained no theology or doctrine. It was practical, they said; just an ethical manifesto, which contained no doctrine or dogma. There is nothing quite so sad as that, because this Sermon on the Mount is full of doctrine. We have it here in this paragraph. The important thing is not so much that I turn the other cheek, as that I should be in a state in which I am ready to do so. The doctrine involves my whole view of myself.

No man can practise what our Lord illustrates here unless he has finished with himself, with his right to himself, his right to determine what he shall do, and especially must he finish with what we commonly call the 'rights of the self'. In other words we must not be concerned about ourselves at all. The whole trouble in life, as we have seen, is ultimately this concern about self, and what our Lord is inculcating here is that it is something of which we must rid ourselves entirely. We must rid ourselves of this constant tendency to be watching the interests of self, to be always on the lookout for insults or attacks or injuries, always in this defensive attitude. That is the kind of thing He has in mind. All that must disappear, and that of course means that we must cease to be sensitive about self. This morbid sensitiveness, this whole condition in which self is 'on edge' and so delicately and sensitively poised and balanced that the slightest disturbance can upset its equilibrium, must be got rid of. The condition which our Lord is here describing is one in which a man simply cannot be hurt. Perhaps that is the most radical form in which one can put that statement. I reminded you in the last chapter of what the apostle Paul says about himself in 1 Corinthians 4:3. He writes: 'With me it is a very small thing that I should be judged of you, or of man's judgment: yea, I judge not mine own self.' He has committed the whole question of his judgment to God, and thus he has entered into a state and condition in which he just cannot be hurt. That is the ideal at which we should be aiming — this indifference to self and its interests.

A statement which the great George Müller once made about himself seems to illustrate this very clearly. He writes like this: 'There was a day when I died, utterly died, died to George Müller and his opinions, preferences, tastes and will; died to the world, its approval or censure; died to the approval or blame of even my brethren and friends; and since then I have studied only to show myself approved unto God.' That is a statement to be pondered deeply. I cannot imagine a more perfect or adequate summary of our Lord's teaching in this paragraph than that. Müller was enabled to die to the world and its approval or censure, to die even to the approval or censure of his friends and most intimate companions. And we should notice the order in which he put it. First, it was the approval or censure of the world; then the approval or censure of his intimates and friends. But he said he had succeeded in doing both, and the secret of it, according to Müller, was that he had died to himself, to George Müller. There is no doubt that there is a very definite sequence in this matter. The furthest removed is the world, then come his friends and associates. But the most difficult thing is for a man to die to himself, to his own approval or censure of himself. There are many great artists who treat with disdain the opinion of the world. The world does not approve of their work? 'So much the worse for the world', says the great artist. 'Men are so ignorant they do not understand.' You can become immune to the opinion of the mass and the mob, to the world. But then there is the approval or censure of those who are near and dear to you, those who are intimately associated with you. You value their opinion more highly, and you are therefore more sensitive to it. But the Christian must reach the stage in which he surmounts even that and realizes that he must not be controlled by it. And then he goes on to the last, the ultimate stage which concerns what a man thinks of himself — his own assessment, his own approval of himself and his own judgment of himself. You will find, in many a biography, stories of men who have delivered themselves from sensitivity to the world and to intimates, but who have found that it means a terrible battle, an almost impossible fight not to be concerned about one's self, and one's own judgment of one's self. And as long as we are concerned about that we are not really safe even from the other two. So the key to it all, as George Müller reminds us, is that we must die to ourselves. George Müller had died to himself, to his opinion, his preferences, his likes and dislikes, his tastes, his will. His one concern, his one idea, was to be approved unto God.

Now that is our Lord's teaching here, that the Christian is to get into such a state and condition that he can say that.

The next point is obviously that only the Christian can do this. That is where we find doctrine in this paragraph. No man can possibly attain to this except a Christian. It is the very opposite and antithesis of what is true of the natural man. It is difficult to imagine anything further removed from what the world generally describes as a gentleman. A gentleman, according to the world, is one who fights for his honour and his name. Although he no longer challenges to a duel the moment he is insulted because it is prohibited by law, this is what he would do if he could. That is the world's idea of a gentleman and of honour; and it always means self-defence. It applies not only to man individually but to his country and to everything that belongs to him. It is surely true to say that the world despises a man who does not do that, and it admires the aggressive kind of person, the person who asserts himself and is always most ready to defend himself and his so-called honour. We say, therefore, plainly and without apology, that no man can implement this teaching who is not a Christian. A man must be born again and be a new creature before he can live like this. No man can die to himself except the man who can say, 'I live; yet not I, but Christ liveth in me.' It is the doctrine of the rebirth. In other words our Lord says: 'You have to live like that, but you can do so only when you have received the Holy Spirit and there is a new life in you. You have to become utterly different; you have to become entirely changed; you have to become a new being.' The world dislikes this teaching and would have us believe that in various ways man can approximate to it unaided. We used to hear a great deal about the 'word of a sportsman', about being 'a sport' and so on. We do not hear quite so much about that these days, for the obvious reason that we have found men who are famous as 'sportsmen' and who, when they are playing games, are full of a sense of honour and ready to stand aside and not consider themselves, figuring in divorce court cases, and displaying there a complete lack of honour, even a lack of ordinary decency, truthfulness, and the sense of right and fair play. Oh no, by being a 'sportsman' you cannot live like this. This is something utterly removed from the world and its sport even at its very highest and best. It is something that is only possible for one who is regenerate, who has received the Spirit of the Lord Jesus Christ.

Having thus stated the doctrine, we must now ask a practical question. How am I to live like that? Someone may say: 'You have confronted us with teaching; but I find it difficult, I tend to fail in practice. How can one live that kind of life?'

Let us, first of all, approach the matter on a purely practical level. The first thing we must do is to face this whole problem of the self in an honest manner. We must cease to make excuses, cease trying to evade and circumvent it. It is to be faced honestly and squarely. We must hold all this teaching before us and examine ourselves in the light of it. But it is not enough that we should do that in general only; we must do it in particular also. Whenever I notice in myself a reaction of self-defence, or a sense of annoyance or a grievance, or a feeling that I have been hurt and wronged and am suffering an injustice — the moment I feel this defensive mechanism coming into play, I must just quietly face myself and ask the following questions. 'Why exactly does this thing upset me? Why am I grieved by it? What is my real concern at this point? Am I really concerned for some general principle of justice and righteousness? Am I really moved and disturbed because I have some true cause at heart or, let me face it honestly, is it just myself? Is it just this horrible, foul self-centredness and self-concern, this morbid condition into which I have got? Is it nothing but an unhealthy and unpleasant pride?' Such self-examination is essential if we are to conquer in this matter. We all know this by experience. How easy it is to explain it in some other way. We must listen to the voice that speaks within us, and if it says: 'Now you know perfectly well it is just yourself, that horrid pride, that concern about yourself and your reputation and your own greatness' — if it is that, we must admit and confess it. It will be extremely painful, of course; and yet, if we want to rise to our Lord's teaching, we have to pass through such a process. It is the denial of self.

Another thing on the practical level which is of the very greatest importance is to realize the extent to which self controls your life. Have you ever tried doing that? Examine yourself and your life, your ordinary work, the things you do, the contacts you have to make with people. Reflect for a moment upon the extent to which self comes into all that. It is an amazing and terrible discovery to note the extent to which self-interest and self-concern are involved, even in the preaching of the gospel. It is a horrible discovery. We are concerned about doing it well. Why? For the glory of God, or for our own glory? All the things we do and say, the impression we make even when we meet people casually — what are we really concerned about? If you analyse the whole of your life, not only your actions and conduct, but your dress, your appearance, everything, it will amaze you to discover the extent to which this unhealthy attitude towards self comes in.

But let us go one step further. I wonder whether we have ever realized the extent to which the misery and the unhappiness and the failure and the trouble in our lives is due to one thing only, namely self. Go back across last week, consider in your mind and recall to your conscience the moments or the periods of unhappiness and strain, your irritability, your bad temper, the things you have said and done of which you are now ashamed, the things that have really disturbed you and put you off your balance. Look at them one by one, and it will be surprising to discover how almost every one of them will come back to this question of self, this self-sensitivity, this watching of self. There is no question about it. Self is the main cause of unhappiness in life. 'Ah', you say, 'but it is not my fault; it is what somebody else has done.' All right; analyse yourself and the other person, and you will find the other person probably acted as he did because of self, and you are really feeling it for the same reason. If only you had a right attitude towards the other person, as our Lord goes on to teach in the next paragraph, you would be sorry for him and would be praying for him. So ultimately it is you who are to blame. Now it is a very good thing on the practical level just to look at it honestly and squarely. Most of the unhappiness and sorrow, and most of our troubles in life and in experience, arise from this ultimate origin and source, this self.

Let us come to a higher level, however, and look at it doctrinally. It is a very good thing to look at self in a doctrinal and theological manner. According to the teaching of Scripture, self was responsible for the fall. But for it, sin would never have entered into the world. The devil was subtle enough to know its power, so he put it in terms of self. He said: 'God is not being fair to you; you have a legitimate grudge and a grievance.' And man agreed, and that was the whole cause of the fall. There would be no need of International Conferences to try to solve the problems of the nations at the present time if it were not for the fall. And the whole trouble is just self and self-assertion. That is self regarded doctrinally. But self always means defiance of God; it always means that I put myself on the throne instead of God, and therefore it is always something that separates me from Him.

All moments of unhappiness in life are ultimately due to this separation. A person who is in real communion with God and with the Lord Jesus Christ is happy. It does not matter whether he is in a dungeon, or whether he has his feet fast in the stocks, or whether he is burning at the stake; he is still happy if he is in communion with God. Is not that the experience of the saints down the centuries? So the ultimate cause of any misery or lack of joy is separation from God, and the one cause of separation from Him is self. Whenever we are unhappy it means that in some way or other we are looking at ourselves and thinking about ourselves, instead of communing with God. Man, according to the Scriptures, was meant to live entirely to the glory of God. He was meant to love the Lord God with all his heart, with all his soul, with all his mind and with all his strength. The whole of man was meant to glorify God. Therefore, any desire to glorify self or safeguard the interests of self is of necessity a sin, because I am looking at myself instead of looking at God and seeking His honour and glory. And it is that very thing in man which God has condemned. It is that which is under the curse of God and the wrath of God. And as I understand the teaching of the Scriptures, holiness eventually means this, deliverance from this self-centred life. Holiness, in other words, must not be thought of primarily in terms of actions, but in terms of an attitude towards self. It does not mean essentially that I do not do certain things and try to do others. There are people who never do certain things that are regarded as sinful; but they are full of pride of self. So we must look at it in terms of self and our relationship to ourselves, and we must realize again that the essence of holiness is that we should be able to say with George Müller that we have died, died completely, to this self that has caused so much ruin in our lives and experience.

261

Now, lastly, let us come to the highest level and look at the problem of self in the light of Christ. Why did the Lord Jesus Christ the Son of God ever come into this world? He came ultimately in order to deliver mankind from self. We see this selfless life so perfectly in Him. Look at His coming from the glory of heaven to the stable in Bethlehem. Why did He come? There is only one answer to that question. He did not consider Himself. That is the essence of the statement that Paul makes in Philippians 2. He was eternally the Son of God and was 'equal with God' from eternity, but He did not consider that; He did not hold on to that and to His right to the manifestation of that glory. He humbled Himself and denied Himself. There would never have been the incarnation had it not been that the Son of God put self, as it were, aside.

Then look at His selfless life here upon earth. He often said that the words He spake He did not speak of Himself, and the actions He performed He said 'are not mine; they have been given to me of the Father'. That is how I understand Paul's teaching of the self-humiliation of the cross. It means that, coming in the likeness of man, He deliberately made Himself dependent upon God; He did not consider Himself at all. He said: 'I have come to do thy will, O God,' and He was wholly dependent upon God for everything, for the words He spoke and for everything He did. The very Son of God humbled Himself to that extent. He did not live for Himself or by Himself in any measure. And the apostle's argument is, 'Let this mind be in you, which was also in Christ Jesus.'

We see it supremely of course in His death upon the cross. He was innocent and guiltless, He had never sinned or done anyone any harm, yet 'when he was reviled, (he) reviled not again; when he suffered, he threatened not; but committed himself to him that judgeth righteously' (1 Pet. 2:23). That is it. The cross of Christ is the supreme illustration, and the argument of the New Testament is this, that if we say we believe in the Lord Jesus Christ and believe that He has died for our sins, it means that our greatest desire should be to die to self. That is the final purpose of His dying, not merely that we might be forgiven, or that we might be saved from hell. Rather it was that a new people might be formed, a new humanity, a new creation, and that a new kingdom be set up, consisting of people like Himself. He is 'the firstborn among many brethren', He is the pattern. God has made us, says Paul to the Ephesians: 'We are his workmanship, created in Christ Jesus.' We are 'to be conformed to the image of his Son'. That is the language of Scripture. So that we may say that the reason for His death on the cross is that you and I might be saved and separated from that life of self. 'He died for all', says the apostle again in 2 Corinthians 5. We believe 'that if one died for all, then were all dead; and that he died for all.' Why? For this reason, says Paul: 'that they which live should not henceforth live unto themselves, but unto him which died for them, and rose again.' That is the life to which we are called. Not the life of self-defence or self-sensitivity, but such a life that, even if we are insulted, we do not retaliate; if we receive a blow on the right cheek we are ready to turn the other also; if a man sues us at the law and takes away our coat we are ready to give our cloak also; if we are compelled to go a mile, we go twain; if a man comes and asks something of me I do not say, 'This is mine'; I say rather, 'If this man is in need and I can help him, I will'. I have finished with self, I have died to myself, and my one concern now is the glory and honour of God.

That is the life to which the Lord Jesus Christ calls us and He died in order that you and I might live it. Thank God the gospel also goes on to tell us that He rose again and that He has sent into the Church, and into every one who believes on Him, the Holy Spirit with all His renovating and energizing power. If we are trying to live this kind of life in and of ourselves, we are doomed; we are damned before we start. But with the blessed promise and offer of the Spirit of God to come and dwell in us and work in us, there is hope for us. God has made this life possible. If George Müller could die to George Müller, why should not every one of us who is a Christian die in the same way to that self that is so sinful, that leads to so much misery and wretchedness and unhappiness, and which finally is such a denial of the blessed work of the Son of God upon the cross on Calvary's hill?

Chapter Twenty-nine

Love Your Enemies

W E come now to verses 43-48 in which we have the last of the six illustrations which our Lord has used to explain and display His teaching with
regard to the meaning of God's holy law for man, as contrasted with the perversion of it by the Pharisees and scribes. There is just one textual point which we
must dismiss first. You will notice that in the Revised Version there is a slight
difference in verse 44. In the Authorized Version we read: 'But I say unto you,
Love your enemies, bless them that curse you, do good to them that hate you,
and pray for them which despitefully use you, and persecute you.' In the Revised Version it is just: 'Love your enemies, and pray for them that persecute
you.' The Authorized Version is therefore fuller than the Revised Version and
contains a number of clauses which the latter lacks. The explanation of course
is simply a matter of textual criticism. There are many ancient manuscripts
containing the Gospels, and there are slight variations in them here and there,
not with regard to any vital matter of doctrine, but with regard to certain details such as this. Now many of the recognized best manuscripts do not contain
this fullness which is to be found in the Authorized Version, and that is why
these statements are absent from the Revised. However, as the same teaching is
certainly to be found elsewhere, I think it is best for us to take the teaching as
given in the Authorized Version.

Once more, the way to approach this statement is to start with the teaching of
the Pharisees and scribes. They said: 'Thou shalt love thy neighbour, and hate
thine enemy.' That was actually what they taught. The question at once arises in
one's mind, where did they find this in the Old Testament? Is there anywhere
there a statement to that effect? And the answer is, of course, 'No'. But that was
the teaching of the Pharisees and scribes and they interpreted it like this. They

264

said that the 'neighbour' meant only an Israelite; so they taught the Jews to love the Jews, but they told them at the same time to regard everybody else not only as an alien but as an enemy. Indeed they went so far as to suggest that it was their business, almost their right and their duty, to hate all such people. We know from secular history of the hatred and the bitterness which divided the ancient world. The Jews regarded all others as dogs and many Gentiles despised the Jews. There was this terrible 'middle wall of partition' dividing the world and causing intense animosity in that way. Thus there were many amongst the zealous Pharisees and scribes who thought they were honouring God by despising everybody who was not a Jew. They thought it was their business to hate their enemies. But these two statements are not found in juxtaposition anywhere in the Old Testament.

Nevertheless, there does seem to be a certain amount to be said for the teaching of the Pharisees and scribes. It is not surprising in a sense that they taught what they did and tried to claim justification for it from the Scriptures. We must say this, not by any means because we are anxious to mitigate the crimes of the Pharisees and scribes, but because this point has often caused, and still causes, considerable difficulty in the minds of many Christian people. Nowhere in the Old Testament, I repeat, do we find 'Love your neighbour and hate your enemy'; but we do find many statements that may have encouraged people to hate their enemies. Let us consider some of them.

When the Jews entered the Promised Land of Canaan, they were commanded by God, you will remember, to exterminate the Canaanites. They were literally told to exterminate them, and though they did not in fact do this, they should have done so. Then they were told that the Amorites, the Moabites and the Midianites were not to be treated with kindness. That was a specific command from God. Later we read that the memory of the Amalekites was to be blotted out from under heaven because of certain things they had done. Not only that, it was part of God's law that if any man murdered another, the relative of the murdered man was allowed to kill the murderer if he could catch him before he had entered one of the cities of refuge. That was part of the law. But perhaps the main difficulty which people encounter as they face this subject is the whole problem of the so-called imprecatory Psalms in which curses are called down upon certain people. Perhaps one of the most famous examples of this is Psalm 69 in which the Psalmist says: 'Let their eyes be darkened, that they see not; and make their loins continually to shake. Pour out thine indignation upon them, and let thy wrathful anger take hold of them. Let their habitation be desolate; and let none dwell in their tents,' and so on. There can be little question but that it was Old Testament teaching of that type and order that seemed to the Pharisees and scribes to justify their injunction to the people that, while they were to love their neighbours, they must hate their enemies.

What is the answer to this problem? Surely there is only one way of facing it and that is to regard all these various injunctions, including the imprecatory Psalms, as always being judicial and never something individual. In writing his Psalms, the Psalmist is not so much writing about himself as about the Church; and his Psalms, you will find, are concerned in every single instance, in every imprecatory Psalm, with the glory of God. As he talks about the things that are being done to him, he is speaking of things that are being done to God's people and to God's Church. It is the honour of God that he is concerned about, it is his zeal for the house of God and for the Church of God that moves him to write these things.

But perhaps it can best be put like this. If you do not accept that principle which says that all these imprecations are always judicial in character, then at once you are involved in an insoluble problem with regard to the Lord Jesus Christ Himself. Here He is telling us we are to love our enemies. Turn then to Matthew 23 and listen to Him thundering out woes upon the heads of the Pharisees. How do you reconcile the two things? How do you reconcile the exhortation to love your enemies with these woes pronounced upon the Pharisees, and all the other things that He said with respect to them? Or, indeed, let us look at it in this way. Here our Lord tells us to love our enemies, because, He says, that is exactly what God does: 'That ye may be the children of your Father which is in heaven: for he maketh his sun to rise on the evil and on the good, and sendeth rain on the just and on the unjust.' There are people who have foolishly interpreted this to mean that the love of God is universal absolutely, and that it does not matter whether a man sins or not. Everybody is going to heaven because God is love; because God is love He can never punish. But that is to deny the teaching of Scripture from beginning to end. God punished Cain, and the ancient world in the flood; He punished the cities of Sodom and Gomorrah; and He punished the children of Israel when they were recalcitrant. Then the whole teaching of the New Testament from the lips of Christ Himself is that there is to be a final judgment, that, finally, all the impenitent are going to a lake of fire, to the place where 'their worm dieth not, and the fire is not quenched'. If you do not accept this judicial principle, you must just say that there is a contradiction running right through not only the teaching of the Bible, but even through the teaching of the Lord Jesus Christ Himself; and that is an impossible position.

The way to resolve the problem, therefore, is this. We must recognize that, ultimately, there is this judicial element. While we are in this life and world,

God does indeed cause His sun to rise on the evil and on the good, He blesses people who hate Him, and He does send rain upon those who defy Him. Yes, God goes on doing that. But at the same time He announces to them that, unless they repent, they shall finally be destroyed. Therefore there is no ultimate contradiction. People like the Moabites and the Amorites and the Midianites had deliberately rejected the things of God, and God, as God and as the righteous judge Eternal, pronounced judgment upon them. It is the prerogative of God to do that. But the difficulty with the Pharisees and scribes was that they did not draw that distinction. They took this judicial principle and put it into operation in their ordinary affairs and in their daily lives. They regarded this as a justification, on their own part, for hating their enemies, hating anybody they disliked, or anybody who was offensive to them. Thus they deliberately destroyed the principle of God's law, which is this great principle of love.

Let us now consider this positively and perhaps it will throw still further light upon the matter. Our Lord, again contrasting the perverted teaching of the Pharisees and the scribes with His own teaching, says: 'But I say unto you, Love your enemies.' Then, as an illustration: 'Bless them that curse you, do good to them that hate you, and pray for them which despitefully use you, and persecute you.' Once more we are dealing with exactly the same principle as we had in verses 38-42. It is a definition of what the attitude of the Christian should be towards other people. In the previous paragraph we had that in a negative form, here we have it positively. There the position was that of a Christian man subjected to insults by others. They come and strike him a blow, and inflict other kinds of injury upon him. And all our Lord says in the previous paragraph is that you must not hit back. 'Ye have heard that it hath been said, An eye for an eye, and a tooth for a tooth: But I say unto you, That ye resist not evil.' That is the negative. Here, however, our Lord leaves that and goes on to the positive and it is, of course, the very climax of Christian living. Here He leads us on to one of the greatest and most glorious things that are to be found even in His own teaching. The principle that guides and governs our exposition, once more, is this simple and yet profound one of our attitude towards ourselves. It was the principle with which we expounded the previous paragraph. The only thing that enables a man not to hit back, to turn the other cheek and to go the second mile, to give his cloak as well as his coat when that is forcibly demanded, and to help others in desperate need, the vital thing is that a man should be dead to himself, dead to self-interest, dead to a concern about self. But our Lord goes very much further here. We are told we must positively love these people. We are even to love our enemies. It is not simply that we are not to strike back at them, but that we must be positive in our attitude towards them. Our Lord is at

267

pains to have us see that our 'neighbour' must of necessity include even our enemy.

The best way of facing this is to see it in the form of a number of principles. It is the most exalted teaching that we can find anywhere, for it ends on this note: 'Be ye therefore perfect, even as your Father which is in heaven is perfect.' It all concerns this matter of love. What we are told, therefore, is that you and I in this world of time, faced as we are by problems and difficulties and people and many things that assail us, are to behave as God behaves, are to be like Him, and to treat others as He treats them. Do this, says Christ, 'that ye may be the children of your Father which is in heaven: for he maketh his sun to rise on the evil and on the good, and sendeth rain on the just and on the unjust.' You are to be like that, He says, and to behave like that.

What does this mean? The first thing, of necessity, is that our treatment of others must never depend upon what they are, or upon what they do to us. It must be entirely controlled and governed by our view of them and of their condition. Clearly that is the principle which He enunciates. There are people who are evil, foul and unjust; nevertheless God sends rain upon them and causes the sun to shine upon them. Their crops are fructified like the crops of the good man; they have certain benefits in life, and experience what is called 'common grace'. God does not bless only the efforts of the Christian farmer; no, at the same time He blesses the efforts of the unjust, the evil, the unrighteous farmer. That is a common experience. How does He do so? The answer must be that God is not dealing with them according to what they are or according to what they do to Him. What is it, if one may ask such a question with reverence, that governs God's attitude to them? The answer is that He is governed by His own love which is absolutely disinterested. In other words, it does not depend upon anything that is in us, it is in spite of us. 'For God so loved the world, that he gave his only begotten Son, that whosoever believeth in him should not perish, but have everlasting life.' What made Him do it? Was it something loving, or lovely, or lovable in us or in the world? Was it something that stimulated the eternal heart of love? Nothing whatsoever. It was entirely and altogether in spite of us. What moved God was His own eternal heart of love unmoved by anything outside itself. It generates its own movement and activity — an utterly disinterested love.

This is a tremendously important principle, because according to our Lord that is the kind of love that we are to have, and the love that we are to manifest with respect to others. The whole secret of living this kind of life is that man should be utterly detached. He must be detached from others in the sense that his behaviour is not governed by what they do. But still more important, he should be detached from himself, for until a man is detached from himself he will never be detached from what others do to that self. As long as a man is living for himself, he is sensitive, watchful and jealous; he is envious and is therefore always reacting immediately to what others do. He is in intimate contact with them. The only way to detach yourself from what others do to you is that you first of all detach yourself from yourself. That is the principle that governs not only this paragraph but the previous one also, as we have already seen. The Christian is a man who is taken out of this present evil world. He is placed in a position apart and lives on a higher level. He belongs to a different kingdom. He is a new man, a new creature, a new creation. Because of that, he sees everything differently, and therefore reacts in a different manner. He is no longer of the world, but outside it. He is in a position of detachment. 'There', says Christ, 'you can become like God in this respect, that you will no longer be governed exclusively by what other people do to you; you will have something within you that will determine your conduct and behaviour.'

We must not linger over this; but I think that, if we examine ourselves, we shall see at a glance that one of the most tragic things about us is that our lives are so much governed by other people and by what they do to us and think about us. Try to recall a single day in your own life. Think of the unkind and cruel thoughts that have come into your mind and heart. What produced them? Somebody else! How much of our thinking and acting and behaviour is entirely governed by other people. It is one of the things that make life so wretched. You see a particular person and your spirit is upset. If you had not seen that person you would not have felt like that. Other people are controlling you. 'Now', says Christ in effect, 'you must get out of that condition. Your love must become such that you will no longer be governed and controlled by what people say. Your life must be governed by a new principle in yourself, a new principle of love.'

The moment we have that, we are enabled to see people in a different way. God looks down upon this world and sees all the sin and shame, but He sees it as something that results from the activity of Satan. There is a sense in which He sees the unjust man in a different way. He is concerned about him and about his good and welfare, and He therefore causes the sun to shine upon him and sends the rain upon him. Now we must learn to do that. We must learn to look at other people and say: 'Yes, they are doing this, that and the other to me. Why? They are doing it because they are dupes of Satan; because they are governed by the god of this world and are his helpless victims. I must not be annoyed. I see them as hell-bound sinners. I must do everything I can to save them.' That is God's way of doing it. God looked at this sinful, arrogant, foul world, and He sent His only begotten Son into it to save it because He saw its condition. What was the explanation of that? He did it for our good and our welfare. And we must learn to do this for other people. We must have a positive concern for their good. The moment we begin to think of it like this it is not so difficult to do what He asks us to do. If we know in our hearts something of this compassion for the lost and the sinful and those who are perishing, then we shall be able to do it.

Why should we do this? There is often a great deal of sentimentalizing about this. People say we should do it in order to turn them into friends. That is often the basis of pacifism. They say: 'If you are nice to people they will become nice to you.' There were people who thought that could be done even with Hitler. They thought that you simply had to speak to him across a table and he would soon become nice if you were nice to him. There are people who still think that way; but let us be realists, not sentimentalists, because we know that that is not true and it does not work. No, our action is not aimed at turning them into friends.

Others say, 'God regards and treats them not so much as they actually are, but in terms of what they are capable of becoming.' That is the modern psychological view of this matter. It governs the way in which some schoolteachers handle children. They must not punish them or exercise discipline. They must not treat children as they are, but rather as they ought to be and as they are capable of becoming, in order that they may become that. Some would like to see the same principle put into operation more widely with regard to the treatment of prisoners in prison. We must not punish, we must just be nice. We must see in that man what he can become, and we must draw it out of him. But what of the results? No; it is not because our action will somehow change these people psychologically and turn them into what we want them to be, that we are to do these things. We must do them for one reason only, not that we can ever redeem or make anything of them, but that in this way we can display to them the love of God. It is not looking for that spark of divinity in the heart which would save it, and then fanning it into a flame. No, men are born in sin and shapen in iniquity, they are not capable, in and of themselves, of becoming anything that is right. But God has so ordained it that His wonderful gospel of redemption has sometimes been conveyed to men and women in the following manner. They look at a person and ask: 'What has made that person different?' and that person says: 'I am what I am by the grace of God. It is not because I am born different, it is because God has done something to me. And what the love of God has done to me, it can do for you.'

How then may we manifest this love of God in our contact with other people? Here it is: 'Bless them that curse you', which, in more ordinary language, we put like this: reply to the bitter words with kind words. When people say harsh and unkind things we all tend to reply in kind — 'I told him; I answered him; I gave it to him'. And so we put ourselves on their level. But our rule must be kind words instead of bitter words.

Secondly: 'Do good to them that hate you', which means benevolent actions for spiteful actions. When somebody has been really spiteful and cruel to us we must not be the same to them. Rather we must respond with actions of benevolence. Though that farmer may hate God, and is unjust, and is a sinner, and has rebelled against Him, God causes His sun to shine upon him and sends the rain that is going to fructify the crops. Benevolent actions for cruel ones.

Lastly: 'Pray for them which despitefully use you, and persecute you.' In other words, when we are being cruelly persecuted by another person, we must pray for them. We must get on our knees, and talk to ourselves before we talk to God. Instead of being bitter and harsh, instead of reacting in these terms of self and in a desire to get our own back, we must remind ourselves that in everything we do we are under God, and before God. Then we must say: 'Well now; why should this person be behaving like this? What is it? Is it something in me, perchance? Why do they do it? It is because of that horrible, sinful nature, a nature which is going to lead them to hell.' Then we should go on thinking, until we see them in such a way that we become sorry for them, until we see them as going to their terrible doom, and at last become so sorry for them that we have no time to be sorry for ourselves, until we are so sorry for them, indeed, that we begin to pray for them.

This is the way in which we should test ourselves. Do you pray for people who persecute you and who use you despitefully? Do you ask God to have mercy and pity upon them, and not to punish them? Do you ask God to save their souls and open their eyes before it is too late? Do you feel a great concern? It is that which brought Christ to earth and sent Him to the cross. He was so concerned about us that He did not think about Himself. And we are to treat other people like that.

In order that we may be quite clear as to what this means and involves we must understand the difference between loving and liking. Christ said: 'Love your enemies', not 'Like your enemies'. Now liking is something which is more natural than loving. We are not called upon to like everybody. We cannot do so. But we can be commanded to love. It is ridiculous to command anyone to like another person. It depends upon the physical constitution, temperament and a thousand and one other things. That does not matter. What does matter is that we pray for the man whom we do not like. That is not liking but loving him.

People have stumbled at this. 'Do you mean to say that it is right to love and not to like?' they ask. I do. What God commands is that we should love a man and treat him as if we do like him. Love is much more than feeling or sentiment. Love in the New Testament is very practical — 'For this is the love of God, that we keep his commandments.' Love is active. If, therefore, we find we do not like certain people, we need not be worried by that, so long as we are treating them as if we did like them. That is loving, and it is the teaching of our Lord everywhere. We have some glorious examples of it in the New Testament. You remember the parable of the Good Samaritan told by our Lord in response to the question 'who is my neighbour?' The Jews traditionally hated the Samaritans and were their bitter enemies. However our Lord tells us in the parable that when the Jew was attacked by thieves and robbers on the road between Jericho and Jerusalem, several Jews passed by and did not help him. But the Samaritan, the traditional enemy, went across the road and cared for him and did everything for him. That is loving our neighbour and our enemy. Who is my neighbour? Any man who is in need, any man who is down through sin or anything else. We must help him, whether he is a Jew or a Samaritan. Love your neighbour, even if it means loving your enemy. 'Do good to them that hate you.' And our Lord, of course, not only taught it, but He did it. There we see Him dying upon the cross, and what has He to say about those men who condemned Him to that, and who drove in the cruel nails? These are the blessed words that come from His holy lips: 'Father, forgive them; for they know not what they do.'

It also became the teaching and the practice of the apostles everywhere in the New Testament. How foolish to say that the Sermon on the Mount does not apply to Christians now but refers to the future, when the kingdom comes. No, it is for us now. Paul says: 'If thine enemy hunger, feed him; if he thirst, give him drink', which is exactly the same teaching. It is everywhere. And the apostles not only taught it; they lived it. Look at that wonderful man, Stephen, being stoned to death by cruel, foolish enemies. These were his last words: 'Lord, lay not this sin to their charge.' He has reached the level of his Master; he is loving, as God in heaven loves this sinful world. And, thank God, the saints throughout the centuries have done the same. They have manifested the same, glorious, wonderful spirit.

Are we like that? This teaching is for us. We are meant to love our enemies and to do good to them that hate us and to pray for those that despitefully use and malign us; we are meant to be like this. I go further; we can be like this. The Holy Spirit, the Spirit of love and joy and peace, is given to us, so that, if we are not like this, we are without excuse and we are doing great dishonour to our great and gracious Lord.

But I have a word of comfort for you. For unless I am greatly mistaken, every person confronted by these things feels at this moment condemned. God knows I feel condemned; but I have a word of comfort at this point. I believe in a God who 'maketh his sun to rise on the evil and on the good, and sendeth rain on the just and on the unjust'. But the God whom I know has done more than that; He has sent His only begotten Son to the cruel cross of Calvary that I might be saved. I fail; we all fail. But, 'If we confess our sins, he is faithful and just to forgive us our sins, and to cleanse us from all unrighteousness.' Do not feel that you are not a Christian if you are not living this kind of life fully. But, above all, having received this comfort, do not presume upon it, but rather feel that it breaks your heart still more because you are not like Christ, and not as you ought to be. If only we all might begin to love like this, and every Christian in the world were loving in this way! If we did, revival would soon come, and who knows what might happen even in the whole world.

'Love your enemies, bless them that curse you, do good to them that hate you, and pray for them which despitefully use you, and persecute you,' and then you will be like your Father who is in heaven.

Chapter Thirty

What Do Ye More than Others?

I N our study of this paragraph concerning our attitude towards our enemies, let us now concentrate in particular upon one phrase, 'What do ye more than others?', which is to be found in verse 47: 'And if ye salute your brethren only, what do ye more than others? do not even the publicans so?' Having given His detailed exposition of how His people should treat and regard their enemies, our Lord, as it were, brings the entire section and the whole teaching to a grand and glorious climax. All along, as we have seen, He has not been concerned so much about the details of their behaviour; rather, His desire has been that they should understand and grasp who they are and how they are to live. And here He sums it all up in this amazing statement that comes right at the very end: 'Be ye therefore perfect, even as your Father which is in heaven is perfect.' That is to be the quality of life we are to live.

There is no attitude with regard to the Sermon on the Mount which is quite so ridiculous as that which regards it as if it were but an ethical programme, a kind of social scheme. We have already considered that, but we must return to it, because it seems to me that this paragraph alone is enough to explode once and for ever any such false notion with respect to this great Sermon. This one paragraph contains what we might call the most essential characteristic of the New Testament gospel in its entirety, and that is the paradox which runs right through it. The gospel of Jesus Christ, though I object to much modern use of the term, is essentially paradoxical; there is an apparent contradiction in it from the beginning to the very end. We find that here, in the very essence of this message.

The paradoxical character of the gospel was first stated by that ancient man, Simeon, when he had the Infant Jesus in his arms. He said, 'This child is set for the fall and rising again of many in Israel.' There is the paradox. At one and the same time He is set for the fall and for the rising again. The gospel always does these two things, and unless our view of it contains these two elements, it is not a true one. Here is a perfect illustration of it. Have we not felt that as we have been working our way through this Sermon? Is there anything known to us that is more discouraging than the Sermon on the Mount? Take this passage from verse 17 to the end of this fifth chapter — these detailed illustrations given by our Lord as to how we are to live. Is there anything more discouraging? We feel that the Ten Commandments, the ordinary moral standards of decency, are difficult enough; but look at these statements about not even looking with lust, about going the second mile and throwing in the cloak together with the coat, and so on. There is nothing more discouraging than the Sermon on the Mount; it seems to throw us right out, and to damn our every effort before we have started. It seems utterly impossible. But at the same time do we know of anything more encouraging than the Sermon on the Mount? Do we know of anything that pays us a greater compliment? The very fact that we are commanded to do these things carries with it an implicit assertion that it is possible. This is what we are supposed to be doing; and there is a suggestion, therefore, that this is what we can do. It is discouraging and encouraging at the same time; it is set for the fall and rising again. And nothing is more vital than that we should always be holding those two aspects firmly in our minds.

The trouble with that foolish, so-called materialistic view of the Sermon on the Mount was that it did not see either side of the Sermon clearly. It reduced both of them. In the first place it reduced the demands. Those who held it said: 'The Sermon on the Mount is something practical, something that we can do.' Well, the answer to such people is that what we are asked to do is to be as perfect as God, as perfect in this matter of loving our enemies as He is. And the moment we face the actual demands, we see that they are quite impossible to the natural man. But these people have never seen that. What they have done, of course, is just to isolate certain statements and say: 'This is all we have to do.' They do not believe in fighting under any circumstances. They say, 'We are to love our enemies'; so they just become passive resisters. But that is not the whole of the Sermon on the Mount. The Sermon on the Mount includes this injunction: 'Be ye therefore perfect, even as your Father which is in heaven is perfect.' They have never faced the stringency of the demand.

At the same time they have never seen the other side, which is that we are children of God, and are unusual and exceptional. They have never seen the glory and grandeur and the uniqueness of the Christian position. They have always thought of the Christian as just a man who makes a greater moral effort than anyone else and disciplines himself. In other words, most of the trouble experienced by such people with this Sermon on the Mount, as indeed with the whole of the New Testament teaching, is that they never truly understand or grasp what it means to be a Christian. That is the fundamental trouble. People who are in difficulty about salvation in Christ are in this difficulty because they have never understood what a Christian really is.

In this phrase we have, once more, one of those perfect definitions as to what constitutes a Christian. The dual aspect is displayed; discouragement and encouragement; the fall and the rising again. Here it is: 'What do ye more than others?' Now here there is real value in Dr. Moffatt's translation, 'If you only salute your friends, what is special about that?' That is the key to it all. We find this thought not only here but also in verse 20. Our Lord started by saying: 'I say unto you, That except your righteousness shall exceed the righteousness of the scribes and Pharisees. . . .' The Pharisees and scribes had a high and exalted standard, but the righteousness in view here is more than their righteousness; there is something special about it.

Let us consider this great principle in the form of three subsidiary principles. *The Christian is essentially a unique and special kind of person.* This is something which can never be emphasized sufficiently. There is nothing more tragic than the failure on the part of many professing Christians to realize the uniqueness and the special character of a Christian. He is a man who can never be explained in natural terms. The very essence of the Christian's position is that he is an enigma. There is something unusual, something inexplicable and something elusive about him from the standpoint of the natural man. He is something quite distinct and apart.

Now our Lord tells us here that this special characteristic, this uniqueness, is twofold. First of all it is a uniqueness that separates him from everybody who is not a Christian. 'If ye love them which love you, what reward have ye? do not even the publicans the same?' They can do that, but you are different. 'And if ye salute your brethren only, what do ye more than others? do not even the publicans so?' (So reads the Authorized Version; the Revised Version has 'Do not even the Gentiles the same?') The Christian, you see, is a man who is different from others. He does what other people do, yes; but he does more than they do. That is what our Lord has been emphasizing all along. Anyone can go the first mile, but it is the Christian who goes the second. He is always doing more than anybody else. This is obviously tremendously important. The Christian at once, and by primary definition, is a man who stands out in society, and you cannot explain him in terms of the natural man.

However, we must go beyond that. The Christian, by our Lord's definition, and it is repeated elsewhere right through the New Testament, is not only a man who is doing more than others; he does what others cannot do. That is not to detract from the capacity and ability of the natural man; but the Christian is a man who can do things which nobody else can do. We can emphasize that still more by putting it like this. The Christian is a man who is above, and goes beyond, the natural man at his very best and highest. Our Lord showed that here in His attitude towards the standard of morality and behaviour of the Pharisees and scribes. They were the teachers of the people, and they exhorted everybody else. He says to those who listened: 'You must go beyond all that.' And we must go beyond it also. There are many people in the world who are not Christian but who are very moral and highly ethical, men whose word is their bond, and who are scrupulous and honest, just and upright. You never find them doing a shady thing to anybody; but they are not Christian, and they say so. They do not believe on the Lord Jesus Christ and may have rejected the whole of the New Testament teaching with scorn. But they are absolutely straightforward, honest and true. As someone once said of the late Lord Morley, who spelled the name of God with a small 'g', you could ring a gold coin on his conscience. Now the Christian, by definition here, is a man who is capable of doing something that the best natural man cannot do. He goes beyond and does more than that; he exceeds. He is separate from all others, and not only from the worst among others, but from the very best and highest among them. He strives in his daily life to show this capacity of the Christian to love his enemies and to do good to them that hate him, and to pray for them which despitefully use him and persecute him.

The second aspect of this uniqueness of the Christian is that he is not only unlike others, but *he is meant to be positively like God and like Christ.* 'That ye may be the children of your Father which is in heaven. . . . Be ye therefore perfect, even as your Father which is in heaven is perfect.' This is stupendous, but it is the essential definition of the Christian. The Christian is meant to be like God, he is meant to manifest in his daily life in this cruel world something of the characteristics of God Himself. He is meant to live as the Lord Jesus Christ lived, to follow that pattern and to imitate that example. Not only will he be unlike others. He is meant to be like Christ. The question which we must ask ourselves, then, if we want to know for certain whether we are truly Christian or not, is this: Is there that about me which cannot be explained in natural terms? Is there something special and unique about me and my life which is never to be found in the non-Christian? There are many people who think of the Christian as a man who believes in God, a man who is morally good, just, and upright and all the rest. But that does not make a man a Christian. There are people who deny Christ, Mohammedans for example, who believe in God and who are highly ethical, just and straight in their dealings. They have a code of morality and they observe it. There are many who are in that position. They tell you that they believe in God, and they are highly ethical and moral; but they are not Christian, they specifically deny Christ. There are many men, like the late Mr. Gandhi and his followers, who are undoubtedly believers in God, and again, if you look at their lives and actions, there are scarcely any grounds you can find for criticism; but they are not Christians. They said they were not Christians; they still say that they are not Christians. Therefore we deduce that the characteristic of the Christian is just this quality (I will put it in the form of a question). As I examine my activities, and look at my life in detail, can I claim for it that there is something about it which cannot be explained in ordinary terms and which can only be explained in terms of my relationship to the Lord Jesus Christ? Is there anything special about it? Is there this unique characteristic, this 'plus', this 'more than'? That is the question.

Let us now turn to the second principle, which will elucidate the first. Let us look at some of the ways or respects in which the Christian does manifest this uniqueness and special quality. He does so, of course, in the whole of his life because, according to the New Testament, he is a new creation. 'Old things are passed away; behold, all things are become new,' so he is going to be altogether different. First of all, the Christian is different from the natural man, and goes beyond the natural man in his thinking. Take, for example, his attitude towards the law, morality and behaviour. The natural man may observe the law, but he never goes beyond it. The characteristic of the Christian is that he is still more concerned with the spirit than he is with the letter. Your moral, ethical man wants to live within the law, but he does not consider the spirit, the ultimate essence of the law. Or put it in a different way, the natural man gives a grudging obedience, the Christian man delights 'in the law of God after the inward man'.

Or look at it in terms of morality. The natural man's attitude towards morality is generally negative. His concern is that he should not do certain things. He does not want to be dishonest, unjust or immoral. The Christian's attitude towards morality is always positive; he hungers and thirsts after a positive righteousness like that of God Himself.

Or again, consider it in terms of sin. The natural man always thinks of sin in terms of actions, things that are done or not done. The Christian is interested in the heart. Did not our Lord emphasize that in this Sermon, when He said, in effect: 'As long as you are not guilty of physical adultery you think you are all right. But I ask, What about your heart? What about your thoughts?' That is the view of the Christian man. Not actions only, he goes beyond that to the heart.

What about the attitude of these two men towards themselves? The natural man is prepared to admit that perhaps he is not entirely perfect. He says: 'You know I am not a complete saint, there are certain defects in my character.' But you will never find a man who is not a Christian feeling that he is all wrong, that he is vile. He is never 'poor in spirit', he never 'mourns' because of his sinfulness. He never sees himself as a hell-deserving sinner. He never says, 'Were it not for the death of Christ on the cross, I would have no hope of seeing God.' He will never say with Charles Wesley, 'Vile and full of sin I am'. He regards that as an insult, because he claims that he has always tried to live a good life. He therefore resents that and does not go as far as that in his self-condemnation.

Then what about the attitude of these two men towards other people? Your natural man may regard others with tolerance; he may bring himself to be sorry for them and say that we must not be too hard on others. But the Christian goes beyond that. He sees them as sinners, and as the dupes of Satan; he sees them as the terrible victims of sin. He does not merely see them as men for whom allowances are to be made; he sees them as dominated by 'the god of this world' and held captive by Satan in all his various forms. He goes beyond the other.

The same is true of their respective views of God. The natural man thinks of God primarily as Someone who is to be obeyed, and Someone whom he fears. That is not the essential view of the Christian. The Christian loves God because he has come to know Him as Father. He does not think of God as One whose law is grievous and hard. He knows He is a holy yet loving God, and he enters into a new relationship with Him. He goes beyond everybody in his relationship to God, and desires to love Him with all his heart, and mind, and soul, and strength, and his neighbour as himself.

Then in the matter of living, the way in which the Christian does everything is different. The great motive to Christian living is love. Paul puts it in a remarkable way when he says: 'Love is the fulfilling of the law.' The difference between your naturally good, moral man and the Christian is that the Christian has an element of grace in his actions; he is an artist, while the other man acts mechanically. What is the difference between the Christian and the natural man in doing good? Well, the natural man often does a great deal of good in this world, but I hope I am not being unfair to him when I say that he generally likes to keep a record of it. He is rather subtle sometimes in the indirect way in which he refers to it, but he is always conscious of it, and keeps an account of it. One hand always knows what the other hand is doing. Not only that, there is always a limit to what he does. He generally gives out of his superabundance. It is the Christian who gives without counting the cost, who gives sacrificially and in such a way that each hand does not know what the other is doing.

But look at these two men as they react to what happens to them in this life and world. What about the trials and tribulations that come, as they must come, such as sickness or war? The good, natural, moral man often faces these

279

things with real dignity. He is always a gentleman. Yes; by exercising an iron willpower, he faces it with a stoical kind of resignation. I do not want to detract from his qualities, but he is always negative, he is just holding himself in check. He does not complain, he is just bottling it up as it were. Does he ever know what it is to rejoice in tribulation? The Christian does. The Christian rejoices in tribulations for he sees a hidden meaning in them. He knows that 'all things work together for good to them that love God', and that God allows things to happen at times in order to perfect him. He can wrestle with the storm, he can rejoice in the midst of his tribulation. The other man never rises to that. There is something special about the Christian. The other man just maintains his calm and dignity. You see the difference?

Our Lord puts it here finally in the matter of injuries and injustice. How does your natural man behave when he suffers these? Again, he may face it with this calm and iron will. He just manages not to hit back and retaliate. He merely ignores it all, or cynically dismisses the person who misunderstands him. But the Christian deliberately takes up the cross, and holds to Christ's injunction which tells him to 'deny himself, and take up his cross'. 'He who will come after me', says Christ in effect, 'is certain to get persecution, and to suffer injuries. But take up the cross.' And here He tells us how we are to do these things. He says: 'Whosoever shall smite thee on thy right cheek, turn to him the other also. And if any man will sue thee at the law, and take away thy coat, let him have thy cloke also. And whosoever shall compel thee to go a mile, go with him twain. Give to him that asketh thee, and from him that would borrow of thee turn not thou away.' And he is to do it all gladly and willingly. That is the Christian. There is something special about him, he is always going further than anybody else.

The same is true of our attitude towards our neighbour, even if he is our enemy. The natural man can sometimes be passive. He can decide not to strike back and hit back, but not easily. Once more, there has never been a natural man who has been able to love his enemy, to do good to them that hate him, to bless them that curse him, and to pray for them that despitefully use him and persecute him. I do not want to be unfair in what I am saying. I have known men who call themselves pacifists and who would not hit back, or kill; but I have sometimes known bitterness in their hearts against men who have been in the Forces and against certain prime ministers, which was simply terrible. Loving your enemy does not just mean that you do not fight and kill. It means that you are positively loving that enemy and praying for him and for his salvation. I have known men who would not fight, but who do not love even their brethren. It is the Christian alone who can rise to this. Your natural ethics and morality can make a passive resister; but the Christian is a man who positively loves his enemy, and goes out of his way to do good to them that hate him, and to pray for them that use him despitefully and malign him.

But finally let us look at these two men as they die. The natural man, again, may die with dignity. He may die on his deathbed, or on the field of battle, without a grumble, or without complaining. He maintains the same general attitude to death as he had to life, and he goes out with stoical calm and resignation. That is not the Christian's way of facing death. The Christian is one who should be able to face death as Paul faced it, and he should be able to say: 'To me to live is Christ, and to die is gain', and: 'having a desire to depart, and to be with Christ; which is far better.' He is entering into his eternal home, going into the presence of God. Even more, the Christian not only dies gloriously and triumphantly; he knows where he is going. He is not only not afraid; there is a sense of anticipation. There is always something special about him.

What is it that thus makes the Christian a special person? What is it that accounts for this uniqueness? What makes him do more than others? It is his whole outlook on sin. The Christian man has seen himself as utterly hopeless and condemned; he has seen himself as a man who is utterly guilty before God and who has no claim whatsoever on His love. He has seen himself as an enemy of God and an outsider. And then he has seen and understood something about the free grace of God in Jesus Christ. He has seen God sending His only begotten Son into the world, and not only that, sending Him even to the death of the cross for him, the rebel, the vile and guilty sinner. God did not turn His back on him, He went beyond that. The Christian knows that all this happened for him, and it has changed his whole attitude towards God and to his fellowmen. He has been forgiven when he did not deserve it. What right then has he, not to forgive his enemy?

Not only that, he has an entirely new outlook towards life in this world. He comes to see that it is only an antechamber to real life and that he himself is a sojourner and a pilgrim. Like all the men of faith described in Hebrews 11 he is seeking that 'city which hath foundations'. He says: 'Here have we no continuing city, but we seek one to come.' That is his whole view of life, and it changes everything. He has also a hope of glory. The Christian is a man who believes he is going to look into the face of Christ. And when that great morning comes, when he looks into the face of One who endured the cruel cross for him in spite of his vileness, he does not want to remember, as he looks into those eyes, that he refused to forgive someone while he was here on earth, or that he did not love that other person, but despised and hated him and did everything he could against him. He does not want to be reminded of things like that. So, knowing all this, he loves his enemies and does good to them that hate him, because he is conscious of what has been done for him, what is coming to him, and of the glory that remains. His whole outlook has been changed; and this has happened because he himself has been changed.

What is a Christian? A Christian is not a man who reads the Sermon on the Mount and says: 'Now I am going to live like that, I am going to follow Christ and emulate His example. There is the life I am going to live and I shall do so by my great willpower.' Nothing of the kind. I will tell you what a Christian is. He is one who has become a child of God and is in a unique relationship to God. That is what makes him 'special'. 'What do ye more than others?' He should be special, you should be special, because you are a special person. You say breeding counts. If this is so, what is the breeding of a Christian? It is this, he has been born again, he has been born spiritually and he is a child of God. Did you notice the way our Lord puts it? 'I say unto you, Love your enemies, bless them that curse you, do good to them that hate you, and pray for them which despitefully use you, and persecute you.' Why? 'That you may be like God'? No: 'That ye may be the children' — and not even of God — 'ye may be the children of your Father which is in heaven'. God has become Father to the Christian. He is not the Father of the non-Christian; He is God to them and nothing else, the great Law-Giver. But to the Christian, God is Father. Then, again, our Lord does not say, 'Be ye therefore perfect, even as God in heaven is perfect.' No, thank God, but 'Be ye therefore perfect, even as your Father which is in heaven is perfect.' If God is your Father you must be special, you cannot help it. If the divine nature is in you, and has entered into you through the Holy Spirit, you cannot be like anybody else; you must be different. And that is what we are told about the Christian everywhere in the Bible, that Christ dwells in his heart richly through the Holy Ghost. The Holy Spirit is in him, filling him, working His mighty power in the depths of his personality, teaching him His will. 'It is God which worketh in you both to will and to do.' And, above all, the love of God has been shed abroad in his heart through and by the Holy Spirit. He is bound to be special, he must be unique, he cannot help it.

How can a man who has never had the love of God shed abroad in his heart love his enemy and do all these other things? It is impossible. He cannot do it; and furthermore he does not do it. There never has been a man outside Christ who can do this. The Sermon is not an exorbitant demand of this kind. When you first read it, it discourages you and casts you down. But then it reminds you that you are a child of your Father in heaven, that you are not just left to yourself but that Christ has come to dwell in you and to take up His abode in you. You are but a branch of the Vine. Power and life and sustenance are there; you are simply to bear the fruit.

I end, then, with this searching question. It is the most profound question a man can ever face in this life and world. Is there anything special about you? I am not asking whether you are living a good, moral, upright life. I am not asking whether you say your prayers, or whether you go to church regularly. I am asking none of these things. There are people who do all that and still are not Christians. If that is all, what do ye more than others, what is there special about you? Is there anything of this special quality about you? Is there something of your Father about you? It is a fact that children sometimes do not resemble their parents very closely. People look at them and say: 'Yes, there is something of his father there after all,' or 'I see something of the mother; not very much, but there is something.' Is there just that much of God about you? That is the test. If God is your Father, somewhere or another, in some form or other, the family likeness will be there, the traces of your Parentage will inevitably appear. What is there special about you? God grant that as we examine ourselves we may discover something of the uniqueness and the separateness that not only divides us from others, but which proclaims that we are children of our Father which is in heaven.

VOLUME TWO

Preface

A S this volume consists of a continuation of the Studies in the Sermon on the Mount begun in Volume I, it does not call for any special word of introduction. All that was said in the Preface to that volume applies here and, from my standpoint, it is important that it should be borne in mind.

Each chapter is a sermon in and of itself and yet each can be understood only in the light of the whole.

The fact that there are thirty sermons in this volume, as in the previous one, is quite accidental and not planned nor contrived. It has never been my custom to divide up a portion of Scripture into a number of parts and then to issue a syllabus announcing what will be done each week. That seems to me to limit the freedom of the act of preaching, quite apart from the fact that in actual practice I sometimes find that I succeed in doing only about half of what I had planned and purposed. In other words expository preaching must always be *preaching* and not merely mechanical exposition.

It was never my intention to preach sixty sermons on the Sermon on the Mount; I just went on from Sunday to Sunday and this turned out to be the result. I can but hope and pray that God will bless it.

I would again thank all whom I mentioned in Volume I for their invaluable help and encouragement.

Westminster Chapel,   D. M. LLOYD-JONES
Buckingham Gate, London   *March 1960*

Chapter One

Living the Righteous Life

OUR consideration of this Sermon on the Mount began with an analysis and division of its contents.[1] We saw that here in chapter 6 we come to a new section. The first section (vv. 3-12) contains the Beatitudes, a description of the Christian as he is. In the next section (vv. 13-16), we find this Christian man, who has thus been described, reacting to the world and the world reacting to him. The third (vv. 17-48) deals with the relationship of the Christian to the law of God. It gives a positive exposition of the law and contrasts it with the false teaching of the Pharisees and scribes. It ends with the great exhortation in the closing verse: 'Be ye therefore perfect, even as your Father which is in heaven is perfect.'

We come now to quite a new section, and it runs right through this sixth chapter. Here we have what we may well call a picture of the Christian living his life in this world in the presence of God, in active submission to God, and in entire dependence upon Him. Read this sixth chapter and you will find that this reference to God the Father keeps on recurring. We have been looking at this Christian man who has been told something of his characteristics, who has been told how he is to behave in society, and who has been reminded of what it is that God expects of him and demands from him. Here we have a picture of him going on to live that life in this world; and the greatest thing that is ever emphasized is that he does it all in the presence of God. That is something of which he should constantly be reminded. Or, to put it in another way, this section presents a picture of the children in relationship to their Father as they wend their way on this pilgrimage called life.

The chapter reviews our life as a whole, and it considers it under two main

---

1. See pp. 17-19 in this volume.

aspects. This is something very wonderful, for in the last analysis the life of the Christian in this world has two sides, and both of them are covered here. The first one is dealt with in verses 1 to 18; the second from verse 19 to the end of the chapter. The first is what we may call our religious life, the culture and nurture of the soul, our piety, our worship, the whole religious aspect of our life, and everything that concerns our direct relationship to God. But of course that is not the only element in the life of the Christian in this world. He is reminded by it that he is not of this world, that he is a child of God and a citizen of a kingdom that cannot be seen. He is but a journeyman, a sojourner, a traveller in this world. He is not a worldling and does not belong to this world as other people do; he is in this unique relationship to God. He is walking with Him. Nevertheless he is in this world, and though he is not of it any longer this world keeps doing things to him, and he is in many senses subject to it. And, after all, he does have to walk through it. So that the second picture is that of the Christian in his relationship to life in general, not so much as a purely religious being now, but as a man who is subject to 'the slings and arrows of outrageous fortune', a man who is concerned about food and drink, clothing and shelter, who may have a family and children to bring up, and who therefore is subject to what is called in the Scriptures 'the cares of this world'.

Those are the two great divisions of this chapter, the directly religious part of the Christian life, and the mundane. Both these aspects are taken up by our Lord and dealt with in considerable detail. In other words, it is vital for the Christian that he should be absolutely clear about both these matters, and he needs instruction about both. There is no greater fallacy than to imagine that the moment a man is converted and becomes a Christian, all his problems are solved and all his difficulties vanish. The Christian life is full of difficulties, full of pitfalls and snares. That is why we need the Scriptures. They would have been unnecessary but for that. These detailed instructions given by our Lord and in the Epistles would be unnecessary were it not for the fact that the life of the Christian in this world, as John Bunyan and others have been very careful to point out in their great Christian classics, is a life beset by problems. There are pitfalls associated with our practice of the Christian life, and associated also with our living our lives in this world together with other people. You will find as you analyse your own experience, and still more as you read the biographies of God's people, that many have got into difficulties, and many have for the time being found themselves in great misery and unhappiness and have lost their experience of joy and happiness in the Christian life, because of their neglect of one aspect or the other. There are some people who are wrong in their religious life as we shall see; and there are others who seem to be all right in that respect, but who, because they are tempted in a very subtle manner on the more practical side, tend to go wrong in that way. So we have to face both these matters. Here, in the teaching of our Lord, they are dealt with right down to the minutest detail.

We may as well realize at the outset that this chapter 6 is again a very searching one; indeed, we can go further and say that it is a very painful one. I sometimes think that it is one of the most uncomfortable chapters to read in the entire Scriptures. It probes and examines and holds a mirror up before us, and it will not allow us to escape. There is no chapter which is more calculated to promote self-humbling and humiliation than this particular one. But thank God for it. The Christian should always be anxious to know himself. No other man truly wants to know himself. The natural man thinks he knows himself, and thereby reveals his basic trouble. He evades self-examination because to know one's self is ultimately the most painful piece of knowledge that a man can ever acquire. And here is a chapter that brings us face-to-face with ourselves, and enables us to see ourselves exactly as we are. But, I repeat, thank God for it, because it is only the man who has truly seen himself for what he is who is likely to fly to Christ, and to seek to be filled with the Spirit of God who alone can burn out of him the vestiges of self and everything that tends to mar his Christian life and living.

Here, as in the previous chapter, the teaching is given, in a sense, partly by way of contrast with that of the Pharisees. You remember there was a kind of general introduction to this when our Lord said: 'Except your righteousness shall exceed the righteousness of the scribes and Pharisees, ye shall in no case enter into the kingdom of heaven.' There we were looking at and contrasting the teaching of the Pharisees and scribes, and the teaching that should govern the life of the Christian. Here the emphasis is not so much on teaching as on practical living, including piety, and our whole religious demeanour and behaviour.

As we come to this first section, we find that verse 1 is an introduction to the message of verses 2 to 18. It is indeed astounding to notice the perfect arrangement of this Sermon. Those who are musical, and are interested in the analysis of symphonies, will see that there is something still more wonderful here. The theme is stated, then comes the analysis, after which the particular themes and sections — the various 'leit motifs', so called — are taken up, until eventually all is drawn together and gathered up in a final statement. Our Lord employs a similar method here. In the first verse He lays down the general principle governing the religious life of the Christian. Having done that, He goes on to give us three illustrations of that principle, in the matters of almsgiving, praying and fasting. There, ultimately, is the whole of one's religious life and practice. If we analyse the religious life of a man we find that it can be divided into these three sections, and into these three sections only: the way I do my almsgiving, the nature of my prayer life and contact with God, and the way in which I should mortify the flesh. Again we must point out that the three are but illustrations. Our Lord illustrates what He lays down as a general principle exactly as we found Him doing in His exposition of the law in chapter 5.

The fundamental principle is laid down in the first verse. Here there is no doubt at all but that the Revised Version is, at this point, superior to the Authorized Version which reads like this: 'Take heed that ye do not your alms before men.' It should be: 'Take heed that ye do not your righteousness (or, if you prefer it, your piety) before men, to be seen of them: else ye have no reward with your Father which is in heaven.' This again is just a question of a textual difference in the manuscripts. Without doubt the second is the better version, and all good commentators are agreed in saying that this word should be 'righteousness' rather than 'alms'. Almsgiving is one of the particular illustrations, whereas in this first verse our Lord is concerned to lay down a general principle. The word 'righteousness' governs the three aspects of righteous living. We look first at piety itself and then come to consider the various manifestations of piety. The general principle is this: 'Take heed that ye do not your righteousness before men, to be seen of them: else ye have no reward with your Father which is in heaven.' Let us consider this in the form of a number of subsidiary principles.

The first of these is this — *the delicate nature of the Christian life.* The Christian life is always a matter of balance and poise. It is a life that gives the impression of being self-contradictory, because it seems to be dealing at the same time with two things which are mutually exclusive. We read the Sermon on the Mount and we come across something like this: 'Let your light so shine before men, that they may see your good works, and glorify your Father which is in heaven.' Then we read, 'Take heed that ye do not your righteousness before men, to be seen of them: else ye have no reward with your Father which is in heaven.' And a man looking at that says, 'Well, what am I to do? If I am to do all these things in secret, if I am not to be seen of men, if I am to pray in my closet having locked the door, if I am to anoint my face and wash myself, thus giving the appearance that I am not fasting, how can men know I am doing these things, and how can they possibly see this light which is shining in me?'

But, of course, that is obviously only a superficial contradiction. You notice how the first statement puts it: 'Let your light so shine before men, that they may see your good works, and glorify your Father which is in heaven.' In other words there is no contradiction here, but we are called to do both these things at one and the same time. The Christian is to live in such a way that men looking at him, and seeing the quality of his life, will glorify God. He must always remember at the same time that he is not to do things in order that he may attract attention to himself. He must not desire to be seen of men, he is never to be self-conscious. But, clearly, this balance is a fine and delicate one; so often we tend to go to one extreme or the other. Christian people tend either to be guilty of great ostentation or else to become monks and hermits. As you look at the long story of the Christian Church throughout the centuries you will find this great conflict has been going on. They have either been ostentatious, or else they have been so afraid of self and self-glorification that they have segregated themselves from the world. But here we are called to avoid both extremes. It is a delicate life, it is a sensitive life; but if we approach it in the right way, and under the leading of the Holy Spirit, the balance can be maintained. Of course, if we just take these things as rules which we have to put into operation we shall go wrong on the one side or the other. But if we realize that what matters is the great principle, the spirit, then we shall be saved from the error on the right hand and on the left. Let us never forget this, the Christian at one and the same time is to be attracting attention to himself, and yet not attracting attention to himself. That will be seen more clearly as we proceed.

The second subsidiary principle is that *the ultimate choice is always the choice between pleasing self and pleasing God.* That may sound very elementary, and yet it seems necessary that we should emphasize it for this reason. 'Take heed that ye do not your alms before men, to be seen of them.' 'Surely, then,' we may think, 'the choice is between pleasing men and pleasing God.' I suggest that is not the choice: the ultimate choice is the choice between pleasing self and pleasing God, and that is where the subtlety of this matter comes in. Ultimately our only reason for pleasing men around us is that we may please ourselves. Our real desire is not to please others as such; we want to please them because we know that, if we do, they will think better of us. In other words, we are pleasing ourselves and are merely concerned about self-gratification. That is where the insidious character of sin is seen. What appears to be so selfless may be just a very subtle form of selfishness. According to our Lord it comes to this: man by nature desires the praise of man more than the praise of God. In desiring the praise of man, what he is really concerned about is his good opinion of himself. In the last analysis it always comes to this, we are either pleasing ourselves or else we are pleasing God. It is a very solemnizing thought, but the moment we begin to analyse ourselves and see the motives of our conduct we shall agree that it comes to that.

That brings us to the next subsidiary principle which perhaps is the most important of all. *The supreme matter in this life and world for all of us is to realize our relationship to God.* One almost apologizes for making such a statement, and yet I suggest that the greatest cause of all our failures is that we constantly forget our relationship to God. Our Lord puts it like this. We should realize that our supreme object in life should be to please God, to please Him only, and to please Him always and in everything. If that is our aim we cannot go wrong. Here, of course, we see the outstanding characteristic of the life of our Lord Jesus Christ. Is there anything that stands out more clearly in His life? He lived entirely for God. He even said that the words that He spoke were not of Himself and that the works He did were the works which the Father had given Him to do. His whole life was given to glorifying God. He never thought of Himself; He did nothing for Himself, He did not obtrude Himself. What we are told of Him is this, 'A bruised reed shall he not break, and smoking flax shall he not quench.' He did not raise His voice aloft. In a sense He seems to be there unseen and trying to hide Himself. We are told about Him that 'he could not be hid', but He seemed to be trying always to do this. There was a complete absence of ostentation. He lived entirely and always and only for the glory of God. He said constantly in various ways: 'I seek not My own honour but the honour of Him who has sent Me.' And He put it negatively in this way: 'How can ye believe, which receive honour one of another and seek not the honour that cometh from God only?' 'That is your trouble', He says in effect. 'You are so concerned about man. If only you had a single eye to the glory and honour of God, then all would be well.'

The second thing which we have to remember in this connection is that we are always in the presence of God. We are always in His sight. He sees our every action, indeed our every thought. In other words, if you believe in having texts placed before you in a prominent position on your desk or on the wall of your house, there is no better one than this: 'Thou God seest me'. He is everywhere. 'Take heed that ye do not your righteousness before men.' Why? 'Else ye have no reward with your Father which is in heaven.' He sees it all. He knows your heart; other people do not. You can deceive them, and you can persuade them that you are quite selfless; but God knows your heart. 'Ye', said our Lord to the Pharisees one afternoon, 'ye are they which justify yourselves before men; but God knoweth your hearts; for that which is highly esteemed amongst men is abomination in the sight of God.' Now this is obviously a fundamental principle for the whole of our life. I sometimes feel that there is no better way of living, and trying to live, the holy and sanctified life than just to be constantly reminding ourselves of that. When we wake up in the morning we should immediately remind ourselves and recollect that we are in the presence of God. It is not a bad thing to say to ourselves before we go any further: 'Throughout the whole of this day, everything I do, and say, and attempt, and think, and imagine, is going to be done under the eye of God. He is going to be with me; He sees everything; He knows everything. There is nothing I can do or attempt but God is fully aware of it all. "Thou God seest me". It would revolutionize our lives if we always did that.

In a sense the many books which have been written on the devotional life all concentrate on this. You remember that famous little book of Brother Lawrence's, *The Practice of the Presence of God.* I am not recommending it, but I am recommending the principle behind it. We have to learn, if we want to live this life fully, that we have to discipline ourselves and speak to ourselves. This is the fundamental thing, the most serious thing of all, that we are always in the presence of God. He sees everything and knows everything, and we can never escape from His sight. Those men who wrote the Psalms knew all about it, and there are instances of where men have cried out in desperation: '"Whither shall I flee from thy presence!" I cannot get away from You. You are there "if I make my bed in hell. . . . If I take the wings of the morning, and dwell in the uttermost parts of the sea. . . ." I cannot get away from You.' If we only remembered that, hypocrisy would vanish, self-adulation and all we are guilty of by way of feeling ourselves above others, would immediately disappear. It is a cardinal principle that we cannot get away from God. In this matter of the ultimate choice between self and God, we must always remember that God knows all about us. 'All things are naked and opened unto the eyes of him with whom we have to do.' He knows the thoughts and intents of the heart. And He can divide to the separating of the joint and marrow and the very soul and spirit. There is nothing hid from His sight. We have to start with that postulate.

If we were all to practise this it would be revolutionary. I am quite certain a revival would start at once. What a difference it would make to church life, and the life of every individual. Think of all the pretence and sham, and all that is unworthy in us all. If only we realized that God is looking at all, and is aware of it all, and is recording it all! That is the teaching of the Scriptures, and that its method of preaching holiness — not offering people some marvellous experience which solves all problems. No, it is just realizing that we are always there in the presence of God. For the man who starts with a true realization of that is soon to be seen flying to Christ and His cross, and pleading to be filled with the Holy Spirit.

The next subsidiary principle concerns rewards. This whole question of rewards seems to trouble people, and yet our Lord continually makes statements like those in verses 1 and 4. Here He indicates that it is quite right to seek the reward which God gives. He says, 'Otherwise ye have no reward of your Father which is in heaven.' If you do the right thing, then 'thy Father which seeth in secret himself shall reward thee openly.' There was a teaching (we do not hear so much of it now) towards the beginning of the century which used to say that one should live the Christian life for its own sake, and not for the reward. It was such a good thing in and of itself that one should not be animated by any motive such as desire for heaven or fear of hell. We should be disinterested and altruistic. The teaching was often put in the form of a story, an illustration. A poor man was walking along an Eastern road one day with a bucket of water in one hand and a bucket of fire in the other. Somebody asked him what he was going to do with these buckets, and he replied that he was going to burn heaven with the bucket of fire and drown hell with the bucket of water — he was not interested in either. But that is not the New Testament teaching. The New Testament teaching would have us see that it is a good thing to desire to see God. That is the *summum bonum*. 'Blessed are the pure in heart: for they shall see God.' It is a right and legitimate desire, it is a holy ambition. We are told this about our Lord Himself. 'Who for the joy that was set before him endured the cross, despising the shame' (Heb. 12:2). And we are told about Moses that he did what he did because he had his eye on 'the recompence of the reward'. He was farsighted. Why did the people whose lives we read of in Hebrews 11 live the life they did? The answer is this — they saw certain things afar off, they were seeking for 'a city which hath foundations', they had their eye on that ultimate objective.

Concern about rewards is legitimate and is even encouraged by the New Testament. The New Testament teaches us that there will be a 'judgment of rewards'. There are those who shall be beaten with few stripes, and there are those who shall be beaten with many stripes. Every man's work shall be judged whether it be of wood or hay or stubble or silver or gold. All our works are going to be judged. 'We must all appear before the judgment seat of Christ; that every one may receive the things done in his body, according to that he hath done, whether it be good or bad.' We *should* be interested therefore in this matter of rewards. There is nothing wrong in it as long as the desire is the reward of holiness, the reward of being with God. The second thing about rewards is this. There is no reward from God for those who seek it from men. This is a terrifying thought but it is an absolute statement. 'Take heed that ye do not your alms before men, to be seen of them: otherwise ye have no reward of your Father which is in heaven.' If you have your reward from men in that particular respect, you will have nothing whatever from God. Let me put it like this very bluntly. If I am concerned as I preach this gospel as to what people think of my preaching, well that is all that I will get out of it, and nothing from God. It is an absolute. If you are seeking a reward from men you will get it, but that is all you will get. Work through your religious life, think of all the good you have done in the past, in the light of that pronouncement. How much remains to come to you from God? It is a terrifying thought.

Those are the principles with regard to the general statement. Let us now consider briefly what our Lord has to say about this particular matter with respect to almsgiving. It follows of necessity from the principles we have been laying down. He says there is a wrong and a right way of almsgiving. Almsgiving, of course, means helping people, giving a helping hand in case of need, giving money, time, anything you like which is going to help people.

The wrong way to do this is to announce it. 'Therefore when thou doest thine alms, do not sound a trumpet before thee.' Of course they did not actually do that; our Lord is painting a picture. In effect they are engaging a trumpeter to go before them to say: 'Look at what this man is doing.' The wrong way to do these things is to proclaim them, and to draw attention to them. We could spend much time showing the subtle ways in which this can be done. Let me give one illustration. I remember a lady who felt called of God to start a certain work, and she felt called to do this on what is called 'faith lines'. There was to be no collection or appeals for funds. She decided to inaugurate this work by having a preaching service and I was given the privilege of preaching at the service. Halfway through the meeting, when the announcements came, this good lady for ten minutes told that congregation of people how this work was to be done entirely on faith lines, how no collection was to be taken, how she did not believe in collections or asking for money and so on. I thought it was the most effective appeal for funds that I had ever heard! I am not suggesting she was dishonest; I am quite sure she was not, but she was very apprehensive. And in a spirit of fearfulness we may likewise be doing this kind of thing quite unconsciously. There is a way of saying that you do not announce these things which just means that you are announcing them. O how subtle it is! You know the sort of man who says, 'Of course I do not believe in announcing the number of converts when I take a mission. But, after all, the Lord must be glorified, and if people do not know the numbers, well, how can they give glory to God?' Or, 'I do not like these long reports in my anniversary meeting, but if God is to be glorified how can people do that unless . . ?' You see the subtlety. It is not always that there is an obvious trumpeter. But when we truly come to examine our hearts we find that there are very subtle ways in which this selfsame thing can be done. Well, that is the wrong way and the result of that is this: 'Verily I say unto you, They have their reward.' People praise and say, 'How wonderful, how marvellous; terrific, isn't it?' They get their reward, they get their praise. They get their names in the paper; articles are written about them; there is a great deal of talk about them; people write their obituary notices; they get it all. Poor men, that is all they will get; they will get nothing from God. They receive their reward. If that is what they wanted they have got it; and how they are to be pitied. How we ought to pray for them, how we ought to feel sorry for them.

What is the right way? The right way, says our Lord, is this. 'When thou doest alms, let not thy left hand know what thy right hand doeth: that thine alms may be in secret: and thy Father which seeth in secret himself shall reward thee openly.' In other words, Do not announce to others in any shape or form what you are doing. That is obvious. But this is less obvious: Do not even announce it to yourself. That is difficult. It is not so difficult for some people not to announce it to others. I think that any man with even an element of decency in him rather despises a man who advertises himself. He says it is pathetic, it is so sad to see men advertising themselves. Yes, but what is so difficult is not to pride yourself because you are not like that. You can despise that kind of thing, you can dismiss it. Yes, but if that leads you now to say to yourself. 'I thank God I am not like that', immediately you become a Pharisee. That is what the Pharisee said, 'Thank God I am not like that, and especially like this publican.' Note that our Lord does not stop at saying you must not sound a trumpet before you and announce it to the world; you do not even announce it to yourself. Your left hand must not know what your right hand is doing. In other words, having done it in secret you do not take your little book and put down: 'Well, I have done that. Of course I haven't told anybody else that I have done it.' But you put an extra mark in a special column where exceptional merit is recorded. In effect our Lord said: 'Don't keep these books at all; don't keep spiritual ledgers; don't keep profit and loss accounts in your life; don't write a diary in this sense; just forget all about it. Do things as you are moved by God and led by the Holy Spirit, and then forget all about them.' How is this to be done? There is only one answer, and that is that we should have such a love for God that we have no time to think about ourselves. We shall never get rid of self by concentrating on self. The only hope is to be so consumed by love that we have no time to think about ourselves. In other words, if we want to implement this teaching we must look at Christ dying on Calvary's Hill, and think of His life and all He endured and suffered, and as we look at Him realize what He has done for us.

And what is the result of all this? It is glorious. This is how our Lord puts it. He says, 'You must not keep the account. God does that. He sees everything and He records it all, and do you know what He will do? He will reward you openly.' What utter fools we are to keep our own accounts, not realizing that if we do so we shall get no reward from God. But if we just forget all about it and do everything to please Him, we shall find that God will have an account. Nothing we have done will be forgotten, our smallest act will be remembered. Do you remember what He said in Matthew 25? 'When I was in prison you visited me, when I was thirsty you gave me drink.' And they will say, 'When did we do all this? We are not aware we have done this.' 'Of course you have done it,' He will reply, 'it is there in the Book.' He keeps the books. We must leave the account to Him. 'You know,' He says, 'you did it all in secret; but I will reward you openly. I may not be rewarding you openly in this world, but as certainly as you are alive, I will reward you openly at the Great Day when the secrets of all men shall be disclosed, when the great Book shall be opened, when the final pronouncement shall be made before the whole world. Every detail of all you have done to the glory of God will be announced and proclaimed and you will be given the credit and the honour and the glory. I will reward you openly, and I will say, "Well done, thou good and faithful servant; . . . enter thou into the joy of thy lord."'

Let us keep our eyes upon the ultimate, let us remember that we are always in the presence and sight of God, and let us live only to please Him.

Chapter Two

How to Pray

IN verses 5-8 we come to the second example taken by our Lord to illustrate His teaching concerning piety or the conduct of the religious life. This, as we have seen, is the theme which He considers in the first eighteen verses of this chapter. 'Take heed', He says in general, 'that ye do not your righteousness before men, to be seen of them: else ye have no reward with your Father which is in heaven.' Here is His second illustration of this. Following the question of almsgiving comes the whole question of praying to God, our communion and our fellowship with God. Here, again, we shall find that the same general characteristic which our Lord has already described is, alas, far too much in evidence. This portion of Scripture, I sometimes think, is one of the most searching and humbling in the entire realm of Scripture. But we can read these verses in such a way as really to miss their entire point and teaching, and certainly without coming under condemnation. The tendency always when reading this is just to regard it as an exposure of the Pharisees, a denunciation of the obvious hypocrite. We read, and we think of the kind of ostentatious person who obviously is calling attention to himself, as the Pharisees did in this matter. We therefore regard it as just an exposure of this blatant hypocrisy without any relevance to ourselves. But that is to miss the whole point of the teaching here, which is our Lord's devastating exposure of the terrible effects of sin upon the human soul, and especially sin in the form of self and of pride. That is the teaching.

Sin, He shows us here, is something which follows us all the way, even into the very presence of God. Sin is not merely something that tends to assail and afflict us when we are far away from God, in the far country as it were. Sin is something so terrible, according to our Lord's exposure of it, that it will not only follow us to the gates of heaven, but — if it were possible — into heaven itself. Indeed, is not that the Scripture teaching with regard to the origin of sin? Sin is not something which began on earth. Before man fell there had been a previous Fall. Satan was a perfect, bright, angelic being dwelling in the heavenlies; and he had fallen before ever man fell. That is the essence of the teaching of our Lord in these verses. It is a terrible exposure of the horrible nature of sin. Nothing is quite so fallacious as to think of sin only in terms of actions; and as long as we think of sin only in terms of things actually done, we fail to understand it. The essence of the biblical teaching on sin is that it is essentially a disposition. It is a state of heart. I suppose we can sum it up by saying that sin is ultimately self-worship and self-adulation; and our Lord shows (what to me is an alarming and terrifying thing) that this tendency on our part to self-adulation is something that follows us even into the very presence of God. It sometimes produces this result; that even when we try to persuade ourselves that we are worshipping God, we are actually worshipping ourselves and doing nothing more.

That is the terrible nature of His teaching at this point. This thing that has entered into our very nature and constitution as human beings, is something that is so polluting our whole being that when man is engaged in his highest form of activity he still has a battle to wage with it. It has always been agreed, I think, that the highest picture that you can ever have of man is to look at him on his knees waiting upon God. That is the highest achievement of man, it is his noblest activity. Man is never greater than when he is there in communion and contact with God. Now, according to our Lord, sin is something which affects us so profoundly that even at that point it is with us and assailing us. Indeed, we must surely agree on the basis of New Testament teaching that it is only there we really begin to understand sin.

We tend to think of sin as we see it in its rags and in the gutters of life. We look at a drunkard, poor fellow, and we say: There is sin; that is sin. But that is not the essence of sin. To have a real picture and a true understanding of it, you must look at some great saint, some unusually devout and devoted man. Look at him there upon his knees in the very presence of God. Even there self is intruding itself, and the temptation is for him to think about himself, to think pleasantly and pleasurably about himself, and really to be worshipping himself rather than God. That, not the other, is the true picture of sin. The other is sin, of course, but there you do not see it at its acme; you do not see it in its essence. Or, to put it in another form, if you really want to understand something about the nature of Satan and his activities, the thing to do is not to go to the dregs or the gutters of life; if you really want to know something about Satan, go away to that wilderness where our Lord spent forty days and forty nights. That is the true picture of Satan where you see him tempting the very Son of God.

All that comes out in this statement. Sin is something that follows us even into the very presence of God.

Before we come to our analysis of this, I would make one other preliminary observation which seems to me to be quite inevitable. If this picture does not persuade us of our own utter sinfulness, of our hopelessness as well as our helplessness, if it does not make us see our need of the grace of God in the matter of salvation, and the necessity of forgiveness, rebirth and a new nature, then I know of nothing that ever can persuade us of it. Here we see a mighty argument for the New Testament doctrine about the absolute necessity of being born again, because sin is a matter of disposition, something that is so profound and so vitally a part of us that it even accompanies us into the presence of God. But follow that argument beyond this life and world, beyond death and the grave, and contemplate yourself in the presence of God in eternity for ever and ever. Is not the rebirth something which is a bare essential? Here, then, in these instructions about piety and the conduct of the religious life, we have implicit in almost every statement this ultimate New Testament doctrine of regeneration and the nature of the new man in Christ Jesus. Indeed we can go on even beyond that and say that even if we are born again, and even if we have received a new life and a new nature, we still need these instructions. This is our Lord's instruction to Christian people, not to the non-Christian. It is His warning to those who have been born again; even they have to be careful lest in their prayers and devotions they become guilty of this hypocrisy of the Pharisees.

First, then, let us take this subject in general before coming to a consideration of what is commonly called 'the Lord's Prayer'. We are looking merely at what we might call an introduction to prayer as our Lord teaches it in these verses, and I think that once more the best way of approaching the subject is to divide it into two sections. There is a false way of praying and there is a true way of praying. Our Lord deals with them both.

The trouble with the false way is that its very approach is wrong. Its essential fault is that it is concentrating on itself. It is the concentrating of attention on the one who is praying rather than on the One to whom the prayer is offered. That is the trouble, and our Lord shows that here in a very graphic and striking way. He says: 'When thou prayest, thou shalt not be as the hypocrites are: for they love to pray standing in the synagogues and in the corners of the streets, that they may be seen of men.' They stand in the synagogue in a prominent position, they stand forward. You remember our Lord's parable of the Pharisee and the publican who went into the temple to pray. He makes exactly the same point there. He tells us that the Pharisee stood as far forward as he could in the most prominent place, and there he prayed. The publican, on the other hand, was so ashamed and full of contrition that 'standing afar off' he could not even so much as lift up his face to heaven, but just cried out, 'God be merciful to me a sinner.' In the same way our Lord says here that the Pharisees stand in the synagogues and in the corners of the street, in the most prominent position, and pray in order that they may be seen of men. 'Verily I say unto you, They have their reward.'

According to our Lord, the reason for their praying in the street corners is something like this. A man on his way to the temple to pray is anxious to give the impression that he is such a devout soul that he cannot even wait until he gets to the temple. So he stands and prays at the street corner. For the same reason, when he reaches the temple, he goes forward to the most prominent position possible. Now what is important for us is to extract the principle, so I put that as the first picture.

The second is put in the words: 'When ye pray, use not vain repetitions, as the heathen do: for they think that they shall be heard for their much speaking.' If we take these two pictures together, we shall find that there are two main errors underlying this whole approach to God in prayer. The first is that my interest, if I am like the Pharisee, is in myself as the one who is praying. The second is that I feel that the efficacy of my prayer depends upon my much praying or upon my particular manner of prayer.

Let us look at these separately. The first trouble, then, is this danger of being interested in myself as one who prays. This can show itself in many different ways. The first and the basic trouble is that such a person is anxious to be known amongst others as one who prays. That is the very beginning of it. He is anxious to have a reputation as a man of prayer, anxious and ambitious in that respect. That in itself is wrong. One should not be interested in oneself, as our Lord goes on to show. So if there is any suspicion of interest in ourselves as praying people we are already wrong, and that condition will vitiate everything we are proposing to do.

The next step in this process is that it becomes a positive and actual desire to be seen praying by others. That, in turn, leads to this, that we do things which will ensure that others do see us. This is a most subtle matter. We saw in the matter of almsgiving that it is not always blatant and obvious. There is a type of person who parades himself and puts himself in a prominent position and is always calling attention to himself. But there are also subtle ways of doing this selfsame thing. Let me give an illustration of that.

There was a man who wrote quite a well-known book on the Sermon on the Mount in the early days of the present century. In dealing with this section he points out this subtle danger and how it comes to a man without his knowing it — this demonstrative tendency even in the matter of prayer. And of course it is the obvious comment to make. But I remember that when I was reading the biography of this commentator, I came across this interesting statement. The biographer, who was anxious to show the saintliness of his subject, illustrated it like this. Nothing was quite so characteristic of him, he said, as the way in which, when he was walking from one room to another, he would suddenly in the corridor fall down on his knees and pray. Then he would get up and go on his way again. That was to the biographer a proof of the saintliness and devoutness of this particular man.

I do not think I need explain what I mean. The trouble with the Pharisees was that they tried to give the impression that they could not wait until they got to the temple; they had to stand where they were at the street corners to pray, at once, blatant and obvious, Yes, but if you fall down on your knees in a corridor in a house it is rather wonderful! I want to show on the basis of our Lord's teaching that that man would have been a greater saint if he had not dropped on to his knees, but rather had offered up his prayer to God as he was walking along that corridor. It would have been an equally sincere prayer, and nobody would have seen it. How subtle this is! The very man who warns us against the thing is guilty of it himself. 'Let every man examine himself.'

Another very subtle form which it takes is this. A man may say to himself, 'Of course I am not going to drop on my knees in a corridor as I go from one room to another; I am not going to stand at the corners of the street; I am not going to parade myself in the temple or in the synagogue; I am going to pray always in secret. Our Lord said, "Enter into thy closet, and . . . shut thy door." My prayer is always going to be the secret prayer.' Yes, but it is possible for a man to pray in secret in such a way that everybody knows he is praying in secret, because he gives the impression that by spending so much time there he is a great man of prayer. I am not romancing. Would to God I were. Do you not know something about this? When you are in the secret closet with the door shut, what are the thoughts that come to you, thoughts about other people who know you are there, and what you are doing and so forth? We must get rid of the notion that this only works in the blatant and obvious way of the Pharisees of old. It is the same thing, however subtle or hidden the form.

Of course we must not be overscrupulous about these matters, but the danger is so subtle that we must always bear it in mind. I remember people talking about a man who attended certain conferences and remarking with great admiration that they noticed that he always slipped away after the meetings, climbed a high rock away from everybody else, and then got down on his knees and prayed. Well, that good man certainly did that, and it is not for me to judge him. But I wonder whether in that great effort of climbing there was not a little admixture of this very thing our Lord here denounces. Anything that is unusual ultimately calls attention to itself. If I go out of my way, metaphorically, *not* to stand at the street corners, but become famous as the man of the lonely rock, I may be calling attention to myself. That is the trouble; the negative becomes the positive in a very subtle manner before we realize what we are doing.

But let us follow it a little further. Another form which this takes is the terrible sin of praying in public in a manner which suggests a desire to have an effect upon the people present rather than to approach God with reverence and godly fear. I am not sure, for I have frequently debated this matter with myself, and therefore speak with some hesitancy, whether all this does not apply to the so-called 'beautiful prayers' that people are said to offer. I would question myself whether prayers should ever be beautiful. I mean that I am not happy about anyone who pays attention to the form of the prayer. I admit it is a highly debatable question. I commend it to your consideration. There are people who say that anything that is offered to God should be beautiful, and that therefore you should be careful about the phrasing and the diction and the cadence of your sentences. Nothing, they say, can be too beautiful to offer to God. I admit there is a certain force in that argument. But it does seem to me that it is entirely negatived by the consideration that prayer is ultimately a talk, a conversation, a communion with my Father; and one does not address one whom one loves in this perfect, polished manner, paying attention to the phrases and the words and all the rest. There is surely something essentially spontaneous about true communion and fellowship.

This is why I have never believed in the printing of so-called pulpit prayers. Of course it ultimately rests on very much larger issues into which we cannot now enter. I am simply raising the question for your consideration. I would suggest, however, that the controlling principle is that the whole being of the person praying should be intent upon God and should be centred upon Him, and that he should be oblivious of all other things. Far from desiring people to thank us for our so-called beautiful prayers, we should rather be troubled when they do so. Public prayer should be such that the people who are praying silently and the one who is uttering the words should be no longer conscious of each other, but should be carried on the wings of prayer into the very presence of God. I think if you compare and contrast the eighteenth and nineteenth centuries in this respect you will see what I mean. We have not many of the recorded prayers of the great evangelists of the eighteenth century; but we have many of the popular prayers of the so-called pulpit giants of the nineteenth century. I am not at all sure but that it was not just there that the change took place in the life of the Christian Church, which has led to the present lack of spirituality and the present state of the Christian Church in general. The Church became polished and polite and dignified, and the supposed worshippers were unconsciously occupied with themselves and forgetful that they were in communion with the living God. It is a very subtle thing.

The second trouble in connection with this wrong approach arises when we tend to concentrate on the form of our prayers, or on the amount or length of time spent in prayer. 'When ye pray', He says, 'use not vain repetitions, as the heathen do: for they think that they shall be heard for their much speaking.' You are familiar with what is meant by this term 'vain repetitions'. It is to be seen still in practice in many Eastern countries where they have prayer wheels. The same tendency is shown also in Roman Catholicism in the counting of beads. But again it comes to us in a much more subtle way. There are people who often attach great importance to having a set time for prayer. In a sense it is a good thing to have a set time for prayer; but if our concern is primarily to pray at the set time rather than to pray, we may as well not pray. We can get so easily into the habit of following a routine and forgetting what we are really doing. As the Mohammedan at certain hours of the day falls down on his knees, so many people who have their set time for prayer rush to God at this particular time, and often lose their tempers in doing so should anyone hinder them. They must get on their knees at this particular hour. Regarded objectively, how foolish it seems! But again, let every man examine himself.

It is not only the question of the set time, however; the subtle danger shows itself in yet another way. Great saints, for instance, have always spent much time in prayer and in the presence of God. Therefore we tend to think that the way to be a saint is to spend much time in prayer and in the presence of God. But the important point about the great saint is not that he spent much time in prayer. He did not keep his eye on the clock. He knew he was in the presence of God, he entered into eternity as it were. Prayer was his life, he could not live without it. He was not concerned about remembering the length of time. The moment we begin to do that, it becomes mechanical and we have ruined everything.

What our Lord says about the matter is: 'Verily I say unto you, They have their reward.' What did they desire? They wanted the praise of men, and they had it. And similarly today they are spoken of as great men of prayer, they are spoken of as those who offered wonderful, beautiful prayers. Yes, they get all that. But, poor souls, it is all they will get. 'Verily I say unto you, They have their reward.' Their obituary notices will refer to them as wonderful people in this matter of prayer, but, believe me, the poor heartbroken soul who cannot frame a sentence, but who has cried out in agony to God, has reached God in a way, and will have a reward, the other will never know. 'They have their reward.' The praise of man is what they wanted, and that is what they get.

Let us turn from them to the true way. There is a right way of praying, and again the whole secret is in the matter of the approach. That is the essence of our Lord's teaching. 'Thou, when thou prayest, enter into thy closet, and when thou hast shut thy door, pray to thy Father which is in secret; and thy Father which seeth in secret shall reward thee openly. But when ye pray, use not vain repetitions, as the heathen do: for they think that they shall be heard for their much speaking. Be not ye therefore like unto them: for your Father knoweth what things ye have need of, before ye ask him.' What does it mean? Stated in terms of the essential principle it is this: the one thing that is important when we pray anywhere is that we must realize we are approaching God. That is the one thing that matters. It is simply this question of 'recollection', as it is called. If only we would realize that we are approaching God everything else would be all right.

But we need a little more detailed instruction, and fortunately our Lord gives it. He divides it up like this. First of all there is the process of exclusion. To make sure that I realize I am approaching God I have to exclude certain things. I have to enter into that closet. 'When thou prayest, enter into thy closet, and when thou hast shut thy door, pray to thy Father which is in secret.' Now what does this mean?

There are some people who would fondly persuade themselves that this is just a prohibition of all prayer meetings. They say, 'I do not go to prayer meetings, I pray in secret.' But it is not a prohibition of prayer meetings. It is not a prohibition of prayer in public, for that is taught of God and commended in the Scriptures. There are prayer meetings recorded in the Scriptures, and they are of the very essence and life of the Church. That is not what He is prohibiting. The principle is that there are certain things which we have to shut out whether we are praying in public or whether we are praying in secret. Here are some of them. You shut out and forget other people. Then you shut out and forget yourself. That is what is meant by entering into thy closet. You can enter into that closet when you are walking alone in a busy street, or going from one room to another in a house. You enter into that closet when you are in communion with God and nobody knows what you are doing. But if it is an actual public act of prayer the same thing can be done. I am referring to myself and to all preachers. What I try to do when I enter a pulpit is to forget the congregation in a certain sense. I am not praying to them or addressing them; I am not speaking to them. I am speaking to God, I am leading in prayer to God, so I have to shut out and forget people. Yes; and having done that, I shut out and forget myself. That is what our Lord tells us to do. There is no value in my entering into the secret chamber and locking the door if the whole time I am full of self and thinking about myself, and am priding myself on my prayer. I might as well be standing at the street corner. No; I have to exclude myself as well as other people; my heart has to be open entirely and only to God. I say with the Psalmist: 'Unite my heart to fear thy name. I will praise thee, O Lord my God, with all my heart.' This is of the very essence of this matter of prayer. When we pray we must deliberately remind ourselves that we are going to talk to God. Therefore other people, and self also, must be excluded and locked out.

The next step is realization. After exclusion, realization. Realize what? Well, we must realize that we are in the presence of God. What does that mean? It means realization of something of who God is and what God is. Before we begin to utter words we always ought to do this. We should say to ourselves: 'I am now entering into the audience chamber of that God, the almighty, the absolute, the eternal and great God with all His power and His might and majesty, that God who is a consuming fire, that God who is "light and in whom is no darkness at all", that utter, absolute Holy God. That is what I am doing.' We must recollect and realize all that. But above all, our Lord insists that we should realize that, in addition to that, He is our Father. 'When thou hast shut thy door, pray to thy Father which is in secret; and thy Father which seeth in secret shall reward thee openly.' The relationship is that of Father and child, 'for your Father knoweth what things ye have need of, before ye ask him.' O that we realized this! If only we realized that this almighty God is our Father through the Lord Jesus Christ. If only we realized that we are indeed His children and that whenever we pray it is like a child going to its father! He knows all about us; He knows our every need before we tell Him. As the father cares for the child and looks at the child, and is concerned about the child, and anticipates the needs of the child, so is God with respect to all those who are in Christ Jesus. He desires to bless us very much more than we desire to be blessed. He has a view of us, He has a plan and a programme for us, He has an ambition for us, I say it with reverence, which transcends our highest thought and imagination. We must remember that He is our Father. The great, the holy, the almighty God is our Father. He cares for us. He has counted the very hairs of our head. He has said that nothing can happen to us apart from Him.

Then we must remember what Paul puts so gloriously in Ephesians 3: He 'is able to do exceeding abundantly above all that we ask or think.' That is the true notion of prayer, says Christ. You do not go and just turn a wheel. You do not just count the beads. You do not say: 'I must spend hours in prayer, I have decided to do it and I must do it.' You do not say that the way to get a blessing is to spend whole nights in prayer, and that because people will not do so they cannot expect blessing. We must get rid of this mathematical notion of prayer. What we have to do first of all is to realize who God is, what He is, and our relationship to Him.

Finally we must have confidence. We must come with the simple confidence of a child. We need a childlike faith. We need this assurance that God is truly our Father, and therefore we must rigidly exclude any idea that we must go on repeating our petitions because it is our repetition that is going to produce the blessing. God likes us to show our keenness, our anxiety and our desire over a thing. He tells us to 'hunger and thirst after righteousness' and to seek it; He tells us to 'pray and not to faint'; we are told to 'pray without ceasing'. Yes; but that does not mean mechanical repetitions; it does not mean believing that we shall be heard for our 'much speaking'. It does not mean that at all. It means that when I pray I know that God is my Father, and that He delights to bless me, and that He is much more ready to give than I am to receive and that He is always concerned about my welfare. I must get rid of this thought that God is standing between me and my desires and that which is best for me. I must see God as my Father who has purchased my ultimate good in Christ, and is waiting to bless me with His own fullness in Christ Jesus.

So, we exclude, we realize, and then in confidence we make our requests known to God, knowing He knows all about it before we begin to speak. As a father delights that his child should come repeatedly to ask for a thing rather than that the child should say, 'Father has always done this', as the father likes the child to keep on coming because he likes the personal contact, so God desires us to come into His presence. But we must not come with doubtful minds; we must know that God is much more ready to give than we are to receive. The result will be that 'thy Father which seeth in secret shall reward thee openly.' O the blessings that are stored at the right hand of God for God's children. Shame on us for being paupers when we were meant to be princes; shame on us for so often harbouring unworthy, wrong thoughts of God in this matter. It is all due to fear, and because we lack this simplicity, this faith, this confidence, this knowledge of God as our Father. If we but have that, the blessings of God will begin to fall upon us, and may be so overwhelming that with D. L. Moody we shall feel that they are almost more than our physical frames can bear, and cry out with him, saying, 'Stop, God.'

God is able to do for us exceeding abundantly above all that we can ask or think. Let us believe that and then go to Him in simple confidence.

Chapter Three

Fasting

W E turn now to consider the third illustration given by our Lord of the way in which we should conduct ourselves in this matter of personal righteousness. In chapters 4 and 5 we shall return to our detailed study of His teaching concerning prayer, especially as it is given in what is commonly called 'The Lord's Prayer'. But before doing that, it seems to me that we should have these three particular illustrations of personal righteousness clearly in our minds.

You remember that in this section of the Sermon on the Mount our Lord is talking about the question of personal righteousness. He has already described the Christian in his general attitude to life — his thought life, if you like. Here, however, we are looking more at the Christian's conduct. Our Lord's general statement is this: 'Take heed that ye do not your righteousness (or your piety) before men, to be seen of them: else ye have no reward with your Father which is in heaven.'

We have already pointed out how our Lord shows that our Christian lives can be divided up into three main sections. There is that aspect or portion of our lives in which we do good to others — almsgiving. Then there is the question of our intimate personal relationship with God — our prayer life. The third is the one we shall look at now as we consider verses 16-18 — the question of personal discipline in one's spiritual life, considered especially in terms of fasting. It is important, however, that we should realize that what our Lord says here about fasting is equally applicable to the whole question of discipline in our spiritual lives. I have my contacts with men and women; I have my contact with God; and I have also my contact with myself. Or we can put this threefold division in terms of what I do with others, what I do with God, what I do with myself. The last is the subject which our Lord takes up in this short paragraph.

We cannot approach this statement about fasting without making a few general preliminary remarks. I think we must all be struck at once by the fact that there is constantly a need of variation of emphasis, not only in our preaching of the gospel, but also in our whole approach to the gospel and in our thinking about it. Though truth is one and always the same, nevertheless, because of its many-sided character, and because human nature is what it is as the result of sin, particular eras in the history of the Church need a special emphasis on particular aspects of truth. This principle is found in the Bible itself. There are those who would have us believe that there is a great quarrel in the Old Testament as between the priests and the prophets, those who emphasized works and those who emphasized faith. The truth is, of course, that there is no quarrel as such, there is no contradiction. There were people who gave a false emphasis to particular aspects of truth, and they needed correction. The point I am making is that at a time when the priestly emphasis has been much in vogue, what is needed especially is the emphasis on the prophetic element. Or, at other times, when the emphasis has been excessively on the prophetic, then it is time to redress the balance and to remind people of, and to emphasize, the priestly.

You find the same thing occurring in the New Testament. There is no ultimate contradiction between James and Paul. It is a particularly superficial view of the New Testament which says that these two men contradict each other in their teaching. They do not; but each one, because of certain circumstances, was led by the Holy Spirit to put a certain emphasis upon the truth. James is evidently dealing with people who tended to say that, as long as you say you believe on the Lord Jesus Christ, all is well, and you need not worry about anything else. The only thing to say to such people is: 'Faith without works is dead.' But if you are dealing with people who are always drawing attention to what they do, and who put their stress upon works, then you have to emphasize to them this great aspect and element of faith.

I am reminded of all that in this context because, particularly for Evangelicals, this whole question of fasting has almost disappeared from our lives and even out of the field of our consideration. How often and to what extent have we thought about it? What place does it occupy in our whole view of the Christian life and of the discipline of the Christian life? I suggest that the truth probably is that we have very rarely thought of it at all. I wonder whether we have ever fasted? I wonder whether it has even occurred to us that we ought to be considering the question of fasting? The fact is, is it not, that this whole subject seems to have dropped right out of our lives, and right out of our whole Christian thinking.

There is no difficulty in tracing the cause of that. It is obviously a reaction against the Catholic teaching, so-called, in all its various forms. The Catholic teaching, whether it be Anglo-, or Roman-, or anything else, always does give

311

great prominence to this question of fasting. And Evangelicalism is not only something in and of itself; it is always, in addition, a reaction against Catholic teaching. The tendency of a reaction is always to go too far. In this instance, because the false Catholic emphasis on fasting is disliked, we tend to swing to the other extreme and to leave fasting out of account altogether. Is not that why the vast majority of us have never seriously even considered this question of fasting? But I have observed certain indications that it is a subject which is gradually coming back into consideration amongst Evangelicals. I cannot say that I have noticed it hitherto in the evangelical religious literature of Great Britain; but certainly in evangelical literature that comes from across the Atlantic there is increased prominence being given to this whole question of fasting. As men and women are beginning to consider the days and the times through which we are passing with a new seriousness, and as many are beginning to look for revival and reawakening, the question of fasting has become more and more important. You will probably find that our attention is going to be directed increasingly to this subject, so it is a good thing for us to face it together. Quite apart from that, however, here it is in the Sermon on the Mount; and we have no right to pick and choose with Scripture. We must take the Sermon on the Mount as it is, and here is the question of fasting confronting us. So we must consider it.

Our Lord at this point was primarily concerned with only one aspect of the subject, and that was the tendency to do these things in order to be seen of men. He was concerned about this exhibitionist aspect, which we must therefore of necessity consider. But I feel that, in view of the neglect of the subject amongst us, it is right and profitable for us also to consider it in a more general manner, before we come to this particular point which our Lord emphasizes.

Let us approach it in this way. What is really the place of fasting in the Christian life? Where does it come in according to the teaching of the Bible? The answer is roughly like this. It is something that is taught in the Old Testament. Under the law of Moses the children of Israel were commanded to fast once a year, and this was binding upon that nation and people for ever. Further on we read that, owing to certain national emergencies, the people themselves appointed certain additional fasts. But the only fast that was directly commanded by God was that one great, annual fast. When we come to New Testament times, we find that the Pharisees fasted twice in the week. They were never commanded to do so by God, but they did so, and made it a vital part of their religion. It is always the tendency of a certain type of religious person to go beyond the Scriptures; and that was the position with the Pharisees.

When we come to look at our Lord's teaching we find that though He never taught fasting directly, He certainly taught it indirectly. In Matthew 9 we are told that He was asked a question specifically about fasting. They said to Him, 'Why do we and the Pharisees fast oft, but thy disciples fast not? And Jesus said unto them, Can the children of the bridechamber mourn, as long as the bridegroom is with them? but the days will come, when the bridegroom shall be taken from them, and then shall they fast.' It seems to me that there, quite clearly, is implicit teaching of, and almost an advocacy of fasting. It is clear, at any rate, that He never prohibited it. Indeed, in this teaching which we are now considering, His approval of it is obviously implied. What He says is, 'when thou fastest, anoint thine head, and wash thy face;' so that quite clearly it was something that was regarded by our Lord as right and good for Christian people. And we remember that He Himself fasted for forty days and forty nights when He was in the wilderness being tempted of the devil.

Then, going on beyond our Lord's teaching and practice to that of the early Church, we find it was something that was practised by the apostles. The church at Antioch, when it sent out Paul and Barnabas on their first preaching tour, did so only after a period of prayer and of fasting. Indeed, on any important occasion, when faced with any vital decision, the early Church always seemed to give themselves to fasting as well as to prayer, and the apostle Paul, in referring to himself and his life, talks about being 'in fastings oft'. It was clearly something that was a regular part of his life. Now those who are interested in matters of textual criticism will remember that in Mark 9:29, where our Lord is reported as saying, 'This kind can come forth by nothing, but by prayer and fasting,' it is probably true to say that 'fasting' should not be there according to the best documents and manuscripts, but that is quite immaterial as regards the general question because there is all this other teaching which shows quite clearly that the New Testament definitely teaches the rightness and the value of fasting. And when we enquire into the subsequent history of the Church we find exactly the same thing. The saints of God in all ages and in all places have not only believed in fasting, they have practised it. It was true of the Protestant Reformers, it was certainly true of the Wesleys and Whitefield. I admit that they tended to do it more before they were truly converted than they did afterwards; but they did nevertheless continue to fast after their conversion. And those of you who are familiar with the life of that great Chinese Christian, Pastor Hsi of China, will remember how Pastor Hsi, when confronted by some new or exceptional difficulty or problem, invariably had a period of fasting as well as of prayer. God's people have felt that fasting is not only right, but is of great value and of great importance under certain conditions.

If, then, that is the historical background, let us approach it a little more directly and ask this question. What exactly is fasting? What is its purpose? There can be no doubt that ultimately it is something which is based upon an understanding of the relationship between the body and the spirit. Man is body, mind and spirit, and these are very intimately related to one another and interact very closely upon one another. We distinguish them because they are different, but we must not separate them because of their interrelationship and interaction. There can be no question whatever but that physical bodily states and conditions do have a bearing upon the activity of the mind and of the spirit, so that the element of fasting must be considered in this peculiar relationship of body, mind and spirit. What fasting really means, therefore, is abstinence from food for spiritual purposes. That is the biblical notion of fasting which must be separated from the purely physical. The biblical notion of fasting is that, for certain spiritual reasons and purposes, men and women decide to abstain from food.

This is a very important point, so we must put it also in a negative form. I was reading recently an article on this subject, and the writer referred to that statement of the apostle Paul in 1 Corinthians 9:27 where he says: 'I keep under my body'. The apostle says that he does this in order that he may do his work more efficiently. The writer of the article said that this is an illustration of fasting. Now I suggest that, of necessity, it has nothing whatsoever to do with fasting. That is what I would call a part of man's general discipline. You should always keep under your body, but that does not mean you should always fast. Fasting is something unusual or exceptional, something which a man does now and again for a special purpose, while discipline should be perpetual and permanent. I therefore cannot accept such texts as: 'I keep under my body', and 'Mortify your members that are upon the earth', as being a part of fasting. In other words, moderation in eating is not fasting. Moderation in eating is a part of discipline of the body, and it is a very good way of keeping the body under; but that is not fasting. Fasting means an abstinence from food for the sake of certain special purposes such as prayer or meditation or the seeking of God for some peculiar reason or under some exceptional circumstance.

To make the matter complete, we would add that fasting, if we conceive of it truly, must not only be confined to the question of food and drink; fasting should really be made to include abstinence from anything which is legitimate in and of itself for the sake of some special spiritual purpose. There are many bodily functions which are right and normal and perfectly legitimate, but which for special peculiar reasons in certain circumstances should be controlled. That is fasting. There, I suggest, is a kind of general definition of what is meant by fasting.

Before we come to consider the ways in which we fast, let us consider how we are to regard and approach the whole question. Here again the division is simple, for finally we have but the wrong and the right way. There are certain wrong ways of fasting. Here is one of them. If we fast in a mechanical manner, or merely for the sake of doing so, I suggest that we are violating the biblical teaching with regard to the whole matter. In other words, if I make fasting an end in itself, something of which I say, 'Well now, because I have become a Christian, I have to fast on such a day and at such a time in the year because it is part of the Christian religion', I might as well not do it. The special element in the act goes right out of it when that is done.

This is something which is not peculiar to fasting. Did we not see exactly the same thing in the matter of prayer? It is a good thing for people, if they can, to have certain special times for prayer in their lives. But if I make up my programme for the day and say that at such and such an hour every day I must pray, and I just pray in order to keep to my programme, I am no longer praying. It is exactly the same with regard to the question of fasting. There are people who approach it in precisely that way. They become Christians; but they rather like to be under a kind of law, they rather like to be under instruction. They like to be told exactly what they must or must not do. On one particular day in the week they must not eat meat, and so on. It is not the thing to do in the Christian life; you do not eat on a particular day. Again at a certain period of the year you abstain from food, or you eat less, and so forth. Now there is a very subtle danger in that. Anything we do merely for the sake of doing it, or as a matter of rule or rote, is surely an entire violation of the scriptural teaching. We must never regard fasting as an end in itself.

But we must add to that something at which I have already hinted, and which can be put in this form: we should never regard fasting as a part of our discipline. Some people say it is a very good thing that on one day in the week we should not eat certain things, or that at a given period in the year we should abstain from certain things. They say that it is good from the standpoint of discipline. But discipline is surely something which must be permanent, discipline is something which is perpetual. We should always be disciplining ourselves. That is something about which there can be no discussion at all. We should always keep our body under, we should always be holding the reins tightly upon ourselves, we must always be in a disciplined condition in every respect. So it is wrong to reduce fasting merely to a part of the process of discipline. Rather is it something that I do in order to reach that higher spiritual realm of prayer to God, or meditation, or intense intercession. And that puts it into an entirely different category.

Another false way of regarding fasting I would put like this. There are some people who fast because they expect direct and immediate results from it. In other words they have a kind of mechanical view of fasting; they have what I have sometimes called, for lack of a better illustration, the 'penny in the slot' view of it. You put your penny in the slot, then you pull out the drawer, and there you have your result. That is their view of fasting. If you want certain benefits, they say, fast; if you fast you will get the results. This attitude is not confined to the question of fasting. We saw earlier in dealing with prayer that there are many people who regard prayer in that way. They read accounts of how certain people at one time decided to have an all-night prayer meeting, how they went on praying right through the night, and how, as a result of that, a revival broke out. So they decide that they will have an all-night prayer meeting, and they expect a revival to follow. 'Because we pray, revival must come.' Or you can find it in connection with holiness teaching. Certain people say that if you only obey certain conditions you will get a blessing, that there will be an immediate and direct result. Now I never find that anywhere in the Bible, in connection with fasting or anything else. We must never fast for the sake of direct results.

Let me put it even more pointedly like this. There are people who advocate fasting as one of the best ways and methods of obtaining blessings from God. Some of this recent literature to which I have referred, I regret to say, seems to be guilty of that. People write an account of their life and they say, 'You know, my Christian life was one which always seemed to be "bound in shallows and in miseries"; I was never truly happy. My life seemed to be a series of ups and downs. I was a Christian but I did not seem to have what certain other people whom I knew seemed to possess. I was like that for years. I had gone the round of all the conventions, I had read the prescribed books on this subject, but I never seemed to get the blessing. Then I happened to come across teaching which emphasized the importance of fasting, and I fasted and I received the blessing.' Then the exhortation is: 'If you want a blessing, fast.' That seems to me to be a most dangerous doctrine. We must never speak like that about anything in the spiritual life. These blessings are never automatic. The moment we begin to say, 'Because I do this, I get that', it means that we are controlling the blessing. That is to insult God and to violate the great doctrine of His final and ultimate sovereignty. No, we must never advocate fasting as a means of blessing.

Let us consider another illustration of this point. Take the question of tithing. Here we have another subject that is coming back again into prominence. Now there is very good scriptural basis for tithing; but there are many who tend to teach the question of tithing like this. A man writes an account of his life. Again he says that his Christian life was unsatisfactory. Things did not go well with him; indeed he was having financial troubles in his business. Then he came across the teaching of tithing and he began to tithe. At once great joy flooded his life. Not only that, but his business also began to be successful. I have read books which actually go so far as to say this: 'If you really want to be prosperous, begin tithing'. In other words, 'You do the tithing, and the result is bound to follow; if you want the blessing — tithe'. It is exactly the same as with fasting. All such teaching is quite unscriptural. Indeed it is worse than that; it derogates from the glory and the majesty of God Himself. Therefore we should never advocate, indulge in, or practise fasting as a method or a means of obtaining direct blessing. The value of fasting is indirect, not direct.

The last thing to consider under this heading is that we must obviously be very careful not to confuse the physical with the spiritual. We cannot consider this fully now, but, having read some accounts of people who have practised fasting, I do feel that they cross the borderline from the physical to the spiritual in this way. They describe how, after the preliminary physical misery of the first three or four days, and after the fifth day especially, a period of unusual mental clarity comes in; and sometimes some of these friends describe this as if it were purely spiritual. Now I cannot prove that it is not spiritual; but I can say this, that men who are not Christian at all and who undergo a period of fasting, invariably testify to the same thing. There is no doubt whatsoever that fasting, purely on the physical and bodily level, is something which is good for one's physical frame as long as it is done properly; and there is no doubt that clarity of mind and brain and understanding does result from it. But we must always be very careful that we do not attribute to the spiritual what can be adequately explained by the physical. Here again is a great general principle. It is what some of us would say to those who make claims in the matter of faith and holiness, as also to those who are over-ready to claim something as miraculous when it is not certainly or unmistakably so. We do harm to the cause of Christ if we claim as miraculous something which can be easily explained on a natural level. The same danger is present in this question of fasting — a confusion between the physical and the spiritual.

Having considered, then, some of the false ways of viewing this matter of fasting let us now look at the right way. I have already suggested it. It should always be regarded as a means to an end, and not as an end in itself. It is something that a man should do only when he feels impelled or led to it by spiritual reasons. It is not to be done because a certain section of the Church enjoins fasting on a Friday, or during the period of Lent, or at any other time. We should not do these things mechanically. We must discipline our lives, but we must do so all the year round, and not merely at certain stated periods. I must discipline myself at all times, and must fast only when I feel led by the Spirit of God to do so, when I am intent on some mighty spiritual purpose, not according to rule, but because I feel there is some peculiar need of an entire concentration of the whole of my being upon God and my worship of Him. That is the time to fast, and that is the way to approach the subject.

But let us come to the other aspect. Having looked at it in general, let us look at the way in which it is to be done. The wrong way is to call attention to the fact that we are doing it. 'When ye fast, be not, as the hypocrites, of a sad countenance: for they disfigure their faces, that they may appear unto men to fast.' Of course, when they did it in this way, people saw they were undergoing a fasting period. They did not wash their faces or anoint their heads. Some of them went even further; they disfigured their faces and put ashes upon their head. They wanted to call attention to the fact that they were fasting, so they looked miserable and unhappy and everybody looked at them and said, 'Ah, he is undergoing a period of fasting. He is an unusually spiritual person. Look at him; look at what he is sacrificing and suffering for the sake of his devotion to God.' Our Lord condemns that root and branch. Any announcing of the fact of what we are doing, or calling attention to it, is something which is utterly reprehensible to Him, as it was in the case of prayer, and of almsgiving. It is exactly the same principle. You must not sound a trumpet proclaiming the things you are going to do. You must not stand at the street corners or in a prominent place in the synagogue when you pray. And in the same way you must not call attention to the fact that you are fasting.

But this is not only a question of fasting. It seems to me that this is a principle which covers the whole of our Christian life. It condemns equally the affecting of pious looks, it condemns equally the adoption of pious attitudes. It is pathetic sometimes to observe the way in which people do this even in the matter of singing hymns — the uplifted face at certain points and the rising on tiptoe. These things are affected, and it is when they are affected that they become so sad.

May I put a question for your consideration and for your interest at this point? Where does the question of dress come into all this? To me this is one of the most baffling and perplexing things in connection with our Christian lives, and I find myself halting between two obvious opinions. There is much in me that not only understands, but likes, the practice of the early Quakers who used to dress differently from other people. Their idea was that they wanted to show the difference between the Christian and the non-Christian, between the Church and the world. They said that we must not even look like the world; we must look different. Now in every Christian there must be something that heartily says 'Amen' to that. I cannot understand the Christian who wants to look like the typical, average, worldly person in appearance, in dress or in anything else — the loudness, the vulgarity, the sensuality of it all. No Christian should want to look like that. So there is something very natural about this reaction against it and this desire to be quite different.

But that, unfortunately, is not the only aspect of the subject. The other aspect is that it is not of necessity true that 'the apparel doth proclaim the man' in this respect. The dress does proclaim the man up to a point, but not completely so. The Pharisees wore a particular dress and 'made broad their phylacteries', but it did not guarantee true righteousness. Indeed, the Bible teaches that ultimately that is not the way in which the Christian is differentiated from the non-Christian. It seems to me that it is what I *am* that shows the difference. If I myself am right, the rest is likely to follow. So that I do not proclaim that I am a Christian by dressing in a particular way so much as by being what I am. But think it out. It is an interesting and a very fascinating question. I think probably the truth is that both statements are right. As Christians we should all desire to be unlike those worldlings, and yet at the same time we must never get into the position of saying that it is our dress that truly proclaims what we are. There, then, is the wrong way of doing it; and the reward is still the same as it is with all those false methods — 'Verily I say unto you, They have their reward.' People think that those who fast in that way are very spiritual and that they are exceptionally holy people. They will get the praise of men but that is all the reward they will get, for God seeth in secret. He sees the heart and 'that which is highly esteemed amongst men is abomination in the sight of God'.

What then is the right way? Let us begin by putting it negatively. The first thing is that it does not mean going out of our way to be as unlike the Pharisees as possible. Many think that, because our Lord says, 'But thou, when thou fastest, anoint thine head, and wash thy face; that thou appear not unto men to fast, but unto thy Father which is in secret.' They say that we must not only not disfigure our faces but that we must go out of our way to conceal the fact that we are fasting, and even give the opposite impression. But this is a complete misunderstanding. There was nothing exceptional about washing the face and anointing the hair. That was the normal, usual procedure. What our Lord is saying here is, 'When you fast be natural'.

We can apply that in this way. There are some people who are so afraid of being regarded as miserable because they are Christians, or afraid of being called foolish because they are Christians, that they tend to go to the other extreme. They say that we must give the impression that to be a Christian is to be bright and happy, and so, far from being dowdy in dress, we must go to the opposite extreme. So they go out of their way not to be drab, and the result is they are quite as bad as those who are guilty of dowdiness. Our Lord's principle is always this: 'Forget other people altogether.' In order to avoid looking sad, don't put a grin on your face. Forget your face, forget yourself, forget other people altogether. It is this interest in the opinions of other people that is so wrong. Don't worry about the impression you are making; just forget yourself and give yourself entirely to God. Be concerned only about God and about pleasing Him. Be concerned only about His honour and His glory.

If our great concern is to please God and to glorify His name, we shall be in no difficulty about these other things. If a man is living entirely to the glory of God, you need not prescribe for him when he has to fast, you need not prescribe the sort of clothes he has to put on or anything else. If he has forgotten himself and given himself to God, the New Testament says that man will know how to eat and drink and dress because he will be doing it all to the glory of God. And thank God the reward of such a man is safe and certain and assured, and it is mighty — 'Thy Father which seeth in secret himself shall reward thee openly.' The one thing that matters is that we be right with God and concerned about pleasing Him. If we are concerned about that, we may leave the rest to Him. He may withhold the reward for years: it does not matter. We shall receive it. His promises never fail. Even though the world may never know what we are, God knows, and at the great Day it will be announced before the whole world. 'Thy Father which seeth in secret himself shall reward thee openly.'

> 'Men heed thee, love thee, praise thee not:
> The Master praises: what are men?'

Chapter Four

'When Ye Pray'

W E return now to a consideration of our Lord's teaching concerning
prayer. In Matthew 6, you remember, we have our Lord's treatment of
the whole question of Christian piety. He divides up the subject into three sections which really cover the whole of our righteousness or religious living. First
of all comes the question of almsgiving — our charity towards others, then the
question of prayer and our relationship to God, and finally the question of personal discipline which He considers under the general heading of fasting. We
have already considered those three aspects of the religious life, or the life of piety, separately; and when considering the subject of prayer, we said that we
would return again to a study of what is commonly known as the Lord's Prayer.
For our Lord clearly found it necessary not only to warn His followers against
certain dangers in connection with prayer, but also to give them positive instruction.

He has already warned them, you remember, not to be as the hypocrites,
who pray standing in the synagogues and on street corners in order to be seen
of men. He has told them that vain repetitions in and of themselves have no
value, and that the mere bulk or quantity of prayer will produce no special benefit. He has also told them that they must pray in secret, and that they must
never be concerned about men or what men might think of them, but that what
is vital and essential in this matter of prayer is not only that they should shut
out other people, but that they should shut themselves in with God, and concentrate upon Him and their relationship to Him. But, as we have said, He
clearly feels that a general warning is not sufficient, and that His disciples need
more detailed instruction. So He goes on to say, 'After this manner therefore
pray ye', and He proceeds to give them this instruction with regard to the
method of prayer.

We are face-to-face here with one of the most vital subjects in connection with our Christian life. Prayer is beyond any question the highest activity of the human soul. Man is at his greatest and highest when, upon his knees, he comes face-to-face with God. Not that we desire to indulge in vain comparisons. Almsgiving is excellent; it is a noble activity, and the man who feels led, and who responds to the leading, thus to help his fellowmen in this world is a good man. Again, fasting in various forms is a very high and noble activity. The man of the world knows nothing about this, nor about self-discipline. He just yields to every impulse, gives himself over to lust and passion, and lives more or less like an animal in a mere mechanical response to the instincts that are within him. He knows nothing about discipline. The man who disciplines himself stands out and has the mark of greatness upon him; it is a great thing for a man to discipline his life at all times, and occasionally to take exceptional measures for his spiritual good.

These things, however, pale into insignificance when you look at a man engaged in prayer. When a man is speaking to God he is at his very acme. It is the highest activity of the human soul, and therefore it is at the same time the ultimate test of a man's true spiritual condition. There is nothing that tells the truth about us as Christian people so much as our prayer life. Everything we do in the Christian life is easier than prayer. It is not so difficult to give alms — the natural man knows something about that, and you can have a true spirit of philanthropy in people who are not Christian at all. Some seem to be born with a generous nature and spirit, and to such almsgiving is not essentially difficult. The same applies also to the question of self-discipline — refraining from certain things and taking up particular duties and tasks. God knows it is very much easier to preach like this from a pulpit than it is to pray. Prayer is undoubtedly the ultimate test, because a man can speak to others with greater ease than he can speak to God. Ultimately, therefore, a man discovers the real condition of his spiritual life when he examines himself in private, when he is alone with God. We saw in chapter 2 that the real danger for a man who leads a congregation in a public act of prayer is that he may be addressing the congregation rather than God. But when we are alone in the presence of God that is no longer possible. And have we not all known what it is to find that, somehow, we have less to say to God when we are alone than when we are in the presence of others? It should not be so; but it often is. So that it is when we have left the realm of activities and outward dealings with other people, and are alone with God, that we really know where we stand in a spiritual sense. It is not only the highest activity of the soul, it is the ultimate test of our true spiritual condition.

Another way of putting that is this. You will find that the outstanding characteristic of all the most saintly people the world has ever known has been that they have not only spent much time in private prayer, but have also delighted in it. We cannot read the life of any saint without finding that that has been true of him. The more saintly the person, the more time such a person spends in conversation with God. Thus it is a vital and all-important matter. And surely there is a greater need for guidance at this point than at any other.

This has been true in the experience of God's people throughout the centuries. We find it recorded in the Gospels that John the Baptist had been teaching his disciples to pray. They obviously had felt the need of instruction, and they had asked him for instruction and guidance. And John had taught them how to pray. Our Lord's disciples felt exactly the same need. They came to Him one afternoon and said, in effect, 'John the Baptist taught his disciples how to pray; Lord, teach us how to pray.' Undoubtedly the desire arose in their hearts because they were conscious of this kind of natural, instinctive, initial difficulty of which we are all aware; but it must also have been greatly increased when they watched His own prayer life. They saw how He would arise 'a great while before dawn' and go up into the mountains to pray, and how He would spend whole nights in prayer. And sometimes, I have no doubt, they said to themselves: 'What does He talk about? What does He do?' They may also have thought, 'I find after a few minutes in prayer that I come to the end of my words. What is it that enables Him to be drawn out in prayer? What is it that leads to this ease and abandonment?' 'Lord', they said, 'teach us how to pray.' They meant by this that they would like to be able to pray as He prayed. 'We wish we knew God as You know Him. Teach us how to pray.' Have you ever felt that? Have you ever felt dissatisfied with your prayer life, and longed to know more and more what it is truly to pray? If you have, it is an encouraging sign.

There is no question but that this is our greatest need. More and more we miss the very greatest blessings in the Christian life because we do not know how to pray aright. We need instruction in every respect with regard to this matter. We need to be taught how to pray, and we need to be taught what to pray for. It is because it covers these two things in a most amazing and wonderful manner that we must spend some time in a consideration of what has become known amongst us as 'The Lord's Prayer'. It is a perfect synopsis of our Lord's instruction on how to pray, and what to pray for.

Now I must make it quite clear at this point that that is all I propose to do. The subject of prayer is a very great and large one, which might indeed engage us for a long time. However, we must not allow it to do so because we are actually working our way through the Sermon on the Mount, and therefore it would be wrong to digress overmuch on this one particular question. All I intend to do is to explain our Lord's teaching in this prayer, and I am not going to do even that in any great detail. I simply intend to underline and emphasize what seem to me to be the great central principles which our Lord was obviously anxious to inculcate.

There are certain general matters with regard to this prayer that certainly need a word or two of comment. 'The Lord's Prayer', as we call it, has often been the subject of much controversy. There are many people who, for various reasons, refuse to recite it in an act of public worship. There are some who seem to object to it on doctrinal grounds, and who feel that it belongs to the realm of law rather than of grace, and that it has nothing to do with Christian people. They stumble over the petition with regard to the forgiveness of sins. We shall deal with that in detail when we come to it, but I am simply mentioning now certain of the preliminary difficulties that various friends experience. They say that forgiveness here seems to be conditional upon our forgiving, and that, they maintain, is law not grace, and so on. It is necessary therefore that we should make a number of preliminary observations.

The first is that this prayer is undoubtedly a pattern prayer. The very way in which our Lord introduces it indicates that. 'After this manner therefore pray ye.' Now, says our Lord in effect, when you come to pray to God, this is the kind of way in which you are to pray. And the amazing and extraordinary thing about it is that it really covers everything in principle. There is a sense in which you can never add to the Lord's Prayer; nothing is left out. That does not mean, of course, that when we pray we are simply to repeat the Lord's Prayer and stop at that, for that is obviously something that was not true of our Lord Himself. As we have already seen, He spent whole nights in prayer; many times He arose a great while before day and prayed for hours. You always find in the lives of the saints that they have spent hours in prayer. John Wesley used to say he held a very poor view of any Christian who did not pray for at least four hours every day.

To say that this prayer is all-inclusive, and is a perfect summary, simply means, therefore, that it really does contain all the principles. We might say that what we have in the Lord's Prayer is a kind of skeleton. Take, for instance, this act of preaching. I have certain notes before me; I have not a complete sermon. I merely have headings — the principles which are to be emphasized. But I do not stop at a mere enunciation of principles; I expound and work them out. That is the way in which we should regard the Lord's Prayer. The principles are all here and you cannot add to them. You can take the longest prayer that has ever been offered by a saint, and you will find that it can all be reduced to these principles. There will be no additional principle whatsoever. Take that great prayer of our Lord's which is recorded in John 17 — our Lord's High-Priestly prayer. If you analyse it in terms of principles, you will find that it can be reduced to the principles of this model prayer.

The Lord's Prayer covers everything; and all we do is to take these principles and employ and expand them and base our every petition upon them. That is the way in which it is to be approached. And as you look at it in that way, I think you will agree with St. Augustine and Martin Luther and many other saints who have said that there is nothing more wonderful in the entire Bible than the Lord's Prayer. The economy, the way in which He summarizes it all, and has reduced everything to but a few sentences, is something that surely proclaims the fact that the speaker is none other than the very Son of God Himself.

Let us go on to another observation, which is one that we have been emphasizing right through our consideration of this Sermon. It is that this prayer is obviously meant not only for the disciples, but for all Christians in all places and at all times. When we were dealing with the Beatitudes we constantly repeated that they are applicable to every Christian. The Sermon on the Mount was not meant only for the disciples at that time and for the Jews in some coming kingdom age; it is meant for Christian people now and at all times, and has always been applicable. Exactly as we have had to judge ourselves by the teaching of the fifth chapter with respect to the relationship of the Christian to the law, so we come face-to-face with this prayer, and with what our Lord says in this matter: 'After this manner therefore pray ye.' He speaks to us today exactly as He spoke to the people who were about Him at that particular time. Indeed, as we have already seen, unless our prayer corresponds to this particular pattern and form, it is not true prayer.

There may be questions in the minds of many with regard to reciting the Lord's Prayer as an act of public worship. That is a point for legitimate debate, a point for legitimate difference of opinion. It seems to me, however, that we can never remind ourselves too frequently of this particular form; and, for myself, I have always been comforted by this thought, that whatever I may forget in my own private prayers, as long as I pray the Lord's Prayer I have at any rate covered all the principles. On condition, of course, that I am not merely mechanically repeating the words, but am really praying from my heart and with my mind and with my whole being.

The next point is that there are some people in trouble about the Lord's Prayer because it does not say 'for Christ's sake', or because it is not offered specifically in Christ's name. They say that it cannot be a prayer for Christian people because Christians should always pray in the name of Christ. The answer to this is, of course, that our Lord, as we have seen, was simply laying down principles which must always govern man's relationship to God. He was not concerned to say everything about that relationship at this point. But He was concerned to say this; that whoever comes into the presence of God must always realize these things. Later on in His life and teaching He will teach them explicitly about praying in His name. But it is surely clear that even in the Lord's Prayer, praying in Christ's name is implicit. No man can truly say 'Our Father which art in heaven', save one who knows the Lord Jesus Christ and who is in Christ. So it is implicit even at the very beginning. But, in any case, that does not affect the principles which our Lord teaches here so plainly.

Concerning the particular difficulty with regard to forgiveness, we shall deal with that in detail when we come to that petition in our consideration of the prayer.

Let us then sum up our general remarks by repeating that there is nothing more exalted, and more elevating, than this wonderful prayer which the Lord Jesus Christ taught His people. Let us also remember that He taught it, not that they might just repeat it mechanically for the rest of their lives, but rather that they should say to themselves, 'Now there are certain things I must always remember when I pray. I must not rush into prayer; I must not start speaking at once without considering what I am doing. I must not merely be led by some impulse and feeling. There are certain things I must always bear in mind. Here are the headings for my prayer; here is the skeleton which I have to clothe; these are the lines along which I must proceed.' I trust therefore that none of us will think that it is the hallmark of true Evangelicalism to speak rather disparagingly of the Lord's Prayer. I trust also that none of us will be guilty of that spiritual pride, not to say arrogance, which refuses to recite the Lord's Prayer with others. Let us rather realize that our Lord here was really telling these people how He Himself prayed, that that was His own method, that these were the things He always had in mind, and that therefore we can never do anything greater or higher than to pray along the lines of the Lord's Prayer. We shall never exceed this prayer if we pray truly, so we must never dismiss it as legalism, and imagine that because we are in the dispensation of grace we have gone beyond that. We shall find as we analyse this prayer that it is full of grace. Indeed the law of God was full of grace, as we have already seen. Our Lord has been expounding the law of Moses and has shown that, when spiritually understood, it is full of the grace of God, and that no man can understand it truly unless he has the grace of God in his heart.

Let us now look briefly at this subject of how to pray and what to pray for. With regard to the first matter we remind ourselves again of the vital importance of the right approach, for this is the key to the understanding of successful prayer. People so often say, 'You know, I prayed and prayed but nothing happened. I did not seem to find peace. I did not seem to get any satisfaction out of it.' Most of their trouble is due to the fact that their approach to prayer has been wrong, that somehow or other they did not realize what they were doing. We tend to be so self-centred in our prayers that when we drop on our knees before God, we think only about ourselves and our troubles and perplexities. We start talking about them at once, and of course nothing happens. According to our Lord's teaching here we should not expect anything to happen. That is not the way to approach God. We must pause before we speak in prayer.

The great teachers of the spiritual life throughout the centuries, whether Roman Catholic or Protestant, have been agreed about this, that the first step in prayer has always been what they call 'Recollection'. There is a sense in which every man when he begins to pray to God should put his hand upon his mouth. That was the whole trouble with Job. In his wretchedness he had been talking a great deal. He felt that God had not been dealing kindly with him, and he, Job, had been expressing his feelings freely. But when, towards the end of the book, God began to deal with him at close quarters, when He began to reveal and manifest Himself to him, what did Job do? There was only one thing for him to do. He said, 'Behold, I am vile; what shall I answer thee? I will lay mine hand upon my mouth.' And, strange as it may seem to you, you start praying by saying nothing; you recollect what you are about to do.

I know the difficulty in this. We are but human, and we are pressed by the urgency of our position, the cares, the anxieties, the troubles, the anguish of mind, the bleeding heart, whatever it is. And we are so full of this that, like children, we start speaking at once. But if you want to make contact with God, and if you want to feel His everlasting arms about you, put your hand upon your mouth for a moment. Recollection! Just stop for a moment and remind yourself of what you are about to do. We can put it in a phrase. Do you know that the essence of true prayer is found in the two words in verse 9, 'Our Father'? I suggest that if you can say from your heart, whatever your condition, 'My Father', in a sense your prayer is already answered. It is just this realization of our relationship to God that we so sadly lack.

Perhaps we can put it in another way like this. There are people who believe it is a good thing to pray because it always does us good. They adduce various psychological reasons. That of course is not prayer as the Bible understands it. Prayer means speaking to God, forgetting ourselves, and realizing His presence. Then again, there are others, and sometimes I think they would claim for themselves an unusual degree of spirituality, who rather think that the hallmark of true prayer life, of ease and facility in prayer, is that one's prayer should be very brief and pointed, and one should just simply make a particular request. That is something which is not true of the teaching of the Bible concerning prayer. Take any of the great prayers which are recorded in the Old Testament or in the New. None of them is what we might call this 'businesslike' kind of prayer which simply makes a petition known to God and then ends. Every prayer recorded in the Bible starts with invocation. It does not matter how desperate the circumstance; it does not matter what the particular quandary might be in which those who pray find themselves. Invariably they start with this worship, this adoration, this invocation.

We have a great and wonderful example of this in the ninth chapter of Daniel. There the prophet, in terrible perplexity, prays to God. But he does not start immediately with his petition; he starts by praising God. A perplexed Jeremiah does the same thing. Confronted by the demand that he should buy a plot of land in a seemingly doomed country, Jeremiah could not understand it; it seemed all wrong to him. But he does not rush into the presence of God for this one matter; he starts by worshipping God. And so you will find it in all the recorded prayers. Indeed, you even get it in the great High-Priestly prayer of our Lord Himself which is recorded in John 17. You remember also how Paul put it in writing to the Philippians. He says, 'in nothing be anxious; but in everything by prayer and supplication with thanksgiving let your requests be made known unto God' (Phil. 4:6, RV). That is the order. We must always start with invocation, before we even begin to think of petition; and here it is once and for ever put to us so perfectly in this model prayer.

It would take too long to expound as I should like the meaning of this statement, 'Our Father'. Let me put it like this, therefore, in what may appear to be a dogmatic form. It is only those who are true believers in the Lord Jesus Christ who can say, 'Our Father'. It is only the people of whom the Beatitudes are true who can say with any confidence, 'Our Father'. Now I know that this is an unpopular doctrine today, but it is the doctrine of the Bible. The world today believes in the universal Fatherhood of God and the universal brotherhood of man. That is not found in the Bible. It was our Lord who said to certain religious Jews that they were 'of their father the devil', and not children of Abraham, not children of God. It is only to 'as many as receive him' that He gives the right (the authority) 'to become the sons of God'.

'But,' says someone, 'what did Paul mean when he said, "we are also his offspring"? Does not that mean we are all His children and He is the universal Father?' Well, if you analyse this passage, you will find that Paul is speaking there, in Acts 17, of God as the Creator of all things and all people, that God in that sense has given life and being to everybody throughout the world. But that is not the meaning of God as Father in the sense in which Paul uses it elsewhere of believers, nor the sense in which, as we have seen, our Lord Himself uses it. The Bible draws a very sharp distinction between those who belong to God and those who do not. You notice it in the Lord's High-Priestly prayer in John 17:9. He said, 'I pray for them: I pray not for the world, but for them which thou hast given me; for they are thine.' It is an utter, absolute distinction; it is only those who are in the Lord Jesus Christ who are truly the children of God. We become the children of God only by adoption. We are born 'the children of wrath', 'the children of the devil'. 'the children of this world'; and we have to be taken out of that realm and translated into another realm before we become the children of God. But if we truly believe on the Lord Jesus Christ, we are adopted into God's family, and we receive 'the Spirit of adoption, whereby we cry, Abba, Father'.

The man of the world does not like this doctrine. He says we are all the children of God; and yet in his heart he has a hatred towards God, and when, in desperation, he prays to God he has no confidence that he is speaking to his Father. He feels God is someone who has set Himself against him. He talks about the Fatherhood of God, but he has not received the Spirit of adoption. It is only the one who is in Christ who knows this.

So when our Lord says, 'Our Father', He is obviously thinking of Christian people, and that is why I say that this is a Christian prayer. A man may say, 'Our Father', but the question is, is he conscious of it, does he believe and experience it? The ultimate test of every man's profession is that he can say with confidence and with assurance, 'My Father', 'My God'. Is God your God? Do you know Him really as your Father? And when you come to Him in prayer, have you that sense of coming to your Father? That is the way to start, says our Lord, to realize that you have become a child of God because of what He has done for you through the Lord Jesus Christ. That is implicit in this teaching of Christ. He suggests and anticipates all that He was going to do for us, all He was going to make possible for His own. They did not understand it yet. Nevertheless, He says, that is the way to pray, that is how I pray, and you are going to pray like this.

You notice, however, that He adds immediately, 'Which art in heaven'. This is a most wonderful thing — 'Our Father which art in heaven.' These two phrases must always be taken together, for this very good reason. Our ideas of fatherhood have often become very debased and have always, therefore, to be corrected. Do you notice how often the apostle Paul in his Epistles uses a most striking phrase? He talks about the 'God and Father of our Lord Jesus Christ'. That is most significant. It is simply calling attention to what our Lord says at this point. 'Our Father.' Yes; but because of our debased conception of fatherhood, He hastens to say, 'Our Father which art in heaven', the 'God and Father of our Lord Jesus Christ'. That is the kind of Father we have.

But there are many people in this world, alas, to whom the idea of fatherhood is not one of love. Imagine a little boy who is the son of a father who is a drunkard and a wife beater, and who is nothing but a cruel beast. That little boy knows nothing in life but constant and undeserved thrashings and kickings. He sees his father spend all his money on himself and his lust, while he himself has to starve. That is his idea of fatherhood. If you tell him that God is his Father, and leave it at that, it is not very helpful, and it is not very kind. The poor boy of necessity has a wrong idea of fatherhood. That is his notion of a father, a man who behaves like that. So our human, sinful notions of fatherhood need constant correction.

Our Lord says, 'Our Father which art in heaven;' and Paul says 'the God and Father of our Lord Jesus Christ'. Anyone like Christ, says Paul in effect, must have a wonderful Father, and, thank God, God is such a Father, the Father of our Lord Jesus Christ. It is vital when we pray to God, and call Him our Father, that we should remind ourselves that He is 'our Father which is in heaven', that we should remind ourselves of His majesty and of His greatness and of His almighty power. When in your weakness and your utter humiliation you drop on your knees before God, in your anguish of mind and heart, remember that He knows all about you. The Scripture says, 'all things are naked and opened unto the eyes of him with whom we have to do.' Remember, also, that if sometimes you rush into the presence of God and want something for yourself, or are praying for forgiveness for a sin you have committed, God has seen and knows all about it. It is not surprising that, when he wrote Psalm 51, David said in the anguish of his heart, 'Thou desirest truth in the inward parts.' If you want to be blessed of God you have to be absolutely honest, you have to realize He knows everything, and that there is nothing hidden from Him. Remember also that He has all power to punish, and all power to bless. He is able to save, He is able to destroy. Indeed, as the wise man who wrote the book of Ecclesiastes put it, it is vital when we pray to God that we should remember that 'He is in heaven and we are upon the earth'.

Then remember His holiness and His justice, His utter, absolute righteousness. Let us remember, says the author of the Epistle to the Hebrews, that whenever we approach Him we must do so 'with reverence and godly fear: for our God is a consuming fire'.

That is the way to pray, says Christ, take these two things together, never separate these two truths. Remember that you are approaching the almighty, eternal, ever-blessed holy God. But remember also that that God, in Christ, has become your Father, who not only knows all about you in the sense that He is omniscient, He knows all about you also in the sense that a father knows all about his child. He knows what is good for the child. Put these two things together. God in His almightiness is looking at you with a holy love and knows your every need. He hears your every sigh and loves you with an everlasting love. He desires nothing so much as your blessing, your happiness, your joy and your prosperity. Then remember this, that He 'is able to do exceeding abundantly above all that we ask or think'. As your 'Father which is in heaven' He is much more anxious to bless you than you are to be blessed. There is also no limit to His almighty power. He can bless you with all the blessings of heaven. He has put them all in Christ, and put you into Christ. So your life can be enriched with all the glory and riches of the grace of God Himself.

That is the way to pray. Before you begin to make any petition, before you begin to ask even for your daily bread, before you ask for anything, just realize that you, such as you are, are in the presence of such a Being, your Father which is in heaven, the Father of our Lord Jesus Christ. 'My God.' 'My Father.'

Chapter Five

Prayer: Adoration

W E come now to the next division of the Lord's Prayer which is that which deals with our petitions. 'Our Father which art in heaven': that is the invocation. Then come the petitions: 'hallowed be thy name. Thy kingdom come. Thy will be done in earth, as it is in heaven. Give us this day our daily bread. And forgive us our debts, as we forgive our debtors. And lead us not into temptation, but deliver us from evil.' There has been much debating and disputing amongst the authorities as to whether you have there six or seven petitions. The answer turns on whether that last statement 'deliver us from evil' is to be regarded as a separate petition, or whether it is to be taken as part of the previous petition and to be read like this: 'Lead us not into temptation but deliver us from evil'. It is one of those points (and there are others in connection with the Christian faith) which simply cannot be decided, and about which we cannot be dogmatic. Fortunately for us, it is not a vital point, and God forbid that any of us should become so absorbed by the mere mechanics of Scripture, and spend so much time with them, as to miss the spirit and that which is important. The vital matter is not to decide whether there are six or seven petitions in the Lord's Prayer but rather to notice the order in which the petitions come. The first three — 'Hallowed be thy name. Thy kingdom come. Thy will be done in earth, as it is in heaven' — have regard to God and His glory; the others have reference to ourselves. You will notice that the first three petitions contain the word '*Thy*', and all have reference to God. It is only after that that the word '*us*' comes in: 'Give us this day our daily bread. Forgive us our trespasses as we forgive those who trespass against us. Lead us not into temptation. Deliver us from evil.' That is the vital point — the order of the petitions, not the number. The first three are concerned about and look only to God and His glory.

But let us observe something else which is of vital importance, the proportion in the petitions. Not only must our desires and petitions with regard to God come first, but we must notice, too, that half the petitions are devoted to God and His glory and only the remainder deal with our particular needs and problems. Of course if we are interested in biblical numerics — an interest which is perhaps not to be entirely discouraged, though it can become dangerous if and when we tend to become too fanciful — we shall see, in addition, that the first *three* petitions have reference to God, and that three is always the number of Deity and of God, suggesting the three blessed Persons in the Trinity. In the same way, *four* is always the number of earth and refers to everything that is human. There are four beasts in the heavens in the book of Revelation, and so on. Seven, which is a combination of three and four, always stands for that perfect number where we see God in His relationship to earth, and God in His dealing with men. That may be true of this prayer, our Lord may have specifically constructed it to bring out those wonderful points. We cannot prove it. But in any case the important thing to grasp is this: that it matters not what our conditions and circumstances may be, it matters not what our work may be, it matters not at all what our desires may be, we must never start with ourselves, we must never start with our own petitions.

That principle applies even when our petitions reach their highest level. Even our concern for the salvation of souls, even our concern for God's blessing upon the preaching of the Word, even our concern that those who are near and dear to us may become truly Christian, even these things must never be given the first place, the first position. Still less must we ever start with our own circumstances and conditions.

It does not matter how desperate they may be, it does not matter how acute the tension, it does not matter whether it be physical illness, or war, or a calamity, or some terrible problem suddenly confronting us: whatever it may be, we must never fail to observe the order which is taught here by our blessed Lord and Saviour. Before we begin to think of ourselves and our own needs, even before our concern for others, we must start with this great concern about God and His honour and His glory. There is no principle in connection with the Christian life that exceeds this in importance. So often we err in the realm of principles. We tend to assume that we are quite sound and clear about principles, and that all we need is instruction about details. The actual truth, of course, is the exact reverse of that. If only we would always start in prayer with this true sense of the invocation; if only we were to recollect that we are in the presence of God, and that the eternal and almighty God is there, looking upon us as our Father, and more ready to bless and to surround us with His love than we are to receive His blessing, we should achieve more in that moment of recollection than all our prayers put together are likely to achieve without that realization. If only we all had this concern about God and His honour and glory!

Fortunately, our Lord knows our weakness, He realizes our need of instruction, so He has divided it up for us. He has not only announced the principle; He has divided it up for us into these three sections which we must proceed to consider. Let us look now at the first petition: 'Hallowed be thy name'.

We realize now that we are in the presence of God, and that He is our Father. Therefore this, says Christ, should be our first desire, our first petition: 'Hallowed be thy name'. What does that mean? Let us look very briefly at the words. The word 'Hallowed' means to sanctify, or to revere, or to make and keep holy. But why does He say 'Hallowed be thy name'? What does this term 'the Name' stand for? We are familiar with the fact that it was the way in which the Jews at that time commonly referred to God Himself. Whatever we may say about the Jews in Old Testament times and however great their failures, there was one respect, at any rate, in which they were most commendable. I refer to their sense of the greatness and the majesty and the holiness of God. You remember that they had such a sense of this that it had become their custom not to use the name 'Jehovah'. They felt that the very name, the very letters, as it were, were so holy and sacred, and they so small and unworthy, that they dare not mention it. They referred to God as 'The Name', in order to avoid the use of the actual term Jehovah. So that the 'name' here means God Himself, and we see that the purpose of the petition is to express this desire that God Himself may be revered, may be sanctified, that the very name of God and all it denotes and represents may be honoured amongst men, may be holy throughout the entire world. But perhaps in the light of the Old Testament teaching it is good for us to enlarge on this just a little. The 'name', in other words, means all that is true of God, and all that has been revealed concerning God. It means God in all His attributes, God in all that He is in and of Himself, and God in all that He has done and all that He is doing.

God, you remember, had revealed Himself to the children of Israel under various names. He had used a term concerning Himself (*El* or *Elohim*) which means His 'strength' and His 'power'; and when He used that particular name, He was giving the people a sense of His might, His dominion, and His power. Later He revealed Himself in that great and wonderful name *Jehovah* which really means 'the self-existent One', 'I am that I am', eternally self-existent. But there were other names in which God described Himself: 'the Lord will provide' *(Jehovah-jireh)*, 'the Lord that healeth' *(Jehovah-rapha)*, 'the Lord our Banner' *(Jehovah-nissi)*, 'the Lord our peace' *(Jehovah-Shalom)*, 'the Lord our Shepherd' *(Jehovah-ra-ah)*, 'the Lord our Righteousness' *(Jehovah-tsidkenu)*, and another term which means, 'the Lord is present' *(Jehovah-shammah)*. As you read the

Old Testament you will find all these various terms used; and in giving these various names to Himself God was revealing Himself and something of His nature and being, His character and His attributes, to mankind. In a sense 'thy name' stands for all that. Our Lord is here teaching us to pray that the whole world may come to know God in this way, that the whole world may come to honour God like that. It is the expression of a burning and deep desire for the honour and glory of God.

You cannot read the four Gospels without seeing very clearly that that was the consuming passion of the Lord Jesus Christ Himself. It is found again perfectly in that great High-Priestly prayer in John 17 when He says, 'I have glorified thee on the earth' and 'I have manifested thy name unto the men which thou gavest me'. He was always concerned about the glory of His Father. He said, 'I have not come to seek mine own glory but the glory of him that sent me.' There is no real understanding of the earthly life of Christ except in these terms. He knew that glory which ever belongs to the Father, 'the glory which I had with thee before the world was.' He had seen that glory and He had shared it. He was filled with this sense of the glory of God, and His one desire was that mankind might come to know it.

What unworthy ideas and notions this world has of God! If you test your ideas of God by the teaching of the Scriptures you will see at a glance what I mean. We lack even a due sense of the greatness and the might and the majesty of God. Listen to men arguing about God, and notice how glibly they use the term. It is not that I would advocate a return to the practice of the ancient Jews; I think they went too far. But it is indeed almost alarming to observe the way in which we all tend to use the name of God. We obviously do not realize that we are talking about the ever blessed, eternal, and absolute, almighty God. There is a sense in which we should take our shoes off our feet whenever we use the name. And how little do we appreciate the goodness of God, the kindness and the providence of God. How the Psalmist delighted in celebrating God as our rock, God as our peace, God as our shepherd who leads us, God as our righteousness, and God as the ever present One who will never leave us nor forsake us.

This petition means just that. We should all have a consuming passion that the whole world might come to know God like that. There is an interesting expression used in the Old Testament with regard to this which must sometimes have astonished us. The Psalmist in Psalm 34 invites everybody to join him in 'magnifying' the Lord. What a strange idea! 'O', he says, 'magnify the Lord with me, and let us exalt his name together'. At first sight that appears to be quite ridiculous. God is the Eternal, the self-existent One, absolute and perfect in all His qualities. How can feeble man ever magnify such a Being? How can we ever make God great or greater (which is what we mean by magnify)? How can we exalt the name that is highly exalted over all? It seems preposterous and quite ridiculous. And yet, of course, if we but realize the way in which the Psalmist uses it, we shall see exactly what he means. He does not mean that we can actually add to the greatness of God, for that is impossible; but he does mean that he is concerned that this greatness of God may appear to be greater amongst men. Thus it comes to pass that amongst ourselves in this world we can magnify the name of God. We can do so by words, and by our lives, by being reflectors of the greatness and the glory of God and of His glorious attributes.

That is the meaning of this petition. It means a burning desire that the whole world may bow before God in adoration, in reverence, in praise, in worship, in honour and in thanksgiving. Is that our supreme desire? Is that the thing that is always uppermost in our minds whenever we pray to God? I would remind you again that it should be so whatever our circumstances. It is when we look at it in that way that we see how utterly valueless much of our praying must be. When you come to God, says our Lord, in effect, even though you may be in desperate conditions and circumstances, it may be with some great concern on your mind and in your heart; even then, He says, stop for a moment and just recollect and realize this, that your greatest desire of all should be that this wonderful God, who has become your Father in and through Me, should be honoured, should be worshipped, should be magnified amongst the people. 'Hallowed be thy name.' And as we have seen, it has always been so in the praying of every true saint of God that has ever lived on the face of the earth.

If, therefore, we are anxious to know God's blessing and are concerned that our prayers should be effectual and of value, we must follow this order. It is all put in a phrase repeated many times in the Old Testament: 'The fear of the Lord is the beginning of wisdom'. That is the conclusion reached by the Psalmist. That is the conclusion, likewise, of the wise man in his proverbs. If you want to know, he says, what true wisdom is, if you want to be blessed and prosperous, if you want to have peace and joy, if you want to be able to live and die in a worthy manner, if you want wisdom with regard to life in this world, here it is, 'the fear of the Lord'. That does not mean craven fear; it means reverential awe. If, therefore, we want to know God and to be blessed of God, we must start by worshipping Him. We must say, 'Hallowed be thy name', and tell Him that, before mentioning any concern about ourselves, our one desire is that He shall be known. Let us approach God 'with reverence and godly fear: for our God is a consuming fire'. That is the first petition.

The second is 'Thy kingdom come'. You notice that there is a logical order in these petitions. They follow one another by a kind of inevitable, divine necessity. We began by asking that the name of God may be hallowed amongst men.

But the moment we pray that prayer we are reminded of the fact that His name is not hallowed thus. At once the question arises, Why do not all men bow before the sacred name? Why is not every man on this earth concerned about humbling himself now in the presence of God, and worshipping Him and using every moment in adoring Him and spreading forth His name? Why not? The answer is, of course, because of sin, because there is another kingdom, the kingdom of Satan, the kingdom of darkness. And there, at once, we are reminded of the very essence of the human problems and the human predicament. Our desire as Christian people is that God's name shall be glorified. But the moment we start with that we realize that there is this opposition, and we are reminded of the whole biblical teaching about evil. There is another who is 'the god of this world'; there is a kingdom of darkness, a kingdom of evil, and it is opposed to God and His glory and honour. But God has been graciously pleased to reveal from the very dawn of history that He is yet going to establish His kingdom in this world of time, that though Satan has entered in and conquered the world for the time being, and the whole of mankind is under his dominion, He is again going to assert Himself and turn this world and all its kingdoms into His own glorious kingdom. In other words, running right through the Old Testament, there are the promises and the prophecies concerning the coming of the kingdom of God or the kingdom of heaven. And, of course, at this particular, crucial point of world history, when our Lord Himself was here on earth, this matter was very much in the forefront of men's minds. John the Baptist had been preaching his message, 'Repent ye: for the kingdom of heaven is at hand'. He called the people to be ready for it. And when our Lord began preaching, He said exactly the same thing; 'Repent: for the kingdom of heaven is at hand.' In this petition He obviously has that whole idea in His mind as He teaches His disciples to offer this particular prayer. At that immediate historical point He was teaching His disciples to pray that this kingdom of God should come increasingly and come quickly, but the prayer is equally true and equally right for us as Christian people in all ages until the end shall come.

We can summarize the teaching concerning the kingdom. The kingdom of God really means the reign of God; it means the law and the rule of God. When we look at it like that we can see that the kingdom can be regarded in three ways. In one sense the kingdom has already come. It came when the Lord Jesus Christ was here. He said, 'If I with the finger of God cast out devils, no doubt the kingdom of God is come upon you'. He said in effect, 'The kingdom of God is here now; I am exercising this power, this sovereignty, this majesty, this dominion; this is the kingdom of God'. So the kingdom of God in one sense had come then. The kingdom of God is also here at this moment in the hearts and lives of all who submit to Him, in all who believe in Him. The kingdom of God is present in the Church, in the heart of all those who are truly Christian. Christ reigns in such people. But the day is yet to come when His kingdom shall have been established here upon the earth. The day is yet to come when

'Jesus shall reign where'er the sun
Does his successive journeys run.'

That day is coming. The whole message of the Bible looks forward to that. Christ came down from heaven to earth to found, to establish, and to bring in this kingdom. He is still engaged upon that task and will be until the end, when it shall have been completed. Then He will, according to Paul, hand it back to God the Father, 'that God may be all in all'.

So our petition really amounts to this. We should have a great longing and desire that the kingdom of God and of Christ may come in the hearts of men. It should be our desire that this kingdom should be extended in our own hearts; for it is to the extent that we worship Him, and surrender our lives to Him, and are led by Him, that His kingdom comes in our hearts. We should also be anxious to see this kingdom extending in the lives and hearts of other men and women. So that when we pray, 'Thy kingdom come', we are praying for the success of the gospel, its sway and power; we are praying for the conversion of men and women; we are praying that the kingdom of God may come today in Britain, in Europe, in America, in Australia, everywhere in the world. 'Thy kingdom come' is an all-inclusive missionary prayer.

But it goes even further than that. It is a prayer which indicates that we are 'Looking for and hasting unto the coming of the day of God' (2 Pet. 3:12). It means that we should be anticipating the day when all sin and evil and wrong and everything that is opposed to God shall finally have been routed. It means that we should have longings in our hearts for the time when the Lord will come back again, when all that is opposed to Him shall be cast into the lake of burning, and the kingdoms of this world shall have become the kingdoms of our God and of His Christ.

'Thy kingdom come, O God;
    Thy rule, O Christ, begin;
Break with Thine iron rod
    The tyrannies of sin.'

That is the petition. Indeed its meaning is expressed perfectly at the very end of the book of Revelation. 'Even so, come, Lord Jesus'. 'The Spirit and the bride say, Come'. Our Lord is just emphasizing here that before we begin to think of

338

our own personal needs and desires, we should have this burning desire within us for the coming of His kingdom, that the name of God may be glorified and magnified over all.

The third petition, 'Thy will be done in earth, as it is in heaven' needs no explanation. It is a kind of logical consequence and conclusion from the second, as that was a logical conclusion from the first. The result of the coming of the kingdom of God amongst men will be that the will of God will be done amongst men. In heaven the will of God is always being done perfectly. We have only some dim and faint figures of it in the Scriptures, but we have sufficient to know that what is characteristic of heaven is that everyone and everything is waiting upon God and anxious to glorify and magnify His name. The angels, as it were, are on the wing all ready and waiting to fly at His bidding. The supreme desire of all in heaven is to do the will of God, and thereby to praise and worship Him. And it should be the desire of every true Christian, says our Lord here, that all on earth should be the same. Here, again, we are looking forward to the coming of the kingdom, because this petition will never be fulfilled and granted until the kingdom of God shall indeed be established here on earth amongst men. Then the will of God will be done on earth as it is done in heaven. There will be 'new heavens and a new earth, wherein dwelleth righteousness'. Heaven and earth will become one, the world will be changed, evil will be burned out of it, and the glory of God will shine over all.

In these words, then, we are taught how we begin to pray. Those are the petitions with which we must always start. We can summarize them again in this way. Our innermost and greatest desire should be the desire for God's honour and glory. At the risk of being misunderstood I suggest that our desire for this should be even greater than our desire for the salvation of souls. Before we even begin to pray for souls, before we even begin to pray for the extension and the spread of God's kingdom, there should be that overruling desire for the manifestation of the glory of God and that all might humble themselves in His presence. We can put it like this. What is it that troubles and worries our minds? Is it the manifestation of sin that we see in the world, or is it the fact that men do not worship and glorify God as they ought to do? Our Lord felt it so much that He put it like this in John 17:25: 'O righteous Father, the world hath not known thee: but I have known thee, and these (referring to the disciples) have known that thou hast sent me.' 'Righteous Father,' He said in effect, 'here is the tragedy, here is the thing that perplexes Me, and saddens Me, that the world has not known Thee. It thinks of Thee as a tyrant, it thinks of Thee as a harsh Lawgiver, it thinks of Thee as Someone who is opposed to it and always tyrannizing over it. Holy Father, the world has not known Thee. If it had but known Thee it could never think of Thee like that.' And that should be our attitude, that should be our burning desire and longing. We should so know God that our one longing and desire should be that the whole world should come to know Him too.

What a wonderful prayer this is. O the folly of people who say that such a prayer is not meant for Christians, but that it was meant only for the disciples then and for the Jews in some coming age. Does it not make us feel in a sense that we have never prayed at all? This is prayer. 'Our Father which art in heaven, Hallowed be thy name'. Have we arrived at that yet, I wonder? Have we really prayed that prayer, that petition, 'Hallowed be thy name'? If only we are right about that, the rest will follow. 'Thy kingdom come. Thy will be done in earth, as it is in heaven'. We need not turn to Him and ask Him, 'Lord, teach us how to pray'. He has done so already. We have but to put into practice the principles He has taught us so plainly in this model prayer.

Chapter Six

Prayer: Petition

A NY man who attempts to preach on the Lord's Prayer must surely find himself in great difficulties. There is a sense in which it is almost presumption to preach on it at all. One should simply repeat these phrases and meditate upon them and consider them from the heart. For they themselves say everything, and the more I study this prayer the more I believe that if only one used these phrases as our Lord intended them to be used, there is really nothing more to be said. But, on the other hand, we are all frail and fallible, we are sinful creatures, and the result is that we need to have these things analysed and enforced.

We have been trying to do so and we come now to the last section (verses 11-15). We have already considered whether there are three petitions here, or four. On the whole, and in spite of the interesting possibility from the standpoint of biblical numerics, I would say there are *three*, and these last three petitions have reference to ourselves and our own needs and desires. It seems to me that the words our Lord uses in verse 13 really determine this: 'And', He says — that is the word that introduces each new petition — 'And lead us not into temptation, but deliver us from evil'. If there were four petitions it would probably read like this: 'And lead us not into temptation, and deliver us from evil'. His use of 'but' seems to indicate that it is really one petition offered from two angles or two different sides.

Before we comment on these three petitions individually, there are two or three general statements which must be made. The first concerns the all-inclusiveness of these petitions. All our great needs are summed up in them. 'Give us this day our daily bread'. 'Forgive us our debts, as we forgive our debtors'. 'And lead us not into temptation, but deliver us from evil'. Our whole life is found there in those three petitions, and that is what makes this prayer so utterly amazing. In such a small compass our Lord has covered the whole life of the believer in every respect. Our physical needs, our mental needs and, of course, our spiritual needs are included. The body is remembered, the soul is remembered, the spirit is remembered. And that is the whole of man, body, soul and spirit. Think of all the activities going on in the world at this moment, the organizing, the planning, the legislation and all other things; they are for the most part concerned with nothing but the body of man, his life and existence in this world of time. That is the tragedy of the worldly outlook, for there is another realm, the realm of relationships — the soul, the thing whereby man makes contact with his fellow man, the means of communication with one another and all social life and activity. It is all here. And above all, we have the spiritual, that which links man with God, and reminds him that he is something other than dust, and that as Longfellow says, 'Dust thou art, to dust returnest, was not spoken of the soul'. Man has been made this way; he cannot escape it, and our Lord has provided for it. We cannot fail to be impressed by the all-inclusiveness of these petitions. That does not mean that we should never enter into details; we must, we are taught to do so. We are taught to bring our life in detail to God in prayer; but here we have only the great headings. Our Lord gives us these and we fill in the details, but it is important for us to be sure that all our petitions should belong under one or other of the headings.

The second general comment concerns the wonderful order in which these petitions are put. How often, when we have thought about this prayer and meditated upon it, have we felt a sense of surprise that the first should be what it is? Let us look at it again in its setting: 'Our Father which art in heaven, Hallowed be thy name. Thy kingdom come. Thy will be done in earth, as it is in heaven' — a wonderful, exalted, spiritual level. We would have expected that immediately after that would come the spiritual needs of man followed in a descending order by the needs of his soul and at the very end some remembrance of the body and its needs. But that is not how our Lord puts it. Immediately after those exalted petitions about God and His glory, He says: 'Give us this day our daily bread'. He starts with the body. There is indeed something surprising about that at first sight, but the moment we stop to think about it we shall realize that the order is absolutely right. Our Lord is now considering our needs, and clearly the first thing that is necessary is that we must be enabled to continue our existence in this world. We are alive and we must be kept alive. The very fact of my existence and being are involved, so the first petition deals with the needs of our physical frame, and our Lord starts with that. He then goes on to deal with the need of cleansing from the defilement and guilt of sin; and, lastly, with the need for being kept from sin and its power. That is the true way to look at man's life. I am alive and I must be kept alive. But then I am conscious of guilt and unworthiness, and feel the need to be cleansed from that. Then I think of the future and realize that I need to be delivered from certain things that face me there.

Another way is to put it like this. Life in a physical sense, or in a biological sense, is the basis upon which all depends, so I must pray about my existence. But the moment I do so I come to realize that the physical is only one side of my life. There is another side. I remember that our Lord said, 'This is life eternal, that they might know thee the only true God, and Jesus Christ, whom thou hast sent'. He also said that He had come 'that they might have life, and that they might have it more abundantly'. Having been concerned only with my bare physical existence, I now begin to learn that what really makes life, *life,* is that I should be walking in fellowship and communion with God.

That, according to John in his First Epistle, is the real way of facing life in a world such as this. There are contradictions and difficulties; there are all sorts of things to get me down. But John said he was writing that letter in order that 'your joy may be full' in spite of it all. How is my joy to be full in such a world? By having fellowship with the Father and with His Son Jesus Christ. That is real living. But the moment I realize that, I know there are certain things that tend to interrupt that fellowship. I am sinful; therefore I need forgiveness of sins in order that I may enjoy that life of God. And when my communion with God has been restored the only other thing I need is to continue to enjoy that fellowship without interruption, without anything ever coming between me and the face of God who has become my Father in the Lord Jesus Christ.

So that is the order — daily bread; forgiveness of sins; to be kept from anything that may cast me again into sin, to be delivered from everything that is opposed to my higher interests and to my true life. The sum of it all is that ultimately there is nothing in the whole realm of Scripture which so plainly shows us our entire dependence upon God as does this prayer, and especially these three petitions. The only thing that really matters for us is that we know God as our Father. If we only knew God like this our problems would be solved already and we would realize our utter dependence upon Him and go to Him daily as children to their Father.

There, then, are our general observations. Let us now look briefly at the separate petitions in the order in which they appear. If we were interested in the mechanics of Scripture we could stay for some time considering the meaning of the term 'our daily bread'. It is said to be one of the most difficult terms in the whole of the Bible. What is the exact meaning of the expression? I am not going to weary you with all the views and theories. It must at least mean this. 'Give us this day what is necessary for us'. Some would say it should read: 'Give us this day our bread for tomorrow', which means exactly the same thing. In other words, all we are to ask for is sufficient, or what is necessary, for each day. It is a prayer for necessities. Bread is the staff of life; and I agree with those who say it should not be confined to the matter of food. It is meant to cover all our material needs, everything that is necessary for the life of man in this world.

Having said that, we must make a number of further comments. In the first place is there not something extraordinary and wonderful about the connection between this request and the previous requests? Is not this one of the most wonderful things in the whole of Scripture, that the God who is the Creator and Sustainer of the universe, the God who is forming His eternal kingdom and who will usher it in at the end, the God to whom the nations are but as 'the small dust of the balance' — that such a God should be prepared to consider your little needs and mine even down to the minutest details in this matter of daily bread! But that is the teaching of our Lord everywhere. He tells us that even a sparrow cannot fall to the ground without our Father, and that we are of much greater value than many sparrows. He says that 'the very hairs of your head are all numbered'. If only we could grasp this fact, that the almighty Lord of the universe is interested in every part and portion of us! There is not a hair of my head that He is not concerned about, and the smallest and most trivial details in my little life are known to Him on His everlasting throne. This is something you find only in Scripture. You go straight from 'Thy will be done in earth, as it is in heaven', to 'Give us this day our daily bread'. But that is the way of God, 'the high and lofty One that inhabiteth eternity, whose name is Holy'; who nevertheless, as Isaiah tells us, dwells with him also 'that is of a contrite and humble spirit'. That is the whole miracle of redemption; that is the whole meaning of the incarnation which tells us that the Lord Jesus Christ takes hold of us here on earth and links us with the almighty God of glory. The kingdom of God, and my daily bread!

It must be emphasized, of course, that all we pray for must be absolute necessities. We are not told to pray for luxuries or superabundance, nor are we promised such things. But we are promised that we shall have enough. David looking back in his old age could say, 'I have not seen the righteous forsaken, nor his seed begging bread'. The promises of God never fail. But they refer to necessities only, and our idea of necessity is not always God's. But we *are* told to pray for necessities.

Let us come, however, to another matter that is perhaps more perplexing. There are some people who see an apparent contradiction here. Our Lord asks us to make our requests; but He has just said that we are not to be like the heathen who think they shall be heard for their much speaking, because 'your Father knoweth what things ye have need of, before ye ask him'. 'Very well,' says some-one; 'if God knows before we ask Him, why should we express our needs to Him? Why tell Him about things that He knows already?' This brings us to the heart of the meaning of prayer. We do not tell God these things because He is not aware of them. No, we must think of prayer more as a relationship between father and child; and the value of prayer is that it keeps us in touch and contact with God.

An illustration once used by Dr. A. B. Simpson gave me great help when I first read it, and it continues to do so in this connection. He said that so many of us tend to think that God as our Father gives us the great gift of grace in one great lump sum, and that, having received it, we just go on living on it. 'But', he said, 'it is not like that. That would be very dangerous for us. If God just gave us all His glorious gifts of grace in one lump sum, we would be in danger of enjoy-ing the gift and forgetting all about God.' For though we cannot understand it, God wants us, and as our Father, He likes us, to speak to Him. He is like an earthly father in that respect. The earthly father is grievously wounded by the son who is content to enjoy the gift the father has given him but who never seeks his company again until he has exhausted his supplies and needs some more. No, the father likes the child to come and speak to him; and this is God's way of doing it. It is, says Dr. Simpson, exactly as though a father put a great de-posit for his son into the bank, and the son can only receive a supply each time by writing a cheque. Each time he needs another instalment he has to write a cheque. And that is how God deals with us. He does not give it to us all at once. He gives it to us in instalments. God is there in grace offering His guarantee, and all we have to do is to sign our cheques and present them. That is prayer, it is presenting our cheque, just going to God and asking Him to honour it.

This, surely, is the marvellous thing, that God likes us to come to Him. The God who is self-existent, the great Jehovah, the God who is not dependent upon anybody, who is from eternity to eternity, who exists in Himself apart from all — this is the astounding thing, that because we are His children He likes us to come to Him, and likes to hear us. The God who made heaven and earth, and orders the stars in their courses, likes to hear our lisping praises, likes to hear our petitions. That is because God is love; and that is why, though He knows all about our needs, it gives Him great pleasure, if we can so put it, when He sees us coming to Him to ask for our daily bread.

But we must emphasize next another aspect: we must all realize our utter dependence upon God, even for our daily bread. If God willed it so, we should have no daily bread. He could withhold the sun and its influence; He could stop the rain; He could make our land absolutely barren so that the farmer with all his modern implements and chemicals could not raise a crop. He could blast the crop if He wanted to. We are absolutely in the hand of God, and the supreme folly of this twentieth century is the folly of thinking that because we have acquired a certain amount of knowledge of the laws of God, we are independent of Him. We cannot live for a day without Him. Nothing would continue were it not sustained and kept going by God. 'Give us this day our daily bread.' It is a good thing for us at least once a day, but the oftener the better, to remind ourselves that our times, our health, and our very existence, are in His hands. Our food and all these necessary things come from Him, and we depend upon His grace and mercy for them.

We come now to the second division, which is often a great cause of difficulty. 'And forgive us our debts, as we forgive our debtors.' There are two main difficulties about this. There are those who feel that there is no need for a Christian to ask for forgiveness, and these people are divided into two groups. Some of them say that Christians need not ask for forgiveness, because we are justified by faith, by which they mean, of course, that we are justified by faith in the presence of God. What does it mean to be 'justified by faith'? It is God's declaration that He has dealt with our sins in full in the Person of the Lord Jesus Christ, the sins we have committed and the sins we shall commit, that He has imputed to us the righteousness of Jesus Christ, and regards and declares us to be righteous in Him. That is justification by faith. In that case, they argue, if all my sins were dealt with there, what need have I to ask for forgiveness?

Others say there is no need to ask for forgiveness because of their view of sanctification. Their position is that they do not sin any longer; they are perfect. They hold the holiness theory which teaches that sin has been eradicated, and that they are perfect, and sinless. So that for them it would be wrong to pray for forgiveness of sins; neither need they do so, for they do no wrong. But the answer to this error is that our Lord tells us to pray for forgiveness of our debts, trespasses, sins (or whichever word you prefer). He is not talking about justification; He is not dealing here with the case of a sinner who has just awakened to the fact that he needs to have his sins forgiven and so comes to God and receives the gift of salvation and realizes his justification in Christ — that is not what we have here. Here, rather, is what our Lord speaks of in John 13. You remember that as He washed the disciples' feet, Peter said to Him, 'Lord, not my feet only, but also my hands and my head'. 'No,' said Christ, 'he that is washed needeth not, save to wash his feet, but is clean every whit.' There is only one washing of the entire person — that is our justification. But having been justified, as we walk through this world we become soiled and tarnished by sin. That is true of every Christian. Though we know we have been forgiven, we need forgiveness still for particular sins and failures. It is all stated briefly in chapter 1 of John's

First Epistle, where we see that the Christian, though walking in the life of faith, may yet fall into sin. What are we to do about it? John tells us to 'confess our sins'. And 'if we confess our sins, he is faithful and just to forgive us our sins, and to cleanse us from all unrighteousness'. John is not writing to unbelievers; it is a letter to believers. He is writing to Christians, and our Lord was speaking to believers here.

Who is the man who can pray, 'Forgive us our debts, as we forgive our debtors'? He is the man who already has a right to say, 'Our Father'. And the only man who has a right to say 'Our Father' is the one who is in Christ Jesus. It is 'The Children's Prayer'. It is not a prayer for anybody, but only for those who have become the children of God in the Lord Jesus Christ. It is the relationship of the child to the Father, and the moment we realize we have offended, or grieved or sinned against the Father, we confess it and ask to be forgiven, and we are sure that we are forgiven.

With regard to those who claim that they are so sanctified that they do not need forgiveness, we learn again from John's Epistle that 'If we say we have no sin, we deceive ourselves, and the truth is not in us'. The man who does not know the blackness of his own heart, but is simply concerned with his own theories, is a man who is not examining himself truly. The greater the saint the greater is the sense of sin and the awareness of sin within.

But let us look at the second great difficulty in connection with this petition. 'Forgive us our debts, as we forgive our debtors.' There are people who say that this prayer should never be used by Christian people, for to do so, they say, is to go back to the law. These words apply, they maintain, only to those people to whom our Lord was actually speaking, and it will apply again only to those who will live in the future 'Kingdom Age'. These alone are the people who will pray, 'Forgive me because I forgive others'. They will be back on legal ground. 'It does not say "for Christ's sake",' say these interpreters; they say, 'there is no mention of the atonement; therefore it does not apply to Christians'. What do we say to this?

The first comment is that the text does not say, 'Forgive us our debts because we forgive our debtors'; it does not say, 'Forgive us on the ground of the fact that we forgive our debtors'. It says rather 'even as', 'even as I forgive those who are my debtors'. Or let us look at it like this. Take that argument which says that because the Lord's Prayer does not say 'for Christ's sake', and because the atonement is not specifically mentioned, it contains no gospel. To be consistent they must never again use the parable of the Prodigal Son for it also does not mention the atonement. It does not say anything about 'for Christ's sake'. It just gives an amazing picture of God as Father. It simply says that the son came back and that the father freely forgave him everything and showered his love upon him. But such an attitude towards the parable and towards this petition is quite ridiculous and pathetic. As the parable is concerned to point out one great central truth, so our Lord here was simply concerned to remind us of the need for forgiveness and to assure of the fact of forgiveness. He is not so much concerned about the mechanism or the way of forgiveness here, any more than He is in the parable of the Prodigal Son. We must take our Scriptures as a whole and compare Scripture with Scripture.

Now take this idea that there was ever a time when men were forgiven on strictly legal grounds, or that there is to be some time in the future when men will be on strictly legal grounds before God, and will be forgiven even as they forgive. Do we realize what that means? It means, of course, that such people will never be forgiven. Paul says that the law condemns everybody. 'There is none righteous, no, not one.' 'All have sinned, and come short of the glory of God.' The whole world lies guilty before God, and has been condemned. And I can assure you that there will never be anyone in any coming 'Kingdom Age', or in any other age, who can ever be forgiven by God apart from the death of the Lord Jesus Christ upon the cross. How absurd is this theory that in some coming kingdom age forgiveness will be strictly on legal grounds or that at any time it has been procured on such grounds. The only way of forgiveness before Christ, after Christ and always, is through Christ and Him crucified. The way of salvation in Him was ordained 'before the foundation of the world', and that fact is implicit in this and in every similar statement everywhere in the Scriptures. We must learn to take our Scriptures together, and to compare Scripture with Scripture, and to realize that here our Lord was simply concerned about the relationship of Father and child. He could not at this point explain the doctrine of the atonement. He even said at the end of His life that there were certain truths which He had to teach them but which they could not bear then. The truth concerning the way of forgiveness is implicit here, but the great fulfilment was to come.

We must not allow ourselves to be misled in this way. What we have here is what we find so clearly taught in Matthew 18, in the parable of the steward who would not forgive his underling although he had been forgiven by his master. It means that the proof that you and I are forgiven is that we forgive others. If we think that our sins are forgiven by God and we refuse to forgive somebody else, we are making a mistake; we have never been forgiven. The man who knows he has been forgiven, only in and through the shed blood of Christ, is a man who must forgive others. He cannot help himself. If we really know Christ as our Saviour our hearts are broken and cannot be hard, and we cannot refuse forgiveness. If you are refusing forgiveness to anybody I suggest that you have never been forgiven. 'Forgive us our debts, as we forgive our debtors.' I say to the glory of God and in utter humility, that whenever I see myself before God and realize even something of what my blessed Lord has done for me, I am ready to forgive anybody anything. I cannot withhold it, I do not even want to withhold it. That is what our Lord is saying here. We have a right therefore to pray like that. Pray to God and say, 'Forgive me O God as I forgive others because of what Thou hast done for me. All I ask is that Thou shouldst forgive me in the same manner; not to the same degree, because all I do is imperfect. In the same way, as it were, as Thou hast forgiven me, I am forgiving others. Forgive me as I forgive them because of what the cross of the Lord Jesus Christ has done in my heart.'

This petition is full of the atonement, it is full of the grace of God. We see how important it is by the fact that our Lord actually repeats it. Having finished the prayer He goes back and says (in vv. 14 and 15), 'For if ye forgive men their trespasses, your heavenly Father will also forgive you; but if ye forgive not men their trespasses, neither will your Father forgive your trespasses.' The thing is absolute and inevitable. True forgiveness breaks a man, and he must forgive. So that when we offer this prayer for forgiveness we test ourselves in that way. Our prayer is not genuine, it is not true, it is of no avail, unless we find there is forgiveness in our heart. God give us grace to be honest with ourselves, and never to repeat these petitions in the Lord's Prayer in a mechanical way.

Now just a word about the last petition, 'Lead us not into temptation, but deliver us from evil'. That is the final request and it means this. We are asking that we should never be led into a situation where we are liable to be tempted by Satan. It does not mean that we are dictating to God what He shall or shall not do. God does test His children, and we must never presume to tell God what He is or is not to do. He knows that we need much training in our preparation for glory. But though it does not mean that we are to dictate to God, it does mean that we may request of Him that, if it be in accordance with His holy will, He should not lead us into positions where we can be so easily tempted, and where we are liable to fall. It means that we should request Him to preserve us from this, and not to lead us in this way. This is what our Lord meant when He said to His disciples at the end, 'Watch and pray, that ye enter not into temptation'. There are situations which will be dangerous to you; watch and pray, always be on guard lest you fall into temptation. And coupled with that is this other aspect of the petition, that we pray to be delivered from evil. Some would say 'from the evil one', but I think that limits the meaning, for 'evil' here includes not only Satan but evil in every shape and form. It certainly includes Satan; we need to be delivered from him and his wiles. But there is evil also in our hearts, so we need to be delivered from that, and from the evil in the world as well. We need to be delivered from it all. It is a great request, a comprehensive petition.

Why should we ask that we may be kept from evil? For the great and wonderful reason that our fellowship with God may never be broken. If a man merely wants to be holy as such, there is something wrong with him. Our supreme desire should be to have a right relationship with God, to know Him, to have uninterrupted fellowship and communion with Him. That is why we pray this prayer, that nothing may come between us and the brightness and the radiance and the glory of our Father which is in heaven. 'Lead us not into temptation, but deliver us from evil.'

Then, you remember, there is a postscript: 'For thine is the kingdom, and the power, and the glory, for ever.' It is in some of the old versions; it is not in others. We do not know for certain whether our Lord did actually utter it at this point or not; but whether He did or not, it is very appropriate. What can one say after facing such a prayer, and such words? There must be a kind of final thanksgiving, there must be some sort of doxology. As we consider our needs, our dependence upon Him, our relationship to Him, we cannot stop by saying, 'Deliver us from evil'. We must end as we began, by praising Him. The measure of our spirituality is the amount of praise and of thanksgiving in our prayers. 'Thine is the kingdom, and the power, and the glory.' Our daily food is assured us, we have as our Father One who can keep us from hell, from Satan, from ourselves, from all. 'Thine is the kingdom, and the power' — And Thine must be, and, as far as we are concerned, shall be, the glory for ever and ever. Amen.

Chapter Seven

Treasures on Earth and in Heaven

T HE theme of this section of the Sermon on the Mount is, you remember, the relationship of the Christian to God as his Father. There is nothing more important than this. The great secret of life according to our Lord is to see ourselves and to conceive of ourselves always as children of our heavenly Father. If only we do that we shall be delivered immediately from two of the main temptations that attack us all in this life.

These temptations He puts in this way. The first is the very subtle one that comes to every Christian in the matter of his personal piety. As a Christian I have my private, personal life of devotion. In that connection our Lord says that the one thing that matters, and the one consideration for me, should always be that God's eye is upon me. I must not be interested in what people say, neither must I be interested in myself. If I give alms, I must not give them in order to be praised of men. The same is true of my prayers. I must not want to give the impression that I am 'a great man of prayer'. If I do, my prayer is useless. I must not be interested in what people think of me as a man of prayer. All that He denounces. I must pray as under God and in the presence of God. Exactly the same principles obtain with the question of fasting; and you remember how we worked it out in detail in chapter 3. These considerations have brought us to the end of verse 18 of Matthew 6.

We come now to verse 19 where our Lord introduces the second aspect of this great question of the Christian living his life in this world in relationship to God as his Father, involved in its affairs and feeling its cares, its strains and its stresses. It is, in fact, the whole problem of what is so often called in the Bible, 'the world'. We frequently say that the Christian in this life has to contend with the world, the flesh and the devil; and our Lord recognizes that threefold description of our problem and conflict. In handling this question of personal piety He deals first with the temptations that come from the flesh and the devil. The devil is particularly watchful when a man is pious, and when he is engaged in the manifestations of his piety. But having dealt with that, our Lord proceeds to show that there is another problem, and that is the problem of the world itself.

Now what do the Scriptures mean by the expression 'the world'? It does not mean the physical universe, or merely a collection of people; it means an outlook and a mentality, it means a way of looking at things, a way of looking at the whole of life. One of the most subtle problems with which the Christian ever has to deal is this problem of his relationship to the world. Our Lord frequently emphasizes that it is not an easy thing to be a Christian. He Himself when He was here in this world was tempted of the devil. He was also confronted by the power and subtlety of the world. The Christian is in precisely the same position. There are attacks which come upon him when he is alone, in private. There are others which come when he goes out into the world. You notice our Lord's order. How significant it is. You prepare yourself in the secrecy of your own chamber. You pray and do various other things — fasting and almsgiving and doing your good deeds unobserved. But you also have to live your life in the world. That world will do its best to get you down, it will do its utmost to ruin your spiritual life. So you have to be very wary. It is a fight of faith, and you need the whole armour of God, because if you have not got it, you will be defeated. 'We wrestle not against flesh and blood.' It is a stern battle, it is a mighty conflict.

Our Lord teaches that this attack from the world, or this temptation to worldliness, generally takes two main forms. First of all there may be a positive love of the world. Secondly, there may be anxiety, or a spirit of anxious care with respect to it. We shall see that our Lord shows that one is as dangerous as the other. He deals with the love of the world from verses 19 to 24, and He deals with the problem of being conquered by anxiety and care with respect to the world and its life and all its affairs, from verse 25 to the end of the chapter.

Again, however, we must remember that He treats both aspects of the problem still in terms of our relationship to our heavenly Father. So, as we enter into the details of His teaching, we must never forget the great principles which govern everything. We must again be very careful that we do not reduce this teaching to a number of rules and regulations. If we do that, we shall fall immediately into the whole error of monasticism. There are some people who are so worried about the cares and the affairs of this life that for them there is only one thing to do, that is to get out of it. So they shut themselves up in monasteries and become monks, or live as hermits in their lonely cells. But that is the false view which is found nowhere in the teaching of the Bible, where we are shown how to overcome the world while living in the midst of it.

Our Lord puts His teaching first of all in the form of a blunt assertion, which is also an injunction. He lays down a law, a great principle. And having given the principle, He then, in His infinite kindness and condescension, supplies us with various reasons and considerations which will help us to carry out His injunction. As we read words like these, we must surely again be amazed and impressed by His condescension. He has a right to lay down laws and then leave us with them. But He never does that. He states His law, He gives us His principle, and then in His kindness He gives us reasons, He supplies us with arguments which will help us and strengthen us. We are not meant to rely upon them, but they are a great help, and sometimes when our faith is weak, they are of inestimable value.

First and foremost then, here is the injunction: 'Lay not up for yourselves treasures upon earth . . . but lay up for yourselves treasures in heaven'. That is the injunction, that is the exhortation. The remainder, you see, goes into the realm of reason and explanation. 'Lay not up for yourselves treasures upon earth, where moth and rust doth corrupt, and where thieves break through and steal; but lay up for yourselves treasures in heaven, where neither moth nor rust doth corrupt, and where thieves do not break through nor steal.' But look first of all at the exhortation itself. It is a twofold one — negative and positive. Our Lord puts the truth in such a way that we are left without excuse. If any of us Christian people find ourselves receiving a very poor reward when we come to the great judgment of rewards, we shall have no excuse at all.

Negatively, then, He says, 'Lay not up for yourselves treasures upon earth'. What does He mean by this? First of all we must avoid interpreting this only with respect to money. Many have done that, and have regarded this as a statement addressed only to rich people. That, I suggest, is foolish. It is addressed to all others also. He does not say, 'Lay not up for yourselves money', but, 'Lay not up for yourselves treasures'. 'Treasures' is a very large term and all-inclusive. It includes money, but it is not money only. It means something much more important. Our Lord is concerned here not so much about our possessions as with our attitude towards our possessions. It is not what a man may have, but what he thinks of his wealth, what his attitude is towards it. There is nothing wrong in having wealth in and of itself; what can be very wrong is a man's relationship to his wealth. And the same thing is equally true about everything that money can buy.

Indeed we go further. It is a question of one's whole attitude towards life in this world. Our Lord is dealing here with people who get their main, or even total, satisfaction in this life from things that belong to this world only. What He is warning against here, in other words, is that a man should confine his ambition, his interests and his hopes to this life. That is what He is concerned about, and viewed in that way, it becomes a much bigger subject than the mere possession of money. Poor people need this exhortation about not laying up treasures upon earth quite as much as the rich. We all have treasures in some shape or form. It may not be money. It may be husband, wife or children; it may be some gift we have which in actual worth and monetary value is very small. To some people their treasure is their house. That whole danger of being house proud, of living for your house and home is dealt with here. No matter what it is, or how small it is, if it is everything to you, that is your treasure, that is the thing for which you are living. This is the danger against which our Lord is warning us at this particular point.

That gives us some idea of what He means by 'treasures upon earth', and you see it is almost endless. Not only love of money, but love of honour, the love of position, the love of status, the love of one's work in an illegitimate sense, whatever it may be, anything that stops with this life and this world. These are the things of which we must be wary, lest they become our treasure.

Having said that, we come to a very practical question. How does one 'lay up' treasures on earth with respect to these things? Once more we can merely give some general indications as to what it means. It may mean living to hoard and amass wealth as wealth. Many people do that, and our Lord may have had that chiefly in mind. But surely it has a wider reference. Our Lord's injunction means avoiding anything that centres on this world only. It is, as we have just seen, all-inclusive. It applies to people who, though they may not be interested in wealth or money at all, are yet interested in other things which are entirely worldly in the last analysis. There are people who have often been guilty of sad and serious lapses in their spiritual life because of this very thing we are considering. They cannot be tempted by money, but they can be tempted by status and position. If the devil comes and offers them some material bribe they will smile at it. But if he comes with guile, and, in connection with their Christian work, offers them some exalted position, they persuade themselves that their one interest is in the work, and they accept and receive it, and you soon begin to observe a gradual decline in their spiritual authority and power. Promotion has done endless harm in the Church of God to men who have been quite honest and sincere, but who have not been on guard against this danger. They have been laying up treasures on earth without knowing it. Their interest has suddenly been moved from that one centre of pleasing God and working for His honour and His glory, and has turned, almost without their knowing it, to themselves and their own engagement in the work.

In such ways a man can be laying up treasures on earth, and it is so subtle that even good people can be a man's greatest enemy. Many a preacher has been ruined by his congregation. Their praise, their encouragement of him as a man, has almost ruined him as the messenger of God, and he has become guilty of laying up treasures on earth. He tends almost unconsciously to be controlled by the desire to have his people's good opinion and praise, and the moment that happens a man is laying up treasures on earth. The possible examples are almost endless. I am simply trying to give you some slight indication of the realm and scope of this amazing injunction. 'Lay not up for yourselves treasures on earth.' Whatever the *form* may be, it is the *principle* that matters.

Let us look now at the positive side of the injunction, 'Lay up for yourselves treasures in heaven'. It is very important that we should be clear about this. Some people have interpreted it as meaning that our Lord is teaching that a man can achieve his own salvation. 'Treasure in heaven,' they say, 'means a man's salvation and his eternal destiny. Therefore, is not our Lord exhorting a man to spend his whole life in making sure of his eternal destiny?' Patently that is wrong. That is to deny the great central New Testament doctrine of justification by faith only. Our Lord cannot mean that, because He is addressing people of whom the Beatitudes are true. It is the man who is poor in spirit, who has nothing, who is blessed. It is the man who mourns because of his sinfulness who knows that, at the end, in spite of all he may or may not have done, he can never achieve his own salvation. That interpretation, therefore, is clearly wrong. What then does it mean? It means something that is taught in many places in the Scriptures, and two other passages will help us to understand the teaching here. The first is in Luke 16 where our Lord deals with the case of the unjust steward, the man who made a quick and clever use of his position. You remember He sums it up like this. 'Make to yourselves', He says, 'friends of the mammon of unrighteousness; that, when ye fail, they may receive you into everlasting habitations.' Our Lord teaches that the children of this world are wiser in their generation than the children of light. They make sure of their own ends. Now, says our Lord in effect, I am going to take that as a principle and apply it to you. If you have money, so use it while you are here in this world that, when you arrive in glory, the people who benefited by it will be there to receive you.

The apostle Paul expounds this in 1 Timothy 6:17-19: 'Charge them that are rich in this world, that they be not high-minded, nor trust in uncertain riches, but in the living God, who giveth us richly all things to enjoy; that they do good, that they be rich in good works, ready to distribute, willing to communicate; laying up in store for themselves a good foundation against the time to come, that they may lay hold on eternal life.' In other words, if you have been blessed with riches, use them in such a way in this world that you will be building up a balance for the next. Our Lord says exactly the same thing at the end of Matthew 25 where He talks about the people who gave Him meat when He was hungry and who visited Him in prison. They ask, 'When saw we thee an hungred, and fed thee? . . . or in prison, and came unto thee?' And He says, 'Inasmuch as ye have done it unto one of the least of these my brethren, ye have done it unto me.' You do not realize it, but in doing these good deeds to these people, you have been building up your balance in heaven, there you will receive your reward and enter into the joy of your Lord.

That is the principle which our Lord constantly emphasizes. He said to His disciples after His encounter with the rich young ruler, 'How hard is it for them that trust in riches to enter into the kingdom of God'. It is this trusting in riches, it is this fatal self-confidence, that makes it impossible for you to be poor in spirit. Or again, as He put it to the people one afternoon when He said, 'Labour not for the meat which perisheth, but for that meat which endureth unto everlasting life'. That is the kind of thing He meant by 'laying up treasures in heaven'.

How do we do this in practice? The first thing is to have a right view of life, and especially a right view of 'the glory'. That is the principle with which we started. The great fact of which we must never lose sight is that in this life we are but pilgrims. We are walking through this world under the eye of God, in the direction of God and towards our everlasting hope. That is the principle. If we always think of ourselves in that way, how can we go wrong? Everything will then fall into position. That is the great principle taught in Hebrews 11. Those mighty men, those great heroes of the faith had but one purpose. They walked 'as seeing him who is invisible'. They said they were 'strangers and pilgrims on the earth', they were making for 'a city which hath foundations, whose builder and maker is God'. So when God called out Abraham he responded. He turned to a man like Moses who had amazing prospects in the Egyptian court and commanded him to leave it all and to become a miserable shepherd for forty years, and Moses obeyed, 'for he had respect unto the recompence of the reward'. And so with all of them. What made Abraham ready to sacrifice his beloved son Isaac? What made all the other heroes of the faith prepared to do the things they did? It was that they desired 'a better country, that is, an heavenly'.

We must always start with that great principle. If we have a right view of ourselves in this world as pilgrims, as children of God going to our Father, everything falls into its true perspective. We shall immediately take a right view of our gifts and our possessions. We begin to think of ourselves only as stewards who must give an account of them. We are not the permanent holders of these things. It matters not whether it is money, or intellect, or ourselves, or our personalities, or whatever gift we may have. The worldly man thinks he himself owns them all. But the Christian starts by saying, 'I am not the possessor of these things; I merely have them on lease, and they do not really belong to me. I cannot take my wealth with me, I cannot take my gifts with me. I am but a custodian of these things'. And, at once, the great question that arises is: 'How can I use these things to the glory of God? It is God I have to meet, it is God I have to face, it is He who is my eternal judge and my Father. It is to Him that I shall have to render up an account of my stewardship of all the things with which He has blessed me.' 'Therefore,' the Christian says to himself, 'I must be careful how I use these things, and of my attitude towards them. I must do all the things He tells me to do in order that I may please Him.'

There, then, is the way in which we can lay up treasures in heaven. It all comes back to the question of how I view myself and how I view my life in this world. Do I tell myself every day I live, that this is but another milestone I am passing, never to go back, never to come again? I am pitching my moving tent 'a day's march nearer home'. That is the great principle of which I must constantly remind myself — that I am a child of the Father placed here for His purpose, not for myself. I did not choose to come; I have not brought myself here; there is a purpose in it all. God has given me this great privilege of living in this world, and if He has endued me with any gifts, I have to realize that, although in one sense all these things are mine, ultimately, as Paul shows at the end of 1 Corinthians 3, they are God's. Therefore, regarding myself as one who has this great privilege of being a caretaker for God, a custodian and a steward, I do not cling to these things. They do not become the centre of my life and existence. I do not live for them or dwell upon them constantly in my mind; they do not absorb my life. On the contrary, I hold them loosely; I am in a state of blessed detachment from them. I am not governed by them; rather do I govern them; and as I do this I am steadily securing, and safely laying up for myself, 'treasures in heaven'.

'But what a selfish outlook', says someone. My reply is that I am but obeying the exhortation of the Lord Jesus Christ. He tells us to lay up for ourselves treasures in heaven, and the saints have always done so. They believed in the reality of the glory that awaited them. They hoped to get there and their one desire was to enjoy it in all its perfection and in all its fulness. If we are anxious to 'follow in their train' and to enjoy the same glory we had better listen to our Lord's exhortation, 'Lay not up for yourselves treasures upon earth . . . but lay up for yourselves treasures in heaven.'

Chapter Eight

God or Mammon

I N our analysis of verses 19-24 we have seen that our Lord first of all lays down a proposition or a commandment, 'Lay not up for yourselves treasures upon earth . . . but lay up for yourselves treasures in heaven.' In other words, He tells us that we are so to live in this world, and so to use everything we have, whether our possessions, or gifts, or talents, or propensities, that we shall be laying up for ourselves treasures in heaven.

Then, having given us the injunction in that way, our Lord proceeds to supply us with reasons for doing this. I would remind you again that here we have an illustration of the wonderful condescension and understanding of our blessed Lord. He has no need to give us reasons. It is for Him to command. But He stoops to our weakness, mighty as He is, and He comes to our aid and supplies us with these reasons for carrying out His commandment. He does so in a very remarkable manner. He elaborates the reasons and presses them upon our consideration. He does not merely give us one reason; He gives us a number. He works it out for us in a series of logical propositions, and, of course, there can be no doubt at all but that He does this, not only because He is anxious to help us, but also, and still more perhaps, because of the desperate seriousness of the subject with which He is dealing. Indeed, we shall see that this is one of the most serious matters which we can ever consider together.

Again we must remember that these words were addressed to Christian people. This is not what our Lord has to say to the unbeliever out in the world; this is the warning that He gives to the Christian. We are dealing here with the subject of worldliness, or worldly-mindedness, and the whole problem of the world; but we must cease to think of it in terms of people who are in the world outside. This is the peculiar danger of *Christian* people. At this point our Lord is dealing with them and nobody else. You can argue if you like that if all this is true for the Christian, it is much more so for the non-Christian. That is a perfectly fair deduction; but there is nothing so fatal and tragic as to think that words like these have nothing to do with us because we are Christians. Indeed, this is perhaps the most urgent word that is needed by Christian people at this very moment. The world is so subtle, worldliness is such a pervasive thing, that we are all guilty of it, and often without realizing it. We tend to label worldliness as meaning certain particular things only, and always the things of which we are not guilty. We therefore argue that this has nothing to say to us. But worldliness is all-pervasive, and is not confined to certain things. It does not just mean going to theatres or cinemas, or doing a few things of that nature. No, worldliness is an attitude towards life. It is a general outlook, and it is so subtle that it can come into the most holy things of all, as we saw earlier.

We might digress here for a moment and look at this subject from the standpoint of the great political interest in this country, particularly, for example, at the time of a General Election. What, in the last analysis, is the real interest? What is the real thing that people on both sides and all sides are concerned about? They are interested in 'treasures upon earth', whether they be people who have treasures or whether they be people who would like to have them. They are all interested in the treasures; and it is most instructive to listen to what people say, and to observe how they betray themselves and the worldliness of which they are guilty, and the way in which they are laying up for themselves treasures upon earth. To be very practical (and if the preaching of the gospel is not practical it is not true preaching), there is a very simple test which we can apply to ourselves to see whether these things apply to us or not. When, at the time of a General or local Election, we are called on to make a choice of candidates, do we find ourselves believing that one political point of view is altogether right and the other altogether wrong? If we do, I suggest we are somehow or another laying up for ourselves treasures on earth. If we say that the truth is altogether on one side or the other, then if we analyse our motives we shall discover it is because we are either protecting something or anxious to have something. Another good way of testing ourselves is to ask ourselves quite simply and honestly why we hold our particular views. What is our real interest? What is our motive? What, when we are quite honest and truthful with ourselves, is really at the back of these particular political views that we hold? It is a most illuminating question if we are really honest. I suggest that most people will find if they face that question quite honestly, that there are some treasures upon earth about which they are concerned, and in which they are interested.

The next test is this. To what extent are our feelings engaged in this matter?

How much bitterness is there, how much violence, how much anger and scorn and passion? Apply that test, and again we shall find that the feeling is aroused almost invariably by the concern about laying up treasures upon earth. The last test is this. Are we viewing these things with a kind of detachment and objectivity or not? What is our attitude towards all these things? Do we instinctively think of ourselves as pilgrims, and mere sojourners in this world, who of course have to be interested in these things while we are here? Such an interest is certainly right, it is our duty. But what is our ultimate attitude? Are we controlled by it? Or do we stand apart and regard it objectively, as something which is ephemeral, something which does not really belong to the essence of our life and being, something with which we are concerned only for a while, as we are passing through this life? We should ask ourselves these questions in order that we may make quite certain whether this injunction of our Lord is speaking to us. Those are some of the ways in which we can find out very simply whether we are or are not guilty of laying up for ourselves treasures upon earth, and not laying up for ourselves treasures in heaven.

When we come to consider our Lord's arguments against laying up treasures on earth, we find that the first is one which we may very well describe as the argument of common sense, or of ordinary observation. 'Lay not up for yourselves treasures upon earth.' Why? For this reason: 'where moth and rust doth corrupt, and where thieves break through and steal'. But why should I lay up treasures in heaven? For this reason: 'where neither moth nor rust doth corrupt, and where thieves do not break through nor steal'. Our Lord is saying that worldly treasures do not last; that they are transitory, passing, ephemeral. 'Change and decay in all around I see.' 'Where moth and rust doth corrupt.'

How true it is. There is an element of decay in all these things, whether we like it or not. Our Lord puts it in terms of the moth and rust that tend to lodge themselves in these things and destroy them. Spiritually we can put it like this. These things never fully satisfy. There is always something wrong with them; they always lack something. There is no person on earth who is fully satisfied; and though in a sense some may appear to have everything that they desire, still they want something else. Happiness cannot be purchased.

There is, however, another way of looking at the effect of moth and rust spiritually. Not only is there an element of decay in these things; it is also true that we always tend to tire of them. We may enjoy them for a while, but somehow or other they begin to pall or we lose interest in them. That is why we are always talking about new things and seeking them. Fashions change; and though we are very enthusiastic about certain things for a while, soon they no longer interest us as they did. Is it not true that as age advances these things cease to satisfy us? Old people generally do not like the same things as young people, or the young the same as the old. As we get older these things seem to become different, there is an element of moth and rust. We could even go further and put it more strongly and say that there is an impurity in them. At their best they are all infected. Do what you will you cannot get rid of the impurity; the moth and rust are there and all your chemicals do not stop these processes. Peter says a wonderful thing in this very connection: 'Whereby are given unto us exceeding great and precious promises; that by these ye might be partakers of the divine nature, having escaped the corruption that is in the world through lust' (2 Pet. 1:4). There is corruption in all these earthly things; they are all impure.

The last fact, therefore, about these things is that they inevitably perish. Your most beautiful flower is beginning to die immediately you pluck it. You will soon have to throw it away. That is true of everything in this life and world. It does not matter what it is, it is passing, it is all fading away. Everything that has life is, as the result of sin, subject to this process — 'moth and rust doth corrupt'. Things develop holes and become useless, and at the end they are gone and become utterly corrupt. The most perfect physique will eventually give way and break down and die; the most beautiful countenance will in a sense become ugly when the process of corruption has got going; the brightest gifts tend to fade. Your great genius may be seen gibbering in delirium as the result of disease. However wonderful and beautiful and glorious things may be, they all perish. That is why, perhaps, the saddest of all failures in life is the failure of the philosopher who believes in worshipping goodness, beauty and truth; because there is no such thing as perfect goodness, there is no such thing as unalloyed beauty; there is an element of wrong and of sin and a lie in the highest truths. 'Moth and rust doth corrupt.'

'Yes,' says our Lord, 'and thieves break through and steal.' We must not stay with these things, they are so obvious, and yet we are so slow to recognize them. There are many thieves in this life and they are always threatening us. We think we are safe in our house; but we find thieves have broken in and ransacked it. Other marauders are always threatening us — illness, a business loss, some industrial collapse, war and finally death itself. It matters not what it is that we tend to hold on to in this world, one or other of these thieves is always threatening and will eventually take it from us. It is not only money. It may be some person for whom you are really living, your pleasure is in that one person. Beware, my friends; there are robbers and thieves who are bound to come and eventually rob you of these possessions. Take our possessions at their highest as well as their lowest; they are all subject to these robbers, these attacks. 'The thieves break through and steal', and we cannot prevent them. So our Lord appeals to our common sense, and reminds us that these worldly treasures never last. 'Change and decay in all around I see.'

But look at the other, positive side. 'Lay up for yourselves treasures in heaven, where neither moth nor rust doth corrupt, and where thieves do not break through nor steal.' This is wonderful and full of glory. Peter puts it in a phrase. He says 'to an inheritance incorruptible, and undefiled, and that fadeth not away, reserved in heaven for you' (1 Pet. 1:4). 'The things which are not seen are eternal,' says St. Paul; it is the things which are seen that are temporal (2 Cor. 4:18). These heavenly things are imperishable and the thieves cannot break through and steal. Why? Because God Himself is reserving them for us. There is no enemy that can ever rob us of them, or can ever enter in. It is impossible because God Himself is the Guardian. Spiritual pleasures are invulnerable, they are in a place which is impregnable. 'I am persuaded, that neither death, nor life, nor angels, nor principalities, nor powers, nor things present, nor things to come, nor height, nor depth, nor any other creature, shall be able to separate us from the love of God, which is in Christ Jesus our Lord' (Rom. 8:38, 39). Furthermore, there is nothing impure there; naught that corrupts shall enter in. There is no sin there, nor element of decay. It is the realm of eternal life and eternal light. He dwells 'in the light which no man can approach unto', as the apostle Paul puts it (1 Tim. 6:16). Heaven is the realm of life and light and purity, and nothing belonging to death, nothing tainted or polluted can gain admission there. It is perfect; and the treasures of the soul and of the spirit belong to that realm. Lay them up there, says our Lord, because there is no moth nor rust there, and no thief can ever break through nor steal.

It is an appeal to common sense. Do we not know that these things are true? Are they not true of necessity? Do we not see it all as we live in this world? Take up your morning newspaper and look at the death column; look at all that is happening. We know all these things. Why do we not practise them and live accordingly? Why do we lay up treasures on earth when we know what is going to happen to them? And why do we not lay up treasures in heaven where we know that there is purity and joy, holiness and everlasting bliss?

That, however, is merely the first argument, the argument of common sense. But our Lord does not stop at that. His second argument is based upon the terrible spiritual danger involved in laying up treasures on earth and not in heaven. That is a general heading, but our Lord divides it into certain subsections. The first thing against which He warns us in this spiritual sense is the awful grip and power of these earthly things upon us. You notice the terms He uses. He says, 'Where your treasure is, there will your heart be also.' The heart!

Then in verse 24 He talks about the mind. 'No man can serve two masters' — and we should notice the word 'serve'. These are the expressive terms He uses in order to impress upon us the terrible control that these things tend to exercise over us. Are we not all aware of them the moment we stop to think — the tyranny of persons, the tyranny of the world? This is not something we can think about at a distance as it were. We are all involved in this; we are all in the grip of this awful power of worldliness which really will master us unless we are aware of it.

But it is not only powerful; it is very subtle. It is the thing that really controls most men's lives. Have you seen the change, the subtle change, that tends to take place in men's lives as they succeed and prosper in this world? It does not happen to those who are truly spiritual men; but if they are not, it invariably happens. Why is it that idealism is generally associated with youth and not with middle age and old age? Why do men tend to become cynical as they get older? Why does the noble outlook upon life tend to go? It is because we all become victims of 'treasures on earth', and if you watch you can see it in the lives of men. Read the biographies. Many a young man starts out with a bright vision; but in a very subtle way — not that he falls into gross sin — he becomes influenced, perhaps when he is at college, by an outlook that is essentially worldly. Though it may be highly intellectual, he nevertheless loses something that was vital in his soul and spirit. He is still a very nice man and, moreover, just and wise; but he is not the man he was when he began. Something has been lost. Yes; this is a familiar phenomenon: 'Shades of the prison house begin to close upon the growing boy.' Do we not all know something about it? It is there; it is a prison house, and it fastens itself upon us unless we are aware of it. This grip, this power, masters us and we become slaves.

However, our Lord does not stop at the general. He is so anxious to show us this terrible danger that He works it out in detail. He tells us that this terrible thing that grips us tends to affect the entire personality; not merely part of us, but the whole man. And the first thing He mentions is the 'heart'. Having laid down the injunction He says, 'For where your treasure is, there will your heart be also.' These things grip and master our feelings, our affections and all our sensibility. All that part of our nature is absolutely gripped by them and we love them. Read John 3:19. 'This is the condemnation, that light is come into the world, and men loved darkness rather than light, because their deeds were evil.' We love these things. We pretend that we only like them, but really we love them. They move us deeply.

The next thing about them is a little more subtle. They not only grip the heart, they grip the mind. Our Lord puts it in this way: 'The light of the body is the eye: if therefore thine eye be single, thy whole body shall be full of light. But if thine eye be evil, thy whole body shall be full of darkness. If therefore the light that is in thee be darkness, how great is that darkness!' (vv. 22, 23). This picture of the eye is just His way of describing, by means of an illustration, the way in which we look at things. And according to our Lord, there are but two ways of looking at everything in this world. There is what He calls the 'single' eye, the eye of the spiritual man who sees things really as they are, truly and without any double view. His eye is clear and he sees things normally. But there is the other eye which He calls the 'evil' eye, which is a kind of double vision, or, if you like, it is the eye in which the lenses are not clear. There are mists and opacities and we see things in a blurred way. That is the evil eye. It is coloured by certain prejudices, coloured by certain lusts and desires. It is not a clear vision; it is all cloudy, coloured by these various tints and taints. That is what is meant by this statement which has so often confused people, because they do not take it in its context. Our Lord in this picture is still dealing with the laying up of treasures. Having shown that where the treasure is, the heart will be also, He says that it is not only the heart but the mind as well. These are the things that control man.

Let us work out this principle. Is it not amazing to notice how much of our thought is based upon these earthly treasures? The divisions in thought in almost every realm are almost entirely controlled by prejudice, not by pure thought. How very little thinking there is in this country at the time of a general election for example. None of the protagonists reason; they simply present prejudices. How little thought there is on every side. It is so obvious in the political realm. But alas, it is not confined to politics. This blurring of the vision by love of earthly treasures tends to affect us morally also! How clever we all are at explaining that a particular thing we do is not really dishonest. Of course if a man smashes a window and steals jewellery he is a robber; but if I just manipulate my income tax return. . . . ! Certainly that is not robbery, we say, and we persuade ourselves that all is well. Ultimately there is but one reason for our doing these things, and that is our love of earthly treasures. These things control the mind as well as the heart. Our views and our whole ethical outlook are controlled by these things.

Even worse than that, however, our religious outlook is controlled by these things also. 'Demas hath forsaken me', writes Paul. Why? 'Having loved this present world.' How often this is seen in the matter of service. These are the things that determine our action, though we do not recognize it. Our Lord says in another place: 'Take heed to yourselves, lest at any time your hearts be overcharged with surfeiting, and drunkenness, and cares of this life, and so that day come upon you unawares. For as a snare shall it come on all them that dwell on the face of the whole earth. Watch ye therefore, and pray always, that ye may be accounted worthy to escape all these things that shall come to pass, and to stand before the Son of man' (Luke 21:34-36). It is not only evil doing that dulls the mind and makes us incapable of thinking clearly. The cares of this world, settling down in life, enjoying our life and our family, any one of these things, our worldly position or our comforts — these are equally as dangerous as surfeiting and drunkenness. There is no doubt but that much of the so-called wisdom which men claim in this world is nothing, in the last analysis, but this concern about earthly treasures.

But lastly, these things not only grip the heart and mind, they also affect the will. Says our Lord, 'No man can serve two masters'; and the moment we mention the word 'serve' we are in the realm of the will, the realm of action. You notice how perfectly logical this is. What we do is the result of what we think; so what is going to determine our lives and the exercise of our wills is what we think, and that in turn is determined by where our treasure is — our heart. So we can sum it up like this. These earthly treasures are so powerful that they grip the entire personality. They grip a man's heart, his mind and his will; they tend to affect his spirit, his soul and his whole being. Whatever realm of life we may be looking at, or thinking about, we shall find these things are there. Everyone is affected by them; they are a terrible danger.

But the last step is the most solemn and serious of all. We must remember that the way in which we look at these things ultimately determines our relationship to God. 'No man can serve two masters: for either he will hate the one, and love the other; or else he will hold to the one, and despise the other. Ye cannot serve God and mammon.' This is indeed a very solemn thing, and that is why it is dealt with so frequently in Scripture. The truth of this proposition is obvious. Both make a totalitarian demand upon us. Worldly things really do make a totalitarian demand as we have seen. How they tend to grip the entire personality and affect us everywhere! They demand our entire devotion; they want us to live for them absolutely. Yes, but so does God. 'Thou shalt love the Lord thy God with all thy heart, and with all thy soul, and with all thy mind, and with all thy strength.' Not in a material sense necessarily, but in some sense or other He says to us all, 'Go, sell all that thou hast, and come, follow me.' 'He that loveth father or mother more than me is not worthy of me: and he that loveth son or daughter more than me is not worthy of me.' It is a totalitarian demand. Notice it again in verse 24: 'Either he will hate the one, and love the other; or else he will hold to the one, and despise the other.' It is 'either — or'; compromise is completely impossible at this point. 'Ye cannot serve God and mammon.'

This is something which is so subtle that many of us miss it completely at the present time. Some of us are violent opponents of what we speak of as 'atheistic materialism'. But lest we may feel too happy about ourselves because we are opponents of that, let us realize that the Bible tells us that all materialism is atheistic. Ye cannot serve God and mammon; it is impossible. So if a materialistic outlook is really controlling us, we are godless, whatever we may say. There are many atheists who speak religious language; but our Lord tells us here that even worse than atheistic materialism is a materialism that thinks it is godly — 'if the light that is in thee be darkness, how great is that darkness!' The man who thinks he is godly because he talks about God, and says he believes in God, and goes to a place of worship occasionally, but is really living for certain earthly things — how great is that man's darkness! There is a perfect illustration of that in the Old Testament. Study carefully 2 Kings 17:24-41. Here is what we are told. The Assyrians conquered some area; then they took their own people and settled them in that area. These Assyrians of course did not worship God. Then some lions came and destroyed their property. 'This', they said, 'has happened to us because we do not worship the God of this particular land. We will get priestly instruction on this.' So they found a priest who instructed them generally in the religion of Israel. And then they thought that all would be well. But this is what Scripture said about them: they 'feared the Lord, and served their graven images'.

What a terrible thing that is. It alarms me. It is not what we say that matters. In the last day many shall say, 'Lord, Lord, have we not done this, that and the other?' But He will say unto them, 'I never knew you'. 'Not every one that saith unto me, Lord, Lord, shall enter into the kingdom of heaven; but he that doeth the will of my Father.' Whom do you serve? That is the question, and it is either God or mammon. There is nothing in the last analysis that is so insulting to God as to take His name upon us and yet to show clearly that we are serving mammon in some shape or form. That is the most terrible thing of all. It is the greatest insult to God; and how easily and unconsciously we can all become guilty of this.

I remember once hearing a preacher tell a story which he assured us was simple, literal truth. It illustrates perfectly the point which we are considering. It is the story of a farmer who one day went happily and with great joy in his heart to report to his wife and family that their best cow had given birth to twin calves, one red and one white. And he said, 'You know I have suddenly had a feeling and impulse that we must dedicate one of these calves to the Lord. We will bring them up together, and when the time comes we will sell one and keep the proceeds, and we will sell the other and give the proceeds to the Lord's work.' His wife asked him which he was going to dedicate to the Lord. 'There is no need to bother about that now,' he replied, 'we will treat them both in the same way, and when the time comes we will do as I say.' And off he went. In a few months the man entered his kitchen looking very miserable and unhappy. When his wife asked him what was troubling him, he answered, 'I have bad news to give you. The Lord's calf is dead.' 'But', she said, 'you had not decided which was to be the Lord's calf.' 'Oh yes,' he said; 'I had always decided it was to be the white one, and it is the white one that has died. The Lord's calf is dead.' We may laugh at that story, but God forbid that we should be laughing at ourselves. It is always the Lord's calf that dies. When money becomes difficult, the first thing we economize on is our contribution to God's work. It is always the first thing to go. Perhaps we must not say 'always', for that would be unfair; but with so many it is the first thing, and the things we really like are the last to go. 'Ye cannot serve God and mammon.' These things tend to come between us and God, and our attitude to them ultimately determines our relationship to God. The mere fact that we believe in God, and call Him, Lord, Lord, and likewise with Christ, is not proof in and of itself that we are serving Him, that we recognize His totalitarian demand, and have yielded ourselves gladly and readily to Him. 'Let every man examine himself.'

Chapter Nine

Sin's Foul Bondage

IN our consideration of this particular passage we have so far been dealing with what we might call the direct and explicit teaching of our Lord concerning this matter of treasures upon earth and treasures in heaven. But we cannot leave it at that, because there is surely something else here. In these verses 19-24, there is indirect teaching, there is implicit teaching; and we fail to pay attention to such teaching in Scripture always at our peril. Our Lord is concerned with the practical aspect of this matter, but obviously there is something else involved as well. In warning us about this very practical matter, He also deals incidentally with most important doctrine, although He does not set out primarily to do that. We can put it like this. Why is it that these instructions are necessary? Why is it that the Bible is full of this kind of warning? It is to be found everywhere; this is only one example, but there are many others which we could take. What is it that makes it so necessary for our Lord, and the apostles afterwards, to warn us as Christian people about these things?

Surely there is only one answer to that question. All this is simply due to sin and its effects. There is a sense in which one is astounded when one reads a passage such as this. One tends to say, 'I am a Christian; I have a new view of things, and I do not need this'. And yet we see it is necessary, and we all need it. In various ways all of us are not only being attacked by this, but are being conquered by it. There is only one thing that explains that, and that is sin, the terrible power and effect of sin upon mankind. So that here we can see that, as our Lord expounds His teaching, gives His commandment and states His reasons, He is incidentally telling us a great deal about sin and what it does to man.

I

The first thing we must note is that sin is obviously something that has an entirely disturbing and upsetting effect upon the normal balance in man, and the normal functioning of his qualities. There are three parts to man. He was made by God, body, mind and spirit, or, if you prefer it, body, soul and spirit; and the highest is the spirit. Next to that comes the soul, and next to that the body. Not that there is anything wrong with the body, but that is the relative order. The effect of sin is that the normal functions of man have been entirely disturbed. There is no doubt that, in one sense, the highest gift that God has given to man is the gift of mind. According to the Scripture man was made in the image of God; and a part of the image of God in man is undoubtedly the mind, the ability to think and to reason, especially in the highest sense and in a spiritual sense. Man, therefore, was obviously meant to function in the following way. His mind, being the highest faculty and propensity that he possesses, should always come first. Things are perceived with the mind and analysed by it. Then come the affections, the heart, the feeling, the sensibility given to man by God. Then thirdly there is that other quality, that other faculty, called the will, the power by which we put into operation the things we have understood, the things we have desired as the result of apprehension.

That is the way in which God made man, and that is how man was meant to function. He was meant to understand and to be governed and controlled by his understanding. He was to love that which he thus understood to be best and truest for himself and for all concerned; and then he was to put all that into practice and into operation. But the effect of the Fall and of sin upon man has been to upset that order and balance. You notice how our Lord puts it here. He lays down His instruction: 'Lay not up for yourselves treasures upon earth, where moth and rust doth corrupt, and where thieves break through and steal: but 'Lay up for yourselves treasures in heaven, where neither moth nor rust doth corrupt, and where thieves do not break through nor steal. For where your treasure is, there will your heart be also.' The heart comes first. Then He goes on to the mind and says, 'The light of the body is the eye: if therefore thine eye be single, thy whole body shall be full of light. But if thine eye be evil, thy whole body shall be full of darkness.' The heart is first, the mind second, and the will third; for 'No man can serve two masters: for either he will hate the one, and love the other; or else he will hold to the one, and despise the other. Ye cannot serve God and mammon.'

We have already considered the way in which these earthly treasures and possessions tend to master and control the entire personality — heart, and mind, and will. Then we were not concerned about the order; but this time we are very concerned about the order in which our Lord puts these things, for what He says here is nothing but the simple truth about us all by nature. Man, as the result of sin and the Fall, is no longer governed by his mind and understanding; he is governed by his desires, his affections and his lusts. That is the teaching of Scripture. Thus we see that man is in the terrible predicament of being no longer governed by his highest faculty, but by something else, something subsidiary.

There are many Scriptures which prove this. Take that great statement in John 3:19: 'This is the condemnation (this is the final condemnation of mankind), that light is come (or has come) into the world.' What, then, is the matter with man? Does he not believe it? Does he not accept it? No, 'This is the condemnation, that light is come into the world, and men loved darkness rather than light, because their deeds were evil'. Man, in other words, instead of looking at life with his mind, looks at it with his desires and affections. He prefers darkness; he is controlled by his heart instead of by his head. We must be quite clear about this. This is not to say that man as God made him should not have a heart, and should not feel things. The important thing is that no man should be governed by his emotions and desires. That is the effect of sin. A man should be *governed* by his mind, his understanding.

This surely is the final answer to all those people who are not Christian, and who say they are not Christian because they think and because they reason. The simple truth about them is that they are governed, not by their minds, but by their hearts and by their prejudices. Their elaborate attempts to justify themselves intellectually is nothing but an attempt to camouflage the godlessness of their hearts. They are trying to justify the kind of life they are living by putting up an intellectual position; but the real trouble is that they are governed by desires and by lusts. They do not approach the truth with the mind, they approach it with all these prejudices which come from the heart. As the Psalmist puts it so perfectly: 'The fool hath said in his heart, There is no God.' That is what the unbeliever always says, and that is why he says it; and then he tries to find an intellectual reason to justify what his heart wants to say.

Our Lord here reminds us of this plainly. It is the heart that covets these worldly things, and the heart in sinful man is so powerful that it governs his mind, his understanding and his intellect. Man likes to think of himself as a gigantic intellect. Scientists are often fond of claiming this; but I can assure you that scientists are sometimes the most prejudiced men you can meet. Some of them are prepared to manipulate facts in order to buttress their theory. They often start their books by saying that a certain idea is but a theory, but a few pages later you find them referring to it as a fact. That is the heart in operation and not the mind. This is one of the greatest tragedies about sin and its effects. In the first instance it upsets the order and the balance; and the greatest and supreme gift becomes subservient to the lesser. 'Where your treasure is, there will your heart be also.'

II

The second thing that sin does is to blind man in certain vital respects. Of course that follows by a kind of inevitable logic. If the mind is not always in control there is of necessity going to be a kind of blinding. The apostle Paul's way of putting it is this: 'If our gospel be hid, it is hid to them that are lost: in whom the god of this world hath blinded the minds of them which believe not' (2 Cor. 4:3 and 4). That is precisely what sin does and it does it through the heart. We can see how our Lord illustrates that principle in this short paragraph at which we are looking. Sin blinds the mind of man to things which are perfectly obvious; and so, though they are so obvious, man in sin does not see them.

Take this question of worldly treasures. It is a simple fact that none of them continue. There is no need to argue about that; it is the obvious truth. We looked at some of these treasures in our last chapter. People pride themselves on personal appearance. It is bound to deteriorate. They are going to be desperately ill one day and die, and decay will set in. It is bound to happen; yet people pride themselves on this, and may even sacrifice their belief in God for it. The same thing applies to money. We cannot take it with us when we die, and we are always liable to lose it. All these things pass away; they are all bound to go. If a man sits down and really faces that, he must admit that it is the simple truth; yet all people who are not Christian tend to live on the opposite assumption. They are jealous and envious of one another, they will sacrifice everything for these things — these things that are bound to come to an end and which they are bound to leave behind them. The real situation is so obvious, and yet they do not seem to see the obvious. If a man just sits down and says, 'Well, now; here I am today living in this world. But what is going to happen to me? What is my future?', he is bound to say in reply, 'I may go on living like this for a number of years, or I may not; I do not know. I may not be alive tomorrow; I may not be alive a week from today; I do not know. But I know for certain that this is bound to come to an end. There will be an end to my life in this world. I have to die; and when I die I have to leave all these things. I shall have to leave my house, my loved ones, my possessions. I have to leave it all behind and go on without them.' We know that that is the simple fact. But how often do we face that fact? How often do we live in the realization of it? Is our whole life controlled by the consciousness of that obvious truth? The answer is that it is not; and the reason for this is sin which blinds the mind of man to that which is absolutely obvious. 'Change and decay in all around I see' we often sing. Yet though I do see it, I do not seem to perceive it.

In the same way sin blinds us to the relative values of things. Take time and eternity. We are creatures here in time and we are going on to eternity. There is no comparison between the relative importance of time and eternity. Time is limited and eternity is endless and absolute. Yet do we live as realizing these relative values? Is it not again a simple fact that we give ourselves to things that belong to time and entirely ignore the things that are eternal? Is it not true that all the things about which we bother so much belong to a very short span of time, and though we know that there are other things that are eternal and endless, we scarcely stop to think about them at all? That is the effect of sin — relative values are not appreciated.

Or take darkness and light. There is no real comparison between them. There is nothing more wonderful than light. It is one of the most amazing things in the universe. God Himself is light and 'in him is no darkness at all'. We know the kind of deeds that belong to darkness, the things that happen in the dark, and under the cover of night. But there will be no darkness and no night in heaven. It is all light and glory there. But how slow we are to appreciate the relative value of light and darkness. 'Men love darkness rather than light, because their deeds are evil.'

Then think again of the value of man and of God. The whole of life apart from Christianity is evaluated in terms of man. He is the one to be considered, his being and his welfare. All who are not Christian are living for man, for themselves and others like themselves. God in the meantime is being forgotten and ignored. He is told to wait until we have a little more time for Him. This is surely characteristic of the life of all mankind as affected by sin. We do not hesitate to turn our backs upon God and say, in effect, 'When I am ill, or on my deathbed I will turn to God; but now I am living for myself'. Our worldly life is being put before God. This is blindness. The mind is blind to relative values. Think of men coveting earthly wealth and earthly riches, position and status, and putting all that before becoming 'heirs of God, and joint-heirs with Christ', before becoming inheritors of the whole world! 'Blessed are the meek: for they shall inherit the earth.' But men do not consider that, and do not covet it, so intent are they upon the immediate.

Consider yet another respect in which sin and evil blind the mind of man. They blind him to the impossibility of mixing opposites. It is all here. Man is always trying to mix things which cannot be mixed. Still worse is the fact that he persuades himself that he can do it successfully. He is quite sure this compromise is possible, and yet our Lord tells us it is not. If you want it stated philosophically, you have but to turn to Aristotle and his axiom to the effect that 'there is no mean between two opposites'. Opposites are opposites, and you will never get a mean between them. Here it is. There is no possible mixing of light and darkness. It is no longer light if you do, and it is no longer darkness. Neither can you mix God and mammon, for no man can serve two masters. It is one or the other, 'for either he will hate the one, and love the other; or else he will hold to the one, and despise the other.' These are absolutes, and if we were capable of thinking clearly we should recognize them as such. They are both totalitarian. Both demand our entire allegiance, and therefore they cannot be mixed. But man in sin and in his supposed cleverness sees two things at one and the same time; and he glories in this double vision. Our Lord, however, tells us here that it cannot be done. We cannot love two opposite things at the same time. Love is exclusive; it is demanding, and always insists upon the absolute. It is either one or the other; it must be light or darkness. The eye is single or not single; it is either God or mammon.

Is not the failure to recognize this the whole trouble with the world today? I fear it is no longer the trouble with the world only. Is it not the trouble with the Church also? The Church of God for many a day has been trying to mix certain incompatibles. If it is a spiritual society, then we cannot mix the world with it in any shape or form. It does not matter what the form is. 'The world' does not mean gross sin only; it means things which are quite legitimate in and of themselves. It is this constant compromising in the life of the Church that has been her ruination ever since the days of Constantine. Once you have lost the division between the world and the Church, the Church ceases to be truly Christian. But, thank God, there have been revivals, there have been people who have seen this truth and who have refused to compromise. It is the only hope for the Church. We have been trying to sustain her by worldly methods, and it is not surprising that she is as she is. And she will continue to be like this as long as we continue to attempt the impossible. It is only when we come to realize that we are God's people, and a spiritual people, and that we live in the realm of the spirit, that we shall be blessed and shall begin to see a revival. We can introduce our worldly methods, and we may appear to be having success, but the Church will not improve. No! the Church is spiritual, and her spiritual life must be nurtured and sustained in a purely spiritual manner.

III

The next effect of sin upon man is to make him a slave of things that were meant to serve him. This is one of the terrible, tragic things about it. According to our Lord here, these earthly, worldly things tend to become our god. We serve them; we love them. Our heart is captivated by them; we are at their service. What are they? They are the very things that God in His kindness has given man in order that they might be of service to him, and in order that he may enjoy life while he is in this world. All these things that can be so dangerous to our souls because of sin were given to us by God, and we were meant to enjoy them — food and clothing, family and friends and all such things. These are all but a manifestation of the kindness and the graciousness of God. He has given them to us that we might have a happy and enjoyable life in this world; but because of sin, we have become their slaves. We are mastered by appetites. God has given us our appetites; hunger, thirst and sex are God-created. But the moment a man is dominated by them, or is mastered by them, he is a slave to them. What a tragedy; he bows down and worships at the shrine of things that were meant to be at his service. Things that were meant to minister to him have become his master. What a terrible, awful thing sin is!

IV

The last point, however, is the most serious and the most solemn of all. The final effect of sin upon mankind is that it entirely ruins man. That is the teaching of the Bible from beginning to end. This thing which came into life through the serpent in the Garden of Eden is intent upon nothing but our final ruination. The devil hates God with the whole of his being, and he has but one object and one ambition; it is to ruin and spoil all that God has made, and in which He delights. In other words, he is intent especially upon the ruination of man and of the world.

How does sin ruin man? Here is the answer as we find it in these verses. It ruins man in the sense that, having spent his lifetime in laying up certain things here on earth, he finds himself at the end with nothing. After laying up for himself treasures on earth where moth and rust doth corrupt, and thieves break through and steal, he finds himself face-to-face with the most powerful adversary of all which is death itself. Then this poor wretched man who has been living for these things suddenly finds himself with absolutely nothing — stripped with nothing at all but his naked soul. It is utter ruination. 'What shall it profit a man, if he shall gain the whole world, and lose his own soul?'

That is what sin eventually leads to, and there are many scriptural passages to prove this. Look at Luke 16:19-31. There it is perfectly; you need not go beyond that. This is a matter of understanding and common sense to which we need to apply our minds. Think of all the things for which you tend to be living at this moment, the things that really count, the things that really matter in your life. Then ask yourself this simple question: 'How many of these things will I be able to take with me when I die?' That is the test. How many of them will still be with you in the River of death and beyond the River? Sin is final ruination which leaves a man with nothing at the end.

Still worse in a sense is this, that at the end he also finds that he has been entirely and utterly wrong all his life. Our Lord puts it like this: 'The light of the body is the eye: if therefore thine eye be single, thy whole body shall be full of light. But if thine eye be evil, thy whole body shall be full of darkness. If therefore the light that is in thee be darkness, how great is that darkness!' That is a picture which means this. As we have seen, the light of the body is, in a sense, the mind, the understanding, this extraordinary faculty that God gave to man. If, as the result of sin and evil, and because of the control of the heart and of lust and passion and desire, this supreme instrument has become perverted, how great is that darkness! Is anything worse than that, or more terrible than that?

We can look at it like this. Man today, as we have been saying, and as we know full well, not only believes he is being led by his mind; he rejects God because of his mind and understanding. He laughs at religion, he laughs at those who denounce this worldly view of life. He lives for the present; it is the one thing that counts. And he believes that to be a rational point of view to take. He proves it to his own satisfaction and is convinced that he is led by his mind. He does not realize that the light that is in him has become dark. He does not see that his faculties have become upset because of sin. He does not see that various forces are controlling and drugging his mind which is therefore no longer operating freely and rationally. But at the end he will come to see it; at the end he will come to himself like the Prodigal Son of old. Suddenly he will see that the things in which he trusted were dark, and have misled him, and that he has lost everything — the light in him is darkness and how great is that darkness! There is nothing worse than that, to discover at the end that the very thing to which you pinned your faith is the one thing that has let you down.

All this can be seen in that picture of Dives and Lazarus in Luke 16. That man, I am sure, justified himself day by day and said, 'It is all right'. But after he died and found himself there in hell, he suddenly saw it. He saw that he had been a fool all his life. He had done it all deliberately, and it had led him to this. He saw what a fool he had been, and he pleaded with Abraham to send somebody to his brethren who were doing the same thing. He discovered that the light that was in him was darkness and that it was great darkness. That is one of the most subtle deeds of Satan. He persuades a man that by denying God he is being rational; but, as we have seen already several times, what is really happening is that he makes him a creature of lust and desire whose mind is blinded and whose eye is no longer single. The greatest faculty of all has become perverted.

If you are not a Christian do not trust your mind; it is the most dangerous thing you can do. But when you become a Christian your mind is put back in the centre and you become a rational being. There is no more pathetic illusion than for a man to think of the Christian faith as sob-stuff, the dope of the people, something purely emotional and irrational. The true view of it is stated perfectly by the apostle Paul in Romans 6:17. You have 'obeyed from the heart that form of doctrine which was delivered you'. The doctrine was preached to them, and when they came to see it they liked it, believed it, and put it into practice. They received the truth of God first of all with the mind. Truth must be received with the mind, and the Holy Spirit enables the mind to become clear. That is conversion, that is what happens as the result of regeneration. The mind is delivered from this bias of evil and darkness; it sees the truth and loves and desires it above everything else. That is it. There is nothing more tragic than for a man to find at the end of his life that he has been entirely wrong all the time.

A final word. This wretched man who is ruined by sin not only finds he has nothing, he not only discovers that he has entirely fooled himself and been misled by his supposed light, he finds himself also to be outside the life of God and under His wrath. 'Ye cannot serve God and mammon.' So if a man has served mammon in this life until he dies, he will find himself beyond death outside God. He has not served God, so there is only one thing to say about him, according to Scripture, and that is that 'the wrath of God abideth on him' (John 3:36). All he has lived for has gone; there in eternity he is a naked soul having to face God, the God who is love and who is gracious and kind. The Father, the One who counts the very hairs of the Christian's head, is a stranger to him. He is without God, and not only without God in the world but without God in eternity, without hope, facing an eternity of wretchedness and remorse, of misery and regrets. Sin is a total loss. If you are not living to serve Him, then that will be your fate. You will have nothing at all, and you will dwell in that negativity, that hopeless negativity through all eternity. God forbid that that should be the fate of anyone within reach of these words. If you want to avoid it, go to God and confess to Him that you have been serving earthly things, and laying up for yourselves treasures upon earth. Confess it to Him, give yourself to Him, place yourself unreservedly in His hands and above all ask Him to fill you with His Holy Spirit who alone can enlighten the mind, clear the understanding, make the eye single and enable us to see the truth — the truth about sin, and the only way of salvation by the blood of Christ — the Holy Spirit who can show us how to be delivered from the perversion and the pollution of sin, and to become new men and women, created after the fashion and pattern of the Son of God Himself, loving the things of God and serving Him, and Him alone.

Chapter Ten

Be Not Anxious

A T verse 25 we start a new section in this consideration of the Sermon on the Mount. It is a subsection, in reality, of the major theme which is being considered in this sixth chapter, namely, the Christian walking and living in this world, in his relationship to the Father.

There are two main aspects to be considered — what the Christian does in private, and what he does in public. You see how practical this Sermon is. It is far from being something remote and theoretical. It deals with the practicalities of the personal, private life — all I do, my life of prayer, my life of attempting to do good, my life of fasting, my personal devotion, the nurture and culture of my own spiritual life.

But I do not spend the whole of my time in these occupations. That would be to become a monk or a hermit. I do not segregate myself. No; I live in the world, and am engaged in business and in affairs, and have these multitudes of problems pressing in upon me. Above everything else our Lord reminds us in the second section, starting at verse 19, that the big problem that confronts us is that of worldliness, which is always there and always attacking us. That is the theme from verse 19 to the end of the chapter. But we have seen that it is divided into subsidiary sections. First of all there is the section we have already considered, consisting of verses 19-24. Here now, from verse 25 to the end of the chapter, we come to the second section. It is still the one theme, the danger of worldliness, the danger of mammon, the danger of being defeated by the mind, outlook and life of this present world.

There are perhaps two main ways of looking at the difference between verses 19-24 and this section. One way is to say that in the previous subdivision our Lord was chiefly emphasizing the danger of laying up treasures upon earth, hoarding them, amassing them, living to do that. Here, He is concerned not so much with our laying them up, as with our worrying about them, being anxious concerning them. And of course the two things are different. There are many people who may not be guilty of laying up treasures upon earth, but who nevertheless can be very guilty of worldliness, because they are always thinking about these things, being anxious about them and dwelling upon them constantly. That is the main difference between these two subsections. But it can be put in another way. Some people say that in verses 19-24 our Lord was chiefly addressing rich people, people who are well-off in this world's goods, and who therefore are in a position to lay them up and to amass them. But they suggest that from verse 25 to the end of the chapter He is thinking more of people who are either actually poor, or else those who cannot be described as rich, those who just manage to make both ends meet, those who are face-to-face with the problem of making a living and keeping things going in a material sense. To these people the main danger is not the danger of laying up treasures, or worshipping treasures in some shape or form, but the danger of being burdened by these things and being anxious about them. It does not really matter which interpretation you take. Both are true, for it is possible for a man who is really wealthy to be worried and burdened by these worldly matters; so we need not press the antithesis between rich and poor. The great thing is to concentrate on this danger of being oppressed and obsessed by the things that are seen, the things that belong to time and to this world alone.

Here, we are reminded once more of the terrible subtlety of Satan and of sin. It does not matter very much to Satan what form sin takes as long as he succeeds in his ultimate objective. It is immaterial to him whether you are laying up treasures on earth or worrying about earthly things; all he is concerned about is that your mind should be on them and not on God. And he will assail and attack you from every direction. You may think you have won this great battle against Satan because you conquered him when he came in at the front door and talked to you about laying up treasures on earth. But before you are aware of it, you will find he has come in through the back door and is causing you to have anxious concern about these things. He is still making you look at them, and so is perfectly content. He can transform himself into 'an angel of light'. There is no end to the variety of his methods. His one concern is that we should keep our minds on these things instead of centring them upon God and holding them there. But fortunately for us, we are led by One who knows him and his methods, and if we can say with St. Paul that 'we are not ignorant of his devices', it is because we have been taught and instructed by the Lord Jesus Christ Himself. How subtle was the devil's threefold temptation of Him in the wilderness! 'If thou be the Son of God.' We are subject to similar attacks but, thank God, our Lord has instructed us concerning it here, and His teaching is given in a very plain and explicit manner.

Our Lord continues His warning, He takes nothing for granted. He knows how frail we are; He knows the power of Satan and all his horrible subtlety, so He comes down to details. Again we shall see here, as we saw in the previous section, that He is not content merely to lay down principles or to give a command or injunction. He provides us with arguments and gives us reasons, He puts it to our common sense. We are reminded again that He puts the truth to our minds. He is not concerned to produce a certain emotional atmosphere only, He reasons with us. That is the great thing we need to grasp. So He again starts with a 'therefore' — 'Therefore I say unto you'.

He is carrying on the main argument, but He is going to put it in a slightly different manner. The theme of course is still this, the need of the single eye, the need of looking centrally at the one thing. You find Him repeating it, 'Seek ye first'. That is just another way of saying that you must have the single eye, and serve God and not mammon. At all costs we must do this. He therefore puts it three times over, introducing it by means of the word 'therefore'. 'Therefore I say unto you, Take no thought for your life, what ye shall eat, or what ye shall drink; nor yet for your body, what ye shall put on. Is not the life more than meat, and the body than raiment?' Then in verse 31, He says it again: 'Therefore take no thought, saying, What shall we eat? or, What shall we drink? or, Wherewithal shall we be clothed?' Then in verse 34, He says it again finally: 'Take therefore no thought for the morrow: for the morrow shall take thought for the things of itself. Sufficient unto the day is the evil thereof.' There was never a Teacher in this world like the Lord Jesus Christ! The great art of teaching is the art of repetition; the true teacher always knows that it is not enough to say a thing once, but that it needs to be repeated. So He says it three times, but each time in a slightly different form. His method is particularly interesting and fascinating, and as we proceed to consider it we shall see exactly what it is.

The first thing we must do is to consider the terms which He uses, and particularly this expression 'Take no thought', which people have often misunderstood, and over which many have tripped and stumbled. The Authorized Version puts it like this: 'Take no thought for your life, what ye shall eat . . .', and it goes on repeating that expression. But, of course, the real meaning of 'Take no thought' has changed since this Authorized Version was introduced in 1611. If you consult the authorities, you will find that they give quotations from Shakespeare to show that 'taking thought' was then used in the sense of 'being anxious', or tending to worry. So that the real translation at this point should be, 'Be not anxious', or 'Have no anxiety', or if you prefer it, 'Do not worry', about your life, what you shall eat or what you shall drink. That is the real meaning of the word. Indeed the actual word that was used by our Lord is a very interesting one; it is the word used to indicate something which divides, separates or distracts us, a word used very frequently in the New Testament. If you turn to Luke 12:29, a corresponding passage to this, you will find that the expression used there is 'neither be ye of doubtful mind'. It is a mind which is divided into sections and compartments, and which is not functioning as a whole. We cannot do better therefore than say that it is not 'a single eye'. There is a kind of double vision, a looking in two directions at one and the same time, and therefore not really seeing anything. That is what it means to be anxious, to be worried, to be 'taking thought' in this sense.

A still better illustration of the meaning of the term is to be found in the story of Martha and Mary when our Lord was in their house (Luke 10:38-42). Our Lord turned to Martha and rebuked her. He said, 'Thou art careful and troubled about many things.' Poor Martha was 'distracted' — that is the real meaning of the expression; she did not know where she was nor what she really wanted. Mary, on the other hand, had a single purpose, a single aim; she was not distracted by many things. What our Lord is warning us against, therefore, is the danger of thus being distracted from the main objective in life by care, by this anxiety about earthly, worldly things, by looking so much at them that we do not look at God — this danger of living the double life, this false view, this dualism. That is what He is concerned about.

Perhaps it is important to put in the negative at this point. Our Lord is not teaching us here that we must not think about these things at all. 'Taking no thought' does not mean that. Many times in the history of the Church there have been zealous, misguided people who have taken this literally, and have felt that to live the life of faith they must not think about the future in any sense, they must make no provision at all. They just 'live by faith', they just 'pray to God' and do nothing about it. That is not the meaning of 'Take no thought'. Quite apart from the exact meaning of these words, the context alone, surely, and the plain teaching of the New Testament elsewhere should have saved them from that error. A knowledge of the exact meaning of the words in the Greek is not the sole essential to true interpretation; if you read the Scriptures, and if you watch the context, you should be safeguarded from these errors. Surely the context here, the very illustration that our Lord uses, proves that these people must be wrong. He takes the argument of the birds of the air. It is not true to say that they just have to perch themselves upon the trees or upon a pole, and wait until food is mechanically brought to them. That is not true. They search for it busily. There is real activity in the fowls of the air, so that the very argument our Lord uses at this point entirely precludes the possibility of interpreting it as a kind of passive waiting upon God and doing nothing. Our Lord never condemns farmers for ploughing and harrowing and sowing and reaping and gathering into barns. He never condemns that, for it was God's command that man should live in that way, by the sweat of his brow. So these arguments put in the form of illustrations and including also that of the lilies of the field — how they draw their sustenance from the earth in which they are planted — taken especially in the light of the teaching of the Bible everywhere, should have saved men from this ridiculous misinterpretation. The apostle Paul put it very explicitly in his second letter to the Thessalonians where he says that if a man 'would not work, neither should he eat'. There were people then, misguided and somewhat fanatical, who said, 'The Lord is going to return at any moment; therefore we must not work; we must spend our time waiting for His return.' So they ceased to work and imagined they were being exceptionally spiritual. And that is Paul's laconic remark respecting them: 'If a man will not work, neither shall he eat.' There are certain fundamental principles governing life, and that is one of them.

We find an exposition of this commandment in that great saying of the apostle Paul in Philippians 4:6, 7, where he says, 'Be careful for nothing; but in every thing by prayer and supplication with thanksgiving let your requests be made known unto God. And the peace of God, which passeth all understanding, shall keep your hearts and minds through Christ Jesus.' Or, if you like, 'Do not be careful ('do not be full of care') about anything.' Again, that is not an injunction to idleness, it is a warning against care and anxiety, this tendency to worry that so constantly afflicts us in this life.

There can be no question at all about the real danger of this whole matter. The moment we stop to consider and examine ourselves, we shall find that we are not only open to this danger, but that we have often succumbed to it. Nothing seems to be more natural to mankind in this world than to become anxious, to become burdened and worried. It is the peculiar temptation, some would say, of women, especially of those who are responsible for the care of the home; but it is not by any means confined to them. The danger confronting the husband or father, or anyone who has responsibility towards loved ones and other people, in a world like this, is to spend the whole of life oppressed by these things, and weighed down by them. They tend to master and control us, and we go through life enslaved by them. That is the thing with which our Lord is concerned, and He is so concerned about it that He repeats this warning three times over.

First we shall look at His argument in a very general manner. Let us paraphrase what He actually says. 'Take no thought for your life, what ye shall eat, or what ye shall drink; nor yet for your body, what ye shall put on.' Here again He starts with a general statement and injunction, as He did in the previous section. There He began by laying down a law and then proceeded to give us reasons for keeping it. It is exactly the same here. There is the general statement; we are not to be anxious or worried about what we shall eat or what we shall drink, nor yet for our body what we shall put on. That of course is as comprehensive as anything can be. He is dealing with our life, our existence, our being in this body in which we live. Here we are, distinct personalities; we have this gift of life, and we live our life, in this world and through our bodies. So that when our Lord considers our life and our bodies He is, as it were, considering our essential personality and our life in this world. He puts it broadly; it is comprehensive and it includes the whole of man. He maintains that we must never be anxious either about our lives as such, or about the clothing of our bodies. It is as fully comprehensive as that, and it is very important that we should realize that, because this is a very thoroughgoing injunction. It does not apply only to certain aspects of our life; it takes in the whole of life, our health, our strength, our success, what is going to happen to us — that which is our life in any shape or form. And equally it takes the body as a whole, and tells us that we must not be anxious about our clothing, or any of these things that are part and parcel of our life in this world.

Having given the commandment, He then gives us a general reason for observing it and, as we shall see, having done this, He proceeds to subdivide it and to give particular reasons under two headings. But He starts with the general reason in these words: 'Is not the life more than meat, and the body than raiment?' That takes in the life and the body. Then He subdivides it and takes the life, and gives His argument; then He takes the body and gives His argument. But let us first look at the form of the general argument, which is very striking and important. The logicians would tell us that the argument He uses is one based upon a deduction from the greater to the lesser. He says in effect, 'Wait a minute; consider this before you become anxious. Is not your life more than meat, the sustenance, the food? Is not the body itself more important and greater than the raiment?'

What does our Lord mean by this? The argument is a very profound and powerful one; and how prone we are to forget it! He says in effect, 'Take this life of yours about which you are tending to worry and become anxious. How have you got it? Where has it come from?' And the answer, of course, is that it is a gift of God. Man does not create life; man does not give being to himself. Not one of us ever decided to come into this world. And the very fact that we are alive at this moment is entirely because God willed and God decided it. Life itself is a gift, a gift from God. So the argument which our Lord uses is this. If God has given you the gift of life — the greater gift — do you think He is now suddenly going to deny Himself and His own methods, and not see to it that that life is sustained and enabled to continue? God has His own ways of doing that, but the argument is that I need never become anxious about it. Of course I am to plough and sow and reap and gather into barns. I am to do the things that God has ordained for man and life in this world. I must go to work and earn money and so on. But all He says is that I need never be concerned or worried or anxious that suddenly there will not be sufficient to keep this life of mine going. That will never happen to me; it is impossible. If God has given me the gift of life, He will see to it that that life is kept going. But this is the point: He is not arguing as to *how* this will be done. He is just saying that it will be.

I commend to your study, as a matter of great interest and vital importance, the frequency with which that argument is used in the Scriptures. We have a perfect illustration of it in Romans 8:32, 'He that spared not his own Son, but delivered him up for us all, how shall he not with him also freely give us all things?' It is a very common biblical argument, the argument from the greater to the lesser, and we must always be watching for it and applying it. The Giver of the gift of life will see that the sustenance and support of that life will be provided. We must not stay now to take the argument from the birds of the air, but that is exactly what God does with them. They have to find their food, but it is He who provides it for them; He sees that it is there for them.

Exactly the same, of course, applies to the body. The body is a gift from God, and therefore we can be quite happy and certain in our minds that He will somehow or other provide the means whereby these bodies of ours can be covered and clothed. Here we come to one of His great principles, one of the great central principles of the Bible. There is nothing of which this modern generation needs to be reminded so much as just this. The main trouble with most of us is that we have forgotten first principles, and especially this vital one that the things we enjoy in this life are the gift of God. For instance, how often do we thank God for the gift of life itself? We tend to think that with our scientific knowledge we can understand the whole origin and essence of life. So we think of these things in terms of natural causes and inevitable processes. Quite apart, however, from the fact that all such theories are nothing but theories which cannot be proved, and are lacking at the most vital point, how tragic they are in the lack of understanding of biblical teaching which they reveal. Where does life come from? Read your modern scientists on the origin of life and you will find that they cannot explain it. They cannot bridge the gulf from the inorganic to the organic. They have their theories; but they are nothing more than this, and even so they disagree amongst themselves. That, however, is the fundamental problem. Where has this principle called life come from? What is its origin? If you say it started with the inorganic somehow becoming organic, I ask where did the inorganic come from? You are bound to go back to the life principle. And there is only one satisfactory answer — God is the Giver of life.

But we must not take this in just a general way. Our Lord was particularly interested in our individual case and condition, and what He is really teaching us here is that it is God who has given us the gift of life and being and existence. It is a tremendous conception. We are not merely individuals thrown up or thrown out by an evolutionary process. God is concerned about us one by one. We should never have come into this world if God had not willed it. We must take a firm hold and grasp of this great principle. There should never be a day in our lives when we fail to thank God for the gift of life and food and existence, and the marvel and the wonder of the body that He has given us. These things are solely and entirely His gift. And, of course, if we fail to realize that, we shall fail everywhere.

It may be well for us at this point to stop and meditate upon this great principle, before going on to our Lord's subsidiary argument. He sums up His central teaching in these words: 'O ye of little faith'. Faith there, as we shall see, does not mean some vague principle; He has in mind our failure to understand, our lack of comprehension of the biblical view of man and of life as it is to be lived in this world. That is the real trouble with us, and our Lord's purpose in giving the illustrations which we shall consider later, is to show us how we fail to think as we ought. He asks: 'How is it that you do not see inevitably that this must be true?' And of all the things I have mentioned which we fail to grasp and to understand truly, this preliminary, fundamental point about the nature and being of man himself is most important. Here it is in all its simplicity. It is God Himself who gives us life, and the body in which we live it; and if He has done that we can draw this deduction, that His purpose with respect to us will be fulfilled. God never leaves unfinished any work He has begun; whatever He starts, whatever He has purposed, He will most surely fulfil. And therefore we come back to this, that there is a plan for every life in the mind of God. We must never regard our lives in this world as accidental. No. 'Are there not twelve hours in the day?' Christ said one day to his timorous and frightened disciples. And we need to say that to ourselves. We can be certain that God has a plan and a purpose for our lives, and it will be carried out. So we must never be anxious about our life and about its sustenance and its support. We must not be anxious if we find ourselves in a storm at sea, or in an aeroplane, and things seem to be going wrong, or if in a railway train we suddenly remember that there was an accident on that line the previous week. That sort of thing is abolished if we really get this right view about life itself and the body as gifts of God. They are from Him and are given by Him. He does not just start a process like that and then allow it to continue anyhow, somehow. No; once He starts it He keeps it going. God who decreed all things at the beginning is carrying them out; and God's purpose for mankind and God's purpose for the individual are certain and always sure.

We cannot do better than remind ourselves again of something we have already mentioned, and that is the faith of God's people throughout the centuries. That is the faith and teaching to be found, for example, in the hymns of Philip Doddridge. A typical example is found in his great hymn:

> 'O God of Bethel! by whose hand
>   Thy people still are fed;
> Who through this weary pilgrimage
>   Hast all our fathers led.'

That is his great argument, based ultimately upon the sovereignty of God, that God is the Ruler of the universe, and we are known to Him one by one, and are in a personal relationship to Him. It was the faith of all the great heroes of the faith described in Hebrews 11. That is what kept those men going. Quite frequently they did not understand but they said, 'God knows and God undertakes'. They had this final confidence that He who had brought them into being, and who had a purpose for them, would not leave them nor forsake them. He would surely sustain and lead them all the journey through, until their purpose in this world had been completed, and He would receive them into their heavenly habitation where they would spend their eternity in His glorious presence. 'Be not anxious about your life, what ye shall eat, or what ye shall drink; nor about your body, wherewithal it shall be clothed. Is not the life more than meat, and the body than raiment?' Argue it out, start with first principles and draw the inevitable deduction. The moment you do so, care and worry and anxiety will vanish, and as a child of your heavenly Father you will walk with peace and serenity in the direction of your everlasting home.

Chapter Eleven

Birds and Flowers

W E have been considering in these verses 25-30 our Lord's general statement concerning the terrible danger that confronts us in this life arising
from our tendency to be over-interested in various ways in the things of the
world. We tend to become anxious about our life, about what we shall eat, and
what we shall drink, and also about our body, what we shall put on. It is appalling to notice how many people seem to live entirely within that compass; food,
drink and clothing is the whole of their life. They spend the whole of their time
thinking about these things, talking about them, discussing them with others,
arguing about them, and reading about them in various books and magazines.
And the world today is doing its utmost to get us all to live on that level. Take a
casual glance at the books on the bookstalls and you will see how all these
things are catered for. That is the mind of the world, and that is the circle of its
interest. People live for these things, and become concerned and worried about
them in all sorts of different ways. Knowing this and being aware of the dangers, our Lord first of all gives us an omnibus reason for avoiding that particular snare.

But having warned us that we must not be anxious about what we shall eat
or drink, or what we shall put on, He now goes on to give each aspect of the
question separate consideration. The first is considered in verses 26 and 27, and
deals with our existence, the continuation and sustaining of our life in this
world. Here is the argument: 'Behold the fowls of the air: for they sow not, neither do they reap, nor gather into barns; yet your heavenly Father feedeth them.
Are ye not much better than they? Which of you by taking thought can add one
cubit unto his stature?' Some people would say that the statement in verse 27
belongs to the following section, but it seems to me perfectly clear that it must,
for reasons which will emerge in a moment, belong to this first section.

With regard to the whole question of food and drink and the maintenance of life, our Lord provides us with a double argument, or, if you like, with two main arguments. The first is derived from the birds of the air. You notice that at this point the argument is no longer from the greater to the lesser; rather is it the other way round. Having established the proposition on a lower level He then raises it to the higher level. First of all He starts by making a general observation, by calling our attention to something that is a fact of life in this world. 'Behold the fowls of the air.' Look at them. 'Behold' does not always carry the meaning of intense gazing. He is just asking us to look at something that is staring us in the face. See what is before your eyes — these birds, these fowls of the air. What is the argument we can deduce from them? It is that these birds are obviously provided with food.

There is a great deal of difference between the way the life of the birds is sustained and that of man. In the case of the birds it is provided for them. In the case of man a certain process is clearly involved. He sows the grain, and later on reaps the crop that has grown from the seed sown. Then he proceeds to gather it into barns and to put it aside until he needs it. That is man's way, and it is the right way; it was the way that God commanded man after the Fall, 'In the sweat of thy face shalt thou eat bread' (Gen. 3:19). Away back at the beginning of history seedtime and harvest were determined by God, not by man, so that sowing and reaping and gathering into barns is absolutely right for him. He is supposed to do that, and that is how he is to live. That is why the injunction not to 'take thought' cannot mean that we are to sit down and expect our bread to arrive miraculously in the morning. That is not scriptural, and all who imagine that that is the life of faith have misunderstood the teaching of the Bible.

But man is never to be worried about these things. He must not spend the whole of his time looking at the sky, wondering what the weather is going to be, and whether he will have something to put into his barn. That is what is condemned by our Lord. Man has to sow; he is commanded by God to do so. But he is to rely upon God who alone can give the increase. Our Lord draws attention to the birds. There is nothing more obvious about them than the fact that they are kept alive and that food is provided for them in nature — worms and insects and all the things on which birds live. It is there for them. Where does it come from? The answer is that God provides it for them. There, is a simple fact of life, and He tells us to look at it. These little birds who make no provision in the sense of preparing or producing food for themselves, have it provided for them. God looks after them and takes care of them. He sees to it that there is something for them to eat. He sees to it that their life is sustained.

That is a simple statement of the fact. Our Lord now takes that fact and draws two vital deductions from it. God deals thus with the animals and the birds of the air only in and through His general providence. He is not their Father; 'Behold the birds . . . yet your heavenly Father feedeth them'. That is a very interesting statement. God is the Maker and the Creator and the Sustainer of everything in the world; and He deals with the whole world, not only man, through His general providential arrangements, and only in that way. Then you notice the subtle change, introducing the profoundest argument of all: 'your heavenly Father feedeth them'.

God is our Father, and if our Father takes this great care of the birds to whom He is related only in His general providence, how much greater, of necessity, must be His care for us. An earthly father may be kind, for instance, to the birds or to animals; but it is inconceivable that a man should provide sustenance for mere creatures and neglect his own children. If this is true of an earthly father, how much more is it true of our heavenly Father. Here is our first deduction.

You see our Lord's method of reasoning and arguing; every word is important and must be noted carefully and closely. Observe the subtle transition from God caring providentially for the birds of the air, to 'your heavenly Father'. And as we follow His argument in these verses we shall see that this is something absolutely basic and vital. As we go through life in this world we notice and observe these facts of nature as we call them. But because we are Christians we must look at them with a deeper understanding and say to ourselves, 'No; things do not just happen in nature. They have not just come into being anyhow, somehow, fortuitously, as so many modern scientists would have us believe. Not at all. God is the Creator, and God is the sustainer of all things that are. He provides even for the birds, and the birds know instinctively that it is there, and He sees to it that it is there. Very well then; but what about myself? I now remind myself that I am a child of God, that He is my heavenly Father. God is not to me merely a Creator. He is the Creator, but He is more than that; He is my God and Father in and through the Lord Jesus Christ.' We should reason thus with ourselves, according to our Lord; and the moment we do that, care and anxiety and worry are quite impossible. The moment we begin to apply these truths to our minds fear goes out immediately and of necessity.

That, then, is our first deduction from this general observation of nature, and we must hold on to it. God is our heavenly Father if we are truly Christian. We must add that, because all that we are considering applies only to Christians. Indeed we can go further and say that, although God does deal in a providential manner with the whole of mankind — as we have seen in the previous chapter where He says that God 'maketh his sun to rise on the evil and on the good, and sendeth rain on the just and on the unjust' — these specific statements of our Lord's here are for God's children only, for those who are children of their heavenly Father in and through our Lord and Saviour Jesus Christ. And it is only the man who is a Christian who knows God to be his Father. The apostle Paul in the Epistle to the Romans says that no man but a Christian can say 'Abba, Father'. No man, unless the Holy Spirit dwells in him, really knows God as his Father and can rely upon Him. But, says our Lord, if you are in that relationship, then you must realize it is a sin for you to be anxious and worried, because God is your heavenly Father, and if He takes care of the birds, how much greater will be His care for you.

Our Lord puts His second deduction in these words, 'Are ye not much better than they?' Here again is this argument from the lesser to the greater. It means, as it is put elsewhere, 'of how much greater value are you than the birds of the air'. This is the argument which derives from the true greatness and dignity of man, and especially the Christian man. Here we can only work out the mechanics of the argument. We shall have to take it on a deeper level later, but we must say now that there is nothing more remarkable in the whole of biblical doctrine than the doctrine of man, this emphasis on the greatness and dignity of man. One of the ultimate objections to the godless, sinful, unchristian life is that it is an insult to man. The world thinks that it is making much of man. It talks about human greatness and suggests that the Bible and its teaching humble and humiliate human nature. The truth is, of course, precisely the opposite. True human greatness has tended to disappear as the biblical view of man has waned, for even at its best and highest the worldly, naturalistic view of man is unworthy. Here is true greatness and dignity; man made in the image of God, and therefore in some sense like God the Master and Lord of Creation. Our Lord comes in a humble, lowly manner; but it is as you look at Him that you see the true greatness of man. Though He was born in a stable and placed in a manger it is there, not in king's palaces, that we see the true dignity of man.

The world has a false idea of greatness and dignity. To find the true conception of man you must go to Psalm 8 and other places in Scripture. Above all, you must look at the Lord Jesus Christ, and look also at the New Testament picture of a man 'in Christ' made after His image. Then you will see the true relevance of this argument from the lesser to the greater — 'Are ye not much better than they?' But God takes care of these birds; they have a value, they are precious in His sight. Has He not said that not one of them can fall to the ground without 'your heavenly Father' knowing? If that is true, then look at yourself and realize what you are in the sight of God. Remember that He sees you as His child in the Lord Jesus Christ, and once and for ever you will cease to be concerned and worried and anxious about these things. When you see yourself as His child, then you will know that God will inevitably care for you.

There is, however, a second argument implied in this first one, an argument based upon the uselessness and futility of worry. These are our Lord's words: 'Which of you by taking thought can add one cubit unto his stature?' This is an argument which we must follow very carefully. To begin with, we must determine what exactly the statement is saying, and here we have two main opinions. When we ask what is the meaning of this term 'stature', we find that there are two possible answers. Half the authorities say that 'stature' means height, and normally when we talk about stature we think of height. But the Greek word used for 'stature' also means length or duration of life. And it is used in both senses in scriptural as well as in classical Greek. So it is no use asking, 'What does the Greek say?' because it does not say; the word may be used in either sense. So we cannot decide it in terms of the Greek.

How then do we approach it? The context surely must determine and decide this matter. What is a cubit? It happens to be eighteen inches, and bearing that in mind this mention here of 'stature' simply cannot mean height. It is quite impossible, for the reason that our Lord is again working from the lesser to the greater. Can you imagine anybody being anxiously concerned to add eighteen inches to his height! The suggestion is ridiculous. It cannot refer to height; it must refer to duration of life. This is what our Lord is saying: 'How many of you by taking all this trouble and care, and by being so worried and anxious, can extend the length of your life even by a moment.' We talk about the span of life, and that is the argument which our Lord is using, for He is still concerned here about our life in this world. The original statement is, 'Take no thought for your life'. He is not considering the body, He is considering existence, the continuance of life in this world. The introduction of the idea of height into the teaching here would be a complete irrelevance. No; our Lord is referring in this verse to the duration and extension of life, and it is because of their obsession with this that so many people become worried about their bodily needs. They desire to extend their life.

Now then, says our Lord in effect, face this question; face this argument. With all that you do, with all your tremendous efforts, with all your trouble and anxiety, is there any one of you that can extend the span of life by even a moment? And the answer to that question is that we cannot. That is one of the things which are so obvious, but which we all tend to forget. We do not remind ourselves of it as we should; but it is incontrovertibly true. The fact is that we cannot extend our lives in this world though we may try to do so in various ways. The millionaire can buy all the food and drink he wants, but he cannot extend his life. We are told that 'Money is power!' Perhaps it is in many respects, but not in this. The millionaire has no advantage over the most wretched pauper in existence.

We can go further. Medical knowledge and skill cannot extend life. We think they can, but that is because we do not know. These things are all determined by God, and thus even medical men are often bewildered and frustrated. Two patients who appear to be in the same condition are given identical treatment. One recovers; the other dies. What is the answer? The answer is that 'no man can add one cubit to his duration of life'. It is a great mystery, but we cannot escape it. Our times are in the hands of God, and do what we will, with all our food and drink, and our medical profession, and all our learning and science and skill, we cannot add a fraction to the duration of a man's life. In spite of all modern advances in knowledge, our times are still in the hands of God. And so, our Lord argues, why all the fuss and bother, why all the excitement, why all this worry and anxiety? Life is a gift from God. He starts it and He determines the end of it. He sustains it, and we are in His hands. Therefore, when you tend to become worried and anxious, just pull yourself up at once and say, I cannot start, or continue or end life; all this is entirely in His hands. If that greater thing is there in His control, I can leave the lesser also to Him. You cannot extend your life even by one cubit; therefore recognize the utter futility and waste of time and energy involved in worrying about these things. Do your work; sow, reap and gather into barns; but remember that the remainder is in the hands of God. You may have the finest seed you can buy on the market; you may have the best plough and everything necessary in the sowing; but if God withheld the sun and the rain you would not have a crop. God is ultimately behind it all. Man has his place and his work, but it is God that giveth the increase. This is what we must always remember, and it applies always and in all circumstances.

But we must now turn our attention to the section which starts at verse 28. 'And why take ye thought for raiment?' Here is the second matter — the body and its clothing. 'Consider the lilies of the field, how they grow; they toil not, neither do they spin: and yet I say unto you, That even Solomon in all his glory was not arrayed like one of these. Wherefore, if God so clothe the grass of the field, which to day is, and to morrow is cast into the oven, shall he not much more clothe you, O ye of little faith?' Again the argument is from the lesser to the greater. Again we are asked to observe a fact of nature. But this time He uses a slightly stronger term. It was 'behold the fowls'; now it is '*consider* the lilies of the field'. He means, of course, that we must meditate about these things and consider them on a deeper level.

Our Lord puts the argument as before. First of all look at the facts, the lilies of the field, the natural wild flowers, the grass. The authorities again spend many pages in trying to decide exactly what a 'lily' means. But surely He is referring to some common flowers which were growing in the fields of Palestine, and with which they were all perfectly familiar. And He says, Look at these things — consider; these do not toil, neither do they spin, and yet look at them. Look at the marvel, look at the beauty, look at the perfection. Why, even Solomon in all his glory was not arrayed like one of these. The glory of Solomon was proverbial amongst the Jews. You can read of his magnificence in the Old Testament, the marvellous clothing and all the wonderful vestures of the king and his court, his palaces of cedarwood with their furniture overlaid with gold and encrusted with precious stones. And yet, says our Lord, all that pales into insignificance when compared with one of these. There is an essential quality in the flowers, in the form, in the design, in the texture and substance, and in the colouring that man, with all his ingenuity, can never truly imitate.

> 'To me the meanest flower that blows can give
> Thoughts that do often lie too deep for tears.'

That is what *He* sees. He sees the hand of God; He sees the perfect creation; He sees the glory of the Almighty. The little flower that is never perhaps seen during the whole of its brief existence in this world, and which seemingly 'wastes its sweetness on the desert air', is nevertheless perfectly clothed by God. That is a fact, is it not? If so, draw the deduction from it. 'If God so clothe the grass of the field . . . shall he not much more clothe you, O ye of little faith?' If God does that for the flowers of the field, how much more for you?

But why is this so? Here is the argument. 'If God so clothe the grass of the field, which to day is, and to morrow is cast into the oven, shall he not much more clothe you?' What a mighty argument this is. The grass of the field is transient and passing. In ancient times they used to cut it and use it as fuel. It was the old way of baking bread. You first of all cut the grass and dried it, and then put it in the oven and set it on fire, and it generated great heat. Then you raked it out and put in the bread which you had prepared for baking. That was a common practice, and it was so in our Lord's day. So you see the powerful argument. The lilies and the grass are transient; they do not last very long. How well aware of this we are. We cannot make our flowers last; the moment we cut them they are beginning to die. They are here today with their exquisite beauty and all their perfection, but it is all gone by tomorrow. These beautiful things come and go, and that is the end of them. You, however, are immortal; you are not only a creature of time, you belong to eternity. It is not true to say that you are here today and gone tomorrow in a real sense. God hath 'set eternity' in the heart of man; man is not meant to die. 'Dust thou art, to dust returnest, was not spoken of the soul'. You go on, and on, and on. You not only have natural dignity and greatness, but you also have an eternal existence beyond death and the grave. When you realize that truth about yourself, can you believe that the God who has made you and destined you for that, is going to neglect your body while you are in this life and world? Of course not. 'If God so clothe the grass of the field, which to day is, and to morrow is cast into the oven, shall he not much more clothe you, O ye of little faith?'

Chapter Twelve

Little Faith

O YE of little faith' (Matt. 6:30). We have here our Lord's final argument concerning the problem of anxious care. Or, perhaps, we can describe it as being our Lord's summing up of the warning not to 'take thought' about our lives as to what we shall eat or drink, or about our bodies in the matter of dress. It is the conclusion of the detailed argument which He has worked out in terms of birds and flowers. In effect, He seems to say: This is what it all amounts to. The real cause of the trouble is your failure to draw obvious deductions from the birds and the flowers. But, coupled with that, there is an obvious lack of faith. 'O ye of little faith.' That is the ultimate cause of the trouble.

The question that obviously arises is this: What does our Lord mean by 'little faith'? What is its exact connotation? He does not say, you notice, that they have no faith; He charges them with 'little' faith. It is not the absence of faith on their part that concerns Him; it is the inadequacy of that faith, the fact that they do not have sufficient faith. It is therefore a very striking phrase and our immediate reaction should be to thank God for it. What exactly does it mean? The right way to answer that question is to pay careful attention to the entire context. Who are the people whom He is describing here and against whom this charge is preferred? Once more we must remind ourselves that they are Christian people, and only Christian people. Our Lord is not speaking about everybody in the world. The Christian message really has no comfort and consolation to give to people who are not Christian. Words like these are not addressed to everybody; they are addressed only to those of whom the Beatitudes are true. They are, therefore, addressed to those who are poor in spirit, and those who mourn because of their sense of guilt and of sin, those who have seen themselves as truly lost and helpless in the sight of God, those who are meek and therefore hungering and thirsting after righteousness, realizing that it is only to be obtained in the Lord Jesus Christ. They have faith; the others have no faith at all. So it is spoken of such people only.

Further, it is spoken of people with respect to whom He can use the term 'your heavenly Father'. God is Father only to those who are in Jesus Christ. He is the Maker and the Creator of all men; we are all His offspring in that sense. But, as the apostle John puts it, it is only those who believe on the Lord Jesus Christ who have the right and the authority to become the sons of God (see John 1:12). Our Lord, in addressing the Pharisees, spoke of 'my Father' and 'your father', and said 'you are of your father the devil'. So here. He is not teaching some vague general doctrine about the 'universal fatherhood of God' and the 'universal brotherhood of man'. No; the gospel divides people into two groups, those who are Christian and those who are not. We must assert, and more than ever at a time like this, that the gospel of Jesus Christ has only one thing to say to the non-Christian world, namely that it is under the wrath of God, that it can expect nothing in this world but misery and unhappiness, wars and rumours of wars, and that it will never know any true peace. Put positively, the Christian gospel tells the world that it must believe on the Lord Jesus Christ if it desires to be blessed of God. There is no hope for the world as such; there is only hope for those who are Christian. This is a message only for the people of whom the Beatitudes are true, those who can truly and rightly say that they are the children of God in Jesus Christ. Indeed, in the very next phrase which we shall be considering, He contrasts these people with the Gentiles — 'all these things do the Gentiles seek'. There we see the division, 'the Gentiles' and those who are 'in Christ', those who are outside and those who are inside, God's people and those who are not God's people.

That, then, is the way in which we must understand this phrase. These people have faith, but it is insufficient faith. Surely, therefore, we are entitled to put it like this. Our Lord is speaking here about Christian people who have only saving faith, and who tend to stop at that. Those are the people about whom He is concerned, and His desire is that they should be led, as the result of listening to Him, to a larger and deeper faith. The first reason for this is that people who have saving faith only, and who go no further, rob themselves of so much in this life. And not only that. Because of their lack of a larger faith, they are obviously more prone to the worry and anxiety and to this killing care which attacks us all in this life. Our Lord, indeed, goes so far as to say that worry in a Christian is always due ultimately to a lack of faith, or to little faith. Worry and anxiety, being cast down and defeated, being mastered by life and its attendant circumstances, are always due, in a Christian, to lack of faith.

The thing we must aim at, therefore, is greater faith. The first step in obtaining this is to realize what is meant by 'little faith'. We shall see that this is our

Lord's method in the next little section which begins at verse 31: 'Therefore take no thought, saying, What shall we eat? or, What shall we drink? or, Wherewithal shall we be clothed?' Our Lord gives us positive instruction as to how to increase our faith; but before He does that, He wants us to see exactly what is meant by little faith. You start with the negative, then go on to the positive.

What then is this condition which is described by our Lord as being 'little faith'? What sort of faith is it, and what is wrong with it? First of all, let us consider a general definition. We can say of this type of faith in general that it is one which is confined to one sphere of life only. It is faith that is confined solely to the question of the salvation of our souls, and it does not go beyond that. It does not extend to the whole of life and to everything in life. This is a common complaint among us as Christian people. On the question of the salvation of our souls we are perfectly clear. We have been awakened by the work of the Holy Spirit to see our lost estate. We have been convicted of sin. We have seen how utterly helpless we are to put ourselves right in the sight of God, and that the only way of deliverance is in the Lord Jesus Christ. We have seen that He came into the world, and died for our sins, and thereby reconciled us to God. And we believe on Him, and have that saving faith with regard to the present and to all eternity. That is saving faith, the thing that makes us Christians, and without which we are not Christian at all. Yes; but Christian people often stop at that, and they seem to think that faith is something that applies only to that question of salvation. The result is, of course, that in their daily lives they are often defeated; in their ordinary daily lives there is very little difference to be seen between them and people who are not Christian. They become worried and anxious, and they conform to the world in so many respects. Their faith is something that is reserved only for their ultimate salvation, and they do not seem to have any faith with regard to the everyday affairs of life and living in this world. Our Lord is concerned about that very thing. These people have come to know God as their heavenly Father, and yet they are worried about food and drink and clothing. Their faith is confined; it is a little faith in that way; its scope is so curtailed and limited.

We must start with that. You cannot read the Bible without seeing that true faith is a faith that extends to the whole of life. You see it in our Lord Himself, you see it in the great heroes of the faith we read of in Hebrews 11. We can put it like this. A little faith is a faith which does not lay hold of all the promises of God. It is interested only in some of them, and it concentrates on these. Look at it in this way. Go through the Bible and make a list of the various promises of God. You will find that there are a great number, indeed an astonishing number. Peter talked about the 'exceeding great and precious promises'. It is amazing and astounding. There is no aspect of life that is not covered by these extraordinary promises of God. How guilty we all are in the light of this! We select certain of these promises and concentrate upon them, and somehow or other we never look at the others. We never lay hold of the others, and the result is that, while we triumph in certain respects, we fail so miserably in others. That is 'little faith'. It is faith, which is confined in its relationship to the promises, and does not realize that it is meant to be something that should link up with them all, and appropriate every one of them.

Let us look at it again from a slightly different angle. I once heard a man use a phrase which affected me very deeply at the time, and still does. I am not sure it is not one of the most searching statements I have ever heard. He said that the trouble with many of us Christians is that we believe on the Lord Jesus Christ, but that we do not believe Him. He meant that we believe on Him for the salvation of our souls, but we do not believe Him when He says a thing like this to us, that God is going to look after our food and drink, and even our clothing. He makes such statements as 'Come unto me, all ye that labour and are heavy laden, and I will give you rest', and yet we keep our problems and worries to ourselves, and we are borne down by them and defeated by them, and get anxious about things. He has told us to come to Him when we are like that; He has told us that if we are thirsting in any respect we can go to Him, and He has assured us that whosoever comes to Him will never thirst, and that he that eats of the bread that He shall give shall never hunger. He has promised to give us 'a well of water springing up into everlasting life' so that we shall never thirst. But, we do not believe Him. Take all these statements He made when He was here on earth, the words He addressed to the people around Him; they are all meant for us. They are meant for us today as definitely as when He first uttered them, and so also are all the astounding statements in the Epistles. The trouble is that we do not believe Him. That is the ultimate trouble. 'Little faith' does not really take the Scripture as it is and believe it and live by it and apply it.

So far we have been looking at 'little faith' in general. Let us come now to the details and look at it in a more analytical manner. We must do this in order that we may be essentially practical, for after all this subject is a vital and practical one. There is no greater fallacy than to regard the gospel of Jesus Christ as just something that you think of when you are in church or when you are spending a certain amount of time in meditation. No, it applies to the whole of life. Let us look at it like this. To be 'of little faith' means, first of all, that we are mastered by our circumstances instead of mastering them. That is an obvious statement. The picture given in this entire section is of people who are being governed by life. There they are, as it were, sitting helplessly under a great cloud of concern about food and drink and clothing and many other things. These things are bearing down upon them and they are the victims of them. That is the picture which He gives, and we know how true it is. Things happen to us, and immediately, as we put it, we are 'bowled over', we are mastered by them. That is something which, according to Scripture, should never happen to a Christian. The picture given of him everywhere in the Bible is of one who is above his circumstances. He can even 'rejoice in tribulation', not just stand up to it with a stoical kind of fortitude. He does not give way or whimper; he is not simply, to use the common phrase, 'grinning and bearing it'. No; he rejoices in the midst of tribulation. Only one who has true faith can look down upon life in that way, and can ever rise to such a height: but that, according to the Bible, is possible to the Christian.

Why does the man of little faith allow things to master him and to get him down? The answer to that question is that, in a sense, the real trouble with 'little faith' is that it does not think. In other words, we have to be right in our whole conception of faith. Faith, according to our Lord's teaching in this paragraph, is primarily thinking; and the whole trouble with a man of little faith is that he does not think. He allows circumstances to bludgeon him. That is the real difficulty in life. Life comes to us with a club in its hand and strikes us upon the head, and we become incapable of thought, helpless and defeated. The way to avoid that, according to our Lord, is to think. We must spend more time in studying our Lord's lessons in observation and deduction. The Bible is full of logic, and we must never think of faith as something purely mystical. We do not just sit down in an armchair and expect marvellous things to happen to us. That is not Christian faith. Christian faith is essentially thinking. Look at the birds, think about them, and draw your deductions. Look at the grass, look at the lilies of the field, consider them.

The trouble with most people, however, is that they will not think. Instead of doing this, they sit down and ask, What is going to happen to me? What can I do? That is the absence of thought; it is surrender, it is defeat. Our Lord, here, is urging us to think, and to think in a Christian manner. That is the very essence of faith. Faith, if you like, can be defined like this: It is a man insisting upon thinking when everything seems determined to bludgeon and knock him down in an intellectual sense. The trouble with the person of little faith is that, instead of controlling his own thought, his thought is being controlled by something else, and, as we put it, he goes round and round in circles. That is the essence of worry. If you lie awake at night for hours I can tell you what you have been doing; you have been going round in circles. You just go over the same old miserable details about some person or some thing. That is not thought; that is the absence of thought, a failure to think. That means that something else is controlling your thought and governing it, and it leads to that wretched, unhappy state called worry. So we are entitled to define 'little faith' in the second place as being a failure to think, or of allowing life to master our thought instead of thinking clearly about it, instead of 'seeing life steadily and seeing it whole'.

Little faith, if you like, can also be described as a failure to take scriptural statements at their face value and to believe them utterly. Here is a man who has suddenly found himself in trouble and tried by circumstances. What should he do? He should turn to the Bible, and then say to himself. 'I must take the statements of that Book exactly as they are'. Everything that is in us by nature, and the devil outside us, will do their utmost to prevent our doing this. They tell us that those statements were meant only for the disciples, and that they are not meant for us. Some people, as we have seen, would even relegate the whole of the Sermon on the Mount to the disciples, and to people who are going to live in some future kingdom. Others say that it was all right for the first Christians who had just passed through Pentecost but that now the world has changed. Those are the suggestions that come to us. But I reject all that. We are to read the Scriptures, and we are to say to ourselves, 'Everything I am going to read here is spoken to me; everything our Lord said to the Pharisees He says to me; and if there is anything corresponding to what He said of them in me it means that I am a Pharisee. All these promises likewise are meant for me. God does not change; He is exactly as He was two thousand years ago, and all these things are absolute and eternal.' So I must come to the Bible and remind myself of that. It means that I take it and its teaching as it is, in its context, and know that it is speaking to me. I must not dismiss it in any way. I have to learn to take Scripture at its face value. 'Little faith' means a failure to do that as we ought.

We must go on, however, to something which is still more practical. 'Little faith' really means a failure to realize the implications of salvation, and the position resulting from salvation. That is clearly our Lord's argument and reasoning here. Half our trouble is due to the fact that we do not realize to the full the implications of the doctrine of salvation which we believe. That is the argument of every New Testament Epistle. The first part consists of a doctrinal statement, which is designed to remind us of what we are and who we are as Christians. Then comes a practical second part, which is always a deduction from the first. That is why it generally starts with the word 'therefore'. That is exactly what our Lord is doing here. Here we are, worrying about food and drink and clothing! The trouble with us is that we do not realize that we are children of our heavenly Father. If only we realized that, we should never worry again. If only we had some dim, vague conception of the purposes of God with respect to us, worry would be impossible. Take, for instance, Paul's great prayer for the Ephesians. He tells them that he was praying that 'the eyes of their understanding might be enlightened' — note the word 'understanding'. To what end and for what purpose? 'That ye may know what is the hope of his calling, and what the riches of the glory of his inheritance in the saints, and what is the exceeding greatness of his power to us-ward who believe' (Eph. 1:18, 19). That, according to Paul, is what they needed to know and understand. Read every Pauline Epistle and you will find that kind of statement somewhere.

The trouble with us Christian people is that we do not realize what we are as children of God, we do not see God's gracious purposes with respect to us. We saw that earlier, in passing, when we considered how He contrasted us as children with the grass of the field. The grass is here today in the field, but tomorrow it will be thrown as fuel into the oven to bake bread. But God's children are destined for glory. All the purposes and the promises of God are meant for us and designed with respect to us; and the one thing we have to do, in a sense, is just to realize what God has told us about ourselves as His children. The moment we truly grasp that, worry becomes impossible. A man then begins to apply the logic which argues: 'If, when we were enemies, we were reconciled to God by the death of his Son, much more, being reconciled, we shall be saved by his life' (Rom. 5:10). That is it. Whatever happens to us, 'He that spared not his own Son, but delivered him up for us all, how shall he not with him also freely give us all things?' The mighty argument continues in Romans 8: 'Who shall lay any thing to the charge of God's elect?' . . . (Rom. 8:32ff.). We may have to face problems and distresses and sorrow, but 'in all these things we are more than conquerors through him that loved us'. The vital thing is to see ourselves as His children. The argument follows of necessity. If God so clothe the grass how much more shall He clothe you? Your heavenly Father, who sees the birds, feedeth them. Are ye not much better than they? We have to realize what we are as God's children.

Or, to put it the other way round, we have to realize what God is as our heavenly Father. Here, again, is something which Christian people are so slow to learn. We believe in God; but how slow we are to believe and to realize that He is what He says He is, our heavenly Father. Christ talked about going 'to my Father, and your Father'. He has become our Father in Christ. And what are we to learn about Him? Here are some headings for your consideration.

Think first of the immutable purposes of God with regard to His children, and I would emphasize that word 'immutable'. The children of God have their names written in the Lamb's Book of Life before the foundation of the world. There is nothing contingent about this. It was 'before the foundation of the world' that we were elected. His purposes are immutable and changeless, and they envisage our eternal destiny and nothing less. This is constantly expressed in various ways in the Scriptures. 'Elect according to the foreknowledge of God', 'separated unto Christ Jesus', 'sanctified, set apart by the Spirit', and so on. When people believe things like that they are able to face life in this world in a very different way. That was the secret, once more, of the heroes of the faith in Hebrews 11. They understood something of the immutable purposes of God, and, therefore, whether it was Abraham or Joseph or Moses, they all smiled at calamities. They just went on because God had told them to do so, because they knew that His purposes must surely come to pass. Abraham was put to the supreme test of being asked to sacrifice Isaac. He could not understand it but he said: I will do it because I know God's purposes are sure, and though I have to slay Isaac, I know that God can raise him from the dead. The immutable purposes of God! God never contradicts Himself, and we must remember that He is always behind, beneath and everywhere round about us. 'Underneath are the everlasting arms.'

Then think of His great love. The tragedy of our position is that we do not know the love of God as we should. Paul prayed again for the Ephesians that they might know the love of God. We do not know His love to us. In a sense the whole of the first Epistle of John was written in order that we might know that. If only we knew the love of God to us, and rested in it (1 John 4:16) our whole lives would be different. How easy it is to prove the greatness of that love in the light of what He has already done in Christ. We have already looked at those mighty arguments from the Epistle to the Romans. If while we were yet enemies He has done the greatest thing, how much more, we say it with reverence, is He bound to do the lesser things. The love of God to us!

Then we must meditate upon His concern for us. That is what our Lord is emphasizing here. If He is concerned about the birds, how much more for us? He tells us in another place that even 'the hairs of our head are all numbered'. Yet we worry about things. If only we realized God's loving concern for us, that He knows everything about us, and is concerned about the smallest detail of our lives! The man who believes that can no longer worry.

Then think about His power and His ability. 'Our God', 'my God'. Who is my God who takes such a personal interest in me? He is the Creator of the heavens and the earth. He is the Sustainer of everything that is. Read again Psalm 46 to remind yourself of this: 'He maketh wars to cease unto the end of the earth; he breaketh the bow, and cutteth the spear in sunder'. He controls everything. He can smash the heathen and every enemy; His power is illimitable. And as we contemplate all that, we must agree with the deduction of the Psalmist when, addressing the heathen, he said: 'Be still, and know that I am God'. We must not interpret that 'Be still' in a sentimental manner. Some regard it as a kind of exhortation to us to be silent; but it is nothing of the sort. It means, 'Give up (or 'Give in') and admit that I am God'. God is addressing people who are opposed to Him and He says: This is My power; therefore give up and give in, keep silent and know that I am God.

We must remember that this power is working for us. We have seen it in Paul's prayer for the Ephesians: 'The exceeding greatness of his power' (1:19). He 'that is able to do exceeding abundantly above all that we ask or think, according to the power that worketh in us' (3:20). In the light of such statements is not worry ridiculous? Is it not utterly foolish? It just means that we do not think; we do not read our Scriptures, or, if we do, we do so in a perfunctory manner, or are so controlled by prejudices that we do not take them at their face value. We must face these things and draw out our mighty deductions.

A last thought. This 'little faith', is ultimately due to a failure to apply what we know, and claim to believe, to the circumstances and details of life. I can put that in a phrase. Do you remember that famous incident in our Lord's earthly life and ministry when He was sleeping in the stern of the ship and the water began to come in? The sea had become boisterous, and the disciples became worried and anxious and said, 'Master, carest thou not that we perish?' His reply to them summarizes perfectly all we have said in this chapter. He said: 'Where, where is your faith?' (see Luke 8:23-25). Where is it? You have it, but where is it? Or, if you like, He said: Why don't you apply your faith to this? You see it is not enough to say we have faith; we must apply our faith, we must relate it, we must see that it is where it ought to be at any given moment. It is a poor type of Christianity that has this wonderful faith with respect to salvation and then whimpers and cries when confronted by the daily trials of life. We must apply our faith. 'Little faith' does not do this. I trust that, after looking at this mighty argument of our blessed Lord, we shall not only feel convicted, but shall also see that to be worried is an utter contradiction of our position as children of God. There is no circumstance or condition in this life which should lead a Christian to worry. He has no right to worry; and if he does he is not only condemning himself as being a man of little faith, he is also dishonouring his God and being disloyal to his blessed Saviour. 'Take no thought'; exercise faith; understand the truth and apply it to every detail of your life.

Chapter Thirteen

Increasing Faith

HERE, in verses 31-33, our Lord presents us with the positive approach towards 'little faith'. It is not sufficient that we should realize what it means; the great thing is to have a larger and a bigger faith. He introduces His teaching with His word 'therefore'; it follows on immediately, it is a link in a chain. 'Therefore', He says, 'in the light of all this', 'Take no thought, saying, What shall we eat? or, What shall we drink? or, Wherewithal shall we be clothed?' That is a repetition of the fundamental injunction. There are those who would have us believe that the addition of the word 'saying' means that there is a slight alteration. In the first place, you remember, He said, 'Therefore I say unto you, Take no thought'; here, they point out, He says, 'Therefore take no thought, saying'.

I do not think that it is a material difference. There is no objection to the argument that there *is* a difference, that in the first instance our Lord was giving a general warning against the tendency to worry, but that here He goes a step further and says, in effect, 'You must not even say these things; you may think them, but you must not say them.' Whether that is so or not is immaterial because the point still remains the same. Our Lord shows us here the positive way to increase our faith, and again He puts it in the form of an argument. Let us remind ourselves that His method is always very logical. He does not merely make statements and pronouncements; He reasons them out with us. What marvellous condescension! Look at that word 'for'. 'For after all these things . . .'; 'for your heavenly Father knoweth . . .'; and so on. All we have to do, therefore, is to follow His argument. At this point we observe that three main points are put for our consideration, three main principles which, if we grasp and understand them, will inevitably lead to a greater faith. The way in which our Lord handles this subject is truly remarkable.

His essential argument is that we, as Christians, are to be different from the

Gentiles. That is how He starts. You notice that He puts this statement in brackets as it were: 'For after all these things do the Gentiles seek.' But what a powerful statement it is, and how important! Though negative in form, it leads to a very positive result. If you want to increase your faith, the first thing you have to realize is that to be worried and anxious about food, and drink, and clothing, and your life in this world is, in a sense, to be just like the Gentiles.

What does He mean by this? The word 'Gentile', of course, really means 'heathen'. The Jews were God's chosen people. It was they who had the oracles of God and the special knowledge of God; the others were described as heathen. So we must analyse this word and realize exactly what He means. The statement is that if I am guilty of being worried and anxious about these matters of food and drink and clothing, and about my life in this world, and certain things which I lack — if these dominate me and my life, then I am really living and behaving as a heathen. But let us try to discover the real significance of that.

The heathen were people who had no revelation from God, and who therefore had no knowledge of God. That is the great point made in the Old Testament, that is the thing that differentiated the children of Israel from all others. Paul says in his argument concerning this matter in Romans 3:2 that 'unto them were committed the oracles of God'. God made a special revelation of Himself to the Jews not only in the call of Abraham and other individual instances, but supremely in the giving of the law and the great teaching of the prophets. The heathen knew nothing about that; they had not had this special revelation, nor did they have a knowledge of God. They did not have the Old Testament Scriptures and they were, therefore, without the means of knowing Him. That is the essential point about the heathen, they know nothing about God in a real sense, they are 'without God in the world'.

We can, of course, go further in this connection and say that the heathen know nothing about the revelation of God in Jesus Christ, and know nothing about God's way of salvation. They are entirely ignorant of the view of life which is taught in the Bible. They do not know that 'God so loved the world, that he gave his only begotten Son, that whosoever believeth in him should not perish, but have everlasting life.' They know nothing about the 'exceeding great and precious promises', or about the various pledges that God has given to His own people in this world. The heathen know nothing about that, and have not received it. They are in real darkness about life in this world and how it is to be lived and about their eternal destiny. Their view of life is entirely limited by their own thoughts, and they lack this light that is given from above.

We must not stay with this, but the heathen who hold this pagan view of life generally view the things that happen to us in one of two main ways. There are those amongst them who believe that everything in this life is accidental.

That view is sometimes known as the 'theory of contingency' which teaches that things happen without rhyme or reason, and that you never know what is going to happen next. That, for instance, is the view of life in this world that is held, and is being taught and given considerable prominence at the present time by men like Dr. Julian Huxley, to whom everything is accidental and contingent. There is, they say, no purpose whatsoever in life. There is no design, order or arrangement; the whole thing is fortuitous. It is a very old view. There is nothing new about it, and there are no people in the world today who are more pathetic than those who imagine that to hold such a view is the hallmark of modernity. Half the heathen take that view of life and it is obviously going to affect in a profound sense their whole attitude towards everything that happens.

The other view, commonly called 'fatalism', is the extreme opposite of that. It teaches that what is to be will be. It does not matter what you may do or say, it is going to happen. 'What is to be will be.' Therefore it is utter folly to strive or make any effort. You just go on and trust that things will not go too badly with you, and that somehow or another you will have a fairly easy passage through this world. Fatalism teaches that you can do nothing about life, that there are powers and factors controlling you inexorably, and holding you in the grip of a rigid determinism. So there is no purpose in thought, still less in worry. But fatalism leads to worry all the same, because such people are always worrying as to what is going to happen next. 'Contingency' and 'fatalism', then, are the two main expressions of the heathen view of life.

It is important for us to bear those two views in mind because Christian people often hold one or other of them unconsciously. The Christian view, on the other hand, the one taught in the Bible, and especially at this particular point in the Sermon on the Mount, is what can be described as the doctrine of 'certainty'. Life, it says, is not controlled by blind necessity, but certain things are certain because we are in the hands of the living God. So, if you are a Christian, you put that doctrine of certainty over against the theories of contingency and fatalism. There is a great difference between these views — the Christian view and the pagan; and what our Lord is saying is that, if you are living a life full of anxiety and worry, you are virtually spiritually dead and taking the pagan view of life.

It follows of necessity that if that is our fundamental view of life in this world, it is going to determine our way of living, and to control our whole behaviour. 'As a man thinketh in his heart, so is he.' You can always tell what a man's philosophy of life is by the way in which he lives and by the way he reacts to the things that are happening round about him. That is why a time of crisis always sifts people. We always betray exactly where we stand by what we say.

You remember our Lord said on one occasion that we shall be judged by every idle word we utter (see Matt. 12:36). We proclaim a great deal about ourselves as Christians by our ordinary remarks and by our ordinary comments about life. Our view of life comes out in our every expression.

Moreover, if a man has a pagan view of life in this world, he will also have a pagan view of life in the next world. The pagan view of that life is that it is a realm of shadows. You will find that in Greek and other pagan mythologies. Everything is uncertain. If a man, therefore, has that view, this world is going to be everything to him and he is going to make the best of this life because it is the only life about which he has any knowledge. Furthermore, he is either trying to anticipate contingency, or else he is trying somehow to elude this fatalism that is gripping him. What he does is this. He says, Here I am at this moment; I am going to get the most out of this because I do not know what is going to happen next. Therefore his philosophy is 'Let us eat, drink, and be merry': let us live for the hour. I have this hour, let me extract out of it everything that I can.

That is what we are seeing all around us; that is the way in which the majority of people seem to be living today. They argue that, since you do not know what is going to happen next month or next year, the essence of wisdom is to say, 'Well; let's spend all we have; let's get the maximum pleasure out of life now.' Thus they are quite negligent of consequences and quite heedless about their eternal destiny. Our Lord sums it all up by putting it like this, 'For after all these things do the Gentiles (the heathen, the pagans) seek.' And this word 'seek' is a very strong one. It means that they seek earnestly, that they are continually seeking these things, that they really live for them. Let us say this about them. They are perfectly consistent; if that is their view of life, then they are doing the right thing. They live for these things, they seek them earnestly and continually.

From all this, however, arises the vital and important question. Are we like that? If these things are first in our lives, says our Lord, and if they monopolize our lives and our thinking, then we are nothing better than the heathen, we are worldlings with worldly minds. This word comes to us with terrible power and significance. There are so many people who can be described as spiritual worldlings. If you talk to them about salvation they have the correct view; but if you talk to them about life in general they are worldlings. When it is a matter of the salvation of the soul they have the correct answer; but if you listen to their ordinary conversation about life in this world you will discover a heathen philosophy. They are worried about food and drink; they are always talking about wealth and position and their various possessions. These things really control them. They are made happy or unhappy by them; they are put out by them or pleased by them; and they are always thinking and talking about them. That is to be like the heathen, says Christ; for the Christian should not be controlled by these things. Whatever may be his position with respect to them, he is not finally to be controlled by them. He should really not be made unhappy or happy by these things, because that is the typical condition of the heathen, who is dominated by them in his whole outlook upon life and in his living in this world.

This is a very good way, therefore, of increasing our faith and of introducing ourselves to the biblical conception of the life of faith. God's people, God's children in this world, are meant to live the life of faith; they are meant to live in the light of that faith which they profess. I suggest, therefore, that there are certain questions which we should always be putting to ourselves. Here are some of them. Do I face the things that happen to me in this world as the Gentiles do? When these things happen to me, when there seem to be difficulties about food, or drink, or clothing, or difficulties in some relationship in life, how do I face them? How do I react? Is my reaction just that of the heathen, and of people who do not pretend to be Christian? How do I react during a war? How do I react to illness and pestilence and loss? It is a very good question to ask.

But let us go further. Does my Christian faith affect my view of life and control it in all matters? I claim to be Christian, and hold the Christian faith; the question I now ask myself is, Does that Christian faith of mine affect my whole detailed view of life? Is it always determining my reaction and my response to the particular things that happen? Or, we can put it like this. Is it clear and obvious to myself and to everybody else that my whole approach to life, my essential view of life in general and in particular, is altogether different from that of the non-Christian? It should be. The Sermon on the Mount begins with the Beatitudes. They describe people who are altogether different from all others, as different as light from darkness, as different as salt from putrefaction. If, then, we are different essentially, we must be different in our view of, and in our reaction to, everything. I know of no better question that a man can ask himself in every circumstance in life than that. When something happens to upset you, do you ask, 'Is my reaction essentially different from what it would be if I were not a Christian?' Let us remind ourselves of the teaching we have already considered at the end of the fifth chapter of this Gospel. You remember that our Lord put it like this: 'If ye salute your brethren only, what do ye more than others?' That is it. The Christian is a man who does 'more than others'. He is a man who is absolutely different. And if in every detail of his life this Christianity of his does not come in, he is a very poor Christian, he is a man 'of little faith'.

Or, let us put it in a final question like this: Do I always place everything in my life, and everything that happens to me, in the context of my Christian faith, and then look at it in the light of that context? The heathen cannot do that. The heathen has not got the Christian faith. He does not believe in God, or know anything about Him; he has not this revelation of God as his Father and himself as His child. He does not know anything about God's gracious purposes so, poor man, he turns in upon himself and reacts automatically and instinctively to what happens. But what really proves that we are Christians is that, when these things come to us, or happen to us, we do not see them just as they are; as Christians we take them and put them immediately into the context of the whole of our faith and then look at them again.

We ended the last chapter by describing faith as being essentially active. Our Lord asked His disciples, 'Where is your faith? Why are you not applying it?' This time we can put it the other way round. Something happens to us that tends to upset us. The heathen in the natural man makes him lose his temper, or become hurt and sensitive. But the Christian stops and says, 'Wait a minute. I am going to take this thing and put it into the context of everything I know and believe about God and my relationship to Him'. Then he looks at it again. Then he begins to understand what the author of the Epistle to the Hebrews means when he says, 'whom the Lord loveth he chasteneth'. Because the Christian knows that, he is able to enjoy it, in a sense, even while it is happening, because he puts it into the context of his faith. He is the only man who can do that; the heathen cannot do it, he is incapable of it. So we ask that general question. Is it evident to me and to everybody else that I am not a heathen? Is my conduct and my behaviour in life such that it shows I am a Christian? Do I show plainly and clearly that I belong to a higher realm, and that I can raise everything about me to that realm? 'After all these things do the Gentiles seek,' says our Lord. But you are not Gentiles. Realize what you are; remember who you are and live accordingly. Rise to the level of your faith; be worthy of your high calling in Christ Jesus. Christian people, watch your lips, watch your tongues. We betray ourselves in our conversation, in the things we say, in the things that come out in our unguarded moments. Such behaviour is typical of the heathen; the Christian exercises discipline and control because he sees everything in the context of God and of eternity.

The second argument is really a repetition of that which our Lord has already pressed upon us several times. He does not rush these things. He says, 'For your heavenly Father knoweth that ye have need of all these things'. He has already been telling us this in the argument about the birds and the lilies of the field. But He knows us; He knows how prone we are to forget things. So He says it again: 'Your heavenly Father knoweth that ye have need of all these things'. We can put it in this form. The second principle by which you can increase and enlarge your faith is that, as a Christian, you should have implicit faith in and reliance upon God as your heavenly Father. We have already considered it,[1] so we need only summarize it here. It means something like this. Nothing can happen to us apart from God. He knows all about us. If it is true to say that the very hairs of our head are all numbered, then we must remember that we are never in any position or situation outside God's knowledge or care. He knows it much better than we do ourselves. This is the argument of our blessed Lord Himself. 'Your heavenly Father knoweth that ye have need of all these things.' There is no more blessed statement in the whole of Scripture than that. You will never be anywhere but that He sees you; there will never be anything in the depths of your heart, in the innermost recesses of your being but that He knows all about it. The author of the Epistle to the Hebrews puts this same truth in a different connection: 'All things are naked and opened unto the eyes of him with whom we have to do' (4:13). He is a discerner of the thoughts and intents of the heart. He says that in order to warn those Hebrew Christians. We must remember that we are not only to live in the fear of the Lord, but we are to live in the comfort and the knowledge of God. He not only sees what is happening to you when you are taken ill, He not only knows when you are suffering bereavement and sorrow, He knows every pang of the heart, He knows every heartache. He knows everything; there is nothing outside His omniscience. He knows all about us in every respect and He therefore knows our every need. From that our Lord draws this deduction. You need never be anxious, you must never be worried. God is with you in this state, you are not alone, and He is your Father. Even an earthly father does this in a measure. He is with his child, protecting, doing everything he can for him. Multiply that by infinity, and that is what God is doing with respect to you, whatever your circumstance.

If we were but to grasp this, it would surely cause worry and strain and anxiety to be banished once and for ever. Never allow yourself for a moment to think that you are left to yourself. You are not. You and I must learn to say what our Lord Himself said under the very shadow of the cross: 'The hour cometh, yea, is now come, that ye shall be scattered . . . and shall leave me alone: and yet I am not alone, because the Father is with me.' And that is His promise to us also: 'I will never leave thee, nor forsake thee'. But above all else rely upon this, that He knows everything about us, every circumstance, every need, every wound; and therefore we can rest quietly and confidently in that blessed and most glorious assurance.

That, in turn, brings us to the third argument, which is that we are to concentrate upon perfecting our relationship to God as our heavenly Father. We, unlike the heathen, are to rely implicitly upon our knowledge of Him as our

---

1. See pp. 398ff. in this volume.

heavenly Father, and we are to concentrate upon perfecting this knowledge and our relationship to Him. 'But seek ye first the kingdom of God, and his righteousness; and all these things shall be added unto you.' I wonder whether I dare suggest that there is an element of humour introduced at this point. It seems to me, in effect, that our Lord is saying this: He has said twice over, and then has repeated in various forms: Do not worry about food and drink and clothing; do not worry about your life in this world; do not worry as to whether God is trying you or not. And then, as it were, He says: If you want to worry, I will tell you what to worry about. Worry about your relationship to the Father! That is the thing to concentrate on. The Gentiles are seeking these other things, and so are many of you, but 'Seek ye rather'. That is the thing to seek.

Again we should remember that 'seek' carries the meaning of seeking earnestly, seeking intensely, living for it. And He even enforces it by adding another word, 'first'. 'Seek ye first.' That means, generally, principally, above everything else; give that priority. Once more we find our Lord repeating Himself. He says: You are concerned about these other things, and you are putting them first. But you must not. What you have to put first is the kingdom of God and His righteousness. He has already said that in the model prayer which He taught these people to pray. You remember the teaching. You come to God. Of course you are interested in life and in this world; but you do not start by saying, 'Give us this day our daily bread'. You start like this: 'Our Father which art in heaven, Hallowed be thy name. Thy kingdom come. Thy will be done in earth, as it is in heaven.' And then, and only then, 'Give us this day our daily bread'. 'Seek ye first' — not 'your daily bread', but, 'the kingdom of God and his righteousness'. In other words, you must bring yourself to that position in mind and heart and desires. It must take absolute priority over everything else.

What does our Lord mean by saying: 'Seek ye first the kingdom of God'? Obviously He is not telling His hearers how to make themselves Christian; but He is telling them how to behave because they are Christian. They are in the kingdom of God, and because they are in it they are to seek it more and more. They are, as Peter puts it, to 'make their calling and election sure'. In practice it means that, as children of our heavenly Father, we should be seeking to know Him better. Now the author of the Epistle to the Hebrews puts that perfectly when he says in 11:6, 'He that cometh to God must believe that he is, and that he is a rewarder of them that diligently seek him.' Put your emphasis on the 'diligently'. Many Christian people miss so many blessings in this life because they do not seek God diligently. They do not spend much time in seeking His face. In His courts they drop on their knees to pray, but that is not of necessity seeking the Lord. The Christian is meant to be seeking the face of the Lord daily, constantly. He takes and makes time to do so.

Furthermore, it means that we must think more about the kingdom and our relationship to God, and especially about our eternal future. It was because he did this that Paul was able to say to the Corinthians, 'Our light affliction, which is but for a moment, worketh for us a far more exceeding and eternal weight of glory; while we look not at the things which are seen, but at the things which are not seen: for the things which are seen are temporal; but the things which are not seen are eternal' (2 Cor. 4:17, 18). Notice that 'while'. The apostle only rejoices in spite of these things — 'while', 'as long as'. He puts it as a positive exhortation and injunction to the Colossians when he says, 'Set your affection on things above, not on things on the earth'. That is the meaning of seeking the kingdom of God.

But He says, 'Seek ye first the kingdom of God, and his righteousness'. Why the addition of this 'righteousness'? Again, this is a very important addition. This means holiness, the life of righteousness. You are not only to seek the kingdom of God in the sense that you set your affections on things above; you must also positively seek holiness and righteousness. Once more we get the repetition of 'Blessed are they which do hunger and thirst after righteousness: for they shall be filled.' Yes, that is it. The Christian is seeking righteousness, seeking to be like Christ, seeking positive holiness and to be more and more holy, growing in grace and in the knowledge of the Lord. This is the way to increase your faith. It works like this. The more holy we are, the nearer we shall be to God. The more holy we are, the greater will be our faith. The more sanctified and holy we are, the greater will be our assurance and therefore our claims and our reliance upon God. This is experience, is it not? Have you not known this many times? Suddenly something goes wrong in your life and you turn to God in prayer; and the moment you do so you are reminded of your slackness in the past weeks or months. Something says within you, 'Surely you are behaving just like a cad? How many days and weeks and months have passed when you have not sought the face of God? You have said your prayers mechanically; but now you are seeking God, you are making time to look for Him. But you have not done that regularly.' You feel condemned, and you have lost confidence in your prayers. There are absolute rules in this spiritual life, and it is the man who seeks the kingdom of God and His righteousness who has the greatest confidence in Him. The nearer we live to God the less we are aware of the things of this life and this world, and the greater our sense of assurance about Him. The more holy we are, the better we shall know God. We shall know Him as our Father, and then nothing that happens to us will upset our equanimity, because our relationship to Him is so close.

We can paraphrase our Lord's words thus: If you want to seek anything, if you want to be anxious about anything, be anxious about your spiritual condition, your nearness to God and your relationship to Him. If you put that first, worry will go; that is the result. This great concern about your relationship to God will drive out every lesser concern about food and clothing.

The man who knows himself to be a child of God and an heir of eternity has a very different view of things in this life and world. This is true of necessity, and the greater that faith and knowledge, the smaller will these other things become. Moreover he has a definite specific promise. Let us lay hold on this promise and grasp it firmly. The promise is that, if we do truly seek these things first and foremost, and almost exclusively, these other things shall be added unto us, they will be 'thrown into the bargain'. The heathen does nothing but think about these things. There are spiritual worldlings also who are praying about these things and nothing else, but they never find satisfaction. The man of God prays about and seeks the kingdom of God, and these other things are added unto him. It is a specific promise of God.

You have a perfect illustration of this in the story about Solomon. Solomon did not pray for riches and length of days; he prayed for wisdom. And God said in effect: Because you have not prayed for these other things I will give you wisdom; and I will give you these other things as well. I will give you riches and length of days into the bargain (see 1 Kings 3). God always does that. It is not an accident that the Puritans of the seventeenth century, especially the Quakers, became wealthy people. It was not because they hoarded wealth, it was not because they worshipped mammon. It was just that they were living for God and His righteousness, and the result was that they did not throw away their money on worthless things. In a sense, therefore, they could not help becoming wealthy. They held on to the promises of God and incidentally became rich.

Put God, His glory and the coming of His kingdom, and your relationship to Him, your nearness to Him and your holiness in the central position, and you have the pledged word of God Himself through the lips of His Son, that all these other things, as they are necessary for your well-being in this life and world, shall be added unto you. That is the way to increase your faith. Be unlike the heathen; remember that God knows all about you as your Father, and is watching over you. Therefore seek to be more like Him and to live your life nearer to Him.

Chapter Fourteen

Worry: Its Causes and Cure

IN Matthew 6:34 our Lord brings to a conclusion the subject with which He has been dealing in this entire section of the Sermon on the Mount, namely, the problem which is created for us by our relationship to the things of this world. It is a problem that confronts us all. It does so in different ways as we have seen. Some people are tempted to be governed by worldly possessions in the sense that they want to hoard and amass them. Others are troubled by them in the sense that they are worried about them; it is not the problem of super-abundance in their case, but the problem of need. But, essentially, according to our Lord, it is one and the same problem, the problem of our relationship to the things of this world, and of this life. As we have seen, our Lord takes great trouble to work out the argument with respect to this matter. He deals with both aspects of the problem and analyses both.

Here, in this verse, He brings this consideration to an end and He puts it in this particular form. Three times over He uses this expression, 'Take therefore no thought'. It is so important, that He deliberately states it like that three times, and in particular with regard to the question of food and drink and clothing; and He works out the argument, you remember, with regard to these matters. Here is the conclusion of the whole subject, and I am sure that many, when they first read this verse in its context, must have felt almost a sense of surprise that our Lord should have added it. He seems to have reached such a wonderful climax in the previous verse, the thirty-third, where He has concentrated His positive teaching in the memorable words, 'Seek ye first the kingdom of God, and his righteousness; and all these things shall be added unto you.' That seems like one of those final statements to which nothing can be added, and at first sight the verse at which we are now looking seems to be almost an anticlimax. You cannot imagine anything, higher than, 'Seek ye first the kingdom of God, and his righteousness.' Be right about that, says our Lord, and then you have no need to worry about these other things; they shall be added unto you. You are to be right with God and God will look after you. But then He goes on to say, Do not be anxious about the morrow — the future: for the morrow shall take thought for the things of itself. 'Sufficient unto the day is the evil thereof.'

It is always good when we face a problem like this to ask a question. We can be quite certain that this is not an anticlimax; there is some very good reason for this addition. Our Lord never utters words merely for the sake of doing so. Having given us this wonderful positive teaching He returns to it and puts it in this negative form. He ends on the negative and that is, at first sight, what constitutes the problem. Why did He do that? The moment you face the fact and begin to question it, you will see at once why our Lord did so. It is because this is really an extension of His teaching. It is not mere repetition, or just a summary; it is that, but it is more than that. In adding this He carried the teaching one step further. So far, He has been looking at this problem as it concerns us in the immediate present; now here He takes it on and covers the future also. He extends it, and applies it, to cover the whole of life. And here, if one may use such language and such an expression with regard to our blessed Lord, He shows His profound understanding of human nature and of the problems with which we are confronted in this life. All must agree that you will not find anywhere in any textbook a more thorough analysis of worry, anxiety, and the anxious care that tends to kill man in this world, than you find in this paragraph which we have been considering in detail.

Here our Lord shows His final understanding of the condition. Worry, after all, is a definite entity; it is a force, a power, and we have not begun to understand it until we realize what a tremendous power it is. We so often tend to think of the condition of worry as one which is negative, a failure on our part to do certain things. It is that; it is a failure to apply our faith. But the thing we must emphasize is that worry is something positive that comes and grips us and takes control of us. It is a mighty power, an active force, and if we do not realize that, we are certain to be defeated by it. If it cannot get us to be anxious and burdened and borne down by the state and condition of things that are actually confronting us, it will take this next step, it will go on into the future.

We must have discovered this in ourselves, or perhaps when we have tried to help to deliver other people who are suffering from a condition of worry. The conversation starts with the particular thing that has brought them to you. You then provide the answers and show how unnecessary worry is. You will find, however, that almost invariably they go on and say, 'Yes, but . . .' That is typical of worry, it always gives the impression that it does not really want to be relieved. The person wants to be relieved, but the worry does not; and we are entitled to draw that distinction. Our Lord does it Himself when He talks about the morrow taking thought for the things of itself. That is personalizing worry; He is regarding it as a power, almost a person, that takes hold of you, and in spite of yourself keeps arguing with you and saying one thing and then another. It leads to that curious perverse condition in which one almost desires not to be relieved and not to be delivered: and it often works in the particular form we are considering together now. When you have brought out all the answers and given a full explanation to such persons, then they say, 'Ah yes, that is all right for now; but what about tomorrow? what about next week? what about next year?' And on and on it goes, into the future. In other words, if it cannot work up its case on the facts it has before it, it does not hesitate to conjure up facts. Worry has an active imagination, and it can envisage all sorts and kinds of possibilities. It can envisage strange eventualities, and with its terrible power and activity it can transport us into the future and into a situation that is yet to come. And there we find ourselves worried and troubled and borne down by something which is purely imaginary.

We need not go further into the matter because we all know exactly what it is. But the key to the understanding of how to treat the subject is to realize that we are dealing with a very vital force and power. I do not want to exaggerate it too much. There are cases where this condition is undoubtedly the result of the work of evil spirits; we can see clearly that there is another personality at work. But even short of direct possession we must recognize the fact that our adversary, the devil, does in various ways, through using a lowered physical condition or taking advantage of a natural tendency to overanxiety, thus exercise a tyranny and power over many. We have to understand that we are fighting for our lives against some tremendous power. We are up against a powerful adversary.

Let us see how our Lord deals with this problem, this worry and anxiety about the future. The first thing we must remember, is that what He says now is in the context of His previous teaching. Here again it is fatal to take this statement right out of its context. We must remember all He has been telling us, for it is all still applicable. We continue from that to the further argument that He uses here, where He shows us the folly of being anxious. He shows it for the foolish thing it is as He asks in effect: Why do you allow yourself to be worried thus about the future? 'The morrow shall take thought for the things of itself. Sufficient unto the day is the evil thereof.' If the present is bad enough as it is, why go to meet the future? To go on from day to day is enough in and of itself; be content with that. But not only that. Worry about the future is so utterly futile and useless; it achieves nothing at all. We are very slow to see that; yet how true it is.

Indeed we can go further and say that worry is never of any value at all. This is seen with particular clarity as you come to face the future. Apart from anything else, it is a pure waste of energy because however much you worry you cannot do anything about it. In any case its threatened catastrophes are imaginary; they are not certain, they may never happen at all.

But above all that, says our Lord, can you not see that, in a sense, you are mortgaging the future by worrying about it in the present? Indeed, the result of worrying about the future is that you are crippling yourself in the present; you are lessening your efficiency with regard to today, and thereby you are reducing your whole efficiency with regard to that future which is coming to meet you. In other words, worry is something that is due to an entire failure to understand the nature of life in this world. Our Lord seems to picture life like this. As the result of the Fall and sin there is always a problem in life, because when man fell, he was told that henceforward he was going to live and eat his bread 'by the sweat of his brow'. He was no longer in Paradise, he was no longer just to take the fruit and live a life of ease and enjoyment. As the result of sin, life in this world has become a task. Man has to labour and must meet trials and troubles. We all know that, for we are all subject to the same tribulations and trials.

The great question is, how are we to face them? According to our Lord, the vital thing is not to spend every day of your life in adding up the grand total of everything that is ever likely to happen to you in the whole of your life in this world. If you do that, it will crush you. That is not the way. Rather, you must think of it like this. There is, as it were, a daily quota of problems and difficulties in life. Every day has its problems; some of them are constant from day to day, some of them vary. But the great thing to do is to realize that every day must be lived in and of itself and as a unit. Here is the quota for today. Very well; we must face that and meet it; and He has already told us how to do so. We must not go forward and tack tomorrow's quota on to today's, otherwise it may be too much for us. We have to take it day by day. You remember how our Lord turned upon His disciples when they were trying to dissuade Him from going back to unfriendly Judaea to the house where Lazarus lay dead? They pointed out to Him the possible consequences, and how it might shorten His life. His answer to them was 'Are there not twelve hours in the day?' You have to live twelve hours at a time and no more. Here is the quota for today; very well, face that and deal with that. Do not think of tomorrow. You will have tomorrow's quota, but then it will be tomorrow, and not today.

It is very easy to deal with this matter solely on that level and very tempting to do so. That is what you might call, if you like, psychology. Not the so-called new psychology but the old psychology of life which has been practised by mankind

417

from the very beginning. And it is very profound psychology; it is the essence of commonsense and wisdom, purely on the human level. If you want to go through life without crippling yourself and burdening yourself and perhaps losing your health and the control of your nerves, these are the cardinal rules. Do not carry yesterday or tomorrow with you; live for today and for the twelve hours you are in. It is very interesting to notice as you read biographies how many men have failed in life because they have not done that. Most men who have been successful in life have been characterized by this wonderful capacity for forgetting the past. They have made mistakes. 'Well,' they say, 'I have made them and I cannot undo them. If I meditated upon them for the rest of my life, it would make no difference. I am not going to be a fool, I will let the dead past bury its dead.' The result is that when they make a decision they do not spend the night worrying about it afterwards. On the other hand, the man who cannot help referring back keeps himself awake saying, 'Why did I do that?' And so he saps his nervous energy, and wakes up after poor and broken sleep feeling tired and unfit. As a consequence he makes more mistakes, completing the vicious circle of worry by saying, 'If I am making these mistakes now, what about next week?' The poor man is already down and defeated.

Here is our Lord's answer to all that. Do not be foolish, do not waste your energy, do not spend your time thus in worrying over what has passed, or about the future; here is today, live to the maximum today. But of course we must not stop at that level. Our Lord does not. We must take this statement in the whole context of this teaching. So, having reasoned it out on a natural line, and having seen the essential wisdom of that, we go on to see that we must learn not only to rely on God in general, but also in particular. We must learn to realize that the God who helps us today will be the same God tomorrow, and will help us tomorrow.

This is perhaps the lesson which many of us need to learn, that not only must we learn to divide up our life in this world into these periods of twelve or twenty-four hours; we must divide up our whole relationship to God in exactly the same way. The danger is that, while we believe in God in general, and for the whole of our life, we do not believe in Him for the particular sections of our life. Thereby many of us go wrong. We must learn to take things to God as they arise. Some people fail very grievously in this matter because they are always trying to anticipate God; they are always sitting down, as it were, and asking themselves, 'Now I wonder what God is going to ask me to do tomorrow or in a week's time or in a year? What is God going to ask of me then?' That is utterly wrong. Never try to anticipate God. As you must not anticipate your own future, do not anticipate God's future for you. Live day by day; live a life of obedience to God every day; do what God asks you to do every day. Never allow yourself to indulge in thoughts such as these, 'I wonder when tomorrow comes whether God will want me to do this or to do that.' That must never be done, says our Lord. You must learn to trust God day by day for every particular occasion, and never try to go ahead of Him.

There is a sense in which we commit ourselves to God once and for ever; there is another sense in which we have to do it every day. There is a sense in which God has given us everything in grace once and for ever. Yes; but He gives grace to us also in parts and portions day by day. We must start the day and say to ourselves, 'Here is a day which is going to bring me certain problems and difficulties; very well, I shall need God's grace to help me. I know God will make all grace to abound, He will be with me according to my need — "as thy days, so shall thy strength be".' That is the essential biblical teaching with regard to this matter; we must learn to leave the future entirely in God's hands.

Take, for instance, that great statement of it in Hebrews 13:8. The Hebrew Christians were passing through troubles and trials, and the author of that Epistle tells them not to worry, and for this reason: 'Jesus Christ the same yesterday, and to day, and for ever.' In effect he says you need not worry, for what He was yesterday, He is today, and He will be tomorrow. You need not anticipate life; the Christ who takes you through today will be the same Christ tomorrow. He is changeless, everlasting, always the same; so you must not think about tomorrow; think instead about the changeless Christ. Or consider the way in which Paul puts it in 1 Corinthians 10:13: 'There hath no temptation taken you but such as is common to man: but God is faithful, who will not suffer you to be tempted above that ye are able; but will with the temptation also make a way to escape'. That is certain with regard to the whole of your future. There will be no trial that will come to you but that God will always provide that way of escape. It will never be above your strength; there will always be the remedy.

We can sum it all up by saying that, as we learn in wisdom to take our days one by one as they come, forgetting yesterday and tomorrow, so we must learn this vital importance of walking with God day by day, of relying upon Him day by day, and applying to Him for the particular needs of each day. The fatal temptation to which we are all prone is that of trying to store grace against the future. That means lack of faith in God. Leave it with Him; leave it entirely with Him, confident and assured that He will always be going before you. As the Scripture puts it, He will 'prevent' you. He will be there before you to meet the problem. Turn to Him and you will find that He is there, that He knows all about it, and knows all about you.

That, then, is the essence of the teaching. But if we are to explain it honestly and fully, we are compelled at this point to consider a problem. Ordinary people reading this verse have always tended to ask two questions. 'Take therefore no thought for the morrow: for the morrow shall take thought for the things of it-self. Sufficient unto the day is the evil thereof.' Is it wrong, therefore, they ask, for a Christian to save, to save money, to put something by, as we say, for a rainy day? Is it right or is it wrong for a Christian to take out an insurance policy? The answer is exactly the same as it was when we dealt with the first part of this sec-tion. There we saw that the answer is that 'take no thought' does not literally mean that you should not think at all, but that you are not to worry. This should always be translated as 'Do not be anxious about', 'do not be agitated about', 'do not worry about' tomorrow. We saw, you remember, that our Lord does not tell us that, because the birds of the air are fed without ploughing and sowing and reaping and gathering into barns, therefore man should never plough or sow, and should never reap and gather into barns. That is to make the thing ridiculous, because it is God Himself who ordained seedtime and harvest. And the farmer when he ploughs is in fact taking proper thought for the mor-row because he knows that his crop is not going to grow automatically. He has to plough the earth and to look after it, and eventually he reaps and gathers into his barn. In a sense that is all a preparation for the future, and of course that is not condemned by the Scriptures. On the contrary, it is even commended by Scripture. That is how man is to live his life in this world according to the ordi-nance of God Himself. So this verse must not be taken in that foolish and ridic-ulous sense. We are not just to sit and wait for food and clothing to come to us; that is to ridicule the teaching.

That entitles us, I think, to take the next step and to say that our Lord's teaching throughout is that we are to do that which is right, that which is rea-sonable, that which is legitimate. But — and this is where the teaching of this verse comes in — we are never to take so much thought about these things, or to be so concerned about them, as to allow them to dominate our life, or limit our usefulness, in the present. That is the point at which we cross the line from reasonable thought and care to anxious care and worry. Our Lord is condemn-ing not the man who ploughs the earth and sows the seeds, but the man who, having done that, sits down and begins to get worried about it and has his mind always centred on it, the man who is obsessed by the problem of life and living, and by fear of the future. That is the one thing He condemns, for not only is that man limiting his usefulness in the present, not only is he crippling the present with fears for the future, but above all he is allowing these cares to dom-inate his life. Every man in this life, as the result of sin and the Fall, has his prob-lems. Problems are inevitable; existence in itself is a problem. I shall therefore have to meet and face problems but I am not to allow myself to be dominated and crushed by that thought. The moment I am dominated by a problem I am in this state of worry and anxiety which is wrong. So I may take reasonable thought and care, and make reasonable provision, and then think no more about it. Even necessary affairs must not become my life. I must not spend all my time with them, and they must not always be occupying my thought.

We must go a step further still. I must never allow thought with regard to the future to inhibit in any way my usefulness in the present. Let me explain. There are various good causes in this world that need our help and assistance, and they have to be kept going from day to day. And there are certain people who are so concerned about how they are going to be able to live in the future that they have no time to help the causes which are in need at this moment That is what is wrong. If I allow my concern about the future to cripple me in the present I am guilty of worry; but if I make reasonable provision, in a legitimate manner, and then live my life fully in the present, all is well. Furthermore there is nothing in the Scripture which indicates that it is wrong to save or to be insured. But if I am always thinking about this insurance, or my bank balance, or as to whether I have saved enough and so on, then that is something which our Lord is concerned about and condemns. This could be illustrated in many different ways.

The danger with this text is for people to take one of two extreme positions. There are those who say that the Christian should live his life fully but should make no provision at all for the future. In the same way there are those who say that it is wrong to take up a collection in a church service, that these things should be done by faith. But it is not quite as simple as that because the apostle Paul teaches the members of the church at Corinth not only to take up collections, but he even tells them to put it aside on the first day of the week. He gives them detailed instructions; and there is much in the New Testament about the collection for the saints.

There must be no misunderstanding at this point; the teaching of Scripture is perfectly clear and explicit. There are two ways of maintaining God's work, and what applies to God's work applies to all our lives as Christians in this world. There are some men who are undoubtedly called to a special ministry of faith. Read for instance 1 Corinthians 12, and amongst the gifts that the Holy Spirit dispenses according to His own will to man you will find there is the so-called gift of faith. It is not the gift of miracles; it is the gift of faith, it is a special gift. What is this faith then? It is not saving or believing faith, for all Christians have that. What then is it? It is clearly the sort of faith that was given, for instance, to George Müller and Hudson Taylor. Those men were given a special gift by God in order that God might manifest His glory through them in that particular way. But I am equally certain that God called Dr. Barnardo to do the same sort of work and told him to take up collections and make appeals. The same God works in sanctified men in different ways; but both methods are obviously equally legitimate. Or take another illustration. It would be very difficult to find two holier or more dedicated men than George Müller and George Whitefield. Müller was definitely called to found an orphanage which was to be supported by faith and prayer, while Whitefield was called to start his orphanage in America and to keep it going by direct appeals for money to God's people.

That is clearly the truth concerning the conduct of the life of the Church as taught in the Scriptures; and we should apply exactly the same principles to our own personal lives. There are certain people who may be definitely called of God to live that particular kind of life which manifests that gift of faith. There are certain people for whom to put money aside or to take out an insurance policy would be quite wrong. But to say that anybody who takes up an insurance policy or who saves is therefore not a Christian is error. 'Let every man be fully persuaded in his own mind'; let every man examine himself in this matter; let not one condemn the other. All we must say is this; the Scripture certainly does allow this reasonable care, unless you are certain that God has called you to live your life in the other way. It is, therefore, quite wrong, and unscriptural, to condemn saving and insurance in the light of this text. But on the other hand, we must always be careful to maintain and preserve this balance.

Let us now summarize this teaching by putting it in the form of a number of general principles.

The first is this: All the things we have been dealing with in the last four or five chapters apply only to Christians. Somebody once said to me, 'How can that teaching about God's care for men be true? With all the need and poverty that exists in the world, with all the suffering of homeless and displaced men, women and children, how can you assert that?' The answer is that the promises are only to Christian people. What is the commonest cause of poverty? Why are the children ragged and without food? Is it not usually because of the sins of the parents? The money had been spent on drink or squandered on vain or evil things. Analyse the cases of poverty and you will find the results illuminating. These promises are made only to Christian people; they are not universal promises to everybody. Take that great statement of David, 'I have been young, and now am old; yet have I not seen the righteous forsaken, nor his seed begging bread.' Applied to the righteous I think this is literally true; but let us be careful that we recognize the meaning of the word 'righteous'. He does not say, 'I have never seen a professing Christian forsaken, nor his seed begging bread.' He says the 'righteous'. I suggest if you examine your experience you will have to agree with David that you have never seen the righteous man forsaken nor his seed begging bread. Now the important word there is 'seed'. How far does it extend? Does it extend to the posterity and the seed of this man for ever and for ever? I do not think so. I think it extends only to his immediate seed, because the grandson may be a profligate and an unrighteous man; therefore the promise does not hold good. God does not say that He is going to bless a man who is living an ungodly life. It is to the righteous and his seed — that is the promise — and we can challenge anybody to give us an example to the contrary. These promises are only to God's people. They are always based on full Christian doctrine; if you do not believe the doctrine, they do not apply to you.

Second, worry is always a failure to grasp and apply our faith. Faith does not work automatically. How often have we seen that during these studies. Never think of faith as something put inside you to work automatically; you have to apply it. Faith does not grow automatically either; we must learn to talk to our faith and to ourselves. We can think of faith in terms of a man having a conversation with himself about himself and about his faith. Do you remember how the Psalmist puts it in Psalm 42? Look at him turning to himself and saying, 'Why art thou cast down, O my soul? and why art thou disquieted within me?' That is the way to make faith grow. You must talk to yourself about your faith. You must question yourself as to what is the matter with your faith. You must ask your soul why it is cast down, and wake it up! The child of God talks to himself; he reasons with himself; he shakes himself and reminds himself of himself and of his faith, and immediately his faith begins to grow. Do not imagine that because you became a Christian all you have to do is to go on mechanically. Your faith does not grow mechanically, you have to attend to it. To use our Lord's analogy, you have to dig round and about it, and pay attention to it. Then you will find it will grow.

Finally, a large part of faith, especially in this connection, consists of just refusing anxious thoughts. That to me is perhaps the most important and the most practical thing of all. Faith means refusing to think about worrying things, refusing to think of the future in that wrong sense. The devil and all adverse circumstances will do their utmost to make me do so, but having faith means that I shall say: 'No; I refuse to be worried. I have done my reasonable service; I have done what I believed to be right and legitimate, and beyond that I will not think at all.' That is faith, and it is particularly true with regard to the future. When the devil comes with his insinuations, injecting them into you — all the fiery darts of the evil one — say, 'No; I am not interested. The God whom I am trusting for today, I will trust for tomorrow. I refuse to listen; I will not think your thoughts.' Faith is refusing to be burdened because we have cast our burden upon the Lord. May He, in His infinite grace, give us wisdom and grace to implement these simple principles and thereby rejoice in Him day by day.

Chapter Fifteen

'Judge Not'

WE come now to the last major section of the Sermon on the Mount. There is much disagreement as to the right way of approaching it. Some would regard chapter 7 of Matthew's Gospel as just a collection of aphoristic statements with very little internal connection between them. But it seems to me that that is quite a mistaken view of this section of the Sermon, because there is quite clearly an underlying theme in the entire chapter, that of judgment. It is the theme that constantly recurs as our Lord proceeds with His teaching, and which He puts in different ways.

It is not difficult to trace the connection between this section and the previous one. Indeed, as we have seen repeatedly, it is very important that we should always regard the Sermon as a whole before we attempt a particular interpretation of any section, or any statement in a section. So it is good for us to review the whole again very hurriedly. First we get the description of the Christian man, his character. Then we are shown the effect upon him of all that happens in the world in which he lives and his reaction to that world. Then he is reminded of his function in the world as the salt of the earth and as a light set for all to see, and so on. Then, having thus described the Christian as he is and in his setting, our Lord goes on to give him particular instructions with regard to his life in this world. He starts with his relationship to the law. That was especially necessary because of the false teaching of the Pharisees and scribes. That is the theme of that long section in chapter 5 in which our Lord, in terms of six main principles, enunciates His view and interpretation of the law over against that of the Pharisees and scribes. So the Christian man is taught how he is to behave in general, how the law applies to him, and what is expected of him.

Having done that, in chapter 6 our Lord looks at this Christian man who has thus been described, living his life in this world, and living it, especially, in fellowship with his Father. He has to remember always that the Father is looking upon him. He has to remember this when he is in private and when he is deciding what good he is going to do — his almsgiving, his prayer, his fasting, everything designed to bring about the growth and nurture and culture of his inner spiritual life and being. It has always to be done as realizing that the Father's eye is upon him. There is no value or merit in it if we do not realize that; if we are out to please ourselves or to impress others we may as well do nothing.

Then we come to another section, in which our Lord shows us the danger of the impact of the life of this world upon us, the danger of worldliness, the danger of living for the things of this life and this world, whether we have too much or too little, and especially the subtlety of that danger.

Having dealt with all that He now comes to this final section. And here, it seems to me, He is enforcing again the all-importance of our remembering that we are walking under the Father's eye. The particular subject He handles is one which is mainly concerned with our relationship with other people; but still the important thing to realize is that our relationship to God is the fundamental matter. It is as if our Lord were saying that the final thing which matters is not what men think of us, but what God thinks of us. In other words, we are reminded all along that our life here is a journey and a pilgrimage, and that it is leading on to a final judgment, an ultimate assessment, and the determination and proclamation of our final and eternal destiny.

All must agree that this is something of which we constantly need to be reminded. Half our troubles are due to the fact that we live on the assumption that this is the only life and the only world. Of course we know that is not true; but there is a great difference between knowing a thing and really being governed and guided by that knowledge in our ordinary life and outlook. If we were questioned and asked whether we believe that we go on living after death, and that we shall have to face God in judgment, we would undoubtedly say 'yes'. But as we live from hour to hour are we mindful of that? We cannot read the Bible without coming to the conclusion that the thing that really differentiates God's people from all others is that they have always been people who walk in the consciousness of their eternal destiny. The natural man does not care about his eternal future; to him this is the only world. It is the only world he thinks about; he lives for it and it controls him. But the Christian is a man who should walk through this life as conscious that it is but transient and passing, a kind of preparatory school. He should always know that he is walking in the presence of God, and that he is going on to meet God; and that thought should determine and control the whole of his life. Our Lord is at pains to show us here, as He was in the last section, that we ever need to be reminded of that, and that we need to be reminded of it in detail. We have to remember this fact in every part of our lives; we must remember that every section of our existence must be brought into that relationship. We are undergoing a process of judgment the whole time, because we are being prepared for the final judgment; and as Christian people we should do all things with that idea uppermost in our minds, remembering that we shall have to render an account.

That is the controlling theme in this chapter. Our Lord handles it in various ways, leading up to the great climax in that striking picture of the two houses. These represent two men listening to these things; one puts them into practice and the other does not. Once more we are reminded of the greatness of this Sermon on the Mount, its searching character, the profundity of its teaching, indeed its truly alarming character. There never has been such a Sermon as this. It finds us all somehow, somewhere. There is no possibility of escape; it searches us out in all our hiding places and brings us out into the light of God. There is nothing, as we have seen several times before, which is so unintelligent and fatuous as the statement of those who are fond of telling us that what they really like in the New Testament is the Sermon on the Mount. They dislike the theology of Paul and all this talk about doctrine. They say, 'Give me the Sermon on the Mount, something practical, something a man can do himself.' Well here it is! There is nothing that so utterly condemns us as the Sermon on the Mount; there is nothing so utterly impossible, so terrifying, and so full of doctrine. Indeed, I do not hesitate to say that, were it not that I knew of the doctrine of justification by faith only, I would never look at the Sermon on the Mount, because it is a Sermon before which we all stand completely naked and altogether without hope. Far from being something practical that we can take up and put into practice, it is of all teaching the most impossible if we are left to ourselves. This great Sermon is full of doctrine and leads to doctrine; it is a kind of prologue to all the doctrine of the New Testament.

Our Lord opens His consideration of this great question of our walking in this world under a sense of judgment in terms of the particular matter of judging one another. 'Judge not'. Our Lord still uses, you notice, the same method that He has used right through this Sermon. He makes an announcement and then gives reasons for it; He lays down a principle and then reasons with us concerning it, or puts it to us in a more logical manner in detail. That is His method. It has been His method with regard to worldliness; and here again He comes back to it. He makes His deliberate pronouncement — 'Judge not'.

We are confronted here by a statement which has often led to a great deal of confusion. Admittedly it is a subject that can be very easily misunderstood, and it can be misunderstood on two sides and from two extremes, as is almost invariably the case with truth. The question is, what exactly does our Lord mean when He says, 'Judge not' — Don't judge? The way to answer this question is not to seek a dictionary. Merely to look at the word 'judge' cannot satisfy us at this point. It has many different meanings so it cannot be decided in that way. But it is of vital importance that we should know exactly what it means. Never, perhaps, was a correct interpretation of this injunction more important than at this present time. Different periods in the history of the Church need different emphases, and if I were asked what in particular is the need of today, I should say that it is a consideration of this particular statement. This is so because the whole atmosphere of life today, and especially in religious circles, is one that makes a correct interpretation of this statement quite vital. We are living in an age when definitions are at a discount, an age which dislikes thought and hates theology and doctrine and dogma. It is an age which is characterized by a love of ease and compromise — 'anything for a quiet life', as the expression goes. It is an age of appeasement. That term is no longer popular in a political and international sense, but the mentality that delights in it persists. It is an age that dislikes strong men because, it says, they always cause disturbance. It dislikes a man who knows what he believes and really believes it. It dismisses him as a difficult person who is 'impossible to get on with'.

This can easily be illustrated, as I have suggested, in the political sphere. The man who is now acclaimed and almost idolized in Great Britain is the man who, before the war, was severely criticized as being an impossible person. He was excluded from office because he was said to be an individualist who had extreme views and with whom it was impossible to work. The same mentality that led to such treatment of Winston Churchill in the thirties is in control in the realm of Christian affairs and in the realm of the Christian Church today. There have been ages in the history of the Church when men were praised because they stood for their principles at all costs. But that is not so today. Such men today are regarded as being difficult, self-assertive, non-cooperative and so on. The man who is now glorified is the man who can be described as being in 'the middle of the road', not at one extreme or the other, a pleasant man, who does not create difficulties and problems because of his views. Life, we are told, is sufficiently difficult and involved as it is, without our taking a stand on particular doctrines. That surely is the mentality today, and it is not unfair to say that it is the controlling mentality. It is very natural in a sense, because we have experienced so much trouble, so many problems, and disasters. It is only natural, also, that people should be ready to turn away from men with principles who know where they stand, and should seek ease and peace. Just cast your minds back to the twenties and the thirties of this century in the political and international spheres and you will see exactly what I am describing. The cry was for tranquillity and ease; and evasion of problems followed naturally and inevitably. Eventually, peace at almost any price, even that involving the humiliation and betrayal of others, became the controlling idea.

At a time like this, then, it is of the utmost importance that we should be able to interpret correctly this statement concerning judging, because there are many who say that 'judge not' must be taken simply and literally as it is, and as meaning that the truly Christian man should never express an opinion about others. They say that there must be no judging whatsoever, that we must be easy, indulgent and tolerant, and allow almost anything for peace and quiet, and especially unity. This is not a time for these particular judgments, they say; what is needed today is unity and fellowship. We must all be one together. This is often argued in terms of the danger of Communism. Some people are so alarmed at Communism that they say that, at all costs, all who in any sense use the name Christian should be accepted. We should all agree because of that common danger and common enemy.

The question arises therefore as to whether that is a possible interpretation. I suggest, in the first instance, that it cannot be; and it cannot be, quite clearly, because of Scripture teaching itself. Take the very context of this statement and you will surely see at once that that interpretation of 'judge not' is quite impossible. Look at verse 6, 'Give not that which is holy unto the dogs, neither cast ye your pearls before swine, lest they trample them under their feet, and turn again and rend you'. How can I put that into practice if I do not exercise judgment? How do I know which kind of person can be described as a 'dog' in this way? In other words, the injunction that immediately follows this statement about judging at once calls upon me to exercise judgment and discrimination. Then again, take the more remote connection in verse 15: 'Beware of false prophets, which come to you in sheep's clothing, but inwardly they are ravening wolves.' How is that to be taken? I cannot 'beware of false prophets' if I am not to think, and if I am so afraid of judging that I never make any assessment at all of their teaching. These people come 'in sheep's clothing'; they are very ingratiating and they use Christian terminology. They appear to be very harmless and honest and are invariably 'very nice'. But we are not to be taken in by that kind of thing — beware of such people. Our Lord also says, 'Ye shall know them by their fruits'; but if I am not to have any standard or exercise discrimination, how can I test the fruit and discriminate between the true and the false? So, without going any further, that cannot be the true interpretation which suggests that this just means being 'free and easy', and having a flabby and indulgent attitude towards anybody who vaguely uses the designation Christian. That is quite impossible.

This view, however, is held so tenaciously that we must not even leave it at that.

We must go further and put it like this: the Scripture itself teaches us that judgment has to be exercised in connection with affairs of State. It is Scripture which teaches us that judges and magistrates are appointed of God and that a magistrate is called upon to deliver and pronounce judgment, that it is his duty to do so. It is part of God's way of restraining evil and sin and their effects in this world of time. So, if a man says he does not believe in police courts he is contradicting Scripture. It does not always mean the use of force, but judgment has to be exercised, and for a man not to do so, or to be unprepared to do so, is not merely to fail in fulfilling his duty, it is to be unscriptural.

But you also find the same teaching in the Scriptures with regard to the Church. They show very clearly that judgment is to be exercised in the realm of the Church. This is worthy of an entire study on its own, because, owing to our flabby ideas and notions, it is almost true to say that such a thing as discipline in the Christian Church is nonexistent today. When did you last hear of a person being excommunicated? When did you last hear of a person being kept back from the Communion Table? Go back to the history of Protestantism and you will find that the Protestant definition of the Church is, 'that the Church is a place in which the Word is preached, the Sacraments are administered, and discipline is exercised'.

Discipline, to the Protestant Fathers, was as much a mark of the Church as the preaching of the Word and the administration of the Sacraments. But we know very little about discipline. It is the result of this flabby, sentimental notion that you must not judge, and which asks, 'Who are you to express judgment?' But the Scripture exhorts us to do so.

This question of judging applies, also, in the matter of doctrine. Here is this question of false prophets to which our Lord calls attention. We are supposed to detect them and to avoid them. But that is impossible without a knowledge of doctrine, and the exercise of that knowledge in judgment. Paul writing to the Galatians says, 'But though we, or an angel from heaven, preach any other gospel unto you than that which we have preached unto you, let him be accursed.' That is a clear pronouncement. Then you remember what the apostle has to say in 1 Corinthians 15 about those people who were denying the resurrection. He says the same thing in 2 Timothy 2 when he says that some deny the resurrection, saying it is past already, 'of whom is Hymenaeus and Philetus'; and he again expresses judgment with regard to that and exhorts Timothy to do so. In writing to Titus he says, 'A man that is an heretick after the first and second admonition reject.' How do you know whether a man is a heretic or not if your view is that, as long as a man calls himself a Christian, he must be a Christian, and you do not care what he believes? Then go on to John's Epistles, John 'the apostle of love'. In the First Epistle he gives his instructions with regard to the false teachers and the anti-Christs who were to be avoided and rejected. Indeed, in his second Epistle, he puts it very strongly in these words: 'If there come any unto you, and bring not this doctrine, receive him not into your house, neither bid him God speed: for he that biddeth him God speed is partaker of his evil deeds.' You see what the apostle is saying. If a man comes to you who does not hold the true doctrine, you must not receive him into your house, you must not bid him God speed and provide him with money to preach his false doctrine. But today it would be said that that is a lack of charity, that it is being over-punctilious and censorious. This modern idea, however, is a direct contradiction of the Scripture teaching with regard to judging.

Then you find the same thing in our Lord's words to the Jews elsewhere: 'Judge not according to the appearance, but judge righteous judgment' (John 7:24). He looks at the Pharisees and says, 'Ye are they which justify yourselves before men; but God knoweth your hearts: for that which is highly esteemed among men is abomination in the sight of God' (Luke 16:15). You remember His injunction as to what we are to do if our brother trespass against us; we are to go to our brother and tell him his fault 'between thee and him alone'. If he will not listen we are to take witnesses, that in the mouth of two or three witnesses every word may be established; but if he still does not listen then we are to take it to the Church, and if he will not listen to the Church we are to regard him as a heathen man and a publican. We are to have nothing more to do with him. In 1 Corinthians 5 and 6 you will find that Paul gives exactly the same teaching. He tells the Corinthians not to keep company with a man who is an idolater, but to withdraw themselves. That is judgment the whole time. The simple question is thus: how can we put all these injunctions into practice if we are not exercising judgment, if we are not thinking, if we have not a standard, if we are not prepared to make an assessment? These are a few selections out of a large number of Scriptures which we could quote, but they are sufficient to prove that our Lord's statement cannot be interpreted as meaning that we must never judge, never arrive at conclusions and apply them.

If, then, it does not mean that, what does it mean? Surely our Lord's emphasis is this. He is not telling us that we are not to make these assessments based on judgment, but He is very concerned about the matter of condemning. In trying to avoid this tendency to condemn, people have swung right over to the other extreme, and so again they are in a false position. The Christian life is not quite as easy as that. The Christian life is always one of balance. There is a great deal to be said for the point of view that to walk by faith means to walk on a knife edge. You can fall on this side or that; you have to keep on the dead centre of truth, avoiding the error on the one side and on the other. So that while we say that it does not mean the refusal to exercise any discrimination or thought or judgment, we must hasten to say that what it does warn against is the terrible danger of condemning, of pronouncing judgment in a final sense.

The best way to illustrate this is to think of the Pharisees. In this Sermon on the Mount our Lord had the Pharisees in His mind most of the time. He was telling His own people to be very careful not to become like the Pharisees in their view of the law and in their way of living. They misinterpreted the law. They were boastful and demonstrative in their giving of alms; they were demonstrative in their praying at the street corners and in making broad their phylacteries; and they announced that they were fasting. They were, at the same time, mercenary and materialistic in their outlook with regard to the things of this world. Now our Lord has them in His mind at this particular point also. You remember the picture which He gives in Luke 18:9-14 of the Pharisee and the publican who both went up to the temple to pray. The Pharisee said, 'God, I thank thee, that I am not as other men . . . or even as this publican.' It was that judging and condemning attitude of the Pharisees towards others that was so wrong.

But the New Testament makes it painfully clear that that attitude was not confined to the Pharisees. It was something that constantly troubled the early Church; and it has been troubling the Church of God ever since. It is something that troubles the Church of God today, and as we approach this subject we should remember our Lord's statement in this connection when He said: 'He that is without sin among you, let him first cast a stone.' I suppose there is nothing in the whole of the Sermon on the Mount that comes to us with such a sense of condemnation as this statement which we are studying. How guilty we all are in this respect! There is a tendency for this thing to spoil all our lives and to rob us of our happiness! What havoc it has made, and does make, in the Church of God! It is a word to every one of us; it is a painful subject, but a very necessary one. This Sermon comes and speaks to us, and we ignore it, as our Lord reminds us here, at our peril. It is so important a subject that we must analyse it still further, though it is going to be painful. The way to treat a wound is not just to ignore it or to give it some superficial treatment; the right treatment is to probe it. It is painful, but it has to be done. If you want it to be cleansed and purified and healthy you have to apply the probe. Let us therefore probe this wound, this putrefying sore that is in the soul of every one of us, in order that we may be cleansed.

What is this danger against which our Lord is warning us? We can say first of all that it is a kind of spirit, a spirit which manifests itself in certain ways. What is this spirit that condemns? It is a self-righteous spirit. Self is always at the back of it, and it is always a manifestation of self-righteousness, a feeling of superiority, and a feeling that we are all right while others are not. That then leads to censoriousness, and a spirit that is always ready to express itself in a derogatory manner. And then, accompanying that, there is the tendency to despise others, to regard them with contempt. I am not only describing the Pharisees, I am describing all who have the spirit of the Pharisee.

It seems to me, further, that a very vital part of this spirit is the tendency to be hypercritical. Now there is all the difference in the world between being critical and being hypercritical. True criticism is an excellent thing. Unfortunately there is very little of it. But true criticism of literature, or art, or music, or anything else, is one of the highest exercises of the human mind. Criticism in a true sense is never merely destructive; it is constructive, it is appreciation. There is all the difference in the world between exercising criticism and being hypercritical. The man who is guilty of judging, in the sense in which our Lord uses the term here, is the man who is hypercritical, which means that he delights in criticism for its own sake and enjoys it. I am afraid I must go further and say that he is a man who approaches anything which he is asked to criticize expecting to find faults, indeed, almost hoping to find them.

The simplest way, perhaps, of putting all this is to ask you to read 1 Corinthians 13. Look at the negative of everything positive which Paul says about love. Love 'hopeth all things', but this spirit hopes for the worst; it gets a malicious, malign satisfaction in finding faults and blemishes. It is a spirit that is always expecting them, and is almost disappointed if it does not find them; it is always on the lookout for them, and rather delights in them. There is no question about that, the hypercritical spirit is never really happy unless it finds these faults. And, of course, the result of all this is that it tends to fix attention upon matters that are indifferent and to make of them matters of vital importance. The best commentary in this connection is found in Romans 14 where Paul tells the Romans at great length to avoid judging one another in matters like food and drink, and regarding one day above another. They had been exalting these matters to a supreme position, and judging and condemning in terms of these things. But Paul tells them that that is all wrong. 'The kingdom of God is not meat and drink; but righteousness, and peace, and joy in the Holy Ghost', he says (Rom. 14:17). One may observe one day, and another, another. 'Let every man be fully persuaded in his own mind.' But the thing to remember, he says, is that you are all being judged by God. The Lord is the judge. Furthermore, you do not decide whether a man is a Christian or not by regarding his views on matters such as these, which are unimportant, and matters of indifference. There are essential matters in connection with the faith, matters about which there must be no doubt, while others are matters of indifference. We must never elevate the latter into matters of vital importance.

That is more or less the spirit of the man who is guilty of judgment. I am not applying all this as we go along. I trust that the Holy Spirit is enabling us to do so. If we ever know the feeling of being rather pleased when we hear something unpleasant about another, that is this wrong spirit. If we are jealous, or envious, and then suddenly hear that the one of whom we are jealous or envious has made a mistake and find that there is an immediate sense of pleasure within us, that is it. That is the condition which leads to this spirit of judgment.

But look at it in practice. It shows itself in a readiness to give judgment when the matter is of no concern to us at all. How much of our time do we spend in expressing our opinion about people who really have no direct dealings with us? They are nothing to us, but we experience a malicious pleasure in doing so. That is part of the way in which it shows itself in practice.

Another manifestation of this spirit is that it puts prejudice in the place of principle. We are to judge in terms of principle, because otherwise we cannot discipline the Church. But if a man takes his own prejudices and puts them up as principles, he is guilty of this spirit of judgment.

Another way in which it shows itself is in its tendency to put personalities in the place of principles. We all know how easy it is for a discussion to drift to persons or personalities and away from principles. It is true to say that people who object to doctrine are generally those who are most guilty at this particular point. Because they do not have a grasp and understanding of doctrine they can talk only in terms of personalities; so the moment a man stands for principles or doctrine, they begin to say that he is a difficult person. The person is obtruded into the place where principle should come, and that, in turn, leads to the tendency to impute motives. Because they cannot understand why another man stands for principles, motives are imputed to him; and to impute motives is always a manifestation of this spirit of judgment.

A further way in which we may know whether we are guilty of this, is to ask if we habitually express our opinion without a knowledge of all the facts. We have no right to pronounce any judgment without being aware of these facts, without going to the trouble of becoming acquainted with them. We should search for all the facts and then judge. To do otherwise is to be guilty of this pharisaical spirit.

Another indication of it is that it never takes the trouble to understand the circumstances, and is never ready to excuse; it is never ready to exercise mercy. A man who has a charitable spirit possesses discrimination and is ready to exercise it. He is prepared to listen and to see if there is an explanation, if there is an excuse, to discover if there may be mitigating circumstances. But the man who judges says, 'No, I require nothing further'. Therefore he rejects any explanation, and does not listen to argument or reason.

But perhaps we can end the description and bring it to its awful revolting climax by putting it like this: This spirit really manifests itself in the tendency to pronounce final judgment upon people as such. This means that it is not a judgment so much on what they do, or believe, or say, as upon the persons themselves. It is a final judgment upon an individual, and what makes it so terrible is that at that point it is arrogating to itself something that belongs to God. You remember how, when our Lord sent messengers into the villages of the Samaritans to make ready for His arrival, and they would not receive them, that James and John hearing this said: 'Lord, wilt thou that we command fire to come down from heaven, and consume them?' That is it; they wanted to destroy those Samaritans. But our Lord turned and rebuked them and said, 'Ye know not what manner of spirit ye are of. For the Son of man is not come to destroy men's lives, but to save them.' They were guilty of forming and passing a final judgment on those people and proposing to destroy them. There is all the difference in the world between doing that and expressing an enlightened, intelligent criticism of a man's views and theories, his doctrine, his teaching or his mode or manner of life. We are called upon to do the latter; but the moment we condemn and dismiss the person we are assuming a power that belongs to God alone and to no one else.

It is a painful subject, and so far we have looked only at the injunction. We have not yet considered the reason which our Lord adds to the injunction. We have just taken the two words, and I trust we shall always remember them. 'Judge not'. As we do so let us thank God that we have a gospel which tells us that 'while we were yet sinners, Christ died for us', that not one of us stands in his own righteousness, but in the righteousness of Christ. Without Him we are damned, utterly lost. We have condemned ourselves by judging others. But then God the Lord is our judge, and He has provided a way whereby we pass 'from judgment unto life'. The exhortation is that we should live our lives in this world as people who have passed through the judgment 'in Christ', and who now live for Him and live like Him, realizing that we have been saved by His wondrous grace and mercy.

Chapter Sixteen

The Mote and the Beam

W E have already considered the meaning of our Lord's command 'Judge not' and what it involves in practice. Now we come, in verses 1-5, to the reasons which He gives for not judging. Again we cannot but feel, as we look at them, that His case is unanswerable, His logic inevitable. At the same time we shall feel our sinfulness and see the ugliness of sin.

Let us look at His reasons. The first is: 'Judge not, that ye be not judged.' Do not judge, in order that you yourselves may not be judged. That is a very practical and personal reason, but what exactly does it mean? There are those who would have us believe that it means something like this. Do not judge other people if you dislike other people judging you. Do not judge other people if you do not wish to be judged yourself by them. They say that what this really means is that, as you do to others, they will do to you, or, as the phrase puts it, you will be paid back in your own coin. They say that it amounts to this, that the person who is always critical and censorious of others, is always a person who is likely to bring criticism upon himself. And of course that is true and perfectly right. It is further true to say that there are no people who are more sensitive to criticism than those who are always criticizing others. They dislike it and complain when it happens to them; but they never seem to remember this when they do it with respect to others. We must agree, then, that that statement is true, that the kind of person who is always criticizing is criticized in turn, and that therefore, if they wish to avoid this painful criticism, they must be less critical and censorious of others. And, on the other hand, it is true to say that the person who is less critical is appreciated by others, and is not subject to criticism in the same way as that more critical kind of person.

But surely it is quite wrong to interpret this statement as meaning that and that alone. While we must accept that in general, it seems that our Lord goes very much further. We say this, not only on the basis of what we have in this entire chapter, which, as we have seen, is meant to hold us face-to-face with the judgment of God, but also because of other statements in Scripture which are parallel to this, and which explain and therefore reinforce it. Surely it means this: 'Judge not, that ye be not judged' — by God. There are many evangelical Christians who immediately react against such an exposition in terms of the great teaching of the Scripture with regard to justification by faith only. They point out that John 5:24 teaches that, if we believe on the Lord Jesus Christ, we have passed through judgment or from judgment unto life. They add that the first verse of Romans 8 says, 'There is therefore now no condemnation to them which are in Christ Jesus.' Surely, they say, this means that because we are Christians we are taken entirely outside the realm of judgment. There is no longer any judgment, they argue on the basis of such teaching, for the man who is a true Christian.

This criticism calls for attention and a reply, and we do so in this way. We remind ourselves again that the words we are considering are addressed to believers, not to unbelievers. They are addressed to people of whom the Beatitudes are true, to those who are the children of God and born again of the Spirit. It is quite clear, therefore, that in some respect such people are still subject to judgment.

But, in addition to that, we must approach the question also in terms of the parallel teaching of Scripture elsewhere. Perhaps the best way to deal with it is to put it like this. In the Scriptures we are taught that there are three types or kinds of judgment, and it is the failure to isolate and distinguish these that causes this confusion. We should be concerned about this subject for many reasons. One is that many of us who claim to be evangelical Christians are not only guilty of glibness in these matters, but are also curiously lacking in what used to be called the 'fear of God'. There is a lightness, a boisterousness, a superficiality about many of us which seems to me to be far removed from the character of truly Christian, godly people as it is to be seen in the Bible and in the Church throughout the centuries. In our anxiety to give the impression that we are happy, we are often lacking in reverence and what the Scripture means by 'reverence and godly fear'. The whole idea of 'the fear of the Lord' and of godliness somehow or other has become lost amongst us. That is partly due to this failure to realize the scriptural teaching with regard to judgment. We are so anxious to assert the doctrine of justification by faith only, that very often we are guilty of minimizing the other doctrines of Scripture which are equally a part of our faith and therefore equally true. So it is important for us to understand this doctrine with regard to judgment.

First of all there is a judgment which is final and eternal; that is the judgment which determines a man's status or his standing before God. This determines the great separation between the Christian and the non-Christian, the sheep and the goats, those who are going on to glory and those who are going to perdition. That is a kind of first judgment, a basic judgment which establishes the great dividing line between those who belong to God and those who do not. That is clearly taught everywhere in Scripture from beginning to end. That is the judgment which determines and settles man's final destiny, his eternal condition, whether he is to be in heaven or in hell.

But that is not the only judgment which is taught in the Scriptures; there is a second, which I would call the judgment to which we are subject as God's children, and because we are God's children.

In order to understand this we should read 1 Corinthians 11, where Paul expounds the doctrine concerning the Communion Service. He says, 'Whosoever shall eat this bread, and drink this cup of the Lord, unworthily, shall be guilty of the body and blood of the Lord. But let a man examine himself, and so let him eat of that bread, and drink of that cup. For he that eateth and drinketh unworthily, eateth and drinketh damnation to himself, not discerning the Lord's body' (vv. 27-29). Then — 'For this cause many are weak and sickly among you, and many sleep (which means 'many have died'). For if we would judge ourselves, we should not be judged. But when we are judged, we are chastened of the Lord, that we should not be condemned with the world' (vv. 30-32).

That is a most important and significant statement. It indicates clearly that God judges His children in this way, that if we are guilty of sin, or of wrong living, we are likely to be punished by Him. The punishment, says Paul, may take the form of sickness or illness. There are those who are sick and ill because of their wrong living. It does not mean of necessity that God has sent sickness upon them, but it probably means that God withholds His protection from them and allows the devil to attack them with illness. You have the same statement in the same Epistle where he talks about handing a man over to Satan in order that he may correct him in that way (chap. 5). It is a most serious and important doctrine. Indeed, Paul goes further and says that some of those Corinthians had died because of their wrong living; judgment had come upon them in that way. He is talking of the judgment of God, and therefore we can interpret it thus, that God allows Satan, who controls the power of death, to remove these people because of their refusal to judge themselves and to repent and turn back to God. His exhortation, therefore, is that we should examine ourselves, we should judge ourselves and condemn that which is wrong in ourselves in order that we may escape this other judgment. So it is very wrong for the Christian to trip lightly through life saying that he believes in the Lord Jesus Christ and that therefore judgment has nothing to do with him, and all is well. Not at all; we must walk warily and circumspectly, we must examine ourselves and search ourselves lest this kind of judgment descend upon us.

All this is confirmed in Hebrews 12, where the doctrine is put in this form: 'Whom the Lord loveth he chasteneth, and scourgeth every son whom he receiveth.' The argument at that point is designed to comfort and encourage those Hebrew Christians in the difficult times through which they were passing. It is this: We must be careful to look at trials in the right way. In a sense a man ought to be more frightened if nothing ever goes wrong with him in this world than if things do go wrong, because 'whom the Lord loveth he chasteneth'. He is bringing His sons, His children, to perfection, and He therefore disciplines them in this world. He judges their sins and their blemishes in this world in order to prepare them for the glory. Those who are not saints — well, they are 'bastards' and He allows them to flourish. You find the same thing again in Psalm 73, where we find the Psalmist very perplexed by this fact. He says: 'I do not understand God's ways. Look at those ungodly, evil people. Their eyes stand out with fatness; there are no bands in their death; they always seem to be flourishing. Verily I have washed my hands in vain.' But he came to see that this way of thinking was very wrong, for it was viewing the life of the ungodly only in this world. They may have their enjoyment in this life; but that is all they get, and judgment will suddenly descend upon them, and it will be final and eternal. God judges His people in this world in order to spare them from that. 'If we judge ourselves,' says Paul, 'we shall not be condemned with the world.' That, then, is the second way of looking at judgment, and it is a very important way. We are all along under the eye of God, and God is watching our lives and judging our sinfulness, all for our benefit.

But we must look at the third kind of judgment taught in Scripture, the judgment which is often referred to as 'the judgment of rewards'. Whether that is a true designation or not does not matter, but that there is a judgment for God's people after death is very clearly taught in the Scriptures. You find it in Romans 14 where he says, 'We shall all stand before the judgment seat of Christ.' Do not judge another man or another man's servant about these questions of observing particular days, and eating particular meats, and so on, says the apostle, for every man will have to bear his own judgment, and is responsible to God — 'for we shall all stand before the judgment seat of Christ'. You have exactly the same thing in the Corinthian Epistles. There is the passage in 1 Corinthians 3 where he says: 'Every man's work shall be made manifest' and 'the day shall declare it'. Whatever a man has built upon the foundation — gold, silver, precious stones, wood, hay, stubble — it will all be judged by fire. Some of it will be entirely destroyed, the wood, hay, stubble, etc., but the man himself shall be saved, 'yet so as by fire'. But it all indicates a judgment, a judgment of our work since we have become Christian, and, particularly in this passage, of course, the preaching of the gospel and the work of ministers in the Church.

Then, in 2 Corinthians 5, the judgment is clearly not only for ministers but for all — 'For we must all appear before the judgment seat of Christ; that every one may receive the things done in his body, according to that he hath done, whether it be good or bad.' 'Knowing therefore', says Paul, 'the terror of the Lord, we persuade men.' That is not addressed to unbelievers; it is addressed to Christian believers. Christian believers will have to appear before this judgment seat of Christ, and there we shall be judged according to what we have done in the body, whether good or bad. This is not to *determine* our eternal destiny; it is not a judgment which decides whether we go to heaven or to hell. No, we have passed through that. But it is a judgment which is going to *affect* our eternal destiny, not by determining whether it is heaven or hell, but by deciding what happens to us in the realm of glory. We are not given any further details about this in Scripture, but that there is a judgment of believers is very clearly and specifically taught.

You find it again in Galatians 6:5: 'Every man shall bear his own burden'. That is a reference to the same judgment. 'Bear ye one another's burdens, and so fulfil the law of Christ.' But also 'Every man shall bear his own burden'; every one of us is responsible for his own life, his own conduct and behaviour. It does not, let me emphasize again, determine my eternal destiny, but it is going to make a difference to me, it is a judgment of my life since I have become a Christian. And then there is that moving statement in 2 Timothy 1:16-18 where, in referring to Onesiphorus, Paul thanks God for this man who had been so kind to him when he was in prison. This is what he prays for him: 'The Lord grant unto him that he may find mercy of the Lord in that day'; in that day when judgment is going to be exercised, may the Lord have mercy upon him. And in Revelation 14:13 there is the statement about all those that die in the Lord: 'Blessed are the dead which die in the Lord . . .; and their works do follow them.' Our works follow us.

The chief reason, then, why Christian people must not judge, is that we be not judged ourselves by the Lord. We shall see Him as He is; we shall meet Him, and this judgment will take place. If we do not want to be ashamed, as John puts it (1 John 2:28), on that occasion, let us be careful now. If we would have 'boldness in the day of judgment', then we must be careful as to how we live in the here and now. If we judge, we shall be judged in terms of that very judgment. Here, therefore, is something of which we must never lose sight. Though we are Christians, and are justified by faith, and have an assurance of our salvation, and know we are going to heaven, we are yet subject to this judgment here in this life, and also after this life. It is the plain teaching of the Scripture, and it is summarized here in this first statement by our Lord in this section of the Sermon on the Mount: 'Judge not, that ye be not judged.' It is not simply that if you do not want other people to say unkind things you must not say unkind things about them. That is all right; that is quite true. But much more important is the fact that you are exposing yourself to judgment, and that you will have to answer for these things. You do not lose your salvation, but you are evidently going to lose something.

That brings us to the second reason for not judging which is adduced by our Lord. It is in the second verse: 'For with what judgment ye judge, ye shall be judged: and with what measure ye mete, it shall be measured to you again.' We can put that in the form of a principle. The second reason for not judging is that, by so doing, we not only produce judgment for ourselves, we even set the standard of our own judgment — 'With what measure ye mete, it shall be measured to you again.' Once more, this does not merely indicate what other people may do to us. We say a man is always 'paid back in his own coin', and that is perfectly true. Men who have been so careful to scrutinize and examine others, and to talk about minor blemishes in them, are often amazed when those same people judge them. They cannot understand it, but they are being judged by their own yardstick and their own measure.

But we cannot leave this statement at that; we must go beyond it, because Scripture does so. Our Lord is really declaring that God Himself, in this judgment which I have been describing, will judge us according to our own standards. Let us look at some scriptural authority for this interpretation. Consider our Lord's statement as recorded in Luke 12, where He talks about being 'beaten with many stripes' or 'with few stripes', and says 'unto whomsoever much is given, of him shall be much required: and to whom men have committed much, of him they will ask the more' (v. 48). He teaches that God acts on that principle. Then read the statement in Romans 2:1, 'Therefore thou art inexcusable, O man, whosoever thou art that judgest: for wherein thou judgest another, thou condemnest thyself, for thou that judgest doest the same things.' You are proving, says Paul, by your judging of others that you know what is right; so, if you do not do that which is right, you are condemning yourself.

But perhaps the clearest statement of this is given in James 3:1, a verse which is of vital importance, but which is frequently ignored because we do not like the Epistle of James, imagining as we do that he does not teach justification by faith only. This is how he puts this particular matter: 'My brethren, be not many masters, knowing that we shall receive the greater condemnation.' In other words, if you set yourself up as an authority, if you become a master, if you are thus acting as masters and authorities, remember you will be judged by your own authority; by the very claim you make, you yourself will be judged. You are setting yourself up as an authority? Very well; that will be the very standard applied to you in your own judgment.

Our Lord puts it here plainly in the words we are considering: 'With what judgment ye judge, ye shall be judged: and with what measure ye mete, it shall be measured to you again.' It is one of the most alarming statements in the whole of Scripture. Do I claim that I have exceptional knowledge of the Scripture? If I do I shall be judged in terms of the knowledge that I claim. Do I claim that I am a servant who really knows these things? Then I must not be surprised if I am beaten with many stripes. We should be very careful, therefore, how we express ourselves. If we sit as an authority in judgment upon others, we have no right to complain if we are judged by that very standard. It is quite fair, it is quite just, and we have no ground whatsoever for complaint. We claim we have this knowledge; and if we have that knowledge we must show it by living up to it. By the claim that I myself make, I myself shall be judged. If, therefore, I am careful in my scrutiny of other people and their lives, that very standard comes back upon myself, and I have no ground at all for complaining. The answer to me if I complain would be this: You knew it, you were able to exercise it with regard to others, why did you not exercise it in your own case? It is a very surprising and alarming thought. There is nothing I know of that is so likely to deter us from the sinful practice of condemning others and from that foul and ugly spirit that delights in doing so.

That brings us in turn to the last reason with which our Lord supplies us. He puts it in verses 3-5: 'And why beholdest thou the mote that is in thy brother's eye, but considerest not the beam that is in thine own eye? Or how wilt thou say to thy brother, Let me pull out the mote out of thine eye; and, behold, a beam is in thine own eye? Thou hypocrite, first cast out the beam out of thine own eye; and then shalt thou see clearly to cast out the mote out of thy brother's eye.' Was there ever such sarcasm? Was there ever a more perfect example of irony? How richly we deserve it. We can summarize the argument in this way in the form of a number of principles. Our Lord is teaching us that the third reason for our not judging others is that we are incapable of judgment. We cannot do it. Therefore, as we cannot do it properly, we must not try to do it at all. He says that our spirit is such that we are not entitled to judge. Not only must we remember that we ourselves shall be judged and that we determine the standards of that judgment, but furthermore He says: Stop a moment; you cannot judge because you are incapable of judging.

Our Lord proves it in this way. He first of all points out that we are not concerned about righteousness and true judgment at all, because if we were, we should deal with it in ourselves. We like to persuade ourselves that we are really concerned about truth and righteousness, and that that is our only interest. We claim that we do not want to be unfair to people, that we do not want to criticize, but that we are really concerned about truth! Ah, says our Lord in effect, if you were really concerned about truth, you would be judging yourself. But you do not judge yourself; therefore your interest is not really in truth. It is a fair argument. If a man claims that his only interest is in righteousness and truth, and not at all in personalities, then he will be as critical of himself as he is of other people. A really great artist is always the severest critic of himself. It matters not what walk of life it is, whether it is singing, or acting, or painting, or anything else, a really great artist and true critic is as critical of himself as he is of the work of other people, perhaps more so, because he has an objective standard. But you, says our Lord, have no objective standard. You are not interested in truth and righteousness, otherwise you would never pass yourselves, as you are doing, and only criticize others. That is the first statement.

Then we can take it further and say that He also shows that such people are not concerned about the principles as such but simply about persons. The spirit of hypercriticism, as we have seen, is one which is concerned with personalities rather than with principles. That is the trouble with many of us in this respect. We are really interested in the person we are criticizing, not in the particular subject or principle; and our real desire is to condemn the person, rather than to get rid of the evil that is in the person. That, of course, at once renders us incapable of true judgment. If there is bias, if there is personal feeling and animus, we are no longer true examiners. Even the law recognizes this. If it can be proved that there is some connection between any member of a jury and the person on trial, that member of the jury can be disqualified. What is desiderated in a jury is impartiality. There must be no prejudice, there must be nothing personal; it must be unbiased, objective judgment. The personal element must be entirely excluded before there can be true judgment. If we apply that to our judgment of other people, I fear we shall have to agree with our Lord that we are quite incapable of judgment, because we are so interested in the person or the personality. There is so often an ulterior motive in our judgment; so often we fail to differentiate between the person and his action.

But let us follow our Lord in His analysis. His next argument is in verse 4: 'How wilt thou say to thy brother, Let me pull out the mote out of thine eye; and, behold, a beam is in thine own eye?' That is sarcasm at its highest. He says that our own condition is such that we are quite incapable of helping others. We affect to be very concerned about these people and their faults, and we try to give the impression that we are concerned only about their good. We say that we are troubled about this little blemish that is in them, and that we are anxious to get rid of this mote. But, says our Lord, you cannot do it, because it is such a delicate process. This beam that is in your own eye makes you incapable of doing so.

I once read a very acute remark which put this perfectly. It said that there is something very ridiculous about a blind person trying to lead another blind person, but that there is something much more ridiculous than that, and that is a blind oculist. A blind oculist cannot possibly remove a speck out of another man's eye. If a blind man in general is useless in helping others, how much more useless is a blind oculist? That is what our Lord is saying at this point. If you want to be able to see clearly to remove this minute speck out of the sensitive eye of that other person in whom you affect an interest, make certain your own eye is quite clear. You cannot be a help to another while you are blinded by the beam in your own eye.

Finally, He actually condemns us as hypocrites. 'Thou hypocrite, first cast out the beam out of thine own eye; and then shalt thou see clearly to cast out the mote out of thy brother's eye.' How true it is. The fact of the matter is that we are not really concerned about helping this other person; we are interested only in condemning him. We pretend to have this great interest; we pretend that we are very distressed at finding this blemish. But in reality, as our Lord has already shown us (and this is the horrible part), we are really glad to discover it. It is hypocrisy. One person goes to another as a would-be friend and says, 'It is such a shame that this defect is in you.' But oh, the malice that is often displayed by such action, and the pleasure that such a person often enjoys! No, says our Lord, if you really want to help other people, if you are genuine and true in this matter, there are certain things you have to do yourself. First — and we must notice this — first cast the beam out of thine own eye, and then thou shalt see clearly to cast out the mote out of thy brother's eye.

That can be interpreted in this way. If you really do want to help others, and to help to rid them of these blemishes and faults and frailties and imperfections, first of all realize that your spirit and your whole attitude has been wrong. This spirit of judging and hypercriticism and censoriousness that is in you is really like a beam, contrasted with the little mote in the other person's eye. 'You know,' says our Lord in effect, 'there is no more terrible form of sin than this judging spirit of which you are guilty. It is like a beam. The other person may have fallen into immorality, some sin of the flesh, or may be guilty of some little error here and there. But that is nothing but a little mote in the eye when compared with this spirit that is in you, which is like a beam. Start with your own spirit,' He says in other words; 'face yourself quite honestly and squarely and admit to yourself the truth about yourself.' How are we to do all this in practice? Read 1 Corinthians 13 every day; read this statement of our Lord's every day. Examine your attitude towards other people; face the truth about yourself. Take the statements you make about another person; sit down and analyse them, and ask yourself what you really mean. It is a very painful and distressing process. But if we examine ourselves and our judgments and our pronouncements honestly and truly, we are on the high road to getting the beam out of our eye. Then having done that we shall be so humbled that we shall be quite free from the spirit of censoriousness and hypercriticism.

What a wonderful piece of logic this is! When a man has truly seen himself he never judges anybody else in the wrong way. All his time is taken up in condemning himself, in washing his hands and trying to purify himself. There is only one way of getting rid of the spirit of censoriousness and hypercriticism, and that is to judge and condemn yourself. It humbles us to the dust, and then it follows of necessity that, having thus got rid of the beam out of our own eyes, we shall be in a fit condition to help the other person, and to get out the little mote that is in his eye.

The procedure of getting a mote out of an eye is a very difficult operation. There is no organ that is more sensitive than the eye. The moment the finger touches it, it closes up; it is so delicate. What you require above everything else in dealing with it is sympathy, patience, calmness, coolness. That is what is required, because of the delicacy of the operation. Transfer all that into the spiritual realm. You are going to handle a soul, you are going to touch the most sensitive thing in man. How can we get the little mote out? There is only one thing that matters at that point, and that is that you should be humble, you should be sympathetic, you should be so conscious of your own sin and your own unworthiness, that when you find it in another, far from condemning, you feel like weeping. You are full of sympathy and compassion; you really do want to help. You have so enjoyed getting rid of the thing in yourself that you want him to have the same pleasure and the same joy. You cannot be a spiritual oculist until you yourself have clear sight. Thus, when we face ourselves and have got rid of this beam, and have judged and condemned ourselves and are in this humble, understanding, sympathetic, generous, charitable state, we shall then be able, as the Scripture puts it, to 'speak the truth in love' to another and thereby to help him. It is one of the most difficult things in life, it is one of the last things to which we attain. God have mercy upon us. But there are people, thank God, who can 'speak the truth in love', and when they have spoken it to you, you not only know they are speaking the truth, you thank them for it. There are other people who tell you the same truth, but in such a manner as to lead you to defend yourself at once, and to hate them for doing so. It is because they have not 'spoken the truth in love'. Let every man, therefore — again I quote James — 'let every man be swift to hear, slow to speak, slow to wrath' (James 1:19).

'Judge not' for these three reasons. God have mercy upon us. How good it is that we can face such a truth in the light of Calvary and the shed blood of Christ. But if you want to avoid chastisement in this life, and the suffering of loss — that is the scriptural statement — in the next life, judge not, except you judge yourself first.

Chapter Seventeen

Spiritual Judgment and Discrimination

IN Matthew 7:6 our Lord brings to an end what He has to say concerning the difficult and involved subject of punishment. The Authorized Version puts this verse in a special paragraph on its own; but I suggest that that is not right. It is not a statement on its own with no connection with what precedes it. It is rather the conclusion of that matter, the final statement in that connection.

It is an extraordinary statement and one which generally comes with a great shock of surprise to people. Here our Lord has been telling us in the most solemn manner not to judge, and that we should cast the beam out of our own eye before we begin to think about the mote that is in our brother's eye; He has been warning us that with what judgment we judge, we shall be judged. Then suddenly He says, 'Give not that which is holy unto the dogs, neither cast ye your pearls before swine, lest they trample them under their feet, and turn again and rend you.' It seems incongruous; it seems to come as an entire contradiction of all that we have been considering. And yet, if our exposition of the first five verses has been right, it is not surprising at all; indeed, it follows as an almost inevitable corollary. Our Lord tells us that we must not judge in the sense of condemning; but He reminds us here that that is not the total statement with regard to this matter. In order to have a right balance and a complete statement on the subject, this further observation is essential.

If our Lord had finished His teaching with those first five verses, it would undoubtedly have led to a false position. Men and women would be so careful to avoid the terrible danger of judging in that wrong sense that they would exercise no discrimination, no judgment whatsoever. There would be no such thing as discipline in the Church, and the whole of the Christian life would be chaotic. There would be no such thing as exposing heresy and pronouncing judgment with regard to it. Because everybody would be so afraid of judging

446

the heretic, they would turn a blind eye to the heresy; and error would come into the Church more than it has done. So our Lord goes on to make this further statement here, and we cannot fail, once more, to be impressed by the wonderful balance of scriptural teaching, its amazing perfection. That is why I am never tired of pointing out that a detailed, microscopic study of any one section of Scripture is generally much more profitable than a telescopic view of the whole Bible; because if you make a thorough study of any one section, you will find that you will meet all the great doctrines sooner or later. We have done so in considering this Sermon on the Mount. It shows the importance of looking at the details, of paying attention to everything, for as we do so, we discover this wonderful balance which is to be found in Scripture. We go to extremes and become unbalanced because we are guilty of isolating statements instead of taking them in their context. It is because they forget this addition to our Lord's teaching on judging that so many people show a lack of discrimination and are ready to praise and recommend anything that is put before them which vaguely claims the name Christian. They say that we must not judge. That is regarded as a friendly and charitable spirit, and so men and women fall unchecked into grievous errors and their immortal souls are thrown into jeopardy. But all that is avoided if we just take the Scripture as it is, and remember that in it this perfect balance is always to be found.

Take this statement which seems, when looked at superficially, to be so surprising in view of what our Lord has just been saying. How do we reconcile these two things? The simple answer is that, while our Lord exhorts us not to be hypercritical, He never tells us not to be discriminating. There is an absolute difference between these two things. What we are to avoid is the tendency to be censorious, to condemn people, to set ourselves up as the final judge and to make a pronouncement on persons. But that, of course, is very different from exercising a spirit of discrimination, to which Scripture is ever exhorting us. How can we 'prove' and 'test the spirits', how can we, as we are exhorted to do later, 'beware of false prophets', if we do not exercise our judgment and our discrimination? In other words, we are to recognize the error, but we are to do so, not in order to condemn, but in order to help. And it is just there that we find the connecting link between this statement and what has preceded it. Our Lord has been dealing with the question of helping our brother to get rid of the mote that is in his eye. If we wish to do that in the right way, and He has already told us the right way, then, of course, we must have a spirit of discrimination. We must be able to recognize motes and beams and to discriminate between person and person.

Our Lord now proceeds to instruct us with regard to the whole question of dealing with people, handling them, and discriminating between person and person. And He does it in these words: 'Give not that which is holy unto the dogs, neither cast ye your pearls before swine, lest they trample them under their feet, and turn again and rend you.' What does He mean by this? Obviously He is referring to the truth, which is holy, and which can be likened to pearls. What is this holy thing, this pearl to which He is referring? It is clearly the Christian message, the message of the kingdom, the very thing about which He is speaking Himself in this incomparable Sermon. What, then, does He mean? Are we here exhorted not to present the Christian truth to unbelievers? What kind of persons can those be who are described as being dogs and swine? What extraordinary terminology to use! The dog was not regarded in Palestine as we are accustomed to do in this country; it was the scavenger of the village, its very name a term of opprobrium; not the domestic pet to which we are accustomed, but a fierce and dangerous, half-wild animal. While the swine in the Jewish mind stood for all that was unclean and outside the pale.

And these are the two terms our Lord uses in teaching us how to discriminate between people and people. We have to recognize that there is a class of person who, with respect to the truth, can be described as a 'dog' or as belonging to the 'swine'. 'Does He mean', asks someone, 'that this is to be the attitude of Christian people to unbelievers, to those who are outside the kingdom?' Clearly it cannot mean that, for the good reason that you could never convert the unconverted if you are not to present truth to them. Our Lord Himself went out preaching to such people. He sent out His disciples and apostles to preach to them, He sent the Holy Spirit upon the early Church in order that she might testify and preach the truth to them. So it clearly cannot mean that.

What, then, does it mean? The best way to approach the problem is to look at it first of all in the light of our Lord's own practice. What did He Himself do? How did He Himself implement this particular teaching? The answer of Scripture is that He very clearly differentiated between person and person and type and type. If you read the four Gospels you will see that He does not handle any two people in exactly the same way. Fundamentally it is the same, but on the surface it is different. Take His way of handling Nathanael, and Nicodemus, and the woman of Samaria. At once you see certain differences. Look at the entire difference in His manner and method when He was confronting the Pharisees and when He was confronting the publicans and sinners. See the difference in His attitude towards the self-righteous, proud Pharisee and the woman caught in sin. But perhaps one of the best illustrations of all is the one that we encounter in Luke 23. When examined by Pilate, our Lord answered; but when He was questioned by Herod, who should have known better, and who just had a morbid, unhealthy curiosity and was looking for signs and wonders, He answered him nothing, He just would not speak to him (see vv. 3 and 9). Thus you see that our Lord, when dealing with people in terms of the same truth, dealt with them in different ways and accommodated His way of teaching to the person. He did not vary the truth, but He varied the particular method of presentation, and that is what you will find as you read the four Gospels.

Then when you come on to the practice of the apostles, you will find that they do precisely the same as their Lord, and carry out the injunction that is given here. Take, for instance, that statement in Acts 13:46, where Paul was preaching at Antioch in Pisidia and meeting the jealousy and envy and opposition of the Jews. We read that Paul and Barnabas were bold and said, 'It was necessary that the word of God should first have been spoken to you: but seeing ye put it from you, and judge yourselves unworthy of everlasting life, lo, we turn to the Gentiles.' Paul is not going to preach to them any longer; he is not going to continue presenting this holy thing to them. But then you find exactly the same thing in his conduct at Corinth. This is what we read in Acts 18:6: 'And when they opposed themselves, and blasphemed, he shook his raiment, and said unto them, Your blood be upon your own heads; I am clean: from henceforth I will go unto the Gentiles.' Here, you see, are people to whom the truth has been presented; but they did the very thing our Lord prophesied. As dogs and swine, they turned again and they opposed, they blasphemed, and they stamped the truth under their feet. The reaction of the apostle is to turn away from them; he no longer presents the gospel to them. He turns his back upon the Jews who thus reject and show their inability to appreciate the truth, and he turns to the Gentiles and becomes the great apostle to the Gentiles.

There, it seems to me, is the right way to approach this statement which at first sight is somewhat perplexing. But we cannot leave it at that. Let us pursue the exposition a little more in detail, because we must remember that this statement is made to us. It is not something that was relevant only to that particular time, or to some future kingdom. We have seen that it is meant, like the whole of the Sermon, for Christians now, and it is therefore an exhortation to us. We are told: 'Give not that which is holy unto the dogs, neither cast ye your pearls before swine, lest they trample them under their feet, and turn again and rend you.' How do we interpret this? What does it mean to us?

First and foremost it means that we must recognize the different types and persons, and we must learn to discriminate between them. There is nothing so pathetic or so unscriptural as a mechanical way of testifying to others. There are some Christians who are guilty of that. They witness and testify, but they do it in a thoroughly mechanical way. They never really consider the person with whom they are dealing; they never try to assess the person, or to discover exactly what his position is. They fail completely to implement this exhortation.

449

They present the truth in exactly the same way to all and sundry. Quite apart from the fact that their testifying is generally quite useless, and that the only thing they achieve is a great feeling of self-righteousness, it is utterly unscriptural.

There is no higher privilege in life than to be a witness for Jesus Christ. I understand that in these days men who would become commercial travellers generally have to attend a course of training in the psychology of salesmanship. It is felt to be necessary and important, if they are to sell their particular commodity, that they should know something about people. They must know how to approach people. We are all so different, and the same thing must be presented to different people in correspondingly different ways. Although the commodity is the same, they have discovered that it is important that the salesman should know something about people and the psychology of salesmanship. It is not for us to pronounce judgment as to whether such a course is necessary, but we can use it to emphasize the fact that the New Testament has always taught the necessity for preparation. Not that we need a course in psychology! No; but we need to know our New Testament. If we know our New Testament we know that people are all different; and if we really are concerned about winning souls, and not simply anxious to bear our own witness and testimony, then we shall realize the importance of discriminating and understanding. We must not say, 'Well; I am like this, and this is my temperament, and this is my way of doing things.' No; with the apostle Paul we must become 'all things to all men' that we may by all means save some. To the Jew he became as a Jew, to the Gentile as a Gentile, to them that were under the law as under the law, to this end.

That is the first point, and we must surely agree that we often fall into this trap with regard to witnessing. It tends to be mechanical, and it may even be that we are almost pleased when somebody does behave with us in the manner of the dog and the swine, for then we feel we have been persecuted for Christ's sake, when in reality it is not that at all, but simply that we have not known our Scriptures and have not witnessed in the right way.

The second principle is that we must not only learn to distinguish between one type and another; we must also become expert in knowing what to give to each type. You do not handle a Pilate and a Herod in exactly the same way; you answer the questions of a Pilate, but you say nothing to a Herod. We must see people as they are and be sensitive to them. We have taken the beam out of our own eye, we have got rid of everything that is censorious, and we really are concerned about helping the other. In that spirit, we try to find precisely the right thing for that person. It is curious to note how readily we become slaves to words. I have known people who, when they preach on the text about becoming 'fishers of men', are always careful to say that we must know which bait to use; but when they come to a text like this they seem to be oblivious of the fact that the same principle applies, and is equally true, here. We must know what is appropriate for each person in each particular situation. That is one reason why it is difficult for a raw convert to be a good witness. We can understand more clearly in the light of this teaching why Paul says that no novice must be given a prominent position in the Church. How far we have departed in our practice from the New Testament! Our tendency is to lay hands on the raw convert and immediately put him into some prominent position. But Scripture tells us not to push a man into prominence at once. Why? Partly for this reason, that the novice may not be an expert in the things we are considering.

Our third principle is that we should be very careful as to the way in which we present the truth. Apart from the truth itself the method of presentation must vary from person to person. We must learn to assess people. There are some to whom certain things are offensive though they are not offensive to others. We must be careful not to put truth in a way that is likely to be offensive to any type of person. For instance, to go to every unbeliever and say, 'Are you saved?' is not the scriptural method. There is a type who, if you say that to him, will take offence at it, and will not be led on to the truth. The effect of such a question on him will be to produce this response that our Lord is describing, the reaction of the dog and the swine, the trampling and the rending, the blasphemy and the cursing. And we must always be careful not to give anyone cause to blaspheme or to curse. There are those, of course, who will do that however perfect our method. Then we are not responsible and we can say with Paul, 'Your blood be upon your own heads.' But, if the offence is in us, God have mercy upon us. A man who is preaching the truth can be guilty of preaching the truth in an unworthy manner. You and I must never be the cause of antagonism; we must always preach the truth in love, and if we cause offence, it should always be 'the offence of the cross', not anything offensive in the preacher. Our Lord was teaching that.

There is one final principle under this heading. It is that we must learn to know which particular aspect of the truth is appropriate in particular cases. This means that in the case of an unbeliever we should never present to him anything but the doctrine of justification by faith only. We should never discuss any other doctrine with an unbeliever. He will often be anxious to discuss other doctrines, but we must not allow it. The account given in John 4 of our Lord's interview with the woman of Samaria is a perfect illustration of this point. She wanted to discuss various matters, such as the Being of God, how and where to worship, and the differences which separated the Jews and the Samaritans. But our Lord would not allow it. He kept bringing her back to herself, to her sinful life, to her need of salvation. And we must do the same thing. To discuss election and predestination, and the great doctrines of the Church, and the present need of the Church, with a man who is an unbeliever is obviously quite wrong. The man who is not born again cannot understand these other doctrines and therefore you must not consider them with him. It is for us to decide what to discuss with him.

But this applies not only to unbelievers; it applies also to believers. Paul tells the church at Corinth that he cannot give them strong meat; he had it, but he could not give it to them because they were still babes. He says that he had to feed them with milk because they were not yet fit for meat. 'We speak wisdom', he says, 'among them that are perfect.' To give this perfect wisdom of God to a babe in spiritual understanding is obviously ridiculous, so we are called upon to exercise this discrimination in all directions. If we really are to be witnesses and presenters of the truth we must pay some attention to these things.

We should now draw some general deductions from all these considerations. If you consider the implications of this verse you will find that they are of grave importance. Do you notice the first obvious implication on the surface? There is not a single statement in Scripture that gives a more awful picture of the devastating effect of sin upon man as this verse. The effect of sin and evil upon man as the result of the Fall is to make us, with respect to the truth of God, dogs and swine. That is the effect of sin upon man's nature; it gives him an antagonism to truth. 'The carnal mind', says the apostle Paul, 'is enmity against God', the nature of the dog and the swine. Sin makes man hate God and, also, 'hateful (or full of hate), and hating one another,' says Paul in Titus 3:3. Yes, God-haters and 'not subject to the law of God, neither indeed can be'. 'Enemies and aliens,' outside the kingdom, at enmity with God. What a terrible thing sin is! You can see the same reactions in the world today. Present the truth to certain people and they snarl at it. Talk about the blood of Christ, and they laugh and make jokes about it, and spit upon it. That is what sin does to man; that is what it does to his nature; that is how it affects his attitude towards the truth. It is something that gets into the very depths and vitals of man's being, and turns him into something that is not only hateful, but utterly opposed to God, and purity, to cleanness, and holiness, and truth.

I emphasize this because I feel that we are all guilty at this point. When we are dealing with others we often do not realize their true condition. We tend to become impatient with people when they do not become Christians immediately. We do not see that they are so much under the dominion of sin and of Satan, they are so much the dupes of the devil, they are so twisted, and perverted, and polluted — that is the word — inwardly by sin, that they really are in a spiritual sense in this condition of dog and swine. They do not appreciate that which is holy; they do not attach any value to spiritual pearls; even God Himself is hateful to them. If we do not start by realizing that, we shall never be able to help them. And as we realize the truth about them we shall begin to understand why our Lord had a great compassion for the people, and a great sorrow in His heart as He looked upon them in pity. We shall never really help anybody until we have the same spirit and mind in us, and realize that in a sense they cannot help it. They need a new nature, they must be born again. The Sermon on the Mount just legal teaching for some Jews in the future? Out, out, upon the suggestion! Here is a doctrine that leads directly to the grace of God; nothing but the rebirth can ever enable any man to appreciate and receive the truth. Dead in trespasses and sins, we must be quickened by the Holy Spirit before we can ever give a true response to divine instruction. You see the number of profound doctrines that are hidden away in this one text.

Then there is a second matter; the nature of the truth. We have dealt with it to some degree, so we need only touch upon it now. Truth is very varied, truth is very full. It is not all exactly the same; there are different varieties, such as milk and strong meat. There is truth in the Scripture which is appropriate to the very beginner; but, as the author of the Epistle to the Hebrews says, we must also 'go on unto perfection'. He seems to say, 'We do not want to go back again and lay a foundation of first principles; we ought to have finished with that. If you but exercise yourselves I can take you on to this great Melchizedek doctrine; but I cannot do it now because you are slow to hear and to learn.' That shows us that there is this great composite character to the truth. The question we must ask ourselves is, am I growing in my knowledge? Am I hungering and thirsting after this higher doctrine, this wisdom that Paul has for them that are perfect? Do I feel that I am proceeding, as it were, from the Epistle to the Galatians to the Epistle to the Ephesians? Am I going on to these profounder truths? They are only for the children of God.

There are certain secrets in the Bible which only God's children can appreciate. Read the introduction to the Epistle to the Ephesians, just the first nine or ten verses, and there you will find doctrine that only the children of God can understand; indeed, only those children who are exercising their spiritual senses and growing in grace. People in spiritual ignorance may argue about the doctrines of God's calling and election, and questions like that, without having any understanding of them. But if we are growing in grace, these doctrines will become more and more precious. They are secrets which are given only to those who can receive them — 'he that hath ears to hear, let him hear'. If you find that some of these great and mighty expositions of truth which you have in the Epistles say nothing to you, examine yourself, and ask yourself why you are not growing, and why you cannot take in these truths. There is a great distinction to be drawn between first principles and more advanced principles. There are people who spend their lifetime in the realm of apologetics and who never go on to deeper spiritual truths. They remain as babes in the Christian life. 'Let us go on unto perfection' and try to develop an appetite for these deeper aspects of truth.

Lastly, there is a question which we might ask here. And I deliberately put it in the form of a question because I admit quite frankly that I am not quite clear in my own mind what the answer should be. Is there, I wonder, a query, a question, perhaps a warning, in this verse regarding the indiscriminate distribution of the Scriptures? I am simply raising a question for you to consider and for you to discuss with others. If I am told that I have to discriminate in speaking to people about these things, if I have to differentiate between type and type and person and person, and about the particular truth I give to each, is it a good thing to put the whole Bible within the reach of people who can be described as spiritual dogs and swine? May it not sometimes lead to blasphemy and cursing and to behaviour and conduct of swinish character? Is it always right, I wonder, to put certain texts of Scripture on placards, especially those referring to the blood of Christ? I have often, myself, heard those very things leading to blasphemy. I simply put the questions. Think of the eunuch in Acts 8 going back from Jerusalem. He had his Scriptures and was actually reading them, when Philip approached him and said: 'Understandest thou what thou readest?' And he replied, 'How can I, except some man should guide me?' Exposition is generally necessary, and you cannot do away with the human instrument as a general rule.

'But,' we protest, 'look at the wonderful effect of the distribution of the Scriptures.' If we could discover the exact facts, I wonder how many people we should find who have been converted apart from human agency? I know there are wonderful, exceptional cases. I have read stories of people who have been converted in that way. Thank God that kind of thing can happen. But I suggest that it is not the normal method. Does not the fact that we have to be careful in our choice of aspects of truth as we deal with different people raise a query in our minds? Sometimes of course, we try to avoid the duty of speaking, by giving a Gospel or Scripture portion, but that is not God's normal way. The way of God has always been the presenting of the truth immediately through personality, man expounding the Scriptures. If you have a conversation with a man and are able to point out the truth to him, he may then ask for a copy of the Scriptures, or you may feel you should give him one. That is right and good. Give him your Scripture. The query I am raising has reference to the indiscriminate placing of the Bible where there is no one to explain it, and where a man, in the condition described by our Lord in the verse of our text, is facing this great and mighty truth without a human guide.

This probably comes as a surprise to many, but I suggest that we need to think again carefully about some of these matters. We become slaves to custom and to certain habits and practices, and very often we become quite unscriptural as we do so. I thank God that we have this great written word of God; but I have often felt that it would not be a bad thing to experiment for a while with the idea of not allowing anybody to have a copy of the Scriptures unless he showed signs of spiritual life. That may be going too far, but I have felt sometimes that doing this would impress upon people the precious nature of this Book, its wonderful character, and the privilege of being allowed to possess it and to read it. It might not only be a good thing for the souls of those who are outside; it would certainly give the Church a completely new conception of this priceless treasure that God has put into our hands.

We are the custodians and the expositors of the Bible; and if we gain nothing else as the result of our study, we must all feel that we have been lazy, that we have not prepared ourselves as we should have done for such a responsible, such a great task. It is not quite as easy as we sometimes seem to think, and if we take the Word of God seriously, we shall see the vital need of study and preparation and prayer. We must, then, consider this question; but above all, let us remember those other aspects of the truth which we have seen so clearly, and never forget the absolute need of regeneration for the reception and understanding of spiritual truth. The mere distribution of Scripture as such is not the key to the solution of the problem today. God still needs men and women like ourselves to expound, to explain the truth, to act as a Philip to those who have the Word but cannot understand it. Let us maintain a true balance and a due sense of proportion in these things, for the good of souls and in order that we may give a balanced, full-orbed representation of the truth of God.

Chapter Eighteen

Seeking and Finding

I CANNOT imagine a better, more cheering or a more comforting statement with which to face all the uncertainties and hazards of our life in this world of time than that contained in verses 7-11. It is one of those great comprehensive and gracious promises which are to be found only in the Bible. There is nothing that can be more encouraging as we face life with all its uncertainties and possibilities, our 'future all unknown'. In such a situation, this is the essence of the biblical message from beginning to end, this is the promise that comes to us: 'Ask, and it shall be given you; seek, and ye shall find; knock, and it shall be opened unto you.' In order that we might be quite certain about it, our Lord repeats it, and puts it in an even stronger form, for He says: 'Every one that asketh receiveth; and he that seeketh findeth; and to him that knocketh it shall be opened.' There is no doubt about it, it is certain; it is an absolute promise. What is more, it is a promise made by the Son of God Himself, speaking with all the fullness and authority of His Father.

The Bible teaches us everywhere that that is the one thing that matters in life. The biblical view of life, in contradistinction to the worldly view, is that life is a journey, a journey full of perplexities, problems and uncertainties. That being the case, it emphasizes that what really matters in life is not so much the various things that come to meet us, and with which we have to deal, as our readiness to meet them. The whole of the biblical teaching with regard to life is in a sense summed up in that one man Abraham, of whom we are told, 'he went out, not knowing whither he went'. But he was nevertheless perfectly happy, at peace and at rest. He was not afraid. Why? An old Puritan who lived 300 years ago answers that question for us: 'Abraham went out, not knowing whither he went; but he did know with whom he went.' That is the thing that matters, he knew that he went out on that journey with Another. He was not alone, there

456

was One with him who had told him that He would never leave him, nor forsake him; and though he was uncertain as to the events that were coming to meet him, and the problems which would arise, he was perfectly happy because he knew, if I may so put it, his Travelling Companion.

Abraham was like the Lord Jesus Christ Himself who, under the shadow of the cross, and knowing that even His most trusted disciples were suddenly going to leave Him and forsake Him in their fear and concern about saving their own lives, nevertheless was able to say this: 'The hour cometh, yea, is now come, that ye shall be scattered, every man to his own, and shall leave me alone: and yet I am not alone, because the Father is with me' (John 16:32). According to the Bible, that is the one thing that matters. Our Lord does not promise to change life for us; He does not promise to remove difficulties and trials and problems and tribulations; He does not say that He is going to cut out all the thorns and leave the roses with their wonderful perfume. No; He faces life realistically, and tells us that these are things to which the flesh is heir, and which are bound to come. But He assures us that we can so know Him that, whatever happens, we need never be frightened, we need never be alarmed. He puts all that in this great and comprehensive promise: 'Ask, and it shall be given you; seek, and ye shall find; knock, and it shall be opened unto you.' That is just one of the biblical ways of repeating this message which runs through the Scriptures as a golden cord from beginning to end.

If we are to derive the full benefit from such wonderful, gracious words, we must look at them a little more closely. It is not enough just to repeat a great phrase like this. The Bible must never be used as a form of psychological treatment. There are people who do that. There are people who think that the best way to go through life triumphantly is to read and repeat wonderful verses to oneself. Of course that can help you up to a point; but it is not the biblical message and the biblical method. That kind of psychological treatment gives only temporary ease. It is like the teaching which tells us that there is no such thing as disease, and that you cannot be ill, and that because there is no disease there is no pain. That sounds most helpful and may lead to a temporary improvement; but there *are* diseases, and diseases lead to death, as even the adherents of such cults eventually discover for themselves. That is not the biblical way. The Bible conveys truth to us, and wants us to consider this truth. So, when we come to a phrase like this, we do not just say, 'all is well'. We must know what it means, and we must apply it in detail to our lives.

As we come to analyse this great statement, we are reminded again of that canon of interpretation which we have often had to heed which warns us of the danger of extracting a text from its context. We must avoid the terrible danger of wresting the Scriptures to our own destruction through not taking them in their setting, or failing to observe particularly what they say, or failing to note their qualifications as well as their promises. This is particularly important with a statement such as this. There are people who say, 'Scripture says, "Ask, and it shall be given you; seek, and ye shall find; knock, and it shall be opened unto you". Very well,' they go on; 'does not that say explicitly, and does it not mean of necessity, that whatever I want or desire, God is going to give to me?' And because they think that it does, and because they think that that is the scriptural teaching, they ignore all the other teaching and just go to God with their requests. Their requests are not granted, and then they are down in the depths of depression and despair. Their case is even worse than it was before. They say, 'God does not seem to be fulfilling His promise', and they are wretchedly unhappy. We have to avoid that. Scripture is not something that works automatically. It pays a great compliment to us by regarding us as intelligent people, and it presents truth to our minds by the Holy Spirit. It asks us to take it as it is, and as a whole, in all its promises. That is why, you notice, we are not looking at verses 7 and 8 only. We are considering verses 7-11 because we must take this statement as a whole if we are not to go seriously astray in considering its various parts.

There is no difficulty in showing that this statement, far from being a universal promise that God is pledged to do for us anything that we may ask of Him, is actually something very much bigger than that. I thank God — let me put it like this bluntly — I thank God that He is not prepared to do anything that I may chance to ask Him, and I say that as the result of my own past experience. In my past life I, like all others, have often asked God for things, and have asked God to do things, which at that time I wanted very much and which I believed were the very best things for me. But now, standing at this particular juncture in my life and looking back, I say that I am profoundly grateful to God that He did not grant me certain things for which I asked, and that He shut certain doors in my face. At the time I did not understand, but I know now, and am grateful to God for it. So I thank God that this is not a universal promise, and that God is not going to grant me my every desire and request. God has a much better way for us, as we shall now see.

The right way to look at this promise is this. First of all let us ask this obvious question. Why did our Lord utter these words at this particular point? Why do they come at this particular stage in the Sermon on the Mount? We have reminded ourselves that there are certain people who say that this seventh chapter of Matthew, this final portion of the Sermon on the Mount, is nothing but a collection of statements which our Lord just delivers one after another as they happen to occur to Him. But we have already agreed that that is a very false analysis, and that there is a theme running right through the chapter. The theme is that of judgment, and we are reminded that in this life we are always living under the judgment of God. Whether we like it or not, the eye of God is upon us, and this life is a kind of preparatory school for the great life that is awaiting us beyond death and time. So everything we do in this world is of tremendous significance, and we cannot afford to take anything for granted. That is the theme, and our Lord applies it immediately. He starts with the question of judging other people. We must be careful about that because we ourselves are under judgment. But, why then does our Lord utter this promise of verses 7-11 at this point? Surely the answer is this. In verses 1-6 He has shown us the danger of condemning other people as if we were the judges, and of harbouring bitterness and hatred in our hearts. He has also told us to see to it that we remove the beam out of our own eye before trying to extract the mote out of our brother's eye. The effect of all that upon us is to reveal us to ourselves and to show us our terrible need of grace. He has held us face-to-face with the tremendously high standard by which we shall be judged — 'With what judgment ye judge, ye shall be judged: and with what measure ye mete, it shall be measured to you again.' That is the position at the end of verse 6.

Immediately we realize that, we are humbled and begin to ask, 'Who is sufficient for these things? How can I possibly live up to such a standard?' Not only that; we realize also our need of cleansing, we realize how unworthy and sinful we are. And the result of all this is that we feel utterly hopeless and helpless. We say, 'How can we live the Sermon on the Mount? How can anybody come up to such a standard? We need help and grace. Where can we get it?' Here is the answer: 'Ask, and it shall be given you; seek, and ye shall find; knock, and it shall be opened unto you.' That is the connection, and we should thank God for it, because standing face-to-face with this glorious gospel we must all feel undone and unworthy. Those foolish people who think of Christianity only in terms of a little morality which they themselves can produce have never really seen it. The standard by which we are confronted is that found in the Sermon on the Mount, and by it we are all crushed to the ground and made to realize our utter helplessness and our desperate need of grace. Here is the answer; the supply is available, and our Lord repeats it for the sake of emphasis.

As we look at this there are a number of questions which should be asked. Why are we all what we are in view of such promises? Why is the quality of our Christian living so poor? We are left entirely without excuse. Everything we need is available; why then are we what we are? Why are we not exemplifying this Sermon on the Mount more perfectly? Why are we not conforming more and more to the pattern of the Lord Jesus Christ Himself? All that we need is offered us; it is all promised us here in this comprehensive promise. Why are we not availing ourselves of it as we should? Again, fortunately, that question is also answered, and that is the real meaning of this verse. Our Lord analyses these words and He shows us why we have not received, why we have not found, why the door has not been opened to us as it should have been. He realizes what we are, and He encourages us to avail ourselves of the gracious promise. In other words, there are certain conditions which must be observed before we can rejoice in these great benefits that are offered us in Christ. What are they? Let us note them simply and briefly.

If we want to go through life triumphantly, with peace and joy in our hearts, ready to face whatever may come to meet us, and to be more than conquerors in spite of everything, there are certain things we have to realize, and here they are. The first is, we must realize our need. It is strange, but some people seem to think that all that is necessary is that the promises of God should be held before us. That is not enough, however, because the central trouble with the whole of mankind is that we do not realize our need. There are many who preach about the Lord Jesus Christ to no effect and we can see why. They have no doctrine of sin, they never convict or convince people of sin. They always hold Christ before men and say that that is enough. But it is not enough; for the effect of sin upon us is such that we shall never fly to Christ until we realize that we are paupers. But we hate to regard ourselves as paupers, and we do not like to feel our need. People are ready to listen to sermons which present Christ to them, but they do not like to be told that they are so helpless that He had to go to the cross and die before they could be saved. They think that that is insulting. We must be brought to realize our need. The first two essentials to salvation and to rejoicing in Christ are the consciousness of our need, and the consciousness of the riches of grace that are in Christ. It is only those who realize these two things who 'ask' truly, because it is only the man who says 'O wretched man that I am' who seeks for deliverance. The other man is not aware of his need. It is the man who knows that he is 'down and out' who begins to ask. And then he begins to realize the possibilities that are in Christ.

What our Lord emphasizes here at the beginning is the paramount importance of the realization of our need. He puts that by using these three terms — ask, seek, knock. When you consult the commentators you will find great discussions as to whether seeking is stronger than asking, and knocking stronger than seeking. They spend much of their time in dealing with such matters. And, as usual, you find that they tend to contradict each other. Some say that asking represents a faint desire, seeking a greater desire, and knocking something very powerful. Others say that the man who knocks is the man who is right outside and that the supreme thing is asking, not knocking. The unbeliever, they say, must knock at the door, and having entered in at the door he begins to seek, and at last face-to-face with his Lord and Master he can ask.

But, surely, all that is quite irrelevant. Our Lord is simply at pains to emphasize one thing, that is that we are to show persistence, perseverance, importunity. This comes out clearly when we notice the setting of this selfsame passage in Luke 11. There we have the parable of the man upon whom a guest suddenly landed at midnight, and as he had no bread to set before him, he went and knocked at the door of a friend who was already in bed. And because of his importunity the friend gave him some bread. The same thing is taught in the parable of the importunate widow in Luke 18. That is precisely what we have here. These three words emphasize the element of persistence. There are times of stocktaking in life when we pause for a moment and say: 'Life is moving on; I am moving on. What progress am I making in this life and world?' We begin to take stock of ourselves and say: 'I am not living the Christian life as I should; I am not as diligent in my reading of the Bible and in prayer as I know I should be. I am going to change all this. I see there is a higher level to which I must attain, and I want to get there.' We are honest; we are quite sincere; we fully intend to do it. And so, during the first few days of a new year, we read the Bible regularly, we pray and we ask God for His blessing. But — and this is surely true of all of us — we soon begin to slacken and to forget. At the very moment we thought of reading or praying something comes in, quite 'out of the blue', as we say, something we never anticipated, and our whole scheme and programme is upset. In a week or two we find that we have entirely forgotten our excellent resolve. That is what our Lord is concerned about. If you and I are really to obtain these blessings which God has for us, we must go on asking for them. 'Seeking' simply means going on asking; 'knocking' is just the same thing. It is an intensification of the word 'ask'. We go on, we persist; we are like the importunate widow. We keep on asking the judge, as it were, just as she did, and our Lord tells us that the judge said, 'I had better do something about this woman or else she is going to worry me with her persistence.'

The importance of this element of persistence cannot be exaggerated. You find it not only in biblical teaching, but also in the lives of all the saints. The most fatal thing in the Christian life is to be content with passing desires. If we really want to be men of God, if we really want to know Him, and walk with Him, and experience those boundless blessings which He has to offer us, we must persist in asking Him for them day by day. We have to feel this hunger and thirst after righteousness, and then we shall be filled. And that does not mean that we are filled once and for ever. We go on hungering and thirsting. Like the apostle Paul, leaving the things which are behind, we 'press toward the mark'.

'Not as though I had already attained', says Paul, 'but I follow after'. That is it. This persistence, this constant desire, asking, seeking and knocking. This, we must agree, is the point at which most of us fail.

Let us then hold on to that first principle. Let us examine ourselves in the light of these Scriptures and the pictures given of the Christian man in the New Testament. Let us look at these glorious promises and ask ourselves, 'Am I experiencing them?' And if we find we are not, as we all must confess, then we must go back again to this great statement. That is what I mean by the possibilities. While I must begin by asking and seeking, I must go on doing so until I am aware of an advance and a development and a rising to a higher spiritual level. We must keep on at it. It is a 'fight of faith'; it is 'he that endureth to the end' that will be saved in this sense. Persistence, continuance in well-doing, 'always to pray, and not to faint.' Not just pray when we want a great blessing and then stop; always pray. Persistence; that is the first thing. The realization of the need, the realization of the supply, and persistence in seeking after it.

Let us now look at the second principle, which is the realization that God is our Father. Our Lord talks about that in verse 9 and He puts it like this: 'Or what man is there of you, whom if his son ask bread, will he give him a stone?' This, of course, is the central principle of all — the realization that God is our Father. That is what our Lord is concerned to emphasize in all He says here. He is using His familiar method of arguing from the lesser to the greater. If an earthly father does so much, how much more so God? This is one of our main troubles, is it not? If you should ask me to state in one phrase what I regard as the greatest defect in most Christian lives I would say that it is our failure to know God as our Father as we should know Him. That is our trouble, not difficulties about particular blessings. The central trouble still is that we do not know, as we ought to, that God is our Father. Ah yes, we say; we do know that and believe it. But do we know it in our daily life and living? Is it something of which we are always conscious? If only we got hold of this, we could smile in the face of every possibility and eventuality that lies ahead of us.

How then are we to know this? It is certainly not something based on the notion of the 'universal Fatherhood of God' and the 'universal brotherhood of man'. That is not biblical. Our Lord says something here that ridicules that and proves such an idea to be nonsense. He says, 'If ye then, being evil'. You see the significance? Why did He not say, 'If *we* then, being evil'? He did not say it because He knew He was essentially different from them. The speaker is the Son of God; not a man who is called Jesus, but the Lord Jesus Christ, the only begotten Son of God. He does not include Himself in that 'ye'. But He does include the whole of mankind. 'Ye being evil' means that we not only do things which are evil, but that we *are* evil. Our natures are corrupt and evil, and those who are essentially corrupt and evil are not the children of God. There is no such thing as the universal Fatherhood of God in the generally accepted sense of that term. Christ says of certain people: 'Ye are of your father the devil, and the lusts of your father ye will do.' No; by nature we are all the children of wrath, we are all evil, we are all enemies of God; by nature we are not His children. So this does not entitle all men to say, 'Well now; I rather like this doctrine. I am rather afraid of all that lies ahead of me, and I like to be told that God is my Father.' But God is your Father only when you satisfy certain conditions. He is not the Father of any one of us as we are by nature.

How then does God become my Father? According to the Scriptures it is like this. Christ 'came unto his own, and his own received him not. But as many as received him, to them gave he power (i.e., authority) to become the sons of God' (John 1:11, 12). You become a child of God only when you are born again, when you receive a new life and a new nature. The child partakes of the nature of the Father. God is holy, and you and I are not children of God until we have received a holy nature; and that means we must have a new nature. Being evil, and even conceived in sin (Ps. 51:5), we do not have one; but He will give it to us. Now that is what is offered to us. And there is no contact and communion with God, nor are we heirs to any of these promises of God, until we become His children. In other words, we must remember that we have sinned against God, that we deserve the wrath and punishment of God, but that He has dealt with our sin and guilt by sending His Son to die on the cross of Calvary for us. And believing in Him, we receive a new life and nature and we become children of God. Then we can know that God is our Father; but not until then. He will also give us His Holy Spirit, 'the Spirit of adoption, whereby we cry, Abba, Father'; and the moment we know this we can be certain that God as our Father adopts a specific attitude with respect to us. It means that, as my Father, He is interested in me, that He is concerned about me, that He is watching over me, that He has a plan and purpose with respect to me, that He is desirous always to bless and to help me. Lay hold of that; take a firm grasp of that. Whatever may happen to you, God is your Father, and He is interested in you, and that is His attitude towards you.

But that does not exhaust the statement. There is a very interesting negative addition. Because God is your Father He will never give you anything that is evil. He will give you only that which is good. 'What man is there of you, whom if his son ask bread, will he give him a stone? Or if he ask a fish, will he give him a serpent?' Multiply that by infinity and that is God's attitude towards His child. In our folly we are apt to think that God is against us when something unpleasant happens to us. But God is our Father; and as our Father he will never give us anything that is evil. Never; it is impossible.

The third principle is this. God, being God, never makes a mistake. He knows the difference between good and evil in a way that no one else does. Take an earthly father; he does not give a stone for bread, but he sometimes makes a mistake. The earthly father at his best sometimes thinks at the moment that he is acting for the good of his child, but discovers later that it was bad. Your Father who is in heaven never makes such a mistake. He will never give you anything which will turn out to be harmful to you, but which at first seemed to be good. This is one of the most wonderful things we can ever realize. We are the children of a Father who not only loves us but looks upon us and keeps His eye upon us. He will never give us anything evil. But beyond all, He will never lead us astray, He will never make a mistake in what He gives us. He knows everything; His knowledge is absolute. If we but knew we were in the hands of such a Father, our outlook upon the future would be entirely transformed.

Lastly, we must remember increasingly the good gifts which He has for us. 'How much more shall your Father which is in heaven give good things to them that ask him?' This is the theme of the whole Bible. What are the good things? Our Lord has given us the answer in that passage in Luke 11. There, you remember, it reads like this: 'If ye then, being evil, know how to give good gifts unto your children: how much more shall your heavenly Father give the Holy Spirit to them that ask him?' That is it. And in giving the Holy Spirit He gives us everything; every fitness we require, every grace, every gift. They are all given to us in Him. Peter summing it up says, 'his divine power hath given unto us all things that pertain unto life and godliness' (2 Pet. 1:3). You see now why we should thank God that asking, and seeking and knocking, do not just mean that if we ask for anything we like we shall get it. Of course not. What it means is this. Ask for any one of these things that is good for you, that is for the salvation of your soul, your ultimate perfection, anything that brings you nearer to God and enlarges your life and is thoroughly good for you, and He will give it you. He will not give you things that are bad for you. You may think they are good but He knows they are bad. He does not make a mistake, and He will not give you such things. He will give you things that are good for you, and the promise literally is this, that if we seek these good things, the fullness of the Holy Spirit, the life of love, joy, peace, long-suffering, etc., all these virtues and glories that were seen shining so brightly in the earthly life of Christ, He will give them to us. If we really want to be more like Him, and like all the saints, if we really ask for these things, we shall receive; if we seek them, we shall find them; if we knock, the door will be opened unto us and we shall enter into their possession.

The promise is, that if we ask for the good things our heavenly Father will give them to us.

That is the way to face the future. Find out from the Scriptures what these good things are and seek them. The thing that matters supremely, the best thing for all of us, is to know God, 'the only true God, and Jesus Christ, whom (he) hath sent'; and if we seek that above everything else, if we 'seek first the king-dom of God, and his righteousness', then we have the word of the Son of God for it that all these other things shall be added unto us. God will give them to us with a bounty that we cannot even imagine. 'Ask, and it shall be given you; seek, and ye shall find; knock, and it shall be opened unto you.'

Chapter Nineteen

The Golden Rule

A S we approach the great statement of 7:12, which is generally described as the 'Golden Rule for Life and Living', the first matter which must engage our attention is what we may describe as a question of mechanics, namely, the relationship of this statement to the rest of this Sermon on the Mount. Here at the beginning of this twelfth verse we meet the word 'therefore'. Why 'therefore'? Obviously, it tells us that it is not a detached statement, that it clearly has a connection with what has gone before. 'Therefore all things whatsoever ye would that men should do to you, do ye even so to them: for this is the law and the prophets.' In other words, our Lord is still dealing with the subject of our judgment of others. He has never left that. If we regard verses 7-11 as a parenthesis we must be careful to remember that they are there to remind us that we need this supply of grace because of this question of judgment. Having shown us how to be blessed and rendered capable of helping one another, and of living the Christian life in its fullness, He comes back again to the original subject and says 'Therefore', in this matter of judgment, in this whole question of your relationship to other people, let this be the rule. We are still looking at this general subject of our judgment of others. That justifies us in saying that there is this definite internal unity in this chapter; and, furthermore, it justifies us in the view we took of the instructions with regard to prayer. It is not a detached statement, but part of a great argument which is designed to bring us into this right position with regard to this subject.

But someone may say: 'If you argue that this verse is a continuation of the theme of our judgment of others, why did He not put this statement immediately after verse 6? Why did He introduce the subject of prayer and so on? Why not rather put it like this: "Give not that which is holy unto the dogs, neither cast ye your pearls before swine, lest they trample them under their feet, and

466

turn again and rend you; therefore all things whatsoever ye would that men should do to you, do ye even so to them"?'

The answer, when you seek for it, is again not difficult. The statement at which we are now looking, which is the summing up of this whole matter of judgment, comes with much greater force and cogency when we look at it in the light of that brief statement about prayer. It is only after He has reminded us of what God has done for us in spite of our sins, and of God's attitude towards us and God's dealings with us, that the tremendous argument of this exhortation really comes home to us. We shall consider that point further when we come to study the exhortations in detail.

Here, then, we stand face-to-face with our Lord's final dictum with regard to this whole matter of judging others and of our relationship to them. It is well described as the 'golden rule'. What an extraordinary and remarkable statement it is. It is nothing, of course, but an epitome of the commandments which our Lord has summed up elsewhere in the words, 'Love thy neighbour as thyself'. He is really saying that, if you are in trouble at all as to how you should deal with others, and behave with respect to them, this is how you should act. You do not start with the other person; you start by asking yourself, 'What is it I like? What are the things that please me? What are the things that help and encourage me?' Then you ask yourself. 'What are the things I dislike? What are the things that upset me, and bring out the worst in me? What are the things that are hateful and discouraging?' You make a list of both these things, your likes and dislikes, and you work them out in detail — not only in deeds, but also in thoughts and in speech — with respect to the whole of your life and activities. 'What do I like people to think about me? What is it that tends to hurt me?'

Our Lord goes right down into the details and, therefore, it is essential that we also should deal with a matter like this in detail. We all know how easy it is to read such a statement, or to listen to an exposition of it, or to read an exposition of it in a book, or to see some great picture which conveys it, and to say, 'Yes; wonderful, marvellous,' and yet to fail completely to put it into practice in actual life and living. So our Lord, the incomparable moral and ethical Teacher, knowing that, teaches that the first thing we have to do is to lay down a rule for ourselves about these matters. And this is how we do so. Having drawn up this list of all our likes and dislikes, when we come to deal with other people we have nothing to do but to say quite simply: 'That other person is exactly as I am in these matters'. We must put ourselves constantly in their position. In our conduct and behaviour with respect to them we must be careful to do, and not to do, all the things which we have found to be pleasing or displeasing to ourselves. 'Therefore all things whatsoever ye would that men should do to you, do ye even so to them.' If you only do that, says our Lord, you can never go wrong. You do not like unkind things said about you? Well, do not say them about others. You do not like people who are difficult, and who make your life difficult, and bring problems into your life, and constantly put you on edge? Well; in exactly the same way, do not let your behaviour be such that you become like that to them. It is quite as simple as that, according to our Lord. All the great text-books on ethics and social relationships and morality, and on all the other subjects which deal with the problems of human relationships in the modern world can really be reduced to that.

This is something which is of urgent importance at the present time. All thinkers agree that the great problem of the twentieth century is after all the problem of relationships. Sometimes we foolishly tend to think that our international and other problems are economic, social or political; but in reality they all come down to this, our relationships with people. It is not money. Money does come into it, but it is only a kind of counter that is used. No; it is a question of what I myself want, and what the other person wants; and ultimately all the clashes and disturbances and unhappinesses in life are due to this. And our Lord here in this curious, laconic statement puts the whole truth concerning this matter: 'All things whatsoever you would that men should do to you, do ye even so to them.' That is the final statement about this question. If only we approached it like that, starting with self and then applying it to others, the entire problem would be solved.

But unfortunately we cannot leave it at that. There are people, as we shall see, who seem to think that this is all that is necessary. There are still people (and it is amazing that there can be such, but there are) who believe that all you have to do is just to hold up a standard before people and they will say: 'That is perfectly right; now we will proceed to do this.' But the world today is proving clearly that that is not the case, so we must go on with our consideration.

The gospel of Jesus Christ starts on the very basis which we have just been enunciating, that it is not enough merely to tell people the right way. That is not the problem; it is much deeper than that. Let us follow our Lord's way of putting it. You notice His comment on the golden rule; 'This', He says, 'is the law and the prophets'. In other words, that is a summary of the law and the prophets; it is their whole object and purpose. What does He mean by putting it like that? It is just another example of the way in which He calls attention, as He has done so frequently in this Sermon on the Mount, to the tragic manner in which God's law has been misunderstood. He still probably has His eye on the Pharisees and the scribes, the doctors of the law and the instructors of the people. You remember how at great length in the fifth chapter He took up many points of which He could say, 'Ye have heard that it was said by them of old time . . . but I say unto you'. His great concern there was to give these people the right view of the law; and He comes back to it here once more. Half our troubles are due to the fact that we do not understand the meaning of God's law, its true character and intent. We tend to think that it is just a number of rules and regulations which we are supposed to keep; we constantly forget the spirit. We think of a law as something which is to be observed mechanically, as something which is detached and almost impersonal; we regard it very much as if it were a series of regulations issued by a machine. You buy the machine, and you get your rules and regulations and all you have to do is to carry them out. Our whole tendency is to regard God's law with respect to life in some such way as that. Or, to put it in another form, the danger always is to regard the law as a thing in and of itself, and to think that all we have to do is to keep those regulations and that, if we do so and never deviate from them, or go beyond or stop short of them, all will be well. Now all those are entirely false views of the law.

Perhaps we can go further and say that our danger is to think of the law as being something negative, something prohibitive. Of course there are aspects of the law which are negative; but what our Lord is emphasizing here is — as He has said at great length in the fifth chapter — that the law which God gave to the children of Israel through the medium of angels and of Moses is a very positive thing, is a spiritual thing. It was never meant to be mechanical, and the whole fallacy of the Pharisees and the scribes, and all who followed them, was that they reduced something that was essentially spiritual and living to the realm of the mechanical, to something that was an end in itself. They thought that as long as they had actually not murdered somebody they had kept the law concerning murder, and that as long as they had not committed physical adultery they were all right in a moral sense. They were guilty of complete failure to see the spiritual intent, to see the spiritual character of the law, and above all to see the great end and object for which the law had been given.

Here, our Lord puts all that in this perfect summary. Why does the law tell us not to covet our neighbour's goods and possessions, or his wife, or anything else? Why does the law tell us 'Thou shalt not kill'; 'Thou shalt not steal'; 'Thou shalt not commit adultery'? What does it mean by all this? Is it designed simply that you and I should uphold these things as rules and regulations, or as subsections in Acts of Parliament which govern and control us and keep us within certain limits? No, that is not the object at all. The whole purpose and the real spirit behind it all is this, that we are to love our neighbour as ourselves, that we are to love one another.

Being the creatures that we are, however, it is not enough just to tell us to love one another; the matter has to be broken up for us. As the result of the Fall we are sinful; so it is not enough just to say, 'Love one another'. Our Lord breaks it up, therefore, and says: As you yourself value your life, remember that the other man also values his life, and that if your attitude towards that man is right, you will not kill that man, because you know he values his life as you do yours. The vital thing, after all, is that you love that man, that you understand him and desire the well-being of your neighbour even as you desire your own well-being. That is the law and the prophets. It all comes to that. All the detailed regulations given in the law in the Old Testament — what it tells you to do, for example, if you see your neighbour's ox straying, how you are to bring it back to him, or if you see anything going wrong in his farm, how you are to inform him at once and do your utmost to help him — are not just meant to lead you to say: 'The law says that if I see my neighbour's ox straying I am to take it back, therefore I must do so'. Not at all; it is rather that you may say to yourself: 'This man is like myself, and it will be a grievous matter and a loss to him if he is going to lose that ox. Well, he is a man like myself, and how grateful I would be if someone returned my ox to me. Therefore I will do that for him.' In other words, you are to be interested in your neighbour, you are to love him, and to desire to help him, and to be concerned about his happiness. The object of the law is to bring us to that, and these detailed regulations are nothing but illustrations of that great central principle. The moment we cease to realize that that is the spirit of the law and the purpose of the law, we go hopelessly astray.

That, then, is our Lord's own exposition of it. It was very necessary in His own day; it is very necessary today. We so constantly forget the spirit of the law and of life as God meant us to live it.

We must now apply all this to the modern world and to ourselves. People hear this golden rule and they praise it as marvellous and wonderful, and as a perfect summary of a great and involved subject. But the tragedy is that, having praised it, they do not implement it. And, after all, the law was not meant to be praised, it was meant to be practised. Our Lord did not preach the Sermon on the Mount in order that you and I might comment upon it, but in order that we might carry it out. That will be impressed upon us later on when He says that the man who hears these sayings and does them is like a person who builds his house upon a rock, but the other man who 'hears and does not' is like one who builds his house upon the sand. The modern world is like that; it admires these wonderful statements of Christ but it does not put them into practice. That brings us to the crucial question. Why do men forsake this golden rule? Why do they not keep it? Why do they not live their lives in this way? Why are there troubles and disputes not only between nations, but also between different classes within the nations; yes, even in families; yes, even between two people?

Why is it that there is any dispute or quarrelling or unhappiness? Why do we ever hear of two persons who do not speak to each other, and who avoid looking at each other? Why is there jealousy and backbiting, and all the other things which we know to be so true of life?

What is the matter? The answer is theological, and profoundly biblical. Foolish people, as we have seen, have so often said that they dislike theology, and especially the theology of the apostle Paul. They say that they like the simple gospel and especially the Sermon on the Mount, because it is practical and has no theology in it. Now this one verse proves how unutterably hollow the view is which says that all you have to do is to give people instruction, and tell them what to do, to hold before them the golden rule, and give them intelligent training, and that they will recognize it and rise up and put it into practice. The simple answer to that is that the golden rule has been confronting mankind for nearly two thousand years, and for the last hundred years in particular we have done everything we can by legislation and education to improve men, but still they are not obeying it.

Why is this so? It is just at this point that theology comes in. The first statement of the gospel is that man is sinful and perverted. He is a creature that is so bound and governed by evil that he cannot keep to the golden rule. The gospel always starts with that. The first principle in theology is the Fall of man and the sin of man. It can be put like this. Man does not implement the golden rule, which is a summary of the law and the prophets, because his whole attitude towards the law is wrong. He does not like the law; in fact he hates it. 'The carnal (natural) mind is enmity against God: it is not subject to the law of God, neither indeed can be' (Rom. 8:7). So it is useless to hold the law before such people. They hate the law, they do not want it. Of course, when they sit back in their armchair and listen to an abstract statement about life as it should be, they say that they like it. But if you apply the law to them, they immediately hate it and react against it. The moment it is applied to them they dislike and resent it.

But why should they be like this? According to the Bible we are all like this by nature because, prior to our dislike of the law, and prior to our wrong attitude to the law, is our wrong attitude towards God Himself who has given the law. The law is an expression of God's holy will; it is an expression in a sense of God's own person and character. And man dislikes the law of God because he is a natural hater of God. That is the New Testament argument: 'The natural mind is enmity against God'. The natural man, man as he is as the result of the Fall, is an enemy, an alien from God. He is 'without God in the world'; he dislikes God, and hates Him and everything that comes from Him. And why is this so? The ultimate answer is that his attitude towards himself is wrong. That is why all men do not by instinct and by nature hurry to carry out this golden rule.

The whole thing can be brought down to one word, 'self'. Our Lord expresses it by saying that we should 'love our neighbour as ourselves'. But that is the one thing we do not do, and do not want to do, because we love self so much in a wrong way. We do not do unto others as we would wish them to do unto us, because the whole time we are thinking only about ourselves, and we never transfer our thought to the other person. That is, in other words, the condition of man in sin as the result of the Fall. He is entirely self-centred. He thinks of nothing and no one but himself, he is concerned about nothing but his own well-being. This is not my dictum; it is the truth, the simple, literal truth about everybody in the world who is not a Christian; and, alas, it very often remains true even of Christians. Instinctively we are all self-centred. We are resentful of what is said and thought of us, but we never seem to realize that other people are the same, because we never think of the other person. The whole time we are thinking of self, and we dislike God because God is Someone who interferes with this self-centredness and independence. Man likes to think of himself as completely autonomous, but here is Someone who challenges that, and man by nature dislikes Him.

So the failure of man to live by, and to keep, the golden rule is due to the fact that he is self-centred. That, in turn, leads to self-satisfaction, self-protection, self-concern. Self is in the forefront the whole time, for man wants everything for himself. In the last analysis is not that the real cause of the trouble in your labour disputes? It all really comes to that. One side says: 'I am entitled to have more'. The other side says, 'Well, if he has more, I shall have less'. And so they both object to each other and there is a quarrel, because each one is thinking only of himself. I am not entering into the particular merits of particular disputes. There have been cases where men have been entitled to much more, but the bitterness always comes in because of sin and self. If we were only honest enough to analyse our attitude towards all these questions, whether political, social, economic, national or international, we should find that it all comes back to that. You see it in the nations. Two nations want the same thing, so each one is watching the other. All nations try to see themselves simply as the guardians and the custodians of the general peace of the world. There is an element of selfishness in patriotism always. It is 'my country', 'my right'; and the other nation says the same; and because we are all so self-centred there are wars. All disputes and quarrelling and unhappinesses, whether between individuals, or between divisions of society, or between nations or groups of nations, all in the end come down to just that. The solution for the problems of the world today is essentially theological. All the conferences and all the proposals about disarmament and everything else will come to nothing while there is sin in the human heart controlling individuals and groups and nations. The failure to implement the golden rule is due solely to the Fall and to sin.

Let us now put that positively. How is it possible for anyone to implement this golden rule? The question really is, how can our attitude and conduct ever conform to what our Lord says here? The answer of the gospel is that you must start with God. What is the greatest commandment? It is this: 'Thou shalt love the Lord thy God with all thy heart, and with all thy soul, and with all thy mind, and with all thy strength.' And the second is like unto it: 'Thou shalt love thy neighbour as thyself'. You notice the order. You do not start with your neighbour, you start with God. And relationships in this world will never be right, whether between individuals, or groups of nations, until we all start with God. You cannot love your neighbour as yourself until you love God. You will never see yourself or your neighbour aright until you have first of all seen both in the sight of God. We have to take these things in the right order. We must start with God. We were made by God and for God, and we can function truly only in relationship to God.

So then we start with God. We turn from all the quarrelling and disputes and problems and we look into His face. We begin to see Him in all His holiness and almightiness, and in all the power of His creatorship, and we humble ourselves before Him. He is worthy to be praised, and He alone. And, knowing that in His sight even nations are but as grasshoppers and like 'the small dust of the balance', we soon begin to realize that all the pomp and glory of man becomes as nothing when we truly see God. And, in addition, we begin to see ourselves as sinners. We see ourselves as such vile sinners that we forget that we ever had a right. We certainly see that we have no rights at all before God. We are wretched, foul and ugly. That is not only the teaching of Scripture; it is amply confirmed by the experiences of all who have come to know God in any real sense. It is the experience of every saint, and if you have not seen yourself as a worthless creature I should be very doubtful whether you are a Christian at all. No man can really come into the presence of God without saying, 'I am unclean'. We are all unclean. The knowledge of God humbles us to the dust; and in that position you do not think about your rights and your dignity. You have no need any longer to protect yourselves, because you feel you are unworthy of everything.

But, in turn, it also helps us to see others as we should see them. We see them now, no longer as hateful people who are trying to rob us of our rights, or trying to beat us in the race for money, or position or fame; we see them, as we see ourselves, as the victims of sin and of Satan, as the dupes of 'the god of this world', as fellowcreatures who are under the wrath of God and hell-bound. We have an entirely new view of them. We see them to be exactly as we are ourselves, and we are both in a terrible predicament. And we can do nothing; but both of us together must run to Christ and avail ourselves of His wonderful grace. We begin to enjoy it together and we want to share it together. That is how it works. It is the only way whereby we can ever do unto others as we would that they should do unto us. It is when we are really loving our neighbour as ourselves because we have been delivered from the thraldom of self, that we begin to enjoy 'the glorious liberty of the children of God'.

And of course, finally, it works like this. When we look to God and realize something of the truth about Him, and ourselves in our relationship to Him, the one thing we are conscious of is that God never deals with us according to our deserts. That is not His method. That is what our Lord was saying in the previous verses: 'What man is there of you, whom if his son ask bread, will he give him a stone? Or if he ask a fish, will he give him a serpent? If ye then, being evil, know how to give good gifts unto your children, how much more shall your Father which is in heaven give good things to them that ask him?' That is the argument. God does not give us what we deserve; God gives us His good things in spite of our being what we are. He does not merely look at us as we are. Were He to do so we should all be condemned. If God saw us only as we are, every one of us would be utterly condemned for ever. But He is interested in us in spite of these externals; He sees us as a loving Father. He looks upon us in His grace and mercy. So He does not deal with us merely as we are. He deals with us in grace.

That is why our Lord kept back this argument and put it after that wonderful prayer. That is how God deals with us. 'Now', He says in effect, 'you deal like that with your fellow men. Do not merely see the offensive and the difficult and the ugly. See behind all that'. Let us then observe human beings in their relationship to God, destined for eternity. Let us learn to look at them in this new way, in this divine way. 'Look at them', says Christ in effect, 'as I have looked upon you, and in the light of the thing that brought Me from heaven for you, to give My life for you.' Look at them like that. The moment you do so you will find that it is not difficult to implement the golden rule, because at that point you are delivered from self and its terrible tyranny, and you are seeing men and women with a new eye and in a different way. You will be able to say with Paul, 'Henceforth know we no man after the flesh'. You see everybody in a spiritual way. It is only when we come to this, after having started with God and sin and self and others, that we shall indeed be able to implement this amazing summary of the law and the prophets: 'Whatsoever ye would that men should do to you, do ye even so to them'. That is the thing to which we are called in Christ Jesus. We are to implement it, we are to practise it. And as we do so we shall be showing the world the only way in which its problems can be solved. We shall at the same time be missionaries and ambassadors for Christ.

Chapter Twenty

The Strait Gate

THE remarkable and striking statement of verses 13 and 14 is, judged from every standpoint, a most important and vital one. In terms of the mechanics of an analysis of the Sermon on the Mount it is crucial, because anyone who analyses the Sermon must agree that at this point we reach one of its main divisions. Here we can safely say that our Lord really has finished the Sermon as such, and that from here on He is rounding it off, and applying it, and urging upon His listeners the importance and necessity of practising it and implementing it in their daily lives.

We have seen in our studies that the section of the Sermon occupying the seventh chapter has an essential unity, it has a common theme, namely the theme of judgment. Strictly speaking, the Sermon as such has come to an end at the close of verse 12. By the end of that verse our Lord has laid down all the principles which He was concerned to inculcate.

His object in this Sermon, as we have seen, is to bring Christian people to realize first of all their nature, their character as a people, and then to show them how they are to manifest that nature and character in their daily life. Our Lord, the Son of God, has come from heaven to earth in order to found and establish a new kingdom, the kingdom of heaven. He comes into the midst of the kingdoms of this world, and His purpose is to call out a people unto Himself from the world and to form them into a kingdom. Therefore it is essential that He should make it quite plain and clear that this kingdom He has come to establish is entirely different from anything that the world has ever known, that it is to be the kingdom of God, the kingdom of light, the kingdom of heaven. His people must realize that it is something unique and separate; so He gives them a description of it. We have been working through that description. We have looked at His general portrait of the Christian in the Beatitudes. We have listened to Him telling these people that, because they are that kind of person, the world will react to them in a particular way; it will probably dislike them and persecute them. Nevertheless they are not to segregate themselves from the world and become monks or hermits; they are to remain in society as salt and as light. They are to keep society from putrefaction and from falling to pieces, and they are to be its light; that light, apart from which the world remains in a state of gross darkness.

Having done that, He then comes to the practical application and out-working of it all. He reminds them at once that the kind of life they have to live is to be entirely different even from the best and most religious that was known at that time. He contrasts it with the teaching of the Pharisees and scribes and doctors of the law. They were considered to be the best people, the most religious people, and yet He shows His people that their righteousness is to exceed the righteousness of the scribes and Pharisees. And He proceeds to show how this is to be done by giving detailed instruction as to how we are to do our almsgiving, and how to pray and how to fast. Finally He deals with our whole attitude towards life in this world, and our attitude towards other people in the matter of judgment. He has been laying down all these principles.

'There', He says in effect, 'is the character of this kingdom which I am forming. That is the type of life I am going to give you, and I want you to live and manifest it.' He has not only laid down principles; He has worked them out for us in detail. Now, having done that, He pauses, as it were, and looks at His congregation and says, 'Well now; there is My purpose. What are you going to do about it? There is no point in listening to this Sermon, there is no purpose in your having followed Me through all this delineation of the Christian life, if you are only going to listen. What are you going to do about it?' He comes, in other words, to exhortation, to application.

Here once more we are reminded that our Lord's method must ever be the pattern and example for all preaching. That is not true preaching which fails to apply its message and its truth; nor true exposition of the Bible that is simply content to open up a passage and then stop. The truth has to be taken into the life, and it has to be lived. Exhortation and application are essential parts of preaching. We see our Lord doing that very thing here. The remainder of this seventh chapter is nothing but a great and grand application of the message of the Sermon on the Mount to the people who first heard it, and to all of us at all times who claim to be Christian.

So He proceeds now to test His listeners. He says, in effect, 'My Sermon is finished. Now at once you must ask yourselves a question, "What am I doing about this? What is my reaction? Am I to be content to fold my arms and say with so many that it is a marvellous Sermon, that it has the grandest conception of life and living that mankind has ever known — such exalted morality, such wonderful uplift — that it is the ideal life that all ought to live?"' The same applies to us. Is that our reaction? just to praise the Sermon on the Mount? If it is, according to our Lord, He might as well never have preached it. It is not praise He desires; it is practice. The Sermon on the Mount is not to be commended, it is to be carried out.

Then He goes on and says that there is a further test, the test of fruit. There are many people who have praised this Sermon but who have not manifested it in their lives. Beware of such people, says our Lord. It is not what a tree looks like that matters; you test it by its fruit.

Then there is a final test, and that is the test applied to us by circumstances. What happens to us when the wind begins to blow, and the hurricane threatens, the rain descends and the floods come and beat upon the house of our life? Does it stand? That is the test. In other words, our interest in these things is quite useless and valueless unless it means that we have something that will enable us to stand in the darkest and most critical hours of our lives. That is the way in which He puts His application. Listening to these things, hearing them, praising them is not only not enough; according to our Lord, it is extremely dangerous. This Sermon is practical; it is meant to be lived. It is not merely an ethical idea; it is something that we are meant to implement and put into practice. We have been reminding ourselves of that as we have gone through it in detail; but the whole purpose of the remainder of this chapter is just to exhort us to do that in a most serious and solemn manner, and always in the light of judgment. And, of course, that is not only the teaching of the Sermon on the Mount; it is the teaching of the whole of the New Testament. Take a portion of Scripture such as the Epistle to the Ephesians, chapters 4 and 5. There you have exactly the same thing. The apostle gives them practical injunctions, tells them not to lie, and not to steal, to be loving and kind and tenderhearted. That is just a reiteration of this Sermon on the Mount. The Christian message is not some theoretical idea; it is something that really is to become characteristic of our daily life and living. That is the purpose of the remainder of this Sermon.

We must now examine particularly verses 13 and 14 in which our Lord begins this application of His own message. Let us look at them like this. He tells us that the first thing we must do after we have read this Sermon is to look at the type and kind of life to which He calls us, and realize what it is. We have seen time and again that the danger in dealing with the Sermon on the Mount is to become lost in details, or to be sidetracked by particular things that interest us. That is the false approach. So our Lord exhorts us to wait a moment and to look at the Sermon as a whole and to reflect upon it. What would we say is its outstanding characteristic? What is the thing that emerges as being of supreme importance? What is the one thing above all others that we have to grasp as a principle? He answers His own question by saying that the outstanding characteristic of the life to which He calls us is 'narrowness'. It is a narrow life, it is a 'narrow way'. He puts it dramatically before us by saying: 'Enter ye in at the strait gate'. The gate is narrow; and we must also walk along a narrow way.

His illustration is a very useful and practical one. He puts it in a dramatic form and the scene is immediately conjured up in our mind's eye. Here we are, walking along, and suddenly we find two gates confronting us. There is one on the left which is very wide and broad, and a great crowd of people are entering in. On the other hand there is a very narrow gate which takes only one person at a time. We see as we look through the wide gate that it leads to a broad way and that a great crowd is surging along it. But the other way is not only narrow at the beginning, it continues to be narrow, and there are but few to be seen walking along it. We can see the picture quite clearly. That, says our Lord in effect, is what I have been talking about. That narrow road is the way along which I want you to walk. 'Enter ye in at the strait gate.' Come on to this narrow way where you will find Me walking before you. At once we are reminded of some of the outstanding characteristics of this Christian life to which our Lord and Saviour Jesus Christ calls us.

The first thing we notice is that it is a life which is narrow or strait at the very beginning. Immediately it is narrow. It is not a life which at first is fairly broad, and which as you go on becomes narrower and narrower. No! The gate itself, the very way of entering into this life, is a narrow one. It is important to stress and impress that point because, from the standpoint of evangelism, it is essential. When worldly wisdom and carnal motives enter into evangelism you will find that there is no 'strait gate'. Too often the impression is given that to be a Christian is after all very little different from being a non-Christian, that you must not think of Christianity as a narrow life, but as something most attractive and wonderful and exciting, and that you come in in crowds. It is not so according to our Lord. The gospel of Jesus Christ is too honest to invite anybody in that way. It does not try to persuade us that it is something very easy, and that it is only later on that we shall begin to discover it is hard. The gospel of Jesus Christ openly and uncompromisingly announces itself as being something which starts with a narrow entrance, a strait gate. At the very beginning it is absolutely essential that we should realize that. Let us look at this in a little more detail.

We are told at the very outset of this way of life, before we start on it, that if we would walk along it there are certain things which must be left outside, behind us. There is no room for them, because we have to start by passing through a strait and narrow gate. I like to think of it as a turnstile. It is just like a turnstile that admits one person at a time and no more. And it is so narrow that there are certain things which you simply cannot take through with you. It is exclusive from the very beginning, and it is important that we should look at this Sermon in order to see some of the things which must be left behind.

The first thing we leave behind is what is called worldliness. We leave behind the crowd, the way of the world. 'Wide is the gate, and broad is the way, that leadeth to destruction, and many there be which go in thereat: because strait is the gate, and narrow is the way, which leadeth unto life, and few there be that find it.' You must start by realizing that, by becoming a Christian, you become something exceptional and unusual. You are making a break with the world, and with the crowd, and with the vast majority of people. It is inevitable; and it is important that we should know it. The Christian way of life is not popular. It never has been popular, and it is not popular today. It is unusual, exceptional, strange, and it is different. On the other hand, crowding through the wide gate and travelling along the broad way is the thing that everybody else seems to be doing. You deliberately get out of that crowd and you start making your way towards this strait and narrow gate, alone. You cannot take the crowd with you into the Christian life: it inevitably involves a break.

We can put this best, perhaps, by emphasizing that it is something that is always intensely personal. Nothing, after all, is more difficult in this life than to realize that we are individual persons. We are all of us so much slaves of 'the done thing'. We come into a world full of traditions and habits and customs to which we tend to conform. It is the easy and obvious thing to do; and it is true to say of most of us that there is nothing we hate so much as being unusual or different. There are exceptions of course, some who are eccentric by nature and others who affect eccentricity; but it is true of the vast majority of us that we all like to be the same. Children are like that. They want their parents to be the same as other parents; they do not want anything unusual. It is amazing to observe how people instinctively like to conform to pattern in custom, habit, and behaviour; and indeed, at times, it is even amusing. We hear certain people objecting to the tendency in modern legislation to regimentation. They voice their objections to it strongly, as they do their belief in individuality and freedom. Yet they themselves are often just typical representatives of the particular section or group in which they have been brought up, or to which they like to belong. You can tell almost at once the school or university they have attended; they conform to pattern.

We all tend to do this, with the result that one of the most difficult things that many people have to face when they become Christian is that it is going to involve them in being unusual and exceptional. But it has to happen. In other words, one of the first things that happens to a person who becomes alive to the message of the gospel of Christ is that he says to himself. 'Well; whatever may be happening to the majority, I myself am a living soul and I am responsible for my own life'. 'Every man shall bear his own burden.' So when a man becomes a Christian he first begins to see himself as a separate unit in this great world. Formerly he had lost his individuality and identity in the great crowd of people to whom he belonged; but now he stands alone. He had been rushing madly with the crowd, but he suddenly halts. That is always the first step in becoming a Christian. And he realizes, furthermore, that if his soul, his eternal destiny, is to be made safe, he must not only stand for a moment in the surge of that crowd, he must separate himself from it. He may find it difficult to extricate himself, but he must do it; and while the majority are going in one direction he must go in the other. He leaves the crowd. You cannot get a crowd through that turnstile all together, it only takes one person at a time. It makes a man realize that he is a responsible being before God, his judge Eternal. The gate is strait and narrow, it brings me face-to-face with judgment, face-to-face with God, face-to-face with the question of life and my personal being, my soul and its eternal destiny.

But I not only have to leave the crowd, the world and the 'jollity' outside. Still more difficult, and still straiter and narrower, is the realization that I have to leave the *way* of the world outside. We are all familiar with this in practice and in our Christian lives. It is one thing to leave the crowd, but it is a very different thing to leave the *way* of the crowd. That, of course, is the ultimate and final fallacy of monasticism. Monasticism is really based upon the idea that if you leave people, you leave the spirit of the world. But you do not. You can leave the world in a physical sense, you can leave the crowd and the people; but there in your lonely cell the spirit of the world may still be with you. That is something that is equally true in connection with Christian life and living. There are people who have segregated themselves from the group to which they belonged, and yet you find the spirit of worldliness left in them still, perhaps even evident in their deportment. They have not left the spirit of the world and the way of the world. But we must. Living the way of the world and the life of the world in a different setting does not make us Christian. In other words, we must leave outside the gate the things that please the world. This cannot be evaded. We have only to read the Sermon on the Mount to come to the conclusion that the things that belong to and that please our unregenerate nature must be left outside that strait gate.

We can illustrate this. You remember that we have heard in this Sermon that we must check the spirit that demands 'an eye for an eye, and a tooth for a tooth', that we must not resist evil, — 'whosoever shall smite thee on thy right cheek, turn to him the other also'. We do not do that sort of thing instinctively; it does not come naturally to us and we do not like it. 'If any man . . . take away thy coat, let him have thy cloke also.' 'Whosoever shall compel thee to go a mile, go with him twain.' 'Ye have heard that it hath been said, Thou shalt love thy neighbour, and hate thine enemy. But I say unto you, Love your enemies, bless them that curse you, do good to them that hate you, and pray for them which despitefully use you, and persecute you.'

To obey those injunctions is not instinctive, indeed it is something we do not like. The instinctive thing is to hit back, to defend our rights, to love those who love us, and to hate those who hate us. But our Lord has been telling us that if we are really to be His people and to live in His kingdom, we must leave outside the depraved, the instinctive, and the worldly, the things liked and done by our fallen nature. There is no room for such things. We should realize at the beginning that that kind of luggage cannot be admitted. Our Lord is warning us against the danger of an easy salvation, against the tendency to say: 'Just come to Christ as you are and all is going to be well'. No, the gospel tells us at the outset that it is going to be difficult. It means a radical break with the world; it is an entirely different type of life. So we leave not only the world, but also the way of the world outside.

Yes, but still narrower and still straiter; if we really want to come into this way of life, we have to leave our 'self' outside. And it is there of course that we come to the greatest stumbling block of all. It is one thing to leave the world, and the way of the world; but the most important thing in a sense is to leave our self outside. Yet it is obvious, is it not? We are not to take our self with us on this way. That is not being foolish; it is typical New Testament language. Self is the Adamic man, the fallen nature; and Christ says that he must be left outside. 'Put off the old man', that is, leave him outside the gate. There is no room for two men to go through this gate together, so the old man must be left behind. Every illustration breaks down somewhere, and even this illustration used by our Lord Himself cannot cover the whole truth. There is a sense in which the Christian has not left the old man outside and so needs the exhortation of the apostle to 'put off the old man'. Nevertheless we are told at the very outset that self has no place in this kingdom.

The New Testament gospel is very humbling to self and to pride. At the beginning of the Sermon we are confronted by: 'Blessed are the poor in spirit'. No natural man born into this world likes to be poor in spirit. We are by nature the exact opposite to that; we are all born with a proud nature, and the world does its utmost to encourage our pride from our very birth. The most difficult thing in the world is to become poor in spirit. It is humbling to pride, and yet it is essential. At the entrance to that strait gate there is a notice that says: 'Leave yourself outside'. How can we bless them that curse us, and pray for them which despitefully use us, unless we have done this? How can we possibly follow our Lord, and be children of our Father which is in heaven, and love our enemies, if we are self-conscious and always defending and watching self and being concerned about it. We have gone through all this already in detail; but we must look at it again in general, as our Lord calls upon us to do so in this invitation to enter the strait gate. Self cannot possibly exist in this atmosphere; all along it must be crucified. 'Judge not, that ye be not judged.' Do unto others as you would that all men should do unto you, and so on. Our Lord tells us that at the very beginning. Have no illusion about this. If you think it is a life in which you are going to make a great name, and be praised, and one in which you are going to be made wonderful, you may as well stop at this point and go back to the beginning, for he who would enter by this gate must say goodbye to self. It is a life of self-abasement, self-humiliation. 'If any man will come after me' — what happens? 'Let him deny himself (the first thing always), and take up his cross, and follow me.' But self-denial, denial of self, does not mean refraining from various pleasures and things that we may like; it means we deny our very right to our self, we leave our self outside, and go in through the gate saying: 'Yet not I, but Christ liveth in me'.

That then is the first thing. This gate is narrow; the very beginning of the Christian life is strait because we have to leave certain things outside.

But I would also emphasize that it is strait and narrow in another way, namely, that it is difficult. The Christian way of life is difficult. It is not an easy life. It is too glorious and wonderful to be easy. It means living like Christ Himself, and that is not easy. The standard is difficult — thank God for it. It is a poor kind of person who wants only the easy and avoids the difficult. This is the highest life that has ever been depicted to mankind, and because of that it is difficult, and it is strait and narrow. 'Few there be that find it.' Of course! There are always fewer consulting doctors of medicine than general practitioners; there are never as many experts as there are ordinary workers. It does not matter what realm or department of life you are thinking of, you will always find that the real experts are few in number. When you come to the topmost level in any walk in life the company is always smaller. Anybody can follow the ordinary; but the moment you want to do something unusual, the moment you want to reach the heights, you will find that there are not many trying to do the same. It is exactly the same with respect to the Christian life; it is such an exalted life and such a wonderful one, that there are but few who find it and enter it, simply because it is difficult. We need not emphasize this. Consider what we have been told as we have gone through the Sermon in detail. Look at this kind of life as our Lord has depicted it, and you will see that it must be narrow because it is so difficult. It is the highest, it is the acme of perfection in living.

In addition it is strait and narrow because it always involves suffering, and because, when it is truly lived, it always involves persecution. 'Blessed are ye, when men shall revile you, and persecute you, and shall say all manner of evil against you falsely, for my sake. Rejoice, and be exceeding glad: for great is your reward in heaven: for so persecuted they the prophets which were before you.' They have always done that, the world has always persecuted the man who follows God. You see it perfectly in the case of our Lord Himself. He was rejected by the world. He was hated by men and women because He was what He was. 'Yea,' says Paul, 'and all that will live godly in Christ Jesus shall suffer persecution.' But who likes being persecuted? We do not like to be criticized or to be dealt with harshly. We really do like all people to speak well of us, and it is very galling to us to know that we are being hated and criticized; but Christ has warned us that we will be, if we come into this narrow way. It is strait and difficult; and as we enter, therefore, we must be ready for suffering and persecution.

You must be ready to be misunderstood; you must be ready, perhaps, even to be misunderstood by your nearest and dearest. Christ has told us that He came 'not to send peace, but a sword', a sword that may divide mother from daughter, or father from son, and those of your own household may be your greatest enemies. Why? Because you have been set apart. You have been set apart from your family, and have entered by this strait gate that does not admit us by families, but one by one. It is very hard, it is very difficult. But the Lord Jesus Christ is honest with us; and if we see nothing else, God grant that we may see the honesty and the truthfulness of this gospel which tells us at the very outset that we may have to come apart from husband or from wife for the sake of becoming a Christian and following Christ. You are not called upon to separate actually and in fact, but spiritually. But you can only come one by one, for it is a strait and narrow gate.

So far we have seen how narrow and strait this life is at the beginning. But it is not only strait at the beginning; it continues to be strait. It is not only a strait gate, it is a narrow way also. The Christian life is narrow from the beginning to the end. There is no such thing as a holiday in the spiritual realm. We can take a holiday from our usual work; but there is no such thing as a holiday in the spiritual life. It is always narrow. As it starts, so it continues. It is a 'fight of faith' always, right to the end. It is the narrow way, and on each side there are enemies. There are things oppressing us and people attacking us all along to the very end. You will have no easy pathway in this world and in this life, and Christ tells us that at the beginning. If you have an idea that the Christian life is going to be difficult at the commencement and that later it becomes quite easy, you have an entirely false view of the teaching of the New Testament. It is narrow all the way; there will be foes and enemies attacking you right to the last minute.

Am I discouraging? Does anyone feel like saying: 'Well, if it is like that, I am going back'? But I would remind you before you decide to do that, that we are told something about the end to which this road leads. Yet apart from that, is it not the most glorious thing to go on following Him? Even so, let us be under no illusion; the wrestling against principalities and powers, against the darkness of this world, and the spiritual wickedness in high places, continues while man is in this life and world. There will be subtle temptations on the road of life, and you will have to watch and be on guard, from the beginning to the end. You will never be able to relax. You will always have to be careful; you will have to walk circumspectly, as Paul puts it; you will have to watch your every step. It is a narrow way, it starts as such and so it continues.

These then are the things that we have to bear in mind as we contemplate this Sermon as a whole. It is most dangerous, as well as being quite unscriptural, to fail to realize them at the very beginning. To divorce forgiveness of sins from the remainder of the Christian life and to regard it as if it were the whole is clearly heresy. True evangelism, as I understand it, is one that presents to men and women the Christian life as a whole, and we must be very careful about giving the impression that people can crowd, as it were, to Christ, can try to rush the strait gate without considering the narrow way to which it leads. It was our Lord Himself who spoke those parables about the foolish people who did not count the cost — the man who started to put up a tower, without counting the cost, and so had to leave his building unfinished. The same was true of the king who went to fight another king, without assessing the strength of the enemy. It is our Lord who tells us to count the cost and to face what we have to do before we start. He shows us the whole life. He has not merely come to save us from punishment and from hell; He has come to make us holy, and to 'purify unto himself a peculiar people, zealous of good works'. He came into this world to prepare the way of holiness, and His ambition and His purpose for us is that we shall walk in that way in His steps, in this high calling, in this glorious life, that we should live even as He Himself lived it, resisting even unto blood if necessary. That was His life, a straight and thorny road; but He trod it. And your privilege and mine is the privilege of coming out of the world and entering into this life, and following Him all the way.

'Christian! seek not yet repose,
    Cast thy dreams of ease away;
Thou art in the midst of foes:
        Watch and pray.'

Chapter Twenty-one

The Narrow Way

W E return to a further consideration of this statement in verses 13 and 14 because our Lord in these words does not ask us merely to contemplate the nature of the kingdom or the Christian life in general. It is not an invitation to come and view a wonderful prospect, to sit as it were in the gallery and look at the arena. We are meant to be participators in this; it is a call to action. You notice the words: 'Enter ye'; they are an invitation and an exhortation at one and the same time. Having contemplated it in general, we have to do something about it.

That then is the first principle which we must elaborate a little. It is a call to action. What does this mean? First, it means that the gospel of Jesus Christ, this enunciating of the principles of the kingdom, is something that demands a decision and a committal. This is quite unavoidable; it is something which is a part of the warp and woof of the New Testament presentation of the truth. It is not a philosophy that you look at and compare and contrast with other philosophies. You can never maintain a detached attitude to this; and if our concern about these things is a purely intellectual one, which has never affected our lives, then the New Testament says we are just not Christian. It is, of course, a wonderful philosophy, but the temptation is to regard it as just that, as something to be read about, and to be interested in. But the gospel refuses to be taken like that; it is essentially something that comes to us demanding to control our lives. It comes to us in much the same way as our Lord Himself approached men. You remember how, as He walked along, He came across a man like Matthew, and said to him, 'Follow me', and Matthew got up and followed Him. The gospel does something like that. It does not say: 'Consider Me; admire Me'. It says: 'Follow Me; believe Me'. It always calls for a decision, for a committal. This is obviously something that is quite vital. There is no purpose in describing the glories and the wonders and the beauties of that narrow way if we are still going to look at it only from a distance. It is a road that is to be trodden; it is something we are to enter into. Nothing is more remarkable than the way in which we succeed in persuading ourselves for so long that an interest in the gospel without a decision and a committal is possible. But it is not.

So we ask ourselves a very simple question at this point. My ultimate test of myself, and of my profession of the Christian faith, can be put like this: Have I committed myself to this way of life? Is it the thing which controls my life? We have seen what it tells us to do; have we then put ourselves under its teaching? Is it dominating our lives? Is it governing and controlling us in our actual decisions and practice? This, of course, involves a very definite act of the will. It calls upon me to say: 'Recognizing this as God's truth and as the call of Christ, I am going to give myself to it, come what may. I am not going to consider the consequences. I believe it, I will act upon it; this henceforth is going to be my life.'

There was a time when some of our forefathers used to teach that it was a good thing for every Christian to make a covenant with God. Having considered the truth like this, they would sit down and solemnly write out on paper the covenant which they made with God, and they would put their signature to it and the date, exactly as if it were a business transaction. They would sign away themselves, and their right to themselves and all they had, and their right to live as they chose. They would henceforth give themselves to God, much as a man joining an army surrenders the right to himself and the control of his life. They would enter into a contract like that, a covenant with God, and they would sign, seal and settle it, and there it was. There is something to be said for that practice. Some of us suffer so much from the tendency just to contemplate the Christian life without doing anything about it, that it would be a good thing for us deliberately and definitely to make an act of committal such as this, and thus enter in at the strait gate. It demands a decision.

That in turn leads to the second principle. Having looked at the truth and having decided that I have to do something about it, I now begin to seek for this strait gate. You notice how our Lord puts it. He says, 'because strait is the gate, and narrow is the way, which leadeth unto life, and few there be that find it'. Why is this? It is because there are few that seek it. This is a gate which must be sought deliberately. In other words, the essence of wisdom in these matters is to move from the general to the particular. It is surely true of the experience of all of us to say that one of the greatest dangers confronting us is the danger of listening to the truth, or reading it, and nodding our head in agreement with it but of never doing anything at all about it. We do not seek for the strait gate.

Seeking the strait gate means something like this. Having seen the truth, and having expressed my agreement, I should then say to myself, 'What exactly must I do to make this operative?' That is seeking the strait gate. There is a way of seeking truly and we must discover in detail exactly what it means for us. That is seeking the strait gate — really to put the truth into operation. I am concerned to impress the point that the gate really has to be sought. It is not easy; it is difficult. You have to go out of your way to find this gate. You will have to analyse yourself and be very honest with yourself, and, having refused to hold back, say: 'I am going on with this until I discover exactly what I have to do.' There are so many who do not find this way of life because they have never sought the gate and entered in. If you read the biographies of some of God's great saints in past times you will find that they sought this strait gate for many a long day. Look at Martin Luther. There he is in his cell, fasting, sweating and praying. Read again about men like George Whitefield and John Wesley. These men were seeking this strait gate. They did not know what they had to do, they were wrong in their ideas, but at long last, by diligent seeking they found it, and when they found it they entered in. Now in some way or another we must all do that. In other words, we must give ourselves no rest or peace until we know for certain that we are on this way. That is 'entering the strait gate'. You enter it only after you have sought and after you have found it.

The third step is that, having decided that you are going to enter and having sought the gate and entered through it, you then go right on; you commit yourself, and you say certain things to yourself. It is surely true to say that the solution to many of our problems in this Christian life is that we should talk more to ourselves. We should constantly remind ourselves of who we are and what we are. That is what is meant by not only entering in but continuing along this way. The Christian man should remind himself every morning as he wakes up, 'I am a child of God; I am a unique person; I am not like everybody else; I belong to the family of God. Christ has died for me and has translated me from the kingdom of darkness into His own kingdom. I am going to heaven, I am destined for that. I am but passing through this world. I know its temptations and trials; I know the subtle insinuations of Satan. But I do not belong to him. I am a pilgrim and a stranger; I am one who is following Christ along this road.' You remind yourself of that, you commit yourself, and you go on doing so. And the result will be that you will find yourself walking along this narrow way. That is the first general principle upon which we must act. When we have seen the truth we must do something about it; we must bring ourselves into a practical relationship to it.

The second principle stands out very clearly. It is the consideration of some reasons for doing this. Once more, as we have found so often in our study of this Sermon, our blessed Lord stoops to our weakness. We have found almost invariably that it is His method, His technique if you like, to lay down a principle or to give an injunction; and then, having done that, to give us some reasons for carrying it out. He need not have done so. There we see something of His great pastoral heart and His sympathy with us as His people. He is a High Priest who is able 'to sympathize with us'. He understands us. He knows that we are so fallible and imperfect as a result of sin that it is not enough merely to show us the way. We need to be supplied with reasons. 'Enter ye in at the strait gate: *for* wide is the gate, and broad is the way that leadeth to destruction, and many there be which go in thereat: *because* strait is the gate, and narrow is the way, which leadeth unto life, and few there be that find it.'

What then are the reasons? Let us just summarize them. The first reason He gives us for entering in at this strait gate is the character of the two types of life that are open to us and possible for us. There is the broad way which you enter through the wide gate, and there is the other way which is entered through the strait gate, a way which is narrow the whole time. If we only realized the truth concerning the character of these two ways there would be no hesitation. Of course, it is so difficult for us to detach ourselves from life in this world, and yet the essence of this matter is that we should do so. That is why, if one may say so, God in His infinite wisdom ordained that one day in seven should be set apart for the contemplation of these things, and that men should meet together in public worship. When we meet for worship we are stepping out of this world in which we live in order that we may look upon it all objectively. It is so difficult to do that when you are in it; but once you come out, and sit apart and look at it objectively, you really begin to see things as they are.

Look for a moment at that worldly life which those people live who are on the broad way. Look at it, for instance, as you see it in the newspapers. Take any one of them. They represent the typical worldly life at its best and at its worst. Look at that life which has such a fascination for so many people, that life which so fascinates them that they are prepared to risk their eternal soul for it, if they believe in the soul at all. What is it that holds them? Look at the life and analyse it. What is there in it ultimately with all its pomp and its glory and its luxury? Can you imagine anything that is so utterly empty finally? What real satisfaction is there in such a life? You remember those famous questions which the apostle Paul puts to the Romans, which, it seems to me, summarize this perfectly. At the end of Romans 6:21, he asks, 'What fruit had ye then in those things whereof ye are now ashamed? for the end of those things is death.' Now that you have become a Christian, he says, as you look back across your life, you are ashamed of it. But what fruit did you have in it even then?

This is a question that all people should face, especially those who live from one round of pleasure to another, and who regard honest work as just a nuisance, or merely as a means of getting money in order to go back to have more pleasure. What is there in it? What is the gain? What is the satisfaction? What have they of ultimate value intellectually, apart from anything else? What is there uplifting and ennobling in dressing in a particular way and having their photographs in the so-called society papers, in being known for their fashionable attire or personal appearance, or for the figure they cut, and all the rest of it? What real value is there in the praise and adulation of man? Look at the people who live for such things, analyse their lives, and especially their end. That is not cynicism, it is realism. As the hymn puts it,

> 'Fading is the worldling's pleasure,
> All his boasted pomp and show.'

How empty it is. The apostle Peter describes the same thing as 'vain conversation'. There is nothing in it, it is so superficial and empty. It is very difficult, apart from Christianity, to understand the mentality of people who live on such a level. They have minds and brains, but they do not seem to be much in evidence in this life of make-believe and delusion and folly and self-hypnotism. What an utterly empty life it is, even looked at as it is in and of itself, this life of pomp and show and shadow and appearance.

Then look at the other life and see how essentially different it is in every respect. The broad way is empty and useless, intellectually, morally, and in every other respect. It leaves man with a nasty taste in his mouth even at the time, and leads to jealousy and envy and all sorts of things that are unworthy. But look at the other, and immediately you see a striking contrast. Read the Sermon on the Mount again. What a life! Take this New Testament. What food for your intellect! Here is something to engage your mind. Read books about it. Can you imagine a higher intellectual occupation, apart from anything else? Here you have something to think about, something to grapple with intellectually, something that gives you real and lasting satisfaction. How ethical, how uplifting, how large and noble it is.

The trouble ultimately with all who are not Christian is that they have never seen the glory and the magnificence of the Christian life. How noble and pure and upright it is! But they have never seen it. They are blind to it. As the apostle Paul says, 'The god of this world hath blinded the minds of them which believe not' (2 Cor. 4:4). But once a man gets a glimpse of the glory and majesty and privilege of this high calling I cannot imagine that he would ever desire anything else. Let us be very practical and blunt about this. Anybody who calls this Christian life 'narrow' (in the usual sense of that term) and hankers after the other, is just proclaiming that he has never seen this truly. He is like those people who say that they find Beethoven rather boring, and that they prefer jazz music. What they are really saying is they do not understand Beethoven; they do not hear him, they know nothing about him. They are ignorant musically. As someone has said, they tell us nothing about Beethoven, but a great deal about themselves!

There, then, is the character and the nature of the two lives. The New Testament constantly presents this argument. This is to be found repeatedly in the Epistles. The writers describe the life, and then say, in effect: 'Surely, having seen that, you do not want to go back to anything else?' That is their argument. They remind you of these two lives; 'Wide is the gate, and broad is the way, that leadeth to destruction.' But 'strait is the gate, and narrow is the way, which leadeth unto life.' The man who does not consider his destination is a fool. The man who makes travelling an end in itself is illogical and inconsistent. That is the great argument of the Bible from beginning to end. 'Consider your latter end'; consider your destination and whither that sort of life leads. If only the world could be persuaded to ask that question, all would soon be changed. We have seen how the apostle Paul tells us that the broad way is certain to lead to shame and misery and destruction. 'The wages of sin is death' — spiritual death and separation from God as well as suffering, agony, despair and useless remorse; 'but the gift of God is eternal life through Jesus Christ our Lord' (Rom. 6:23). If ever, therefore, you feel that the Christian way of life is rather irksome, just remind yourself of the destination to which it leads. Then look at the world with its apparent joy and happiness; look at the people who are loving and enjoying it, and try to picture them when they will be decrepit with old age, and 'the last enemy' comes to meet them. Suddenly they are taken ill. They can no longer drink, and smoke, and dance, and gamble, and do the things on which they have lived. On their deathbed what have they? Nothing; nothing to look forward to except fear, and horror, and torment, and destruction. That is the end of that life. We know that well; it has always been true. Read the biographies of the world's great men, statesmen and others, who are not Christian, and notice again the eclipse which they experience. And remember that we are never given details of the actual end. How can it lead to anything else? It leads 'to destruction'.

But this other life leads to a life more abundant. It starts by giving new life, a new outlook, new desires, new everything; and as you go on it becomes greater and more wonderful. However much you may have to suffer in this life and world, you are destined for a glory which is indestructible. You are going on to an inheritance, according to the apostle Peter, which is 'incorruptible, and undefiled, and that fadeth not away', reserved in heaven by God for you.

Another argument our Lord uses is that not to enter in at the strait gate means that we are already on the broad way. It has to be one or the other. 'There is no mean between two opposites.' The Christian is confronted by two ways only, and if we are not on the strait and narrow way, we are on the wide and broad way. So indecision and a failure to commit ourselves means that we are not on the narrow way. Passive resistance is resistance; if we are not for Him we are against Him. That is a very powerful argument. Indecision is fatal, because it means wrong decision. There is no alternative. It is either the narrow or the broad way.

The greatest inducement of all, however, to enter in at the strait gate and to walk the narrow way, is this. There is Someone on that road before you. You have to leave the world outside. You may have to leave many who are dear to you, you have to leave yourself, your old self, and you may think as you go through that gate that you are going to be isolated and solitary. But it is not so. There are others on this road with you — 'few there be that find it'. There are not as many as there are on the other way, but they are a very choice and separate people. But above all look at the One who is treading that road ahead of all, the One who said, 'Follow me', the One who said, 'Let him deny himself, and take up his cross, and follow me'. If there were no other inducement for entering in at the strait gate, that is more than enough. To enter this way means to follow in the footsteps of the Lord Jesus Christ. It is an invitation to live as He lived; it is an invitation to become increasingly what He was. It is to be like Him, to live as He lived whose life we read of in these Gospels. That is what it means; and the more we think of it in that way the greater will the inducement be. Do not think of what you have to leave; there is nothing in that. Do not think of the losses, do not think of the sacrifices and sufferings. These terms should not be used; you lose nothing, but you gain everything. Look at Him, follow Him, and realize that ultimately you are going to be with Him, and to look into His blessed face and enjoy Him to all eternity. He is on this way, and that is enough.

Before we leave this matter there is one other principle that we should consider. We have decided to enter, and we have found the reasons for entering. There are, however, certain problems that people constantly mention when they consider this text. One is that the theology of this teaching presents a stumbling block to certain people. The first difficulty is this. Does our Lord teach here that there is a kind of neutral position in life? Here we are pictured as standing on a road with a wide and a narrow gate before us. Is there ever a time in a man's life when he is neither good nor bad? Are we all born in innocency and neutrality? Do we deliberately enter one or the other? It seems to teach that.

The answer, of course, is that we must always compare Scripture with

Scripture, and take any particular Scripture in the light of the whole. Scripture teaches us plainly that we are all born into this world the children of sin and wrath. We are all, as descendants of Adam, born in guilt and shame, born in sin and shapen in iniquity, born, indeed, 'dead in trespasses and sins'. Actually, therefore, we are all born on the broad way. Why then did our Lord put it like that? For this reason. He is teaching here the importance of entering in upon His way of life, and He uses an illustration. He dramatizes and objectifies the situation and asks us to regard it as if we were confronted by the choice of one of two ways. In other words, He asks: Are you committed for ever to that worldly life in which you were born, or are you going to leave it and come into Mine? It is perfect teaching technique and one cannot imagine a better illustration. Yet every illustration has its limits. He is concerned about our committal of ourselves, so He puts it like that. So there is no teaching here which contradicts the plain teaching of Scripture to the effect that we must all be born again, that we all need a new nature, that we are all children of this world, and the children of Satan, until we become the children of God. Our Lord Himself teaches that, does He not? He gives power to all who receive Him to 'become' the children of God. That is the teaching everywhere in the Gospels, as it is the teaching of all the Epistles also. So, as we look at it like that, we see that it is an illustration to stress one great point only.

But there is another question. Does our Lord teach that it is our decision and action that saves us? 'Enter ye in at the strait gate', He seems to say, 'and if you do so, and walk along the narrow way, you will arrive at life; whereas if you enter in at the other you will land in destruction.' Does this teach, then, that a man saves himself by his decision and by his action?

Again we approach the problem in the same manner. We must always compare Scripture with Scripture, and realize that it never contradicts itself. And Scripture teaches that all are justified by faith, and saved by the death of the Lord Jesus Christ on our behalf. He came 'to seek and to save that which was lost.' 'There is none righteous, no, not one.' The whole world is guilty before God. No man by his own action can save himself; his righteousness is but as 'filthy rags'. We are all saved by the grace of the Lord Jesus Christ and by nothing that we do. Then what about this text? asks someone. The answer can be put in this form. I do not save myself by entering in at the strait gate, but by doing so I announce the fact that I am saved. The only man who does enter in at the strait gate is the man who is saved; the only people on the narrow way are those who are saved; otherwise they would not be there. 'The natural man receiveth not the things of the Spirit of God'; 'The carnal (natural) mind is enmity against God', and therefore against the narrow way. It is 'not subject to the law of God, neither indeed can be.' So no man, as he is, is ever going to choose to enter in at the strait gate because it is foolishness to him. No; what our Lord is saying here is this. It is not because I make myself 'poor in spirit' that I am 'blessed'; but when I become poor in spirit as the result of the working of the Holy Spirit upon me, I am truly blessed. By being and doing these things we proclaim what we are, we are announcing gladly and readily that we are His. It is only Christian people who are to be found along the narrow way, and you do not make yourself a Christian by entering in. You are entering in and walking upon it because you are saved.

We can put that the other way round; Does a failure to live the Christian life fully prove that we are on the broad way? We have spent time in considering the characteristics of the strait and the narrow way, and we have a clear picture of the Christian life everywhere in the Sermon on the Mount. But we fail in so many respects; we do not turn the other cheek, and so on. Does that mean, therefore, that we are still on the broad way? The answer is 'No'. No picture must be pressed in all its detail, otherwise, as we have seen so many times, it becomes ridiculous. The questions that have to be asked in the light of this text are these: Have you decided for this way of life? Have you committed yourself to it? Have you chosen it? Is this what you want to be? Is this what you are endeavouring to be? Is this the life you are hungering and thirsting after? If it is, I can assure you that you are in it. It is our Lord Himself who said, 'Blessed are they which do hunger and thirst after righteousness: for they shall be filled.' The man who hungers and thirsts after righteousness is not a man who is absolutely sinless and perfect. There is no such person in this life. What our Lord is saying in effect is, 'My people are the people who want to follow Me, those who are striving to do so.' They have entered in at the strait gate and are walking the narrow way. They often fail and fall into temptation but they are still on the way. Failure does not mean that they have gone back on to the broad way. You can fall on the narrow way. But if you realize that you have done so, and immediately confess and acknowledge your sin, He is 'faithful and just' to forgive you your sin and to cleanse you from all unrighteousness. John has put it all for us in the first chapter of his first Epistle: 'If we walk in the light, as he is in the light, we have fellowship one with another, and the blood of Jesus Christ his Son cleanseth us from all sin.' 'In him is no darkness at all'; but we stumble into sin and break the fellowship and communion. We are on the way still, but we have lost the communion. And we have nothing to do but to confess it, and at once the blood of Jesus Christ will cleanse us from that sin and every other unrighteousness. The communion is restored and we go on walking with Him. This picture of the narrow way is designed to stress and impress this one great principle — our desire, our ambition, our committal, our decision, our hungering and thirsting to be like Him, and to be walking with Him.

The last question is this. 'Wide is the gate, and broad is the way, that leadeth to destruction, and many there be which go in thereat: because strait is the gate, and narrow is the way, which leadeth unto life, and few there be that find it.' 'Does that mean,' says someone, 'that only a few are going to be saved? Are the vast majority of mankind to be damned?' I need do nothing by way of reply but give our Lord's answer to that question. People curious about theological problems, and who had often debated the question among themselves, came to our Lord one day (Luke 13:23), and asked, as their modern counterparts are so fond of asking, 'Are there few that be saved?' You remember our Lord's answer. He looked straight into the eyes of these philosophers, these speculative gentlemen, and said: 'Strive to enter in at the strait gate.' Leave a question like that to God; God, and God alone, knows how many are going to be saved. It is not your business or mine to discover how many are going to be saved. Our business is to strive to enter, to make certain that *we* are in it; and if we make certain that we are in it, one day in glory, and not until then, we shall find out how many companions we have. And it may very well be that we shall have a great surprise. But it is not our business now. Our business is to enter in, to strive to enter in, to make certain. Enter in, and you will find yourself amongst the saved, amongst those who are to be glorified, amongst all who look unto Jesus, 'the author and finisher of our faith'.

Chapter Twenty-two

False Prophets

IN verses 15 and 16, and to the end of this chapter, our Lord is concerned with just one great principle, one great message. He is emphasizing but one thing, the importance of entering in at the strait gate, and making quite certain that we are truly walking along the narrow way. In other words, it is a kind of enforcement of the message of verses 13 and 14. There He puts it in the form of an invitation or exhortation, that we are to enter in at this strait gate, and to walk and to keep on walking that narrow way. Here He elaborates that. He shows us some of the dangers, hindrances and obstacles that meet all who attempt to do that. But all along He keeps on emphasizing this vital principle, that the gospel is not just something to be listened to, or to be applauded, but ever to be applied. As James puts it, the danger is to look into the mirror, and immediately to forget what we have seen, instead of looking steadily into the mirror of that perfect law and remembering it and putting it into practice.

That is the theme our Lord continues to emphasize right until the end of the Sermon. First of all He puts it in the form of two particular and special dangers that confront us. He shows us how to recognize them and, having recognized them, how to deal with them. Then, having dealt with these two dangers, He winds up the argument, and the entire Sermon, by putting it in a plain, blunt, unvarnished statement in terms of the picture of the two houses, the one built upon the rock and the other upon the sand. But it is the same theme from beginning to end, and the thing that is common to the three divisions in the general statement is the terrible warning about the fact of judgment. That, as we have seen, is the theme right through this seventh chapter of Matthew's Gospel and it is most important that we should realize that. It is the failure to grasp this that accounts for most of our troubles and problems. It accounts for the light and superficial evangelism that is far too common today. It accounts also for the lack of holiness and sanctified living that is true of most of us. It is not that we need special teaching about these things. What we all seem to be forgetting is that the whole time the eye of God is upon us, and that we are all moving steadily and certainly in the direction of the final judgment.

So our Lord goes on repeating that. He puts it in different forms, but all along He emphasizes the fact of judgment, and the character of the judgment. It is not a superficial one, not a mere examination of the externals, but a searching of the heart, an examination of the whole nature. Above all He stresses the absolute finality of the judgment, and the consequences that follow upon it. He has already told us in verses 13 and 14 why we should enter in at the strait gate. The reason is, He says, that the other gate is a broad one which 'leadeth to destruction', the destruction that follows the final judgment upon the ungodly. Our Lord, clearly, was so concerned about this that He continually repeats it. This shows again the perfection of His method as a teacher. He knew the importance of repetition. He knew how dull we are, how slow we are, and how ready to think we know a thing, when in reality we do not, and how therefore we need to be reminded constantly of the same fact. We all know something of the difficulty of remembering these vital principles. People in past ages resorted to all sorts of means and methods to aid themselves in doing this. You find in many Anglican churches that the Ten Commandments were painted on the wall. It was their realization of the tendency to forget that led our forefathers to do that.

Our Lord, then, reminds us again of these things, first of all by putting before us two special warnings. The first is this one about the false prophets. 'Beware of false prophets, which come to you in sheep's clothing, but inwardly they are ravening wolves.' The picture which we should hold in our minds is something like this. Here we are, as it were, standing outside this strait gate. We have heard the Sermon, we have listened to the exhortation, and we are considering what to do about it. 'Now,' says our Lord in effect, 'at that point one of the things you have to beware of most especially is the danger of listening to false prophets. They are always there, they are always present, just outside that strait gate. That is their favourite stand. If you start listening to them you are entirely undone, because they will persuade you not to enter in at the strait gate and not to walk in the narrow way. They will try to dissuade you from listening to what I am saying.' So there is always the danger of the false prophet who comes with his particular subtle temptation.

The question that immediately arises for us is, What are these false prophets? Who are they, and how are they to be recognized? This is not as simple a question as it would appear to be. Its interpretation is one that is full of interest, indeed fascination. There have been two main schools of thought with regard to this statement about the false prophets, and some of the great names in the history of the Church are to be found on each side. The first is the school which says that this is a reference only to the teaching of the false prophets. 'Ye shall know them by their fruits', says our Lord, and the fruit, we are told, refers to teaching and doctrine, and to that alone. There are those who would confine the interpretation of the meaning of false prophets solely to that. Protestant expositors belonging to this group have generally thought of the Church of Rome as the supreme illustration of this.

The other group, however, disagrees entirely. It says that this reference to the false prophets really has nothing at all to do with teaching, that it is purely a question of the kind of life that these people live. A well-known expositor like Dr. Alexander MacLaren, for instance, says this: 'It is not a test to detect heretics, but rather to unmask hypocrites, and especially unconscious hypocrites.' His argument is, and there are many who follow him, that it has nothing to do with the teaching. The whole difficulty concerning these people is that their teaching is right, but their lives are wrong, and that they are not conscious that they are hypocrites.

There are, then, these two schools of thought, and obviously we have to face their different ways of explaining and expounding this statement. In the last analysis it does not matter very much which of the two we believe. Indeed, I suggest that they are both right and both wrong, and that the error is to say that the true exposition is either the one or the other. This is not to be guilty of compromise; but simply a way of saying that one cannot satisfactorily explain and expound this statement except by including the two elements. You cannot say that it is only a matter of teaching, and that it is a reference to heretical teaching only, for the reason that it is not really very difficult to detect such teaching. Most people who have any modicum of discrimination can detect a heretic. If a man came into a pulpit and seemed to be doubtful about the being of God, and denied the deity of Christ and the miracles, you would say that he was a heretic. There is not much difficulty about that, or anything very subtle about it. And yet, you notice, our Lord's picture suggests that there is a difficulty, and that there is something subtle about this. You notice the very terms in which He puts it, this picture of the sheep's clothing. He suggests that the real difficulty about this kind of false prophet is that at first you never imagine that he is such. The whole thing is extremely subtle, so much so that God's people can be misled by it. You notice how Peter puts it in the second chapter of his second Epistle. These people, he says, 'creep in unawares'. They look like the right people; they have sheep's clothing on, and no one suspects anything false. Now the Bible, in the Old Testament and in the New, always brings out that characteristic of the false prophet. It is his subtlety that really constitutes the danger. Any true exposition of this teaching, therefore, must give due weight to that particular element. For this reason, then, we cannot accept it as being merely a warning about heretics and their teaching. But the same thing applies to the other side. It is obviously not something outrageous in conduct. There again everybody could recognize it, and it would not be subtle, or constitute a difficulty.

The picture we need to have in our minds, therefore, should rather be this. The false prophet is a man who comes to us, and who at first has the appearance of being everything that could be desired. He is nice and pleasing and pleasant; he appears to be thoroughly Christian, and seems to say the right things. His teaching in general is quite all right and he uses many terms that should be used and employed by a true Christian teacher. He talks about God, he talks about Jesus Christ, he talks about the cross, he emphasizes the love of God, he seems to be saying everything that a Christian should say. He is obviously in sheep's clothing, and his way of living seems to correspond. So you do not suspect that there is anything wrong at all; there is nothing that at once attracts your attention or arouses your suspicion, nothing glaringly wrong. What then can be wrong, or may be wrong, with such a person? My suggestion is that finally this person may be wrong both in his teaching and in his type of life for, as we shall see, these two things are always indissolubly linked together. Our Lord puts it by saying, 'Ye shall know them by their fruits.' The teaching and the life can never be separated, and where there is wrong teaching in any shape or form it always leads to a wrong type of life in some respect.

How then can we describe these people? What is wrong with their teaching? The most convenient way of answering this is to say that there is no 'strait gate' in it, there is no 'narrow way' in it. As far as it goes it is all right, but it does not include this. It is a teaching, the falseness of which is to be detected by what it does *not* say rather than by what it *does* say. And it is just at this point that we realize the subtlety of the situation. As we have already seen, any Christian can detect the man who says outrageously wrong things; but is it unfair or uncharitable to say that the vast majority of Christians today do not seem to be able to detect the man who seems to say the right things but leaves out vital things? We have somehow got hold of the idea that error is only that which is outrageously wrong; and we do not seem to understand that the most dangerous person of all is the one who does not emphasize the right things.

That is the only way to understand rightly this picture of the false prophets. The false prophet is a man who has no 'strait gate' or 'narrow way' in his gospel. He has nothing which is offensive to the natural man; he pleases all. He is in 'sheep's clothing', so attractive, so pleasant, so nice to look at. He has such a nice and comfortable and comforting message. He pleases everybody and everybody speaks well of him. He is never persecuted for his preaching, he is never criticized severely. He is praised by the Liberals and Modernists, he is praised by the Evangelicals, he is praised by everybody. He is all things to all men in that sense; there is no 'strait gate' about him, there is no 'narrow way' in his message, there is none of 'the offence of the cross'.

If that is the description of the false prophet in general, let us put this question: What do we mean exactly by this 'strait gate' and 'narrow way'? What do we mean by saying that there is nothing offensive in his preaching? We can best answer this in terms of an Old Testament quotation. You remember how Peter argues in the second chapter of his second Epistle. He says, 'There were false prophets also among the people (the children of Israel in the Old Testament), even as there shall be false teachers among you.' So we must go back to the Old Testament and read what it says about the false prophets, because the type does not change. They were always there, and every time a true prophet like Jeremiah or someone else came along, the false prophets were always there to question him, and to resist him, and to denounce and ridicule him. But what were they like? This is how they are described: 'They have healed the hurt of the daughter of my people slightly (or lightly), saying, Peace, peace; when there is no peace.' The false prophet is always a very comforting preacher. As you listen to him he always gives you the impression that there is not very much wrong. He admits, of course, that there is a little; he is not fool enough to say that there is nothing wrong. But he says that all is well and will be well. 'Peace, peace,' he says. 'Don't listen to a man like Jeremiah,' he cries; 'he is narrow-minded, he is a heresy hunter, he is non-co-operative. Don't listen to him, it is all right.' 'Peace, peace.' Healing 'the hurt of the daughter of my people slightly, saying, Peace, peace; when there is no peace.' And, as the Old Testament adds devastatingly and with such terrifying truth about religious people then and now, 'my people like to have it so'. Because it never disturbs and never makes you feel uncomfortable. You carry on as you are, you are all right, you do not have to worry about the strait gate and the narrow way, or this particular doctrine or that. 'Peace, peace.' Very comforting, very reassuring always is the false prophet in his sheep's clothing; always harmless and nice, always, invariably, attractive.

In what way does this show itself in practice? I suggest that it does so generally by an almost entire absence of doctrine as a whole in its message. It always talks vaguely and generally; it never gets down to particularizing about doctrine. It does not like doctrinal preaching; it is always so vague. But someone may ask: 'What do you mean by this particularizing about doctrine, and where do the strait gate and the narrow way come in?' The answer is that the false prophet very rarely tells you anything about the holiness, the righteousness, the justice, and the wrath of God. He always preaches about the love of God, but those other things he does not mention. He never makes anyone tremble as he thinks of this holy and august Being with whom we all have to do. He does not say that he does not believe these truths. No; that is not the difficulty. The difficulty with him is that he says nothing about them. He just does not mention them at all. He generally emphasizes one truth about God only, and that is love. He does not mention the other truths that are equally prominent in the Scriptures; and that is where the danger lies. He does not say things that are obviously wrong, but he refrains from saying things that are obviously right and true. And that is why he is a false prophet. To conceal the truth is as reprehensible and as damnable as to proclaim an utter heresy; and that is why the effect of such teaching is that of a 'ravening wolf'. It is so pleasing, but it can lead men to destruction because it has never confronted them with the holiness and the righteousness and the justice and the wrath of God.

Another doctrine which the false prophet never emphasizes is that of the final judgment and the eternal destiny of the lost. There has not been much preaching about the Last Judgment in the last fifty or sixty years, and very little preaching about hell and the 'everlasting destruction' of the wicked. No, the false prophets do not like teaching such as you have in the second Epistle of Peter. They have tried to deny its authenticity because it does not fit in with their doctrine. They say that such a chapter should not be in the Bible. It is so strong, it is so blasting; and yet there it is. And it is not an isolated case. There are others. Read the Epistle of Jude, read the so-called gentle apostle of love, the apostle John, in his first Epistle, and you will find the same thing. But it is here also in this Sermon on the Mount. It comes out of the mouth of our Lord Himself. It is He who talks about the false prophets in sheep's clothing that are ravening wolves; it is He who describes them as rotten, evil trees. He deals with the judgment in exactly the same way as did Paul when he preached to Felix and Drusilla of 'righteousness, temperance, and judgment to come'.

In the same way the false prophet's teaching does not emphasize the utter sinfulness of sin and the total inability of man to do anything about his own salvation. It often does not really believe in sin at all, and certainly does not emphasize its vile nature. It does not say that we are all perfect; but it does suggest that sin is not serious. Indeed, it does not like to talk about sin; it talks only about individual or particular sins. It does not talk about the fallen nature, or say that man himself in his totality is fallen, lost and depraved. It does not like to talk about the solidarity of the whole of mankind in sin, and the fact that we have 'all sinned and come short of the glory of God'. It does not emphasize this doctrine of the 'exceeding sinfulness of sin' as you find it in the New Testament. And it does not emphasize the fact that man is 'dead in trespasses and sins', and utterly helpless and hopeless. It does not like that; it does not see the necessity of doing that. What I am emphasizing is that the false prophet does not say these things, so that an innocent believer listening to him assumes that he believes them. The question that arises concerning such teachers is, do they believe these things? The answer, obviously, is that they do not, otherwise they would feel compelled to preach and to teach them.

Then there is the expiatory aspect of the atonement, and the substitutionary death of the Lord Jesus Christ. The false prophet talks about 'Jesus'; he even delights to talk about the cross and the death of Jesus. But the vital question is, What is his view of that death? What is his view of that cross? There are views being taught which are utterly heretical and a denial of the Christian faith. The one test is this: Does he realize that Christ died on the cross because it was the only way to make expiation and propitiation for sin? Does he really believe that Christ was there crucified as a substitute for him, that He was bearing 'in his own body on the tree' his guilt and the punishment of his guilt and sin? Does he believe that if God had not punished his sin there in the body of Christ on the cross, I say it with reverence, then even God could not have forgiven him? Does he believe that it was only by setting forth His own Son as a propitiation for our sins on the cross that God could be 'just, and the justifier of him which believeth in Jesus' (Rom. 3:25, 26)? Merely to talk about Christ and the cross is not enough. Is it the biblical doctrine of the substitutionary penal atonement? That is the way to test the false prophet. The false prophet does not say these things. He talks around the cross. He talks about the people round the cross and sentimentalizes about our Lord. He does not know anything about Paul's 'offence of the cross'. His preaching of the cross is not 'foolishness to the Greeks', it is not a 'stumbling block to the Jew'. He has made the cross 'of none effect through his philosophy'. He has made it a rather beautiful thing, a wonderful philosophy of love and heartbreak because of a world that is not interested. He has never seen it as a tremendous, holy transaction between the Father and the Son in which the Father has 'made' the Son to be 'sin for us', and has laid our iniquity upon Him. There is none of that in his preaching and teaching, and that is why it is false.

In the same way it does not emphasize repentance in any real sense. It has a very wide gate leading to salvation and a very broad way leading to heaven. You need not feel much of your own sinfulness; you need not be aware of the blackness of your own heart. You just 'decide for Christ' and you rush in with the crowd, and your name is put down, and is one of the large number of 'decisions' reported by the press. It is entirely unlike the evangelism of the Puritans and of John Wesley, George Whitefield and others, which led men to be terrified of the judgment of God, and to have an agony of soul sometimes for days and weeks and months. John Bunyan tells us in his *Grace Abounding* that he endured an agony of repentance for eighteen months. There does not seem to be much room for that today. Repentance means that you realize that you are a guilty, vile sinner in the presence of God, that you deserve the wrath and punishment of God, that you are hell-bound. It means that you begin to realize that this thing called sin is in you, that you long to get rid of it, and that you turn your back on it in every shape and form. You renounce the world whatever the cost, the world in its mind and outlook as well as its practice, and you deny yourself, and take up the cross and go after Christ. Your nearest and dearest, and the whole world, may call you a fool, or say you have religious mania. You may have to suffer financially, but it makes no difference. That is repentance. The false prophet does not put it like that. He heals 'the hurt of the daughter of my people slightly', simply saying that it is all right, and that you have but to 'come to Christ', 'follow Jesus', or 'become a Christian'.

Finally, therefore, we can put it like this. The false prophet does not emphasize the absolute necessity of entering this strait gate and walking along this narrow way. He does not tell us that we must practise this Sermon. If we only listen to it without practising it we are damned; if we only comment on it, without carrying it out, it will rise in judgment against us and condemn us. The false teaching is not interested in true holiness, in biblical holiness. It holds on to an idea of holiness such as the Pharisees had. You remember that they picked out certain sins of which they were not guilty themselves, as they thought, and said that as long as you were not guilty of those you were all right. Alas, how many Pharisees there are today! Holiness has just become a question of not doing three or four things. We no longer think of it in terms of 'love not the world, neither the things that are in the world . . . the lust of the flesh, and the lust of the eyes, and the pride of life' (1 John 2:15, 16). 'The pride of life' is one of the greatest curses in the Christian Church. The false teaching desires a holiness like that of the Pharisees. It is just a question of not doing certain things that we ourselves have agreed upon because they do not happen to appeal to us in particular. Thus we have reduced holiness into something that is easy, and we crowd into that broad way and try to practise it.

Those are some of the characteristics of these false prophets that come to us in sheep's clothing. They offer an easy salvation, and an easy type of life always.

They discourage self-examination; indeed, they almost feel that to examine oneself is heresy. They tell you not to examine your own soul. You must always 'look to Jesus', and never at yourself, that you may discover your sin. They discourage what the Bible encourages us to do, to 'examine' ourselves, to 'prove our own selves', and to face this last section of the Sermon on the Mount. They dislike the process of self-examination and mortification of sin as taught by the Puritans, and those great leaders of the eighteenth century — not only Whitefield and Wesley and Jonathan Edwards, but also the saintly John Fletcher, who put twelve questions to himself every night as he retired to bed. It does not believe in that, for that is uncomfortable. It is an easy salvation and easy Christian living. It knows nothing about Paul's feeling, when he says 'we that are in this tabernacle do groan, being burdened'. It does not know anything about fighting 'the good fight of faith'. It does not know what Paul means when he says that 'we wrestle not against flesh and blood, but against principalities, against powers, against the rulers of the darkness of this world, against spiritual wickedness in high places' (Eph. 6:12). It does not understand that. It does not see any need for the whole armour of God, because it has not seen the problem. It is all so easy.

We do not like this kind of teaching against false prophets today. We are living in days when people say that, as long as a man claims to be a Christian at all, we should regard him as a brother and go on together. But the reply is that our Lord said, 'Beware of false prophets.' These awful, glaring warnings are there in the New Testament because of the very kind of thing to which I have been referring. Of course, we must not be censorious; but neither must we mistake friendliness and affability for saintliness. It is not a question of personalities. We must not despise these people. Indeed, Dr. Alexander MacLaren is right when he says that they are unconscious hypocrites. It is not that they are not nice and pleasing; they are. In a sense that is their greatest danger, and that is what makes them such a source of danger. I am emphasizing this matter because, according to our Lord, we should always be facing it. There is a way that leads to 'destruction', and the false prophet does not believe in 'destruction'.

Is it not true to say that the explanation of the present state of the Christian Church is this very thing we have been considering? Why has the Church become so weak and ineffective? I have no hesitation in answering and saying that it is due to the type of preaching that came in as the result of the higher critical movement of the last century, and which utterly condemned doctrinal preaching. Its advocates preached morality and general uplift. They took their illustrations from literature and poetry, and Emerson became one of the High Priests. That is the cause of the trouble. They still talked about God; they still talked about Jesus; they still talked about His death on the cross. They did not stand out as obvious heretics; but they did not say those other things that are vital to salvation. They gave this vague message that never upsets anybody. They were so pleasant and 'modern' and up-to-date. They suited the popular palate, and the result is not only the empty churches about which we are hearing so much at the present time, but, as we shall see, the poor quality of Christian living of which most of us are so guilty. These things are distasteful and unpleasant, and whether you believe me or not, in honesty I have to confess that if I had not pledged myself to preach like this through the Sermon on the Mount, I would never have chosen these words as a text. I have never preached on it before. I have never heard a sermon on it. I wonder how many of you have done so? It is not liked; it is unpleasant; but our business is not to choose what we like. It is the Son of God who said this, and He puts it into the context of judgment and of destruction. So, at the risk of causing myself to be known as a heresy hunter, or as a peculiar person who is sitting in judgment on his brethren and everybody else, I have tried honestly to explain the Scripture. And I ask you to consider it again prayerfully in the presence of God as you value your own immortal soul and its eternal destiny.

Chapter Twenty-three

The Tree and the Fruit

OUR previous examination of this difficult paragraph 7:15-20 emphasized particularly the element of subtlety in the false prophets, those men who come to us in sheep's clothing, but who inwardly are ravening wolves. To many people this is a difficult section because of its context, because it comes after those words: 'Judge not, that ye be not judged. For with what judgment ye judge, ye shall be judged.' Yet these words were uttered by our Lord Himself. The false prophets are always unhappy about certain statements of our Lord. They are never happy about Matthew 23, for example, where our Lord described the Pharisees as 'whited sepulchres'. Our modern false prophets try to find nice things to say even about the Pharisees. The sheep's clothing prophet teaches that we must never say anything which is at all critical or severe. But the words are uttered by our Lord Himself, therefore we must face them. Again, let us repeat, we must avoid censoriousness; but we cannot expound the Sermon on the Mount fully unless we face them, and try to deal with them quite honestly, realizing as we do so that we are setting up a standard by which we ourselves shall be judged.

Our Lord, clearly, was concerned to emphasize this matter. He has said that the false prophets are to be known by their fruits, and then He goes on to elaborate this by drawing this further picture. He says, 'Do men gather grapes of thorns, or figs of thistles? Even so every good tree bringeth forth good fruit; but a corrupt tree bringeth forth evil fruit. A good tree cannot bring forth evil fruit, neither can a corrupt tree bring forth good fruit. Every tree that bringeth not forth good fruit is hewn down, and cast into the fire. Wherefore by their fruits ye shall know them.' You notice He starts and ends with 'Ye shall know them by their fruits', and 'Wherefore by their fruits ye shall know them' — repetition for the sake of emphasis.

First we must be quite clear on one purely technical point, and that is the meaning of this word 'corrupt'. 'Every good tree bringeth forth good fruit; but a corrupt tree bringeth forth evil fruit.' 'Corrupt', of course, does not mean rotten, because a decayed or rotten tree does not bring forth fruit at all. That is very important, because if we fail to notice it we shall again be missing this element of subtlety which is the main thing in our Lord's emphasis. He is calling attention to the fact that trees which resemble each other in that they look perfectly all right, do not of necessity produce the same kind of fruit. One tree may produce good fruit, the other tree may produce poor fruit. What is called 'evil fruit' does not mean entirely 'rotten' either; it, means it is poor in quality, it is not good fruit. So the contrast which our Lord brings out is between two types of tree which to look at may be almost identical, but which, when you come to judge the fruit, you find to be entirely different. One you can use, and the other you cannot. Clearly there is very profound teaching here. Having considered the question of the doctrine we can now come to the matter of the life, the conduct and the behaviour.

Before, however, we come to the details we must emphasize the great principle which our Lord is here inculcating. It is that to be a Christian is something central to personality, something vital and fundamental. It is not a matter of appearance on the surface either with regard to belief or life. In using this picture of the character, the nature, the real essence of these trees and the fruit which they produce, our Lord is placing very great emphasis upon that. And surely this is the point which we must always be looking for in ourselves and in others. He seems to be drawing attention to the danger of being misled by appearances. It is precisely the same as in that other figure of the false prophets which come to us in sheep's clothing. In other words, it is the danger of appearing to be Christian without really being so. We have already seen that that can happen in the matter of teaching and doctrine. A man may appear to be preaching the gospel when, in reality, and as judged by the true tests, he is not doing so at all. It is exactly the same with regard to conduct and life. The danger here is to try to make ourselves Christian by adding certain things to our lives, instead of *becoming* something new, instead of receiving life within, instead of the very nature which is within us being renewed after the image of the Lord Jesus Christ Himself.

The whole emphasis in our Lord's teaching here is upon the man himself, and He is really saying that what matters in the last analysis is just that. A man may speak in the right way, he may apparently live in the right way, and yet, according to our Lord, he may be a false prophet the whole time. He may be assuming the appearance of the Christian life without really being Christian. This has been a constant source of trouble and of danger in the long history of the

Christian Church. But our Lord has warned us right at the beginning that we must grasp this principle, that to be a Christian means a change in a man's very life and nature. It is the doctrine of the rebirth. No man's service is of any value unless his nature is changed. We shall presently be dealing with that statement: 'Many will say to me in that day, Lord, Lord, have we not prophesied in thy name? and in thy name have cast out devils? and in thy name done many wonderful works?' There we are looking at a man who has been doing many things in his life; but he himself is not changed. He was saying and doing the right things, but they are of no value.

Exactly the same thing can happen with life and conduct. Christianity is unique in this respect, that it is concerned primarily about the state of the heart. And in Scripture the heart is generally not the seat of the emotions, but the centre of the personality. Take, for instance, Matthew 12:33-37. There, surely, our Lord puts it quite clearly and specifically: 'Either make the tree good, and his fruit good; or else make the tree corrupt, and his fruit corrupt: for the tree is known by his fruit.' The emphasis is again upon the character or the nature of the tree. 'It is that', He says in another place, 'which cometh out of the heart that defiles a man'. It is not merely the things you do on the surface; it is not a question of washing the outside of the cups and the platters; it is not that which goes in, it is that which comes out; it is the man himself that really counts. Our Lord is at great pains to emphasize in this picture that what is in the centre of the heart is certain to proclaim itself. It will proclaim itself in its beliefs, in its teaching and doctrine. It will proclaim itself also in its life. It is not always easy to see that, but our Lord tells us that if we have eyes illuminated by the teaching of the New Testament, we shall always be able to recognize it. We saw about doctrine, for instance, that if you only watch to see whether a man is going to say things that are outrageously wrong you will probably never detect the false prophets because they do not say such things. But if you realize that there are certain things a true Christian must always emphasize, and if you watch for them, then you will discover that they are omitted, and you will see that the man you thought was a Christian is really a false prophet, and therefore a grievous danger. It is exactly the same with regard to the life. We can show this in a number of principles.

The first principle is that there is an indissoluble link between belief and life — the nature will out. That which a man is ultimately in the depths is always going to reveal and manifest itself, and it does so in belief and life. The two things are indissolubly linked together. As a man thinks, so eventually he is. As a man thinks, so he does. In other words, we inevitably proclaim what we are and what we believe. It does not matter how careful we are, it is bound to come out. Nature must express itself. You do not get 'grapes of thorns' or 'figs of thistles'; 'a good tree cannot bring forth evil fruit, neither can a corrupt tree bring forth good fruit.' You are not in the realm of appearances; you are now examining in a more critical manner. Our Lord lays these things down as absolutes; and if we observe ourselves and others, and the whole of life carefully, we must agree that this is perfectly true.

We may be deceived for a while. Appearances can be very deceptive, as we all know; but they do not last. The Puritans were very fond of dealing at great length with what they called 'temporary believers'. They meant by that, people who seemed to come under the influence of the gospel, and who gave the appearance of being truly and soundly converted and regenerate. Such people said the right things and there was a change in their lives; they appeared to be Christian. But the Puritans called them 'temporary believers' because those people gave clear, unmistakable evidence afterwards that they had never truly become Christian at all. That kind of thing often happens during revivals. Whenever there is a religious awakening, or any religious excitement, you generally find people who are, as it were, carried along by the flood. They do not know quite what is happening, but they come under the general influence of the Holy Spirit and are clearly affected for the time being. But, according to this teaching, they may never become truly Christian.

There is a discussion of this in 2 Peter 2 where the apostle describes such cases clearly and graphically. He talks about certain people who had come into the Church and had been accepted as Christians, but who had gone out. He describes them in these terms. 'The dog is turned to his own vomit again, and the sow that was washed to her wallowing in the mire.' You see what has happened. To use his illustration, even the sow can be washed, and can appear to be clean on the surface; but there is no change in nature. This becomes yet clearer when we compare it with what the apostle Peter says in verse 4 of chapter 1 of that same Epistle. He says that the Christian has been 'delivered from the corruption that is in the world through lust'. But when he comes to these temporary believers in the second chapter he says that they have been washed from — not 'the corruption', but 'the pollution'. There is a kind of superficial cleansing which does not change the nature. Washing is of real value, but it can be very misleading. A man who has washed on the surface only may give all the appearance of being a Christian. But our Lord's argument is that what really decides whether he is one or not is the nature within. And that nature within is bound to express itself.

You may have to wait before you can see any true evidence. God sees it from the beginning, but we are very slow to see these things. But what a man is, he is bound to show. He will show it in his teaching for certain, he will show it in his life also. It is quite inevitable. We can say, therefore, that true Christian belief must of necessity produce that characteristic type of living. That is, surely, the meaning of this question: 'Do men gather grapes of thorns, or figs of thistles?' These things can never be separated; the inner nature is bound to express itself. A man's final belief is bound to manifest itself, sooner or later, in his life. We must be careful, therefore, that we do not mistake for the real thing that which looks like true Christianity, but which is in reality merely sham and only outward appearance. The exhortation is that we should teach and discipline ourselves always to look carefully for the fruit.

We must now consider in detail the nature or the character of the good fruit. We must look for it in ourselves and in others. We must be very careful because there are people standing outside the narrow and strait gate, who say to us, 'You need not do all that. This is the way'. And we can be misled by them. Therefore we must learn to discriminate; and once more, as we come to examine the fruit, we must bear this element of subtlety in mind. There are types of life which can closely simulate true Christianity, and they are obviously the most dangerous of all. It seems more and more clear that the greatest enemies of the true Christian faith are not those who are right out in the world militantly persecuting Christianity, or flagrantly ignoring its teaching; but rather those who have a false and spurious Christianity. They are the people who will receive the condemnation which our Lord pronounces here on the false prophet. If you look at the history of the Church throughout the centuries you will find that this has always proved to be the case. It is a false and counterfeit Christianity that has always been a hindrance to, and the greatest enemy of, true spirituality. And surely the greatest trouble at this present moment is the worldly state of the Church. We should be much more concerned about the state of the Church herself than about the state of the world outside the Church. It seems increasingly evident that the explanation of the present state of Christendom is to be found inside the Church and not outside. We must bear in mind the question of the subtlety of this whole matter, and therefore we must apply certain delicate tests.

The tests can be both general and particular. Here we are, as it were, looking at someone who makes a profession of Christianity. He does not say anything obviously wrong, and appears to be living a good Christian life. How do we test such a person? You can have good, ethical, moral people with a high code and standard of personal life and living, who look remarkably like Christians but who may not be Christian at all. How do you tell the difference? Here are some of the questions for which you must seek an answer. First of all, why is the man living this sort of life? Take the case of a modern good man who makes no pretence of Christianity, or that of a man who attends a place of worship regularly but who, as judged by New Testament standards, is not a Christian. Why do they live as they do? There are many reasons for this. It may be purely a matter of temperament. There are certain people who have been born nice. They have an equable temperament and character; they are quiet, there is nothing naturally vicious or offensive about them. They have to make no effort to be like this; they were born like that, it is the kind of person they are. It is something purely physical and natural.

Secondly, does this man live this kind of life because he holds certain beliefs or subscribes to certain moral teaching? There are men, in other words, who are what may be called good pagans. They are admirably delineated and analysed in a book called *The Failure of the Good Pagan,* by Rosalind Murray. Such men have very high standards, and they live up to them in their daily practice. A man may do all that quite apart from Christianity. So if you are going to judge merely by the general appearances of a man's life and living then obviously you may well be deceived. It is often said that there are better Christians outside the Christian Church than inside. What that means is that you may find good morality outside the Church. But good morality may have nothing to do with Christianity. It has no essential connection with it. Greek pagan philosophers propounded their great moral teaching before Christ came. Still more significantly, Greek philosophers were sometimes the most bitter opponents of the Christian gospel; they were the very men who regarded the preaching of the cross as 'foolishness'.

So you do not merely look at the man and his life in general. You must try to discover reasons and motives for his actions. From the Christian standpoint there is only one vital test at this point. Does this man give the impression that he is living this sort of life because he is a Christian and because of his Christian faith? If he does not live this life because he is a Christian there is no value in it; it is what our Lord calls corrupt fruit. The Old Testament puts it very strongly when it says: 'All our righteousnesses are as filthy rags'. It was righteousness in the world's eyes, but it was as filthy rags in the sight of God. It is only that which is the outcome of Christian character, and springs from the new nature, which is of any value ultimately in the sight of God.

There then is our general test. Let us now look at certain particular tests. Here we must be careful lest again we expose ourselves to the charge of censoriousness, and we must be fully aware that what we are saying is a judgment upon ourselves. The particular tests of this life are both negative and positive. By negative we mean that if a man is not a true Christian, and if he has not the true Christian doctrine, we shall inevitably find somewhere in his life a certain slackness, a certain failure to conform to the true Christian character. He does not do anything outrageously wrong. We cannot convict him of drunkenness or murder, etc. But unless a man believes those essential tenets of the Christian faith which we emphasized earlier we shall find a slackness somewhere in his life. If a man is not conscious of the utter, absolute holiness of God and the exceeding sinfulness of sin, if he does not see that the real message of the cross of Calvary is that all man's righteousness is worthless and that he is an utter, helpless, foul sinner, he is going to show this in his life. It is bound to show, and in fact it does, though he may conform to a general moral code. There is always somewhere in a man who rejects this high doctrine of salvation a failure to walk the narrow way, and a conformity at some point or other to the world and its outlook. His way of life may look remarkably like the Christian's, but if you watch and observe it in detail you will find that it fails. It is very difficult to put this in a clear and explicit manner. There are certain people about whom all you can say is that, while you find nothing wrong with them in particular, you nevertheless feel that they are wrong centrally. You cannot find anything specific to condemn but at the same time you feel that their outlook is secular and not spiritual, that though they never do anything that is outrageously worldly, their whole attitude is worldly. There is in them a lack of tone and an absence of that peculiar 'aura' which is always present in the man who is truly spiritual.

But, to put it positively, what we look for in anybody who claims to be Christian is evidence of the Beatitudes. The test of fruit is never negative, it is positive. Certain apples may look all right, but you begin to eat them and you will find that they are sour. Now that is the positive kind of test. A true Christian must exemplify the Beatitudes, because you do not get grapes from thorns or figs from thistles. A good tree must bring forth good fruit; it cannot help itself, it is bound to. A man who has the divine nature within himself must produce this good fruit, the good fruit which is described in the Beatitudes. He is poor in spirit, he mourns because of sin, he is meek, he hungers and thirsts after righteousness, he is a peacemaker, he is pure in heart, and so on.

These are some of the tests, and they are tests which always exclude the 'good pagan'. They also always exclude false prophets and temporary believers, because these are the tests of a man's ultimate nature and his real being. Or it can be put in terms of the fruit of the Spirit described in Galatians 5. The fruit that is formed in us and manifests itself is love, joy, peace, long-suffering, gentleness, goodness, meekness, temperance, faith — that is the fruit, and that is what we must look for in a man's life. It is not found in the man who is just morally good: this is the fruit that only a good tree produces. A Christian can generally be known by his very appearance. The man who really believes in the holiness of God, and who knows his own sinfulness and the blackness of his own heart, the man who believes in the judgment of God and the possibility of hell and torment, the man who really believes that he himself is so vile and helpless that nothing but the coming of the Son of God from heaven to earth, and His going to the bitter shame and agony and cruelty of the cross could ever save him, and reconcile him to God — this man is going to show all that in his whole personality. He is a man who is bound to give the impression of meekness, he is bound to be humble. Our Lord reminds us here that if a man is not humble, we are to be very wary of him. He can put on a kind of sheep's clothing, but that is not true humility, that is not true meekness. And if a man's doctrine is wrong, it will generally show itself at this point. He will be affable and pleasant, he will appeal to the natural man, and to the things that are physical and carnal; but he will not give the impression of being a man who has seen himself as a hell-bound sinner, and who has been saved by the grace of God alone. Truth within must of necessity affect a man's appearance. The New Testament man is a sober man, he is grave and humble, he is a meek man. He has the joy of the Lord in his heart, yes, but he is not effusive, he is not boisterous, he is not carnal in his life. He is a man who says with Paul, 'We that are in this tabernacle do groan, being burdened' (2 Cor. 5:4). To say and to believe that is bound to affect the whole man, even his very dress as well as his demeanour. He is not interested in pomp and show and externalities, he is not interested in making an impression; he is meek and concerned about God and his relationship to Him, and the truth of God.

The ultimate test of all, however, is humility. If we have the pride of life and of the world in us, of necessity we do not know much about the truth; and we should examine ourselves again to make sure that we have the new nature within us. What is within is going to show itself. If I am a worldly minded person, though I may preach a great doctrine, though I may have given up certain things, it will come out in my 'idle speech'. Our Lord says that we shall be judged by our 'idle words' (see Matt. 12:36). It is when we are off guard that we really show what we are. We can make ourselves appear to be Christian; but it is what comes out suddenly that reveals our real nature. So everything about this man is going to proclaim what he is. The way in which a man preaches is often much more significant than what he says, because the way in which he speaks displays what the man really is. A man's methods sometimes deny the message that he is preaching. A man who preaches judgment and salvation and yet laughs and jokes is denying his own doctrine. Self-confidence, self-assertion, reliance upon human ability and 'personality', proclaim that the man has a nature within him which is far removed from that of the Son of God who was 'meek and lowly in heart'. Such a man is unlike the apostle Paul, who when he was preaching in Corinth did not come to them with self-confidence and self-assertion, but 'in weakness, and in fear, and in much trembling'. How we give ourselves away, how we proclaim by our unguarded actions what we really are!

Finally we must remember that whatever we may think of these things, and however wrongly we may judge, and however much we may be deceived by false prophets, God is the judge, and God is never deceived. 'Every tree therefore which bringeth not forth good fruit is hewn down, and cast into the fire.' God have mercy upon us. May He awaken us to these vital principles, and enable us to exercise this discrimination with regard to our selves, and with regard to all others who may be a danger to our souls, and who are grievously misrepresenting the cause of our blessed Lord in this sinful and needy world. Let us concentrate upon being certain that we have the divine nature, that we are partakers of it, that the tree is good; because if the tree is good, the fruit also must of necessity be good.

Chapter Twenty-four

False Peace

W E consider now the section 7:21-23. These, surely, are in many ways the
most solemn and solemnizing words ever uttered in this world, not only
by any man, but even by the Son of God Himself. Indeed, were any man to utter
such words we should feel compelled not only to criticize but even to condemn
him. But they are words spoken by the Son of God Himself, and therefore demand our most earnest attention. How often, I wonder, have we considered
them, or heard a sermon on them? Must we not all plead guilty to the fact that,
though we claim to believe the whole of Scripture, in practice we frequently
deny much of it by ignoring it, simply because it does not pander to the flesh, or
because it disturbs us. But if we really believe that this is the Word of God, we
must consider it all; and especially must we be careful to avoid those specious
arguments by which certain people endeavour to avoid the plain teaching of
Scripture. These words are extremely solemn, and the only way in which we can
consider them truly is to do so in the light of the fact that a day is coming 'when
all earthly scenes shall pass away'. It is a word addressed to men and women
who are conscious of the fact that they will have to stand before God in final
judgment.

It is clear that in this paragraph our Lord is continuing the theme with
which He dealt in the previous paragraph, where He warned the people against
false prophets. To our Lord this is such a desperately serious matter that He
comes back to it again. He is not content with one warning. He has really finished the teaching of the Sermon, and has worked it out in great detail. Now He
is applying it. He began the application in the exhortation about entering in at
the strait gate, and walking in the narrow way. But He is so concerned that none
should be misled about this matter that He repeats the warning time and again.

Having shown us the subtlety of the false prophets in His two remarkable analogies, our Lord now makes His warning concerning that matter still more explicit. This time it is even more blunt than the previous one, and our Lord undoubtedly puts it like this because of the desperate seriousness of the matter and the terrible danger that confronts us at this point. His method, you observe, is the same as it has been right through the Sermon on the Mount. He starts always by making a blunt assertion, then He takes it up and illustrates, elaborates and amplifies it. That is exactly what we have in this particular paragraph. First of all He says, 'Not every one that saith unto me, Lord, Lord, shall enter into the kingdom of heaven; but he that doeth the will of my Father which is in heaven.' That is the proposition. But then He goes on to illustrate and elaborate it. 'Many will say to me in that day, Lord, Lord,' etc.

The most important thing from the standpoint of exposition is that we should take these two parts together, that we should not isolate verse 21 from verses 22 and 23, as some have been tempted to do, but that we take all these verses together and regard them as the laying down of the proposition, and the demonstration of its implication. The importance of doing so is seen when we are reminded that certain people, taking verse 21 on its own, have argued that what our Lord is really teaching there is that, in the last analysis, what matters is not so much what a man believes as what he does. It is a quotation often used by people who like to put up faith and works as opposites. They ask: 'Did not He say, "Not every one that saith unto me, Lord, Lord, shall enter into the kingdom of heaven; but he that doeth the will of my Father which is in heaven"?' The emphasis, they maintain, is upon the doing. And then they propound their whole doctrine of salvation by works. 'Some people', they say, 'are always concerned about doctrine, and everlastingly talking about it; but it is not a man's doctrine, but what he does, that really matters'. They misuse verse 21 in that way because they isolate it from verses 22 and 23. But the moment you put them together you see that the object of the statement cannot be to contrast belief and works, because our Lord says about the works in verses 22 and 23 precisely what He says about the belief in verses 21 and 22. It is important, therefore, to take the text in its context and not to isolate it.

No, the message here is not to emphasize works at the expense of belief; it is something much more serious than that. It is, rather, to open our eyes again to the terrible danger of self-deception and self-delusion. That is what our Lord is concerned about here. It was the same general theme in the previous paragraph. There the danger was considered in terms of our being misled by the false prophets because of their sheep's clothing, and the attractive character of their doctrine which is so deceiving, and so subtle. Here, our Lord proceeds to show us the same thing, not now in the false prophets, but in ourselves. It is the danger, the terrible danger of self-deception and self-delusion. Or, to put it positively, our Lord is emphasizing once more that nothing avails in the presence of God but true righteousness, true holiness, the 'holiness, without which no man shall see the Lord' (Heb. 12:14). And if our idea of justification by faith does not include that, it is not the scriptural teaching, it is a dangerous delusion. Scripture, it must be repeated again, must be taken as a whole, and our Lord at this point is simply warning us that whatever we may say or do, we cannot stand in the presence of God if we are not truly righteous and holy. It is what Scripture teaches from beginning to end. It is the teaching of the Lord Himself; it is not human legalism. He is showing once more what true faith really means, and He does so in a new way.

We can put it like this. Our Lord shows us some of the false and wrong things on which men tend to rely. He gives us a list of them. First we shall work through this list; then later we can consider the general lessons and principles which can be deduced from this detailed teaching. But we are bound to face squarely the things which our Lord puts before us for our consideration. The general principle behind the teaching is that self-deception with regard to the soul and its relationship to God is generally due to our relying upon false evidences of salvation. Or, to put it in another way, our Lord shows us what is actually possible in the experience of a man who is finally reprobate and damned. That is the alarming thing. He shows us that a man can get so far and yet be altogether wrong. It is certainly one of the most astounding statements that is to be found anywhere in the Scriptures.

The first piece of false evidence on which some people tend to rest is rather surprising. It is none else than a correct belief. 'Not every one that saith unto me, Lord, Lord, shall enter into the kingdom of heaven; but he that doeth the will of my Father which is in heaven.' There are certain people, says our Lord in effect, who say to Me, 'Lord, Lord', and yet they shall never enter the kingdom of heaven. We must handle this very carefully. He is not criticizing people for saying: 'Lord, Lord'. Everybody should say: 'Lord, Lord'. He is referring to people who are right in their doctrine concerning His nature and about His Person, to people who have recognized Him, and who come to Him, and say 'Lord, Lord'. They say the right things to Him, they believe the right things about Him. Our Lord is not criticizing them for that. What He is saying is that not everyone who does say that shall enter the kingdom of heaven.

The negative is very important at this point. A man who does not say 'Lord, Lord' shall never enter the kingdom of heaven. That is, of course, the starting-point in this whole question of salvation. No man is a Christian unless he says 'Lord, Lord' to the Lord Jesus Christ. Paul says that no man can say that apart from the Holy Spirit (1 Cor. 12:3). Orthodoxy, in other words, is absolutely essential. So what we have here is not a criticism of orthodoxy; it cannot possibly be. But it is a statement of the fact that, if you rely only upon your orthodoxy, you may be damned. Orthodoxy is absolutely vital and essential. Unless we believe that Jesus of Nazareth is indeed the Son of God, unless we recognize Him as the eternal Son, 'substance of the eternal substance', made flesh and dwelling amongst us, unless we believe the New Testament doctrine that He was sent by God to be the Messiah, the Saviour of the world, and that because of that He has been exalted and is Lord of all, to whom every knee shall eventually bow, we are not Christian at all (see Phil. 2:5-11). We *must* believe that. To be a Christian is primarily a matter of believing certain truths concerning the Lord Jesus Christ; in other words, believing on Him. There is no such thing as Christianity apart from that. To be a Christian means that we rest our entire case, our whole salvation, our whole eternal destiny entirely upon the Lord Jesus Christ. That is why a true Christian says, 'Lord, Lord'; that is the content of the statement. It does not just mean saying the right words, it indicates that we mean those things when we say them.

But the alarming and terrifying thing which our Lord says is that not everyone who does say 'Lord, Lord', shall enter into the kingdom of heaven. Those who do go in say it; anyone who does not say it can never enter into the kingdom of heaven; but not all who do say it shall enter in. This is clearly something that should arrest us and cause us to pause. James, in his Epistle, puts the very same point. He warns us to be careful against merely relying upon our belief of certain things, and he puts it like this in a rather startling manner by saying, 'The devils also believe, and tremble' (James 2:19). An instance of this is found in the Gospels where we read that certain devils recognized Him and said 'Lord, Lord', but remained devils. We are all in danger of being content with an intellectual assent to the truth. There have been people throughout the centuries who have fallen into this trap. They have read the Scriptures and accepted their teaching. They believed the teaching, and sometimes they have been exponents of the truth, and have argued against heretics. And yet their whole character and life have been a denial of the very truth they have claimed to believe.

It is a terrifying thought and yet Scripture so often teaches us that it is a dreadful possibility. A man who is unregenerate and not born again may accept the scriptural teaching as a kind of philosophy, as abstract truth. Indeed, I would not hesitate to say that I always find it very difficult to understand how any intelligent man is not compelled to do that. If any man comes to the Bible with an intelligent mind and faces its evidence, it seems almost incredible that he should not arrive at certain inevitable logical conclusions. And a man may do that and still not be a Christian. The historical evidence for the Person of Jesus Christ of Nazareth is beyond question. You cannot explain the persistence of the Christian Church apart from Him; the evidence is overwhelming. So a man may face that and say: 'Yes, I accept that argument'. He may subscribe to the truth and say: 'Jesus of Nazareth was none other than the Son of God'. He may say that and still be unregenerate, and not a Christian. He may say 'Lord, Lord', and yet not enter the kingdom of heaven. Our forefathers, in days when they realized these dangers, used to emphasize this tremendously. Read the works of the Puritans and you will find that they devoted not only chapters but volumes to the question of 'false peace'. Indeed, this danger has been recognized throughout the centuries. There is the danger of trusting your faith instead of Christ, of trusting your belief without really becoming regenerate. It is a terrible possibility. There are people who have been brought up in a Christian home and atmosphere, who have always heard these things, and in a sense have always accepted them, and have always believed and said the right thing; but still they may not be Christians.

The second possibility is that these people may not only be believers of the truth, but also fervent and zealous. You notice the repetition of the word 'Lord', they do not merely say 'Lord', they say 'Lord, Lord'. These people are not intellectual believers only; there is an element of feeling; emotion is involved. They seem keen and anxious and they are full of fervour. Yet our Lord says that even that may be quite false, and that there are many who thus zealously and fervently say the right things about Him, and to Him, who still shall not enter into the kingdom of God. How is this to be explained?

It is to be explained in the following manner. One of the most difficult things, all Christians must surely admit, is to differentiate between a truly spiritual fervour and a carnal, fleshly, animal zeal and enthusiasm. Natural animal spirits and temperament may very well make a man fervent and zealous. A man may be born with an energetic nature and a fervent enthusiastic spirit — some of us have to be more careful at this point than others. There is nothing of which a preacher needs to be more sure than that the zeal and fervency in his preaching is not produced by his natural temperament or his sermon, but by real belief in Christ. It is a very subtle matter. A man prepares a message and, having prepared it, he may be pleased and satisfied with the arrangement and order of the thoughts and certain forms of expression. If he is of an energetic, fervent nature, he may well be excited and moved by that and especially when he preaches the sermon. But it may be entirely of the flesh and have nothing at all to do with spiritual matters. Every preacher knows exactly what this means, and anybody who has ever taken part in public prayer knows the same. You can be carried away by your own eloquence and by the very thing you yourself are doing and not by the truth at all. There are some people who seem to think it is their duty to be fervent and emotional. Some people never pray in public without crying, and some tend to think that they feel more than others. But it does not follow for a moment. The emotional type of person is always more liable to weep when he prays, but it does not mean of necessity that he is more spiritual.

Our Lord, then, is emphasizing that though they say 'Lord, Lord', and are fervent and zealous, it may be nothing but the flesh. Great enthusiasm in these things does not of necessity imply spirituality. The flesh may account for that; it can counterfeit almost everything. We can perhaps emphasize this point best by quoting something which was written by Robert Murray McCheyne. That man of God, when he merely entered the pulpit, caused people to break down and weep. People felt that he had come straight from an audience with God, and they were humbled by his very appearance. This is what he said in his diary one day: 'Today, missed some fine opportunity of speaking a word for Christ. The Lord saw that I would have spoken as much for my own honour as for His, and therefore He shut my mouth. I see that a man cannot be a faithful, fervent minister until he preaches just for Christ's sake, until he gives up trying to attract people to himself, and seeks to attract them to Christ. Lord', he ends, 'give me this.' Robert Murray McCheyne there recognizes this terrible danger of doing things in the flesh and imagining that we are doing them for Christ's sake.

That, then, is the first part of our Lord's analysis. Nothing is more dangerous than to rely only upon a correct belief, and a fervent spirit, and to assume that, as long as you believe the right things and are zealous and keen and active concerning them, you are therefore of necessity a Christian.

In the verses which follow He goes further and includes works also — that is what makes the supposed antithesis between faith and works so foolish and ridiculous. What then are the works, which, according to the Lord, a man may perform and still be outside the kingdom? It is really an alarming and terrifying list. The first thing He says is: 'Many will say to me in that day, Lord, Lord, have we not prophesied in thy name?' To prophesy means to deliver a spiritual message. You find much about prophecy in the New Testament. Paul discusses it at some length in 1 Corinthians, in connection with the various gifts that were exercised in the Church. Those were the days before the New Testament was written, when certain members of the Church were given messages and the ability to speak them by the Holy Spirit. That is what is meant by prophesying; and our Lord says that there will be many people who will come to Him in the day of judgment and say that they have prophesied in His name — not in their own name, but in His name — but He will say unto them: 'I never knew you: depart from me, ye that work iniquity'. We can interpret that for our own age in this way. It is possible for a man to preach correct doctrine, and in the name of

Christ, and yet himself remain outside the kingdom of God. That is the statement, nothing less. If anyone other than the Lord Jesus Christ had said this we would not believe it. Moreover, we would feel that he was a censorious, narrow-minded person. But it is the Lord Himself who says it.

This is something that is taught frequently in the Scriptures. Was not that, for example, the exact position of a man such as Balaam? He delivered the right message, and yet he was a hireling prophet and a reprobate. He gave, in a sense, the right message and teaching, yet he himself was outside. Did not God use Saul in this kind of way? The spirit of prophecy came upon him from time to time, yet Saul, too, was outside. When you come to the New Testament, you find these things stated still more explicitly. Paul, knowing these terrible dangers, says: 'I keep under my body . . . lest that by any means, when I have preached to others, I myself should be a castaway' (1 Cor. 9:27). When he talks about 'keeping under the body' he is not only thinking, as people often imagine, about certain sins of the flesh, he is referring to the whole of his life. A man has to keep under his body in a pulpit as well as on the street. To keep under the body means to keep curbing and controlling everything that the flesh is anxious to do. The flesh thrusts itself into the forefront. The apostle Paul tells us, in this very context of preaching, that he pounded and pummelled his body and bruised it, in order that having preached to others, he might avoid becoming a castaway himself.

Or take the marvellous statement of this truth which we have in 1 Corinthians 13:1-3. 'Though I speak with the tongues of men and of angels, and have not charity, I am become as sounding brass, or a tinkling cymbal'. Or again: 'Though I have the gift of prophecy, and understand all mysteries, and all knowledge; . . . and have not charity, it profiteth me nothing.' The apostle Paul says in effect, 'I may preach like an angel, I may produce the most wonderful eloquence and oratory; I may be considered by people to be the greatest speaker the world has ever heard, and I may speak about the things of God; and yet I may be outside the kingdom. All is useless if I lack these qualities that really make a man a Christian.' So a man can prophesy and be outside. Think also of his statement in Philippians 1:15 where he says of certain people that they 'preach Christ even of envy and strife'. Their motive is wrong, their thoughts are wrong; but they are preaching Christ, they are saying the right things about Him. Paul glories in their right preaching, but they themselves are wrong because they are doing it in a wrong spirit moved by envy and desiring to score over the apostle. We must realize, then, that it is actually possible for a man to be preaching correct doctrine and yet to be outside the kingdom. Our Lord said on one occasion to the Pharisees, 'Ye are they which justify yourselves before men; but God knoweth your hearts: for that which is highly esteemed among men is abomination in the sight of God'. It is a very terrifying thought, and I understand it to mean this, that at the day of judgment we shall all have great surprises. We shall find men who have been lauded and praised as preachers outside the kingdom. They said the right things, and said them marvellously; but they never had the life and truth within them. It was all carnal.

But not only do these people prophesy, they even cast out devils. Again you notice the repetition of 'in thy name' — 'and in thy name have cast out devils'. It is possible for a person to do even that and still to be outside the kingdom! To prove this is simple. Is it not clear from the New Testament that even Judas had this power? Our Lord sent out His disciples to preach and to cast out devils, and they came back and said to Him in great elation on one occasion, 'Even the devils are subject unto us'. It is quite clear that that applied equally to Judas. Our Lord may give power to a man, and yet the man himself may be lost. There are other powers also that can enable us to do remarkable and astounding things. You remember on one occasion when the people charged our Lord with doing miracles by the power of Beelzebub, He retorted by saying, 'If I by Beelzebub cast out devils, by whom do your sons cast them out?' They were Jewish exorcists. In Acts 19 you will find certain people described as sons of Sceva who had the selfsame power. We see, then, that people may even drive out devils in Christ's name and yet be outside the kingdom.

Finally our Lord comes to the climax which He puts in this form. These people will be able to say to Him that in His name they have done 'many wonderful works' — works of power, miracles, amazing things, almost incredible things. They have done many wonderful works in His name, and yet they are outside the kingdom. How do we prove that this is possible? Part of the proof undoubtedly is found in the case of the magicians of Egypt. You remember when Moses was sent to deliver the children of Israel and to work his miracles, the magicians of Egypt were able to counterfeit and repeat them up to a certain point. They did many marvellous works. But we need not rely only upon that. Our Lord says in Matthew 24:24: 'For there shall arise false Christs, and false prophets, and shall shew great signs and wonders; insomuch that, if it were possible, they shall deceive the very elect.' These are the words of Christ. But take Paul's words in 2 Thessalonians 2:8: 'And then shall that Wicked be revealed, whom the Lord shall consume with the spirit of his mouth, and shall destroy with the brightness of his coming: even him, whose coming is after the working of Satan with all power and signs and lying wonders'. These things are prophesied.

In other words, a man may be able to point to great results such as healings and so on, and yet they may signify nothing. And we should not be surprised at this. Are we not learning more and more in these days about the powers that are innate in man even in a natural sense? There is such a thing as a natural gift of healing; there is a kind of natural, almost magical power in certain people. For instance the whole question of electricity in the human frame is most interesting. We are merely beginning to understand it. There are people such as water-diviners who possess certain curious gifts. Then there is the whole question of telepathy, transference of thought and extra-sensory perception. These things are just coming into our ken. As the result of such gifts and powers many can do marvellous and wondrous things, and yet not be Christian. The natural power of man can simulate the gifts of the Holy Spirit, up to a point. And, of course, we are reminded by Scripture that God, in His own inscrutable will, sometimes decides to give these powers to men who do not belong to Him in order to bring to pass His own purposes. He raises up men for His own particular purpose, but they themselves remain outside the kingdom. It was God who called and used the pagan Cyrus.

Above all we must remember the power of the devil. The devil, as Paul teaches in 2 Corinthians 11:14, can transform himself even into an angel of light, and the devil as an angel of light sometimes persuades people that they are Christian when they are not. If the devil can keep a man outside the kingdom by making him say 'Lord, Lord', he will certainly make him do so. He will do anything to keep a man outside the kingdom; so if a false belief or a true belief held in the wrong way will do this, he will make him have it, and he will give him power to work signs and wonders.

It has all been prophesied, it is all in the Bible; and that is why our Lord warns us so solemnly to pay heed to it. He once summed it up to His disciples like this: 'In this', He says, 'rejoice not, that the spirits are subject unto you; but rather rejoice, because your names are written in heaven'. They had been sent out to preach and to cast out devils, and had been highly successful. They came back full of pride because of the things that had happened, and our Lord said to them in effect: 'Did I not tell you in the Sermon on the Mount that people who are outside the kingdom can preach in My name, and cast out devils and do many wonderful works? Do not be misled by these things; make certain of yourself. It is your heart that matters. Is your name written in heaven? Do you really belong to Me? Have you this holiness, this righteousness which I am teaching? "Not every one that saith unto me, Lord, Lord, shall enter into the kingdom of heaven; but he that doeth the will of my Father which is in heaven"'. The way to test yourself, the way to test any man, is to look below the surface. Do not look at the apparent results, do not look at the wonders and the marvels, but discover whether he conforms to the Beatitudes. Is he poor in spirit; is he meek; is he humble; does he groan in his spirit as he sees the world; is he a holy man of God; is he grave; is he sober; does he say with Paul, 'We that are in this tabernacle do groan, being burdened'? Those are the tests, the tests of the Beatitudes, the tests of the Sermon on the Mount — the man's character, the man's nature. Not the appearances only, but the reality itself alone counts with God.

Let us remember again that it is the Lord who says these things, and it is He who will judge. The words 'Many will say to me in that day' refer to the day of judgment, when He will be the judge, so do not be deceived. 'Ye are they', He says again of this type, 'which justify yourselves before men; but God knoweth your hearts: for that which is highly esteemed among men is abomination in the sight of God.' The New Testament Christian is a definite type of character; he is unmistakable. Read your New Testament, put down the marks of the New Testament man, put them on paper, learn them, meditate upon them, apply them to yourself and to everybody else. Do that, says our Lord, and you will never be led astray, you will not be left outside that strait gate and narrow way. These then are the tests and they may all be summed up in the phrase, 'he that doeth the will of my Father which is in heaven'.

May God grant us honesty as we face this terrifying truth, this truth we shall have to answer for when 'all earthly scenes have passed away', and we stand before Christ and face Him. If you feel you are condemned, confess it to God, hunger and thirst after righteousness, turn believingly to the Lord Jesus Christ, ask Him to give it you, cost what it may, whatever its effects and results, and He will give it to you, for He has said: 'Blessed are they which do hunger and thirst after righteousness: for they shall be filled.'

Chapter Twenty-five

Unconscious Hypocrisy

W E have already considered the general message conveyed by these solemn and solemnizing verses. As we return to them it is important that we should bear in mind that in this little paragraph our Lord is dealing with those who are orthodox. It is not a statement about those who are heterodox, those who hold false teaching or doctrine. Here, the teaching is correct. They prophesy in His name; it is in His name that they cast out devils; and it is in His name that they do many wonderful works. And yet He tells us that they are finally reprobate. So much then is possible for one who is nevertheless finally lost. That is why these words in many ways are more solemnizing and, indeed, alarming than anything we find in the whole extent of Holy Writ.

After that preliminary survey, we can now proceed to draw certain lessons and deductions from it. Surely nothing can be more important than that we should do so. Our Lord goes on repeating these warnings as He exhorts men and women to enter in at the strait gate and to walk in the narrow way, and here again He warns us of the terrible dangers and possibilities that confront us. The one great lesson to be learnt from this passage is the danger of self-deception, and this is emphasized in several ways. For instance our Lord uses the word 'Many'. 'Many will say to me in that day, Lord, Lord, have we not done this and that?' We must not exaggerate the force and strength of this word 'many', but it is a word that carries a very definite meaning. He does not say 'an odd person here and there', but 'many' — self-deception is a danger to the 'many', and His warnings against it are frequent. It is there in the picture that follows about people who build their houses upon the sand. It is the same warning that we find also in the parable of the ten virgins. The five foolish virgins are a straightforward case of self-deception, nothing more. It occurs again in that final picture in Matthew 25, where Christ portrays the final judgment and speaks of those who will confidently come and tell Him of the things they have done for Him. The same warning is being given in all these cases; it is the warning against the terrible danger of self-deception. In other words, as we read what He says here, we are given the impression that these people to whom He is referring will be amazed and astonished at the day of judgment — 'that day'. As we have seen, the whole paragraph is spoken with the day of judgment clearly in mind. Indeed, the whole chapter, as we have constantly seen, is concerned to enforce the fact that the Christian must live his whole life in the light of that coming day. Read through the New Testament and observe how frequently 'that day' is spoken of. 'The day will declare it', says Paul, as if to say: It is all right. I am going on with my ministry, I am doing everything with my eye on that day; people may criticize and say this or that about me, but I shall not allow that to worry me. I have delivered myself and my whole eternal future into the hand of the Lord my judge, and the day of His judgment is going to make everything manifest.

It is clear from the words in this passage that these people, according to our Lord, are going to be astonished at the day of judgment. They have assumed that they are safe, and seem quite sure of their own salvation. Upon what grounds? Because they were saying, 'Lord, Lord'. They were orthodox; they said the right things; they were fervent; they were zealous. They prophesied in His name; they cast out devils; they did many wonderful works. And they were praised of men; they were in fact regarded as outstanding servants. So they were perfectly happy about themselves, quite assured about their whole position, and they never suspected for a second that there was any fault to find in them. They could turn to our Lord in the day of judgment and say: 'Surely, Lord, You know our record? Don't You remember all we said and did in Your name?' They had no doubt about themselves; they were perfectly happy; they were quite assured. It had never crossed their minds even to contemplate the possibility that they could be anything but Christians and saved people, heirs of glory and of eternal bliss. And yet what our Lord says to them is that they are lost. He will 'profess' to them — He plays upon words here, they make their profession, He too will make a profession — He will profess unto them: 'I never knew you, I never had anything to do with you. Though you were always saying "Lord, Lord", and doing things in My name, I never recognized you, there was never any contact between us. You have been deceiving and fooling yourselves the whole time. Depart from Me, ye that work iniquity.'

There can be no doubt about it, the day of judgment is going to be a day of many surprises. How often does our Lord tell these people, His contemporaries, and tell us through them, that He does not judge as they judge. 'Ye are they which justify yourselves before men; but God knoweth your hearts: for that which is highly esteemed among men is abomination in the sight of God.' That kind of false judgment is found at times in the Church, as well as in the world. So often our judgments are carnal. Listen to the comments people make as they go from a place of worship. So often they are about the man, about his very physical appearance, or what they call 'personality', rather than about the message. Those are the things that attract. Our judgments are so carnal. Thus our Lord teaches us to beware of this terrible, alarming possibility of deceiving ourselves. We are all quite clear about conscious hypocrisy. The conscious hypocrite is not a problem; he is obvious and self-evident. What is so much more difficult to discern is unconscious hypocrisy, when a man not only misleads others but also deceives himself, when a man not only persuades others wrongly about himself, but persuades himself wrongly about himself. That is the very thing with which our Lord is dealing here, and we must repeat again, that if we believe the New Testament is true, then there is nothing more important than that we should examine ourselves in the light of a statement such as this.

If, then, what we are describing is unconscious hypocrisy, does it not follow that we can do nothing about it? Is it not by definition something with which a man cannot deal? If it is a condition in which a man is deluding himself, how can he possibly safeguard himself against it? The answer is that, on the contrary, a great deal can be done. The first and most important thing is to consider the causes of self-deception. That is the way to discover it in ourselves. If we can arrive at a list of the causes of self-delusion and self-deception, and then examine ourselves in the light of these causes, we shall be in a position to deal with them. And the New Testament is full of instruction with respect to that. That is why it is always exhorting us to test and to examine ourselves; that is why it is always exhorting us to prove and try the spirits, and indeed to prove all things. It is a great book of warning. That is not popular today. People say that that is being negative; but the New Testament always emphasizes the negative aspect of truth as well as the positive.

What, then, are the common causes of self-deception in this matter? First: there is a false doctrine of assurance. This is the tendency to base our assurance only upon certain statements which we ourselves make. There are those who say, 'Scripture says, "He that believeth on him is not condemned" but shall receive "everlasting life"; "Believe on the Lord Jesus Christ, and thou shalt be saved"; "Whosoever believeth in his heart and confesseth with his mouth shall be saved".' They interpret such statements as meaning that as long as they acknowledge and say certain things about the Lord Jesus Christ, they are automatically saved. Their error is surely this: the man who is truly saved and who has a genuine assurance of salvation does make, and must make, these statements, but the mere making of these statements does not of necessity guarantee, or assure, a man of his salvation. The very people with whom our Lord is dealing *do* say: 'Lord, Lord,' and they seem to put the right content into that statement; but, as we have seen, James reminds us in his Epistle that 'the devils also believe, and tremble'. If we read the Gospels, we discover that the evil spirits, the devils, recognize the Lord. They refer to Him as 'the Holy One of God'. They know who He is; they say the right things about Him. But they are devils and they are lost. So we must be wary of that very subtle temptation, and remember the way in which people wrongly persuade themselves. They say: 'I do believe, and I have said with my mouth that I believe Jesus of Nazareth was the Son of God, and that He has died for my sins, therefore . . .' — but the argument is incomplete. The believer, the Christian, does say these things, but he does not stop at merely saying them. That is what is sometimes described as 'fideism' or 'believeism', which means that a man is really putting his final trust in his own faith and not in the Lord Jesus Christ. He is relying on his own belief, and on his mere assertion of it.

The whole object of this paragraph, surely, is to warn us against the terrible danger of basing our assurance of salvation upon a repetition of certain statements and formulae. We can think of other illustrations of this danger of being a merely formal Christian. What in fact is the difference between what we have just described and basing our assurance of salvation upon the fact that we are members of a church, or that we belong to a certain country, or that we were christened when we were infants? There is no difference. It is possible for a man to say all the right things and yet to live such an evil life that it is quite plain that he is not a Christian. 'Be not deceived', says the apostle Paul in writing to the Corinthians; 'neither fornicators, nor idolaters, nor adulterers . . . shall inherit the kingdom of God.' It is therefore quite possible for a man to say the right things and yet to be living an evil life. 'Let no man deceive himself.' The moment we begin to rest our faith solely upon repeating a formula, without being sure that we are regenerate and that we have evidence of the life of God within us, we are exposing ourselves to this terrible danger of self-delusion. And there are many who state and defend their doctrine of assurance in that way. They say: Do not listen to your conscience. If you have said that you believe, that is enough. But it is not enough, for 'many will say . . . Lord, Lord'. But He will say: 'I never knew you: depart from me, ye that work iniquity.' A superficial doctrine of assurance, therefore, or a false doctrine of assurance, is one of the most common causes of self-delusion.

The second cause of this condition follows inevitably from the first. It is the refusal to examine oneself. Self-examination is not popular today, especially, strangely enough, amongst evangelical Christians. Indeed, one often finds that evangelical Christians not only object to self-examination, but occasionally even regard it as almost sinful. Their argument is that a Christian should look only to the Lord Jesus Christ, that he must not look at himself at all, and they interpret this as meaning that he should not examine himself. They regard examining oneself as looking to oneself. They say that, if you look at yourself, you will find nothing but blackness and darkness; therefore you must look not at yourself, but to the Lord Jesus Christ. So they look away from themselves and refuse to examine themselves.

But that is not scriptural. Scripture constantly exhorts us to examine ourselves, to 'prove to our own selves whether we are in the faith' or whether we are 'reprobate'. And it does so for the very good reason that there is the terrible danger of drifting into antinomianism; that is, into holding that as long as a man believes on the Lord Jesus Christ it does not matter what he does; that if a man is saved it does not matter what kind of a life he lives. Antinomianism holds that the moment you begin to concentrate on behaviour, you are putting yourself back under the law. Believe on the Lord Jesus Christ, it says, and all is well. But that, again, is surely the very thing against which our Lord is warning us in this paragraph; the fatal danger of trusting only in what we say, and forgetting that the essential thing about Christianity is that it is a life to be lived, that it is 'the life of God in the soul of man', that the Christian is a 'partaker of the divine nature', and that this must of necessity be manifest in his life.

Or let us look at the first Epistle of John, which was written to correct this very danger. It has in mind those people who were very ready to say certain things, but whose lives were a blatant contradiction of what they professed. John produces his famous tests of spiritual life. He says: 'He that saith, I know him, and keepeth not his commandments, is a liar, and the truth is not in him.' 'If we say that we have fellowship with him, and walk in darkness, we lie, and do not the truth.' There were people who were doing just that; they were saying, 'I am a Christian, I am in fellowship with God, I am a believer on the Lord Jesus Christ'; but they were living in sin. That is a lie, says John; it is transgression of the law, it is disobedience to God and His holy commandment. However much a man may *say* he believes on the Lord Jesus Christ, if the habit of his life is persistently sinful he is not a Christian. And clearly the way to discover this is to examine ourselves. We must look at ourselves and examine ourselves in the light of the commandments, in the light of scriptural teaching, in the light of this Sermon on the Mount, and we must do so honestly. And, furthermore, when we come to this question of the works which we do, whether prophesying or casting out devils and doing 'many wonderful works', we must examine our motives. We must ask ourselves honestly, 'Why am I doing this, what is the real urge behind it all?'; because a man who does not realize that he may be doing the right things for a thoroughly wrong motive is a mere tyro in these matters. It is possible for a man to preach the gospel of Christ in an orthodox manner, to mention the name of Christ, to be right in doctrine and to be zealous in the preaching of the Word, and yet really to be doing it the whole time for his own self-interest and his own glory and self-satisfaction. The only way to safeguard ourselves against that is to examine and scrutinize ourselves. It is painful and unpleasant; but it has to be done. It is the only way of safety. A man has to face himself squarely and ask: 'Why am I doing it? What is the thing that, in my heart of hearts, I am really out for?' If a man does not do that he is exposing himself to the terrible danger of self-delusion and self-deception.

But let us now consider another cause of this self-same condition, which is the danger of living on one's activities. We need to be quite clear about this, for there is no doubt that one of the greatest dangers of all in the Christian life is that a man may live on his own activities. I once had a letter from a lady who had been a very active Christian worker for some forty years or so. Then she was taken seriously ill and for six months was unable to leave her house. She was honest enough to tell me that she had found it to be a very severe and try-ing discipline. I know exactly what she meant. I have seen it in others and, alas, know something about it in my own experience. I have seen men who have been indefatigable in the work of the kingdom suddenly laid aside by illness, and scarcely knowing what to do with themselves. What is the matter? They have been living on their own activities. You can be so busy preaching and working that you are not nurturing your own soul. You are so neglecting your own spiritual life that you find at the end that you have been living on yourself and your own activities. And when you stop, or are stopped by illness or cir-cumstances, you find that life is empty and that you have no resources.

This is not confined, of course, to the Christian life. How often have we heard of business or professional men who have been highly successful and per-fectly healthy all their lives. They then decide to retire, and everybody is as-tounded when, in six months or so, they hear that they have suddenly died. What is the matter? Often the real explanation is that the thing which kept them going, which provided the stimulus to living and the purpose to life, is suddenly withdrawn, and they collapse. Or think of the way in which so many people today are kept going solely by entertainments and pleasures. When they are suddenly cut off from these they do not know what to do with themselves; they are utterly bored and helpless. They have been living on their own activi-ties and pleasures. And the same thing can happen in the Christian life. That is why it is a good thing for all of us from time to time to stop and take a rest, and to examine ourselves, and ask 'What am I living on?' What if the meetings you attend so frequently and so regularly were suddenly prohibited to you, how would you find yourself? What if your health broke down and you could not read, or enjoy the company of other people, and you were just left alone? What would you do? We must take time to ask ourselves these questions, for one of the greatest dangers to the soul is just to be living on our own activities and on our own efforts. To be overbusy is one of the highroads to self-deception.

Another fruitful cause of this trouble is the tendency to balance our lives by putting up one thing against another. For instance, if our conscience condemns us about the life we are living, we put over against it some good work we are doing. We recognize that certain things count against us, but then we make a list of the good deeds we are doing, and the account balances with a little credit at the end. We have all done that. Do you recall the classic example of it in the case of Saul, the first king of Israel? Saul had been commanded to exterminate the Amalekites; and he had done so up to a point. But he kept King Agag alive, and he also kept the best of the sheep and oxen and so on. You notice how clever he was when upbraided by Samuel. He said, 'I have kept them in order that we might make a sacrifice unto the Lord.' That is a perfect instance of balancing. And we are all prone to this. Instead of allowing our consciences to do their work, we immediately put positive things over against the negative. A man who judges the condition of his life in that way can have only one end. A man who does that sort of thing in business will soon be bankrupt, and a man who does it in the Christian life will soon be spiritually bankrupt, and in the end will be dismissed by the Lord Himself. We must apply this lesson to ourselves. We must allow conscience to deal with us. We must not excuse ourselves, but listen to its dictates and obey them.

That brings us to the vital principle which underlies all the causes of self-deception. In many ways the root trouble, even among good Evangelicals, is our failure to heed the plain teaching of Scripture. We accept what Scripture teaches as far as our doctrine is concerned; but when it comes to practice, we very often fail to take the Scriptures as our only guide. When we come to the practical side we employ human tests instead of scriptural ones. Instead of taking the plain teaching of the Bible, we argue with it. 'Ah, yes,' we say, 'since the Scriptures were written, times have changed.' Dare I give an obvious illustration? Take the question of women preaching, and being ordained to the full ministry. The apostle Paul, in writing to Timothy (1 Tim. 2:11-15), prohibits it directly. He says quite specifically that he does not allow a woman to teach or preach. 'Ah, yes,' we say, as we read that letter, 'he was only thinking of his own age and time;

but you know times have changed since then, and we must not be bound. Paul was thinking of certain semicivilized people in Corinth and places like that.' But the Scripture does not say that. It says, 'Let the woman learn in silence with all subjection. But I suffer not a woman to teach, nor to usurp authority over the man, but to be in silence.' 'Ah, but that was only temporary legislation,' we say. Paul puts it like this: 'For Adam was first formed, then Eve. And Adam was not deceived, but the woman being deceived was in the transgression. Notwithstanding she shall be saved in child-bearing, if they continue in faith and charity and holiness with sobriety.' Paul does not say that it was only for the time being; he takes it right back to the Fall and shows that it is an abiding principle. It is something that is true, therefore, of the age in which we live. But thus, you see, we argue with Scripture. Instead of taking its plain teaching, we say that times have changed — when it suits our thesis we say it is no longer relevant.

Another way in which we do the same thing is this. The Scripture lays down quite plainly not only that we are to preach the gospel, the true message, but also *how* we are to do so. It tells us that we are to do so with 'sobriety' and with 'gravity', in fear and trembling, in 'demonstration of the Spirit and of power', and not with 'enticing words of man's wisdom'. But today evangelistic methods which are a flagrant contradiction of these words are justified in terms of results. 'Look at the results', men say. 'Such and such a man may not conform to the scriptural method, but look at the results!' And because of 'the results' the plain dictates of Scripture are put on one side. Is that believing the Scriptures? Is that taking the Scriptures as our final authority? Is not that repeating the old error of Saul, who said, 'Yes, I know, but I thought it would be good if I did so and so.' He tries to justify his disobedience by some result he is going to produce. We Protestants, of course, hold up our hands in horror at the Roman Catholics, especially the Jesuits, when they tell us that 'the end justifies the means'. It is the great argument of the Church of Rome. We repudiate it in the Roman Catholic Church, but it is a common argument in evangelical circles. The 'results' justify everything. If the results are good, the argument runs, the methods must be right — the end justifies the means. If you want to avoid terrible disillusionment at the day of judgment, face Scripture as it is. Do not argue with it, do not try to manipulate it, do not twist it; face it, receive it and submit to it whatever the cost.

A further common cause of self-deception is our failure to realize that the one thing that matters is our relationship to Christ. He is the judge, and it is what He thinks of us that matters. It is He who will say to these people, 'I never knew you', and that word 'knew' is very strong. It does not mean that He was not aware of their existence. He knows all things, He sees everything; everything is naked and open to Him. 'Know' means 'taking a special interest in', 'being in a particular relationship to'. 'You only have I known of all the families of the earth,' said God to the children of Israel through Amos. That means that He is in this peculiar relationship to Israel. What our Lord will say on the judgment day to these self-deceived people is that they have done all these things in their own power and energy. He never had anything to do with it. So the most important thing for all of us is not to be interested primarily in our activities or in results, but in our relationship to the Lord Jesus Christ. Do we know Him, and does He know us?

Finally, therefore, we must realize that what God wants, and what our blessed Lord wants, above all, is ourselves — what Scripture calls our 'heart'. He wants the inner man, the heart. He wants our submission. He does not want merely our profession, our zeal, our fervour, our works, or anything else. He wants *us*. Read again the words uttered by the prophet Samuel to Saul, king of Israel: 'Hath the Lord as great delight in burnt offerings and sacrifices, as in obeying the voice of the Lord? Behold, to obey is better than sacrifice, and to hearken than the fat of rams' (1 Sam. 15:22). To Saul's argument: 'We kept the best of the sheep and the oxen in order that we might sacrifice them, in order that we might offer them to the Lord,' this is the answer: God does not want our offerings; He does not want our sacrifices; He wants our obedience, He wants *us*. It is possible for a man to say right things, to be very busy and active, to achieve apparently wonderful results, and yet not to give himself to the Lord. He may be doing it all for himself, and he may be resisting the Lord in the most vital place of all. And that is finally the greatest insult we can offer to God. What can be a greater insult than to say: 'Lord, Lord,' fervently, to be busy and active, and yet to withhold true allegiance and submission from Him, to insist upon retaining control of our own lives, and to allow our own opinions and arguments, rather than those of Scripture, to control what we do and how we do it? The greatest insult to the Lord is a will that is not completely and entirely surrendered; and whatever else we may do — however great our offerings and sacrifices, however wonderful our works in His name — it will avail us nothing. If we believe that Jesus of Nazareth is the only begotten Son of God and that He came into this world and went to the cross of Calvary and died for our sins and rose again in order to justify us and to give us life anew and prepare us for heaven — if you really believe that, there is only one inevitable deduction, namely that He is entitled to the whole of our lives, everything without any limit whatsoever. That means that He must have control not only in the big things, but in the little things also; not only over what we do, but how we do it. We must submit to Him and His way as He has been pleased to reveal it in the Bible; and if what we do does not conform to this pattern, it is an assertion of our will, it is disobedience, and as repellent as the sin of witchcraft. Indeed, it belongs to the type of conduct that makes Christ say to certain people: 'Depart from me, ye that work iniquity'. Workers of iniquity! Who are they? The people who said: 'Lord, Lord,' the people who prophesied in His name and in His name cast out devils and in His name did many wonderful works. He calls them 'workers of iniquity' because, in the last analysis, they were doing it to please themselves and not in order to please Him. Let us then solemnly examine ourselves in the light of these things.

Chapter Twenty-six

The Signs of Self-deception

W E have already considered twice the momentous and alarming words of 7:21-23; but because of their vital importance we must do so once again. This matter of self-deception is a very large subject. If you are interested in so-called Manuals of Devotion, whether Roman Catholic or Protestant, you will find that they always devote a good deal of attention to this particular question. All wise physicians of the soul have always concentrated attention on it. We are called to do so by the Bible itself. It is full, not only of exhortations on this matter, but also of practical illustrations of people who have deluded and deceived themselves. But apart from all that, as we value our souls, and as we realize that we are all passing through this world in the direction of a final judgment, and shall all have to stand before the judgment-throne of Christ, this kind of self-examination becomes quite inevitable. As the apostle John put it: 'Every man that hath this hope in him purifieth himself, even as he is pure' (1 John 3:3). And you cannot purify yourself without examining yourself. Some people devote the season of Lent in particular to this question of self-examination. Others of us believe that it should be done throughout the whole year, and that we should be examining ourselves and disciplining ourselves always. We need not enter into that, however. What is important is to recognize the need of self-examination. It is taught constantly in the Bible.

We have seen that the first step to take if we are anxious to avoid deceiving ourselves is to consider the causes of self-deception, and we have dealt with some of the more common ones. Having thus laid down principles, we now come to deal with a few practical details; these are designed to warn us of the subtle way in which we can deceive ourselves. We start by reminding ourselves that we do not live our Christian life in a kind of vacuum. Quite apart from the fact that we live in society among men and women, we have also to contend with the devil and 'the principalities and powers, the rulers of the darkness of this world, and spiritual wickedness in high places.' Nothing according to Scripture teaching will enable us to stand in that conflict except the putting on of the whole armour of God. One of the ways in which we put on that armour is to beware of the subtlety of the attack. And that, because of its very nature, will have to be considered in some detail. I am a little fearful as I proceed to do this, because I know that to do so exposes one to the risk of being misunderstood. If one uses illustrations attention becomes concentrated on the illustrations and not on the principles.

The first big principle is that there is a sense in which everything in connection with the Christian life can be dangerous. I am not maintaining that everything *is* dangerous but that it can be. The devil in his subtlety, as an angel of light, comes to us and takes hold of things which are legitimate and good, and given to us by God, and he so influences us as to make us turn those very things into the instrument of our own self-deception. The things themselves are all right, but we can abuse them. That is the theme which we must elaborate. In a sense, even the means of grace with which God has provided us can prove to be a source of trouble. I trust I am making this clear. Obviously I am not denouncing the means of grace; I am simply pointing out the terrible danger of turning the means of grace which God Himself has appointed, and given us, into something that may be harmful to our souls. I am concerned with the *abuse* of what is good, and not with the *use* of what is good. It is always a great comfort to any man who preaches to know that even such a great master preacher as the apostle Paul could be misunderstood when he taught and preached. Take, for instance, 2 Corinthians 11 with its superb sarcasm. The apostle deals there with the grievous, childish way in which so much of his teaching had been misunderstood in Corinth.

Here, then, are the controlling principles. Things that are good in and of themselves, unless we are careful, may be the very things that will deceive us about the state of our souls. But how can we know whether we are tending to depart from the simplicity that is in Christ, and getting into this terrible false position that is described in this verse? Here are some of the answers. One clear indication of this tendency reveals itself in the following way. If, when we examine ourselves to discover what our main interest is, we find that it is in attending meetings, we are entering into a dangerous condition. Obviously I believe in attending Christian meetings; but when a man gets into the condition in which he lives on meetings, and they become his primary interest, he is in a very dangerous condition. And there are many people in that position. They are kept going by meetings, and when they are suddenly cut off from them they begin to discover a terrible barrenness in their soul and in their Christian experience.

Another symptom of the same condition is an undue interest in phenomena. There are many phenomena in connection with the Christian life for which we can thank God, certain things that come as blessings in connection with the gospel, such as exalted feelings, guidance, physical healing, and so on. These things are part and parcel of the Christian message, but if we find that our main interest is in these phenomena we are in a position that may lead to self-deception. We must never be more interested in what we may call the by-products of the faith than in the faith itself. We must examine ourselves concerning each of these things. We betray our fundamental interest, of course, by what we say. As we listen to other people we discover their main and their real interests. And the same applies to us. We must ask: 'What is my main interest?' Or, perhaps, it would be wise to get someone else to examine and observe us. I suggest that if we discover in ourselves or in others this tendency for the interest to be absorbed by the means of grace and phenomena rather than by our relationship to the Lord, we are already on the way that ultimately leads to this dread self-deception.

Another sign of this is an undue interest in organizations, denominations, particular churches, or some movement or fellowship. We all know exactly what this means. Man is a social being, and we all like to have some outlet for our social instinct and the social part of our makeup. It is the simplest thing in the world to find an outlet for that natural, social, gregarious instinct in the realm of things Christian. The danger lies in our assuming that because of our interest in these things we are, of necessity, Christian. That is the very thing our Lord is saying. Here is a man who says, 'Lord, Lord'; he casts out devils, he does many wonderful works in the name of Christ, in the realm of the Church, and because of that he assumes that he is a Christian. Yet Christ says he may not be. How easily this can be done! There are people who by nature prefer to be in moral rather than immoral societies, but who are not Christian at all. As natural human beings they like moral, ethical people, and their natural desire to have a social outlet, or an outlet for their active moral nature, is provided by some type of organization in connection with Christianity. Self-deception comes in, because they assume that, as they are doing it in a Christian realm, they must be Christian. But their real interest is in the activity and in the organization, not in the Lord, nor in their own relationship to the Lord. This is a terrible possibility. There are people whose real and ultimate interest is in their particular church, not in Christian salvation, not in the Lord at all. They like the church, they like the people, they have been brought up in that atmosphere, and that is the thing that really holds them — that particular church, that particular denomination, or that particular alignment of people. Again it is always revealed by their talk. You will find that they are greatly interested when you talk about the organization, or the people, or the preacher, but that they become strangely silent if you try to have a spiritual talk with them about their soul or about the Lord. We must examine ourselves by that test. What are we really interested in? Are we interested in our relationship to Him and in His glory, or only in one of these other things?

Another, and a very common, danger at this present time is to be interested in the social and general rather than in the personal aspects of Christianity. This has been particularly important in the present century. Many people today, confronted by the problems of this country and of society, are saying more and more that what is needed is biblical teaching and a Christian attitude towards these national and social problems. Watch the statesmen, and the politicians — even some of the leading ones. Although one is given to understand that they practically never attend a place of worship on Sunday they are using increasingly the words 'religion' and 'Christian'. They seem to think vaguely that Christian teaching can help to solve the problems of State. Though they are not active and practising Christians themselves (and I am referring only to these and not to the Christians among them), and are not giving any personal obedience to the Lord, they seem to think that Christianity can be of help in a general way. We are always on dangerous ground when we begin to talk about 'Christian civilization' and 'Christian' or 'Western' values. This is surely much in evidence at the present time; and it is one of the major dangers confronting the Christian Church. I refer particularly to the tendency to regard Christianity as if it were nothing more than anti-communist teaching. This can be seen in the way in which Christian organizations sometimes advertise, and in their use of slogans such as 'Christ or Communism?', etc. It is not surprising that the Roman Catholic Church should think in such terms, but it is sad to see innocent evangelical people being gradually drawn into that net. It works in a very subtle way. A man persuades himself that, because he is an anti-communist, he must be a Christian. But it by no means follows. We thus persuade and deceive ourselves. We judge ourselves by these general criteria, and assume that we are Christians. The substitution of the social and general for the particular and personal in Christian matters is always a terrible danger. Christendom has often been the greatest enemy of spiritual religion. If I find my interest tends to be more and more general, or social, or political, if that is increasingly my main interest in Christianity, then I am in an extremely dangerous state because I have probably ceased to examine myself.

The next danger is that of those whose main and primary interest is in what we may call apologetics, or the definition and defence of the faith, instead of in a true relationship to Jesus Christ. This is a danger of which every preacher should be particularly aware. Many a man who has persuaded himself that he is a Christian is in reality only interested in apologetics. He spends the whole of his time arguing about the Christian faith, defending it, denouncing evolution, denouncing psychology and various other things that seem to be attacking the very vitals of the faith. This is a very subtle danger because such a man may be completely neglecting his own soul, his own personal holiness and sanctification and his personal relationship to the Lord. But he feels quite happy about himself because he is denouncing evolution and is defending the faith against this or that attack. He may not only be putting this to his own account for righteousness, he may even be using it to evade the task of honest self-examination. Apologetics have their essential place in the Christian life, and it is a part of our business as Christians earnestly to contend for the faith; but if we find ourselves doing nothing but that, we are in a dangerous condition. I knew a man who was much used as an evangelical preacher, perhaps second to none at one time. But he began to spend the time every Sunday in his pulpit attacking the Church of Rome and Modernism, and he ceased to preach a positive gospel. Apologetics had taken the place of central gospel truth. It is a special temptation to those who can reason and argue and debate; and it is one of the most subtle attacks to which the soul can ever be subjected. This is the question, therefore, which some of us should constantly be putting to ourselves. Do I find that most of my time is taken up in arguing with people about the outposts of the Christian position? Do I find that I practically never talk to people about their souls and about Christ and about their experience of Him? Am I always, as it were, going round the outposts of the Citadel? How much of my time is spent in the centre itself? 'Let every man examine himself.'

The next danger is a purely academic and theoretical interest in theology. These dangers are not confined merely to one or two types of Christian; not only are they real to the man who is excessively interested in activities and meetings; but also to the man whose only interest is in theology. His position is just as dangerous as that of the other. It is the simplest thing in the world to be interested in the body of Christian truth, in doctrine as such, merely as an intellectual matter; and it is a particular danger to some of us. There is no view of life and the world today which is in any way comparable to Christian theology; there is nothing more exciting or more interesting as an intellectual pursuit than to be reading theology and philosophy. But, valuable as it is, and wonderful as it is, it may become one of the most subtle dangers and temptations to the soul. A man can be so absorbed in the intellectual apprehension that he forgets that he is alive, and forgets other people. He spends the whole of his time reading and enjoying it, he never makes contact with anybody, and he is useless to everybody. In the history of the Church we find again that this has happened frequently. First there is a great revival. Then there follows a stage which is generally described as that of 'consolidation'. People very rightly feel the need of a state of consolidation after revival. The converts must be built up, so they are taught theology and doctrine. Yet we often find that that has led to a state of intellectual religiosity and spiritual aridity. The classical instance of this is to be found in the sixteenth and seventeenth centuries, after the great Protestant revival and Reformation. After the Reformation in England came the era of the Puritans, with its great teaching of theology. But that was followed by a period of barren intellectualism which continued until the evangelical awakening broke out in the thirties of the eighteenth century. Something similar happened in the Reformed and Lutheran churches. So, again, while we believe that theology is vital and essential, we must remember that the devil may so press us that our interest in it becomes inordinate and unbalanced, with the result that we are 'puffed up' rather than 'edified'. As I look back across some thirty years and more in the Christian ministry I have seen many instances of that. I have watched such people, and have seen a kind of intellectual pride, a pride of knowledge coming in. I have seen the tendency to compromise on the ethical and moral side, I have seen the note of urgency disappearing from their prayers. Though the original interest was right and good, gradually it mastered them. They lost their balance and became intellectualists who were no longer concerned about the idea of holiness and the pursuit of a true and living knowledge of God.

Let us now come to another danger. What we have to say concerning it is particularly liable to be misunderstood, so we must be careful. I have, as the result of much observation, come to the conclusion that one of the most dangerous signs in connection with this matter of self-deception is an over interest in prophetic teaching. The Bible contains a great deal of prophetic teaching, and it is our business to acquaint ourselves with it; but there is nothing that can be so dangerous as an undue interest in prophetic teaching, and especially at a time like this with the world in its present condition. Gradually this interest seems to absorb and to master certain people and they think and talk and preach of nothing but prophecy. There is scarcely anything more dangerous to the spiritual condition of the soul than this over absorption in prophetic teaching. One can so easily be spending all one's time in thinking about Russia and Egypt and Israel and other countries, and in working out times and seasons in terms of Ezekiel 37, 38, Daniel 7-12, and other prophetic passages that one's whole life is given to that. In the meantime you are becoming hard and neglectful of yourself and of other people, in a spiritual sense. You are so interested in the 'times and seasons' that you have forgotten your own soul. Of course prophetic teaching is a vital part of the biblical message, and we should be vitally interested in it; but we must recognize the terrible danger of having such an interest in future world events that we forget that we have a life to live here and now and that at any moment we may die and have to stand before God in judgment. At all points our chief danger is to lose a sense of balance and proportion.

There is a further group of dangers connected with the Bible itself. All Christians should believe in reading the Bible and in studying it diligently and regularly. And yet even the Bible, unless we are very careful, can become a danger and a snare in our spiritual lives. Let me illustrate what I mean. If you ever find yourself approaching the Bible in an intellectual rather than a spiritual manner, you are already on the wrong road. To approach the Bible in a purely intellectual manner, to take it as a textbook, to divide up its chapters exactly as if you were analysing a play by Shakespeare, is a very interesting pursuit. Indeed, nothing can be more exciting to a certain type of person. And yet if you once begin to approach it intellectually only, and not spiritually, it can become the cause of your damnation. The Bible is God's Book and it is a Book of Life. It is a Book that speaks to us a word from God. If, therefore, you find yourself looking down at the Bible instead of looking up at it, you had better examine yourself urgently. If it is a Book which you handle as a master, then it is probably the case that you are being mastered by the devil, who as 'an angel of light' is using the very Word of God to rob you of certain spiritual blessings to your soul. Beware then of becoming a student of the Bible in a wrong sense. Personally, I have always disapproved, for these reasons, of all examinations in biblical knowledge. The moment you begin to approach the Bible as a 'subject', you are already in trouble. We should never approach the Bible theoretically; the Bible should always preach to us, and we must never allow ourselves to come to it in any way but that. Nothing is more dangerous than the expert's or preacher's approach to the Bible. This is so in the case of the preacher because his greatest temptation is to regard the Bible as just a collection of texts on which to preach. So he tends to go to his Bible simply to look for texts and not to feed his soul. The moment a man does that he is in a dangerous condition.

But what is true about reading the Bible is equally true of listening to the preaching of the Bible. Some people simply look for 'points' in sermons, and at the end they make comments about this or that. Let us always be careful not to regard ourselves as experts. Let us ever seek to come under the power of this Word, whether we are reading it or listening to it. When a man comes to me at the close of a service and talks about preaching as such, and as an expert, I know I have failed completely as far as he is concerned. The effect of true preaching should be to make us fear and tremble; it should make us examine ourselves and think more about the Lord Jesus Christ. Beware of becoming interested in the mere letter of the Word. It is something that can happen very easily. Beware of becoming over interested in the mechanics — jumping from text to text, working out comparisons, etc. Of course we are to be interested in everything in the Bible, but we are not to be mastered by the mechanics. It is good to be interested in figures, in biblical numerics for instance; but you can easily spend the whole of your life working at such problems, and thereby forget the true interests of your soul. In particular, beware of too great an interest in the various translations of the Bible. I remember a man, an intelligent man, who was converted by the gospel of Jesus Christ. It was wonderful to see the change in him and to observe his development. Then he came under the influence of a certain teaching, and the first evidence I had of his having been influenced by that teaching was that, when he wrote to me, he began to put as a postscript references to certain passages of Scripture. But he did not just write them as he had done formerly. He now put Matthew 7:21 (Weymouth). Then the next time somebody else, Moffatt or Way. (Now probably it would also be Phillips, Knox, etc.) Thus the poor man became more and more interested in translations and in the mechanics. I remember another man of this type coming to me once at the end of a service which had been highly spiritual and very moving. One of the speakers in stressing a point had read a passage, but from a translation other than the Authorized or Revised versions. This man's one remark about the meeting was to ask the question: 'Whose translation was that?' The particular translation had nothing to do with the message. The passage was equally clear in all versions; but he was interested in translations. Translations, as such, can be most valuable and helpful; but once you become absorbed by an interest in them you have probably become more concerned with the mechanics of the Bible than with the spiritual food which it imparts.

The last danger is the terrible one of playing grace against law and thereby being interested only in grace. There is no saving doctrine at all apart from the doctrine of grace; but we must beware lest we hide ourselves behind it in a wrong way. Again I remember a man who had been converted, but who then fell into sin. I was very ready to help him until I found that he was much too ready to help himself. In other words, he came and confessed his sin, but immediately he began to smile and said: 'After all, there is the doctrine of grace'. I felt he was too healthy; he was healing himself a little too quickly. The reaction to sin should be deep penitence. When a man is in a healthy spiritual condition he does not find relief quite as easily as that. He feels he is hopeless and vile. If therefore you find that you can heal yourself easily, if you find you can jump lightly to the doctrine of grace, I suggest you are in a dangerous condition. The truly spiritual man, while he believes in the doctrine of grace, when he is truly convicted of sin by the Holy Spirit, feels at times that it is almost impossible that God can forgive him. I have put that sometimes in this form by saying that I do not quite understand the Christian who can sit through a truly evangelistic sermon without feeling convicted again. Surely, our feeling should be: 'I almost felt that I went through it once more; I felt I was being put through the whole process again'. That is the true reaction. There is always a convicting aspect to the message; and once we find that we are not reacting in that way because we fly at once to grace, we are in the condition which leads to this tragic self-deception.

In other words, the final question is this — what of the soul? You remember the famous story about William Wilberforce and the woman who went to him at the height of his campaign against slavery and said 'Mr. Wilberforce, what about the soul?' And Mr. Wilberforce turned to the woman and said, 'Madam, I had almost forgotten that I had a soul'. This poor woman came to Wilberforce and asked her vital question, and the great man said that he was so concerned about the liberation of the slaves that he had almost forgotten his soul. But, with all due respect to him, the woman was right. Of course, she may have been a busybody; but there is no evidence that she was. Probably the woman saw that here was a good and fine Christian man, doing a most excellent work. Yes, but she also saw and realized that the danger confronting such a man was that of being so absorbed in the question of antislavery that he might forget his own soul. A man can be so busy preaching in pulpits that he forgets and neglects his own soul. After you have attended all your meetings, and denounced Communism until you can scarcely speak, after you have dealt with your apologetics, and displayed your wonderful knowledge of theology and your understanding of the times, and your complete map of the next fifty years, and after you have read all the translations of the Bible, and have shown your proficiency in a knowledge of its mechanics, I still ask you: 'What about your relationship to the Lord Jesus Christ?' You know a great deal more than you did a year ago; but do you know Him better? You denounce many wrong things; but do you love Him more? Your knowledge of the Bible and its translations has become quite astounding, and you are an expert in apologetics; but are you obeying the law of God and of Christ increasingly? Is the fruit of the Spirit more and more manifest and evident in your life? Those are the questions. 'Not every one that saith unto me, Lord, Lord' (and does many wonderful works), 'but he that doeth the will of my Father which is in heaven.'

Let us all examine ourselves and let us take time to do it thoroughly. Do we really desire to know Him? Paul says in effect that he had virtually forgotten everything else. He had no other care: 'That I may know him, and the power of his resurrection . . .' (Phil. 3:10). Forgetting all the past, and pressing on to that — to 'know' Him, and to 'be like' Him. If anything takes the place of that, we are on the wrong road. All these other things are means to bring us to a knowledge of Him, and if we stay with them they are robbing us of Him. God deliver us from the danger of allowing the means of grace to hide the blessed Saviour from our eyes.

Chapter Twenty-seven

The Two Men and the Two Houses

W E have suggested many times, while studying the words in the previous paragraph, that they are amongst the most solemnizing in the whole range and realm of Scripture. Yet verses 24-27, which we are now considering, seem even more solemn and awe-inspiring. They are words with which we are all familiar. Even in a day like this, when there is such ignorance of the Scriptures, most people are familiar with this particular picture. Our Lord has finished His Sermon on the Mount and has given His detailed instruction, He has laid down all His great and vital principles, and He is now applying the truth. He is confronting His followers with the two possibilities; they must all go in at one or other of the two gates, either at the narrow gate or at the broad gate, and they will walk either the narrow way or the broad way. His purpose has been to help them as they face this choice. To that end He has shown them how to recognize and avoid the subtle temptations and dangers which invariably confront those who are in that situation. In these verses our Lord continues with the same theme. Notice the connection. It is not something new; rather it is a continuation and final clinching of His earlier argument. It is the same warning about the danger of a lack of obedience, of being content with listening to the gospel and not putting it into practice. In other words, it is once more the danger of self-deception. The Scriptures, as we have seen, are full of warnings against this; and we have it here pictured, in a most arresting fashion, in the greatness of the fall of the house that was built upon the sand. We have seen it already in the case of the unconscious hypocrites — these people who were so sure that they were Christian, but who will be so sadly disillusioned in the day of judgment, when the Lord says to them, 'I never knew you: depart from me, ye that work iniquity'. It is, then, the same theme, but with an added lesson. Our Lord never drew a new picture merely for the sake of doing so. There must be some new aspect of the matter, which He is anxious to present; and this arresting picture shows clearly what that new emphasis is.

The best way to approach this particular picture is to look at it as the third in a series. The first, in verses 15-20, concerning the false prophet, was designed to warn us against the danger of being deceived by appearances. Affable men come to us in sheep's clothing who inwardly are ravening wolves. How easily we can be deceived by such people because we are so superficial in our judgments. Our Lord said on one occasion, 'Judge not according to the appearance.' He said that God does not judge by the appearance, but by the heart. That is the first warning. We must not assume, as we stand there outside these two gates, that any man who comes to talk to us, and who is pleasant and affable, and who seems to be a Christian, is of necessity a Christian. We must not judge him by appearances; we must apply another test — 'By their fruits ye shall know them.'

The second picture is one of people who assume that everybody who says 'Lord, Lord' shall enter into the kingdom of heaven. This is a picture designed to warn us against the danger of deceiving ourselves in terms of what we believe, or in terms of our zeal and fervour, and our own activities. 'Many will say to me in that day, Lord, Lord, have we not prophesied in thy name? and in thy name have cast out devils? and in thy name done many wonderful works?' They were resting on these things; but they were quite wrong. He had never had anything to do with them; He had never known them. They were just deceiving and deluding themselves.

We are now going to look at the third and last picture. I suggest at once, in order to concentrate attention, that our Lord's chief concern in this picture is to warn us against the danger of seeking and desiring only the benefits and the blessings of salvation, and resting upon our apparent possession of them. Clearly the words are addressed to those who are professing Christians. They are not addressed to people who have no interest whatsoever in the kingdom; they are addressed to people who have been listening, and who like listening, to teaching concerning it. These words are obviously addressed to members of churches, to those who make the claim of being Christian, who profess discipleship, and who are seeking the benefits and blessings of salvation. Everything about the picture emphasizes that, and we see that it, again, is meant to show us the difference between the false and the true profession of Christianity; the difference between the Christian and the seeming Christian; between the man who really is born again and is a child of God, and the man who only thinks he is.

In order to bring out this distinction our Lord presents us with a comparison; indeed, there is a kind of double comparison in the picture. There are two men and two houses. Obviously, therefore, if we are to arrive at the spiritual truth which is taught here, we must examine the picture in detail. There are similarities and differences to be observed.

First of all let us look at the similarities in the case of the two men. To begin with, they had the same desire. They both desired to build a house, a house in which they could live with their families, dwell at ease and enjoy themselves. They wanted the same thing, they thought about the same thing, and they were interested in the same thing. There is no difference at all at that point. Not only so, but they desired a house in the same locality; indeed, they built their houses in the same locality, for our Lord points out clearly that the two houses were subjected to precisely the same tests and stresses. A strong impression is thus given that the two houses were quite near to one another, and were subject to precisely the same conditions. This is a most important point.

But we can go one step further and say that they obviously liked and designed the same kind of house. We deduce that from the fact that our Lord makes it clear that there was no difference between these two houses except in the foundation. Looked at externally and on the surface there was no difference. The doors, the windows and the chimneys were in the same position; they had the same design, the same pattern — the two houses were apparently identical apart from just this one difference beneath the surface. So we are entitled to deduce that these two men liked the same kind of house. Not only did each want a house; they wanted the same kind of house. Their ideas on the subject were absolutely identical. They had much in common.

In saying that, we have incidentally brought out the similarities in the two houses. We have seen that the two houses look absolutely identical if we merely examine them superficially. Everything seems to be in exactly the same position in the one as in the other. Furthermore, we must remember that they are subject to precisely the same tests. Up to this point, therefore, as we look at the two men and the two houses we find nothing but similarity. Yet we know that the whole point of the picture is to show the difference and the dissimilarity. Indeed, our Lord is concerned to show that the difference is a fundamental and vital one.

As we concentrate our attention therefore upon the differences, we can divide up the matter once more into the difference between the men, and the difference between the houses. Before we come to the details, let us look at the difference in general. The first point is that it is not an obvious one. We need to be reminded of this constantly because there is no point at which the devil in his subtlety seems to trap us so frequently. We cling to the notion that the difference between the true Christian and the pseudo-Christian is obvious. Our

Lord's whole point, however, is that this is a most subtle matter. It is not obvious either in the case of the men or the houses. If we do not stress that point we miss the whole purpose of His teaching in the Sermon on the Mount. Our Lord emphasizes this element of subtlety everywhere. It was there in the first picture of the men in sheep's clothing — the false prophets. The whole difficulty about the false prophet, as we saw, was that on the surface he was so extraordinarily like the true prophet. The false prophet is not of necessity a man who says there is no God and that the Bible is just the product of human thinking, and who denies the miracles and the supernatural. The false prophet can be detected only when you examine him very carefully with a sense of discrimination given only by the Holy Spirit. His condition is such that he deceives himself as well as others. It was precisely the same in that second picture: and it is so here also. The difference is not obvious; it is very subtle. Nevertheless to those who have eyes to see it is perfectly clear. If you interpret this picture by saying that the difference between the two houses and the two men is discovered only when the trials come, when the floods descend and the winds blow, then not only is your exposition wrong, it is of no value. By then it is too late to do anything about it. So if our Lord were teaching that, He would in effect be mocking us. But that is not the case; His whole object is to enable us to detect the difference between the two, so that we may safeguard ourselves against the consequences of the false position while there is still time. If we have our eyes anointed with the eye salve which the Holy Spirit can give, if we have 'that anointing from the Holy One', and the unction which enables us to discriminate, we shall be able to detect the difference between the men and the houses.

Look first at the difference between the two men. At this point the record as given at the end of Luke 6 is particularly helpful. There we are told that the wise man digged deep and laid a foundation for his house, whereas the foolish man did not dig at all, and did not trouble to lay a foundation. In other words, the way to discover the difference between these two men is to make a detailed analysis of the foolish man. The wise man is just the exact opposite. And, of course, the key to the understanding of that man is the word 'foolish'. It describes a particular outlook, a characteristic type of person.

What are the characteristics of the foolish man? The first is that he is in a hurry. Foolish people are always in a hurry; they want to do everything at once; they have no time to wait. How often does Scripture warn us against this! It tells us that the godly, righteous man 'shall not make haste'. He is never subject to flurry and excitement and hurry. He knows God and he knows that the decrees and purposes and plan of God are eternal and immutable. But the foolish man is impatient; he never takes time; he is always interested in shortcuts and quick results. That is the chief characteristic of his mentality and his conduct. We are all familiar with this kind of person in ordinary life and quite apart from Christianity. He is the type of man who says, 'I must have a house at once, there is no time for foundations.' He is always in a hurry.

At the same time, because he has that mentality, he does not trouble to listen to instruction; he does not pay any attention to the rules that govern the construction of a house. The construction of a house is a serious matter, and a man who is anxious to build one should never think merely in terms of having some kind of roof over his head. He should realize that certain principles of construction should be observed if he is to have a satisfactory and durable edifice. That is why men consult architects; and the architect draws up plans and specifications and makes his calculations. The wise man is anxious to know the right way to do things; and so he listens to instruction and is prepared to be taught. But the foolish man is not interested in such things; he wants a house; he cannot be bothered about rules and regulations. 'Put it up,' he says. He is impatient, contemptuous of instruction and teaching, saying that he wants 'to get on with it'. That is the typical mentality of the foolish person, both in ordinary life and in connection with things spiritual.

Not only is he in too much of a hurry to listen to instruction, but this foolish man also considers it unnecessary. In his opinion his ideas are the best. He has nothing to learn from anybody. 'Everything is all right,' he says. 'There is no need to be so cautious and to bother so much about these details.' 'Let us get the house built' is his slogan. He does not care what has been done in the past, but simply follows his own impulses and ideas. I am not caricaturing this type of person. Just think of people you have seen and known going into business, or getting married, or building houses, or anything similar, and you will agree that that is a true picture of this foolish mentality which thinks it knows all, is satisfied with its own opinion, and is always in a hurry to put it into effect.

Finally, it is a mentality that never thinks things right through, it never stops to envisage and consider possibilities and eventualities. The foolish man who built his house without a foundation, and on the sand, did not stop to think or to ask himself, 'Now what may happen? Is it possible that the river which is so pleasant to look at in the summer may, in the winter, suddenly become very swollen as the result of heavy rain or snow and I may be flooded out?' He did not stop to think of that; he just wanted a pleasant house in that particular position, and he put it up without considering any one of these things. And if someone had come along and said, 'Look here, my friend, it is no use putting up a house like that on the sand. Don't you realize what may happen in this locality? You don't know what that river is capable of doing. I have seen it like a veritable cataract. I have known storms here that bring down the best-built houses. My friend, I suggest that you dig deep. Get down to the rock'

— the foolish man would have dismissed it all and persisted in doing what he considered best for him. In a spiritual sense, he is not interested in learning from Church history; he is not interested in what the Bible has to say; he wants to do something, and he believes it can be done in his way, and away he goes and does it. He does not consult the plans and specifications; he does not try to look to the future and envisage certain tests that must inevitably come upon the house that is being built.

The wise man, of course, presents us with a complete contrast to that. He has one great desire, and that is to build durably. So he starts by saying, 'I do not know much about this; I am not an expert in these matters; wisdom dictates therefore that I should consult people who do know. I want to have plans and specifications, I want some guidance and some instruction. I know men can build houses quickly, but I want a house that will last. There are many things that may happen, which will test my ideas of construction and my house.' That is the essence of wisdom. The wise man takes trouble to find out all he can; he holds himself in check, and does not allow his feelings and emotions or his enthusiasm to carry him away. He desires knowledge, truth and understanding; is ready to respond to the exhortation of the book of Proverbs which urges us to seek and to covet wisdom, for 'the gain thereof (is better) than fine gold. She is more precious than rubies'. He is not prepared to take risks, and does not rush off in a hurry; he thinks before he acts.

Turning our attention now to the difference between the two houses, there are but two matters calling for comment. The first is that the time for examination has already passed. When the house is built it is already too late. The time for examination is at the very beginning. These two men and their operations must be watched when they are prospecting and planning and choosing the site and location. The time to watch your jerry-builder is at the beginning, to see what he does as regards laying a foundation. It is not enough just to look at the house when it is completed. Indeed, it may look better than the other. That, in turn, leads to the second point which is that, though the difference between the two houses is not obvious, it is nevertheless vital, for ultimately the most important thing about a house is the foundation. This is a truth which is frequently emphasized in the Bible. The foundation, which seems so insignificant and unimportant because it is out of sight, is nevertheless the most vital and important thing of all. If the foundation is wrong, everything else must be wrong. Was not that Paul's great argument when he said, 'Other foundation can no man lay than that is laid, which is Jesus Christ'? The foundation, the first principles, are more important than anything else. Another reason for the vital significance of this one difference between the houses is brought out by the coming of the tests later. They are certain to come sooner or later. We shall not stay with the application of that to our lives now; but as certainly as we are in this life the tests are going to come for every one of us, and we shall have to face them. They are inexorable and unavoidable; and in view of that nothing matters more than the foundation.

Our Lord drew this graphic and dramatic picture of the difference between the two men and the two houses because it is all of vital importance in the spiritual realm. Everything we have been saying provides us with the means of analysing the difference between the Christian and the pseudo-Christian. Is it not significant that we hear so very little today about what the Puritans called the 'false professor'? Read the history of the Church in this land, and you will find that in great periods such as the Puritan era and the Evangelical Revival they paid great attention to this subject. It is seen in the way in which Whitefield and Wesley and others examined the converts before they admitted them to membership of their classes. The same is seen in the great days of the Church in Scotland, and in the first hundred years of the story of the Presbyterian Church of Wales. Indeed it has always been the most prominent feature among all who think of the Church as 'the gathered saints'.

How are we to exercise this discrimination in practice? Let us adopt exactly the same technique as we have already employed. The first thing we have to say about the Christian and the pseudo-Christian is that they have certain points in common. As there were certain similarities between the two builders and the two houses, so there are certain similarities between these two people. The first is that you tend to find them in the same place. The two men in the picture put up their houses in the same locality, they wanted to be near each other and near the river. It is exactly the same in the realm of religion. The true Christian and his false counterpart are generally to be found in the same sphere. You generally find them both in the Church, as members together. They sit and listen to precisely the same gospel; and both seem to like doing so. They are to all appearance in exactly the same position, having the same general outlook and interested in the same activities. The man who is deluded by the counterfeit is not outside the Church; he is inside it. He likes being connected with the Church and he may be an active member of it. These two men are, on the surface, as like each other as were the two builders and their houses in the picture.

But they are not only found in the same place. As we saw, the two men appear to have the same general desires. And in the spiritual application the essence of the difficulty lies in the fact that the nominal Christian has the same general desires as the true Christian. What are these? He desires forgiveness and wants to believe that his sins are forgiven. He wants peace. He went to a meeting in the first place, because life had made him restless. He was unhappy and could not find satisfaction, so he went to the meeting and began to listen. It is a great mistake to think that the only person who desires peace within and the 'quiet heart' is the true Christian. The world today is hungering and thirsting for this peace, and is searching for it. Many people come into the sphere of Christianity because they desire it, as others turn to the various cults.

The same thing is true, also, of the desire for comfort and consolation. Life is hard and difficult and we all tend to be weary and sad, so the world is longing for comfort. The result is that there are many people who come to the Church just, as it were, to be drugged. They sit in the service and do not even listen to what is said. They say that there is something about the atmosphere of the building which is soothing. They are longing for comfort and consolation. The true and the false share that in common.

The same applies in the matter of guidance and the desire to find a way out of our troubles and difficulties. It is not only the true Christian that is interested in guidance. There are unbelievers who have made great mistakes in life, and who are unhappy as a result. They say, 'I always seem to do the wrong thing; I try to work things out but my decisions are always wrong.' Then suddenly they hear someone speaking about guidance, someone who claims an infallible guidance, who says that if you do what he tells you things can never go wrong, and they jump at the teaching with avidity. We must not blame them; it is very understandable. We all know this longing for guidance, for infallible guidance, so that we may cease from making mistakes and always do the right thing and make the right decision. The 'false professor' desires that quite as much as the true Christian.

In exactly the same way he may have a desire to live a good life. You need not be a true Christian in order to desire to live a better life. There are highly moral, ethical men outside the realm of Christianity who are very concerned to live a better life. That is why they read philosophy and study ethical systems. They want to live a good and moral life. Emerson's teaching is still popular. We cannot hope to discriminate between these two men by these tests alone.

Dare we go further and say that the 'false professor' may be very interested in and desirous of spiritual power? Read again that account in Acts 8 of Simon the sorcerer in Samaria. That man saw Philip working miracles, and he was impressed. He had been doing that kind of thing too, but not with this ease and power; and he joined himself to the Christians. Then when he saw that Peter and John by laying their hands on people gave them the gift of the Holy Ghost, Simon became covetous, and offered them money for the possession of that power. He coveted it, and his spiritual descendants in these days may likewise covet and desire spiritual power. He sees a man preaching with spiritual power, and says, 'I would like to be like that.' He pictures himself standing in a pulpit and apparently exercising great power, and it appeals to his carnal nature. There are many examples of men who were blind to spiritual truth but who nevertheless were most desirous of possessing spiritual power. It is as subtle as that.

Finally, the 'false professor' also desires to get to heaven. He is a man who believes in heaven and hell, and he does not want to go to perdition. He very definitely desires to go to heaven. Have you not known such people? Many can be found outside the Church altogether. They most certainly want to go to heaven, and say that they have always believed in God. If that is true of the man obviously outside, how much more is it true of this nominal Christian who is inside the realm and sphere of Christian interest?

So we find these strange similarities between these two persons. They seem to believe the same things and desire the same things. They are similar also in that not only do they desire the same things, they even seem to have the same things. That is the most alarming thought of all, but the two previous pictures have emphasized that truth quite as much as this one does. The 'false professor' believes he is safe. The people who had cast out devils and done many wonderful works in the name of Christ were quite sure of their salvation. They had no vestige of doubt about it. They believed that they were forgiven; they seemed to be at peace and to be enjoying the comforts of religion; they seemed to have spiritual power and were living a better life; they said, 'Lord, Lord'; and they wanted to spend their eternity with Him. Yet He said to them: 'I never knew you: depart from me, ye that work iniquity.' Do you realize that it is possible to have a false sense of forgiveness? Do you realize that it is possible to have a false peace within you? You say, 'I have not worried about my sins for years.' I can well believe that, if you are only a nominal Christian. The fact that you have not thought about these things for years is an indication in itself that there is something wrong about your sense of security and peace. The man who never knows what it is to have certain fears about himself, fears which drive him to Christ, is in a highly dangerous condition. You can have false peace, false comfort, false guidance. The devil can give you remarkable guidance. Telepathy, and all sorts of occult phenomena and various other agencies can do so too. There are powers that can counterfeit almost everything in the Christian life. And, as we have already seen in the previous paragraph, these people can have a certain spiritual power. There is no doubt about it. They can have power to 'cast out devils' and to do 'many wonderful works'. There was no evident difference between Judas Iscariot and the eleven other disciples, though he was 'the son of perdition'.

According to our Lord's teaching, therefore, the similarities between the true and the false can include such matters and extend even as far as that. Nevertheless our Lord's teaching is that though there are these many similarities between these two men and the two houses in the parable, and in the realm of Christian profession, yet there is a vital difference. It is not obvious on the surface, but if you look for it, it is perfectly clear and unmistakable. If we take the trouble to apply our analysis, we cannot fail to see it. We have already indicated the nature of the tests in our analysis of the foolish man. All we need to do is to apply them to ourselves — this hurry, this mentality that does not listen to warnings, that is not concerned about plans and specifications, that thinks it knows what it wants and what is best and goes all out for it. Let us examine ourselves in the light of these criteria, and then we shall see very clearly to which category we belong. I can sum it up in the form of a question: What is your supreme desire? Are you out for the benefits and blessings of the Christian life and salvation, or have you a deeper and profounder desire? Are you out for the fleshly carnal results, or do you long to know God and to become more and more like the Lord Jesus Christ? Are you hungering and thirsting after righteousness?

Chapter Twenty-eight

Rock or Sand?

S O far we have dealt mainly with the mechanics of our Lord's picture of the
two men and the two houses. Obviously, with a picture like this, the first
thing to do is to look at the picture itself, and discover its meaning. Then that
can be applied to the spiritual condition under consideration. We have already
begun to do this, but we must now proceed with it in detail. What are the characteristics of the merely nominal or pseudo-Christian? We can divide them into
general and particular. In general, they are obviously the very things which we
observed in the foolish man who built his house upon the sand. That is to say,
he is foolish, hasty and superficial. He does not believe very much in doctrine,
or in understanding the Scriptures; he wants to enjoy Christianity without
much trouble. He cannot be bothered with all these doctrines and definitions,
he is in a great hurry, and he is always impatient of instruction, and experience
and guidance. He is, indeed, generally impatient of all true knowledge; that is
his chief characteristic according to our Lord's picture of him. So far we have
considered his mentality; and before going on to our next consideration, I want
to stress the importance of that. There is nothing which provides such a true in-
dex of what a man really is as his general mentality. It is a mistake to ignore this
and to concentrate only on his actions in detail.

But turning now to the particulars — what are the characteristics of the 'false
professor'? The first thing about him is that, like the man in the picture, he is a
man who is out to please himself. Analyse all he does, and listen to what he says,
and you will find that it all revolves around himself. That is really the key to everything he does and everything he says; self is at the centre of his life, and self
controls his outlook and all his actions. He desires ease and comfort and certain
benefits. That is why he is to be found in the realm of the Church. He is anxious

to obtain certain blessings, and in this he differs from the man who is right out in the world, and who does not claim to have any beliefs at all. This man has discovered that there are certain blessings offered in Christianity. He is interested in them, and wants to know something about them and how to obtain them. He is always thinking in terms of: What can I get? What will it give me? What benefits are likely to accrue to me if I go in for it? That is the kind of motive that animates him. And because this is his attitude, he does not really face the full teaching of the gospel, nor want to know the whole counsel of God.

Let us consider this in detail. We saw, in looking at the picture earlier, that the trouble with the man who builds his house hurriedly and without foundations upon the sand, is that he does not believe in consulting manuals on architecture and house building, he does not believe in going to an architect, he does not want plans and specifications. Indeed, all such details seem to him an unnecessary fuss, and he has no interest in them. It is exactly the same with the false believer. He does not really trouble to study the Word of God; he is not a true student of the Bible. He may indeed have a certain interest in the grammar or the mechanics of Scripture, but he is not really concerned to know the message of the Book; he has never really allowed himself to face its full teaching. Paul was able to return to the elders of the church at Ephesus and to say to them that he was very happy about one thing, that he had delivered unto them 'all the counsel of God'. He did not keep anything back. The message he had been given by the risen Lord he had given to them. There were parts of it that hurt; parts that perhaps he would rather not have given, but it was not his message; it was the whole counsel of God, and he had given it to them as from God. The superficial false believer is not interested in that.

Secondly, he picks out what he likes, and concentrates on what appeals to him. For instance, he likes the doctrine of the love of God, but not the doctrine of the justice of God. He does not like the idea of God as a holy God, and a righteous God. The idea of the holiness of God is repellent to him, so he does not read about it. He knows that there are certain great passages in the Bible that manifest the love of God, and he can recite them by heart because he reads them so often. He thinks he knows all about John 3:16, but he does not even read that properly. He emphasizes a portion of it, but he does not like the idea of 'should not perish'. He does not go to the end of that same third chapter where it says, 'The wrath of God abideth on him' — that he does not believe and does not like. He is interested in the love of God, and in forgiveness. He is interested, in other words, in everything that gives him the feeling of comfort, and happiness, and joy and peace within. So, whether consciously or unconsciously, he picks and chooses as he reads the Bible. There are many people who do that. There was quite a vogue in that kind of thing in the early part of this century. There were people who never read the Epistles of the apostle Paul; they read only the Gospels. And they did not read the whole of the Gospels because they felt that there were things that were offensive, so they narrowed it down to the Sermon on the Mount. But even here, in the same way, they did not read the Beatitudes, they simply read about 'loving your enemies', etc. They were pacifists and idealists who did not believe, they said, in striking back, but in turning the other cheek. That is the typical false believer. He extracts and picks out that which pleases him, and ignores the rest. You see it so clearly in the picture of the man who built his house upon the sand, and it is exactly the same in the spiritual realm.

We should examine ourselves constantly in the light of the Word. And if we are not reading it in such a way as to be examined by it, we are not reading it correctly. We must face these things. Do I take the whole message of the Scriptures? Am I taking the whole counsel of God? Do I accept the teaching concerning the wrath of God as I do that concerning the love of God? Am I as ready to believe in the righteousness of God as in His mercy; in the justice and holiness of God as well as in His compassion and long-suffering? That is the question. The characteristic of the false believer is that he does not face it all; he just picks out what he wants and likes, and ignores the rest. In other words his outstanding characteristic always is that he never faces completely and honestly the nature of sin, and the effects of sin, in the light of the holiness of God. The trouble with him is that he never wants to feel unhappy, he never wants to feel a sense of dissatisfaction with himself, or a sense of discomfort. The thing he wants to avoid at all costs is being unhappy or being made to feel uncomfortable. He does not like the people who make him feel uncomfortable, nor the passages in the Bible that do the same, so he picks and chooses. He is always out for ease and comfort and happiness; and he never faces properly the biblical doctrine of sin, because it disturbs him and causes him disquiet.

But in so doing he is evading a vital part of the great message of the Bible. The Bible in the first instance is a terrible exposition and a graphic delineation of the effects of sin. That is why it gives all that history in the Old Testament; why, for instance, it shows a man like David, one of its greatest heroes, falling into gross sin, committing adultery and murder. Why does it do that? It is to impress upon us the effects of sin, to teach us that there is something in all of us that can drag us down to that, that we are all by nature false and foul and vile. The false believer does not like such teaching. He dislikes it so much that he even objects to the distinction which the Bible draws between sin and sins. I knew a man who used to attend a place of worship, but now no longer does so. His main reason for staying away is that he did not like the preacher's constant talk about sin. He did not object to hearing about sins, because he was prepared to admit that he was not absolutely perfect. But when the preacher said that man's very nature was vile and foul, he felt that that was going too far. He was not as bad as that! But the Bible talks about the sinful nature and says of us that we are 'shapen in iniquity, and in sin did my mother conceive me', that we are all 'by nature the children of wrath', that we must say, if we speak truthfully, that 'in me (that is in my flesh) dwelleth no good thing', and that nothing will suffice for us but to be born again and to be given a new nature. The nominal and formal Christian hates that doctrine and avoids it.

In other words, the trouble with him ultimately is that he does not really desire to know God. He wants God's blessing, but he does not want God. He does not really desire to serve God and to worship Him with the whole of his being, he simply wants certain things that he believes God can give him. To sum it up, his real trouble is that he does not know the meaning of the expression 'hungering and thirsting after righteousness'. He is not interested in righteousness; he is not interested in holiness. He really does not want to be like Christ; he simply wants to be made comfortable. He is like the man in the picture who wants to build a house hurriedly, so that he can sit in his armchair and enjoy himself. He wishes all to be well with him in this life and in the life to come, but he wants it on his own terms and in his own way. He is impatient, and dislikes all teaching and instruction that warn him that this is not sufficient if he really wants to have a satisfactory and durable edifice.

What, then, are the characteristics of the true Christian? Put positively, it is that he 'doeth the will of my Father which is in heaven'. Our Lord says: 'Not every one that saith unto me, Lord, Lord . . . but he that doeth the will of my Father which is in heaven.' 'Therefore whosoever heareth these sayings of mine, and doeth them, I will liken him unto a wise man.' What does this mean?

The first part of the answer is to make clear what it does not mean. That is most important. Obviously it does not mean 'justification by works'. Our Lord is not saying here that the man who is truly Christian is the man who, having listened to the Sermon on the Mount, puts it into practice and thereby makes himself a Christian. Why is that interpretation impossible? For the good reason that the Beatitudes make it quite impossible. At the very beginning we emphasized that the Sermon on the Mount must be taken as a whole, and so it must. We start with the Beatitudes, and the first statement is: 'Blessed are the poor in spirit.' We can try from now until we are dead, but we shall never make ourselves 'poor in spirit', and we can never make ourselves conform to any of the Beatitudes. That is a sheer impossibility, so it cannot mean justification by works. Then take that great climax at the end of the fifth chapter: 'Be ye therefore perfect, even as your Father which is in heaven is perfect.' That again is quite impossible to man in his own strength, and proves further that this passage does not teach justification by works. Were it to do so it would contradict the whole message of the New Testament which tells us that what we have failed to do, God has sent His Son into the world to do for us — 'with men this is impossible, but with God all things are possible'. No man shall be justified by the deeds of the law, but only by the righteousness of Jesus Christ.

Neither is it a teaching of sinless perfection. Many people read these pictures at the end of the Sermon on the Mount, and say that they mean that the only man who is allowed or able to enter into the kingdom of heaven is the man who, having read the Sermon on the Mount, puts each detail into practice, always and everywhere. This again is obviously impossible. If that were the teaching, then we could be quite certain that there never has been and there never will be a single Christian in the world. For 'all have sinned, and come short of the glory of God'. We have all failed. 'If we say that we have no sin, we deceive ourselves, and the truth is not in us.' It cannot be sinless perfection, therefore, which is advocated here.

What then is it? It is none other than the doctrine which James, in his Epistle, summarizes in the words, 'Faith without works is dead.' It is simply a perfect definition of faith. Faith without works is not faith, it is dead. The life of faith is never a life of ease; faith is always practical. The difference between faith and intellectual assent is that intellectual assent simply says, 'Lord, Lord', but does not do His will. In other words, though I may say 'Lord, Lord' to the Lord Jesus Christ, there is no meaning in it unless I regard Him as my Lord, and willingly become His bond slave. My words are idle words, and I do not mean 'Lord, Lord', unless I obey Him. Faith without works is dead.

Or, to put it another way, true faith always shows itself in the life; it shows itself in the person in general, and it also shows itself in what he does. Mark the double emphasis — faith shows itself in the person in general, as well as in what he says and does. There must be no contradiction between a man's appearance and general demeanour and what he says and does. The first thing we are told about the Christian in the Sermon on the Mount is that he must be 'poor in spirit', and if he *is* 'poor in spirit', he never *looks* as if he were proud and self-satisfied. Another thing we are told about him is that he mourns because of his sin, and that he is meek. The man who is meek never looks pleased with himself. We are talking of what he looks like before he has said or done anything. True faith always shows itself in a man's general appearance, in the total impression he gives, as well as in what he says and does in particular. You have sometimes seen men saying, 'Lord, Lord,' who almost give the impression that they are patronizing God as they say it, so full of themselves are they, so pleased with themselves, so self-confident. They do not know what Paul meant when he said to the church at Corinth, 'I was with you in weakness, and in fear, and in much trembling.' He preached the gospel with a sense of awe upon him because it was the message of God, and he was aware of his own unworthiness and the seriousness of the situation. So we must not forget that faith shows itself in a man's general bearing as well as in what he says and does.

Faith always shows itself in the whole personality. We can summarize it all in the words we find in the first and second chapters of John's first Epistle, where we read, 'If we say that we have fellowship with him, and walk in darkness, we lie, and do not the truth.' 'He that saith, I know him, and keepeth not his commandments, is a liar, and the truth is not in him.' We can see where those have gone astray who hold that the Sermon on the Mount cannot apply to us, but only to the disciples of our Lord's own day, and to the Jews of some future kingdom which is yet to come. They say it must be so, otherwise we are put under the law and not under grace. But the words just quoted from the first Epistle of John were written 'under grace', and John puts it like that specifically: If any man says, 'I know him' — that is your faith, believing in the grace of Christ and the free forgiveness of sin — if any man says, 'I know him, and keepeth not his commandments, (he) is a liar.' That is simply repeating what our Lord says here about those who shall enter the kingdom of heaven: 'Not every one that saith unto me, Lord, Lord, . . . but he that doeth the will of my Father which is in heaven.' And it is the message of the whole of the New Testament. He 'gave himself for us', says Paul to Titus, 'that he might . . . purify unto himself a peculiar people, zealous of good works.' We have been saved 'unto holiness'. He set us apart in order to prepare us for Himself, and 'every man that hath this hope in him purifieth himself, even as he is pure'. That is the doctrine of the Bible.

But we must apply all this in a yet more detailed manner. What is implied by putting into operation the Sermon on the Mount? How can I know whether I am a 'wise' man or a 'foolish' man? Again let me start with a few simple negatives. One of the best tests is this. Do you resent this Sermon on the Mount? Do you dislike it? Do you object to hearing preaching on it? If you do, you are a 'foolish' person. The foolish person always dislikes the Sermon on the Mount when it is presented as it is, in all its parts. Do you feel it is making things impossible for you? Do you become annoyed at its standard? Do you say it is quite impossible? Do you say, 'It is grim, this preaching is grim, it is making everything hopeless'? Is that your reaction to it? It is always the reaction of the false believer. He is impatient with the Sermon on the Mount; he resents being examined, he hates being examined because it makes him feel uncomfortable.

The true Christian is entirely different; he does not resent it, as we shall see. He does not resent the condemnation of the Sermon on the Mount, and he never defends himself against it. We can put it like this. We know that we betray ourselves by our idle remarks, and we can often tell a man by his immediate reaction. We are all so subtle and clever, that when we take second thoughts and begin to think about a thing, we are a little more guarded and careful in what we say. What really shows what we are is our instinctive answer, our immediate reaction. And if our reaction to the Sermon on the Mount is one of resentment, if we feel it is hard and difficult and makes things impossible, and that it is not the nice sort of Christianity we thought it was, we are not true believers.

Another characteristic of the false believer at this point is that, having heard it, he forgets all about it. He is a forgetful hearer who listens to the message and immediately forgets it. He is interested for a moment, then it goes from his mind, perhaps as the result of a conversation in the vestibule on the way out of church.

Another feature of the false professors is that while, in general, they may admire the Sermon and praise its teaching, they never put it into practice. Or they will approve certain parts of it and ignore others. So many people seem to think that the Sermon on the Mount simply says one thing, such as 'love your enemies'. They do not seem to understand all these other things. But we must take it as a whole, chapters 5, 6 and 7, the Beatitudes, the law, instruction, everything, it is all one Sermon.

But let us turn to the positive characteristics of the true believer. He is a man who does face this teaching, and he faces the whole of it. He does not pick and choose, he allows every part of the Bible to speak to him. He is not impatient. He takes time to read it, he does not rush to a few favourite Psalms and use them as a kind of hypnotic when he cannot sleep at night; he allows the whole Word to examine him and to search him. Far from resenting this searching, he welcomes it. He knows it is good for him, so he does not object to the pain. He realizes that 'no chastening for the present is joyous, but grievous'; but he knows that 'afterward it (invariably) yieldeth the peaceable fruit of righteousness to them that are exercised thereby'. In other words the true Christian humbles himself under the Word. He agrees that what it says of him is true. Indeed, he says, 'it has not said enough about me'. He does not resent its criticism, nor that of other people, but rather he says to himself, 'They do not say the half, they do not know me.' He humbles himself under the Word and all its criticism. He admits and confesses his utter failure and his complete unworthiness. You see, the man who is right with respect to this Sermon is a man who, having humbled himself, submits himself to it, becomes poor in spirit, becomes a mourner for his sins, becomes meek because he knows how worthless he is. He immediately conforms to the Beatitudes because of the effect of the Word upon him, and then, because of that, he desires to conform to the type and pattern set before him. Here is a very good test. Would you *like* to live the Sermon on the Mount? Is that your true desire? Is that your ambition? If it is, it is a very good and healthy sign. Any man who desires to live this type and kind of life is a Christian. He hungers and thirsts after righteousness; that is the big thing in his life. He is not content with what he is. He says, 'O that I might be like the saints I have read about, like Hudson Taylor, or Brainerd, or Calvin. If only I were like the men who lived in caves and dens and sacrificed and suffered everything for His sake. If only I were like Paul. O that I were more like my blessed Lord Himself.' The man who can say that honestly is a man who is building on the rock. He is conforming to the Beatitudes. Observe the nature of the test. It is not asking whether you are sinless or perfect; it is asking what you would like to be, what you desire to be.

Then, of course, the true believer is a man who accepts our Lord's teaching concerning the law. You remember how, in the fifth chapter, our Lord interpreted the ancient law spiritually with regard to certain things. The believer accepts that and believes it is right; he is not content with simply refraining from committing adultery as an act, he does not want to *look* at a woman to lust after her. He says, 'That is right; one must be clean in heart, and not only in actions, and I want to be clean like that.' He accepts fully our Lord's teaching about the law.

In the same way he accepts the teaching about doing our alms in secret. He does not advertise his good deeds — neither does he draw attention to the fact that he does not advertise! His left hand really does not know what his right hand is doing. He also remembers the teaching about prayer, and about not setting our affections on the things of the world, about having a 'single' eye. He remembers that we are not even to worry about our daily bread, but are to leave it all to our Father who feeds the sparrows and will certainly not neglect His children. He remembers the instruction about not judging or condemning our brother, and about taking the beam out of our own eye before dealing with the mote in our brother's eye. He recalls that we are taught to do unto others as we would that they should do unto us; he accepts the whole teaching in its fullness. But not only that, he bemoans his failure to live it out. He wants to, he desires to, he tries to, but he realizes that he fails. But then he believes the next portion of the teaching, and he asks, he seeks, he knocks. He believes the message that tells him that by the Holy Spirit these things are possible, and he remembers that Christ has said in this Sermon, 'Ask, and it shall be given you; seek, and ye shall find; knock, and it shall be opened unto you.' And he goes on until he obtains. That is what is meant by 'doing these things'. It means that a man's supreme desire is to do these things and to be like the Lord Jesus Christ. It means he is a man who not only wants forgiveness, not only wants to escape hell and to go to heaven. Quite as much, in a sense, he wants positive holiness in this life and in this world. He wants to be righteous, he sings from his heart that hymn of Charles Wesley's —

> O for a heart to praise my God,
>   A heart from sin set free;
> A heart that always feels Thy blood
>   So freely shed for me.

That is the man who builds upon the rock. He is a man who desires and prays for holiness and who strives after it. He does his utmost to be holy, because his supreme desire is to know Christ. Not only to be forgiven, not only to go to heaven, but to know Christ now, to have Christ as his Brother, to have Christ as his Companion, to be walking with Christ in the light now, to enjoy a foretaste of heaven here in this world of time — that is the man who builds upon the rock. He is a man who loves God for God's sake, and whose supreme desire and concern is that God's name and God's glory may be magnified and spread abroad.

There, then, are the details of this matter. That is what is meant by 'doing' these things. That is what is meant by practising the Sermon on the Mount. It is to agree with the Shorter Catechism that 'the chief end of man is to glorify God and to enjoy Him for ever'. You know that you will never bring yourself to perfection, but your desire, your effort, is to that end, and all the time you are relying upon the Holy Spirit who has been given you to enable you to do so. That is the doctrine, and anyone who can face these tests, the negative and the positive, in that way can be happy and certain and sure that his house is being built upon the rock. If, on the other hand, you find you cannot answer these tests satisfactorily, there is but one inevitable conclusion: you have been building upon the sand. And your house will collapse. It will do so for certain on the day of judgment; it may well do so before that, when the next war comes, perhaps when the hydrogen bomb is let loose, or when you lose your money, your goods, your possessions. You will see, then, that you have nothing. If you see that now, admit it, confess it to God without a second's delay. Confess it and humble yourself 'under the mighty hand of God'. Acknowledge it and cast yourself upon His love and mercy, tell Him that, at last, you desire to be holy and righteous; ask Him to give you His Spirit and to reveal to you the perfect work of Christ on your behalf. Follow Christ, and He will lead you to this true holiness, 'without which no man shall see the Lord'.

Chapter Twenty-nine

The Trial and the Tests of Faith

W E come now to some final considerations about the picture which is contained in verses 24-27 and also about the two previous pictures which we have already studied. We remind ourselves that the teaching in general is designed to warn us against the terrible and subtle danger of self-deception. It is astonishing to note how much space is given in the New Testament to warnings. How slow we are to observe that and to heed it. There are constant warnings against a light and superficial belief, against the tendency just to say, 'Lord, Lord,' and do no more, warnings against the danger of trusting to works and to our own activities. We have been reminded of that very forcibly in the second picture. It is something that is to be found throughout the New Testament Scriptures; it is seen frequently in the teaching of our Lord Himself, and in the teaching of the apostles afterwards.

But it includes at the same time the danger of trusting to feelings, especially to false feelings. There is nothing that is so surprising to the natural mind as the New Testament expositions on the subject of love. For some reason or other we tend to think of love as being a mere matter of sentiment and feeling; we tend to regard it as simply an emotion. And we tend to carry this over into our thinking concerning the New Testament's great gospel of love, and the announcement of the love of God to offending sinners. Yet think for a moment of John's Gospel and his first Epistle in which so much is said about love, and also of 1 Corinthians 13. You will see that their whole emphasis is upon the fact that love is something which is very practical. How often does our Lord say in various ways, 'He that hath my commandments, and keepeth them, he it is that loveth me.'

That is the precise teaching at this point. All this warning at the end of the Sermon on the Mount is simply designed to emphasize the one thing, that 'not every one that saith unto me, Lord, Lord, shall enter into the kingdom of heaven, but he that doeth the will of my Father'. The recurring emphasis on this point is designed to save us from deluding ourselves into thinking that all is well with us because of some vague, general feeling which we may possess. Our Lord says that it is useless to talk about loving Him unless we keep His commandments. 'He that loves Me truly', He seems to say, 'does what I tell him to do'. Nothing is so fallacious as to substitute feelings and sensibilities for definite obedience. That is something that is stressed very emphatically in this great final word of warning, and that is why we have considered in detail what is meant by doing the will of our Father which is in heaven. The wise man is the man who, having heard these sayings, does them.

But we still have to consider why our Lord put His teaching in this particular form. There is in each one of these pictures, as you observe, a note of warning. We have been making casual reference to that as we have been considering each one. But, clearly, we cannot complete this series of considerations without taking up the question of judgment which He announces in every one of the pictures from verse 13. You remember that it is in the verse where He speaks of entering in at the strait gate that He begins to apply the message of the entire Sermon and to enforce its doctrine; and from there onwards the note of judgment comes in. 'Enter ye in', He says, 'at the strait gate: for wide is the gate, and broad is the way, that leadeth to destruction'. There is the note of warning at once. It is to be found again in exactly the same way in connection with the second picture, where He likens the true Christian to the good tree and the false Christian to the corrupt tree. He tells us that 'every tree that bringeth not forth good fruit is hewn down, and cast into the fire'. In the next picture we get it in the words: 'Many will say to me in that day, Lord, Lord, have we not done these various things in thy name. Then will I profess unto them, I never knew you: depart from me, ye that work iniquity.' And here it is, strikingly, in the last picture of the two houses and the two men, because He tells us that a day came when the houses were tested and that one of them fell, and 'great was the fall of it'. So we are forced to consider this great question of judgment. Indeed, we have seen that not only is it the prominent note in these pictures at the end of the Sermon, it has been the dominant note right through this chapter, beginning with 'judge not, that ye be not judged . . .', in verse 1. The note that runs right through this final exhortation is the tremendous note of judgment.

In a sense the message can be put thus: apart from any other consideration, false religion is useless. It is wrong, of course, just as anything that is false is always wrong; but apart from its being wrong, it is in the last analysis of no value at all. It leads in the end to nothing. It may give temporary satisfaction; but it fails to stand the real tests. That is the thing that is emphasized here. That broad way seems safe enough; that corrupt and evil tree in general looks healthy, and you even imagine its fruit to be good until you examine it and find that it is not. In the same way the house that the foolish man built upon the sand appears to be perfect; it looks sound and durable. But the fact is that in the end none of these things are of any value at all; they fail to stand up to the test. That is surely something about which there can be no disagreement. The real thing we need to know about any view of life, or any situation in life that we may hold, is whether it will stand the test. Is it going to help us and be of value to us in the hour of our greatest need? There is little value in a house, however luxurious and comfortable it may be, if when the storms come and the floods begin to beat upon it, it suddenly collapses. That is what we call living in 'a fool's paradise'. It seemed so wonderful when the sun was shining, and when, in a sense, we had no need of its protection and might have been quite satisfied with a tent. But we need a house that can stand up to the storms and the hurricanes. A house built upon the sand cannot do so and is obviously of no value at all.

The Bible makes much of this. It has some very alarming pictures of the apparent success and affluence of the ungodly, spreading himself 'like a green bay tree', when everything is going well. But it always shows that in the time of trouble, when all his prosperity has gone, he has nothing to fall back upon. The Bible is at pains to show the utter folly of the man who is not a Christian. Apart from anything else, what a foolish man he is, living for, and trusting to things that cannot help him in the hour of his greatest need. Think of our Lord's picture of that rich fool who had his barns bursting with goods and who was thinking of building greater ones, when God suddenly said to him, 'Thou fool, this night thy soul shall be required of thee; then whose shall those things be?' The Bible is full of that kind of teaching.

But this teaching that what is false is worthless is not confined to the Bible; human experience through the centuries confirms and establishes this. We can study that in the light of this particular picture. Our Lord says that everything we build in this world, everything that we are relying upon, every preparation that we make, our whole view of life, is going to be subjected to tests. He pictures the tests in the form of the rain descending and the floods coming and the winds blowing. It is something universal; it is something that is going to happen to the wise and to the foolish alike. Nowhere does the Bible tell us that immediately you become a Christian all your troubles end, and that the remainder of the story is that 'all lived happily ever after'. Nothing of the kind. 'The rain descended, the floods came, the winds blew' on the one house, just as they did upon the other. The whole of humanity is subjected to these tests.

The question as to what our Lord meant exactly by the details in this picture is full of interest. Some teach that they refer only to the day of judgment; but that is a totally inadequate understanding of the picture. It certainly includes the day of judgment; but what our Lord says here applies to life in this world as well as to what will happen to us after death and beyond the grave.

It is a dangerous thing, of course, to press the details of any picture too far, and yet, surely, our Lord did not take the trouble to differentiate between the rain and the flood and the wind to no purpose. Obviously He was anxious to convey certain definite ideas, and we can discover something of what is represented by these pictures. Think of the rain, for instance. This rain that He speaks of is something that is going to meet us all. We are all in one of two positions; we are either like the wise man or the foolish one; we are either, as we saw earlier, doing our utmost to put into practice the teaching of the Sermon on the Mount, or else we are not; either we are Christians, or we are deluding ourselves into thinking that we are Christians, and picking and choosing the things that please us out of the gospel, and saying, 'This is quite enough. You need not take these things too seriously; you must not become narrow. All is well as long as you believe things in general.' But our Lord teaches here that if we are in the wrong position our supposed belief will not help us at all; indeed, it will let us down completely when we need it most. What does He mean by the rain? I think He means things like illness, loss or disappointment, something going wrong in your life; something on which you were banking suddenly collapsing before your eyes; perhaps being let down by somebody else, or experiencing some grievous disappointment, a sudden change for the worse in your circumstances, or overwhelming grief and bereavement. These are the things that, at some time or another, come to all of us. There are certain things in life which are unavoidable; try as we may to evade them, we have to face them in the end. It is very difficult for those who are young and bounding with health and vigour to think of themselves as old people, finding it difficult to move from one room to another, or even from one chair to another. But that is the sort of thing that does happen. Age advances, health and vigour go, illness comes. These things, as our Lord shows here, are inevitable, and when they come they test us. It is no small trial to spend weeks and months in the same room; it tests one to the very foundations. The rain, then, covers things of that kind, and includes these tests that search and try us to the very depths.

But not only did the rain descend; our Lord tells us that the floods came and beat upon the house. I always think that this represents, in general, the world, using that term in its biblical sense, as meaning the worldly outlook, the worldly type of life. Whether we like it or not and whether we are true believers or false, the world comes beating against this house of ours, hurling itself in its full flood tide against us. We all have great trouble with the world — 'the lust of the flesh, and the lust of the eyes, and the pride of life'. As surely as we put up our building in this world, as indeed we are all doing, the world itself will come and test it and try it. Worldliness in its subtlety seeps in everywhere. It comes sometimes with mighty power; at other times it will do equal damage by flooding in silently, unobserved and unsuspected. There is literally no end to the forms it may assume. We all know something of this. Sometimes it comes as an enticement, something that draws us and appeals to us and pleads with us; it paints a glowing picture to attract us. At another time it will come as persecution. The world does not care ultimately what method it uses as long as it attains its object. If it can entice us from Christ and the Church it will do so, but if enticement fails, it will show its teeth and try persecution. Both ways test us, and one is quite as subtle as the other — 'the floods came . . . and beat upon that house'.

We all know something of what it is to feel the house almost rocking at times. It is not so much that the Christian wants to forsake his faith, but the power of the world can be so great that he wonders at times whether his foundation is going to hold. He has a wonderful belief in Christ when he is young, but sooner or later, perhaps in middle life, he begins to think of his future, and his career, and his whole position in life; and he begins to hesitate and to wonder. The slowing down process of age comes in, and a kind of slackness enters — that is the world beating against your house, trying and testing it.

Then there is the wind — 'the rain descended, the floods came, and the winds blew'. What does He mean by this — 'and the winds blew'? I tend to agree with those who would interpret the wind as being definite Satanic attacks. The devil has many different ways of dealing with us. According to the Word of God, he can transform himself into an angel of light and quote Scripture. He can tempt us through the world. But sometimes he attacks us directly; he may hurl doubts and denials at us. He will bombard us with foul, evil and blasphemous thoughts. Read the lives of godly men of old, and you will find that they have been subjected to this kind of thing. The devil makes violent attacks, trying to blow the house over, as it were, and the saints throughout the centuries have suffered from the power of this form of attack. You may have known good men who have been subject to this, fine Christians, who have lived godly lives; then, somewhere before the end, perhaps on their deathbed, they go through a period of darkness, and the devil attacks them violently. Indeed, 'we wrestle not against flesh and blood, but against principalities, against powers, . . . against spiritual wickedness in high places.' In Ephesians 6 the apostle Paul says that the only way to stand is to put on the whole armour of God. And here our Lord says in the same way that nothing but the solid foundation He advocates will enable our house to stand.

These things come to us all. But, finally, of course, certain and inevitable, comes death itself. Some have to endure the rain, others the flood, and others the wind and the hurricane; but we all have to meet and to face the fact of death. It will come to each of us in some shape or form, and will test to the very foundation all we have ever built. What a tremendous thing death is! We have not been through it, so we know nothing about it, although we may sometimes have watched others dying and heard them speak of it. Whether it comes suddenly or gradually, we have to meet it. I say it must be a tremendous thing to pass through that moment when you realize you are going out of this world, and leaving all you have always known, and crossing into that land beyond the veil. There is nothing that so profoundly tests a man as to his foundations as the mighty fact and moment of death.

The real question is, how do we stand up to these things? In many ways the prime business of the preaching of the gospel is to prepare men to stand up to these things. It matters not what your view of life may be, nor what your feelings; if you cannot stand up to those tests which I have enumerated you are an utter failure. Whatever a man's gifts or calling may be, and however noble and good his character, if his view and philosophy of life have not catered for these certainties, he is a fool, and all he has will fail him and collapse beneath his feet just when he most needs help. We have already experienced some of these tests. Here are the questions we must ask ourselves. Do we always find God when we need Him most of all? When these tests come and we turn to Him, do we know He is there? Are we agitated and alarmed? Do we dread His presence, or do we turn as a child to his father, and always know He is there, and always find Him? Are we conscious of His nearness and presence at these critical points, and moments? Have we a deep unshakeable confidence in Him, and an assurance that He will never leave us nor forsake us? Are we able to rejoice in Him at all times, even in tribulation? What is our view of the world at this moment, what is our attitude towards the world? Are we in any hesitancy or doubt as to which of these lives we want to live? Have we any uncertainty? Have we not found the utter uselessness of that worldly life that does not put God and His Christ in the centre? What is death to us? Are we horrified at the thought of it; are we so afraid of it that we are always doing our best to banish it out of our thoughts?

The Bible shows clearly what we should be like in all these respects if we are truly Christian. Psalm 37:37 says: 'Mark the perfect man, and behold the upright: for the end of that man is peace'. There is nothing so wonderful in this world as the death of a good man, the Christian man. 'Mark him', says Scripture. The psalmist was an old man when he wrote that — 'I have been young, and now am old', he says — and this is his experience, this is his advice to young people: 'Mark the perfect man . . . for the end of that man is peace'. Many a man seems to have a good time in this world, but his end is not very peaceful. Poor creature! He has not prepared for it, he is not aware that he is going, he is clutching at anything, and he does not die peacefully. Or listen to this extract from Psalm 112:7: 'He shall not be afraid of evil tidings: his heart is fixed, trusting in the Lord'. He is not afraid of pestilences, he is not afraid if wars should arise, he is not afraid of evil tidings. He does not say: 'What are we going to do tomorrow morning?' Not a bit — 'his heart is fixed, trusting in the Lord'. Again, take this magnificent word in Isaiah 28:16: 'He that believeth shall not make haste' or, if you prefer it, 'He that believeth shall not be confounded', he that believeth shall not be 'taken unawares'. Why? Because he has been paying heed, he has been preparing, so that whatever comes to meet him he has a foundation. He is not in a hurry, he never makes haste. Our Lord Himself has taught it perfectly in the parable of the sower. He tells us that the false believer 'had no root in himself'. He endured for a while, but when persecution came he was finished. 'He also that received seed among the thorns is he that heareth the word; and the care of this world, and the deceitfulness of riches, choke the word, and he becometh unfruitful.' The teaching of Scripture is endless on this theme.

This is something that is taught positively in Scripture and is confirmed by Christian experience. Read again the account of those first Christians who, when they were being persecuted, even being put to death, thanked God that He had counted them worthy to suffer for His name's sake. We have those great stories of the first martyrs and confessors, who though thrown to the lions in the arena, yet praised God. Far from complaining, Paul, as he writes to the Philippians from prison, gives thanks to God for his imprisonment, because it gives him an opportunity to preach the gospel. He could even endure the treachery of false friends. He was perfectly happy, and quite serene through it all, and could even look into the face of death and say that it was kind, because it meant going 'to be with Christ; which is far better'. He tells the Corinthians that 'our light affliction, which is but for a moment, worketh for us a far more exceeding and eternal weight of glory'. Read 2 Corinthians 4; read the list of his trials and tribulations; despite it all he can say that. And then listen to him, in his old age, facing death again, knowing it was coming; 'For I am now ready to be offered, and the time of my departure is at hand. I have fought a good fight, I have finished my course, I have kept the faith.' What a way to die! It has been the same throughout the centuries ever since the days when Paul wrote these words. Christian men have been repeating these experiences in their lives. Read the stories of the saints, read the stories of the martyrs and the confessors, read about those men who advanced to the stake smiling, preaching from the stake as the flames were encircling them. It is the most glorious story in the whole of history. Read again the stories of the Covenanters, of the great Puritans and many others.

The teaching, therefore, comes to this; it is only the men who have done these things of which our Lord speaks in the Sermon on the Mount who have these experiences. The pseudo-Christian finds that when he needs help, what he regarded as his faith does not help. It forsakes him when he needs it most. There is no question about this. The one common factor in the lives of all those who have been able to face the trials of life triumphantly and gloriously, is that they have always been men who have given themselves to living the Sermon on the Mount. That is the secret of the 'perfect' man, the 'righteous' man, the 'good' man, the 'Christian' man. So if you want to be able to face these things as Paul faced them, you must try to live as Paul lived. There is no other way for it; they all conformed to the same pattern.

But beyond all these things which we meet in this life, there is the certain approach of the day of final judgment. This is a constant theme in the teaching of the Bible. Here it is: 'Many will say to me in that day'. The Bible has a great deal to say about 'that day'. There were people who disagreed with Paul as to how the gospel should be preached, and as to how the Church should be built up. 'All right', says Paul in effect, 'I am not going to argue with you; the day will declare it.' 'We must all appear before the judgment seat of Christ.' It is mentioned everywhere in the Bible. Read in Matthew 25 about the ten virgins, and the talents, and the nations. All things come before Him in the final judgment. But remember that 1 Peter 4:17 teaches that 'judgment must begin at the house of God'. What is the book of Revelation but a great announcement of this judgment that is coming, when the books will be opened, and all shall be judged everywhere. All will come to judgment. The Bible is full of this, and it tells us that the day of judgment is certain. It tells us that it will be searching, that it will be inward. Everything is known to Him. These men said, 'Have we not done this and that?' And He said, 'I never knew you'. The whole time He has His eye upon them. They do not belong to Him, and He always knew it. Everything is known to Him. 'All things are naked and opened unto the eyes of him with whom we have to do'. He 'is a discerner of the thoughts and intents of the heart'. Nothing can be hid from His sight. Above all we are told that this judgment is final. There is no teaching in Scripture about a second chance, about a further opportunity. Try to produce the evidence, if you can. It is not there. You can perhaps produce two or three highly debatable statements of whose exposition no one can be certain. But are you going to bank on that while the weight of Scripture everywhere is on the other side? It is final judgment; there is no going back.

How then can we make certain of these things? How am I to live my life here on earth with peace and certainty and assurance? How can I make certain that I am building my house upon the rock? How do I really put these things into practice? It is the greatest question in this world. Nothing is more vital than that we should daily remind ourselves of these things. At the risk of being misunderstood, let me put it like this. I sometimes think that there is nothing more dangerous in the Christian life than a mechanical devotional life. I hear people talking glibly about 'having their Q.T.' in the morning. They do not even say 'Quiet Time', they say 'Q.T.' That attitude, as I understand these things, is absolutely fatal. It means that this person has been taught that it is a good thing for a Christian first thing in the morning to read a certain amount of Scripture and then to offer a prayer, before going to his daily work. You observe your 'quiet time' and off you go. Of course, it is a good thing to do; but it can be most dangerous to one's spiritual life if it becomes purely mechanical. I suggest, therefore, that what we should do is this. Certainly read your Scripture, and certainly pray; but not in any mechanical sense, not because you have been told to do it, not because it is 'the done thing'. Do it because the Bible is God's Word, and because He is speaking to you through it. But having read and prayed, stop and meditate, and in your meditation remind yourself of the actual teaching of the Sermon on the Mount. Ask yourself if you are living the Sermon on the Mount, or really trying to do so. We do not talk to ourselves sufficiently; that is our trouble. We talk too much to other people and not enough to ourselves. We must talk to ourselves, and say 'Our Lord said, in effect, I preach this Sermon to you, but it will be of no value to you if you do not do what I say.' Test yourself by the Sermon on the Mount. Remember these pictures at the end of the Sermon. Say to yourself. 'Yes, I am here now; I am young. But I have to die sometime, and am I ready for it?' What would happen to you if you suddenly lost your health, or lost your good looks, or your money or your possessions? What would happen to you if you became disfigured by some disease? Where are you, what are you going to rest upon? Have you faced the inevitability of judgment beyond death? That is the only safe way. It is not really enough just to be reading the Bible and praying; we have to apply what we learn; we have to face ourselves with it, and hold it before us. Do not rely upon activities. Do not say: 'I am so active in Christian work, I must be all right.' Our Lord said that you may not be all right, though you think you are doing it for Him. Just face these things one after another, and test your life by them; and then make certain that you are really keeping this teaching in the forefront and at the very centre of your life. Make quite sure that you are able to say honestly that your supreme desire is to know Him better, to keep His commandments, to live for His glory. However enticing the world may be, say, 'No; I know that I, as a living soul, have to go to meet Him face-to-face. At all costs that must come first; everything else must fall into the background.' It seems to me that that is the whole purpose of our Lord's picture at the end of this mighty Sermon, namely, that we should be warned against and made aware of the subtle danger of self-delusion, and that we should avoid it by thus examining ourselves daily in His presence, in the light of His teaching. May He grant us grace so to do.

Chapter Thirty

Conclusion

I N the last two verses of this chapter we are told by the sacred writer what effect this famous Sermon on the Mount produced upon its auditors. They thus provide us at the same time with the opportunity of considering in general what effect this Sermon should always produce upon those who read and consider it.

These two verses are by no means an idle or useless kind of epilogue. They are of great importance in any consideration of the Sermon. I have no doubt that that was the reason why the writer was led by the Holy Spirit to record the effect of the Sermon, because we are directed here to the Preacher rather than to the Sermon. We are asked, as it were, having considered the Sermon, to look at the One who delivered it and preached it. We have spent much time in considering in detail the teaching of the Sermon, and in the later chapters, especially, we have been considering the urgent appeal which our Lord addressed to those who had been listening. He besought them to put it into practice. He issued a terrible warning against self-deception, against merely admiring the Sermon and commending certain things in it, and failing to realize that, unless we are indeed practising it, we are outside the kingdom of God, and shall find that all on which we have been resting will suddenly be taken from us on the day of judgment.

But the question many may be tempted to ask is: Why should we practise this Sermon? Why should we pay heed to this terrible warning? Why should we believe that, unless we are indeed making our lives conform to this pattern, we shall be without hope as we come face-to-face with God? The real answer to all that is the subject to which we are directed by these last two verses. It is the Person Himself, the Person who uttered these sayings, the One who has delivered this teaching. In other words, as we consider the Sermon on the Mount as a whole, having gone into its various parts, we must realize that we must not concentrate only upon the beauty of the diction, the perfect structure of the Sermon, the impressive pictures, the striking illustrations and the extraordinary balance which we find in it, both from the standpoint of material and the way in which it is presented. Indeed, we can go further. When we consider the Sermon on the Mount, we are never to stop even with the moral, ethical, spiritual teaching; we are to go beyond all these things, wonderful though they are, and vital as they all are, to the Person of the Preacher Himself.

There are two main reasons for saying that. The first is that, ultimately, the authority of the Sermon derives from the Preacher. That is, of course, what makes the New Testament such a unique book, and gives uniqueness to the teaching of our Lord. With all other teachers that the world has ever known, the important thing is the teaching; but here is a case in which the Teacher is more important even than what He taught. There is a sense in which you cannot divide and separate them from one another; but if we are to give priority to one, we must always put the Preacher first. So these two verses coming at the end of the Sermon direct our attention to that fact.

If any man asks: Why should I pay heed to that Sermon, why should I put it into practice, why should I believe that it is the most vital thing in this life? the answer is, because of the Person who preached it. That is the authority, that is the sanction behind the Sermon. In other words, if we are in any doubt as to the Person who preached this Sermon, that is obviously going to affect our view of it. If we are in doubt about His uniqueness, about His deity, about the fact that here was God in the flesh speaking, then our whole attitude towards the Sermon is undermined. But, conversely, if we do believe that the Man who spoke these words was none other than the only begotten Son of God, then they have an awful solemnity and added authority, and we must take the teaching as a whole with all the seriousness which must ever be given to any pronouncement that comes from God Himself. There, then, we have a very good reason for considering this matter. The ultimate sanction behind every expression in the Sermon is to be found there. When we read it, therefore, and are tempted perhaps to argue against it or to explain certain things away, we must remember that we are considering the words of the Son of God. The authority and the sanction are derived from the Speaker, from the blessed Person Himself.

But quite apart from such a general deduction, our Lord Himself insists upon our paying attention to it. He calls attention to Himself in the Sermon. He repeats tests which are obviously designed to focus our attention upon Himself. That is the point at which so much that passes for gospel differs from the real gospel. There is a tendency for some people to create a division between the teaching of the New Testament and the Lord Himself. That is an essential error. He is always calling attention to Himself, and we find that abundantly illustrated in this particular Sermon. The ultimate trouble, therefore, with people who emphasize the teaching of the Sermon on the Mount at the expense of doctrine, and at the expense of theology, is that they never realize that point. We have often referred, in passing, to the case of those who say they like the Sermon on the Mount, and who put the Sermon on the Mount over against the teaching about the atonement and the death of Christ and all the high doctrines of the Epistles, because, they say, the Sermon on the Mount is something practical, something that can be applied to life and become the basis of the social order, and so on. The real trouble with such people is that they have never truly read the Sermon on the Mount, for, if they had done so, they would have found that they were being directed continually to this Person. And immediately that raises crucial doctrine. In other words, the Sermon on the Mount, as we have seen so many times, is really a kind of basic statement out of which everything else comes. It is full of doctrine; and the idea that it is moral, ethical teaching and nothing else, is an idea that is quite foreign to the teaching of the Sermon, and particularly to the point which is emphasized here in these last two verses.

We see, then, that our Lord Himself calls attention to Himself, and, in a sense, there is nothing in the Sermon which is quite so remarkable as the way in which He does that. So, having looked at the whole Sermon, we find that all the instructions He gave become focused together in Him. We look at Him in a special way in the Sermon on the Mount; and any study of it should always lead us to that. Here in these two verses we have a very wonderful way of doing so. We are told about the reaction of these people who had the great and high privilege of looking at Him and listening to the Sermon. And we are told that their reaction was one of astonishment. 'It came to pass, when Jesus had ended these sayings, the people were astonished at his doctrine (or at his teaching): for he taught them as one having authority, and not as the scribes.'

Let us try to recapture this if we can, for there is nothing that we should enjoy — I use the term advisedly — so much as looking at Him. There is no value in all other teaching if we are not right about Him. Essentially the vital point of all teaching, of theology, and of the whole Bible is to bring us to a knowledge of Him and into relationship with Him. So we look at the blessed Person, and we must try to picture this scene. Here is a great crowd of people. First of all it was just our Lord and His disciples when He sat down to teach; but by the end it is obvious that there was a great crowd. Here, sitting before all these people on that mountain, is this young Man, apparently just a carpenter from a little place called Nazareth in Galilee, an artisan, a common, ordinary person. He had had no training in the schools, He was not a Pharisee, or a scribe; He had not been sitting at the feet of Gamaliel or any of the great authorities or teachers. Apparently He was just a very ordinary person, who had lived a very ordinary life. But suddenly He bursts forth upon the countryside in an extraordinary ministry, and here He sits and begins to teach and to preach and to say the things we have been considering together. It is not surprising that these people were astonished. It was all so unexpected, so unusual in every way, so different from everything they had ever known. How difficult it is for us, because of our sheer familiarity with these facts and details, to realize that these things actually happened nearly two thousand years ago, and to realize what the effect must have been upon our Lord's contemporaries. Try to imagine their utter astonishment and amazement as this carpenter from Galilee sits and teaches and expounds the law, and speaks in this extraordinary manner. They were amazed and astonished and dumbfounded.

The thing for us to discover is exactly what caused the astonishment. The first thing, clearly, is the general authority with which He spoke — this Man who talked to them with authority and not as the scribes. That negative is very interesting — that His teaching was not after the manner of the scribes. The characteristic of the teaching of the scribes, you remember, was that they always quoted authorities and never uttered any original thoughts; they were experts, not so much in the law itself, as in various expositions and interpretations of the law which had been put forward since it was first given to Moses. Then, in turn, they were always quoting the experts on these interpretations. As an illustration of what this means, we have but to think of what so often happens in the law courts when a case is being heard. Various authorities are quoted; one authority has said this and another authority has said that; other textbooks are produced and their expositions are given. That was the manner or practice of the scribes, and so they were always arguing; but the chief feature was the endless string of quotations. It is something that still happens today. You can read or hear sermons that seem to be nothing but a series of quotations from various writings. That kind of thing gives the impression of learning and culture. We are told that the scribes and Pharisees were very proud of their learning. They dismissed our Lord with derision, and said, 'How hath this man learning, never having learned?' That points to the fact that the outstanding characteristic of His method was the absence of the endless quotations. In other words, the surprising thing about Him was His originality. He keeps on saying 'I say unto you'; not 'So-and-so has said', but 'I say unto you'. There was a freshness about His teaching. His whole method was different. His very appearance was different. His whole attitude towards teaching was different. It was characterized by this originality of thought and of manner — the way in which He did it as well as what He did.

But, of course, the most astonishing thing of all was the confidence and certainty with which He spoke. That appeared at the very beginning, even as He was uttering those great Beatitudes. He begins by saying: 'Blessed are the poor in spirit' and then, 'for theirs is the kingdom of heaven.' There is no doubt about it, and no question; this is no mere supposition, or possibility only. This extraordinary assurance and authority with which He spoke was something that was manifested from the very beginning.

I imagine, however, that what really astonished these people over and above His general authority was what He said, and in particular what He said about Himself. That, most surely, must have amazed and astonished them. Think again of the things which He said, first of all about His own teaching. He keeps on making remarks which call attention to His teaching, and to His own attitude towards it. Take, for instance, the frequency with which in the fifth chapter He said something like this: 'Ye have heard it said by them of old time . . . but I say unto you'. He does not hesitate to correct the teaching of the Pharisees and their authorities. 'They of old time', you remember we saw, stood for certain Pharisees and their exposition of the Mosaic law. He did not hesitate to put that aside and to correct it. This artisan, this carpenter who had never been to the schools, saying: 'I say unto you'! He claims that authority for Himself and for His teaching.

Indeed, He does not hesitate to assert in that phrase, that He, and He alone, is able to give a spiritual interpretation of the law that was given through Moses. His whole argument is that the people had never seen the spiritual intent or content of the law given by Moses, they were misinterpreting it and reducing it to the physical level. As long as they did not actually commit physical adultery, they thought it did not matter. They did not see that God was concerned about the heart, the desire, the spirit. So He stands before them as the only true interpreter of the law. He says that His interpretation alone brings out the spiritual intent of the law; indeed, He does not hesitate to speak of Himself and to regard Himself as the law giver: 'I say unto you.'

Then you remember how at the end of the Sermon He puts this in a still more explicit manner. 'Therefore', He says, 'whosoever heareth these sayings of mine, and doeth them, . . .' You notice the significance He attaches to His own sayings. As He says that, He is saying something about Himself. He is using this terrifying picture of the two houses. He has already spoken about judgment, and He puts it all in terms of 'these sayings of mine'. He says in effect: 'I want you to listen to these, and I want you to practise them — "these sayings of mine"; do you realize who I am and the importance, therefore, of what I say?' Thus we find that in what He said about His teaching He is making a tremendous pronouncement about Himself. He claims this unique authority.

But we are not left simply with inferences and implications; His references to Himself are not only indirect. Have you ever contemplated the direct references which He makes to Himself in this Sermon on the Mount? Let us take them in the order in which they appear. First, in 5:11, when He has just finished the Beatitudes, He goes on to say: 'Blessed are ye, when men shall revile you, and persecute you, and shall say all manner of evil against you falsely, for my sake.' What an astonishing and amazing thing that is. He does not say, 'Blessed are ye when men shall revile and persecute you for the teaching's sake', or 'Ah, blessed are you people if, in your desire to implement this high and exalted teaching, you suffer persecution and perhaps death itself.' He does not say: 'If you suffer like this for the name of God your Father in heaven, you are blessed.' No, He says 'for my sake'. What unutterable folly it is for people to say that they are interested in the Sermon on the Mount as ethical and moral and social teaching only. Here, before He comes to 'turning the other cheek' and the other things they like so much, He tells us that we ought to be ready to suffer for His sake, and that we are to endure persecution for His sake, and that we may even have to be ready to die for His sake. This tremendous claim comes at the very beginning of the Sermon.

Then He goes on to do the same thing by implication immediately afterwards. 'Ye are the salt of the earth', and 'ye are the light of the world'. Do you see the implication of that? He says in effect, 'You people who are My disciples and My followers, you who have given yourselves to Me even to the extent of enduring persecution for My name's sake, and if necessary death for My sake, you, who are listening to Me and are going to repeat My teaching and propagate it throughout the world, you are the salt of the earth, and the light of the world.' There is only one real deduction to draw from that, that they are going to be a very special and unique people who, because of their relationship to Him, become the salt of the earth and the light of the world. It is the whole doctrine of the rebirth. They are not just people who listen to teaching and then repeat it and so have the effect of salt and light. No, they themselves are going to become salt and light. We have here the doctrine of the mystical relationship to and union of His people with Him, He dwelling in them and imparting His nature to them. Therefore, they in turn become the light of the world as He is the light of the world. So it is again a tremendous statement about Him. He is here asserting His unique deity and His Saviourhood. He is asserting that He is the long expected Messiah.

So, as we look at these two striking statements before we come to His detailed teaching, we are driven to ask, as these people must have asked, Who is this Person who talks like this? Who is this man, this carpenter from Nazareth, who asks us to be ready to suffer for Him, and tells us we shall be blessed indeed of God if we do; who says, 'Rejoice, and be exceeding glad: for great is your reward in heaven' if you suffer injustice and persecution 'for my sake'? Who is this? And who is this who says He can make us the salt of the earth and the light of the world? He gives the answer to the question in 5:17, where He says: 'Think not that I am come to destroy the law, or the prophets: I am not come to destroy, but to fulfil.' Look for a moment at this extraordinary expression, 'I am come'. He speaks of Himself and of His life in this world as being different from that of anybody else. He does not say: 'I have been born, therefore this or that.' He says: 'I am come.' Where Has he come from? He is One who has arrived in this world; He has not only been born, He has come into it from somewhere. He has come from eternity, from heaven, He has come from the bosom of the Father. The law and the prophets had said that He was to come. They said, for instance, 'The Sun of righteousness (shall) arise with healing in his wings.' They were always talking of someone who was to come from the outside. And, here, He says of Himself, 'I am come.' It is not surprising that these people as they sat and listened said: What does He mean; and who is this man, this carpenter who looks like ourselves?

He is always saying: 'I am come.' He is telling them that He does not belong to this realm, but that He has come into this life, and into this world, from glory, from eternity. He is saying: 'I and the Father are one.' He is referring to the incarnation. What tragic folly to regard this Sermon as just a social manifesto, and to see nothing but ethics and morality in it. Listen to what He says about Himself. 'I am come.' This is no human teacher; this is the Son of God.

But furthermore He says that He has come to fulfil, and not to destroy the law and the prophets; which means that He has come to fulfil and to keep God's holy law, that He is also the Messiah. He is claiming here that He is sinless, absolutely perfect. God gave His law to Moses, but not a single human being had ever kept it — 'all the world may become guilty before God', 'there is none righteous, no, not one'. All the saints of the Old Testament had broken the law; none had succeeded in observing it. Yet here is One who stands and says: I am going to keep it; not one jot or one tittle of this law will I break; I am going to fulfil it, I am going to keep and to honour it perfectly. Here is One who claims to be sinless, to be absolutely perfect. Not only that. He does not hesitate to claim for Himself what Paul puts in the words: 'Christ is the end of the law for righteousness to every one that believeth.' In other words, He fulfils the law by carrying it out, He honours it by absolute perfection in His own life. Yes; but He bears the punishment it metes out upon transgressors also. He has satisfied every demand of the law of God, He has fulfilled the law for Himself and others.

But He claims that he is fulfilling the prophets also. He claims that He is the One to whom all the Old Testament prophets pointed. They had been talking about the Messiah; He says, I am this Messiah. He is the One who fulfils in His own Person all the promises. Again the apostle Paul sums it up by putting it like this: 'For all the promises of God in him are yea, and in him Amen.' God's promises are all fulfilled in this wonderful Person who here says of Himself that He is the fulfiller of the law and the prophets. Everything in the Old Testament points to Him; He is the centre of it all. This is the coming One, the One expected. He says all that in the Sermon on the Mount, this Sermon which we are told has no doctrine, and which people like because it is not theological! Can there be a more tragic blindness than that which causes men to speak in such a foolish manner? The whole doctrine of the incarnation of Christ, His Person and His death, is all here. We have seen it as we have gone through the Sermon, and we are looking at it again now.

Another great statement pointing in the same direction is the one we found in 7:21: 'Not every one that saith unto me, Lord, Lord, shall enter into the kingdom of heaven.' He does not hesitate to say that people will address Him as Lord, and that means that He is Jehovah, that He is God. He says here quite calmly that people are going to say to Him, 'Lord, Lord.' They are saying it now, in a sense, and on that great day they will say, 'Lord, Lord', to Him. But the emphasis is upon the fact that they will say that to 'me' — not to the Father who is in heaven, but to 'me', the One speaking there on the mountain. He does not hesitate to ascribe to Himself, and to take to Himself, the highest term used in the whole realm of Scripture for the eternal, absolute, blessed God.

He even went a step further, and announced at the end of the Sermon that He is to be the judge of the world. 'Many will say to me in that day, Lord, Lord,' etc. Notice the repetition — 'And then will I profess unto them, I never knew you: depart from me, ye that work iniquity.' Yes, judgment is being committed to the Son. He is claiming that He is to be the judge of all men, and that what matters is our relationship to Him, His knowledge of us, His concern about us and His interest in us. As someone once put it very well: 'The One who sat there on the Mount to teach, is the One who at the end will sit on the throne of His glory and all the nations of the world shall appear before Him, and He will pronounce the judgment upon them.' Was ever anything more astounding, more astonishing, uttered in this world? Try again to capture the scene. Look at this apparently ordinary Person, this carpenter, sitting there and saying, in effect: 'As

I am sitting here now I shall sit on the throne of eternal glory, and the whole world and the nations and all people will appear before Me, and I will pronounce judgment.' He is indeed the judge eternal.

Thus we have gathered together the main statements He makes about Himself in this famous Sermon on the Mount. As we leave it, therefore, I ask you this simple yet profound question: What is your reaction to it all? We are told that these people 'were astonished at his doctrine: for he taught them as one having authority, and not as the scribes'. We are not told that their reaction went any further than that; but we are told that they were astonished and amazed because of His manner, because of the very form of His teaching, and because of the astounding teaching itself, and especially some of these things which He said about Himself. There are many people who are not even astonished by this Sermon. God forbid that that should be true of any of us. But it is not enough that we should merely be astonished; our reaction must go beyond astonishment. Surely our reaction as He speaks to us should be to recognize that this is none other than the Son of God Himself who has been speaking to us in the words we have considered; the very incarnate Son of God. Our first reaction should be that we recognize again the central truth of the gospel, that God's only begotten Son has entered into this world of time. We are not concerned here with a mere philosophy or outlook upon life, but with the fact that the preacher was the Son of God Almighty here in the flesh.

Why did He come, why did He preach the Sermon? He has not just come to give another law. He was not merely telling people how to live, because the Sermon on the Mount (we say it with reverence) is infinitely more impossible to practise than even the law of Moses, and we have already seen that there had not been a single human being who had been able to keep that. What then is the message? It must be this. In this Sermon our Lord condemns once and for ever all trust in human endeavour and natural ability in the matter of salvation. He is telling us, in other words, that we all have come short of the glory of God, and that however great our efforts and striving from now until our death, they will never make us righteous, or fit us to stand in the presence of God. He says that the Pharisees have been reducing the real meaning of the law, but that the law itself is spiritual. He is saying what Paul came to see and to say later: 'I was alive without the law once; but when the commandment came, sin revived, and I died' (Rom. 7:9). In other words, He is saying that we are all condemned sinners in the sight of God, and that we cannot save ourselves.

Then He goes on to say that we all need a new birth, a new nature, and a new life. We cannot live a life like this as we are by nature; we must be made anew. And what He is saying in this Sermon is that He has come in order to give us this new life. Yes, in relationship to Him, we become the salt of the earth and the light of the world. He has come not merely to outline the teaching. He has come to make it possible. In this Sermon, beginning with the Beatitudes, He has given an account of His people. He has stated what they will be like in general, and given a more detailed account of how they will act. The Sermon is a description of Christian people, people who have received the Holy Spirit; not of natural man striving to make himself right with God, but of God making His people anew. He has given us the gift of the Holy Spirit, the promise made to Abraham, 'the promise of the Father', and having received this promise, we become people conformable to this pattern. The Beatitudes are true of all who are living the Sermon on the Mount, of all who are Christian. That does not mean that we are sinless or perfect; it means that if we look at the general tenor of our life it corresponds to this, or as John puts it in his first Epistle: 'He that is born of God does not continue the practices of sin.' There is this difference. Look at a man's life in general. As you look at the believer he conforms to the Sermon on the Mount. He wants to live it and he does his utmost to do so. He realizes his failure, but prays to be filled with the Spirit; he hungers and thirsts after righteousness, and he has the blessed experience of the promises being realized in his daily life.

This is the true reaction to the Sermon on the Mount. We realize that this was none other than the Son of God, and that in the Sermon He has been saying that He has come to start a new humanity. He is 'the first born among many brethren'; He is 'the last Adam'; He is God's new Man, and all who belong to Him are going to be like Him. It is astounding doctrine, it is astonishing, amazing doctrine; but, thank God, we know it is the truth. We know that He died for our sins, that our sins are forgiven; 'we know that we have passed from death unto life, because we love the brethren'; we know that we belong to Him, because we do indeed hunger and thirst after righteousness. We are conscious of the fact that He is dealing with us, that His Spirit is working within us, revealing to us our shortcomings and imperfections, creating longings and aspirations within us, 'working in us both to will and to do of his good pleasure'. Above all, in the midst of life, with all its trials and problems and tests, indeed amidst all the uncertainties of life in this 'atomic age' and the certain fact of death and the final judgment, we can say with the apostle Paul, 'For the which cause I also suffer these things: nevertheless I am not ashamed: for I know whom I have believed, and am persuaded that he is able to keep that which I have committed unto him against that day' (2 Tim. 1:12).

'In every high and stormy gale
My anchor holds within the veil.

When all around my soul gives way,
He then is all my hope and stay.

On Christ, the solid Rock, I stand;
All other ground is sinking sand.'

'For other foundation can no man lay than that is laid, which is Jesus Christ' (1 Cor. 3:11). 'Nevertheless the foundation of God standeth sure, having this seal, The Lord knoweth them that are his. And, Let every one that nameth the name of Christ depart from iniquity' (2 Tim. 2:19).